MW01029858

Negotiating a Labor Contract

A Management Handbook

Second Edition

Negotiating a Labor Contract

A Management Handbook

Second Edition

Charles S. Loughran

The Bureau of National Affairs, Inc., Washington, D.C.

Seventh Printing, October 1999

Library of Congress Cataloging-in-Publication Data

Loughran, Charles S.
Negotiating a labor contract : a management handbook / Charles S. Loughran. — 2nd ed.
p. cm.
Includes bibliographical references (p.) and index.
ISBN 0-87179-745-3 : $58.00
1. Collective bargaining—Handbooks, manuals, etc. 2. Collective labor agreements—Handbooks, manuals, etc. I. Title.
HD6483.L69 1992
658.3 ' 154—dc20 92-280
CIP

Published by BNA Books
1231 25th St., N.W., Washington, D.C. 20037

Printed in the United States of America
International Standard Book Number: 0-87179-745-3

Summary Table of Contents

Preface xxiii

Acknowledgments xxix

Part I Before Bargaining Begins

Chapter 1 General Assessment of Negotiations 3

Chapter 2 Preparing for Bargaining 50

Chapter 3 Developing a Bargaining Game Plan 93

Chapter 4 The Law Controlling Labor Negotiations 119

Part II The Bargaining Process

Chapter 5 Preliminary Stages of Negotiations 143

Chapter 6 Practical Tips for the Management Spokesperson 177

Chapter 7 Strategies for Bargaining Over Economics 202

Chapter 8 Negotiating Health and Welfare Benefits 243

Chapter 9 Negotiating Pensions 269

Chapter 10 Costing Contract Demands, Offers, and Settlements 291

Chapter 11 Drafting Labor Contract Language 322

Part III Reaching a Final Agreement

Chapter 12 Striving to Reach Agreement 345

Chapter 13 Strike Preparation, Decision Making, and Management 379

Chapter 14 Bringing the Negotiations to a Conclusion 423
Chapter 15 Special Bargaining Situations 458

Appendixes

1. Summary of Labor Contract Provisions 493
2. Labor Cost Recap 498
3. Review of the Development of a Clause 500
4. Negotiations Preparation Checklist 501
5. Strike Contingency Checklist 513
6. Sample Memorandum of Agreement 523
7. Labor Contract Checklist 526

Notes 539
Index 549

Detailed Table of Contents

Preface xxiii
Acknowledgments xxix

Part I Before Bargaining Begins

Chapter 1 General Assessment of Negotiations 3
When to Begin 4
Responsibility for General Assessment 4
Analyzing Previous Negotiations 6
Established Objectives Compared to Negotiation Results 7
Pattern of Negotiations 7
Key Personalities in Previous Negotiations 9
Key Issues 10
Hits, Runs, and Errors 12
Units for Bargaining 13
The Single-Employer–Single-Facility Unit 14
Evaluating the Single-Facility Unit 15
The Proper Economic Fit 15
Work Practice Issues 17
The Single-Employer–Multifacility Unit 18
Evaluating Multifacility Units 18
Multiemployer Bargaining 19
Evaluating Multiemployer Bargaining 20
Multiple-Union Situations 24
Contract Dates 24
The Bell Cow 25
Joint Negotiations 26
Overall Strategy 27
Economic Climate for Bargaining 28
Recent Comparable Settlements 29
Bargaining Leverage 31
Employer Bargaining Power 33
Employer's Financial Condition 33
Anticipated Demand for Product(s) or Service(s) 33

Ability to Supply or Service Customers ... 34
Mutual Aid or Mutual Assistance Pacts ... 38
Union Bargaining Power ... 40
Recent Levels of Employment Hours and Earnings ... 40
Strike Fund ... 41
Availability of Government Subsidies ... 42
Alternative Employment Opportunities ... 42
The Bargaining Leverage Equation ... 43
Institutional and Attitudinal Climate for Bargaining ... 43
Union Organization—Policies, Politics, and Personalities ... 43
Employee Perspective ... 44
Management Perspective ... 46
Labor and Employee Relations ... 46
Importance of Perceptions ... 47
Comparison With Other Employers ... 47
Ability to Change? ... 47
Public and Governmental Perspective ... 48
Summary ... 49

Chapter 2 Preparing for Bargaining ... 50
Assembling Management's Bargaining Committee ... 50
Selecting the Management Spokesperson ... 51
Insider Versus Outsider ... 51
Lawyer Versus Nonlawyer ... 53
The Executive as Negotiator ... 54
Selecting Other Members of the Negotiating Committee ... 56
Operating Expertise ... 56
Cost Specialist ... 57
Note Taker ... 57
Language Draftsperson ... 58
Other Committee Members or Observers ... 59
Establishing the Negotiator's Authority and Management's Expectations ... 60
Gathering Bargaining Data and Information ... 61
How Much Is Necessary? ... 61
Bargaining Book ... 63
Economic Information ... 63
Internal Historical Information ... 63
Current Internal Information ... 66
External Economic Data ... 70
Internal Noneconomic Information ... 75
Work Hours ... 75
Seniority ... 78
Grievances and Arbitration Cases ... 78
Supervisors' Survey ... 79

Development of Contract Clauses 79
Supplemental Agreements 82
External Noneconomic Information 82
Reference to Law 82
Key Contacts 85
Briefing Personnel and Coordinating With Other Management Functions 85
Public and Investor Relations 86
Management Briefing 86
Selecting a Site for Negotiations 87
Formal Notification Preliminary to Bargaining 88
Failure to Reopen 89
Who Has to Reopen 89
Notice to FMCS 90
Checklist for Preparations 92

Chapter 3 Developing a Bargaining Game Plan 93
Establishing Objectives and Setting Economic Parameters 94
Economic Parameters 94
Noneconomic Objectives 95
Models of Bargaining Parameters and Objectives 96
The Role of the Negotiator in Setting Parameters 96
The Simple Model 97
More Direction 98
A Road Map 98
The Target Approach 100
Timing 102
Beginning Negotiations 102
Ending Negotiations 104
Timing of Offers 104
Bargaining Calendar 105
Identifying Key Issues 105
Spotting Hot Issues 107
In-Depth Analysis 107
Dealing With Key Issues 108
Management's Agenda 109
Determining Management's Needs 110
The Running List 110
Grievance and Arbitration Decisions 111
Beyond the Contract 111
Organizing and Prioritizing Management's Needs 112
Avoiding the Major Pitfall of Management Proposals 113
Scope and Strategy of Management Agenda 117

Chapter 4 The Law Controlling Labor Negotiations 119
National Labor Relations Act 119
Good Faith Bargaining 120

Duty to Furnish Information 121
Relevancy 121
Feasibility 123
Confidentiality 123
Waiver 123
Subjects for Bargaining 124
Mandatory vs. Nonmandatory Bargaining Subjects ... 125
Bargaining Over Nonmandatory Subjects 128
Bargaining Over Borderline Mandatory Subjects 128
Avoiding Waiver On a Nonmandatory Subject 129
Bargaining to Impasse Over Nonmandatory Subjects 129
Good Faith in the Conduct of Negotiations 131
An Imprecise Standard 131
"Totality of Conduct" 132
Imposing Conditions 132
Inhibiting or Delaying Meeting 132
Insufficient Authority of Negotiator 133
Surface Bargaining 133
Withdrawal of Accepted Offers 134
Refusal to Put Agreements in Writing 134
Unilateral Changes 135
Bypassing the Union 135
The Effect of Unfair Labor Practices on Bargaining 136
Impact of Board Orders 136
The Significance of an Unfair Labor Practice Strike .. 136
The Right to Strike or Lock Out 138
Caveat—Tip of the Iceberg 139

Part II The Bargaining Process

Chapter 5 Preliminary Stages of Negotiations 143
Ground Rules for Conducting Negotiations 143
Meeting Schedules 144
Pay for Members of the Union Bargaining Committee ... 145
News Media Contacts 146
Order of Addressing Issues 147
Confirming Agreement on Resolved Issues 148
Treatment of Contract Expiration 149
Ascertaining Contract Finalization Requirements 150
Ground Rules for the Management Committee 151
Only the Spokesperson Speaks 151
Method of Calling Caucuses 152
Inadvertent Signals 152
Unauthorized Communications 153
Opening Statement by Management 153

Setting a Tone 153
Theme 154
Presentation 155
Opening Statement by the Union 156
Receiving the Union's Bargaining Agenda 157
Advance Receipt of the Union Agenda 157
Dealing With Pending Grievances 157
Understanding and Clarifying the Union's Proposals 158
Ascertaining Rationale for Proposals 159
The Spokesperson's Notes 159
Pitfalls in Clarifying Union Proposals 160
Avoiding Immediate Substantive Responses 163
Closing Off Further Proposals 163
Presenting Management's Agenda 164
Timing 164
Method of Presentation 165
Accentuate the Positive 165
Evaluating, and Determining Positions on, the Union's Agenda 166
Monetary Issues 166
Nonmonetary Issues 167
Reviewing Each Proposal 167
A Devil's Advocate 168
Developing Management's Positions 169
Initial Response to the Union's Nonmonetary Proposals 172
Kicking the Tires 172
Categorizing Proposals 172
Initial Signaling 173
Eliminating Issues 174
Reflecting Basic Positions 174
Getting Negotiations off the Ground 175

Chapter 6 Practical Tips for the Management Spokesperson 177
Arranging and Conducting Meetings 177
Seating Arrangements 177
Meeting Times 178
Response Timing 179
Caucus Room and Equipment 179
Bargaining Table Talk 180
Setting the Proper Tone 180
Dealing With Abusive Table Talk 180
A Rational Approach 181
A Place for Humor 182
Word Selection 182

The Spokesperson as a Persuader 183
Types of Persuasion 184
Persuasion Based on Factual and Statistical Information 184
Rational Persuasion 186
Emotional Persuasion 187
Limits of Persuasion 188
The Spokesperson as a Listener 189
Listening as an Art 189
Listening for the Source of the Problem 190
Specific Listening Techniques 191
Listening to Everyone 191
Making Concessions 192
Effective Use of the Caucus 193
Tactical Significance 193
Calling for a Caucus 194
Length and Frequency of Caucuses 194
Managing the Caucus 195
Presenting Offers and Proposals 196
Traits and Characteristics of an Effective Management Spokesperson 197
The Other Negotiation 200

Chapter 7 Strategies for Bargaining Over Economics 202
General Forms of Negotiating Wages and Benefits 202
Auction or Traditional Bargaining 202
"Boulwarism" 203
"Ballpark Offer" With Minor Adjustments 203
Piecemeal Approach 203
Pattern-Following Approach 204
Traditional Economic Bargaining: Offer and Counteroffer 204
Management's First Economic Offer 205
Timing of the First Offer 205
Exceptions to the General Rule 206
Timing Factors to Consider 207
Constructing Management's First Economic Offer 208
Credibility of the First Offer 209
Objectives of the First Offer 210
Reviewing the First Offer Before Presentation 212
Presenting Management's First Offer 213
Characterizing the Offer 213
Form of Presentation 214
The Union's Response to Management's First Offer 214
Failure of the Union to Make a Counteroffer 215
Evaluating the Union's First Counteroffer 216

Judging the Union's Economic Expectations 217
Management's Economic Expectations 218
The Potential Early Impasse 219
Applying Pressure 219
Adhering to Conventional Bargaining 220
Formal Response to the Union's First Counteroffer 221
Communicating Through Offers 221
The Need for Candid Dialogue 222
Intermediate Economic Offers 222
Looking Ahead 224
Inching Toward Agreement 224
Complexity of Actual Negotiations 225
Custom Versus Innovation 226
The Trap of Habit 226
Changing the Approach 226
The *Quid Pro Quo* or Tradeoff 227
Advantages of Tradeoffs 228
Disadvantages of Tradeoffs 228
Principle vs. Pragmatism 229
Types of Tradeoffs 230
Direct Tradeoff 230
Concession for Dropping a Demand 230
The "Blocking Issue" 231
The Stalking Horse 232
Timing and Technique of Trading 234
Private Discussions 234
Mediators and Trading 235
Leaving Room to Move 235
The Total-Package or "Bottom-Line" Concept 235
Important Exceptions to the Bottom-Line Concept 236
Policy Issues 237
Loading the Package 237
Contract Term Strategy 238
Avoiding Coincident Contract Expirations 239
A Possible Trap in the Long-Term Contract Offer 239
Discouraging Short-Term Contracts 240
Wage or Other Limited Reopeners 240
Insecurity of Reopeners 241
Tactics of Reopening Clauses 241
Bargaining Strategy—Epilogue 242

Chapter 8 Negotiating Health and Welfare Benefits 243
Use of Experts 243
General vs. Specific Contract Language 244
Employer-Sponsored vs. Joint-Trusteed Plans 245
Advantages 246

Disadvantages 246
Types of Health and Welfare Benefits 247
Life Insurance 247
Accidental Death and Dismemberment 248
Hospital-Surgical-Medical Coverage 248
Indemnity Plans 248
Plan Design 249
Sickness and Nonoccupational Disability Benefits 250
Dental Plans 252
Vision Care 252
Prescription Drug Plans 252
Mental Health Benefits 253
Retiree Medical Benefits 254
Bargaining Obligation—Retiree Benefits 254
FASB 106 255
COBRA 255
Quasi-Health and Welfare Benefits 256
Legal Services 256
Child Care 257
Controlling Costs 258
Self-Insurance 258
Cost Sharing 259
Managed Care 261
Health and Welfare Negotiating Strategies 264
Analyze Experience 264
Negotiating Costs vs. Benefits 265
Design Plan to Encourage Cost Control 266
Retain Key Operating and Administrative Decisions 267
When to Negotiate Health and Welfare Benefits 267
Enlisting Union Cooperation in Cost Control 268

Chapter 9 Negotiating Pensions 269
Comparisons With Health and Welfare 269
Legal Constraints 270
Major Categories of Pension Plans 270
Defined Benefit Plans 271
Principal Features of Defined Benefit Plans 272
Defined Contribution Plans 281
Funding of Defined Contribution Plans 281
401(k) Plans 282
Advantages and Disadvantages of Defined Contribution Plans 282
Hybrid DB/DC Plans—"Target Benefit Plans" 283
Joint-Trusteed or Taft-Hartley Trusts 284
Pension Negotiating Strategies 286
Retain Management Flexibility 286

Avoid Automatic Benefit Increases 287
Beware of Assuming Increases in Past Service Liability 287
Avoid Dual Defined Benefit and Defined Contribution Obligations 288
Beware of Loose Disability Rules and High Disability Benefits 288
Consider Work Group Characteristics When Making Pension Benefit Comparisons 288
Do Not Be Misled by Short-Term Cost Estimates 289

Chapter 10 Costing Contract Demands, Offers, and Settlements 291
The Negotiator as a Cost Estimator 291
Use of Specialists 292
Use of Computers 293
The Necessity of Cost Estimates 293
"New Money" 294
Applying the New Money Concept 295
Management's Needs Must Prevail 296
The "Rollup" Concept 296
What "Rollup" Means 296
Applying the Concept 297
Which Benefits Roll Up 297
The Useful But Deceptive Cents-Per-Hour Measurement 299
The Virtue of Simplicity 299
The Dangers of Simplicity 300
A Handy Shortcut 300
Cents Per Hour and New Money 300
Ascertaining Key Costing Variables 301
Calculating Specific Contract Changes 303
General Wages 303
Bracket or Wage Category Increases 303
Special Job Adjustments 304
Cost-of-Living Adjustments 304
Vacation Benefit Improvements 306
Costing for Multiyear Contracts 306
Costing Concurrent Vacation and Wage Increases 307
Holiday Benefit Improvements 308
Other Paid Leaves 308
Indirect Costs of Paid Leaves 308
Estimating Costs of Premium Payments 310
Noneconomic Provisions 311
Cost Impact Beyond the Bargaining Unit 311
Costing the Total Package 312

A Useful Format 312
Time-Weighting and Present Value Costing 315
Simple Cash Outflow and Wage Negotiating Strategy 315
Present Value Analysis 318
Sharing Cost Estimates With the Union 320

Chapter 11 Drafting Labor Contract Language 322
Language Drafting 322
When Language Should Be Drafted 322
Who Should Draft Language for Management? 324
Nonparticipants as Draftspersons 324
Handling Language Drafted by the Union 325
Writing for the Readers 325
Cosmetic Language Changes 326
General Guidelines for the Draftsperson 327
Simplicity and Clarity 327
Conservative Drafting 332
Considering the Worst Case 332
"Hedge" Phrases 333
Making Contractual Restrictions as Narrow as Possible 343
Watching Out for Borrowed Language 335
Catch-All Terms 336
Pitfalls of Mutual Agreement Clauses 336
Avoiding Agreements to Agree 337
Avoiding Overly General and High-Sounding Clauses 338
Pinpointing the Effective Date 339
Impact of Language Changes on Other Contract Sections 339
Dating and Labeling Each Proposal and Counterproposal 340
The Sidebar Agreement 340
Incorporating Changes 341

Part III Reaching a Final Agreement

Chapter 12 Striving to Reach Agreement 345
Proper Timing 345
Deadlines 346
Signals 346
Pressure to Settle 347
Assessing All Timing Considerations 347
Methods of Moving to a Conclusion 348
Final Offer 348
Precedents to a Final Offer 348

The Credibility Factor 349
Finality as an Aid to Both Sides 349
Exceptions to Finality 350
Piecing the Settlement Together 350
Techniques for Avoiding or Resolving an Impasse 351
Private or Off-the-Record Meetings 351
Ethics of Private Meetings 352
Extension of Formal Meetings 352
Trust Is Crucial 353
Oral Agreements 354
Creative Bargaining 355
Varying the Variables 355
Reaching Beyond the Contract Term 357
Shifting From Wages to Fringes 358
Importance of Appearances 359
Form of Wage Increases 360
Meeting Both Sides' Needs 360
Following an Apparent Pattern 361
Creative Writing 364
Finessing Disagreements 364
Re-examination of Principles 365
Basic Principles 366
Careful Examination 366
Optional Offers 367
Splitting the Difference 368
Contingent Commitment 368
Relate Contingency to Employer's Needs and Capabilities 369
Tying Agreements 369
"Most Favored Nation" Clause 370
Tying to Other Contracts 370
Using Others to Avoid Impasse 372
Mediation 372
Objectives and *Modus Operandi* of Mediators 373
Working With a Mediator 374
Interest Arbitration 375
Limited Scope and Authority of Arbitrator 375
Variations on the Arbitration Theme 376
Bypassing the Union Spokesperson 377

Chapter 13 Strike Preparation, Decision Making, and Management 379
The Role of Strikes in the Bargaining Process 379
Strike Preparations 380
When to Begin 381
Assigning Responsibility 381

Developing a Strike Plan 382
The Strike/Settlement Decision 385
Estimating the Cost of a Strike 386
Assumptions of Operating Levels 386
Intangible Costs 387
Estimating the "Payback" of a Strike 388
Period for Measuring Payback 388
Calculating the Payback 390
Assessing Intangible Paybacks 390
The Long-Term Strike Impact 391
Cost/Benefit Analysis of a Potential Strike 391
Estimating Probability and Duration 392
The Complete Payback Calculation 393
Balancing the Intangibles 394
Beyond Logic 395
Final Offer and Strike Decision Strategy 396
Legal Questions Involving Strikes 397
The Right to Strike and to Picket 397
Secondary Picketing 397
"Common Situs" Picketing 398
"Ally Doctrine" 399
Limits on Violent or Threatening Picketing 399
Legal Rights of Striking Employees 400
"Economic" versus Unfair Labor Practice Strikes 400
Replacing Economic Strikers 400
Unfair Labor Practice Strikes 401
Striker's Misconduct 401
Offer to Return Must Be Unconditional 402
Employers' Rights and Obligations in Strike Situations 402
Unilateral Implementation of Final Offer 402
Communicating With Strikers 403
Continuing Bargaining Obligation 403
Changes in Position 404
Legal Caveats 404
The Decision on Whether to Operate During a Strike 404
Prestrike Bargaining Positions 405
Nature of Struck Operations 405
Feasibility Factors 406
Impact on Labor-Management Relationships 406
Impact on Bargaining Leverage 407
Managing Operations During a Strike 408
Labor Sources 408
Supervisors and Other Salaried Employees 408
Hourly Employees—Other Facilities 409
Use of Strike Replacements 409
Training 411

Care and Feeding of Strike Replacements 412
Scheduling Work 413
Compensation and Benefits 413
Security 413
Services, Supplies, and Deliveries 414
Management's Bargaining Posture During a Strike 416
Initial Bargaining Position 416
Communications 416
Direct Communications 417
Media Communications 418
Resuming Negotiations 418
Bargaining a Strike Settlement Agreement 419
Order of Recall to Work 419
Eligibility for Benefits 420
Seniority Status of Strikers 420
Disciplinary Action for Strike Misconduct 420
Union Disciplinary Action Against Picket Line Violators 421
Pending Litigation 421
Poststrike Posture 422

Chapter 14 Bringing the Negotiations to a Conclusion 423
Applying Pressure to Settle 423
Deadline for Acceptance 424
Deadline on Offer of Retroactivity 425
Added Benefit for Acceptance by Deadline 426
Breaking Off Negotiations 427
Unfair Labor Practice Charge 427
Elimination of Checkoff 428
Strike Preparations 429
Hiring Strike Replacements 430
Representation Election 430
Common Pitfalls in Reaching a Settlement 431
Being Pressured Into Settlement 432
Strike Threat 432
Bargaining Deadline 433
Problems Presented by the Union's Acceptance and Ratification Process 435
Knowing and Dealing With the Union's Ratification Process 436
Final Authority by the Committee 436
Buying a Recommendation 437
Last Minute Add-Ons 439
Premature Implementation 440
Tentative Settlement and Ratification 441
Written Memorandum of Agreement 441

Importance of a Written Summary 442
Memorandum Format 443
Proceeding From Agreement to Ratification 444
Assist in Preparing Written Materials 444
Facilitating Explanatory Meetings and Voting 445
Avoiding Publicity 445
The Publicity Exception 445
The Negative Ratification Vote 448
Preparing and Executing the Revised Contract Document 450
Incorporating Contract Language Changes 450
Incorporating Economic Changes 451
Finalizing the Revised Contract Document 452
Postnegotiation Wrap-Up 453
Informational Meetings for Management and Supervisory Personnel 453
Critique and Analysis 454
Finalizing Minutes and Notes 456
Finalizing Cost Estimates 456
Effect of the Settlement on Other Employee Groups 457

Chapter 15 Special Bargaining Situations 458
Negotiating the Initial Labor Agreement 458
Unique Characteristics 459
Special Preparations 460
Bargaining Suggestions 460
Work From Management's Draft Contract 460
Use Union Security Concessions to Maximum Advantage 461
Specific Contract Language Objectives for an Initial Contract 462
Less Is Usually Best 462
Avoiding Undue Specificity 462
A Strong Management-Rights Clause 462
Avoiding Veto Clauses 463
Automatic Escalators Are Dangerous 464
Zipping Up the Contract 465
Protection Against Strikes 465
Arbitration 466
Perfection Not Attainable 467
Concessionary Bargaining 467
Necessary Ingredients for Concessionary Bargaining ... 468
A Financially Distressed Industry and/or Employer .. 469
The Imminent Threat of Job Loss 469
The Likelihood or Guarantee of More Jobs if Labor Costs Are Lowered 469

Data Sharing 470
Equality of Sacrifice 470
Secure Union Leadership 471
Timing of Concessionary Bargaining 471
Quid Pro Quos 472
Concessionary Bargaining in the Future 474
Negotiating Over the Closure, Sale, or Relocation of a Facility 475
Union Bargaining Waivers 475
Explicit Waivers 475
Failure to Request Bargaining 476
Duty to Bargain Over Work or Facility Relocation 476
Scope of Bargaining Obligation 478
Effects Bargaining 478
Decision Bargaining 478
The Prudent Course 479
Union Bargaining Leverage 480
Economic Action 480
Public Relations 480
Litigation 480
The Timing of Negotiations 481
The Precedential Effect of Agreement 481
Negotiating Joint Union-Management Programs 482
Distinction From Concessionary Bargaining 482
Types of Joint Programs 483
Benefits and Burdens to Management 484
Benefits 484
Burdens 485
Union Perspective 486
Bargaining Strategies and Tactics 487
Separation From Other Negotiations 487
Equal Access to All Information 488
Trial Period 488
Top and Mid-Level Management Support 488
Joint Programs and Traditional Contract Negotiations Not Mutually Exclusive 489

Appendixes

1. Summary of Labor Contract Provisions 493
2. Labor Cost Recap 498
3. Review of the Development of a Clause 500
4. Negotiations Preparation Checklist 501
5. Strike Contingency Checklist 513

6. Sample Memorandum of Agreement 523

7. Labor Contract Checklist 526

Notes **539**

Index **549**

List of Exhibits

2–1. Chronology of Wage and Benefit Changes 64
2–2. Distribution of Bargaining Unit Employees by Wage Brackets 67
2–3. Distribution of Bargaining Unit Employees by Age and Years of Service 68
2–4. Wage Rate Comparison 72
2–5. Employee Benefits Comparison 73
2–6. Summary of Recent Contract Settlements 76
2–7. Grievance Analysis and Arbitration Summary 80
2–8. Labor Agreement Survey—Supervisor's Evaluation 81
2–9. Funeral Leave Clauses 83
2–10. Sample Reopening Letter 90
2–11. FMCS Form F-7 91
3–1. Tentative Bargaining Schedule 106
3–2. MTU Negotiations—Opening Proposal—Article 9—Seniority 113
4–1. Sample Nonwaiver Confirming Letter 130
5–1. Spokesperson's Personal Notes of Negotiations 161
5–2. Worksheet on Union Proposal 170
5–3. Worksheet on Union Agenda 171
10–1. Labor Cost Recap Form 302
10–2. Settlement Summary and Package Cost Estimate ... 313
11–1. Insertion of New Provisions in a Contract 331

List of Tables

10–1. Alternative Wage Offers Under Different Cost Analyses 319
12–1. Strike Settlement Package and Associated Costs Utilizing Bonus 363
13–1. Sample Strike Cost Estimate 387

Preface

This book is intended for a variety of persons who have some responsibility for, or interest in, the employer's side of labor contract negotiations. First, it is designed to guide management's spokesperson or chief negotiator, whose duty it is to represent management at the bargaining table. Second, it is intended to assist the labor relations professional, line management executive, sole entrepreneur, or public agency administrator who may not be a direct participant but is responsible nevertheless for seeing to it that there is a successful outcome from labor contract negotiations. Third, the book is meant to assist students and observers of the collective bargaining process to better understand the procedures, strategy, and tactics which management utilizes to successfully negotiate a labor agreement. While this volume was not originally intended for union negotiators, I have been told by a number of union spokespersons since the initial publication in 1984 that they have read it and have found it of value. In fact, certain passages from this book have been quoted to me by my union counterparts in negotiations. Readers are indeed welcome from either side of the bargaining table.

One of the great difficulties in writing a book such as this is that there is no such thing as a "typical" or "normal" labor contract negotiation. A negotiation for a bargaining unit of ten employees may be settled in a single three-hour meeting between one management negotiator and one union business agent, consummated with a shake of hands, and concluded with nothing more than a promise to send a confirming memorandum of agreement. This is in contast to a negotiation covering thousands of employees in a single-employer–multi-plant or multi-employer bargaining unit which may require months of meetings, bargaining committees composed of dozens of persons, regular press releases, and final contract documents numbering in the hundreds of pages.

Likewise, negotiations in manufacturing industries are somewhat different from those in transportation and service industries, and there is a considerable difference between public employer and private employer collective bargaining. Despite these variations, however, there is sufficient similarity among these various negotiating situations for one volume to be useful to practitioners or students regardless of the size and nature of the bargaining unit or the nature of the employer's enterprise.

Persons who have had experience in other types of negotiations involving such matters as sales contracts, real estate transactions, or litigation settlements may feel that such a background qualifies them to negotiate a labor contract. While such experience is certainly helpful, it would be a serious mistake to conclude that methods and techniques which are successful in other types of bargaining will have direct applicability to contract negotiations with labor unions. Significant differences exist between labor contract negotiations and other types of bargaining.

Unlike a typical sales contract negotiation which is often a one-time event, the relationship between a union and management normally continues over many years. Memories of union negotiators are long. More importantly, the ability of a sales contract negotiator to cease negotiations with a buyer or seller and do business with another buyer or seller is virtually nonexistent in the labor relations arena. Except for very limited situations (e.g., when a union is decertified), the law requires that an employer continue to deal with the union which represents its employees regardless of the degree of difficulty it experiences in reaching an agreement with that union. Other differences exist as well. Labor laws regulate many aspects of bargaining. Parties to a real estate negotiation, for example, are not told by an agency of the state or federal government how they may or may not conduct their negotiations (although it may control what they can agree upon).

Labor negotiations also require a thorough knowledge of work practices within the employer's workplace and within the industry in which the employer competes. The negotiator must also have an understanding of the meaning and effect of typical labor contract clauses as they affect the day-to-day activities in the employer's workplace. The application of the clauses will have evolved through custom and tradition in that industry, past practices in the employer's workplace, as well as decisions of labor arbitrators, the NLRB, and the courts.

Another major difference between labor contract negotiations and other types of bargaining is the relative permanence of language in a labor contract. Unlike commercial contracts or other types of contracts where unduly burdensome provisions can frequently be renegotiated, labor contract clauses covering hours of work, seniority, union security, work jurisdiction, etc., normally remain unchanged from one contract to another. Major changes in these provisions sought by either party usually are attainable only at the risk of a work stoppage.

Because of the variety of contexts within which labor contract negotiations take place, I have made certain assumptions to limit the scope of matters covered to manageable proportions. The first of these assumptions is that employers and the union or unions with which they deal are subject to the National Labor Relations Act (NLRA), sometimes referred to as the "Taft-Hartley Act," as amended. This, of course, is not always the case. Although the NLRA covers the vast majority of employers in manufacturing and service industries, it does not cover airline and railroad employers (who are covered by the Railway Labor Act) or most employers in agriculture or the public sector. However, where federal or state statutes regulate collective bargaining in industries not covered by the NLRA, such statutes have generally been patterned after the NLRA, and therefore have many features in common with the basic labor law in the United States.

A further assumption throughout most of the book is that the negotiations in which management is involved deal with renegotiation of an existing labor contract, rather than with bargaining over terms of a first contract between union and management. Particular attention, however, is given in Chapter 13, "Special Bargaining Situations," to the peculiarities of negotiating a first contract.

Also, it is assumed that the common objective of the negotiating parties is to reach an agreement. This may not be the case, for example, when a resisting employer who has lost a representation election is simply negotiating with a newly certified union with the objective of reaching an impasse in order to fulfill a legal bargaining obligation. If the reader is representing such an employer, this is the wrong book to consult for assistance. The guidance provided in this volume is intended to assist management in reaching an agreement, not in avoiding it.

Much has been written and said about adversarial versus cooperative labor negotiations or, as the academicians would say, "distributive" and "zero-sum" bargaining versus "win-win" negotiations. Stated another way, "do we negotiate over how we will split the pie or how we together will make the pie larger?" This book focuses primarily on process rather than philosophy, and aside from portions of Chapter 18 under subsections on concessionary bargaining and joint union-management programs, little attention is given to a distinct management philosophy on labor contact negotiations. To foreclose the reader's speculation, however, the author believes there is ample room for a range of philosophies and styles of negotiating in most union-management relationships. Not only can the parties work together in a cooperative spirit to make the pie larger, they almost necessarily will have to agree on how the pie (smaller, larger or the same) is to be divided. Negotiating over how to split the pie may be termed "adversarial," but it certainly need not be "hostile." Both parties can be winners even though they may take contrary positions. A more in-depth discussion of union-management and labor negotiating philosophies must be reserved for other treatises, since the negotiation process itself requires all of the pages, and probably more, that are contained within the covers of this book.

It has always struck me that effective labor negotiators are essentially pragmatists with a "hands-on" orientation, and are not particularly given to reflecting upon the process in which they are engaged. A review of available literature about the techniques of labor contract negotiations confirms this impression. My search for books on the subject turned up few titles published within the last 30 years. It was this discovery plus my own fascination and love of the negotiating process which prompted me to write this book.

The process of free collective bargaining as practiced throughout the United States has proven to be a most effective and durable means for employers and unions to set the terms and conditions of employment. Although strikes do occur, the amount of work time lost in the United States due to strikes is extremely small. Differences between unions and management which appear to be completely irreconcilable have a way of being resolved, in the vast majority of cases, in the give-and-take of collective bargaining. It is an amazing and wonderful process to witness and in which to participate.

I hope this volume not only helps the reader make the process work to the reader's advantage but also conveys that sense of amazement and wonder which I have always felt for this subject.

C. S. L.

Seattle, Washington
June, 1992

Acknowledgments

Those who contributed to making this book possible are many.

The laborious task of typing the manuscript with its multiple drafts was performed diligently and cheerfully by my secretaries, Ms. Linda Farris (First Edition) and Ms. Marilyn McGovern (Second Edition changes).

I am deeply indebted to Mr. Lew Scott, a labor attorney in Portland, Oregon with the firm of Lane, Powell, Spears and Lubersky. Lew reviewed and made useful suggestions for Chapters 4 and 11. Messrs. Tom Persely and Paul Gilbert, consulting actuaries with the Seattle Office of William Mercer reviewed and critiqued Chapters 8 and 9 respectively. Their thoughtful ideas were extremely valuable. Notwithstanding the input of Messrs. Scott, Persely, and Gilbert, the author takes full responsibility for any errors and omissions in those chapters.

Lastly, my wife Jo deserves a long and deep bow for her patience, cooperation, and moral support. The lost weekends, diverted vacations, and other inconveniences are part of the price she paid to make this book a reality.

Part I

Before Bargaining Begins

1

General Assessment of Negotiations

Negotiation of a labor contract is an event which usually has a significant impact on the employer whose contract is being negotiated. Because of the potential impact on the employer's customers, suppliers, employees, and the public at large as well as on management and the union, the persons responsible for negotiations have an obligation to thoroughly assess all factors which can influence and be influenced by the negotiations. This assessment process is designed to assist management in properly selecting its bargaining representatives, making adequate preparations, designing a workable bargaining strategy (including realistic economic parameters), and successfully carrying out a bargaining plan. Unfortunately, many employers enter into negotiations with little more advance preparation than if they were negotiating a contract for next year's office supplies. The results of such negotiations usually reflect that lack of preparation.

The assessment process, covered in this chapter, should include a review of previous labor negotiations for the same bargaining unit and an evaluation of the results achieved; consideration of the options available for structuring the unit within which bargaining is to take place; an assessment of the economic climate which is apt to prevail when bargaining begins; an estimate of the relative bargaining leverage possessed by both parties; and a review of the political, institutional, and attitudinal factors which may influence the negotiating parties. The results of this assessment will naturally lead to the production of data and information and to other necessary preparations for the bargaining process. This preparatory stage is covered in Chapter 2. The next step, development of a bargaining strategy, is discussed in Chapter 3.

When to Begin

Planning for negotiations should begin as early as possible, but not so early that relevant conditions are apt to change significantly before negotiations commence. Some employers begin preparations for the next negotiation as soon as the ink is dry on the contract. However, with multiyear contracts, such advance preparation is seldom necessary. For a complex major negotiation of a large corporation, 12 to 18 months of preparation may be necessary. For a simple negotiation involving a single nonpattern-setting unit, four to six months may be sufficient. As a general rule, preparation and planning should normally begin no less than three to six months in advance of the commencement of bargaining, which means that it will be about six to eight months before the contract expiration date. For example, if a contract is set to expire on November 1, and it is anticipated that bargaining will begin on September 15, general assessment and other preparations should generally begin sometime before June 1. If the negotiation is a particularly critical one, more time may be necessary. If the contract to be renegotiated is for a small bargaining unit and no particular difficulties are anticipated, preparations beginning 30 to 60 days in advance may be adequate.

Of course, if the negotiation is for a first contract, the period of time available for advance assessment and planning will be considerably less than what would be considered optimal, since first contracts frequently follow an NLRB election and certification. A bargaining duty is imposed by the certification, and less time will be available before bargaining must begin than if the negotiation was for a renewal of an existing contract.

Responsibility for General Assessment

Organizational structure normally dictates who has the primary responsibility for assessing and planning for negotiations. In corporations or other large organizations, managers specializing in labor and industrial relations normally have such strategic planning responsibilities as part of their portfolio. In smaller organizations these tasks are usually carried out, if at all, by the organization's president or general manager, a line manager, or a personnel administrator. Irrespective of the organization's size and sophistication, the person having primary labor negotiation planning responsibilities should obtain input from, and coordinate with, key managers in other functional areas of the organization. A labor relations specialist who attempts to make an assessment of, and prepare for, labor negotiations without the advice and counsel of the production, sales, and accounting specialists is likely to negotiate a contract that will not truly meet the needs of the organization, and that will be subject to the Monday morning quarterbacking that frequently follows a labor contract negotiation.

The difficulties of assigning planning responsibilities are somewhat complicated when the chief spokesperson in negotiations comes from outside the organization. A labor lawyer, consultant, or association representative can hardly be expected to know the detailed aspects of the employer's business unless he or she has been representing the employer for a considerable period of time. On the other hand, the outside negotiator can assist management in focusing attention on the key aspects of a good bargaining plan and leave to management the essential decisions posed by such a plan. The outside negotiator will want to have a "successful" negotiation, which can often be translated as a crisis-free negotiation. Consequently, he may be reluctant to set negotiating objectives that involve risks. The author is acquainted with a Midwestern labor relations lawyer who represented a number of major corporations. The lawyer would meet with the management of each corporate client prior to negotiations to review the draft agenda of contract changes that would favor management, and after discussing each item on the agenda, would ask the employer's representatives if they were willing to take a strike over each particular item. When the answers were in the negative (and they usually were), the lawyer would persuade them to remove the item from the agenda. In this way the lawyer was able to reduce management's agenda to nothing or to a few inconsequential proposals, which helped to assure a low-risk, "successful" negotiation. However, by making the negotiations a low-risk venture from the spokesperson's standpoint, the employer's potential for achieving favorable bargaining tradeoffs is proportionately reduced. The key here, as in any successful bargaining strategy, is to strike a proper balance between risk and reward.

There is nothing wrong with management's spokesperson, whether an insider or an outsider, taking the lead in assessment and planning. In fact, in most aspects of the plan, he or she is (or should be) the one most qualified to evaluate the pros and cons of a particular course of action. However, the final decision on key aspects of the negotiations, especially on the economic objectives or parameters of the settlement, should be left to the person who has ultimate decision-making authority for such matters in the organization. That person should be the same one who will make the decision whether or not to take a strike if a settlement cannot be reached within the parameters set. This discussion presumes that the top decision maker (e.g., chief executive officer, division vice-president, plant manager) is not the chief spokesperson in negotiations. This presumption is based upon common practice. It is also based on the author's strong feeling that it is bad negotiating policy to have the final decision maker conduct, or even participate directly in, the negotiations. The reasons for this firmly held belief are outlined in detail in Chapter 2 under "The Executive as Negotiator."

Analyzing Previous Negotiations

Unless the negotiation is for a first contract, the formal parties (i.e., employer and union) who are going to be represented at the bargaining table have been there before, although the actual participants may be different. As in almost any other endeavor, much can be learned from previous experience and from history. This is particularly true in labor contract negotiations. Managements and unions have a tendency to (1) follow a particular style of negotiating; (2) react similarly to certain kinds of appeals, pressures, or situations; and (3) be influenced by previous successes and failures. Consequently, much can be learned by looking back and analyzing what happened and why.

In general, the most relevant negotiations to review and analyze will be the most recent. However, there may have been special circumstances such as different participants or other factors which differentiate even the most recent negotiation from the one now at hand. It will probably be useful to go back to at least two or three previous negotiations, which may easily cover a period of 5 to 10 years. Review and analysis will be greatly facilitated if negotiation evaluations and critiques were prepared at the conclusion of previous negotiations as is recommended in Chapter 14. If that has not been done, it will be necessary to rely on available files and the memories of those in management who participated.

Established Objectives Compared to Negotiation Results

The bottom line in any negotiation from management's point of view is whether it met its objectives. This assumes that objectives were established and stated in sufficient detail that an evaluation of performance against those objectives can be made. If objectives were set and not met, it might be concluded that the objectives were not realistic in the first place. This is, in itself, instructive since the setting of unrealistic objectives may lead to as many problems as poor execution.

The review should include pertinent questions, such as "Why was the ultimate settlement X percent higher than the predetermined limit?"; "What necessitated the granting of a cost-of-living clause despite a firm objective to avoid it?"; "How were we able to avoid a strike despite the fact that most of our major competitors were struck?" These are questions which may have been raised during or after the previous negotiations, but if answered, did not have the perspective of time or the benefit of calmer reflection. The key question in this review is "What, if anything, would we do differently if we were in the same situation again?" Evaluation of performance against objectives also should be viewed within the context of the economic environment in which the negotiations took place, the relative bargaining leverage of the negotiating parties, the union's internal political situation at the time, and other relevant factors.

Pattern of Negotiations

Institutions, like people, are creatures of habit. Unions and managements both have a tendency to follow patterns in negotiating style. Consequently, a review of bargaining styles in previous negotiations will be helpful in predicting what can be expected in the forthcoming negotiations. By reviewing the union's opening agenda for the last two or three negotiations, it should be possible to predict at least half of the union's demands which will appear on its bargaining agenda. The number of meetings held in past negotiations before a settlement was reached should give a good clue as to the kind of timetable the next negotiation will follow. Similarly, the number of offers and counteroffers, strike threats posed, typical communications to rank and file, and other patterns are likely to emerge.

This is not to say that historic patterns do not or should not change. New personalities, changing economic conditions, and other variables will cause new negotiating patterns to emerge. Change may in fact be desirable. For example, if management has traditionally allowed itself to be forced into dusk-to-dawn meetings at the eleventh hour to achieve costly settlements, this tradition needs to be changed. Too often, however, management does not review or evaluate previous contract negotiations and consequently cannot appreciate the significance of these traditional patterns or styles of bargaining, how they have influenced the outcome of previous negotiations, or how they might affect forthcoming negotiations.

The types of patterns that should be reviewed include the following:

1. How far in advance of contract expiration date was
   a. the beginning of negotiations?
   b. the first package offer?
   c. the settlement reached?
   d. the ratification vote?
2. Who was the union's spokesperson? Who were other members on the negotiating committee?
3. Was any discernible bargaining strategy followed by the union? If so, what was that strategy?
4. Which constituencies within the union was the leadership attempting to satisfy? Have the union's previous power blocs stayed the same or changed? If they have changed, in what way?
5. What were the key issues in the negotiations? How were they resolved?
6. Were "private" or off-the-record meetings used to facilitate a settlement? If so, how many were held, who requested them, who attended, and what were their results?
7. Was a mediator or third party utilized? If so, did the individual facilitate or inhibit reaching agreement? Was management disadvantaged by the use of a mediator? When did

the mediator enter negotiations? Was this too early, too late, or about the right time?

8. Was information about the negotiations provided to the news media? If so, in what form, by whom, to whom, with what frequency, and with what result?
9. What type, and in what form, has the union made counter-proposals and counteroffers? Written or oral? Realistic or unrealistic?
10. How has the union communicated its "must items"? Has it been directly across the bargaining table, through the media, through counterproposals, by "signals," through private meetings, or by some other means?

By considering these and other factors, management is better able to plan for negotiations and avoid pitfalls which may have hampered previous negotiations.

Key Personalities in Previous Negotiations

While much that emerges from a labor contract negotiation is a result of the interaction of economic forces and the leverage which such forces provide to the respective negotiating parties, it is also true that the persons who conduct the negotiations and the persons who make key bargaining decisions have a great influence on the outcome. In evaluating the results of previous negotiations, attention should be focused on the personalities of the negotiators and their bargaining styles which might have influenced the outcome of negotiations. Also, the chemistry between the union and management negotiators is important. This is evident when one observes a meeting between two seasoned negotiators who have sat across the bargaining table for years, and have learned each other's bargaining styles, "hot buttons," and personalities.

Changes in negotiators and thus in negotiating styles can often have a disruptive effect on the bargaining process. For example, in 1959 the basic steel industry introduced a new management spokesman, R. Conrad Cooper, to replace John Stephens, who had headed the steel industry's bargaining team for some years prior to that time. The Steelworkers' longtime president, David J. McDonald, was not comfortable with the new face, and in his autobiography described some of the factors which later were to cause friction and ultimately contribute to impasse resulting in a lengthy strike:

> In this strained atmosphere, R. Conrad Cooper—the new chairman of the Steel Industry Coordinating Committee—called me early in April, 1959, and asked for a private meeting. This was a normal procedure. John Stephens and I used to meet privately in advance of negotiations to provide one another some idea of the procedures that would be followed in the open meetings. But Cooper instead introduced a new style. He handed me a letter from his committee which I tore open and read in front of him. It called, among other things, for a wage and benefit freeze and the liquidation of the cost-of-living adjustment program in the existing agreements. As I read I could feel the heat creep up my neck, and it came to a boil when Cooper told me the letter had already been released to the newspapers.
>
> . . . From the beginning [in the negotiating meetings] there was none of the horseplay, wisecracks or inside jokes that had always lightened other negotiations and made them bearable. The steel industry members were cold, grim and aloof, and, naturally, after a day or so of this treatment, our team picked up the same attitudes.[1]

The 1959 steel negotiations resulted in a strike involving virtually the entire U.S. steel industry, lasting for more than 4½ months. While it cannot be said that the new and rather hostile relationship between the chief union and management negotiators was the principal cause of that strike, it is difficult to believe that their strained relationship was not at least a contributing factor in that long work stoppage.

In considering the results of previous negotiations, therefore, one must take into account the persons who negotiated those contracts, their personal characteristics, objectives, weaknesses, strengths, and most of all, the chemistry between union and management representatives. The result of these considerations may very well affect management's selection of a spokesperson in the next negotiation. If nothing else, it should help management take advantage of previous successes and avoid the pitfalls of previous failures.

Key Issues

Just as the results of previous negotiations can, in some cases, be traced to the chemistry between the bargainers, so too can the results of a particular negotiation be heavily influenced by one or two key issues. Frequently, an issue, which

---

Note: Endnotes are located at the end of this book.

typically involves a matter of principle, is presented by one side or another and focuses the attention, emotions, and determination of both sides. In such situations, underlying economic interests, clear communication, and good will are often cast aside, and the "burning issues" take precedence. Such issues often precipitate a strike. Even when they do not, the final outcome of the negotiations is apt to be strongly influenced by their presence.

Some years ago the author represented the management of a plant in labor negotiations in which one of the union's major proposals was to prohibit the employer from taking disciplinary action against employees for refusing to perform work which they felt was unsafe. This same issue had been proposed by the union in several prior negotiations, but had always been successfully resisted without great difficulty. However, in the course of the negotiations an employee received an electrical shock while working in a deactivated chamber of an electrostatic precipitator, the safety of which the union's safety committee had previously questioned. Upon investigating the incident, management determined that the shock was caused by harmless static electricity and did not endanger the employee in any way. Nevertheless, it was obvious to the union's bargaining committee, as it was to management, that some problem existed in the chamber and that some action needed to be taken. Unfortunately, the effect of the incident was to focus the union negotiators' attentions on their proposal to permit employees to refuse to perform alleged unsafe work. Management was, of course, concerned that if such a clause were incorporated into the labor contract, employees could refuse to work based ostensibly on safety reasons, when they actually were motivated by other reasons not so legitimate.

As negotiations proceeded, the issue took on an importance far beyond what was merited by the incident of the employee who received the shock or even the proposed contract change itself. The union accused management of being insensitive to the safety of its employees and of endangering their lives, while management felt that the union was attempting to capitalize on an unfortunate incident to usurp management's traditional rights to direct the work of its employees. A strike over the issue was looming.

How that issue was resolved is perhaps less important for present purposes than the understanding of how one sensitive issue can create havoc and influence the outcome of negotiations. However, the result itself provides a useful illustration of how to defuse such a potentially explosive situation. Management directed the union's attention to the particular piece of equipment involved and away from the contract language proposed. A representative of the manufacturer of the defective equipment involved was quickly flown to the plant. He inspected the equipment, determining that faulty wiring existed and that the lockout procedures being used were not foolproof. He then held meetings with management and union safety committees to explain what would be done to correct the problems. Corrective action was taken, and the union's proposed contract language on safety was subsequently withdrawn.

Numerous other examples could be cited of negotiations where one or two explosive issues dominated an entire negotiation. For assessment and planning purposes, if such volatile issues existed in previous negotiations, they should be reviewed with an eye to determine (1) what their impact was on the course of the previous negotiation(s), (2) how they could have been avoided or minimized, (3) whether those same issues or similar issues may be present in the forthcoming negotiations, and (4) whether any other potential issues in the forthcoming negotiations are likely to have a significant impact on the outcome of bargaining.

Hits, Runs, and Errors

No review and analysis of prior negotiations is complete without an in-depth look at what was successful about the negotiations and what mistakes were made. While a critique immediately following negotiations is always recommended, the benefit of two or three years of hindsight can be especially beneficial for assessment purposes. Experience gained during the term of the negotiated contract provides added perspective which could not have been included in the postnegotiation critique.

What factors should be considered in this box-score analysis? For openers, was management's agenda appropriate in terms of what was sought and what was achieved? Were adequate preparations made? If not, what else should have been available? Was the timing of the negotiations advantageous? Could an agreement have been reached at less cost? If so, what could have been avoided and how? Was any language added to, or deleted from, the contract which has proved to be troublesome? Why were the changes agreed to by management, and how can the same mistakes be avoided this time? Were incorrect "signals" given to the union bargainers or the rank and file which hurt management's position?

The list of questions is limited only by the scope of the negotiations themselves. Frequently, this type of analysis can be rather painful in that it requires the negotiators to question their own judgment and skill. It is much easier, but not necessarily more accurate, if the previous negotiations were conducted by persons other than the ones performing the current review and analysis. The essential point here is that one should learn from one's own and others' mistakes and successes.

Units for Bargaining

In a majority of contract negotiations, management will not have an opportunity to alter the unit within which bargaining will take place. For example, no choice is possible in the case of a single employer operating a single facility with only one certified bargaining agent in a geographical area where no other employers have comparable facilities. In such a situation a single-plant unit is the only choice.

Where, however, the employer has several comparable facilities organized by the same union, or a number of other employers in the same general geographical area have comparable facilities, the employer may have an option to select a single-plant unit, a multiplant unit or a multiemployer-multiplant unit. The considerations underlying the choice of a bargaining unit are numerous and are not subject to any type of exact evaluation. What is required are very subjective judgments about the advantages and disadvantages of various bargaining arrangements.

Employers subject to the National Labor Relations Act who have employees that are represented by a labor union are obligated to bargain with the authorized union within the framework of an "appropriate bargaining unit." These are words of legal art and have been the subject of thousands of National Labor Relations Board (NLRB) and court decisions. Without attempting the impossible task of summarizing the results of those cases, it is sufficient for our purposes to say that, in general, the appropriate unit for bargaining purposes meets at least one of the following criteria:

1. The unit is the one certified as appropriate by the NLRB.
2. The unit is the one the employer and union have historically recognized.
3. The unit is the one the employer and union agree to recognize as the appropriate bargaining unit.

More often than not, the legally sufficient bargaining unit will have been determined by the NLRB prior to a certification election or through historical custom well prior to the commencement of bargaining. Management, therefore, is usually not faced with the decision as to what constitutes the *legally determined* appropriate bargaining unit.[2] The key question for assessment and planning purposes is whether or not there is any other appropriate unit within which the bargaining may be conducted which will be more advantageous to management. Stated another way, by agreement with the union(s) and perhaps other employers, can another bargaining arrangement be established which would be superior from management's standpoint to the legally established unit? What are the options available, and what are their advantages and disadvantages?

In this chapter there are numerous references to "plant(s)" and "facility(ies)." The former typically refers to manufacturing whereas the latter normally connotes a service or administrative function. However, the terms are used in this chapter interchangeably with no intent to draw a distinction for bargaining purposes.

The Single-Employer–Single-Facility Unit

The simplest and most common type of negotiating unit is the single-plant or single-facility unit. In making bargaining unit determinations, the National Labor Relations Board presumes that the single facility is the most appropriate unit. This presumption can be rebutted in cases involving multiple facilities of one employer by evidence of bargaining history in another form, interchange of employees from one of the employer's facilities to another, commonality of management among various facilities, similarity of terms and conditions of employment, and other factors. Nevertheless, the presumption applied by the

NLRB denotes a legal preference which makes the single-facility unit the standard negotiating unit.

Evaluating the Single-Facility Unit

The advantages of the single-facility unit appear, on the surface, to be fairly obvious. However, on closer examination, most are two-edged swords, depending upon the facts in each case. The single-facility unit can be the simplest in that it will involve the smallest number of employees, require the negotiators to deal with problems of only one facility, and permit them to deal with economic and working condition issues of a single facility in one geographical area. The advantage of simplicity is lost, however, if an employer has, for example, 20 separate facilities and must conduct 20 separate negotiations. Far and away the principal advantage of single-facility negotiations to such an employer is the minimizing of the damage which can result from a strike caused by an impasse in negotiations at any one facility. In the single-facility negotiation an employer with many facilities has not "put all its eggs in one basket." This advantage is particularly applicable where there is (1) diversity of employee interests and distinct bargaining priorities at the various facilities, (2) poor coordination and support among the local unions involved, (3) differences in contract expiration dates among the facilities, and (4) an absence in the respective labor agreements of contractual rights to observe picket lines established by sister unions. Where one or more of these factors is absent, the advantage of single-facility bargaining diminishes.

The Proper Economic Fit

The single-facility negotiation also allows the bargainers to fit the economic package to the economics of that plant or facility and the products or services produced or rendered therefrom, and to competitive labor costs in that geographical area. A national multiplant bargaining unit stretching from North to South and East to West cannot, for internal union political reasons, usually recognize the labor market cost differentials which exist among those areas. Traditional nationwide bargaining in the automobile, steel, aluminum, rubber, and other heavy industries has caused plants of national employers in these industries in relatively low labor cost areas to become uncompetitive in relation to their independent competitors and employers in other industries in those areas. It may be argued that, no matter what the form of bargaining, major companies such as those in the automobile industry would be forced to pay more or less similar wages and benefits to their employees regardless of whether the employees worked in Michigan or in Texas. It is probably not possible to prove either case beyond question, but it can hardly be disputed that the existence of national multiplant bargaining in the automobile industry and certain other industries has made it virtually impossible to negotiate different labor cost packages based upon regional differences.

The author has had personal experience with a comparable situation in which the employer had a multiplant unit consisting of seven plants in three separate states. While all seven plants were in the same general industry, they manufactured three separate categories of products. Each of the products had different labor/capital ratios, profit levels, and product and labor markets. Notwithstanding such differences, management for many years negotiated the same wage and benefit package for all plants. As a result, several of the seven plants were not competitive with other employers' plants which manufactured the same product. It was only after management finally split up the sole seven-plant unit into seven single-plant units that different settlements could be negotiated which were economically appropriate for the particular plants, locations, and products involved. The error in the traditional arrangement was not so much that there was a single multiplant unit, but that management permitted plants manufacturing different products with different economic factors to be grouped into the same unit for bargaining purposes. This situation was somewhat analogous to one which exists in the automobile industry. Although General Motors assembly plants compete in the passenger car industry with a limited number of domestic and imported models, its subassembly, parts, and accessory plants compete with hundreds and perhaps thousands of independent manufacturers which together constitute an industry very different from that of automobile assembly. Multiplant negotiations which include assembly as well as parts manufacturing plants do not adequately recognize the differences in these industries.

Work Practice Issues

Single-facility negotiations permit the negotiators to address day-to-day working conditions issues (frequently called "local" or "work practice" issues) in greater detail, and allow them to do so in the same negotiation framework in which pure economic issues are bargained. In single-employer–multiplant negotiations or multiemployer negotiations, such issues are typically negotiated in separate meetings which usually occur before or after bargaining on basic wages and benefits. The merging of economic bargaining and working conditions bargaining can be a distinct advantage to management, especially when management is proposing major changes in working conditions. By integrating the bargaining of working conditions with bargaining on economics, management can stress the importance of productivity and efficiency improvements as a condition for settlement, and use wage and benefit improvements as a tradeoff for changes it desires in working conditions. This result is extremely difficult to accomplish in multiplant or multiemployer bargaining since (1) the same working condition improvements are not often applicable to different plants or different companies, and (2) the separation of bargaining levels between economics bargained at the main table and working conditions bargained in another forum or at another time (frequently called "two-level bargaining") precludes the type of *quid pro quo* bargaining necessary for achieving management-proposed changes.

The picture is somewhat less clear when it is the union which is proposing major changes in working conditions. While single-facility negotiations give the union a better opportunity to focus management's attention on such local issues, the union is placed in a position of asking for improvements in wages and benefits as well as in working conditions at the same time. The union may find that it must spend too much bargaining capital on working conditions, thus sacrificing economic gains, or vice versa.

In multiplant or multiemployer bargaining the union is sometimes handicapped in having working conditions issues sufficiently recognized as being important, since economic issues traditionally predominate in such negotiations. In multiemployer bargaining, local issues frequently are "washed out" or forgotten. Nevertheless, if the bargaining format permits, the union may be able to exert considerable pressure on the employer in a multiplant or multiemployer bargaining arrangement by refusing to conclude a settlement until all important local issues are resolved. The classic example of this is the automobile industry's dual-level bargaining which allows the local unions to strike individual plants over local issues after a settlement has been reached on major contract terms on a national level.

The Single-Employer–Multifacility Unit

An employer operating two or more facilities in which the employees are represented by the same union may face the question of whether bargaining is best conducted on a single-facility or multiple-facility basis. The choice does not exist where the sole unit determined by the NLRB to be appropriate is a multifacility unit. However, where single facilities have been determined to be appropriate or the question is in doubt, an important decision needs to be made.

Evaluating Multifacility Units

Many of the advantages and disadvantages of multifacility bargaining were discussed previously in the section on single-facility units. However, some additional considerations need to be mentioned. The multifacility unit makes the most sense from an employer's standpoint where (1) the products or services performed at each facility and the markets for these products or services are identical or nearly identical; (2) management at each facility reports to the same executive; (3) all facilities are located within the same general geographical area; (4) management seeks to establish uniform wages, hours, and working conditions at all facilities; or (5) a disruptive labor relations environment exists at a minority of the facilities involved and that disruptive group is apt to be out-voted by employees in the facilities where the labor relations environment is more favorable.

One of the main advantages of the single-employer–multiplant unit is the prevention of "whip-sawing," the device by which different local unions attempt to achieve better settlement terms than a sister local union by applying strike pressure. This phenomenon frequently appears where single-facility strikes can exert considerable pressure on the employer, or more commonly where the union at a single facility can picket the facilities represented by its sister unions and can count on having such picketing honored. In these cases, the employer is usually at the mercy of each local union and faces a veritable Chinese water torture with each separate negotiation. It is under such circumstances that putting all the eggs in one basket may be the recommended course of action for the employer.

The acceptance of a multiplant unit also can often prevent employees from changing or eliminating their bargaining agent. If the employees wish to decertify their union and/or have another union certified to represent them, they may not be able to have an NLRB election held solely for their plant because the appropriate bargaining unit for election purposes may have been converted to the multiplant unit. This can be a favorable or unfavorable situation from the employer's point of view, depending upon the union involved and the employer's experience with that union.

The multiplant unit can be disadvantageous in that it limits, if not precludes, an employer from "farming out" work from a struck plant to one of its plants that is not on strike. This disadvantage is less serious when one considers that the striking union can easily follow the struck work and picket the plant which is accepting work from the struck plant.

Before agreeing with a union to establish a multiplant unit for bargaining purposes, employers should carefully evaluate their individual situations. Such units have often proven in retrospect to be disadvantageous to employers.

Multiemployer Bargaining

The concept of employers joining together to negotiate a labor agreement is a longstanding one, and this practice has, in many industries, constituted the principal form of bargaining. In the trucking, coal, retail merchandising and construction industries, to name but a few, multiemployer bargaining has been the predominant form of bargaining for many years. It has been particularly popular in service industries for employers in the same geographical area. For example, multiemployer bargaining has been frequently used in the hotel and food service, retail sales, and warehouse and distribution industries in many cities throughout the United States. In a survey of this subject conducted by the U.S. Bureau of Labor Statistics, it was reported that 40 percent of major collective bargaining agreements in the United States were multiemployer agreements.[3]

Evaluating Multiemployer Bargaining

Notwithstanding such popularity, multiemployer bargaining has begun to show signs of diminished importance in recent years, and the decades of the eighties and nineties have brought a growing disenchantment on the part of employers with this form of bargaining. The reasons for the decline vary with the industry and geographical area involved, but some common rationales are present.

Diverse Economic Factors

A major reason for the decline would appear to be the recognition by an increasing number of employers that economic and other labor contract terms which are acceptable to a group of employees in a particular industry are not necessarily appropriate to others in the same industry. Differences in age and type of equipment, customers, market segments, business financing, and other critical elements of an employer's enterprise can place different employers in distinctly different economic situations where a common labor contract settlement is not appropriate for all. And although it may be difficult, even in single-unit bargaining, for one employer to negotiate a settlement significantly different from settlements negotiated by other employers in that same industry, multiemployer bargaining precludes any possibility of doing so.

Lack of Control

An additional disadvantage of multiemployer bargaining which may explain its loss of popularity is the lack of control by any single employer over key management decision making in the bargaining. As with any collective endeavor, the will of each individual person or entity must yield to the will of the majority. In most multiemployer groups, whether they be formal employer associations or merely informal employer groups established solely for the purpose of labor negotiations, no one employer normally determines management's position in negotiations. In the give-and-take of the employers' caucuses, positions emerge which represent the collective desires of the participating employers. Some of these collective positions may be very unpalatable to individual employers. This lack of control has been a traditional feature of this form of bargaining, but it has become more of a problem due to U.S. Supreme Court and lower federal court decisions which have made it virtually impossible for an employer to withdraw from a multiemployer group at any stage of bargaining until a final agreement is obtained, even though impasse has been reached and a strike commenced.[4] These cases have caused individual employers to closely examine their decision to join other employers in collective bargaining, for once they have begun to bargain as part of a multiemployer group, they are "on for the full ride."

Handling Work Rule Issues

Another factor that may explain the diminishing role of multiemployer bargaining is the growing desire of employers to remove inefficient work rules and practices and eliminate restrictive working condition clauses from labor agreements. This is often impossible, or at least extremely difficult, to accomplish in multiemployer bargaining. It is quite common in multiemployer bargaining units for the collective unit to negotiate basic wage and benefit terms, but for individual employers to negotiate their own working condition agreements with the respective local unions that represent their employees. The individual employers often have individual labor agreements or individual supplements to the master agreement which spell out such working conditions as job selection and assignments, hours of work, scheduling, crew sizes, shop practices, and other day-to-day matters. When this is the case, a separate negotiation is usually conducted by each individual employer with the union, or its local union either before, during, or following the master multiemployer negotiations. In a few cases, individual employer issues may be negotiated as part of the main-table bargaining, but working condition issues which are important to one employer are not commonly significant to others. An employer wishing to obtain union concessions on a particular working condition issue or group of issues may find that its position has little in common with the position of its fellow employers, and thus it cannot realistically expect the multiemployer bargaining group to utilize any significant degree of its bargaining leverage to obtain the necessary concession(s) for that employer. In fact, the difficulty of dealing with working condition issues, whether these involve employer-proposed or union-proposed changes, has been one of the traditional stumbling blocks to the formation or continued existence of multiemployer bargaining units. The difficulty, however, became more pronounced for employers in the period of the 1980s due to the increased desire for union concessions and the need to remove inefficiencies created or perpetuated by the labor contract.

Deciding on a Multiemployer Unit

It would be misleading and inaccurate, however, to suggest that multiemployer bargaining is disappearing as a significant form of bargaining in the United States, or that it does not have important advantages to many employers. For example, the small employer in a highly competitive industry cannot often afford the type of economic pressure and strike exposure that can be exerted by a powerful union when bargaining with that employer on an individual basis. In such situations, the union might very well be able to extract higher wages and/or benefits from the individual employer due to the disparate bargaining power. The small employer may be unable or unwilling to take a strike while its eager competitors capture its share of the market. Similarly, the small employer may lack the necessary data and bargaining know-how to conduct effective labor negotiations.

The decision, therefore, whether to join, or maintain participation in, a multiemployer bargaining unit is one that requires careful consideration of a number of questions by the individual employer. Such questions should include the following:

1. *History.* How long has this particular multiemployer group been in existence? Has the composition of the group changed significantly in recent years? If so, why? What is the track record of the unit's bargaining in terms of strikes, reasonable or unreasonable settlements, preservation or sacrifice of management's rights, etc.? Is the future likely to follow the past, or are there likely to be significantly different conditions which will cause changes? What has been the experi-

ence of those employers who have remained outside the unit and negotiated separately?

2. *Composition.* Does the group include most of the major competitors in the industry (and in the area)? If not, why not? Is the lack of substantial representation of the industry a crucial factor? Is your business, product, service, customer base, and/or organization similar to most or all of the other members of the unit? Are the organizations now in the group apt to remain members until negotiations begin? Do the other members of the group have labor relations philosophies and objectives similar to your organization's? If not, how significant are the differences?
3. *Decision Making.* What is the process by which decisions for the multiemployer group are made? If voting is formal, how are votes allocated (e.g., number of facilities represented, number of employees, one vote per employer)? Do some employers control the vote of other employers? Have some employers in the past voted as a block? Have one or more employers dominated decision making in the past? If so, how have, or would have, those decisions affected your organization? What influence is your company likely to have on key bargaining decisions?
4. *Leadership and Expertise.* Who speaks for the multiemployer group and how effective is that individual? How much experience does the spokesman have, and what have been the results of that person's previous negotiations? Who is on the employer's negotiating committee and how is that representation determined? What staff support is available to the negotiators? Could your organization field a better negotiator in your own bargaining than the unit?
5. *Leverage.* Is the multiemployer unit in a good bargaining position (i.e., what is the likelihood that the union will strike the unit), and if so, how vulnerable are the members to a strike? What agreement exists among the members as to the response if the union strikes less than all member employers? How is that agreement to be enforced? Has the union engaged in selective strikes in the past, and if so, what was the result? Can you be sure that you can live up to the multiemployer agreement concerning selective strikes? Would your organization be more likely or less likely to be struck if you negotiated outside the multiemployer unit? If you were to be struck, could you better withstand a strike as a member of the unit or not? What is the likelihood that if you remain outside the unit, the union will attempt to force you to negotiate a higher settlement than the unit? What is the likelihood of obtaining a business advantage by remaining outside the unit if some or all of the members of the unit are struck?

While the above list of considerations is lengthy, it is not exhaustive. Moreover, it does not attempt to place any weights of importance on the respective questions. In reality, an affirmative or negative answer to one or two key questions may be decisive.

If the employer has a realistic option of selecting or negotiating the unit within which it will bargain, that decision is likely to be the single most important decision for management to make during the period prior to bargaining. No employer should be so satisfied with its previous labor contract negotiations that it neglects to consider carefully the unit within which it will bargain. That decision, whether made consciously or by default, will influence every other step taken throughout the negotiations.

Multiple-Union Situations

While not strictly a bargaining unit option, a topic related closely thereto is that of the single-facility–multiple-union situation. In these situations, each union typically represents a separate bargaining unit and negotiates a separate collective bargaining agreement for that unit. Each agreement will normally spell out the jurisdictional limits of the unit covered by the contract. Pity the poor employer who must deal with two or more unions representing different classifications of employees in a single facility! The problems are not unlike those of parents whose children complain that they are not getting treated fairly with respect to their siblings: each child has his own view of equality, and, to compound the problem, in the real world complete equality is seldom, if ever, possible. However, unless the various unions involved merge or employees in the various units vote to certify the same union as their bargaining agent, management must deal with each union in a way which will minimize the employer's strike exposure, and at the same time achieve reasonable economic settlements which maintain the apparent contractual and economic relationships between the employer and the respective bargaining units. In so doing, several considerations are paramount.

Contract Dates

One of the key factors influencing the employer's ability to cope with the multiple-union situation is the schedule of labor contract expiration dates. If the dates are the same, or within reasonable proximity of each other (e.g., within a range of 30 to 45 days in the same year), problems are usually minimized because the negotiations can be handled in sequence during roughly the same period of time. Where, however, the expiration dates are many months or years apart, the employer is unnecessarily exposed to strikes. Furthermore, determining and achieving economic parity among the various unions becomes more difficult. Consequently, if such differences do exist, a prime negotiating objective should be to renegotiate contract expiration dates to get them on the same cycle. If this is not feasible, strong efforts should be made to negotiate tight no-strike clauses which will preclude union members, during the term of the agreements, from honoring picket lines established by the other respective union(s).

The Bell Cow

Where multiple unions represent employees in one facility, it is common for one of the unions to be the lead, pattern-setting or "bell cow" unit. In a manufacturing plant, it is often the union which represents employees in the production department(s) that takes the lead. Once a settlement is reached with that union, the settlement is typically used as a model by the other unions at that facility. However, problems arise where the wage or benefit structures in the existing contracts differ to the extent that uniform contract modifications do not yield uniform results. For example, in an operation with two unions, if one unit is comprised of higher-skilled, higher-paid employees than the other unit, (even though both units may have the same base rate and perhaps the same top rate), a general wage increase in percentage terms will benefit the members of the union with the more skilled workers. Although the same percentage applies to both units, application of that percentage to existing wage rates yields greater wage increases to one than the other.

Such problems can usually be overcome through the use of advance planning to anticipate the impact on all groups and by attempting to maintain a balanced approach over a period of time. To resolve the problem cited in the preceding paragraph, for example, a percentage wage increase can be given in one year of a multiple-year contract and a flat or "across-the-board" increase can be given the next year.

Another problem arises when one of the cows in the herd decides that it is tired of following and seeks to become the bell cow. This amounts to political warfare between the competing unions with the employer caught in the middle. Nothing definitive can be said which will generally apply to such situations. However, it is essential that management keep itself apprised of internal union politics so that such a development can be anticipated. Furthermore, management must keep in close communication with the leaders of the respective unions, and attempt to head off a direct confrontation. In some cases it may be necessary to engage in nearly simultaneous negotiations so that as a final settlement emerges, it is not obvious which negotiation or which union set the pattern.

Joint Negotiations

In some cases employers have been successful, in multiple-union situations, at having all unions sit at the same bargaining table and work toward a uniform settlement. But given the nature of human beings and the politics of the union movement, it is extremely difficult to set up such a bargaining arrangement.

Some years ago the author participated in a single-plant negotiation in the South in which two unions had "joint representation" for one bargaining unit. The employer had agreed to recognize two separate international unions to represent one production and maintenance unit, with each international representing different departments! To make matters worse, one of the international unions had two local unions so that skilled maintenance employees could have their own local union. Each of the two international unions, and each of the three local unions, had their own representatives at the bargaining table. One labor agreement covered the entire plant. Needless to say, the negotiation was a nightmare. The task of achieving relative equality was like trying to level an uneven table top by sequentially shaving off portions of its legs; by the time the table is level, it is too short to be of any use. Based upon that experience and several other multiunion situations, this author has never valued joint negotiations, although it is possible that some unions and managements have developed a sufficiently mature and cooperative relationship within that framework so that this form of negotiation could serve their purposes.

Overall Strategy

In planning for the multiple-union negotiation, management must never take any of the unions for granted by assuming that they will follow the lead union again as they have in the past. Each objective for the negotiations and each possible settlement package with the lead union must be evaluated as to its impact on, and reception by, the other union(s) at that facility. It does not serve management's purpose to achieve a settlement with the lead union to avoid a strike, only to have the same package rejected by one of the other unions at the same facility which may have the power to cause a work stoppage of the entire facility. While it may involve some risks, greater risks might be avoided by having informal or "private" meetings with leaders of the follower union(s) prior to concluding a settlement with the lead union. This is particularly appropriate where the follower union has, in the past, exhibited independence and struck over a settlement offer which was equivalent to that negotiated with the lead union.

Just as damaging to management's position is the granting of "add-ons" to a follower union which were not granted to the lead union. The pressure to do this is often great where a major facility may face a strike over a concession sought by a follower union (but not previously given to the lead union) that involves minimal cost due to the small size of the follower bargaining unit. Once management capitulates to such pressure, however, the lead union is likely, thereafter, to avoid any settlement which does not contain a "most-favored-nation" or other similar clause which assures that it will receive the same additional wages or benefits that may be granted to the follower union. In addition, management loses credibility with the lead union if previously it had made the lead union what was termed its "best and final offer."

In planning for negotiations with two or more unions, management needs to examine the language of its proposals to each union, particularly the lead union, and determine whether it is necessary to "translate" such language into other wording which will be used for the follower unions. Differences in existing contract language in separate contracts can cause the same new proposal to have a different meaning when incorporated into the existing contracts. Consequently, management must keep all bargaining units and all contracts in mind as it is negotiating each one.

To the same extent, when any decisions are made, when proposals or counterproposals are considered, when risks are evaluated, or when any other negotiating action is contemplated, management must ask itself: "What effect will this have on our negotiations with the other union(s)?" While this will not solve all the woes that beset the employer unfortunate enough to be saddled with multiple unions, it may make the misery a little easier to bear.

As will be discussed in later chapters, management must also keep in mind the impact of any given negotiating concession on the employer's salaried work force. This group has no elected representatives to protect its interests, and a management that treats its unionized work force more favorably (for comparable job groups) is asking for trouble. The impact of negotiated wages, benefits, and working conditions on the salaried work forces cannot be ignored.

Economic Climate for Bargaining

As managers look ahead to their next contract negotiation, it is not possible for them to forecast exactly what the economic picture will be at the time the negotiations begin. Nevertheless, a preliminary forecast can be made and subsequently refined as the commencement of bargaining approaches. At the general assessment stage of preparations, what is more important than the exactness of the data is the overall estimate of the general economic climate which is apt to prevail when negotiations are to take place. Although most employers, and most unions for that matter, intuitively consider the economic climate in which they are bargaining, it is usually helpful to consider economic indicators in a somewhat more systematic fashion than is normally done. Certain economic indicia bear particular attention. Among these are the following:

1. *Rate of Unemployment.* Attention should be given not only to the national rate of unemployment but also to the rate in the geographical area in which the bargaining will be con-

ducted. Likewise, the trend should be examined. Is it increasing or decreasing, and how fast has it been rising or falling? Although exact statistics may not be available, some gauges of unemployment in the appropriate industry and in the appropriate geographical area should be consulted. If the overall rate of unemployment in the United States is 6 percent, but in the construction industry the figure is 12 percent in the relevant geographical area, you as a construction employer would want to take that factor particularly into consideration.

2. *Rate of Inflation.* While this statistic is often a misleading indicator as to the rise in prices experienced by a particular work force in a particular facility or group of facilities, it has a very significant psychological impact on most persons. Because of wide publicity given to the Bureau of Labor Statistics' monthly release of Consumer Price Index (CPI) data, union officials and a large percentage of rank and file workers are aware of the current rate of inflation. When it is rising, it raises expectations, and when the rate falls, it tends to moderate, if not lower, expectations. Of course, where cost-of-living adjustment clauses (COLAs) have been in effect, CPI increases have already caused wages to increase. Where no COLAs have been in effect, sharp rises in the CPI build up pressures to negotiate significant wage increases.
3. *Industry Data.* Each industry or activity has certain bellwether statistics it uses to measure the state of economic health of that industry. In the automobile industry it is monthly or annual new car sales. In construction and building products it is housing starts. In the steel industry it is tons produced, and in the newspaper industry it is lines of advertising. Managements and unions in these industries keep a watchful eye on the key data and are careful to note trends. In addition, such factors as inventory levels, new equipment purchases, raw material supplies, airline load factors, government contract awards, and production backlogs are thermometers of the present and barometers of the future economic climate in a particular industry or a particular organization. Reduced to their simplest significance, they reflect the extent to which an employer can afford a particular level of settlement and the extent to which it can or cannot afford to take a strike.

Recent Comparable Settlements

Regardless of the apparent climate in which bargaining will take place, the best predictors of the relative bargaining leverage positions of union and management are the levels of recent settlements made by comparable employers and unions in the appropriate industry or line of activity. Even if "pattern bargaining" is not an established tradition in a particular industry, settlements made by one or more significant employers in an industry are bound to have an impact on other employers in that same industry.

Management should not be misled, however, into believing that it is somehow forced to accept a level of settlement simply because other employers have been willing to, or forced to, accept that level. Different competitive conditions, diverse geographical areas of operations, existing levels of wages and benefits in separate bargaining units, disparate working conditions, or other variables may provide ample rationale for distinguishing the earlier settlements. Similarly, the passage of time and changing economic conditions since the other settlements were negotiated may warrant a different result. Moreover, it may be that the other comparable settlements were simply "bad deals" negotiated by unwise, weak, or intimidated employers. Whatever the reason, other recent settlements in one's industry do not necessarily circumscribe one's own settlement.

But just as it would be erroneous to feel bound by comparable settlements, it would be foolhardy to believe that such settlements have no impact on one's own bargaining picture. Unquestionably they do, if for no other reason than that they reflect the expectations of the union leadership and the rank and file. As the saying goes, "If they can afford it, why can't you?"

Consequently, it is absolutely essential that management accumulate as much information as possible about comparable industry settlements, including preexisting wage/benefit levels, in order to accurately plan for the forthcoming negotiation. Such information is frequently available through employer associations in an industry or geographical area, through private reporting services such as The Bureau of National Affairs, Inc. (BNA), and through government agencies such as the Department of Labor's Bureau of Labor Statistics. Also, direct contact with other employers in one's industry and/or geographical area is an excellent source of information, particularly because frequently a published or authorized statement of a labor contract settlement is not exhaustive as to what was agreed on. Frequently, sidebar agreements, letters of intent, or oral understandings are important ingredients of the settlement which supplement or alter the basic agreements reached. Such information is usually only available from the operative management negotiator, and sometimes not even then.

Once comparable settlements are known, it remains to evaluate their impact upon your negotiation. Has pattern bargaining become an accepted way of life in your industry and/or your area? If not, to what extent have earlier settlements influenced later settlements? Are there different industry segments or other differentiating factors which justify variations from one settlement to another? Are the negotiations on which you are about to embark apt to establish a pattern or set a new direction for other negotiations and if so, how will that affect the results? These and other questions need to be raised at an early stage of the general assessment process.

Bargaining Leverage

The bottom line in any negotiation, whether it be for the sale of a house, a peace treaty between nations, or renewal of a labor agreement, is "bargaining leverage." Bargaining leverage can be gauged by *the relative willingness of each side to incur the consequences of not reaching an agreement.*

The owner of a house who wishes to sell it but would be able and willing to live in it for another year, or who has a number of other prospective buyers, has a rather high tolerance for the failure to reach agreement with a particular prospective buyer. In more common terms, he is not an "anxious seller." Consequently, he has bargaining power. Leverage in a particular negotiation cannot, however, be evaluated solely in terms of the bargaining power of the seller. The conditions faced by the buyer are equally important. If a potential homebuyer is renting a house and his lease is about to expire and/or if there are not many other suitable homes on the market, the buyer may not be willing to incur the consequences of not reaching an agreement with the seller (i.e., sleeping in the street). He is an anxious buyer and therefore has little bargaining power. Under these circumstances, it is clear that the seller has a bargaining advantage over the buyer; i.e., he has "bargaining leverage." This simple and very obvious concept is intuitively understood by virtually all persons regardless of culture or sophistication. Simple bartering between primitive people demonstrates this fact.

What complicates this simple concept and makes the bargaining process interesting is a situation where the bargaining power of the negotiating parties is relatively evenly balanced, and the bargaining power of each party is not well known or well understood by the other party. Returning to the example of the house sale, if the seller has purchased another house and needs to obtain the equity from his old house in order to make the down payment on the new house, and if he does not have any other prospective buyers, his bargaining power has diminished considerably. The negotiation is now on more equal terms. If the seller then does not know that the buyer is about to lose his lease, but the buyer knows that the seller has purchased another house, the buyer has a negotiating advantage. While the buyer may allow his precarious lease situation to influence his offer, he does not have to contend with additional seller resistance which could result from the seller's knowledge of the buyer's plight. In other words, it is not only objective conditions which influence a particular bargain. Leverage is also a function of the parties' perceptions of those conditions.

The basic concept of bargaining leverage applies as much to labor contract negotiations as it does to the sale of a house, except that in labor contract negotiations the conditions faced by the opposite party are usually better known. At least the *opportunity* to know the bargaining power of the other side is usually more available, and it is a foolish employer or union that does not investigate and evaluate the various factors which will influence its own bargaining power and the bargaining power of the other side in order to arrive at an assessment of the relative bargaining leverage possessed by each party.

Most labor contract negotiations in the United States are settled each year without strikes, and most employers and unions have ongoing peaceful collective bargaining relationships. Nevertheless, underlying all negotiations is the economic leverage possessed by each respective party. This leverage ultimately is controlled by the factors discussed in the next sections, that deal with strike pressure and resistance. Discussion of these factors is not included to suggest that an employer must always risk a work stoppage in order to achieve a satisfactory settlement, but merely to indicate that bargaining results between two skilled negotiators are ultimately controlled by bargaining leverage, and that work stoppages are simply the normal means by which that leverage is exerted.

Employer Bargaining Power

By and large an employer's bargaining power is determined by its *ability and willingness* to take and resist a strike. Concurrent with this is the employer's willingness to implement, on a unilateral basis, its last offer to the union, i.e., put its offer into effect without union agreement. Although a union may exert pressure in other ways (e.g., product boycotts, political pressure, or public pressure), for the most part an economic strike is the principal weapon a union has to force an employer to accede to its demands. In certain limited situations, an employer may, as a defensive tactic, lockout its employees. However, an employer's normal means of resisting union demands is to successfully take a strike and/or unilaterally implement its final contract offer. Therefore, in order to evaluate its own bargaining power, management needs to consider each of the factors that will prevent or mitigate damage it is likely to suffer as a result of a strike.

Employer's Financial Condition

In a worst-case analysis, the employer may not be able to operate any struck facilities during the strike, make deliveries from inventories, farm out work to other facilities, or rely on strike insurance or mutual assistance benefits. In such cases, the employer must rely upon its own financial resources to withstand the pressure of the strike. How adequate are these resources? An employer planning for a forthcoming negotiation should develop a best-case–worst-case analysis along the lines of the examples shown in Chapter 13, "Strike Preparation, Decision Making, and Management," in order to gauge its ability to withstand a strike. For example, what will the effect of the strike be on cash flow due to the loss of income? Will borrowing be necessary? Is there a possibility that debt repayment obligations will not be met? Is the strike apt to have a significant effect on the market value of the employer's stock, and if so, to what extent? These kinds of questions must be asked at the outset since they may have a vital effect upon the employer's bargaining power.

Anticipated Demand for Product(s) or Service(s)

The ability of an employer to withstand strike pressure depends, to a large degree, on the market for its products or services at the time a strike might occur. For example, an employer who anticipates that its sales or level of operations are going to drop sharply in the quarter in which the labor contract is due to expire may not be as reluctant to take a strike as it would otherwise be, especially if the anticipated sales or operations decline is apt to require the temporary shutdown of several facilities. Conversely, if the market is growing fast and/or prices are increasing, a strike will be more costly and therefore less palatable to the employer. Stated simply, good markets weaken management's position at the bargaining table and poor markets strengthen it.

Notwithstanding this factor, employers are often reluctant to take strikes even in relatively poor markets because they are afraid of losing market share. The concern is that once a customer uses a competitor's product and/or service the customer may grow to prefer it over the struck employer's product or service, and when the strike is over, the customer may not return. Similarly, an employer that is subject to, and periodically engaged in, strikes may be viewed by customers as an unreliable supplier. For this reason, an employer's bargaining power is greatly enhanced if the supply of the employer's products or services to customers can be maintained during a strike.

Ability to Supply or Service Customers

To the extent that most employers provide a product or a service to a customer, the ability, or lack thereof, to continue providing it is a pivotal issue in determining the employer's bargaining power. Continuity of supply and service to customers is essential not only because it maintains the income stream so necessary to the viability of a business but also because of its effect on long-term customer retention. Customers lost to competition during a strike may not return for a long time, if at all. This factor may not be so great in an industry or activity where there is little competition. If the local telephone service ceases due to a strike, the telephone company has little concern that its customers will be permanently lost. Similarly, an employer which is in the middle of a contract with the U.S. Air Force to build a fleet of bombers need not be too concerned that it will lose its contract due to a strike. These situations are, however, relatively rare in the

U.S. economy. Consequently, the ability to continue to supply the customer is usually vital. This may be done in a number of ways.

Product or Service Inventory

It may be possible for the manufacturer of a commodity or standardized product to build up large inventories prior to a contract expiration date so that customers can be supplied from these inventories during a potential work stoppage. In fact, industries such as the steel, automobile, and rubber industries have done so for many years. However, this technique is not possible in many industries that supply products or services which cannot be inventoried. For example, the airline or live entertainment industries essentially suffer an irretrievable loss unless the strike is industrywide. In these cases, the service must be supplied or performed within a specific time period. Once that period is past, the business is lost forever. A struck airline that is shut down from December 20 to the end of the year is going to lose its heavy Christmas traffic to its competitors, and it will never regain that revenue. Similarly, when a theatrical production run is cut short for a week due to a stagehands' strike, it is not possible to recapture a large portion of those audiences that went that week to see another play, a concert, or a film. Similar inability to inventory occurs in those businesses with a perishable product or service. A tomato crop that does not get picked in the two- to three-week harvest season cannot be recouped. A printing company that is to print the programs for the Super Bowl will not be able to make up the loss of business caused by a strike beginning two days before the print runs are to begin, and ending after Super Bowl Sunday.

This means that the employer must carefully examine its potential ability to inventory its product or service. It may mean that the product to be inventoried may not have all the individual customer special features normally incorporated into the general product but may still be acceptable. The customer may be asked to forego customized features or it may be necessary for the features to be added by the customer or a subcontractor. It may require the employer to innovate or take risks in order to salvage the business. For example, a tomato harvest may be accelerated to avoid a contract expiration, or a theatrical production may open in a different city to avoid a potential stagehand strike. The employer must be inventive and flexible enough to consider new ways of doing business.

Of course, even where building of inventories of a standardized product is possible, it may be difficult to deliver the product due to picketing of production facilities and warehouses. Careful planning here, however, can usually overcome such obstacles. Techniques such as use of remote and unidentified warehouses, carrying the inventories in the customer's warehouse, and transportation by nonunion and highly secure means of transportation can be used to overcome union efforts to disrupt supplies to customers.

Farming Out/Contracting

If an operation is shut down due to a strike, it is often possible to farm out the struck work to another facility of the same employer or contract to a different employer. In such cases, the product or service normally bears the name of the struck employer so as to retain product identification and the relationship with the customer. When this is done, however, the facility which performs the struck work is subject to picketing and a possible work stoppage itself. In most cases, the struck employer's other facility is subject to picketing, regardless of whether it accepts struck work or not, because a union can normally legally picket a struck employer "wherever it can find him."[5] Under normal conditions, a union cannot picket a different employer since this would constitute a secondary boycott (secondary picketing) which is in violation of Section 8(b)(4)D of the National Labor Relations Act. One exception to this rule is the so-called "ally doctrine," whereby a secondary employer assists or becomes an ally of a struck employer by accepting work from that employer which would otherwise be performed by members of the striking union (i.e., "struck work"). Where this occurs, a union may legally picket the employer performing the struck work.[6]

Notwithstanding such picketing risks, farming out or contracting struck work is frequently and successfully done. Many times the union is not aware that the work has been farmed out or contracted, especially when the facility performing the work is far away from the struck facility or where the diversion of operations has begun well in advance of the strike. Also, where the product does not carry a distinctive brand identification (e.g., commodity paper products, bulk chemicals, petroleum), identifying the producer of struck work may be very difficult.

If the struck employer has other facilities which can provide the same or a substitute product or service, those facilities may be utilized to maintain continuity of production, deliveries, and/or services. This avenue becomes a particularly useful technique if the other facilities are nonunion, since the vulnerability to picketing is usually minimal. The capability to farm out struck work to another facility of the struck employer or to contract the work to another employer, greatly enhances the bargaining power of any employer. As with the defensive maneuver of building inventories, the technique of farming and contracting out requires management to be innovative and wiling to take risks.

Operating Struck Facilities

Another means of maintaining the flow of products and/or services to customers is operation of the struck facility with persons hired permanently or temporarily to replace the striking employees or use of salaried employees, including supervisors, to perform the work. This defensive maneuver has a number of advantages over farming out, although it has its disadvantages. It enables the employer to provide essentially the same product and/or service which it normally supplies to the customer. It also permits, at least in the case of a manufacturing facility, the utilization of plant and equipment which would otherwise be idle. It has a significant psychological impact on striking employees and union officials, demonstrating that they are not inflicting significant economic damage on the employer. It also demonstrates that other persons can perform, and are performing, the striking employees' jobs and may (at least in the case of permanent replacements) continue to do so following the strike.

Operating struck facilities is not without its problems. The difficulties of locating and training persons sufficiently skilled to operate the facility may be enormous. Invariably there is hostility and the potential for violence when replacements are hired, especially when the replacements are permanent. These disadvantages are considerably less severe when salaried and/

or supervisory employees are used to operate the struck facility. Such employees usually have the necessary skills to take over from striking employees, and in some cases they are more productive than the striking employees they replace.[7] Having a sufficient number of salaried and/or supervisory employees may, however, be a serious problem, and newly hired replacements may be required.

For many years, managements such as those of the former Bell Telephone System and in the petroleum industry have relied upon salaried and supervisory personnel to replace striking employees. The bargaining power it has given them is reflected in the relatively reasonable level of settlements over the years. Many other industries have not attempted to utilize this device, either out of a belief that it was not operationally feasible or because they were concerned that it would have deleterious effects upon the long-term labor-management relationship. Both concerns are often misplaced. There are many types of manufacturing, processing, and service industries which can be operated with salaried and supervisory personnel—even if at lower than normal levels of operation. As for the effect on long-term labor-management relationships, employers who have operated struck facilities with salaried and supervisory personnel often find that they have gained added (though unexpressed) respect and credibility from union leadership as well as from the rank and file when the strike is terminated.

Whatever the pros and cons may be of operating a struck facility, there can be no question that the ability to do so significantly enhances the bargaining power of the employer. Its effect on bargaining leverage can be decisive.

Mutual Aid or Mutual Assistance Pacts

Another potential weapon in management's arsenal to defend against a strike is the "mutual aid (or mutual assistance) pact" (MAP). In reality, a MAP is simply a form of strike insurance with participating employers being the insureds, and, often, also the insurers. The most widely publicized use of a MAP was in the commercial airline industry, although it has also been used in the construction, newspaper, agriculture, railroad, and pulp and paper industries. Use of MAPs in the airline industry has been prohibited since 1979 as a result of the Airline Deregulation Act.[8]

A MAP is most appropriate where a number of companies in an industry bargain individually with one or several unions, and where the treat of a strike against one or a few employers is likely to result in more costly, or otherwise disadvantageous, settlements which other employers in that industry will be pressured to accept. Mutual assistance is also useful in multiemployer bargaining situations where the union has used selective strikes to force a break in the employers' unified position.

The manner in which MAPs are funded and the manner in which benefits are paid differs considerably from industry to industry. In the newspaper industry, premiums are paid on an annual basis for a specific level of benefits (i.e., a traditional insurance concept). In the airline industry the MAP did not have premium payments, but participating nonstruck carriers were obligated to provide payments to participating struck carriers according to a formula based upon the additional revenue received by the nonstruck carriers during the strike period. In the West Coast Pulp and Paper Industry, employers pledge to make payments to struck employers in an amount related to their normal production during a defined base period; the struck employer is entitled to receive payments based on the amount of production lost as a result of a strike, and no employer forfeits his MAP receipts if he operates his struck mill with replacements.

Virtually all MAPs have a waiting period before benefits are payable, with a common waiting period being one to three weeks. In most cases, benefits are not received until the strike is ended, and in some cases benefits are not paid until all employers have completed their negotiations during a common bargaining cycle.

While a MAP offers an employer some income protection during a strike period, it does not normally provide any relief from the problem of loss of customers, which is always a primary concern. In some industries, employers that form MAPs also cooperate with each other in other ways so that the struck employer may continue to service customers and thereby retain them when the strike ends. Challenges have been made to the legality of MAPs, but thus far they have been held to be permissible except where, as in the airline industry, they are specifically prohibited by law.[9] In addition, the NLRB has held that such plans are not a mandatory subject of bargaining.[10]

The existence of a MAP, or the potential for establishing one, is a key factor in assessing the employer's bargaining power. Moreover, union leaders' awareness of the existence of a MAP is an important ingredient in their estimate of bargaining leverage. For this reason, most employer groups that form MAPs inform the union(s) with which they negotiate of the existence of the MAP, if the matter is not already a subject of public information.

Union Bargaining Power

Just as the employer's bargaining power is determined by its ability and willingness to take and resist a strike, so too is the union's bargaining power based upon its ability and willingness to inflict economic pressure on the employer by stopping all work activity and by pursuing the strike until the union's goals are attained. Of course, one side's weakness is the other side's strength and vice versa. Therefore, to the extent the employer has a small or nonexistent inventory or a heavy demand for its product(s), is unable to operate during a strike, etc., the union's bargaining leverage is enhanced. However, other factors related solely to the resources of the union and its members will largely determine its bargaining power.

Recent Levels of Employment Hours and Earnings

Employees who have been working long hours and receiving overtime-enhanced checks can, other things being equal, usually afford to go without employment for a longer period of time than employees who have been on layoff and/or working short work weeks. This is especially true if those employees have been anticipating a strike and have begun personal savings programs to carry them through the strike.

Beyond the simple economics of this factor is the psychological effect on employees of threatened loss of work when they have been on layoff or reduced work schedules. In addition to recognizing their own need for work, they realize the demand for their employer's product or service is not strong, and therefore their work stoppage is not likely to inflict great harm on their employer. Conversely, where employees have been working overtime for days and weekends without time off, the respite from work offered by a strike may be very appealing. Consequently, the levels of hours and earnings which have existed for the 3-month to 12-month period prior to a contract expiration, compared to normal conditions, will have a bearing on how willing a union and its members are to engage in a strike.

Strike Fund

Most unions maintain a strike fund to provide benefit payments to their members in the event of a strike. The sufficiency of that fund will affect a union's ability, and therefore its willingness, to strike and its ability to sustain the strike. It is sometimes difficult to obtain information about the assets of a strike fund, although some unions make this information known to their members and, therefore, this information can often be obtained by the employer. A review of the federally required "Labor Organization Annual Report (Form LM-2)" may reflect the order of magnitude of the union's strike fund. The LM-2 is a public record and is open to inspection at offices of the Labor-Management Services Administration located in major cities throughout the United States. Unfortunately, these forms are not always current.

Aside from the total value of the strike fund, it is also important to know the amount of weekly benefits payable under the union's strike fund. Some unions' strike benefits are so meager that they would provide little significant assistance to striking members and their families, while others provide meaningful help. By knowing the total value of the fund and the amount of the weekly benefit, the employer can make some rough estimates as to how many weeks the union can provide strike benefits.

Management cannot rely too heavily upon the adequacy of a strike fund or strike benefits as a measure of a union's potential strike endurance, however. Many unions embark upon a strike and continue the strike with little or no strike fund resources, and many unions and their members continue to strike long after their strike funds have been exhausted.

Availability of Government Subsidies

Often government unemployment and welfare benefits subsidize a union's strike. In a number of states, striking employees are eligible for unemployment compensation benefits after a strike has been in progress for a given length of time. In some other states, members of unions who become unemployed due to their observance of sister unions' picket lines are eligible for unemployment compensation. Under federal law, strikers are ineligible for food stamps, and this preclusion has been upheld by the U.S. Supreme Court.[11] An employer attempting to gauge the ability of a union to pursue a strike should become familiar with the laws and government agency practices affecting the eligibility of strikers for unemployment benefits and welfare benefits in the state(s) in which it operates.

Alternative Employment Opportunities

Just as an employer gains bargaining leverage when it has the ability to continue to operate during a strike, so too does a union gain leverage when its members are able to find other work during a strike. The ability of striking employees to match or even approach their prestrike incomes gives them little incentive to terminate a strike until their objectives have been met. The availability of alternative employment has been a particularly significant factor in negotiating with unions representing skilled trades people, especially those in the construction industry. In periods of heavy construction activity, building trades unions have enormous leverage since their striking members need only be referred to another project not involved in the strike or to another city where the strike is not in progress. The leverage factor is magnified because developers usually have high debt service payments to make while a strike is in progress. These considerations have led to the formation of "constructors (or construction users) councils" which attempt to coordinate construction activities in an area so as not to give striking construction workers undue alternative employment opportunities and to reduce pressure placed on contractors to settle unwisely in order to resume construction.

It is not just in the construction industry or other industries using skilled trades people that alternative employment opportunities are a factor. In geographical areas where there are low rates of unemployment, striking workers are often able to find substitute employment in unskilled jobs. In assessing a union's ability to sustain a strike, the prudent employer should examine the labor market demand conditions in the relevant area, as well as consider the types and numbers of skilled employees who will be involved in a possible strike relative to the labor market demand for such employees.

The Bargaining Leverage Equation

A review of factors listed in the preceding pages that determine management and union bargaining power will not yield a quantitative result that tells management the precise extent of its bargaining leverage. At best, these factors give some notion as to which party is likely to feel the greatest economic pressure once a strike begins. However, strikes are not simply disputes between organizations run by rational persons subject only to economic forces. They are usually a test of the wills of the leaders of each side as well as the stamina and determination of all participants and involve emotional, political, interpersonal, and other qualitative considerations. Management can only go so far in assessing its bargaining situation by evaluating the bargaining power equations. Economic leverage forms a backdrop, albeit a crucial backdrop, to the negotiating scenario. But a more complete and realistic assessment requires an examination of the political and institutional climate within which the bargaining will take place.

Institutional and Attitudinal Climate for Bargaining

Union Organization—Policies, Politics, and Personalities

Management should endeavor to know the union with which it is dealing as well as it knows itself. This requires a review of the traditions, personalities, sources of power, institutional characteristics, and other factors which cause the union to act as it has—and as it is likely to act in the future.

Consideration must be given to the personality and characteristics of the union's leader(s). What are the attitudes that affect that person's decisions? What has been his track record in previous negotiations? Has there been a willingness to compromise or not? Are there internal political pressures existing now or anticipated for the future that will affect his decisions? Are there other decision makers or sources of power within the union other than the ostensible leader(s), and if so, who are they? What is the relationship between the ostensible leader(s) and other decision makers, and how should management treat these respective persons relative to each other?

The union, as an organization, should be examined. Is bargaining authority vested in the international, local or regional union organization? What is the relationship between the various levels of the organization, and where does the real power lie with respect to negotiations and strike authority? What is the traditional posture of the union regarding union-management relations? Is it cooperative, hostile, or somewhere in between? Is that tradition continuing or are changes discernible? What is contained in the union's constitution and by-laws relative to collective bargaining, and does this present any problems or require special attention?

Beyond the pure structural aspects of the union, an examination of the union's political and bargaining needs should be made. What pressures are being placed on the union? What are the priority issues—higher wages, more job security, or retirement benefits? How recent was the last strike, and can the union rely on its members to strike this time? In general, the question "What does the Union want and need from these negotiations?" may be the most significant one management can ask. Having some notion of what makes the union, as an institution, and its leaders tick will be most helpful in answering that question.

Employee Perspective

The people on the other side of the bargaining table are union representatives, but the people they are legally obligated to represent are the employer's employees. While some unions are less responsive to their memberships than others, it is vital that management never forget that in the vast majority of negotiations the needs, feelings and demands of rank and file employees will, in the final analysis, be the determining factors in the bargaining posture taken by the union. Therefore, as negotiations are assessed, it becomes necessary to review the perspectives of employees.

Obviously the most thorough way of gaining insight into the perspectives of employees would be to talk to each one of them. This is seldom, if ever, practicable, and even if it were, employees might not be completely candid. There are, however, other ways of gauging the tenor of employee sentiment. A review of grievances filed during the contract term is one measure of the kinds of issues that concern employees. The quantity of grievances filed, the subjects of the grievances, as well as the identity of the grievants are significant. How many grievances were filed, and how many individual grievants were there? How many grievances were filed by the union, its officers, or shop stewards?

The occurrence of work stoppages, slowdowns, demonstrations, or any other concerted activity during the term of the last contract should be considered along with the issue(s) which precipitated the concerted action. If any such actions occurred, the extent of participation should be evaluated.

Measurement tools of good personnel and human resources administration should be utilized to gauge employee sentiment. Examination of rates of absenteeism, tardiness, and turnover can be indicative of employee satisfaction or dissatisfaction. Exit interviews with terminating employees can reveal much about the work atmosphere which would not likely come to light through any other means. Well constructed, carefully administered, and properly timed employee attitude surveys and focus groups can give clues as to specific problem areas and provide a picture of the overall level of employee satisfaction or dissatisfaction.

Attention should also be given to employees' perspectives toward the union. How strong is employee allegiance toward the union, as demonstrated by such indicators as attendance at union meetings and elections of officers? Caution must, however, be exercised here. Attendance at union meetings is not always a reliable gauge of union allegiance. Thus, other questions should also be considered. How many employees volunteer to run for union office? What has been the traditional attitude of rank and file employees toward the union, and has there been any change in that attitude in recent months or years? What comments are made by employees to supervisors about the union and/or its leaders? If dues payment is not required as a condition of employment (i.e., open shop), what percentage of employees pay union dues?

First-line supervisors are apt to be the best sources of information about employee sentiment. Management's failure to take advantage of their proximity to, and familiarity with, rank and file employees is a common mistake.

Management Perspective

The corollary to an examination of employees' attitudes and sentiments is an inward review by management of its own philosophies, policies, and *modus operandi*. These matters are usually taken for granted, and not examined. There is frequently a tacit acceptance of the status quo with regard to an employer's labor relations program, unless such program has been an abject failure. Regardless of how successful management believes it has been in the past, it needs to examine its own labor relations and employee relations philosophies and programs. No record is so outstanding that it cannot be improved.

Labor and Employee Relations

Management's initial inquiry should be directed toward the person or function responsible for union relations and collective bargaining. Is there clear identification of authority and responsibility? Is the person negotiating labor agreements responsible to those who have to administer such agreements? How is the negotiating function linked to the overall management function of the organization? Are the negotiators fully cognizant of line management's business objectives, current problems, and management style? Labor contract negotiations cannot effectively be carried out in a vacuum. Negotiating a labor agreement should aid, not hinder, line management.

The philosophy and attitude of top management regarding employee relations and unions is quite important in the general assessment of negotiations. Top management must be sufficiently consistent and steadfast to stand by a predetermined plan of action, but not so rigid as to reject change when the original plan is doomed to failure. Similarly, management should regard labor contract negotiations as a means of reaching agreement as to wages, hours, and working conditions with a union, not as an opportunity to engage in open warfare with an enemy.

Importance of Perceptions

The image which top management conveys to its employees, the union, and to supervisory and administrative personnel is perhaps as important as the reality of management's philosophy. If management is generally perceived to be weak, it will be difficult to achieve credibility at the bargaining table no matter how persuasive management's spokesperson is. Likewise, if management is regarded as insensitive or cavalier towards employees' interests, it will be difficult to persuade the union or its rank and file that a particular offer is fair. In looking at itself, therefore, management must consider not only how it sees itself, but how it is perceived to be by its employees and the union. Both will vitally affect its bargaining situation.

Comparison With Other Employers

One way to begin this difficult process is for management to compare itself with other employers with whom this same union negotiates. How do other employers—particularly those in the same industry—conduct their labor relations affairs by comparison in matters such as the following:

1. Line vs. staff relationships in labor relations and negotiation matters.
2. General attitude toward unions—are they partners, adversaries, necessary evils, enemies, etc.?
3. Frequency of work stoppages, volume of grievances, and other signs of discontent.
4. Frequency and type of communications to rank and file employees.
5. Type of language in labor agreements with regard to management-rights issues.
6. Image of firmness but fairness in labor-management relationships.
7. Effectiveness and skill of first-level supervision.

Ability to Change?

The process of self-examination will hopefully lead to a greater self-awareness and ideally a strengthening of management's bargaining capabilities. However, notwithstanding the weaknesses revealed by such soul-searching and comparative analysis, change will not always be possible. Some persons and organizations will not adapt regardless of the demonstrated need to do so. For example, a chief executive officer who has a habit of second-guessing his labor negotiator is not likely to change this habit. Similarly, management which has not been willing to take a strike over management-rights issues (as opposed to economic issues) is not likely to change its attitudes so long as key management personnel have not changed. These tendencies may simply have to be factored into the bargaining strategy and accommodated in some way. Nevertheless, by reviewing and evaluating its own labor-management characteristics, management can prepare itself to do a more effective job at the bargaining table.

Public and Governmental Perspective

Although there are normally only two parties to a labor contract negotiation—union and management—a third entity or interest is also frequently involved. That third party is the public affected by the negotiations and/or the community or communities in which the employees work. In a routine negotiation where no threat of a strike exists, or where the bargaining unit is small or not significant, the influence of this third party may be of little concern. Where, however, the employer provides an important public service or a vital consumer product, or employs a significant proportion of the residents of a given community, the negotiations will be influenced by public or consumer concerns as to the effect of the negotiations on the price and continued availability of the product or service or upon the economic welfare of the community in which the strike is taking place.

In many industries, especially those involving a public or quasipublic service, a negotiation which poses a threat of strike or lockout develops a great deal of public or community interest. This interest translates into concern as the strike threat becomes more of a reality, and frequently it is converted into pressure to settle once the strike or lockout occurs. This pressure comes from many sources, such as elected officials, news media, merchants in smaller communities, and citizens at large. Elected officials sometimes engage in "jawboning" or occasionally threaten adverse legislation to encourage one or both sides to compromise and settle. News media outlets can characterize a strike or lockout in such a way as to develop considerable sympathy or antagonism for one or both parties. Merchants in small communities can withhold or extend credit so as to effect the strikers' ability to hold out.

Management cannot afford to overlook the public or community perspective in any labor contract negotiations. The ability of the employer to afford a given settlement, the justification of employees in striking to achieve certain stated objectives, the inconvenience to customers or patrons of a struck employer are all subjects on which the public has, or will form, an opinion. That opinion can be influenced by many sources, including the employer. But whether or not the employer is able to influence public opinion, in a way favorable to it, opinions will be formed and acted upon and will often impact the negotiations.

Management must take time to assess public or community attitudes which bear upon the negotiations. A plan of communications may be developed to assist in the formation of favorable attitudes or it may be concluded that silence is the best policy. In any event, the old saw "The public be damned!" will not suffice.

Summary

Recommendations for analyzing previous negotiations, evaluating the relative bargaining power of the negotiating parties, and considering the institutional and attitudinal climate for bargaining do not, unfortunately, provide conclusive direction for structuring the negotiations, let alone predicting the outcome. At best, such activity provides management with a "feel" as to what type of negotiation to expect and provides some indication as to the type of preparations to make, the framework of a bargaining strategy, and some guidelines as to bargaining goals and economic parameters. Much more, however, needs to be done before negotiations begin.

2

Preparing for Bargaining

Having reviewed the "big picture" through the general assessment procedure outlined in Chapter 1, management now needs to address the more specific and pragmatic chores of getting ready to bargain. The first task is to decide who will speak for management at the bargaining table and what limits, if any, will be placed on his or her authority. Likewise, other members of the management negotiating team need to be selected. Much work will need to be done to gather, organize, and analyze data and information which will be necessary before and during negotiations. In addition, other preparatory steps should be taken, including briefing other management personnel, selecting a site for negotiations, and sending required reopening notices. Each of these steps in organization and preparation will be discussed in detail in this chapter.

Assembling Management's Bargaining Committee

A vital early step in preparing for negotiations is to select those persons who will represent management at the bargaining table (i.e., the spokesperson and those who will assist the spokesperson). For many employers, this selection may be unnecessary if they already have a specialized person or staff of people whose specific responsibility it is to negotiate labor contracts. For other employers, the answer may not be so automatic, and it is especially for these employers that this section has been included.

Selecting the Management Spokesperson

The question of who should speak for management at the bargaining table must be preceded by an inquiry as to what role is envisioned for the spokesperson. Is the individual to be simply a "mouthpiece" to express positions and arguments developed by others and to follow a negotiating game plan formulated by someone else? If so, the selection is not especially difficult. For that, forensic ability, a cool head, and moderate intelligence are about the only qualifications. If, however, the spokesperson is to be a true negotiator—in the sense that he or she is expected to plan the negotiations, develop bargaining strategy and tactics, draft contract proposals, and be a negotiator in every sense of the word—the selection task is considerably more formidable.

The latter is the more common type of spokesperson found at negotiating tables, although some employers still adhere to the belief that their back-room strategists can negotiate more effectively than the spokesperson at the table, and insist that their spokesperson merely "follow the script." For the purposes of this book, it will be assumed that the selection to be made is that of a full-fledged spokesperson who will truly be in charge of the management side of the negotiations.

Insider Versus Outsider

The initial selection issue to be confronted is whether the person should come from within the management organization or should be an outside "expert." No categorical answer is possible. The author has served in both roles and has found that each is valid depending upon the circumstances. The question is not so much whether the person should be from inside or outside the organization as whether he is qualified to do the job.

Perhaps the key ingredient most managements seek in a spokesperson is experience. As is the case with managers of baseball teams, it is often believed that having done the job many times before is more important than the previously achieved results. The rapid turnover of baseball team managers attests to the shallowness of such thinking. Nevertheless, experience is a most important qualification. There are few ways to learn how to conduct labor contract negotiations other than by watching others and actually doing it—except, perhaps, by reading this book. The choice, then, is often between an inexperienced insider and an experienced outsider. It is assumed that in having to make such a choice, management does not have a sufficiently experienced person in its own organization, or otherwise it would not have to look elsewhere. However, there are special situations where time constraints or internal "politics" preclude the use of an insider.

The advantages of the outsider are fairly obvious: experience which includes knowledge of bargaining techniques, traps, and union negotiators' techniques; ability to draft contract language; and a known track record. The outsider may also have considerable knowledge of industry operating and labor practices as well as of labor contracts of other employers in the same industry. The fact that use of an outsider will normally involve a significant cost to the employer is often offset by the fact that most contracts only need to be renegotiated once every two or three years. Of course, the size of the employer's unionized work force and the number of labor contracts the employer needs to have negotiated will heavily influence the decision whether to hire an outsider or use someone within the organization.

Even though he or she may lack experience, the negotiator from within the organization has several ostensible advantages over the outsider. These include familiarity with the organization and its products, services, personnel, and management style as well as a presumed higher level of loyalty to the employer. If a number of contracts need to be negotiated, out-of-pocket cost savings as well as continuity of management's position and consistency of contract terminology from one negotiation to another are additional advantages of using an insider. In addition, it is usually possible to achieve greater credibility and authority of management's position when the spokesperson is a member of management.

Sometimes management goes to an outside organization such as a law firm, labor relations consulting firm, or employer's association and is assigned someone who has little or no greater hands-on experience than a person within its own organization. Therefore, if management does decide to use an outside organization, it should determine the exact individual who will represent it. In all cases where the negotiator has not been used before, the extent of his or her previous experience should be ascertained, and inquiries should be made of other employers who have used the negotiator's services.

The final decision whether to select an outsider should be based on the type and complexity of the negotiations and on how seriously failure to reach a favorable agreement would affect the employer. If there is no clear settlement pattern expected to be followed, if the negotiations are for a large bargaining unit or several facilities, if there is a history of difficult negotiations or strikes, if the union is represented by a seasoned and effective negotiator, management may be prudent to retain a professional negotiator. If, however, none or a few of these conditions exist, an inexperienced negotiator may be perfectly adequate.

If an outsider is selected for his expertise and experience, management should nevertheless assign an inside management person to work alongside the expert, both to learn from the expert and to assure that management positions and philosophies are accurately articulated.

Lawyer Versus Nonlawyer

It is as easy to categorically recommend in favor of, or against, lawyers as negotiators as it is to make a recommendation for or against blue-eyed negotiators, tall or short negotiators, or many other nonrelevant categories of negotiators. Stated simply, some lawyers are excellent negotiators, some are simply terrible, and others are somewhere between these two extremes. While a majority of lawyers should be expected to be very proficient in drafting contract language, it is not essential that the management spokesperson draft language for the contract being negotiated. This chore can be delegated. What cannot be delegated are such requirements as the ability to persuade, to express management's positions clearly and thoughtfully, to plan and execute effective bargaining strategies to resolve stalemates, to control one's temper, and the many other qualities and skills which must be possessed by whoever assumes the role of spokesperson if the task is to be carried out successfully. These characteristics are discussed in some detail in Chapter 6.

In general, the use of a lawyer is more valuable in the negotiation of a first contract than perhaps at any other time. In the first contract, provisions under which management will have to operate for many years to come will be incorporated into a collective bargaining agreement. Changes in contract language in management's favor in subsequent negotiations will be hard-fought. Consequently, it is vital that the terms and language in the first contract be as favorable to management as possible.

Seldom will negotiation of a labor contract actually require the services of a lawyer at the bargaining table, as long as a lawyer is reasonably available for advice and consultation before and during negotiations. Notwithstanding, many employers do not feel comfortable without a lawyer as their spokesperson. Comfort levels aside, employers are best advised to select a person, lawyer or not, who has as many of the characteristics as possible that are listed in Chapter 6 under the heading "Traits and Characteristics of an Effective Management Spokesperson."

The Executive as Negotiator

Some employers feel that it is important that the chief executive or general manager of the organization be the spokesperson in labor negotiations. This is often the case with small employers where there are few managers and there is little or no staff. It is the author's strongly held belief that, regardless of the size of the organization, *the employer's chief decision maker should not sit at the bargaining table.* This is not to say that some management executives are not good negotiators or have not been successful at the bargaining table. But it does say that management places itself at a serious disadvantage by having its chief decision maker at the bargaining table.

"Unseen Authority"

There are several reasons to support this contention, the principal one being the loss of what might be called "unseen authority." This is a phenomenon known to brokers, automobile salespeople, and union negotiators. It is the deferral of final judgment regarding a specific negotiating point or the overall settlement of a negotiation to a third party or group. The broker has a principal who must be satisfied with a tentative deal negotiated by the broker; the automobile salesperson has a sales manager who must approve any lower price; and the union negotiator has a "membership" who must approve or ratify any tentative settlement. By having such an unseen authority (or, if not literally unseen, at least not actually participating in the negotiations), the negotiator has the flexibility of declining a proposal or settlement level on the basis that it is not, or will not be, acceptable to the principal—to use union negotiators' terminology, "The membership won't buy it."

To some, this may appear to be a negative reflection on a negotiator, indicating his or her lack of authority or that he or she is simply "passing the buck." In reality, it is simply an admission that the negotiator is bargaining on behalf of a higher authority than himself, and that such authority will have the final decision as to management's position in the negotiations. Moreover, it is an admission that not all decisions can be rationalized, and that the rejection of a proposal or the refusal to make a higher offer must occasionally be based upon no more profound a reason than "we can't live with it" or "it's final." The fact that someone else has made the determination of what is final does not diminish the negotiator's image as long as the negotiator and the union counterpart recognize that he merely *represents* the employer. Too many negotiators have gotten into trouble by picturing themselves not only as speaking for the employer but also as being the employer. In actuality, even the chief executive officer of a large corporation merely represents the interests of the stockholders, not his own personal interests. Similarly, management's labor negotiator is merely representing the management of the employer.

When the employer's chief decision maker sits at the bargaining table—as the spokesperson or as a member of the bargaining committee—the employer's spokesperson can no longer credibly defer a response or consider the position based upon "management's judgement" since management is right there at the bargaining table. Failure to respond with an authoritative reply then will be interpreted as a sign of weakness or indecision. The "unseen authority" no longer exists because the final authority is seated at the table.

Infrequent Experience

The business executive or ultimate decision maker is often handicapped in labor negotiations to begin with. More often than not he or she only goes to the bargaining table once or twice every several years, whereas the union negotiator has probably negotiated dozens of contracts in the same period of time. Coupling this factor with the loss of the "unseen authority" which occurs when the ultimate decision maker negotiates directly, it is clear that top executives are well advised to select a representative, preferably a skilled professional, to go to the bargaining table as spokesperson.

Selecting Other Members of the Negotiating Committee

In very simple negotiations involving small or inconsequential bargaining units, sometimes one management representative and one union representative will simply sit down and work out an agreement. For more involved negotiations, however, there will normally be a group of management representatives and a group of union representatives who meet for negotiations. Regardless of the limited scope and simplicity of a particular labor negotiation, management should never rely on one person to negotiate its labor agreement, no matter how skillful, trustworthy, and experienced that person might be. The necessity of having careful notes of what was said in meetings is reason alone to have more than one person in attendance. It is advisable to have someone to substantiate what management's spokesperson heard and said in the meetings. Moreover, there are other important functions that are best delegated to others besides the spokesperson. For these reasons, management should select a negotiating committee to assist the spokesperson, and it is wise to make that selection relatively early in the preparatory stage of negotiations.

Operating Expertise

Since the spokesperson will usually be a staff specialist or outsider, he or she will normally not have a detailed knowledge of the day-to-day operations of the enterprise. For this reason, at least one operations person should be on the negotiating committee to advise and counsel the spokesperson on (1) problems imposed by union proposals on working conditions, (2) responses to allegations about working conditions in the facility covered by negotiations, and (3) the operating viewpoint of management-proposed working conditions and/or contractual changes. The person fulfilling this function should not, for the reasons previously set forth, be the ultimate decision maker in the organization. He or she should be, however, high enough in the organization to have a vital role in the management of operations and a sufficient overview of the entire operation in order to understand the impact of contractual changes in all areas of the enterprise. Philosophically, the person providing operating expertise should ideally be about in the middle of the attitudinal spectrum concerning unions (i.e., not a "union hater," but sufficiently cautious and realistic about union-management relationships to avoid harmful agreements).

Cost Specialist

The negotiator will, regardless of his or her computational ability, require some assistance in the preparation of cost data and in estimating cost impacts of proposals and settlement offers. Of all persons on the negotiating team, this person is the one least necessary to have in attendance at the actual negotiations.

Typically this person is a cost accountant, industrial engineer, controller, or other person who has access to the necessary data, and who has experience in preparing cost statements and estimates for the facility or facilities involved. Ideally, the person should be able to conceptualize (i.e., to do more than simply put numbers into and extract them from a computer or calculator), since many proposals have cost implications which are not always obvious on the surface. It is preferable that the person who prepares the basic cost data in advance of the negotiations be the same person who prepares cost estimates during negotiations. The types of cost data preparation and cost estimating which will be required of this person are outlined later in this chapter and in Chapter 10, "Costing Contract Demands, Offers, and Settlements."

Note Taker

The management spokesperson should take brief notes during bargaining meetings for his or her own purposes, but these will seldom be exhaustive enough to serve as an accurate record of negotiations. Consequently, it is recommended that one or more persons be selected to take detailed notes of what is said by both sides in the negotiations. Although some employers prefer to have a secretary or someone else who can take shorthand, this usually requires the attendance of someone totally foreign to the negotiations, adding a tone of formality which can sometimes inhibit the free exchange of ideas. Moreover, the idea that someone is keeping verbatim notes is itself a deterrent to a free and open negotiation. For this same reason, court stenographers and tape recorders are verboten. In fact, the NLRB has held that a party to labor negotiations need not bargain if the other party insists on using a court stenographer or a tape recorder.[1]

Most employers prefer to have a personnel representative or other management representative take notes which can be transcribed in greater detail following the negotiating meetings. These notes are usually unofficial and are for management's future use as an aid in interpreting ambiguous or disputed contract provisions. They are frequently useful in arbitration or other hearings to refresh the recollection of the person taking notes in order to support a particular interpretation of contract language.

It is often advisable to have two management representatives take simultaneous notes and have them collaborate following each negotiating meeting to produce one, hopefully complete, set of management notes. The management spokesman should attempt to review the notes reasonably soon after the negotiations to assure their accuracy.

Language Draftsperson

It is often advisable, though not absolutely necessary, to have someone on the negotiating committee who is proficient in drafting contract language. Normally, the spokesperson carries out this function. In fact, if an outsider is hired to act as spokesperson, he or she will be expected to be a competent language draftsperson. If the spokesperson does not fulfill this role, someone on the negotiating committee, or someone to whom the negotiators have ready access, should be assigned this task.

Frequently, management may desire to have a lawyer, preferably a labor lawyer, approve any language which is to be offered or agreed upon. However, a lawyer is not necessary. Many lay persons can draft contract language that is as carefully drawn as a lawyer's, and frequently not as cumbersome or "legalistic." But whoever is assigned this task, it is important that the person have demonstrated competence in writing labor contract language. Regardless of who prepares the initial draft, it is especially important that the draft be reviewed prior to its use at the bargaining table by several other persons, including those who will have to administer the language.

If the draftsperson is not to be a regular member of the negotiating committee, it is important that the draftsperson be readily accessible. Eleventh-hour negotiations cannot easily be delayed to the following morning until the employer's labor lawyer arrives at the office. As will be pointed out in subsequent chapters, the author has a strong preference for negotiating final contract language at the bargaining table, rather than reaching "agreement in principle" and finalizing contract language after the basic settlement. Too many "agreements" have been scuttled when two parties later try to put into words what they thought they had agreed upon at the bargaining table. Therefore, if final contract language is to be negotiated as part of the substantive bargaining, it is important to have the language draftsperson at the bargaining table or sufficiently accessible on short notice. The availability of modem-equipped computers and fax machines makes it easier to use draftspersons who are not at the bargaining table.

Other Committee Members or Observers

If other persons are on the management negotiating committee, custom will frequently dictate those choices. It may be traditional that certain levels of management be represented at the bargaining table, and regardless of the need for them to be there, great difficulty may be encountered in attempting to change the custom. To many persons, being "in labor negotiations" is a mark of distinction or privilege not easily taken away.

Aside from the constraints imposed by such custom or practice, it is recommended that only persons who need to be in attendance in negotiations actually participate. The more persons who are in attendance, the more difficult will be the spokesperson's job of managing the negotiations and keeping control of the caucuses. Likewise, the more persons who are involved, the more difficult it will be to maintain the confidentiality of management's plans. If, however, custom and tradition prove too strong to limit the attendance in the negotiating meetings, participation at least in management caucuses should be limited to those who are absolutely essential to the caucus.

Establishing the Negotiator's Authority and Management's Expectations

There is perhaps no greater source of conflict and misunderstanding that can arise within the employer's ranks during labor contract negotiations than the failure to establish, at the outset of negotiations, the limits of the negotiator's authority and the expectations management has for the negotiations. Too often, management's principal bargaining representative is assigned to negotiate a labor agreement without specific authority or directions other than perhaps outside cost limits for a final settlement. As a result, the negotiator frequently concedes too much or reaches an impasse too soon because senior management and its negotiator did not have a common understanding. Communication failures on these points have resulted in the termination of some otherwise good negotiators as well as in managements being saddled with unreasonably expensive or restrictive settlements and/or strikes.

Of course, establishing objectives and economic parameters as described in Chapter 3 is a necessary first step. But these steps are not sufficient in themselves because management frequently wishes to monitor or check the progress of the negotiations before prebargaining limits are reached or before certain concessions are made. Therefore, it is important at the outset that questions such as the following be raised and answered:

1. Who in management should the spokesperson report to, or coordinate with, throughout the negotiations? (There should be only one person.)
2. How frequently does management want a report on the progress of negotiations?
3. Are there any possible union proposals or anticipated issues which are totally unacceptable to management (often termed "no-no's" or "strike issues")? These should be reviewed again after the union's agenda has been received.
4. What are the absolute limits (these will be referred to as "the wall") beyond which management will take a strike? Does the negotiator have authority to go to those limits without any further communication? If not, how far can he go without checking further?

5. Assuming that a settlement can be reached for less than the "wall" amounts, within what amount or range would management reasonably like to see a settlement reached?
6. Is there anyone in management outside the negotiating committee who needs to review or approve proposals, contract language, or offers? If so, who is that person, and what specifically needs to be reviewed or cleared?
7. Does management have any negotiating or employee relations policies or philosophies to which the negotiator must adhere in the bargaining?

This listing of potential limitations to the negotiator's authority is not to imply that they are necessarily useful or to be recommended. On the contrary, too many organizations put excessive limitations upon their labor negotiators, sometimes to the point where the spokesperson is little more than a messenger who carries information between the union negotiator and the management decision maker. As a general rule, management should give its representatives in negotiations as much authority and flexibility as possible within overall guidelines established prior to negotiations. While periodic reports may be required, they should be informational, and the negotiator should need to check with, or receive approval from, management only when it is necessary to exceed, or vary from, established guidelines.

Gathering Bargaining Data and Information

The type of data necessary for the negotiations will, to a certain extent, depend upon the nature of the work activity covered by the labor agreement. For example, negotiations covering airline pilots will require extensive data on hours of work (on-duty hours, flight hours, etc.) and scheduling matters, whereas bargaining in the construction industry will focus much more on work rules and work jurisdiction and, therefore, will require more data concerning construction costs, staffing levels, etc. Nevertheless, there are certain types of data and information which apply to negotiations in a wide variety of industries. It is this data that will be covered in this chapter.

How Much Is Necessary?

Similarly, the extent of background information, comparative wage and benefit data, and other necessary information will vary considerably depending upon the scope and complexity of the negotiations. Obviously, preparations for a 50-employee bargaining unit will be dramatically different from that for a 5,000-employee bargaining unit. The approach in this chapter is to describe a rather complete preparation model which would be applicable to a negotiation involving a medium-to large-sized bargaining unit with experienced and somewhat sophisticated union and management negotiators. This model will probably be excessively detailed for many types of less complex negotiations, and conversely it may be too simple for major negotiations in certain industries.

Many corporations have labor relations staffs which regularly prepare information for bargaining. Smaller organizations may have to rely upon accountants, personnel managers, or outside consultants to prepare the information. Regardless of who is responsible for preparing the information, there should be close contact between the management spokesperson and the person(s) responsible for preparing the information to assure that all necessary information is obtained, and that unnecessary information gathering is avoided. The key question that should be asked throughout the data-gathering process is, "How will this information be used?" If a satisfactory answer cannot be found, the information should not be obtained, for it will simply waste precious time and effort that could be devoted to more productive tasks. There is, however, at least one caveat to this statement.

It is not always possible to predict the value of certain information. For example, data is often obtained for the purpose of educating a union negotiating committee about some problem faced by the employer so as to justify an employer's proposal or to resist a union's proposal. Once the data is obtained and analyzed, it often is management which becomes educated, as it discovers that the original problem or concern is either nonexistent, more serious than originally believed, or a manifestation of another underlying problem. Consequently, once data is obtained, it may serve multiple purposes. All of these purposes should be kept in mind when determining how the data will be used, and whether it will be necessary.

The availability of sophisticated computers and specially designed software has greatly expanded the type, amount, and format of bargaining data and information that can be produced. Considerable planning needs to precede the production of this information to ensure its utility for the negotiations.

Bargaining Book

All data and information gathered is best organized in a binder or series of binders commonly called a "bargaining book." By having the information organized by subject matter and separated by dividers with a descriptive tab, the negotiators are able to quickly locate the information sought, extract it from the binder, make copies when necessary, and/or replace it with more current information. The bargaining book is also useful to the spokesperson as a place for storing negotiating documents, including the union's and management's agendas, rough notes taken during negotiations, copies of proposals and counterproposals, and computation sheets of all cost calculations.

Considering that negotiations may proceed for weeks and perhaps even months, it is essential that management properly organize its information. The bargaining book is a convenient way to do so.

Economic Information

Internal Historical Information

It is important to have a historical perspective in wage and benefit negotiations. A chronology of wage and benefit changes concerning the bargaining unit for which negotiations are being conducted is useful for this purpose. The period covered by the chronology should normally be at least 8 to 10 years and preferably 15 to 20 years. Exhibit 2–1 illustrates one example of such a chronology.

Another type of historical data which can prove useful is labor productivity data for the period covered in the labor cost chronology. Although many employers do not have good productivity data, a simple chart showing overall employee-hours per unit of production or unit of service can be very revealing. To the extent that productivity data can be broken down by type of product, department, facility, location, or other meaningful unit it can be even more beneficial. A related, useful item of information is a chronology of prices and costs over the same

Exhibit 2–1. Chronology of Wage and Benefit Changes

Date	Wage Changes	Fringe Items
9/83	3% (21¢ average) plus 10¢ for skilled workers deferred; 12¢ under escalator, 1¢ diverted to fringes	5 paid days off during contract year
10/83		Revised basic pension benefit and retirees' benefits; hearing aid coverage
12/83	8¢ under escalator, 1¢ diverted to fringes	Retiree inflation adjustment of $20 per year of service up to $600. 55% for surviving spouses
3/84	8¢ under escalator, 1¢ diverted to fringes	
6/84	12¢ under escalator, 1¢ diverted to fringes	
9/84	3% (21¢ average) deferred; 18¢ under escalator, 1¢ diverted to fringes	7 paid days off during contract year
10/84		$700 monthly pension income after 30 svc. years, revised retirees' benefits, basic monthly penison benefit ranging from $10.75 to $11.50 per svc. year
12/84	13¢ under escalator plus restoration of 6¢ diverted to fringes	
1/85		Revised company contribution to SUB fund
3/85	13¢ under escalator	
6/85	21¢ under escalator	
9/85	3% plus 24¢; $1.32 of $1.37 in past c-o-l adjustments incorporated into base rates; continued c-o-l with 14¢ diverted to finance fringe benefits	Revised insurance benefits; revised company contribution to SUB fund; revised pension benefits; 8 paid days off during contract year; stock ownership plan
12/85	22¢ under escalator, 1¢ diverted to fringes	Revised pension benefits
3/86	22¢ under escalator, 1¢ diverted to fringes	
6/86	30¢ under escalator, 1¢ diverted to fringes	

Exhibit 2–1. Contd.

Date	Wage Changes	Fringe Items
9/86	3% deferred; 24¢ under escalator, 1¢ diverted to fringes	Nine paid days off during contract year; revised company contribution to SUB fund
12/86	17¢ under escalator, 1¢ diverted to fringes	Vision care for retirees
3/87	22¢ under escalator, 1¢ diverted to fringes	
6/87	23¢ under escalator, 1¢ diverted to fringes	
9/87	3% deferred; 22¢ under escalator, 1¢ diverted to fringes; revised escalator formula to provide 1¢ for each 0.26 CPI rise	Revised company contribution to SUB fund; nine paid days off during contract year; revised pension benefits
12/87	26¢ under escalator, 2¢ diverted to benefits	
3/88	10¢ under escalator, 2¢ diverted to benefits	Guaranteed income stream for senior laid-off workers established
4/88	No general increase; reduced rate for new hires	Revised funding of SUB; revised health care coverage and group life insurance for laid-off workers; expanded tuition refund program for laid-off workers;
12/88	5¢ under escalator	Profit-sharing plan; increased employer contribution to ESOP
3/90	1¢ decrease under escalator	Revised pension benefits
4/90		Prepaid legal services
9/90	2% deferred; 15¢ under escalator, 3¢ diverted to fringes	Profit sharing modified; expanded SUB funding; managed health care instituted
3/91	12¢ under escalator, 2¢ diverted to fringes	
6/91	3¢ under escalator	Revised pension benefits
1/92		Eliminated 2 holidays

period. Have prices kept pace with unit labor costs? What is the relationship between prices and productivity? The chronology allows management to answer such questions. Other data such as capital investment costs and profits may also be useful depending upon the message which management may wish to convey to the union. By including profit data from a sufficiently long period of time, such as 10 to 20 years, management can avoid possible claims that it is now "crying poor mouth" after years of prosperity.

Current Internal Information

Although the contract itself usually contains all necessary information as to current wages and benefits, it is convenient to have that information in summary form for easy reference. Also, the same form can be used to summarize information from the employer's other labor contracts as well as comparable information from competitors' labor agreements. Appendix 1 is an example of an excellent form used by the American Paper Institute for its member companies.

Perhaps the data most necessary when negotiations are in progress is a compilation of labor costs of the negotiating bargaining unit for a representative period prior to the date of contract reopening. Appendix 2 is a form developed by the author some years ago; it has been useful in a large number of negotiations. This labor cost recap form lists all elements of labor costs and reflects gross and hourly payments over a representative 6-month to 12-month period. Because the data-gathering process normally will begin three to six months in advance of the contract expiration date, it will not be possible to obtain data for an entire year at wage rates or benefit levels in effect for the last 12 months of the contract. A representative six-month period extrapolated to a 12-month basis will usually suffice. If that period is not representative, a longer period should be chosen with the rates adjusted to reflect the wages and benefits in effect at the end of the contract.

Cost factors having a "rollup" or multiplying effect are listed on the form separately from those which do not, allowing a simple calculation of the rollup factors. The concept of "rollup" is explained in detail in Chapter 10. Simply stated, it reflects the change in costs of certain benefits which automatically result from a change in wages or salaries. The data in the labor cost recap will serve as a basis for all cost calculations throughout the negotiations.

In addition to current gross average labor costs, it is often helpful to have more detailed data which will facilitate cost estimating as negotiations proceed. The following items are often prepared by employers for this purpose:

1. A list of all job classifications by department with the corresponding wage rates and employee population in each classification. This is useful for estimating the costs of special wage adjustments for particular employee groups. Page 5 of the Summary of Labor Contract Provisions (Appendix 1) lists this information.
2. A list of job wage rate brackets in even increments (e.g., 25 cents or 50 cents each) with the employee population in each bracket (see Exhibit 2–2). This is useful for estimating the cost of wage increases which are granted according to the current wage scale, sometimes called "bracket wage increases."
3. A list of the number of employees in each year of service and a list of the number of employees in different age groups (see Exhibit 2–3). These are useful for calculating vacation im-

Exhibit 2–2. Distribution of Bargaining Unit Employees by Wage Brackets

Wage Ranges	Number of Employees	Wage Ranges	Number of Employees
Below $ 8.00	3	$11.76–$12.00	4
$ 8.00–$ 8.25	8	12.01– 12.25	12
8.26– 8.50	6	12.26– 12.50	15
8.51– 8.75	12	12.51– 12.75	8
8.76– 9.00	20	12.76– 13.00	10
9.01– 9.25	15	13.01– 13.25	6
9.26– 9.50	13	13.26– 13.50	2
9.51– 9.75	21	13.51– 13.75	3
9.76– 10.00	18	13.76– 14.00	10
10.01– 10.25	23	14.01– 14.25	0
10.26– 10.50	30	14.26– 14.50	4
10.51– 10.75	7	14.51– 14.75	1
10.76– 11.00	22	14.76– 15.00	0
11.01– 11.25	37	15.01– 15.25	0
11.26– 11.50	19	15.26– 15.50	2
11.51– 11.75	18	Above 15.50	1
Subtotal	272	Subtotal	350
		Grand Total	622

Exhibit 2–3. Distribution of Bargaining Unit Employees by Age and Years of Service

Years of Service / Age	1	2	3	4	5	6	7	8	9	10	11	12	13	14	15	16	17	18	19	20	21	22	23	24	25	Total
18	–	–	–	–	–	–	–	–	–	–	–	–	–	–	–	–	–	–	–	–	–	–	–	–	–	0
19	2	–	–	–	–	–	–	–	–	–	–	–	–	–	–	–	–	–	–	–	–	–	–	–	–	2
20	1	2	–	–	–	–	–	–	–	–	–	–	–	–	–	–	–	–	–	–	–	–	–	–	–	3
21	5	3	1	–	–	–	–	–	–	–	–	–	–	–	–	–	–	–	–	–	–	–	–	–	–	9
22	2	6	4	2	–	–	–	–	–	–	–	–	–	–	–	–	–	–	–	–	–	–	–	–	–	14
23	3	5	8	1	1	–	–	–	–	–	–	–	–	–	–	–	–	–	–	–	–	–	–	–	–	18
24	–	3	3	4	1	1	–	–	–	–	–	–	–	–	–	–	–	–	–	–	–	–	–	–	–	12
25	–	2	3	–	4	2	–	–	–	–	–	–	–	–	–	–	–	–	–	–	–	–	–	–	–	11
26	4	7	1	5	–	–	1	–	–	–	–	–	–	–	–	–	–	–	–	–	–	–	–	–	–	18
27	2	–	5	4	–	3	–	1	–	–	–	–	–	–	–	–	–	–	–	–	–	–	–	–	–	15
28	–	2	–	3	–	5	1	–	–	–	–	–	–	–	–	–	–	–	–	–	–	–	–	–	–	11
29	2	1	6	2	1	–	2	1	–	–	–	–	–	–	–	–	–	–	–	–	–	–	–	–	–	15
30	–	3	–	6	2	1	–	–	–	–	–	–	–	–	–	–	–	–	–	–	–	–	–	–	–	13
31	3	–	4	2	5	1	2	–	2	–	–	–	–	–	–	–	–	–	–	–	–	–	–	–	–	19
32	1	5	2	3	4	3	–	2	–	1	–	–	–	–	–	–	–	–	–	–	–	–	–	–	–	21
33	4	–	2	2	–	1	2	–	3	–	2	–	–	–	–	–	–	–	–	–	–	–	–	–	–	16
34	1	3	3	–	1	2	1	–	1	2	–	–	1	–	–	–	–	–	–	–	–	–	–	–	–	15
35	–	2	2	5	–	3	–	3	–	2	–	1	–	1	–	–	–	–	–	–	–	–	–	–	–	19
36	3	1	–	3	4	–	2	–	2	–	1	–	–	–	–	1	–	–	–	–	–	–	–	–	–	17
37	2	–	2	–	1	–	3	–	4	–	2	–	2	–	–	–	–	–	–	–	–	–	–	–	–	16
38	1	–	1	–	3	4	5	–	–	3	–	2	1	1	–	1	–	–	–	–	–	–	–	–	–	22
39	–	2	3	–	5	–	2	4	–	4	–	2	1	–	3	–	–	1	–	–	–	–	–	–	–	27
40	1	–	–	3	–	2	–	–	2	–	1	–	3	–	2	–	1	–	–	–	–	–	–	–	–	15
41	2	–	3	–	4	–	2	–	1	–	–	1	2	3	–	2	–	–	1	–	–	–	–	–	–	21

42	–	1	–	4	2	–	1	–	2	–	–	1	–	2	1	1	–	2	–	–	–	–	–	–	–	17
43	–	2	–	2	3	–	1	1	–	–	2	–	1	1	–	2	1	–	–	–	–	–	–	–	–	16
44	–	1	2	–	1	2	3	–	–	2	–	3	–	–	1	–	2	–	–	–	1	–	–	–	–	18
45	1	–	2	–	1	–	–	3	–	1	2	–	3	–	2	–	–	2	–	1	–	–	–	–	–	18
46	–	2	1	3	–	2	4	–	5	–	2	1	1	–	2	–	3	–	2	–	4	–	1	–	–	33
47	–	1	1	2	–	4	–	2	–	1	1	3	–	–	2	–	1	–	1	–	2	–	–	–	–	21
48	–	2	–	1	3	–	2	1	1	–	4	–	2	–	3	–	2	–	–	1	–	3	–	–	–	25
49	1	–	–	2	3	–	1	–	2	2	3	–	4	–	2	1	–	–	2	–	–	–	–	–	–	23
50	1	2	3	–	1	–	1	2	–	1	–	2	2	3	1	4	–	2	3	–	1	–	1	–	–	30
51	–	–	–	2	–	1	–	3	–	4	–	3	2	2	1	–	4	–	2	–	3	–	2	–	–	29
52	–	–	–	1	–	2	–	–	2	3	–	2	1	1	4	–	3	2	1	2	1	2	–	1	–	28
53	–	1	–	1	–	–	2	–	3	–	1	–	2	–	1	2	–	2	1	1	–	–	–	–	–	17
54	–	–	2	–	1	–	2	–	–	3	2	1	1	–	2	–	1	–	2	–	3	–	–	–	–	20
55	–	–	–	–	2	–	2	–	1	–	–	2	–	–	1	–	2	–	1	3	–	2	–	–	–	16
56	–	1	–	1	–	2	–	3	–	–	2	–	1	–	2	2	–	1	–	–	–	–	–	–	–	15
57	–	–	–	–	2	–	–	1	–	2	–	1	1	1	–	1	–	2	–	–	1	–	–	–	–	12
58	–	–	–	2	–	1	1	–	2	–	3	–	–	2	–	1	–	1	–	3	–	–	2	–	–	18
59	–	–	–	–	–	2	–	1	–	2	–	1	1	–	2	–	3	–	2	–	1	1	–	–	–	16
60	–	–	–	–	–	–	–	1	–	1	–	–	–	–	1	2	–	–	–	–	–	2	–	1	–	8
61	–	–	–	–	–	–	–	–	1	–	–	1	–	2	–	–	1	–	2	–	–	–	–	–	–	7
62	–	–	–	–	–	–	–	–	–	–	–	–	–	–	–	1	–	1	–	–	1	–	–	–	1	4
63	–	–	–	–	–	–	–	–	–	–	1	–	1	–	2	–	–	–	1	–	1	–	1	–	–	7
64	–	–	–	–	–	–	–	–	–	–	–	–	–	1	–	–	–	1	–	–	–	–	–	–	1	3
65	–	–	–	–	–	–	–	–	–	–	–	1	–	–	–	–	1	–	–	–	–	–	–	–	–	2
66	–	–	–	–	–	–	–	–	–	–	–	–	–	1	–	–	–	–	–	–	–	–	–	–	–	1
Number of Employees	42	60	64	63	55	44	43	29	34	34	29	28	33	21	35	21	25	17	21	11	19	10	7	2	2	753

provement costs as well as cost changes in pension and other benefits which are related to length of service.

4. Cost data breakdowns and analyses for subgroups of employees, e.g., full time, part time, temporary, regular, leadpersons.
5. Cost breakdowns of selected benefits such as life insurance, hospital costs, professional services, outpatient care, etc.
6. Wage and benefit data for nonunion employees whose wages and benefits are apt to influence, or be influenced by, the forthcoming negotiations.

When the basic data or other information indicates a possible problem (e.g., excessively high overtime costs or medical insurance costs), a more thorough analysis may be necessary. For example, if the problem is excessive overtime, it would be necessary to find the answers to questions such as whether the overtime is occurring primarily in certain job classifications or departments, or on certain days of the week. It may be that excessive amounts of overtime premiums are being paid under one particular section of the contract, and therefore it may be desirable to seek to modify that section in order to reduce overtime costs. Likewise, rising medical insurance costs should be scrutinized to ascertain the causes and propose possible cost containment measures.

In general, once the initial data has been accumulated, it should not simply be placed in the bargaining book for later reference, but should be carefully studied and analyzed to ascertain what implications it has for bargaining and for management in general.

Beyond standard data regarding wages and hours, the scope of data needed for bargaining will be influenced by the bargaining demands of both parties. If management is going to propose, for example, cost control measures in its medical insurance plans, it needs to collect data regarding claims, costs, and other information to support its position. Similarly, if the union is expected to propose additional paid time off (e.g., work breaks, vacations, and holidays), management needs to gather data to show the cost impact of nonproductive time and the effect upon operations. Some of this preparation may have to await receipt of the union's bargaining agenda.

External Economic Data

Competitive or Comparable Wage/Benefit Data

Every employer should know how its wages and fringe benefits compare with those of its competitors and with those of employers in related industries in the same geographical area. It is advisable to have this information on an ongoing basis and it is essential to have it when preparing for negotiations. A spread sheet of wage rate comparisons similar to that shown in Exhibit 2–4 is useful for this purpose. A similar approach is suggested for benefit comparisons as illustrated in Exhibit 2–5. It may not always be easy to obtain this information. Many industries have employer associations which collect, collate, and distribute the data. Where formal associations do not exist, informal coalitions or groups of employers may exchange labor contract information. Consulting firms will usually obtain this data for a fee. If these are not feasible, it will be necessary for an enterprising employer to conduct *ad hoc* surveys of wage and benefit information by direct contact. Offering to make the survey results available to participating employers usually ensures greater cooperation than would otherwise occur. If the participating employers in the survey complete a form such as that shown in Appendix 1, nearly all relevant data will be available.

Comparability of Data

In compiling wage and benefit comparisons, it is important to assure that the data is really comparable, that one is not comparing apples and oranges. In this regard, the following cautionary points should be kept in mind. The individual making the comparison should do the following:

1. Carefully note effective dates of wages and benefits to assure that the data is from comparable periods.
2. Check to see if wages include or exclude any applicable incentive earnings, "red-circle" rates, bonuses, or other premiums.
3. Consider crew sizes for particular operations. Differences in rates may reflect different staffing levels.
4. Determine what skills are required and what duties are being performed by the job classifications which are being compared. Considering job titles alone can be deceptive.
5. Keep in mind, when comparing certain benefits, that it may be important to know the work force makeup, especially the length-of-service profile. For example, five weeks of vacation after 15 years' service may not be very meaningful when the facility only began operating several years ago. This is especially important when comparing vacation and pension benefits.

Exhibit 2–4. Wage Rate Comparison (in dollars)

Company — Contract Expiration	Base Rate	Mainte-nance Journey-man	Multi-craft	Top Helper	Oiler	Combin-ation Power/ Recovery Operator	Top Recovery Operator	Top Power Operator	Turbine Operator	Power Boiler Operator	Top Stock Preparer	Bleach Plant Operator	Automatic Increase
Company A 6/15/93	8.39	—	15.57	—	—	16.05	—	—	—	—	15.26	14.12	—
Company B 5/29/93	8.49	—	12.79	—	11.66	—	12.66	12.66	—	10.84	11.89	12.66	—
Company C 8/31/93	8.69	—	13.12	—	—	13.38	—	—	—	—	12.30	—	—
Company D 6/13/95	6.75	—	13.56	—	—	12.94	—	—	12.94	12.27	12.15	12.43	4%/2%
Company E 10/15/95	8.56	—	—	—	—	—	14.63	—	—	—	12.04	13.48	3%/3%
Company F 6/18/93	8.02	9.25	—	—	9.01	—	—	—	—	—	10.25	—	—
Company G 5/31/93	8.49	—	13.72	—	—	—	14.62	15.21	12.70	12.62	12.44	—	—
Company H 8/14/93	6.97	12.80	—	—	12.29	14.69	—	—	12.92	12.04	14.40	14.31	—
Company I 6/30/93	7.04	—	14.21	—	10.47	16.18	12.56	—	14.42	13.31	13.72	—	—
Company J 7/31/95	7.16	—	13.82	—	10.55	14.98	—	—	—	—	12.19	—	3.5%/2%
Company K 6/19/94	5.98	12.64	—	—	10.35	14.17	—	—	13.30	13.54	13.12	—	—
Company L 7/31/95	7.47	—	14.02	—	10.90	—	14.30	15.40	—	—	13.36	—	4%/1%
Company M 10/22/94	8.95	—	15.42	—	11.24	15.62	—	—	—	11.52	15.86	14.41	5%
Average $	7.77	11.56	14.03	—	10.81	14.75	13.75	14.42	13.26	12.31	13.00	13.57	3.9%/2%

Exhibit 2–5. Employee Benefits Comparison

Company / Contract Expiration	Shift Differential (¢)	Paid Holidays/ Production Restricted	Funeral Leave (Max. No. of Days)	Layoff/ Severance Pay	Meal Allowance ($)	Tool Allowance ($)	Safety Shoes ($/Yr.)	Call Time (Hrs.)	Report Time (Hrs.)	Vacation (Wks./Yrs.) @ Pay Per Week	Pay Option in Lieu of Vacation
Company A 8/31/92	15–20	12/0	1, 3, 5[a]	0	3.00	80	0	4	4	1/1, 2/2, 3/8, 4/15, 5/20, 6/25 @ 48 hrs.	Only at retirement
Company B 6/15/93	15–20	12/4	1, 3, 5[a]	0	3.75	110	0	2[f]	4	1/1, 2/3, 3/6, 4/12, 5/20, 6/30 @ 2%, 44 hrs.	None
Company C 5/29/93	15–21	12/0	3, 5[a]	0	3.50	110	0	2–4	4	1/1, 2/2, 3/8, 4/12, 5/20, 6/25 @ 46 hrs.	Excess of 2 weeks
Company D 8/31/93	15–21	12/3	3	2%	3/4 hr. pay	—[c]	0	2[g]	2	1/1, 2/3, 3/8, 4/15, 5/20, 6/25 @ 45 hrs.	Excess of 1 week
Company E 6/13/93	15–20	12/4	3	2%	3.00	60	20	5	2	1/1, 2/3, 3/8, 4/15, 5/20, 6/30 @ 45 hrs.	All
Company F 10/15/93	16–20	12/3	3	0	3.50	—[c]	30	4	4	1/1, 2/3, 3/8, 4/15, 5/18, 6/25 @ 2%, 44 hrs.	Excess of 2 weeks
Company G 6/18/94	15–25	11/0	3, 4[a]	0	2.15	—[c]	18[d]	4	4	1/1, 2/3, 3/8, 4/15, 5/20, 6/25 @ 2%, 40 hrs.	None
Company H 5/31/93	15–20	13/2	3	0	—[b]	—[c]	30	4[g]	2	1/1, 2/3, 3/8, 4/12, 5/20, 6/25 @ 2%, 40 hrs.	Excess of 3 weeks
Company I 8/14/92	15–20	13/4	3	4–8 wks.	3.50	140	25	4	4	1/1, 2/3, 3/8, 4/12, 5/18, 6/30 @ 2%, 43 hrs.	Excess of 2 weeks
Average/ Trend	15–20	12/2	3	0	3.00	50	13	4	4	1/1, 2/3, 3/8, 4/13, 5/20, 6/27 @ 45 hrs.	Excess of 2 weeks

[a]Varies with degree of kinship. [b]Meal furnished ($3 value). [c]Tools furnished. [d]Two pairs/year ($9 each). [e]Plus time and a half.
[f]Plus time and a half (minimum 4). [g]Plus time worked.

6. Determine which benefits are fully paid by the employer and which, if any, are contributory on the part of the employee.
7. Remember that, except for pension plans to which the employer makes a fixed contribution, comparisons of pension plans and benefits are extremely difficult due to variations in methods of funding, age and service characteristics of the work force, actuarial assumptions, and other factors. While benefit levels may lend themselves to comparisons, seldom will they, in and of themselves, indicate the employer's actual costs.

Nonunion Data

In preparing wage and benefit comparisons, it is important to include comparable nonunion as well as union facilities in the industry concerned. Too often, the nonunion sector is excluded because of an oversight or because of a tacit assumption that it is not relevant. On the contrary, it is most relevant since it reflects what is likely to be a keen source of competition due not only to possible lower wages and fringes but also to the advantage that nonunion facilities have in being able to operate without a labor contract. Considerable difficulty may be encountered in obtaining data from nonunion employers, who may harbor fears that the data will fall into the hands of the union and be used for organizing purposes. In such cases, guarantees of confidentiality are necessary, and even such guarantees might be insufficient to assuage nonunion employers' fears. On the other hand, some nonunion employers provide wages and benefits that are higher than their union competitors, and publicize this fact. In such cases, the data should be readily available. In any event, when gathering external data of wages and benefits, one should include as many nonunion employers as possible.

Recent Settlements

In addition to gathering data on current wage rates and benefit levels, it is especially important to collect copies or summaries of contract settlements in recent comparable negotiations. More than anything else, they reflect the range of a potential settlement the employer is most likely to be facing. While it may be possible to forge a new pattern, the union with which the employer is negotiating will be strongly influenced by what it has, or has not, been able to extract from other employers. A useful format for reflecting these recent comparable settlements is shown in Exhibit 2–6. The employer should be sure to ascertain if the settlement summaries it has been given report *all* significant economic matters which were included in the settlement. It is not too unusual for some employers and some unions to agree to matters that are not publicized. Often these matters are contained in sidebar or memorandum agreements. Certain items may be kept private because of possible embarrassment or out of fear that the concession may spread to other bargaining units. Regardless of whether such nonpublicized agreements are likely to be helpful or harmful to negotiations, it is useful for management to be aware of them.

It is also important to ascertain if any provisions agreed upon in comparable negotiations constituted "buy-outs" or *quid pro quos* for provisions that one of the parties wanted to eliminate from, or have included in, its contract. For example, an employer may have offered additional increases in wages in order to eliminate a wage incentive or production bonus. If not so identified in the settlement summary, an unusually high wage increase can mislead one into believing that the increase was accomplished under normal conditions. Such "buy-outs" can affect any part of a contract settlement.

In major negotiations that set patterns or trends rather than following them, information about previous settlements within the same industry may not be particularly pertinent. In such cases, information about settlements in other industries may be more useful. Care must be taken, however, to put settlements in other industries into the context of the tradition of bargaining and current economic position of the industry in which they occurred. For example, even though the Machinists may have been able to negotiate a 7 percent settlement with the machine tool industry, that level may be completely inappropriate for the aerospace industry, even though the two industries may have much in common. Likewise, a Teamster contract covering over-the-road truck drivers is often not a good benchmark for local delivery trucking or warehousing operations.

Internal Noneconomic Information

Work Hours

A major subject of negotiations in any industry is hours of work which, broadly defined, includes premium pay for overtime or inconvenient schedules, work scheduling procedures, credit for benefits based upon hours worked, and other topics. For this reason the following statistics on work hours can be very useful to have available for negotiations:

Average weekly hours
- For entire bargaining unit
- For each work shift
- For each department
- For each classification (if appropriate)

Work schedules
- For each department
- Continuous operations
- Noncontinuous operations

Paid but unworked hours on the job
- Paid lunch periods
- Paid break periods
- Paid wash-up periods

Exhibit 2–6. Summary of Recent Contract Settlements

Employer / Location	Union	No. of Employees	Term (yrs.)	Contract Dates
Union Machine Tool Skokie, Ill.	IAM #2063	150	3	8/1/90 to 7/31/93
Amax Metals Flint, Mich.	UAW #331	200	2	7/15/90 to 7/15/92
Richmont Fabricators Richmont, Ohio	IBT #6660	75	3	10/1/90 to 9/30/93
Gary Gear Mfg. Gary, Inc.	IAM #256	300	3	2/1/91 to 2/1/94
Hamilton Iron Works Hamilton, Ohio	USW #721	100	1	10/1/91 to 10/1/92
Best Machines Rockford, Ill.	UAW #68	350	3	3/1/91 to 3/1/94
Precision Casting Milwaukee, Wis.	USW #800	60	2	6/1/90 to 5/30/92
Amax Metals Cincinnati, Ohio	UAW #100	150	2	7/15/91 to 7/15/93
Peterson & Sons Indianapolis, Ind.	Indep.	55	3	11/15/91 to 11/15/94

Note: Company names are fictitious.

Exhibit 2–6. Cont.

General Wage Change(s)	Other Wage Change(s)*	Benefit Changes*
+5%, +55¢, +60¢	+25¢: pattern makers +20¢: lead persons	Vacation 3/5 (was 3/7); 13th holiday [3]; major med. $200,000 max.; pension $16 (was $15); add dental plan [2]
+3%, +3% & COLA (40¢ yr. cap)	—	Shift diff. + 10¢/shift each year; 13th holiday [2]; vacation 6/30 (new)
+6%, +4%, +50¢	+1%: tool & die	Pension 1¼% final 5 yrs. avg. (was 1%); vacation pay 2% or 40 hrs. (was flat 40) [2]; weekly S&A $200 (was $175) [2]; maternity benefit—75% of pay
+50¢, +60¢, +70¢ & eliminate COLA	$500 flat bonus (COLA buyout)	Vacations 2/2 (was 2/3) and 5/17 (was 5/20); 12th holiday [2]; shift differential 40¢–45¢ (was 38¢ and 42¢) [3]
—	—	—
+5%, +5%, +5% & COLA	—	13th holiday; vacation 3/5 (was 3/7); vacation 4/12 (was 4/15) [2]; add orthodontia to dental plan—$1,000 maximum
+75¢, +5% (65¢ min.)	+25¢: rates over $14.00	2 × overtime after 8 hrs. on Sunday; pension $17.50 (was $16.50); 12th holiday, 13th holiday [2]
+3%, +3% & COLA (40¢ yr. cap)	—	Vacation 6/30 (new); shift differential 50¢–60¢ (was 45¢–50¢) [2]; weekly S&A—50% of average take-home pay
+25¢, +25¢, +25¢ & profit-sharing	—	Vacation 2/1 (was 2/2); Company to pay full med. (previously paid 75%); 10th holiday [2]

*All changes are effective in the first year of multiyear contracts except where noted in brackets; [2] means second year and [3] means third year.

Overtime hours worked
- For entire bargaining unit
- For each department
- For each job classification (if appropriate)
- Overtime hours offered but refused (if this option is available)

Premium hours worked and paid for based upon
- Over 8 hours per day
- Over 40 hours per week
- Work on holiday
- Work on Saturday or Sunday
- Early call-in or hold-over
- Any other basis for premium pay.

Seniority

Another bargaining subject which competes with hours of work as being among the most discussed noneconomic issues is seniority. Length of service in the bargaining unit is, in a vast majority of contracts, a factor (or *the* factor) in determining job promotions and transfers, shift selection, layoffs, bumping, recall from layoff, etc. In preparing to negotiate on this subject, the employer may find the following pieces of information useful:

- Seniority list(s) by appropriate seniority unit
- Copies of all lines or "ladders" of progression
- Number of jobs filed by job bid procedure
- Number of job bids filled by other than most senior bidding employee
- Periods of layoff and the number and range of seniority dates of employees on layoff during each period
- Frequency and impact of bumping during layoffs
- Average period of layoff for employees who have been laid off.

Grievances and Arbitration Cases

As a means of anticipating the union's bargaining demands as well as for purposes of identifying sections of the labor contract which management may wish to change, many employers find it useful to review and summarize grievances and arbitration cases which arose during the last contract term. A common format for summarizing grievances can be established to allow the employer to identify the section of the contract involved, include a short description of the grievance, state the step in the grievance procedure to which it progressed, and give the final outcome of the grievance. If the employer typically has a lot of arbitration cases, a separate summary of these is useful (see Exhibit 2–7). If it is anticipated that certain of these grievances or arbitration decisions will become specific subjects of discussion in negotiations, it may be useful to have copies of the pertinent grievances, grievance answers, and grievance settlements or arbitration decisions included in the bargaining book.

Supervisors' Survey

Another technique used by many employers to identify possible management proposed contract changes is the supervisors' contract survey. Utilizing a form somewhat like that shown in Exhibit 2–8, supervisors are asked to review the labor agreement, local supplements, or other agreements and note any changes they feel should be made in the contract. This review can also be done in a meeting of supervisors rather than in written survey form. Another option is to have each supervisor review the contract individually, make notes on the form, and then attend a meeting to discuss the proposed changes as a group. The survey of supervisors need not be limited to a review of the labor contract. Other problem areas such as absenteeism, poor workmanship, or low productivity can be ferreted out through the survey technique. Such meetings and surveys can also be used to elicit information about bargaining unit employees and their opinions. Supervisors are good sources of information about employee perceptions and feelings about key issues, internal union politics, and other employee attitudes.

Development of Contract Clauses

The evolution of certain sections or clauses of a labor contract frequently reflects the relative bargaining power of the parties as well as areas of conflict in the parties' relationship. A review of the sequential development of important contract clauses can be helpful in understanding the origin of the current language and in evaluating future proposals for changes

Exhibit 2–7. Grievance Analysis and Arbitration Summary

GRIEVANCE ANALYSIS

Section of Contract Involved	Brief Description of Grievance	Disposed of at Step:				Disposition			Issue Involved—Importance for Negotiations
		1	2	3	4	Dropped by Union	Co. Granted Relief Requested	Compromise	

ARBITRATION SUMMARY

Date of Award	Issue Decided	Section of Contract Involved	Name of Arbi- trator	Party Favored by Award	Summary of the Decision	Significance of Case for Negotiations

Exhibit 2–8. Labor Agreement Survey—Supervisors' Evaluation

Name of Supervisor/Foreman ______________________ Date __________

Department ______________________ Shift __________

Article of Agreement*	Contract Language			Comment**
	Has Not Been a Problem Recom-mend no Changes	Has Caused Minor Problems	Has Caused Major Problems	
I. Agreement				
II. Recognition				
III. Management Rights				
IV. No Strike/ No Lockout				
V. Union Security				
VI. Union Representation				
VII. Grievance Procedure				
VIII. Funeral Leave				
IX. Supervisors				
X. Union Bulletin Board				
XI. Seniority				
XII. Loss of Seniority				
XIII. Hours & Overtime				
XIV. Authorized Leaves of Absence				
XV. Reporting & Call-In Allowances				
XVI. Holidays				
XVII. Vacations				
XVIII. Safety				
XIX. Wages				
XX. Discipline/Discharge				

*Use article or section headings appropriate to contract.
**Attach additional pages to provide more detail.

in those same clauses. Appendix 3 depicts a typical layout of the development of a contract clause.

Supplemental Agreements

Frequently the parties have entered into supplemental agreements, grievance settlements, sidebar agreements, or other understandings during prior negotiations or during the term of the current agreement. Copies of all these agreements should be included in the bargaining book. It is also useful to include an explanation of what prompted the agreement and how it was negotiated.

External Noneconomic Information

In addition to gathering economic summaries of comparable labor contracts in one's own industry, related industries, and/or in the same geographical area, one should attempt to obtain actual copies of those labor agreements. Only by examining the contracts themselves is it possible to ascertain how employees qualify for certain benefits and how provisions are administered, and to note numerous other modifying conditions that cannot be included in a summary.

Actual contract documents also provide tips for the contract draftsperson as to the best means of expressing certain agreements and properly qualifying certain provisions. In some cases, clauses in other labor agreements are useful only to illustrate what should be avoided. In any event, a convenient way of organizing this information is by preparing a "contract clause book." By making copies of the same sections of each comparable contract and organizing these copies by subject matter within tabbed dividers in a single binder, it is possible to quickly flip to one section of the binder and review all contract language on one such subject. Exhibit 2–9 is an example of a page from such a "contract clause book."

Reference to Law

It is not uncommon that bargaining issues arise or are anticipated which have significant legal implications. Subjects such as federal wage and hour laws, affirmative action programs, Occupational Safety and Health Administration

Exhibit 2–9. Funeral Leave Clauses

WESTBROOK MOLDINGS

Section 25—Bereavement Leave

1. When death occurs to a member of any employee's immediate family, the employee, at his request, will be granted reasonable, necessary time off as a bereavement leave of absence. He will be compensated at this regular straight-time hourly rate for hours lost from his regular schedule on any of the days prior to the funeral, the day of the funeral, and the days after the funeral, with a maximum of 3 days.

2. Members of an immediate family shall be employee's spouse, mother, father, brothers, sisters, sons, daughters, grandchildren, mother-in-law, father-in-law, step or foster parents, step or foster brothers, sisters, sons or daughters, son-in-law, daughter-in-law, and the employee's and spouse's grandparents and great grandparents.

3. Compensable hours under the terms of this Section will be counted as hours worked for the purpose of computing vacation and holiday pay and will be counted as hours worked for the purpose of computing weekly overtime.

4. An employee will be given a leave of absence of not to exceed one day without compensation for the purpose of attending a friend's funeral provided he has given not less than 48 hours advance notice to his supervisor and limited to a reasonable number from the same department at the same time.

MID-ATLANTIC POLY PRODUCTS

ARTICLE XX
FUNERAL LEAVE

1. When death occurs to a member of an employee's immediate family, the employee shall be granted necesary time off for the purpose of attending the funeral. Said employee will be compensated at his regular straight-time hourly or piece rate for three consecutive working days, excluding Saturday, Sunday or other days of rest, one of which must be the day of the funeral, subject to the following limitations:
   (a) Members of an employee's immediate family are limited to the employee's spouse, sons, daughters, mother, father, brothers, sisters, step parents, step children, grandfather, grandmother, mother-in-law and father-in-law.
   (b) Proof of relationship and/or death may be required.

ABC PLASTICS

B. Bereavement Leave

1. When death occurs to a member of an employee's immediate family, the employee, if requested, will be granted reasonably necessary time off as bereavement leave of absence. The employee shall be reimbursed at the straight time hourly rate of their scheduled occupation for a total of three (3) days pay.
2. Immediate family includes parents, spouse, brothers, sisters, children, father-in-law, mother-in-law, one step-mother, one step-father, step-children, grandchildren, and grandparents.
3. Hours paid for bereavement leave will be counted as hours worked for the purpose of computing vacation and holiday eligibility, and premium pay.

Contd.

Exhibit 2–9. Contd.

MARYLAND PLASTICS

SECTION 16—FUNERAL LEAVE ALLOWANCE

A. When death occurs to a member of an employee's immediate family the employee, at his request, will be granted reasonably necessary time off as a funeral leave-of-absence for the purpose of attending the funeral, and he will be compensated at his regular straight-time hourly rate for hours lost from his regular schedule on any of the days prior to the funeral, the day of the funeral and the three (3) days after the funeral, with a maximum of four (4) days compensation.

If the funeral is held outside the State of California and the employee does not attend so as to qualify for the funeral leave allowance under this paragraph, the employee, at his request and instead of the funeral leave allowance described above, will be granted reasonably necesary time off within three (3) days of the date of death to attend to matters relating to the death and will be compensated at his regular straight-time hourly rate for hours lost thereby from his regular schedule, with a maximum of one (1) day's compensation.

B. Members of employee's immediate family shall be limited to the employee's spouse, mother, father, brothers, sisters, sons, daughters, mother-in-law, father-in-law, grandmother, grandfather, grandchildren, spouse's stepparents, stepchildren, sons- and daughters-in-law. For the purpose of this Section, an employee shall elect to take funeral leave for either his natural, step or foster parents, or legal guardian.

C. Compensable hours under the terms of this Section will be counted as hours worked for the purpose of computing vacation and holiday pay and will be counted as hours worked for the purpose of computing weekly overtime.

EXTRUSION, INC.

Section 18. Funeral Leave Provision

When death occurs to a member of a regular employee's immediate family, the employee, at his request, will be granted reasonably necessary time off as funeral leave of absence. He will be compensated at his regular straight time hourly rate for the hours lost from his regular schedule on any of the days prior to the funeral, the day of the funeral, and the day after the funeral, with a maximum of three (3) days' compensation.

Members of an employee's immediate family shall be limited to the employee's spouse, mother, father, step-mother, step-father, brothers, sisters, brothers-in-law, sisters-in-law, sons, daughters, grandfather, grandmother, grandchildren, mother-in-law, father-in-law, adopted children, step-children, sons-in-law, and daughters-in-law.

If death in the immediate family occurs while an employee is on his vacation, he may make application for funeral leave pay, up to a maximum of three (3) days compensation, upon his return to work. He will be granted additional days vacation at some later date, when approved by the supervisor. The number of additional vacation days allowed will be equivalent to the number of funeral leave days to which the employee would have been entitled had he not been on vacation, up to a maximum of three (3) days.

Compensable hours under the terms of this Section will be counted as hours worked for the purpose of computing vacation and holiday pay and will be counted as hours worked for the purpose of computing weekly overtime.

Note: Company names are fictitious.

(OSHA) provisions, and the like often become enmeshed in the negotiations. Where these are anticipated, it is sometimes useful to include a copy of pertinent statutes, regulations, and court, NLRB, or OSHA decisions which it is anticipated will bear upon the subject. Copies of arbitration awards involving subjects likely to come up in the negotiations might also be included.

Key Contacts

In the midst of negotiations, it is frequently necessary to contact certain persons for a briefing, to obtain assistance, or for other communications. To conserve valuable time, the bargaining book should contain a list of addresses, telephone numbers and fax numbers, where appropriate, where such persons can be reached, both during business hours and afterward. Such a list might include the following people:

- Key management personnel
- Union representatives
- Mediator
- Legal counsel
- Representatives of other companies
- Public or media relations specialists
- Industry association representatives.

Briefing Personnel and Coordinating With Other Management Functions

As preparations are being made in anticipation of bargaining, it is quite easy for labor relations specialists to overlook the fact that the employer's business is still functioning and may be seriously affected not only by the negotiations themselves, but also by rumors and speculation about the uncertainties created by labor negotiations and the potential for a strike. For example, your competitors' sales personnel may be telling your company's customers about the likelihood of a strike against your company, and advising your customers not to make any order commitments with your company during the period when negotiations are to occur. If your company's sales department has not been briefed in advance and given some information about the potential for a strike, it will not be able to credibly answer inquiries from customers or to scotch misleading information.

Public and Investor Relations

Not only can the negotiations affect other functions of the employer's business, but the converse is equally true: other areas of the employer's organization can affect negotiations. A case in point is in the public and investor relations area. Publicly held companies traditionally want to highlight the organization's financial success for the benefit of stockholders. When they do so just prior to labor negotiations, they make the negotiator's job extremely difficult. A good example of this problem occurred in 1982 when the Chrysler Corporation, just recovering from the verge of bankruptcy and still receiving government loan guarantees, proudly reported a quarterly profit of $100 million, accompanied by statements that Chrysler's "financial recovery was assured." While the profits were real, they represented only the first glimpse of recovery of a very sick corporate patient, a patient not yet ready to donate blood in the form of higher wages and benefits to its employees. Rank and file employees, however, and even local union leaders could not understand why Chrysler could not share its newfound wealth with its employees. An employer cannot present one image to stockholders and another to rank and file employees and expect to have credibility with either group. This is especially true where, as is commonly the case, employees are also stockholders. In most cases, the divergent images are not a result of a duplicitous management, but of uncoordinated public relations and labor relations departments. Each attempts to present the facts in a way that best supports its respective assignment.

Management Briefing

It is vital, therefore, that well before negotiations begin, the management spokesman brief key management people—especially those having responsibility for sales, marketing, public relations, and finance—on the background of negotiations, anticipated key issues, timing of negotiations and crucial deadlines, probabilities of a work stoppage, and contingency plans in the event of a work stoppage. This briefing should include line management personnel and, especially, supervisors. Some information will obviously have to be kept solely within top level management, but other information can be communicated to lower level management, supervisors, and to outsiders where appropriate. In many cases, it may be advisable to prepare a written statement which expresses management's public view of the negotiations and of the probability of a strike-free settlement. Such a statement can be given to key personnel to aid in formulating responses to suppliers, customers, subcontractors, and the like. In some cases where rumors may have a serious impact, a letter to these parties from a high company official is advisable.

The briefing and coordinating conducted prior to negotiations should be followed up periodically during negotiations, subject to the need for maintaining confidentiality.

Selecting a Site for Negotiations

Once a contract is reopened for negotiations the parties need to agree on where they are going to hold their negotiating meetings. While it may seem like a trivial matter, it is not uncommon for negotiating parties, whether they be involved in union/management negotiations or international negotiations, to be at loggerheads over the "shape of the table" or other procedural matters.

The options for meeting places are usually the employer's offices, the union's offices, or a neutral site such as a hotel meeting room. The employer's offices offer the employer the advantage of accessibility to files, personnel, telephones, document duplication and transmission facilities, and the like. Meeting in the employer's offices may also offer a psychological lift in that management is on its own "turf." However, such meetings can be disruptive to the employer's normal business, and the possible easy access of union representatives to rank and file employees could be a disadvantage. Some unions are unwilling to meet in a company facility because it is the management's turf. Union representatives are also aware that if a strike results they will be unable to continue meeting there due to the necessity of crossing a picket line. Although there is a cost advantage to both negotiating parties in using the employer's offices as opposed to a neutral site, this is seldom a significant consideration.

Meeting in the union's offices offers the union many of the same real and psychological advantages that meeting in the employer's offices provide the employer, and many management negotiators in turn have an instinctive aversion to such a practice. The author shares that aversion.

Because of the common difficulty of getting either party to meet on the other's turf, many negotiations are held at a neutral site such as a hotel, fraternal organization hall, Federal Mediation and Conciliation Service (FMCS) office, or other suitable location. A hotel usually offers the maximum in convenience and suitability, but it is not always possible to reserve a suitable room for intermittent and unscheduled negotiations. Consequently, the parties may need to reserve rooms at one or more conveniently located hotels for specific dates well in advance even though they may not meet at those times. Caucus rooms need to be reserved as well. Fraternal organization halls may be available but are often lacking in communications or other facilities. FMCS offices are not recommended unless the negotiations have reached a point where a mediator is desired by management. By meeting at such facilities, the parties are inviting mediation when it is not yet appropriate.

As a general proposition, where meeting size and other circumstances are appropriate, management may wish to invite the union to use the employer's offices for meeting. If this is not acceptable, then management may advise of its willingness to meet at a neutral site.

Formal Notification Preliminary to Bargaining

Most labor contracts contain a clause which sets forth the requirements for reopening that contract for negotiations. A typical clause reads as follows:

> This Agreement may be modified by the party desiring such modifications by mailing to the other party a notice in writing sixty (60) days prior to July 1, 19__, or prior to any subsequent July 1 on which this contract is in effect, that a modification is desired; and if no such sixty (60) days' notice is given prior to any July 1, the earliest time at which such notice may later be so mailed is sixty (60) days prior to July 1 of the next year.

Some provisions allow for reopening only on certain limited issues, such as wages. Typically, a notice for any type of reopening must be sent at least 60 days prior to the contract expiration date. Historically, it was common for the union, rather than the employer, to send a reopening notice, for it was usually the union that sought to bargain improvements in labor contracts. In more recent years, employers have begun to reopen contracts because of their desire to propose contractual changes. Reopening notices should be sent by certified or registered mail with a return receipt requested. It is not necessary for the receiving party to acknowledge receipt of the notice, although out of courtesy and common business practice such acknowledgments are usually sent.

Failure to Reopen

If the notice is not received in a timely manner, contracts typically provide, as does the example shown above, that the contract is closed for one year. The NLRB and the courts have upheld such clauses, and employers who refused to bargain because of not having received a timely reopening notice have not been forced to bargain.[2] It is somewhat unusual for a union not to send a timely reopening notice, and even when such a notice is not received due to an error on the union's part employers often waive the requirement, realizing that failure to negotiate may not work to the advantage of either party.

Who Has to Reopen

A question often raised by employers is whether they must send a reopening notice to the union in order to propose contract changes if the union has already reopened the contract. The answer is no. Unless a contract provides otherwise, once one party (the "initiating party") reopens a labor contract, either party is free to propose changes in the contract.[3] Notwithstanding, if an employer intends to propose contract changes, it is recommended that the employer send its own reopening notice. (Exhibit 2–10 is a sample reopening notice.) This puts the union on notice that the employer has its own agenda of proposed contract changes, and intends to negotiate from its own agenda, regardless of the union's intentions. Unless the contract provides otherwise, it is not necessary that the reopening notice specify what contract changes are proposed or even what sections may be involved in the proposals.

Exhibit 2–10. Sample Reopening Letter

Mr. Harold Stubbs
Business Agent, Local Union No. 268
International Brotherhood of Teamsters
112 Underhill Avenue
Topeka, Kansas 69842

Dear Mr. Stubbs:

In accordance with Article 26 of the labor agreement with your union covering our plant at 10 Miner Road in Topeka, this is a notice of our desire to reopen the agreement for negotitations. We consider all sections of that agreement to be subject to bargaining.

I will contact you within the next month to suggest a time and place to commence negotiations. We look forward to amicable and productive negotiations.

Very truly yours,

Albert C. Mesa
Vice President
Mesa Distribution Co.

It is simply necessary to notify the other party that the contract is reopened for purposes of negotiating changes therein.

Notice to FMCS

In addition to the normal contractual requirement of a 60-day reopening notice, there is a similar requirement contained in Section 8(d) of the National Labor Relations Act before either party can terminate or modify a contract. That section of the Act also requires that the FMCS and the corresponding state conciliation service be notified within 30 days of the reopening notice. The important aspect of Section 8(d) is that no strike or lockout can be commenced until 60 days after the reopening notice has been received. As with the contractual reopening

Exhibit 2–11. FMCS Form F-7

FMCS FORM F-7
REVISED 8/84

NOTICE TO MEDIATION AGENCIES

FORM APPROVED
OMB NO. 3076-0004
EXP. AUG. 31, 1990

MAIL TO: NOTICE PROCESSING UNIT
FEDERAL MEDIATION AND CONCILIATION SERVICE
2100 K STREET, N.W.
WASHINGTON, D.C. 20427

AND

THE STATE OR TERRITORIAL MEDIATION AGENCY

You are hereby notified that written notice of proposed termination or modification of the existing collective bargaining contract was served upon the other party to this contract and that no agreement has been reached.

IF THIS IS A HEALTH CARE INDUSTRY NOTICE PLEASE INDICATE (MARK "X")

① ☐ INITIAL CONTRACT ☐ EXISTING CONTRACT

(MARK ONE "X") AND GIVE APPROPRIATE: MO. DAY YR.

☐ CONTRACT EXPIRATION DATE ___/___/___

② ☐ CONTRACT REOPENER DATE ___/___/___

NAME OF EMPLOYER OR EMPLOYER ASSOCIATION/ORGANIZATION (IF MORE THAN ONE, SUBMIT NAMES AND ADDRESSES ON AN ATTACHED LIST)

③

ADDRESS OF EMPLOYER/ASSOCIATION
NO. STREET CITY STATE ZIP

④

EMPLOYER OFFICIAL TO CONTACT

⑤

(AREA CODE) PHONE NUMBER

⑥

NAME OF INTERNATIONAL UNION OR PARENT BODY

⑦

NAME AND NO. OF LOCAL (IF NOT A LOCAL, GIVE NAME AND NUMBER, IF ANY, OF THE UNION ORGANIZATION INVOLVED IN THE NEGOTIATIONS)

⑧

ADDRESS OF LOCAL UNION
NO. STREET CITY STATE ZIP

⑨

UNION OFFICIAL TO CONTACT

⑩

(AREA CODE) PHONE NUMBER

⑪

A. LOCATION OF AFFECTED ESTABLISHMENT CITY STATE ZIP

B. LOCATION OF NEGOTIATIONS (COMPLETE ONLY IF DIFFERENT FROM 12.A)
CITY STATE ZIP

⑫

TOTAL NUMBER EMPLOYED AT AFFECTED LOCATION(S)

⑬

NUMBER OF EMPLOYEES COVERED BY CONTRACT

⑭

INDUSTRY AND TYPE OF ESTABLISHMENT (E.G., STEEL INDUSTRY — FACTORY; FOOD INDUSTRY — RETAIL CHAIN STORE; EDUCATION — PRIVATE COLLEGE; ELECTRICAL INDUSTRY — PUBLIC UTILITY)

⑮

PRINCIPAL PRODUCT OR SERVICE

⑯

THIS NOTICE IS FILED ON BEHALF OF (MARK "X")

⑰ ☐ UNION ☐ EMPLOYER

TYPE OF NEGOTIATIONS (MARK "X")

☐ SINGLE ESTABLISHMENT
☐ MULTI-PLANT
☐ AREA OR INDUSTRY WIDE
⑱ ☐ OTHER (SPECIFY) ____________

TYPE OF EMPLOYEES COVERED BY CONTRACT (MARK "X" ALL THAT APPLY)

☐ PROFESSIONAL/TECHNICAL
☐ PRODUCTION/MAINTENANCE
☐ CLERICAL
⑲ ☐ OTHER (SPECIFY) ____________

NAME AND TITLE OF OFFICIAL FILING NOTICE

⑳

SIGNATURE DATE

㉑

Receipt of this form does not constitute a request for mediation nor does it commit FMCS to offer its facilities. Receipt of this notice will not be acknowledged in writing by FMCS. FMCS does not forward copies of this notice to state or territorial mediation agencies. While the use of this form is voluntary, it will facilitate our service to respondents.

Public reporting burden for this collection of information is estimated to average 30 minutes per response, including the time for reviewing instructions, searching existing data sources, gathering and maintaining the data needed, and completing and reviewing the collection of information. Send comments regarding this burden estimate or any other aspect of this collection of information, including suggestions for reducing this burden, to FMCS, Administrative Services, Washington, D.C. 20427; and to the Office of Information and Regulatory Affairs, Office of Management and Budget, Washington, D.C. 20503.

notice, only one party, the initiating party, needs to provide the Section 8(d) notice in order for either party to terminate the contract and engage in self-help.[4] FMCS Form F-7 can be used for purposes of this notification, although the notice also may be in the form of a letter or in almost any written form. A copy of the FMCS form is reproduced as Exhibit 2–11.

Checklist for Preparations

Necessary homework in preparing for negotiations begins well in advance of the first bargaining session and continues through the preliminary stages of negotiations. Because of the breadth of such preparations, it is usually helpful to have a checklist of tasks to be undertaken and to assign names of people responsible and completion dates for each task. Appendix 4 is an example of such a checklist. Although it may be more extensive than necessary for most negotiations, it is a useful tool to ensure that all vital steps in the preparation process have been taken.

3

Developing a Bargaining Game Plan

Successful football coaches prepare for an upcoming game by studying films of their opponents' recent games; analyzing the results of their own past games with that opponent, noting strengths and weaknesses at various positions; and determining which selection and order of plays will offer the greatest chance of success. This type of preparation is commonly called a "game plan." In essence, it is a strategy designed to defeat the opponent. As the football team progresses through the game, the coach frequently must adjust the game plan to adapt to the opponent's offensive and defensive formations and plays. Injuries and turnovers (fumbles and interceptions) also will require modification of the game plan. Nevertheless, it is interesting how frequently one hears a winning coach who is interviewed after an important victory declare, "We stayed with our game plan."

The analogy between football games and labor contract negotiations in this regard is rather apt. If management wishes to win—achieve its objectives—it must have a well-conceived game plan or bargaining strategy. It must also be prepared to adapt and modify its strategy to meet its opponent's—the union's—moves. And just as a sophisticated football coach positions one or more of the assistant coaches high in the stands to view the game and evaluate the progress of the game from a more advantageous perspective, so too should management evaluate negotiations, not only on a day-to-day level but "from above" or from a broader perspective. That broader perspective permits management to determine how negotiations are progressing and where they appear to be headed in relation to what was anticipated in the original plan.

A labor contract negotiation can simply "happen" without much direction, or it can be guided in a direction which will better suit the purposes of one of the negotiating parties. Management must realize that it, rather than the union, should control and direct the progress of negotiations. Although the relative bargaining strength will most often determine the final result, the party that has identified its goals and formulated an effective plan for achieving those goals is more likely to control the negotiations and attain its objectives.

Much of the background information necessary for developing an effective game plan has already been stated in Chapters 1 and 2; such tasks as analyzing previous negotiations, identifying key issues, measuring the economic climate, and evaluating the parties' relative bargaining power are necessary preliminaries to constructing a viable bargaining strategy. The game plan itself will necessarily contain the objectives and economic parameters for a final settlement, timing of meetings, critical actions in the negotiations, probable means of dealing with key issues, and the development of management's agenda.

A game plan for labor negotiations cannot generally be completely finalized prior to commencing negotiations. Without some idea of the scope of the union's proposals and the nature and depth of feeling about key issues, development of a final realistic plan may not be possible. Consequently, although the major features of such a plan can be put in place before negotiations begin, other important elements can normally be added only after the union's agenda has been received and some substantive meetings have taken place.

Establishing Objectives and Setting Economic Parameters

Economic Parameters

The process of establishing the economic limits for a negotiation (i.e., that point beyond which an employer will take a strike) is not a scientific one. It usually constitutes an amalgam of analyses, projections, and judgments which usually represent: (1) what economic levels other employers in comparable negotiations have settled for and what the organization has granted in its other comparable negotiations; (2) how much an employer is willing to pay and/or can afford to pay over the next contract term, usually one to three years; (3) what settlement level an employer thinks will be necessary to avoid a strike; and (4) what wage and benefit levels will be necessary to attract and hold a sufficiently skilled work force.

None of these criteria stand in isolation. They are interrelated. For example, the settlement level which may be necessary to avoid a strike is usually determined by settlements reached by other employers in comparable negotiations. Similarly, what an employer is willing to pay is usually no more than what he believes he will have to pay to avoid a strike or to retain a competent work force. The economic climate in which the bargaining takes place will also have a strong influence on which criteria are most significant. In a thriving economy with low unemployment, labor market availability may be quite important, whereas during a recession period it will hardly be considered.

Other things being equal, settlement levels in comparable negotiations will usually be the most significant criterion, for they reveal what a particular union has been willing to settle for and usually represent what amounts an employer's competitors can afford or are willing to spend. Absent significant intra-industry differences, that level should be a good measure of how much an employer can, or should be able to, afford. Other factors also need to be considered. What is the forecast for the employer's business in the next two to three years? What capital expenditures are budgeted for that period? How do the employer's present costs compare with those of his competitors' (union and nonunion)? What, if any, improvements in worker productivity have been experienced during the term of the last contract? The answers to these and similar questions should influence an employer's determination as to what it can and/or is willing to offer.

Noneconomic Objectives

The efficiency of a work force and the employer's unit labor costs can be influenced greatly by the noneconomic provisions of a labor contract. The word "noneconomic" is largely a misnomer. In fact, virtually all labor contract provisions have some economic impact, and many of them have a very substantial influence on employers' labor and operating costs. Labor contract sections containing seniority provisions; staffing levels; rules governing assignment of work, rest periods, or cleanup time; and the like are all immediately translated to the bottom line. Nevertheless, the term "noneconomic" is frequently used because the contract provisions in question involve processes rather than a clearly defined economic payment. In any event, as management prepares to embark upon negotiations, it cannot overlook such noneconomic aspects of the labor agreement. These objectives may be sought by way of management proposals or simply by resisting union proposals for changes in the current agreement.

By analyzing grievance and arbitration case results, consulting with supervisors about troublesome contractual and extracontractual areas, collecting and reviewing other employers' labor contracts, preparing a list of key issues and determining what, if anything, should be included on management's agenda, management will cover all the items which may be appropriate to establish as noneconomic objectives.

Models of Bargaining Parameters and Objectives

Some employers merely instruct their negotiators to negotiate "the best deal they can get." Unfortunately, such directions leave unanswered the question of how much the employer can afford and who will ultimately judge what was the best possible settlement. For any significant labor negotiations, such vague directions are unfair to the negotiator and unwise for management. Objectives, to be meaningful, must be *specific* and *realistic*. They should spell out what is expected with sufficient specificity so that management and its bargaining representative know what constitutes an acceptable settlement and what the outside limits are.

The directions should not be so generous as to allow the negotiator to "give away the store," or so meager as to be unattainable.

The Role of the Negotiator in Setting Parameters

Because employer organizations and management styles differ so greatly, it is not easy to suggest a categorical method for establishing bargaining parameters. Notwithstanding, the author's experience suggests that the most effective way is to have the negotiator (perhaps assisted by one or more members of the negotiating team) develop recommended settlement targets and limits that should be reviewed with, and approved by, executive management. The reasons for this are several. First, the spokesperson has, or should have, the best information as to competitive wages and benefits, labor market availability, bargaining leverage factors, contract strengths and weaknesses, and other relevant information. Second, it is the spokesperson who must ultimately achieve a settlement, and the chances of attaining that objective are enhanced if the spokesperson has played a pivotal role in formulating the bargaining parameters.

This is not to say that top management should accept the negotiator's recommendations without a critical evaluation. Certainly the cost effectiveness, profitability, and viability of the enterprise are the primary responsibilities of top management, and it must exercise the authority to decide what limits and objectives should guide management's negotiations. But the employer's spokesperson needs to be involved from the outset and must be a full participant in setting the bargaining parameters. Once the objectives are established, the negotiator is then following targets that he or she has had a key role in developing and that have been approved by the executive level of management.

The Simple Model

A step up from the simple "best deal" admonition, is the following still simple but slightly more specific set of objectives:

Model A

1. Contract term to be longer than one year.
2. Cost increases no greater than 5.5 percent in any one year.

While general goals such as those shown in Model A may neither appear to be very ambitious nor give the negotiators a great deal of direction, they do provide some framework within which a negotiating plan can be developed. In all of the models in this chapter, it is assumed that avoidance of a strike is a very high priority.

More Direction

A somewhat more detailed and ambitious set of goals could be stated as follows:

<u>Model B</u>

1. Three-year contract term.
2. Limit overall cost increases to a maximum of 5 percent in any one year, and a cumulative cost package of no more than 16 percent for a three-year contract or 10 percent for a two-year contract.
3. Wage increases in any one year to be no greater than 6 percent nor average more than 5 percent in each year of a multiple-year contract.
4. Limit medical insurance cost obligation to a rate of increase no greater than the percentage wage increase in any year.
5. Grant no additional paid time-off benefits.
6. Eliminate restrictive seniority practices in the following areas:
   a. Selection for promotion to skilled trades jobs.
   b. Assignment of overtime requiring additional penalty/premium payments.
   c. Retention of critical skills during layoff periods.
7. Alter grievance/arbitration provisions in order to:
   a. Eliminate current backlog of grievances pending arbitration.
   b. Prevent recurrence of unreasonable backlog.
   c. Prevent grievants and union from circumventing first step of grievance procedure (oral discussion with supervisor).

Model B obviously provides more direction and requires management negotiators to hit a more defined target than Model A, yet gives them sufficient flexibility to structure various packages in order to achieve a settlement. Both Models A and B, however, do not fully take into account the *quid pro quo*s or tradeoffs which are typically necessary in bargaining.

A Road Map

While it may be possible to eliminate restrictive work practices through negotiation, it may not be possible to do so by granting wages and benefits which are no greater than those agreed to by employers that have not achieved union agreement on such concessions. In other words, it may be necessary to trade for, or "buy out," restrictive work practices or contractual provisions that are costly, inefficient, and/or burdensome to management. Consequently, the following model of objectives may be more appropriate:

Model C

1. Lay a foundation through specific actions for a long-term improvement in our labor-management relationship with this union.
2. Term of contract, at least two and preferably three years.
3. Total package cost (wage and fringes):
   a. Two years—maximum increase of 5 percent in any one year and 10 percent cumulative increase over term of contract.
   b. Three years—maximum increase of 6 percent in any one year and 16 percent cumulatively.
   c. "Dividend" of additional package cost increase of up to 1 percent per year if concessions can be attained in items 7 and 8 below which will result in savings over the term of the contract equal to twice the amount of the dividend, based upon conservative cost estimates.[1]
4. Wage increases are to be as follows:
   a. No less than 3 percent and no more than 6 percent in any one year.
   b. Increases in all but one year of the contract must be in percentage terms or otherwise comparably graduated to recognize skill differences.
5. Any increases resulting from COLAs (cost-of-living adjustments) must be taken from amounts available under items 3 and 4 above based upon an assumed increase of 5 percent per year in the national CPI.
6. Any increases in fringe benefits are limited by the following:
   a. No additional holidays.
   b. May grant one additional week of vacation except for employees with less than five years of service, and no employee may receive more than a maximum of five weeks of vacation regardless of service.
   c. No increases in medical insurance benefits except where recommended by benefits consultants, with a maximum of improvements equal to 0.5 percent in total labor cost.
   d. Pension improvements may not result in a monthly benefit rate of more than $20 per year of service.
   e. Fringe benefit improvements in excess of the stated amounts may be increased to the extent they are taken out of the wage package, except that no improvements may

exceed the maximums provided by other comparable employers in our industry in the same geographical area.

7. Change scheduling and overtime provisions to:
   a. Eliminate premium pay for work on Saturday "as such."
   b. Permit scheduling of extra shifts with less than 48 hours notice.
   c. Permit scheduling of split shifts in departments X, Y, and Z when business conditions so require.
8. Change seniority provisions to:
   a. Allow use of part-time employees to avoid scheduled overtime.
   b. Eliminate all "grandfather" agreements (permit buy-outs up to twice annual loss of pay).
   c. Prohibit interdepartmental bidding except in base rate jobs.
9. Strengthen no-strike clause to:
   a. Completely preclude self-help in grievance situations.
   b. Prohibit honoring of stranger picket lines.

Model C provides management negotiators with a rather clear road map of where the negotiations should lead, and what tradeoffs are available.

In Models A, B, and C, the terms "objectives" and "economic parameters" were used. A logical question may arise as to whether these are absolute *maximums* or merely represent settlement *goals*. In other words, will the employer take a strike if a settlement at these levels cannot be attained? Many employers prefer not to be pinned down to an absolute maximum or "wall" before negotiations have commenced. This is sometimes wise, since there are so many variables at this stage that figures which get fixed so early may not be realistic and could result in a tactical miscalculation. Some employers, however, believe that if sufficient data is available and the value of comparable settlements known, the actual amount or cost range of a proper settlement from management's standpoint can be finally determined well before negotiations begin. There is much to be said for this approach as well, so long as management is prepared to adjust its position based upon new information not previously available.

The Target Approach

Another variation of negotiating parameters takes into account the dichotomy between the level of settlement an employer would *like* to have, called here a "target," and the level of settlement to which it is *willing* to agree in order to avoid a strike, i.e., the "wall." An example of this format, covering economic items only, is as follows:

<u>Model D</u>

TARGET

1. Three-year contract term.
2. Maximum average overall cost increase of 6 percent per year with a maximum of 7 percent in any one year.
3. First year general wage increase not to exceed 5.5 percent per year; average annual wage increase over term of contract not to exceed 6.5 percent and a maximum of 7.5 percent in any one year.
4. No medical insurance benefit increases; company contribution to be "capped" each year at a level 10 percent above contribution rate for the preceeding year.
5. No pension improvements.
6. No additional holidays.
7. No additional vacation benefits except for employees who have more than 25 years of service.
8. Eliminate COLA clause; can buy out over term of contract with a lump sum payback equal to a two-year payment assuming an average annual CPI increase of 5 percent.
9. Reduce sick pay benefits by 50 percent—no specific buy-out money available.

WALL

1. Two-year contract term or longer.
2. Total annual average labor cost increase of 8.5 percent per year; maximum of 7 percent in first year.
3. First year general wage increase not to exceed 7 percent, average annual wage increase not to exceed 8.5 percent.
4. Increase medical insurance benefits by no more than $25 per month (composite cost) for each year of contract.
5. No increase in past service benefits under pension plan and limit future service benefits to a rate of increase in percentage terms no greater than the wage increase for that year.
6. Maximum of two additional paid holidays per year for three-year contract; one additional for a two-year contract.
7. Vacation improvement only for employees with more than 15 years service.
8. No increase in COLA formula.

It is obvious that the "target" expectations are higher than the "wall" limitations, showing that the employer is willing to spend an additional amount above the optimum if that is absolutely necessary. Model D can be criticized in that it could lead a negotiator to believe that he or she has obtained a cheap settlement if the target is hit, whereas it might have been possible to settle for less if the "wall" had not been used as a guide as to how much more was available to spend in order to avoid a strike. A competent negotiator, however, will always try to "come back with money in his pocket" (settle for less than he was authorized to offer), regardless of whether he sees the target or wall settlement as his maximum.

The exact format in which the objectives and parameters are displayed is much less important than the fact that they are established. Once established, they should continually be reviewed throughout the negotiation to assure that they are realistic and attainable. But any pressure to adjust them upward must be accompanied by the question, "What has happened since the time the parameters were set to justify a change in them at this time?"

Timing

Another essential ingredient of the bargaining plan is timing—the optimum time for negotiations to begin and end, when key offers will be made, and target dates for reaching certain objectives. While many factors will necessarily complicate adherence to a particular time schedule, this fact should not discourage the preparation of a timetable.

Probably the most logical guide to use when establishing a bargaining timetable is the timing which occurred in previous negotiations, and the favorable or unfavorable results associated with each. If past negotiations have followed a regular pattern and the results have been considered satisfactory, no change would seem indicated. If, however, a strike resulted because the negotiators "ran out of time" or because an explosive issue could not properly be resolved as a result of time constraints, then a change would obviously be warranted.

Beginning Negotiations

It is common practice to begin negotiations 30 to 90 days prior to a contract expiration date. However, a number of factors could vary the time when negotiations commence. These would include the following:

1. Other contract negotiations scheduled for either party.
2. Customer supply deadlines or peak demand periods for employer's product or service.
3. Custom regarding both parties' willingness to negotiate beyond a contract expiration date and their attitudes toward retroactive pay.
4. Availability of key persons on both sides of the table.
5. Relationship of these negotiations to other comparable negotiations in the same industry or firm (i.e., leader/follower role).
6. Complexity of negotiations and number of serious issues which need to be addressed.

Management may also wish to consider some timing innovations. For example, during the middle of a three-year contract, there may be an advantage to reopening the contract to extend it for another several years. This might be warranted in a case where the employer has a major capital construction project or government contract about to begin and does not want the threat of a strike hanging over the project or contract. Similarly, there may be other facilities of the employer with similar contract expiration dates and management may wish to spread out the expiration dates as much as possible. Other innovations might include negotiating a contract extension under a wage reopener clause of an existing contract long before the date set for reopening in order to avoid strike exposure at an undesirable time.

In the normal bargaining situation, it is wise to begin negotiations sufficiently in advance of the expiration date to allow a full discussion of all issues and a normal number of offers and counteroffers. On the other hand, there can be a danger in allowing too much time for bargaining meetings. Where the parties meet on a day-to-day basis too far in advance of the expiration date, pressure is often put on management to "keep the negotiations moving" and avoid an impasse. This normally translates into management concessions. Unless management begins with a large number of its own contract proposals, it can find itself pushed into yielding on smaller issues to keep negotiations headed toward a settlement. Together, these smaller issues can be significant.

Ending Negotiations

Throughout this and other chapters, the term "contract expiration date" is considered as being synonymous with "strike deadline." Contracts in some industries, however, provide for a notice period after the contract expires before a strike can commence. The period is commonly 3 to 10 days. In such cases the deadline is the first day on which a strike can legally occur, and therefore that may be the date upon which management should key its timing strategy.

The ideal time to conclude negotiations is usually thought to be a date sufficiently in advance of the contract expiration date to permit the union to properly present a tentative settlement or management's final offer to its members and conduct a ratification vote. If negotiations are concluded too far in advance of the expiration date, union rank and file may feel that they should reject the offer/settlement since no imminent strike deadline threatens their security, and their negotiators still have time to bargain for more. If the negotiations are not concluded by the expiration date, the employer may be subject to intermittent work stoppages or even a full-blown strike before the final offer can be presented for ratification.

While the normal time for ending negotiations is determined as discussed above, there may be other factors which indicate some innovation in this regard is desirable. For example, the employer may wish to "send a signal" to the rank and file and receive some feedback without being completely exposed to a work stoppage. Thus, negotiations may commence early and a serious offer intended to settle negotiations made well in advance of the contract deadline. The results of a ratification vote then may be some indication of the likelihood of a strike at the contract expiration date, since the union members obviously will be well aware that they too are sending a message.

Timing of Offers

Perhaps no other aspect of bargaining timing is as critical as the timing of economic offers; the timing, as well as the composition, of an offer can influence how it will be received. Of course, the number of economic offers to be made will dictate, to a large extent, the times when they are made. For example, if only two offers are to be made, the times when the first and last are made will usually be quite different from times in negotiations where three or four offers are made.

The timing and frequency of any offers before the first and last offers will be based upon the spread between the positions of the parties, and on any particular roadblocks in the way of a settlement. However, offers made in rapid-fire succession will send an obvious signal to the other party that there is an urgency to settle—perhaps at almost any price. Each offer by management should convey the impression that it has been well thought-out and that it is being made deliberately with the expectation of being accepted, or at least coming very close to acceptance. Frequent offers at short intervals will work against this impression. More thorough considerations concerning the strategy of offers are discussed in Chapter 7.

Bargaining Calendar

A useful way to plan bargaining timing to achieve a strategic advantage is to develop a timetable in calendar format. Such a timetable indicates tentative dates for key events in the negotiation. It is particularly helpful to the management spokesperson to prevent time from slipping by unnoticed, and especially to ensure that a strike deadline does not arrive before essential steps have been taken. A sample bargaining calendar is shown in Exhibit 3–1.

In considering timing as a part of the bargaining plan, employers should allot additional time for contingencies which could delay negotiations. Bargaining never proceeds like clockwork; unanticipated delays inevitably occur. A realistic timetable should make allowance for these delays. Likewise, the timetable will undoubtedly have to be revised a number of times before negotiations are concluded.

Identifying Key Issues

In Chapter 1 it was suggested that a review of key issues in previous negotiations was a useful way to analyze the results of those negotiations. So too, in preparing for forthcoming negotiations it is important to anticipate issues which are likely to emerge as key issues in the negotiations. These issues may

Exhibit 3–1. Tentative Bargaining Schedule

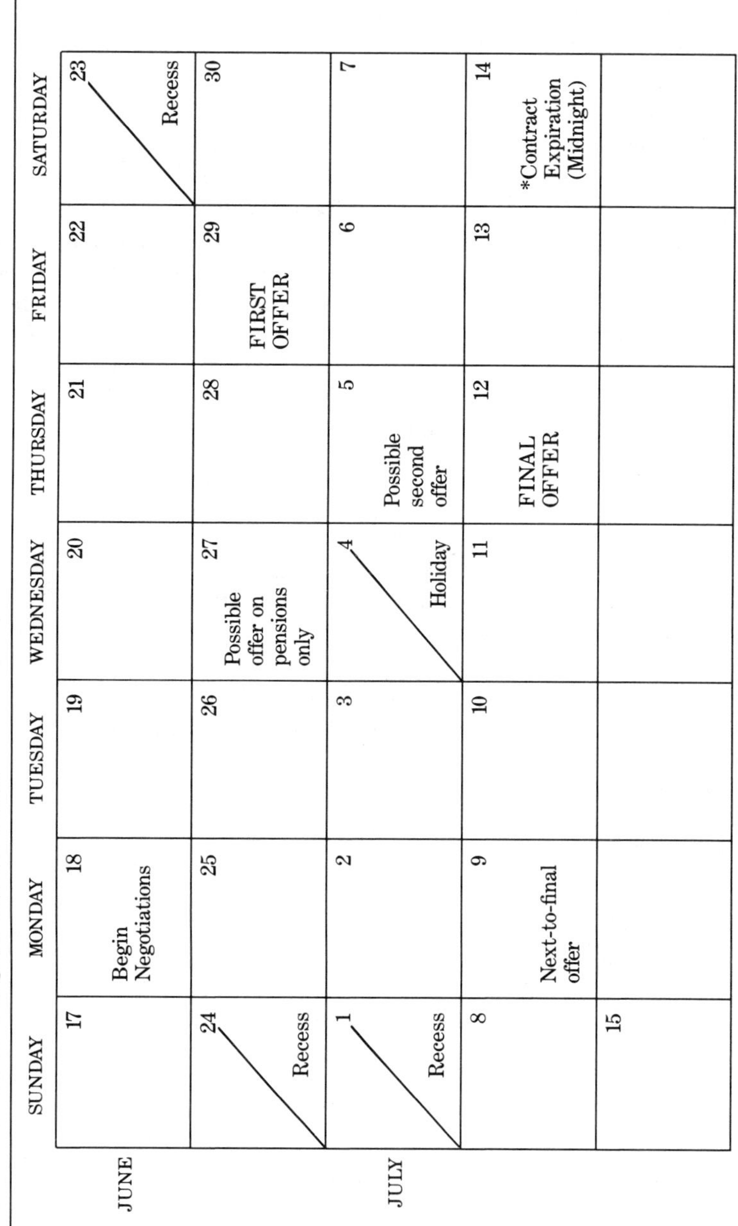

	SUNDAY	MONDAY	TUESDAY	WEDNESDAY	THURSDAY	FRIDAY	SATURDAY
JUNE	17	18 Begin Negotiations	19	20	21	22	23 Recess
	24 Recess	25	26	27 Possible offer on pensions only	28	29 FIRST OFFER	30
JULY	1 Recess	2	3	4 Holiday	5 Possible second offer	6	7
	8	9 Next-to-final offer	10	11	12 FINAL OFFER	13	14 *Contract Expiration (Midnight)
	15						

be originated by the union, by individual employees, by management, or by parties outside the two immediately involved and can arise from a variety of stimuli, including the following:

1. Economic trends during the term of the existing contract (e.g., rampant inflation, recession).
2. Changes in work methods or operations (e.g., skills becoming obsolete, department closure or realignment, seniority disputes resulting from work realignment).
3. Contract interpretation and/or arbitration awards during the term of the agreement.
4. Unpalatable employee or union practices (e.g., excessive absenteeism, wildcat strikes).
5. "Breakthrough" features in settlements involving other employers within the same or a related industry.
6. Notable events in comparable operations (e.g., plant closures, decertification elections).
7. Interpersonal conflicts between management/supervision and the union or employees.

Spotting Hot Issues

These and other factors will often cause controversial or potentially explosive proposals to be advanced by one party or the other. Often these "hot issues" will, prior to negotiations, become a matter of open discussion in the workplace or at least be known through the grapevine. First-line supervisors who have good rapport with their subordinates will, without much effort, be able to pick up issues which are important to the rank and file. Issues likely to be high on the union's priority list will often be highlighted in union publications, casual conversations, and meetings held during the contract term.

Of course, management's spokesperson will be aware, or should be aware, of those issues which are critical to the employer. It remains, however, for the negotiator to ascertain just how high a priority is being attached to those issues by top management, to estimate how attainable they will be in negotiations, and to determine what, if any, alternative solutions may exist to achieve the desired results.

In-Depth Analysis

Once a list of key issues is prepared, it is necessary to devote time to studying and analyzing these issues, developing positions on them, and preparing any backup information or arguments to support or resist them. For example, if it becomes known that the union is seeking to introduce a cost-of-living escalator to apply to pension benefits and that there is strong rank and file support for the concept, considerable time should be devoted to (1) investigating to see if other employers have adopted such a provision and what the results have been; (2) obtaining cost projections of such a benefit; (3) developing arguments and data to resist; (4) developing visual aids to convey the basis for resistance; and (5) formulating alternative proposals which may be more feasible and preparing data and exhibits to support such alternatives. Some negotiators like to have a "white paper" prepared on certain key issues to include the type of information just mentioned. This white paper normally consists of a report by experts presenting factual information, and rational arguments that the negotiator can use at the bargaining table.

Identification of key issues is no guarantee that other issues thought to be insignificant, or perhaps not anticipated at all, might not become prominent in the negotiations. Furthermore, there is usually some wasted effort inherent in such a project, since many anticipated "hot issues" may never materialize or become significant. Nevertheless, because such background work and fact gathering will be difficult if not impossible during the hectic days when negotiations are in progress, it must normally be done in advance if it is to be done at all. Moreover, consideration of key issues is apt to be more thoughtful and rational when done in the unpressured atmosphere preceding negotiations.

Dealing With Key Issues

A viable bargaining plan should include proposed means for dealing with those key issues which have been identified. Some union demands may be successfully resisted merely by a firm negative response, i.e., "No." Other union-sponsored issues may not be so easily disposed of and may require concessions in one form or another. Still others may be unacceptable to management in any form, yet are imperative to the union, and thus present genuine strike issues. Full appreciation of the priorities being placed on these key issues may not be possible until several bargaining sessions have taken place.

The bargaining plan should take each of these issues into account and reflect the following:

- Statement of the issue
- Perceived importance to the union
- Management's position regarding the issue
- Alternatives to the union proposal
- Management's position regarding the alternatives
- Plan for dealing with the issue.

An example of such a plan follows:

1. *Issue.* Union seeks contractual right to honor picket lines of sister locals at facilities X, Y, and Z.
2. *Perceived importance to union.* Very hot issue; two years ago pickets from facility Z came to plant A and caused a three-day work stoppage. Problem at plant Z was over an unresolved grievance delayed in getting to arbitration; two employees were fired and union was enjoined and fined for honoring pickets; could be a strike issue to union.
3. *Management's position.* Our no-strike clause doesn't allow honoring of pickets; must resist at all costs, in fact we are going to propose to tighten the current no-strike clause.
4. *Alternative(s).* None apparent; could possibly agree to put an expedited arbitration clause into all plant contracts for prompt resolution of strike-threatening issues.
5. *Management reaction to alternative.* Don't like expedited arbitration *per se* and especially not in those cases where some hotheads can force it on us.
6. *Dealing with issues.* Resist vehemently—don't believe it's a true strike issue with union, although it could become a rallying point if we can't agree on economics. Will consider limited expedited arbitration if it becomes absolutely necessary to resolve the issue.

A realistic plan for dealing with any key issues should likewise focus on management-sponsored issues. Reaching a final settlement may be impeded by these issues as much as, or more than, by union-sponsored issues, and finding the means of accomplishing the contractual changes desired by management while reaching agreement on all issues requires thoughtful strategic planning.

Management's Agenda

It is often said that "bargaining is a two-way street." Unfortunately, for many years employers either forgot or abandoned that truism. During the period from the end of World War II through the 1970s, collective bargaining in the United States was characterized largely as a "management give—union take" situation. Although some employers sought, and occasionally obtained, union concessions in exchange for improved wages, benefits, and working conditions, the practice of labor negotiations during that period to a great extent was simply a one-way street.

Beginning in the 1980s, and undoubtedly caused primarily by the severe recessionary period affecting most "smokestack industries" (i.e., steel, autos, rubber, heavy manufacturing, etc.), management went on the offensive in contract negotiations, seeking union "give-backs," often proposing contract modifications during the term of multiyear agreements. That type of bargaining came to be known as "concessionary bargaining." A more detailed discussion of this phenomenon follows in Chapter 15.

This chapter discusses the more typical type of two-way bargaining which takes place (or should take place) in conventional collective bargaining. Management has a legitimate right and obligation to seek agreement from the union on matters that will result in cost reduction, product or service improvement, or other advantages to management which will help to offset the cost or loss of efficiency resulting from negotiated improvements sought by the union. Before negotiations commence, therefore, management needs to make the necessary preparations so that bargaining can be a two-way street.

Determining Management's Needs

The Running List

The first order of business is for management to identify those areas of the labor contract which constitute problems for it and which require union agreement in order to be changed. A useful technique is for each person in management who regularly works with a union contract, e.g., a labor relations manager or first-line supervisor, to keep a handy "negotiations file," "problem file," or similarly titled file throughout the term of the labor contract. As grievances are filed, union resistance experienced, or operating problems develop, an appropriate note is made and dropped into the file. As the time arrives to prepare for negotiations, the notes are accumulated and listed in order of importance. In some cases, the passage of time and/or intervening events may have rendered the problem moot or insignificant and, therefore, it need not be included. The completed lists from all management persons are then collected and assembled into a master list as part of management's agenda preparation.

Grievance and Arbitration Decisions

Another means of determining management's needs is to review grievance resolutions and arbitration awards which interpret or apply sections of (1) the contract involved in the negotiations, (2) other contracts of the same employer, and (3) contracts of other employers, especially those in the same industry and/or involving the same union. Such cases give clues as to possible weak points in the contract, areas where the union may have obtained a unique interpretation of a contract clause, or simply areas where management needs to recapture a right it lost in arbitration.

Beyond the Contract

Too often, in attempting to identify problem areas in a labor contract, management personnel merely thumb through the labor agreement in an effort to locate clauses which they feel may need to be changed. Instead of focusing on the day-to-day operational situations or problems, they look at the language in the contract and attempt to remember situations in which the language has caused a problem. The fallacy in that approach, at least as an exclusive approach, is that so many union-related problems originate not because of a clause in the contract but because of an unwritten practice, a side letter or memorandum of agreement, a practice resulting from settlement of a previous grievance, or other limitation not found in the labor contract. Consequently, the review should focus on those situations which have arisen, or potentially could have arisen, when the union thwarted management action, or management refrained from acting, due to a contractual or quasi-contractual limitation.

Organizing and Prioritizing Management's Needs

Once the items have been assembled that are candidates for management's opening proposals, it remains to organize the proposals in a logical fashion and assign them priorities based on the economic value and/or other value to the employer.

A useful way to do this is to prepare a list of possible proposals that reflects the section of the contract involved, a description of the change to be made (or alternatively, the actual change in wording that is contemplated), which department or subdivision of the organization that proposed the change, an estimate of the tangible savings realizable if the change is made, and a priority designation to be assigned to the proposal. Such a list allows key management personnel and the negotiator to seek a meeting of the minds as to what contract changes should be proposed and how strongly they should be pushed for acceptance. Exhibit 3–2 is an example of this type of list.

Because so many contract provisions are not susceptible to clearcut cost analysis, estimated savings calculations are seldom precise. They require reasonable assumptions and rough estimating. Nevertheless, some estimate of cost impact is better than none. In assigning a priority, the author prefers a letter designation approach (A-D) with the letters given some definition such as the ones that follow:

A. Absolutely necessary; don't go home without it.
B. Extremely important; go to great lengths to achieve.
C. Nice to get; obtain if it isn't too costly or disruptive.
D. Minor value; can do without; clarification or possible window-dressing.
E. "Housekeeping"—cleanup language generally for the benefit of both parties.

In some cases, proposed contract changes that have little or no cost impact will be given a higher priority than those offering considerable savings. Some low or no-cost impact items can affect vital aspects of the employer's business and its flexibility to manage. This is why it is important to review the list with key management personnel, and especially to examine the priority designations to make certain that the priorities best meet the employer's most vital needs.

Obviously, a list such as the one here described should be given, or shown to, the most limited number of persons nec-

Exhibit 3–2. MTU Negotiations—Opening Proposals—Article 9—Seniority

Sec.	Para.	Description of Change	Dept.	Prior	Est. $ Savings
9	B	Increase probationary period from 45 calendar days to 6 months.	All	C	NAS
9	D.2	Enable company to select the most qualified, not just the employee who is able to do the job.	H.T	A	NC
9	D.7	Eliminate trial period for successful bidders before determining them to be qualified.	F	B	$150,000
9	F	Eliminate 10-day trial period to demonstrate ability in bumping situation	F	B	$135,000
9	J	Allow employees promoted to supervisors to retain bargaining unit seniority for one year rather than 90 days	S	C	NAS

Code
NAS—no appreciable savings
NC—not calculable

essary, strictly on a need-to-know basis. Since it provides a clear indication of how important management's agenda items are to the employer's negotiators, it would provide union negotiators with an incalculable advantage if it were to fall into their hands.

Avoiding the Major Pitfall of Management Proposals

The Major Pitfall

Once management has identified its needs, it does not necessarily follow that each one should be included on management's agenda of proposals for contractual changes. If management could be guaranteed that it could obtain union agreement on each and every proposal such a strategy would make sense. The reason for this is that *management takes a risk in proposing a change in its labor contract, if it subsequently is not able to obtain the change.*

For example, a labor contract states that in a layoff situation senior employees may bump junior employees in the same department, "provided the senior employees are qualified to perform the jobs held by the junior employees." Management interprets "qualified" to mean that the senior employee must have previously and successfully performed the job held by the junior employee, whereas the union has contended that it simply means that the senior employee must be able to do the job of the junior employee satisfactorily after being given a short trial period to get the knack of the job. Assume further that the company, on several previous occasions, has applied its own interpretation of "qualified" although the union has consistently fought that interpretation, resulting in grievances and much hostility.

First-line supervisors now want management to propose a definition of "qualified" or otherwise modify the seniority clause in order to make it clear that an employee must have demonstrated his qualifications by working on the same job or a similar job before he can bump a junior employee. *Watch out!* If such a proposal is made, and if management is not able to get the union's agreement (and not willing to take a strike in order to unilaterally implement the change), a subsequent dispute pursued to arbitration over the meaning of the word "qualified" could result in an arbitrator's accepting the union's interpretation of that word. The reasoning of the arbitrator would be that if the word "qualified" actually meant what the employer argued it meant, the employer would not have found it necessary to propose that the definition be added. Since the union did not accept the company's proposed change, and since a new agreement was reached without any change in the word "qualified," according to contract construction principles accepted by most arbitrators[2] it must be presumed that the union's interpretation was what both parties originally understood it to mean. Thus, by attempting to clarify some ambiguous language and being unsuccessful, management could lose the benefit of its former interpretation of that section of the contract.

Ways to Avoid or Minimize the Pitfall

Does this mean that management should not propose any contract changes concerning its rights unless it is absolutely clear that management does not already have the right under the language it is proposing to change? Not necessarily. First, however, thoughtful consideration should be given to the advisability of proposing the change at all. If, as in the example given above, management had previously prevailed in its interpretations of "qualified," albeit with some dispute, why not leave well enough alone and simply continue with that interpretation?

If management has good reason to change ambiguous language, there are other and safer ways to do it. One technique is to refrain from including the item in management's original agenda, but to advance it as part of a counterproposal to one of the union's proposals. Referring back to the preceding example concerning bumping, it would not be unusual for the union to propose some change in the seniority article of the contract, perhaps even making a specific proposal for a change in contract language concerning layoffs. As part of a counterproposal or other response to the union's proposal, management can include a clarification of the conditions necessary for senior employees to bump junior employees. The counterproposal, therefore, offers a relatively safe means to propose changes in doubtful language since the proposed change, if not achieved in negotiations, can later be explained in arbitration as simply a response to a union proposal and not something the employer felt compelled to change on its own.

The counterproposal technique, however, is not without its limitations. By not including the desired change as part of management's opening agenda, management may lead the union to later infer that the counterproposal is not one about which management is particularly serious, since otherwise it would not have waited so long to advance it. Consequently, the counterproposal technique is inadequate when management needs to establish in the minds of union representatives a clear necessity for the change. The counterproposal is also not suitable where the language sought to be changed is found in one of the more obscure sections of the contract which is unlikely to be included on the union's agenda of proposed contract changes. A desired change, for example, in the article covering pay for jury duty or in a union recognition clause is not apt to be introduced in response to a union proposal in this regard, since these clauses tend to remain somewhat fixed over time.

In such cases, and even for other more changeable sections of the contract, there is another useful technique, the generalized proposal. Referring again to the earlier example, instead of specifically proposing that the word "qualified" be defined in the desired way, management merely proposes to "Discuss layoff procedures." In this way, management has put the qualification issue "on the table," but in such an indirect way that it cannot easily be argued that it proposed to change specific language. After the issue is on the table and discussed, management negotiators can assess their chances of successfully negotiating the change. If chances appear favorable, a more specific written proposal can be made.

Another danger alleged by some in making proposals when union agreement will be difficult to obtain, is the loss of credibility or "loss of face" if an agreement cannot be reached. Some management negotiators believe that unless management can be absolutely confident of obtaining union acceptance of the proposal, or unless management is willing to take a strike in order to achieve the proposal, it should not be made in the first place. The author does not subscribe to that theory. Assuming that there is no danger of jeopardizing a favorable interpretation of ambiguous contract language, i.e., the pitfall described above or at least assuming that the risk has been minimized by the use of the counterproposal or generalized proposal techniques, there are few good reasons why management should not attempt to correct problem areas in a contract simply because of a concern that the attempt will not be successful. Such an attitude is probably a holdover from earlier years when managements perceived themselves as invincible, and believed that if they proposed a change in the labor contract they had to get it. This philosophy puts much too high a price on obtaining contract changes. If every change needed or desired by management had to pass the strike test (willingness to take a strike to achieve the change), few changes would be proposed by management. Employers, as well as unions, must come to realize that bargaining is, indeed, a two-way street and that in order for unions to receive certain contract improvements, the unions inevitably must make some concessions to enable the employers to afford those improvements. In some cases, unions are more prepared to accept that reality than employers believe, thus reducing the actual risk employers take in proposing changes.

Scope and Strategy of Management Agenda

While the author supports the concept of management-proposed changes and the value of two-way bargaining, he does so with a caveat: management should not emulate some unions' style of bargaining which leads to agendas which look like laundry lists, nor should management propose changes which ask for the moon when it is obviously willing to accept something more like a flashlight. Of course, each firm's management must develop its own style and image in bargaining, but two-way bargaining does not mean that a double standard still does not, or should not, exist; management should not adopt the philosophy adhered to by many unions that having more proposals to "throw away" or trade off means a greater number of proposals will be accepted by the other side. When management proposes contract changes, it should do so seriously and with the intent that they will be obtained. Items of little value or significance should not be placed on the agenda and, if sought at all, should be reserved for counterproposals. Pure "throw-aways" that have no real significance to the employer's enterprise and little or no chance of acceptance should be avoided. While proposals should generally be more extensive than what management is willing to settle for, they should not be so broad or expansive as to be ludicrous. *Management must be credible at the bargaining table.* Making exorbitant, unnecessary, or unrealistic proposals destroys credibility.

In addition to properly framing their proposals, management negotiators must have necessary information, data, and arguments to support them. The information and data must be relevant and accurate and the arguments must be rational, appealing, and persuasive.

One dilemma a management negotiator can encounter in handling management's agenda is indication of the apparent degree of importance management attaches to its proposals. If too much emphasis is placed on the necessity and value of making the change, union negotiators are apt to have an unrealistically high expectation of what management may grant in return. If, however, the necessity of the change is not stressed sufficiently, union representatives may feel that they can reach final agreement without any concession on that point. The middle road is recommended—the management negotiator should explain why the proposal is important while at the same time cautioning that management is not willing to pay an exorbitant amount to buy out an unfavorable benefit or contract provision.

The management negotiator can often enhance management's bargaining position and avoid surprises by informally discussing key management proposals with his or her union counterpart prior to commencing negotiations. In particular cases, bargaining logistics or union-management relationships may not permit this type of informal communication. However, where it is feasible, it should be employed. By informing the union's negotiator in advance that management has one or more critical proposals, and that management is serious about achieving the proposed changes, the negotiator is less likely to encounter hostility and immediate rejection at the bargaining table.

4

The Law Controlling Labor Negotiations

The basic law which governs collective bargaining in the United States is the National Labor Relations Act (NLRA), passed in 1935 (Wagner Act), and amended in 1947 (Taft-Hartley Act) and 1959 (Labor-Management Reporting and Disclosure Act). In the airline and railroad industries, the Railway Labor Act serves as the basic federal statute governing collective bargaining. Many states have statutes and regulations which influence collective bargaining, although these seldom have much effect on employers that operate in interstate commerce. A number of other statutes, including the Norris-La Guardia Act (affecting injunctions in labor disputes), the Sherman Anti-Trust Act and Clayton Antitrust Act (affecting collusive agreements between employers and unions that have an economic impact on other employers), and the Fair Labor Standards Act (establishing minimum wages and overtime premium pay requirements) also influence specific issues in labor contract negotiations, although their influence in the average negotiating situation is quite limited.

National Labor Relations Act

This chapter is restricted to a review of the key elements of the NLRA which specifically influence labor contract negotiations. Numerous other books are available which provide a comprehensive analysis of the NLRA and decisions thereunder.[1] The NLRA as originally enacted was designed to foster collective bargaining. The findings and policies section of the Act (Section 1) states:

> It is hereby declared to be the policy of the United States to eliminate the causes of certain substantial obstructions to the free flow of commerce * * * by encouraging the practice and procedure of collective bargaining * * * , for the purpose of negotiating the terms and conditions of [workers'] employment or other mutual aid or protection.

The principal substantive provisions of the Act which bear directly on labor contract negotiation are Sections 8(d), 8(a)(5), and 8(b)(3), all of which obligate employers and unions to bargain in good faith. Sections 8(a)(5) and 8(b)(3) make it an unfair labor practice for employers and unions, respectively, to "refuse to bargain collectively" with the representatives of the other respective party, and Section 8(d) sets forth the meaning of "bargaining collectively." While the language in the statute is quite short and simple, the ramifications of the duty to bargain are quite extensive.

It would be a mistake, however, to overemphasize the influence of the NLRA on the labor contract negotiating process. Of the hundreds of thousands of labor contracts negotiated in the United States each year, only a small fraction involve the NLRB or ever raise issues of refusing to bargain. The vast majority of contracts are negotiated by parties which have mature and reasonably amicable relationships, and even where economic pressure in the form of strikes or lockouts is necessary, the question of illegal bargaining is usually not involved. Notwithstanding, in order to be adequately equipped, management's representative(s) must understand the scope of the law and the burdens it imposes upon management, as well as the obligations it imposes upon the union, with respect to bargaining.

Good Faith Bargaining

The essence of the obligation to bargain collectively in good faith is set forth in Section 8(d) of the NLRA. It states as follows:

> For the purposes of this section, to bargain collectively is the performance of the mutual obligation of the employer and the

> representative of the employees to meet at reasonable times, and confer in *good faith* with respect to wages, hours, and other terms and conditions of employment, or the negotiation of an agreement, or any question arising thereunder, and the execution of a written contract incorporating any agreement reached if requested by either party, but such obligation does not compel either party to agree to a proposal or require the making of a concession. [Emphasis added.]

The emphasized words "good faith" encompass the spirit of the law as well as the difficulty in applying it. Good faith bargaining requires an honest attempt by both employer and union representatives to reach an agreement, but at the same time does not obligate either party to make a concession or agree to a proposal. Therein lies the difficulty. The concept of good faith bargaining has been applied by the National Labor Relations Board (NLRB or simply "the Board") and the courts in a myriad of situations. Out of those decisions have come a series of obligations imposed on employers, which are reviewed below.

Duty to Furnish Information

Part of the duty to bargain in good faith is the obligation to furnish information which will enable each negotiating party to bargain intelligently. Frequently, data and information pertinent to negotiations (such as overall bargaining unit earnings, hours worked, and costs of benefits) are available only to the employer. Subject to certain conditions which follow, the employer must provide the union with that information. First, the union must request or demand the information; the employer need not supply it unless requested to do so. Second, the information must be relevant to a proper subject of the negotiations.

Relevancy

Relevancy has been very liberally interpreted so that the information need only have possible or potential relevance to issues raised by either party. In one case, an employer was required by the NLRB to furnish information to a union concerning a group of employees at one of the employer's other plants which was nonunion. The union was attempting to bargain about work it felt was being transferred from the plant involved in the negotiations to the nonrepresented plant. The Board ruled that such information was relevant to the negotiations.[2]

What information is relevant can depend on what reasons an employer gives the union for its bargaining position. For example, if an employer denies a wage increase because of decreased business volume, available data on business volume becomes relevant and must be supplied to the union if requested. This brings up an important and frequently occurring question of whether the employer's financial data concerning profit and loss is relevant and whether it must be produced.

"Opening the Books"

A particularly important issue involving the relevancy question develops when an employer, in order to resist a union's demands for wage and/or benefit increases, states that it cannot afford to pay for the improvements sought by the union. Once the employer rejects a union proposal on grounds of an *inability to pay*, the employer's financial condition becomes relevant to the negotiations. The U.S. Supreme Court has ruled that in such cases the union is entitled to information about the employer's financial condition, including statements concerning profit and loss, assets and liabilities, etc.[3] Some employers have no reservations about "opening the books," particularly when the books reveal a very dismal financial picture. On the other hand, most employers, even publicly held corporations, do not wish to have detailed financial information spread out in front of the union, particularly when it may come into the hands of the employer's competitors.

Avoiding Full Disclosure

The simple way to avoid having to open the books is to refrain from taking the position (however stated) that "we can't afford it." Instead, the employer's position can be (again, however stated) that "we're not *willing* to agree." An unwillingness to concede to a union's request may be based upon a number of factors which do not bring the employer's financial condition into the picture. These factors may include the employer's competitive position, labor market conditions, and labor costs in its other plants. By explaining its rationale in terms of an *unwillingness* due to such factors, rather than *inability* based upon poor financial conditions, the obligation to "open the books" can be avoided.

Feasibility

A third condition to the obligation to furnish information is that the requested information should not be unduly burdensome to produce. For example, if a union seeks data from the employer's records which would require hundreds of hours to compile, the employer need not accede to the request, at least in the absence of reimbursement for the cost. However, if the employer can supply the data in some other form that would not be so time consuming to prepare, it is required to do so. If a claim of burdensomeness is raised by the employer, it must be done at the time the request is made in order to allow for some compromise as to the form of the information.

Confidentiality

A fourth condition on supplying requested information concerns the issue of confidentiality. Although employers need not disclose confidential information which is sensitive and of dubious relevancy,[4] the defense of confidentiality is very limited. For example, the NLRB has required employers to provide information about the employer's equipment types and specifications,[5] costs of an insurance plan paid for solely by the employer,[6] time study data on negotiated incentive rates,[7] and copies of aptitude tests given to employees, including actual test papers and scores.[8] The Board has even gone so far as to require an employer to give a union results of the employer's confidential wage surveys in certain geographic areas, requiring the employer to correlate the names of the employers with the corresponding wage data, even though the employer conducting the survey had given assurances to each of the participating employers that the data supplied would not be identified by plant.[9] This decision was upheld on appeal.[10]

Waiver

A fifth condition imposed on the duty to supply information is that the union must not have previously waived its right to request the specific information now sought. The NLRB has ruled that a union's failure to obtain the right to wage information in previous negotiations constitutes a waiver of its right to subsequently demand that information.[11] The Board has also ruled that a contract clause giving management sole discretion over subcontracting meant that the union was not entitled to information concerning use of subcontractors.[12] It would be a mistake, however, to place much reliance on a perceived union waiver of bargaining information, in that the number of situations in which a waiver could be found are so limited as to be almost nonexistent. The waiver must be a very clear one, and in most cases it would have to be shown that the employer relied upon the union's waiver to such an extent that to require the employer to supply the information would be patently unfair (estoppel).

Subjects for Bargaining

In imposing an obligation to bargain collectively, Congress did not require that an employer bargain over all aspects of his business, but only over "wages, hours, and other terms and conditions of employment" (NLRA Section 8(d)). In interpreting this broad guideline, the NLRB has classified the potential subject matter of collective bargaining into three basic categories.

1. *Mandatory*. Subjects over which the parties *must* bargain if requested to do so.
2. *Permissive*. Subjects over which the parties *may* bargain, if they both so desire, but neither is required to do so.
3. *Illegal*. Subjects over which the parties *may not* bargain even if they wish to do so.

For most purposes, the key question in this area that a management negotiator needs to answer is whether a matter is a mandatory subject of bargaining. Does he have to bargain about it or not? If not, the employer can legally refuse to discuss it. If a subject contained in a union proposal is permissive (i.e., the employer may choose, but is not required, to bargain) management will normally elect not to bargain about it. If the subject is illegal, management is prohibited by law from bargaining about it. Consequently, if the subject is permissive or illegal, it is nonmandatory and therefore there is no bargaining obligation.

Mandatory vs. Nonmandatory Bargaining Subjects

The distinction between mandatory and nonmandatory bargaining subjects has significance here not only with respect to union-proposed issues about which management must decide whether or not to negotiate. It also affects the extent to which management may pursue its own bargaining goals. The key rule is that neither party may negotiate to the point of "impasse" over a proposal which is not a mandatory subject of bargaining.

Bargaining to "Impasse"

What constitutes an "impasse" in bargaining is fraught with uncertainty and imprecision. The word "impasse" means a deadlock, a stalemate, or reciprocal unwavering bargaining positions taken by both parties. When neither party will budge one iota from its respective position, impasse has been reached. Occasionaly each party will label its offer or counteroffer as its "last and final" and steadfastly adhere to that position. In such cases, determination of impasse is not difficult. More commonly, however, one or both parties will slightly modify a position in the course of bargaining and cloud the question as to whether true "impasse" has been reached. For this reason, management must be careful to identify all of its contract proposals which fall within the category of nonmandatory bargaining subjects.

Categorizing Bargaining Subjects

As a means of assisting the management negotiator in determining those subjects over which it must bargain and those it may avoid, as well as those over which it may not bargain to an impasse, a list of mandatory and nonmandatory subjects has been prepared. However, several caveats or warnings must be given. First, the facts surrounding the specific proposal, the parties' bargaining history, and the language in the applicable labor agreement can change the category into which the subject matter for bargaining falls. Second, significant differences in categorizing subject matter exist between the NLRB rulings and decisions of the federal appellate courts which hear appeals from the Board. Therefore, even though the

NLRB may mandate bargaining over certain subjects, the federal appellate courts have not always affirmed the Board's decisions. Third, some subjects are in a state of flux so that while as of this writing a subject may be in one category, it may subsequently swing into another category by virtue of a new Board decision. In cases where there is a swing issue for a conflict between the NLRB and the courts, the author has opted for a conservative approach and included the subject in the mandatory category.

Mandatory Subjects of Bargaining

Wage Compensation for Services

- Wages
- Salaries
- Incentive pay or bonus
- Shift premiums
- Overtime premiums
- Premium pay for work on Sundays and holidays
- Merit pay increases
- Equity pay adjustments
- Cost of living adjustments (COLAs)
- Premium payments for undesirable schedules or work
- Red-circle pay
- Longevity pay or premiums
- Pay for training.

Wage Compensation for Nonworked Time

- Holidays
- Vacations
- Jury duty pay
- Funeral or bereavement pay
- Call-in or call-back pay
- Reporting pay or daily/weekly minimum pay
- Standby pay
- Travel pay
- Pay for time spent on union business
- Pay for time spent on safety matters
- Severance pay
- Pay for lost wages due to contract violation.

Nonwage Benefits

- Holiday bonuses or "gifts"
- Pension benefits for current employees when they retire
- Profit-sharing plans

- Stock purchase or bonus plans
- Employer-provided or employer-reimbursed housing, meals, and services
- Medical, life, sickness and accident, dental and vision plans
- Legal services plans
- Discounts on company products
- Leaves of absence (paid or unpaid)
- Clothing and tool allowances or benefits
- Company-provided or employer-reimbursed transportation
- Tuition reimbursement programs.

Working Conditions on the Job

- Hours of work and work schedules
- Rest and lunch periods
- Plant rules of conduct
- Grievance procedures and arbitration
- Promotions, transfers, layoffs, recalls, etc.
- Workloads
- Discharge and discipline
- Safety and safety rules
- Probationary and trial periods
- Testing of employees
- Job-required clothing or equipment
- Job duties
- Job qualifications and certification requirements
- Workplace facilities and conveniences
- Seniority accumulation (loss and application)
- Work assignments.

Management Rights and Union-Management Issues

- Subcontracting
- Management rights clause
- Effects on employees of plant closure, relocation, sale, etc.
- Union shop or other union security agreement (unless state law prohibits)
- Dues checkoff clauses
- Bargaining unit work
- No-strike clause
- Union hiring halls
- Nondiscrimination clauses
- Waiver or "zipper" clauses

- "Most favored nation" clause
- Arrangements for labor contract negotiations.

Nonmandatory Subjects of Bargaining

- Definition of bargaining unit
- Conditions affecting supervisors[13]
- Formal parties to the collective bargaining agreement
- Performance bonds
- Legal liability or indemnification clauses[14]
- Identity of either party's bargaining representatives
- Internal union affairs including contract ratification procedures
- Union label
- Industry promotion funds
- Settlement of unfair labor practice charges
- Multiemployer or multilevel negotiations
- Pension benefits for persons presently retired
- Interest arbitration
- Recording or transcribing of negotiations
- Closed shop (illegal)
- Hot cargo clauses (illegal)
- Clauses which are racially or sexually discriminatory (illegal)
- Union shop clauses (in states with right-to-work laws)
- Strike insurance or mutual aid plans (MAPs).

Bargaining Over Nonmandatory Subjects

The significance of the mandatory/nonmandatory classification of bargaining subjects comes into play when (a) one party proposes a mandatory subject and the other side refuses to bargain about it, and/or (b) one side proposes a nonmandatory subject and bargains to impasse over that issue. In either case, an unfair labor practice can occur. A strike which is caused or prolonged by an employer's refusal to bargain in good faith over a mandatory subject of bargaining, or by an employer's insistence to impasse over a nonmandatory subject, is an unfair labor practice strike.

Bargaining Over Borderline Mandatory Subjects

Consequently, it is frequently advisable for management to voluntarily bargain over a nonmandatory subject proposed by the union (as long as it is not one of the few illegal subjects). This is particularly advisable when the subject proposed for bargaining is a borderline nonmandatory subject. The rationale here is that if the subject proposed for bargaining is disadvantageous to the employer, management will reject it regardless of whether it is required to bargain on that subject or not. Therefore, management can be just as effective, if not more so, by resisting the proposal because it is *unwilling* to agree to it rather than because it *is not required to bargain* about the subject, thus avoiding any risk of an unfair labor practice. (Note the similarity to the previously discussed rationale concerning financial information and inability-to-pay arguments.)

Avoiding Waiver On a Nonmandatory Subject

However, if management elects to voluntarily bargain about a nonmandatory, yet legal, subject of bargaining, a precautionary step should be taken. Management's spokesperson should advise the union's negotiators that he or she believes the subject to be a nonmandatory one, but is willing to proceed to negotiate on it, provided it is agreed that such negotiation does not waive the employer's right to raise the issue of whether the subject is mandatory or nonmandatory at a later time, such as in a case that might be brought before the NLRB. In most cases, the union will agree, since it wants management to begin negotiating on the subject and is willing to let management preserve its legal arguments if the subject causes an impasse in the bargaining. The cautious negotiator will reduce the agreement of nonwaiver to writing in the form of a memorandum agreement signed by both parties or a letter confirming the agreement. A sample letter is included as Exhibit 4–1.

Bargaining to Impasse Over Nonmandatory Subjects

The other major aspect of the mandatory/nonmandatory classification which is important to the management negotiator is that an unfair labor practice is committed by bargaining to impasse over a nonmandatory subject proposed by management. This does not mean that such a subject (as long as it is not one of the few illegal ones) cannot and should not be proposed. For example, if the employer wants to make sure that newly hired, and perhaps disruptive, employees are not on the

Exhibit 4–1. Sample Nonwaiver Confirming Letter

Mr. Raymond T. Flint
President, Local 63
Association of Carpet Weavers
21563 Wendover Avenue
Westchester, N.Y. 30658

Dear Mr. Flint:

In the course of our labor contract negotitations you proposed, on behalf of the union, that our firm enter into an agreement to engage in interest arbitration at the termination of our next collective bargaining contract.

In our meeting, I informed you of our belief that this subject was not a mandatory subject of bargaining under the National Labor Relations Act, as amended. We also stated that we were willing to bargain over this subject, provided it was done with the explicit understanding of both parties that should we fail to reach agreement, the employer reserved all its rights to claim that the subject is not a mandatory subject. In other words, it is agreed that the employer's willingness to engage in bargaining on the subject of interest arbitration will not constitute any waiver of its rights.

If this is not an accurate statement of our agreement, please notify me immediately in writing.

Sincerely,

Ralph T. Biglow
Labor Relations Manager
Woodland Carpet Mills
Raleigh, N.C.

union's grievance committee, it might propose that the labor contract contain a provision requiring that all members of the grievance committee have at least two years of service with the employer. Although the union may refuse to bargain over such a proposal, there is nothing that prevents management from advancing it and seeking union agreement. That particular proposal, or any proposal on a nonmandatory subject, may not, however, legally be pushed to the point of impasse. Careful note should be taken that where an impasse occurs and both mandatory and nonmandatory subjects remain on the bargaining table, it will usually be held that the nonmandatory subject(s) was a sufficient cause of the impasse and that an unfair labor practice has been committed by the party that proposed and insisted on the nonmandatory subject(s).[15] Therefore, if an impasse appears to be imminent, and before a strike occurs, the employer should withdraw any unaccepted nonmandatory proposals it proposed and still has outstanding. If, however, management proposes a nonmandatory subject and the union proceeds to agree on the subject, subsequent failure on the part of the union to sign a contract incorporating the agreement is an unfair labor practice.[16]

Good Faith in the Conduct of Negotiations

Perhaps the most difficult application of the good faith bargaining obligation of the NLRA is in the actual give-and-take at the bargaining table. It is usually easy to ascertain which types of information must be supplied by the parties preparatory to bargaining, and it is not especially difficult to identify those subjects over which unions and employers are required to bargain.

An Imprecise Standard

When it comes, however, to measuring the conduct of the parties in actual negotiations against a "good faith" standard, the NLRB and the courts have encountered such great difficulties and their decisions have been so imprecise and conflicting that employers especially, and unions to a certain extent, have been left with little guidance as to what is, and what is not, legally permissible bargaining. One of the primary reasons for the apparent inconsistencies is that the NLRB and the courts have used a case-by-case approach, choosing to determine good or bad faith bargaining based upon the particular facts in each case. As with so many nebulous legal concepts, it is easier to explain what good faith bargaining *is not* rather than what it *is*, for it is in breaches of the law that the NLRB and the courts have spoken most often.

"Totality of Conduct"

As stated earlier, good faith bargaining means an honest attempt by the negotiating parties to reach an agreement. Conduct which runs counter to that end is normally held to be an unfair labor practice. Rather than considering isolated acts or statements, the NLRB and the courts examine the "totality of conduct" of the negotiations to determine whether good faith bargaining has taken place. In examining the overall bargaining, there are certain categories of conduct which have been held by the NLRB and the courts to lead to the conclusion of bad faith bargaining.

Imposing Conditions

It is generally an unfair labor practice for an employer or a union to impose some precondition for the commencement or continuation of negotiations. A common problem area for employers is the existence of a strike. An employer may not condition negotiations upon the union's agreement to cease an economic strike.[17] Nor may bargaining be withheld until a union agrees to withdraw unfair labor practice charges it has filed.[18] On the other hand, if one party insists that a court reporter or a tape recorder be used to make a transcript of the negotiations, the other party is free to refuse to bargain under such conditions, and the party that insists on the verbatim record will be found to have bargained in bad faith.[19]

Inhibiting or Delaying Meeting

Where a duty to bargain exists, an outright refusal to meet, absent a compelling reason, is clearly a violation. In addition, extended periods of unavailability to meet for negotiations can subject the employer to unfair labor practice violations.[20] However, management representatives may make themselves available to meet only at certain times of the day where other business obligations require attention.[21] If an employer insists on a location for bargaining that is far from the locale of the bargaining unit, a refusal to bargain will usually be found.[22] Delays of several weeks or even months in being available for bargaining may be justifiable depending upon the circumstances, but if there are other indications of an unwillingness to reach an agreement, the delays are more likely to be considered bad faith bargaining.

Insufficient Authority of Negotiator

When a management representative sits down at the bargaining table, it is presumed that he or she has sufficient authority to speak for management, advise the union of management's positions on various issues, accept and reject proposals, make counterproposals, and carry out other functions normally associated with negotiating a labor contract. However the management negotiator need not have authority to make the employer's final decisions. Where the management spokesperson has not been advised of the employer's position, does not have the authority to make proposals or counterproposals on behalf of the employer, or does not exercise apparent authority to conclude a labor agreement, an unfair labor practice is likely to be found.[23]

Surface Bargaining

"Surface bargaining" is a term of art which encompasses a variety of bargaining tactics designed to inhibit agreement, or to serve as a cover for the lack of a willingness to reach an agreement. The word "surface" conveys the negotiator's rationale—it appears on the surface that serious negotiations are taking place, while underneath the intent is to avoid agreement. This type of bargaining without any intent of reaching agreement is an unfair labor practice. Surface bargaining tactics include making counterproposals which do not attempt to reconcile differences;[24] making new and more restricting proposals midway through bargaining;[25] making regressive offers;[26] refusing to take a firm, definite position, resulting in forestalling any agreement;[27] and refusing to make any substantive changes in the employer's position.[28]

There is, however, no legal prohibition against an employer's adhering to its strong management-oriented positions or engaging in "hard bargaining," and Section 8(d) of the NLRA makes clear that there is no requirement that an employer make concessions during bargaining. That section was upheld in an early decision by the U.S. Supreme Court.[29] Moreover, the withdrawal of earlier proposals or the making of less favorable proposals (i.e., regressive) is not, in and of itself, bad faith bargaining.[30] Nevertheless, when an employer refuses to make any significant concessions or backtracks on earlier offers without sufficient, legitimate reasons, it may be taken as some indication of bad faith, and if there is other evidence of attempts by the employer to avoid agreement, these actions may be important factors in assessing the "totality of conduct" that lead to a finding of an unfair labor practice.[31]

A management negotiator should not be fearful, however, of taking adamant stands on any particular issue. As long as there are genuine attempts to reach an overall agreement, the law does not require that an employer back down on any issue.

Withdrawal of Accepted Offers

Closely aligned to surface bargaining, but somewhat more blatant, is the attempted withdrawal of an offer which has been accepted by the union. To be held an unfair labor practice it must be clear, however, that the offer has been accepted prior to the withdrawal.[32] Also, where the accepted offer is coupled with other proposals that are not accepted, the withdrawal is not likely to constitute a violation.[33] The NLRB has also held that no violation occurred where an employer withdrew an accepted proposal as a bargaining tactic to stimulate union movement, but later reinstated the proposal.[34] Likewise, the occurrence of a strike may be grounds for an employer to withdraw concessions previously offered.[35]

Refusal to Put Agreements in Writing

An unfair labor practice is committed when an employer agrees to a provision or a contract but refuses to reduce the agreement to writing. Thus, a violation occurs when a complete contract has been negotiated, and the employer refuses to sign it.[36]

Similarly, when an oral concession is made by an employer but its negotiator refuses to put the concession in written form, an unfair labor practice occurs.[37] However, it must be clear that the employer has, in fact, agreed to the proposal before an obligation arises to put it in writing. As will be pointed out in subsequent chapters, the author recommends, aside from any legal obligation which may require this, that all agreements be put in writing, regardless of how inconsequential they may appear to be.

Unilateral Changes

On matters which are mandatory subjects of bargaining, an employer is prohibited from making unilateral changes therein until good faith bargaining has occurred and impasse has been reached, or until the union has been informed of the employer's desire or intention to make the change and the union declines to bargain about the matter.

Consequently, not only during contract negotiations, but throughout the term of a labor contract, management must be careful to avoid making unilateral changes in any wages, hours, and working conditions without first satisfying this bargaining obligation. There are, however, some conditions that may exist which would permit the employer to institute unilateral changes. For example, if the union after proper notification is dilatory and makes itself unavailable for bargaining on the subject, the unilateral change can be made.[38] Also, when certain conditions have, by prior contract (e.g., management's rights clause) or custom, been considered to be within the control of management (e.g., work procedures, rules of conduct), unilateral changes without prior bargaining are not unlawful.[39] Also, where the unilateral changes are not "material, substantial, or significant," they may be made prior to, or during, bargaining.[40]

Bypassing the Union

An employer may not circumvent the union which is the authorized bargaining agent and deal directly with its employees or some other employee group.[41] This means that the employer may not negotiate directly with employees about terms and conditions of employment. It does not mean, however, that an employer may not communicate with its employees either in preparation for bargaining or during negotiations, as long as the communications do not rise to the level of bargaining. Thus, an employer is permitted to operate a program that permits employees to anonymously express their thoughts and opinions about the workplace and management.[42] Also, management may inform employees either orally or in writing, during labor contract negotiations about any facts relating to the bargaining, including the progress, or lack thereof, of such negotiations, the offers and counteroffers made, and the reasons for the employer's position.[43] The employer may lawfully try to persuade its employees to accept an offer as long as it is clear that the employer is continuing to deal with the union as their exclusive representative.[44]

The Effect of Unfair Labor Practices on Bargaining

Impact of Board Orders

Rules, procedures and case backlogs of the NLRB are such that the agency often cannot force good faith bargaining, or alternatively punish bad faith bargaining, in sufficient time to have an immediate impact on the bargaining. Because the NLRB's machinery for hearing and finally deciding cases is apt to require 6 to 12 months or more, the negotiating parties have often concluded their bargaining by the time a final decision from the agency is rendered. In addition, the Board's decision is subject to review (if appealed) by a federal appeals court, which may take another 6 to 12 months. Even then, any remedial order issued by the NLRB and/or the appeals court for refusing to bargain in good faith is apt to merely order the offending party to bargain in good faith.

Important exceptions to the rather mild bargaining order remedy occur when an employer unilaterally decreases wages or benefits, relocates its plant, subcontracts bargaining unit work, or makes other major changes in mandatory bargaining subjects without first satisfying its bargaining obligation. In such cases the NLRB (and the courts) have frequently ordered the employer to restore the conditions which existed prior to the unilateral change (called the "*status quo ante*"). This can require the reinstatement of employees displaced, restoration and recoupment of wages and benefits lost, or other "make whole" remedies to return affected persons to the position they would have been in but for the unilateral change(s).

The Significance of an Unfair Labor Practice Strike

Despite the rather delayed and normally modest impact of an NLRB finding of bad faith bargaining (not involving a unilateral change), there is a sufficiently serious sanction attached to the finding of employer bad faith bargaining that employers are well advised to avoid engaging in conduct that could reasonably lead to a finding of bad faith bargaining. If an employer is ultimately found to have refused to bargain in good faith, any strike caused or prolonged by bad faith bargaining will be classified as an "unfair labor practice strike." This type of strike is distinguished from the "economic strike" where a work stoppage results from a legitimate disagreement over wages, hours, or working conditions, i.e., anything other than bad faith bargaining. When a strike is caused, even in part, by an employer's unfair labor practices, it will be classified as an unfair labor practice strike even though it was also caused by disagreement over wages, hours, or working conditions. The employer's unfair labor practice need only be a contributing cause of the strike for there to be a finding of an unfair labor practice strike.[45]

The major significance to management of an unfair labor practice classification being attached to a strike is that if the employer elects to replace striking employees, such replacements may only be temporary. That, in turn, means that striking employees in an unfair labor practice strike must be reinstated if they unconditionally offer to return to work.[46] Thus, when an unfair labor practice strike ends, the employer must offer striking employees the opportunity to return to their jobs even though other persons have been hired to fill those jobs. An exception to this rule is made if a striking employee engages in serious misconduct or is discharged for cause in the course of an unfair labor practice strike; such employees need not be reinstated.[47] On the other hand, if the strike is an economic strike (i.e., not caused or prolonged by an employer's unfair labor practice), replacements hired during the strike may be permanent, and if so, may be retained on the employer's payroll following the end of the strike. Economic strikers, who have been permanently replaced, are not entitled to reinstatement, but need only be placed on a recall list for future job vacancies. While on the recall list they continue to be classified as employees, and are entitled to be notified of any job vacancies that occur.[48]

If an NLRB election occurs during the strike, strikers in an unfair labor practice strike are eligible to vote, while replacement employees are not. Permanent replacements of economic strikers may vote in any NLRB election. Economic strikers who have been permanently replaced may only vote in an NLRB election if it is held within 12 months following the beginning of the strike, provided they have not obtained permanent employment with another employer.

An employer who hires permanent replacements with assurances that they will be retained following the end of the strike is legally liable for the damage incurred by such replacement employees if the commitment is not fulfilled. If an employer, as part of a strike settlement agreement, agrees with the union to reinstate striking employees in place of permanent replacement employees, or if the NLRB rules that a strike is an unfair labor practice strike and orders the return of strikers, any permanent replacements who are displaced thereby may sue the employer for breach of contract.[49]

The employer, therefore, who allegedly has committed unfair labor practices during negotiations may not know if such allegations will be upheld as true until many months or even years after the fact. Consequently, any decisions with regard to the hiring of permanent replacements and the retaining of such replacements after the end of a strike must be weighed very carefully.

The Right to Strike or Lock Out

The ultimate weapons in the hands of the negotiating parties to bring economic pressure on the other side are a strike by the union and a lockout by the employer. There are few limitations upon a union's right to strike in the normal bargaining context. The principal legal limitations are as follows:

1. A strike must be waged against the "primary" employer (i.e., the employer of the employees represented by the striking union), not upon some other (secondary) employer for the purpose of bringing economic pressure on the primary employer.
2. The union must, prior to a strike, give the employer written notice at least 60 days in advance, and give federal and state mediation agencies written notice at least 30 days in advance, of its desire to modify or terminate an existing labor agreement.
3. The purpose of a strike may not be to seek recognition of the union by the employer which is being struck, to force the employer to assign work to members of the striking union,

or to force supervisors or self-employed persons to join a union.

4. A union may not strike over a nonmandatory subject of bargaining.
5. A strike imperiling the national health or safety may be enjoined for 80 days if the President of the United States initiates such an injunction.
6. No strike may be legally commenced while there is in effect a collective bargaining agreement which contains a no-strike clause.

Employers may lock out their employees as a means of gaining economic leverage in bargaining with a union, a result of the U.S. Supreme Court's decision in the *American Ship Building* case.[50] Prior to that decision, employers were limited to defensive lockouts to protect their economic interest caused by the threat of a strike or in response to a strike against other employers in a multiemployer bargaining unit. The Supreme Court, however, ruled that employers may use a lockout to bring pressure on the union in negotiations just as a union uses a strike to bring pressure on the employer. The 60-day and 30-day notice provisions applicable to strikes applies equally to lockouts. Employers may hire temporary replacements during a lockout.[51] The law is not clear on the question of whether such replacements may be permanent.

Caveat—Tip of the Iceberg

The thumbnail sketch of the NLRA rules governing contract negotiations provided in this chapter reveals only the tip of the legal iceberg. Although the majority of negotiations are concluded without any legal issues being raised, once such an issue is raised, it is likely to be one without a clearcut answer. It is not necessary that the management negotiator be fully conversant with labor law to be effective. It is essential, however, that the negotiator have a command of the basic concepts underlying NLRB good faith bargaining requirements. The ability to spot potential issues, avoid obvious NLRA violations, and the good sense to seek competent legal advice will suffice in the vast majority of contract negotiations.

Part II

The Bargaining Process

5

Preliminary Stages of Negotiations

The beginning of labor contract negotiations can be a bit like the mating dance of two water buffaloes—both participants are anxious to begin, but not quite sure exactly where to start, with a good deal of time and effort spent by both parties trying to impress each other.

As a general rule, negotiations begin with certain formalities common to most meetings—introductions, small talk, jokes, etc. Frequently, the next step is to discuss what ground rules will apply during the period of negotiations. Ground rules might include such matters as meeting schedules, order of negotiating issues, arrangements for media contacts, and the like. The first day, at least in more formal negotiations, will usually include an opening statement by one or both parties. The major items of concern during the preliminary stage of negotiations will be the presentation and explanation of each side's proposals. The initial response of each party to the proposals made by the other concludes what may be considered the preliminary stage of negotiations, the scope of this chapter.

Ground Rules for Conducting Negotiations

Depending upon the formality of the negotiations and the exposure both parties have had to negotiations with one another, it is often advisable to seek a mutual understanding about certain procedural, and in some cases substantive, aspects of the negotiations. In many cases, where the negotiations are very informal or where the parties have negotiated together over a number of years, both have a pretty good understanding of how they will proceed and ground rule setting is not necessary. Where the relationship is less well established or where the cast of characters on either or both sides has changed, the need to set certain ground rules is likely to exist.

Meeting Schedules

A major point of interest to the parties is when and how often negotiations will take place. Where all participants are from the same geographical area, this may not be much of a problem. However, where either party's spokesperson must travel from a distant city or where management or union representatives must come from scattered locations, the meeting schedules may be of a real concern. It is not unusual for some unions to want to meet on a consecutive day-to-day schedule until an agreement is reached or at least until a final offer is presented. This should be strenuously avoided by management. It is extremely difficult to be adequately prepared to meet and negotiate day in and day out. What tends to happen in such situations is that management makes more concessions than it should and makes errors in judgment, calculations, and contract language drafting which probably would not have been made had more time been available.

There is no magic formula for meeting frequency which is appropriate for all negotiations. As a general rule, however, a frequency rate of more than two to three meetings per week is usually inadvisable, except when the negotiations are winding down to a deadline. (At the wind-up stage of negotiations, obviously, all planned schedules are off and expedience takes over.) Because of travel arrangements or other practical considerations it may be necessary to set a schedule for negotiations that is more frequent than two to three times per week. In such cases, extended caucuses can be held between meetings so that actual face-to-face negotiating meetings do not occur more often than the previously recommended number of times.

The subject of weekend meetings may also be raised at this time. As a general proposition these too should be avoided, except when contract deadlines are at hand. Negotiators, like anyone else, need rest and relaxation. Extended negotiations running through the weekends will simply add to the fatigue and frustration normally encountered in bargaining. The same can be said of evening meetings. Although fatigue factors may adversely affect union as well as management negotiators, management cannot afford to place its representatives in a vulnerable bargaining setting on the chance that they can outlast their union counterparts. Except for the final stages of bargaining, meetings should be kept to normal business hours.

If logistics permit, it is advisable to leave unspecified the time and frequency of meetings. Because the circumstances at each stage of negotiations will vary considerably, it is usually easier to "play it by ear" and set the time of the next meeting at the conclusion of each meeting. Where union agents and management representatives have a number of negotiations running concurrently, their schedules in other negotiations will often dictate the time of meetings. Since the schedules of such concurrent negotiations are not usually known far in advance, fixed meeting schedules are not feasible.

Pay for Members of the Union Bargaining Committee

In certain industries and in certain sections of the country, it is customary for management to pay wages for the time spent in negotiations by employees who lose work time in order to represent the union on its negotiating committee. The author has a definite bias against such payments by management. Employees who are union representatives are serving the needs of their union and are seeking to persuade management to agree to contract changes which will impose greater cost burdens on the employer. It seems justified that the union, not the employer, should assume the cost of the employees when they are performing this function. Moreover, to the extent that management seeks to shorten, rather than lengthen, the time spent in negotiations, the employer's payment for employees' time in negotiations would seem to work at cross-purposes to that objective.

If management feels itself compelled by its own custom or industry practice to pay for such lost time, it is suggested that a limit be placed upon the number of days or the number of hours for which payment is made. A maximum of one or two week's pay is much preferable to an open-ended obligation.

News Media Contacts

One of the subjects which is sometimes raised by union or management negotiators is contact with the news media. Each side is often concerned that the other will, intentionally or by accident, begin negotiating through the newspapers, and/or on radio and television. This is usually a concern where the negotiations cover a large number of persons in a particular community or an industry or otherwise affect vital community services to an extent sufficient to command public interest.

Some unions and managements with mature collective bargaining relationships customarily agree to media contacts only on a joint basis, usually through jointly prepared or jointly authorized press releases. If this arrangement has worked satisfactorily for both parties in the past, it is an excellent way to avoid having the negotiations stray from the bargaining table. Too often, however, these arrangements break down where one or both sides feel that their message is not being heard by their counterparts, or is not being conveyed to the real parties in interest, i.e., top management, rank-and-file union members and their spouses, or the public at large. In such cases one party invariably releases information or speaks to a reporter without joint approval; the other party feels betrayed and the agreement is destroyed. Another difficulty with jointly authorized media contacts is the difficulty in policing them even when both parties have honorable intentions. The resourcefulness and persistence of reporters coupled with the garrulousness of management and union personnel (not necessarily the spokespersons) often results in information leaking out, which can destroy the news media agreement as much as intentional breaches.

A further management consideration regarding joint news releases is whether such an arrangement will be in the employer's best interest. It may be that certain facts need to be known by the union's constituents and there is no other feasible way to get the message across to them. Similarly, there may be cases where the union has spoken freely in opposition to management through the media prior to negotiations, and an agreement on joint releases would simply hamstring management.

As a general proposition, labor negotiations should be confined to the bargaining table and not carried on through the news media. Once arguments, positions, and unfortunately, accusations of either party appear in the media, they are almost impossible to control. Carefully worded statements in negotiations become loosely, if not erroneously, translated in the media. Both parties, as well as the negotiation itself, can be severely damaged. Consequently, it is prudent to avoid media contacts, except perhaps to report on the most superficial aspects of the negotiations. However, before management enters into any agreement with a union to limit its access to the media it should adopt the following guidelines:

1. Have confidence, based upon past experience, that the union can and will live up to the agreement.
2. Consult with internal public relations or corporate communications personnel to assure that vital media relations will not be jeopardized by such an agreement.
3. Ensure that the agreement will no longer be binding if breached by the other side.
4. Establish a means to dissolve the agreement upon a predetermined event or set of circumstances (e.g., rejection of final offer).
5. Draft the agreement clearly and precisely to ensure that any exceptions or conditions are clearly spelled out.

Order of Addressing Issues

Proposals in most union and management agendas can be divided into two broad categories: economic (money) and noneconomic (language). A common ground rule in most labor contract negotiations is to discuss and attempt to resolve language issues first and then to deal with the money proposals. This procedure is usually acceptable to both union and management negotiators and seems to work reasonably well.

As stated elsewhere in this book, it is the rare labor contract provision that does not have economic consequences. Therefore, a division of money and language or "economic" and "noneconomic" subjects is a misnomer. It is probably more apt to say "direct economic" (wages and benefits) and "indirect economic" (seniority, hours of work, scheduling, etc.). Regardless, however, of the terminology, it is usually advantageous to begin with indirect economic or language proposals, attempting to resolve them before addressing the direct economic or money issues.

There are several good reasons for adopting this procedure. First, it permits the negotiations to proceed without the danger of getting stalemated at an early stage on economic issues. Second, contract language issues usually require more time for proposal-counterproposal negotiation, and treating them first and separately makes it less likely that they will become submerged by the more vital economic issues. Third, economic issues usually have to be considered as a package since each economic change affects the total amount of money available for other economic issues. Consequently simultaneous negotiation of economic and noneconomic issues would effectively preclude the item-by-item consideration necessary for most language issues.

As with all rules, there can be exceptions. Where new and perhaps innovative economic issues are introduced into the negotiations (e.g., a productivity bonus plan or a new pension plan), it may be advisable for both parties to agree to begin discussion on these issues at an early point in the talks. Because such matters may call for extraordinary discussion as well as in-depth study and use of outside experts, more time will need to be allocated to them than if only garden-variety economic issues (e.g., a general wage increase or the amount of vacation and holiday time) were involved. The ground rule of "language first–money last" should be flexible enough to accommodate this type of situation.

Confirming Agreement on Resolved Issues

A final agreement on all issues cannot be reached until a complete offer is made by the employer, accepted by the union, and ratified by the union's membership or other ratifying body. Nevertheless, as the negotiations proceed, the bargainers will attempt to conclusively resolve most issues between them, and usually succeed in doing so. This is especially true of the so-called "language" issues. A widely accepted means for confirming these resolutions is for both parties to sign, or place their initials on, the agreed-upon contract language or statement of understanding. This procedure can be established through a ground rule. It should, however, be clearly understood and stated that all such agreements are tentative, being subject to agreement on all other issues. In fact, to ensure that this understanding is part and parcel of the process, a rubber stamp with a legend similar to the one shown below can be used. By stamping this legend on one of the margins of each page of tentatively approved language, the parties can avoid later misunderstanding about what has been resolved and the status (tentative) of that resolution.

TENTATIVE APPROVAL	
SUBJECT TO AGREEMENT ON ALL CONTRACT ISSUES.	
EMPLOYER	UNION
DATE	DATE

It is strongly urged that this method of confirming agreement, or something very similar to it, be used throughout the negotiations, at least for the noneconomic issues. Many negotiations have foundered on the rocks of mistrust and misunderstanding over issues which were apparently resolved, but later resurrected. This technique of signing or initialing tentative agreements does not, of course, guarantee that an issue will not reappear. Nevertheless, it greatly minimizes that possibility.

Treatment of Contract Expiration

Although the issue does not fall, strictly speaking, under the heading of ground rules, it is nevertheless helpful to gain some understanding of how the parties, especially the union, intend to regard the contract expiration date. Some unions follow a strict "no contract–no work" policy so that if an agreement has not been reached by the contract deadline, a strike will be initiated. Other unions customarily continue to negotiate beyond their contract expiration dates, provided there is an agreement or accepted practice of making all economic improvements retroactive to the expiration date. In other cases, unions and managements prefer to have a written contract extension in effect during the period of negotiations following the expiration date. Some labor agreements specifically provide for an automatic extension while negotiations for a renewal of the agreement are continuing.

Raising this sometimes delicate issue at the outset of negotiations may appear to be, and may actually be, premature. An apparent concern, for example, on the part of management for what may happen when the contract expires could lead the union to perceive a weakness in management's bargaining power. For this reason, the subject may be best deferred until the deadline is closer.

Nevertheless, it is still possible in most cases to raise the issue in a strictly businesslike way without leading the union to believe management fears a strike. For example, the management spokesman might say:

> Jim, we haven't negotiated with your local in the past and to make sure that we don't miscalculate, we need to know how your union regards contract expiration dates. What position will your union take if we are still negotiating at the time the contract expires?

If the union has a no contract–no work policy or other settlement constraint, such an inquiry should elicit the desired information. If such a constraint actually exists, the sooner it is known the better. While the union negotiator may use such an inquiry to bring pressure on management, that opportunity will always exist in any case. Moreover, if the expressed constraint is a bluff, the management spokesperson will have the opportunity to probe in order to detect the bluff once the subject is brought up.

Ascertaining Contract Finalization Requirements

If the parties have not dealt with each other in the past, it may not be clear what actions or approvals may be required before a contract settlement is finalized. Typically, management negotiators can make binding commitments on behalf of management so that a tentative settlement is, from management's standpoint, acceptable as a final settlement. An exception to this exists in multiemployer or public employer negotiations where further top management or board approval is often required.

From the union's standpoint, however, a tentative settlement, regardless of the type of labor contract negotiations, must normally be ratified by a vote of the union's membership. Here too, there may be exceptions, as in the case where the union bargaining committee has been given authority to reach a final settlement or as in the case of some unions such as the United Steelworkers where the ratification body is not the entire union membership but a representative body. As a general rule, however, most unions require a ratification vote by the union's rank-and-file membership before a contract settlement is final. The initial period for clarifying bargaining procedures is an ideal time to discuss each bargaining representative's authority to reach an agreement and what, if any, further steps are required to finalize an agreement. Misunderstandings on this subject can cause great turmoil at later stages of negotiations.

Ground Rules for the Management Committee

Although the management committee presumably has had some time together to prepare itself for negotiations, it is quite possible that certain essential internal ground rules have not yet been covered. In any event, at some point prior to the first meeting with the union, important internal guidelines need to be established.

Only the Spokesperson Speaks

As a general policy, the only person on the management committee who should speak at the bargaining table is the spokesperson. The reason for this is that the spokesperson has, or should have, a plan as to how the negotiations are to proceed as well as a definite idea of the image management wants to project in the discussions. If other persons on the management committee speak out, except in special situations, it is difficult for the spokesperson to control and guide the negotiations to the desired result. There are, however, certain exceptions or special situations where this general rule does not apply.

1. When the spokesperson and another member of the management committee arrange, in advance, for the other member to speak.
2. When the spokesperson specifically asks a member of the management committee at a meeting to comment or respond.
3. When a member of the management committee feels he or she can make a significant contribution on a particular point and, by means of a prearranged signal, is given the go-ahead by the management spokesperson (this exception should be used very sparingly).
4. Where the management spokesperson is not sufficiently conversant with some aspect(s) of the labor agreement or work

practices and cannot intelligently speak on the subject. Hopefully, such situations will be rare.

It is often difficult to maintain the discipline of the "spokesperson only speaks" ground rule, especially where a division head, plant manager, or other line management executive is on the management negotiating committee, and persons within that same organization are on the union's negotiating committee. Frequently, questions will be asked or statements will be made which invite, if not beg, for a line management response. Unless one of the above-listed exceptions applies, however, the line manager should hold his or her tongue until the next caucus. At that time he or she can provide the necessary information to the spokesperson and an adequate response can be formulated—to be delivered by the spokesperson or the line manager as appropriate. What the response lacks in timeliness it will more than compensate for in thoughtfulness and precision.

Method of Calling Caucuses

Closely related to the ground rule which precludes committee members from speaking at the bargaining table is the ground rule that no one but the spokesperson calls for a caucus. The reason for this is similar to the previous guideline. The spokesperson is orchestrating the negotiations and has a sense of the timing necessary to achieve this goal. If someone else on the committee calls for a caucus it can destroy the spokesperson's program. Moreover, it takes away from the authority and stature of the spokesperson since the act of calling for a caucus can be of significant tactical importance.

If another member of the negotiating committee feels that a caucus is required, he or she should send a note to the spokesperson or use some prearranged signal (with as little fanfare as possible) to alert the spokesperson that a caucus is desired. The spokesperson can then call for a caucus, if he or she feels it warranted, at the appropriate time.

Inadvertent Signals

Parties to a negotiation frequently give clues to their position, attitudes, or strategies by physical appearances, gestures, and facial expressions. The art of analyzing body language is but one technique of using such information.

Spokespersons are usually experienced enough to avoid expressions which can reveal their underlying feelings except where they want such feelings to be manifest. Other members of the negotiating committee are usually less experienced and are more apt to give telltale signals. Consequently, the spokesperson should instruct the committee to be careful not to give unintended signals through facial expressions, body movements, or other inadvertent means. While they should attempt to be as natural as possible, a personalized "poker face" should be developed.

For the same reason, members of the management committee should be perceptive enough to interpret signals which might be given by members of the union's committee. Just as expressions and gestures by management can reveal certain management feelings, so too can a union position be indicated by inadvertent physical reactions.

Unauthorized Communications

While management personnel should not have to be told, it is nonetheless prudent to establish a ground rule that members of the management negotiating committee are not to communicate with *anyone* outside the management caucus about negotiations unless specifically authorized to do so. Even such innocuous comments as "the negotiations are going pretty well" can be interpreted in ways the speaker had never envisioned. Unless someone else is authorized by the spokesperson, only the spokesperson should speak about the negotiations to others. This includes statements to other members of management, to employees, and to representatives of the news media. In addition, there should be no communications of substance by committee members, other than the spokesperson, to members of the union's negotiating committee unless the spokesperson authorizes it in advance.

Opening Statement by Management

Setting a Tone

As management enters into the substantive phase of negotiations, it can usually enhance its bargaining position by setting a tone as well as a theme for the discussions which are to follow. The tone is essentially an attitude or orientation which management wishes to see prevail in the negotiations. The tone to be conveyed will vary depending upon the employer's labor relations philosophy, the prevailing economic environment, the current state of union-management relations, expectations for the future of the enterprise, and other pertinent considerations. The basic attitude that management should convey to union representatives is that management will take the negotiations seriously and conduct them in a businesslike manner and that management will seek to be fair throughout the negotiations, but that it will not be willing to enter into any agreement which would put an undue burden on the employer's business or take away important management rights. To a large extent, the opening statement may come across as a "motherhood and apple pie" speech. But such flag-waving speeches can serve a useful purpose in setting a proper tone for the balance of the talks.

Theme

From a thematic point of view, the opening statement should address the "big picture" and not get bogged down in details. Nevertheless, it should not be so vague as to leave the union wondering what type of bargaining posture the employer will take in negotiations. While some employers choose to combine their opening statements with a presentation of management's agenda of bargaining proposals, it is advisable to make the two sufficiently distinct so that the message of the opening statement is not lost. If the two are intertwined, the "big picture" aspect and tone-setting objective can be lost among the specific proposals being made. There may be some situations where the employer's situation is so grave, and certain bargaining proposals so critical, that they require mention in the opening statement. Even in these situations, however, it is suggested that they be discussed in broad terms rather than in specific detail.

The type of subjects which are most appropriate for an opening statement include the following topics:

1. The general economic trend in the employer's industry since the last contract negotiations.
2. Productivity trends in the facility or facilities covered by the bargaining unit.

3. Changes in the economy or in the employer's industry which have a bearing on negotiations. These might include product changes, new manufacturing processes, government deregulation, foreign competition, and the like.
4. The employer's competitive position in the relevant industry.
5. Recent collective bargaining settlements by competitors.
6. The positive and/or negative aspects of the labor-management relationship affecting this bargaining unit.

The theme should be more than simply the traditional "poor mouth" message which union representatives are so accustomed to hearing at contract negotiation time. Nevertheless, it is likely to focus on the problems management is now experiencing and anticipates facing in the future. At this threshold phase of bargaining the challenge to management's spokesperson is to accurately portray the positive as well as the negative aspects of the employer's business, and to make the union representatives realize their stake and the stake of their members in the employer's business, while at the same time avoiding the aura of "doom and gloom" (unless, of course, the employer's situation is indeed dire). It is a difficult task, yet well worth the effort, since throughout the negotiations management's spokesperson can explain the employer's position in relation to the points made in the opening statement.

Presentation

In order to substantiate some of the points made in the opening statement, supporting data may be necessary. Unless the parties have a tradition of using sophisticated communications techniques in their presentations and are comfortable with them, it is usually advisable for management to avoid audio-visual presentations to transmit the data. Written handouts and blackboard or other hand-drawn charts are usually more effective. Audio-visual presentations (especially films, slides, or videotapes) are usually regarded as "Public Relations snow jobs" by union representatives. The message which management is trying to convey will be resisted enough without having the additional psychological barrier of a slick presentation.

Regardless of the aids used to transmit the data, the amount of data should be kept to the minimum necessary to convey the message. Similarly, the data should be presented in a clear and simple fashion. Most union representatives are not accustomed to lengthy financial or economic presentations, so clear and simply presented data will usually be more effective than a lengthy, sophisticated presentation.

The opening statement should be kept as short as possible, consistent with the objectives noted above. Only in unusual circumstances should it exceed 10 to 15 minutes. There should be no interruptions tolerated. If union representatives interrupt with questions or statements, they should be politely told to hold their questions or comments until the statement is completed.

Many negotiators do not make an opening statement and simply wade into the nuts and bolts of bargaining. The author believes that management loses an important educational opportunity if it fails to put the negotiations in perspective—the perspective of the employer's enterprise. The optimum time for doing so is at the outset of bargaining. That opportunity should not be lost.

Opening Statement by the Union

Many unions either decline or neglect to make an opening statement. Others include such a statement as part of their presentation of bargaining proposals (bargaining agenda). If an opening statement is made, management representatives should listen attentively and make notes of what is said. During any general statement (as opposed to the presentation of the union's bargaining agenda), no interruptions should be made; management should extend to the union the same courtesy management expects during its opening statement. If the statement contains substantial erroneous information or makes unfair allegations about management, however, little time should be lost following the conclusion of the statement in correcting the errors or refuting the allegations. Although negotiations are not a debating contest, the union spokesperson and committee should know that management will not tolerate significant misstatements in silence. The skillful negotiator can, without creating hostility, "clarify for the record" or "make the union's negotiator aware of information he may not previously have known" so as to signal the union's spokesperson that he or she will not be permitted to get away with inaccuracies, false statements, or innuendo.

Receiving the Union's Bargaining Agenda

The first substantive part of negotiations is the presentation of the union's agenda of contract proposals. Typically this takes place on the first day of negotiations. It is at this point that actual bargaining begins.

Advance Receipt of the Union Agenda

If the union is willing to cooperate, it is a good idea to obtain from union representatives a copy of the union's agenda some time in advance of its formal presentation. Although many unions refuse to release their agenda in advance as a matter of policy, others have no objection, provided it has been completed in sufficient time.

Early receipt of the union's agenda has several advantages. First, it allows management an opportunity to study the proposals, formulate questions to clarify dubious points, complete preliminary cost-estimating, and prepare responses. Second, it can assist management in preparing its own agenda. If the union is proposing to change certain sections or paragraphs of the contract and management desires to make other changes in those same parts of the contract, the management proposals can perhaps be advanced by way of counterproposal rather than as an original proposal. The rationale of this approach, as was pointed out in Chapter 3, is that failure to obtain agreement on a management-proposed change (in a clause subject to several interpretations) can later be interpreted by an arbitrator, court of law, or administrative agency as favoring the union, since management would not have proposed the change if the clause had been favorable to it. By making the proposed change in the form of a counterproposal, it becomes less clear that management felt the need to change that clause absent any other changes proposed by the union.

Dealing With Pending Grievances

Some unions seek to include settlement of pending contract grievances as part of their bargaining agenda or as a supplementary matter to the agenda. Regardless of the form in which this subject is raised, *management should refuse to negotiate on pending grievances as part of contract negotiations*. Grievances should be handled through the grievance procedure set forth in the labor agreement. If that procedure has been exhausted, arbitration normally follows. Labor contract negotiations are for the purpose of negotiating changes in the contract, not for resolving specific disputes arising out of the existing contract. There is, of course, nothing wrong with discussing particular grievances as they relate to certain sections of the contract where proposals for changes in those contract sections have been made. However, the discussion of grievances in such cases is not for the purpose of settling the grievance, but to illustrate the rationale underlying the proposal or otherwise support a proposal made by either side.

If the union insists on seeking to settle pending grievances in negotiations, and management believes that efforts to settle pending grievances would be in its best interest, the grievances may be dealt with, but they should not be discussed as part of contract negotiations. A separate meeting, preferably with a different management spokesperson and representatives, should be scheduled. In such cases, the management representatives should be those who normally handle grievances. Any grievance settlements reached should not be part of the settlement agreement reached in contract negotiations.

As a general rule, however, grievance negotiations have no place in contract negotiations. Once the union finds that it can postpone grievance determinations until the time of contract negotiations, when it has the right to strike and normally possesses greater bargaining leverage, its interest in resolving or dropping grievances will evaporate during the period prior to negotiations. To the extent possible, management should attempt to resolve or give its final position on all pending grievances well in advance of negotiations so as to preclude the subject being raised at all.

Understanding and Clarifying the Union's Proposals

As the union's spokesperson begins to present the union's agenda, management's spokesperson has the responsibility for making sure that he or she understands what it is that is being proposed. As each item is read, questions should be asked if there is any doubt whatsoever about what is intended by the union. One of the oft-repeated key questions should be, "What's the purpose of this proposal or this contract change?"

Ascertaining Rationale for Proposals

Depending upon the custom normally followed by the negotiating parties, the original presentation of the union's agenda can be used as a time for justifying the proposals. Some unions prefer simply to state their proposals during the initial presentation, leaving for a later date arguments or information to support and justify the change. In such cases, management is not greatly disadvantaged by allowing the union to proceed at its own pace. If the union's presentation does not include justification or supporting arguments, one or more separate meetings will need to be held prior to the initial management caucus for considering and evaluating the union's proposals. Where the union does not indicate a preference for deferring justification, however, management's spokesperson should probe certain proposals to determine *why* the union has advanced it and what *justification* exists for management to accept it. The burden for a change in the labor contract must be borne by the party proposing the change. Therefore, the union must be prepared to support its proposals with arguments, examples, and any other rationale which might be persuasive in favor of acceptance. Management should never forget to place the burden where it belongs in such cases.

What is suggested here is that explanation and justification be sought on those particular proposals which are new, unique, strongly felt by the union, or otherwise worthy of inquiry and justification. Certain other proposals may be so onerous to management and the lack of justification so clear that probing by management may only serve to mislead the union into believing that management may take such proposals seriously. For example, a proposal to completely delete a no-strike clause from the contract is one to which management will not normally give any serious consideration. To seek the union's rationale or to invite extended discussion will only make the subject more important in the eyes of the union representatives. Some proposals are best tactfully ignored, and this is an example of one of them.

The Spokesperson's Notes

Throughout the presentation of the union's agenda, management's spokesperson should be taking brief notes. Although complete notes are to be taken by the designated management note taker(s), the spokesperson should have shorthand notes of key points made by the union counterpart. The organization of these notes can be quite important, especially if the negotiations continue over a long period of time. The author likes to keep notes of discussions on specific agenda items according to the item discussed. A convenient and simple form for this purpose is one which lists the proposal at the top together with its numerical or alphabetical designation, the union's comments and/or position on the right side, and management's comments and/or position on the left side, with all entries being dated. Exhibit 5–1 illustrates an example of this type of form. With this type of form it is very convenient for the spokesperson to enter notes of management's prepared response, developed during caucuses, from which he or she can speak during the negotiating meetings.

Pitfalls in Clarifying Union Proposals

Expanding Scope of Proposals

When attempting to clarify a proposal, some management spokespersons make the mistake of asking if a proposal includes items which are not really mentioned in the proposal but which are a logical extension thereof. For example, a proposal may read "Part-time employees to receive full holiday benefits." The proposal does not mention temporary employees, a classification which would usually include summer hires. An unwary management spokesperson might ask if the proposal includes temporary employees. No union spokesperson in his right mind would answer in the negative since the question invites an expansion of the proposal and a union typically feels that more is better. If any clarification is required (although it is not apparent that any is needed in this case), it would be better phrased, "You mean an employee who works less than 40 hours per week?" The point here is to refrain from questions which will allow a union's proposals to be made broader than they might otherwise be. Any questions should be phrased to suggest a limited interpretation. Another way of seeking clarification, yet not inviting an expanded interpretation, is to paraphrase the proposal. Using the above example, the statement would be, "In other words, you want employees who are sched-

Exhibit 5–1. Spokesperson's Personal Notes of Negotiations

Union (circled)

Agenda # 23

Article 7 **Section** B.3

Management

Proposal Description Prohibit scheduling of OT when employees are on layoff

Management	Union
7/22 - Not acceptable. Can't schedule work so precisely to meet this. Could cost us a lot of business if we can't cover peaks & valleys	7/15 Prop. explained. Co. should recall all those on layoff before working O.T. last Oct. Co. abused O.T. with long work weeks while 50 ees on layoff.
7/23 PM reject union C/P as still too restrictive Co. C/P. If weekend O.T. to be scheduled during layoff cond, Co. will meet w/union in advance to see if there's any way to recall to cover extra work.	7/23 AM C/P limit O.T. to 8 hrs./wk./ee when ees on layoff PM will study Co. C/P
7/25 - Reject Union C/P	7/25 reject Co. C/P - doesn't really cover our need C/P - Limit O.T. to 10% per dept. if ees in that dept. are on layoff.
	8/4 - drop proposal

uled for less than 40 hours per week to receive pay for all holidays not worked?" In this way, the management spokesperson asks a leading question that invites a limited interpretation of the proposal.

Unwarranted Curiosity or Interest

It was pointed out earlier that management's spokesperson should avoid questions seeking *justification* about obviously unacceptable union proposals. For the same reason, questions seeking clarification about obviously unacceptable proposals should be avoided. A proposal to "guarantee 40 hours pay per week" could be ambiguous to the extent that it could apply to employees who were not available to work a full week due to illness, injury, or personal reasons as well as employees who were not scheduled for a full work week, i.e., those on layoff. Regardless of the meaning, the proposal is so burdensome and objectionable that even if it only covered employees available for a full work week, it would normally be rejected. Consequently, any inquiry as to its full ramifications is a mistake since it could lead the union into believing that the proposal could be acceptable to management if only certain minor changes were made. Ignoring such ambitious proposals is the safest course of action.

Other Employers' Contracts

Another mistake commonly made at this stage of bargaining is to either (1) ask if any other employers have the provision or language which the union is proposing or (2) resist a proposal on the basis that no other employers have agreed to such an unwise contract provision. A question about, or resistance based upon, other labor contracts almost invariably works in the union's favor. It seems that there is invariably at least one employer who has been foolish enough to agree to unwise contract provisions. An inquiry about such an employer will often be interpreted by union representatives as recognition that acceptance of a provision by some other employer is sufficient justification in the eyes of management for its adoption in this contract. It is quite a different matter if *most* employers in the same industry have adopted such a provision. Nevertheless, if the issue of other employers' labor contracts is raised at all management's spokesperson should let the union bring up the topic if it chooses. A good piece of advice to follow in these situations is "Don't open the door."

Avoiding Immediate Substantive Responses

As the union spokesperson proceeds through his agenda, there is sometimes a temptation to respond, particularly in a negative way, when the proposal is outrageous. In other cases, where the proposal is rather innocuous or inconsequential, the temptation may be to signify immediate acceptance. Both types of responses are discouraged. To indicate immediate rejection of one or even a few proposals, but not of others, could convey an impression of possible acceptance of such other proposals. On the other hand, to indicate immediate acceptance of any union proposals without a studied evaluation or without obtaining any concession(s) in return is to make a serious mistake or at least give away something of value for nothing in return. In fact, as will be stressed in other chapters, *the spokesperson should never make a concession until it has been considered and discussed in the management caucus.* What may appear on the surface to be a simple and innocuous contract change may, on reflection and analysis, be a meaningful and harmful concession.

Consequently, at the initial presentation, management's spokesperson is best advised to simply listen to the union's proposals, ask questions, and avoid substantive responses. As each item is completed, the proper response is not "OK," but rather "I understand your proposal."

Closing Off Further Proposals

When the union's spokesperson has finished the presentation of bargaining proposals, it is expected that the list is complete and that no additions will be made thereafter. Late-blooming or new proposals can be destructive to otherwise progressing negotiations. Management's spokesperson should tie the union down to its agenda with a comment such as "We will proceed on the basis that this represents your complete list of contract proposals." Many unions are not comfortable with this arrangement and seek to keep the door open to add new proposals as the negotiations proceed. In fact, some unions include a statement such as the following on their written bargaining agenda: "The Union reserves the right to make proposals in addition to those included on this agenda."

While one party cannot, as a general rule, legally keep the other from raising additional proposals after bargaining has commenced or refuse to bargain about such proposals,[1] it can place some serious barriers in the way of the late-blooming proposals. If, after receipt of the union's agenda and an appropriate "nail down" statement as previously suggested, there appears to be an effort by the union to keep its options open to introduce new matters, management's spokesperson should put the union on notice by saying, "We will listen to what you may say, but you must understand that we will give little serious consideration to any new proposals made after this point."

Of course, it must be recognized that union negotiators can be very creative and a brand-new proposal can be cleverly disguised as a counterproposal, making it very difficult to label it as a new proposal. Nevertheless, by putting the union on notice about management's abhorrence of new proposals, management can discourage serious abuses.

Presenting Management's Agenda

In Chapter 3, the strategy and preparation of management proposals are discussed. Assuming that management has decided to propose contract changes of its own, it is important that the proposals be properly presented.

Timing

For reasons pointed out earlier it is preferable that management have an opportunity to review the union's agenda prior to presenting its own. Therefore, unless there are compelling reasons for doing otherwise, management is advised to delay presentation of its agenda until sometime following the union's presentation. Beyond that, the presentation should be scheduled in such a way that it does not get sandwiched in among discussion of union proposals. It should be done at a time when it can be presented as the major subject of discussion. Ideally, the entire meeting on a particular day would be devoted to that presentation. The objective here, of course, is to focus the union's attention on management's agenda.

Method of Presentation

The introduction of management's proposed contract changes is essentially a sales presentation. The objective is to introduce the product (proposal) to the customer (union) in such a way that the customer will have a favorable impression of it, and to lay the groundwork for a subsequent sale (acceptance). Except in very unusual circumstances a sale will not be possible on the day of presentation, but the salesperson (spokesperson) should not give the impression that he or she accepts that fact.

Accentuate the Positive

Each proposal should be clearly explained and justified. Examples, data, or any other supporting information should be used to explain why management believes the proposal should be accepted. Not only should the positive features of each proposal be stressed, but any apparent negative aspects should be rationalized or minimized. If the proposal has been adopted and has worked successfully in any other facilities of the employer (especially any others represented by the same union), such facts should be highlighted.

While the sales aspects of the presentation are important, the presentation should not be "hard sell," nor should the impression be given that the proposals are of such high value to the employer that the union will expect management to make significant concessions to achieve them. In this regard, unless the desired changes are extremely far-reaching, management's spokesperson should be careful not to indicate that management is prepared to offer anything more than it would otherwise grant in order to obtain agreement on its proposals. While such concessions may ultimately be necessary, this is not the time to suggest them. For this reason, if management has in mind certain "sweeteners" to offset onerous aspects of its proposal(s), such sweeteners should generally be held in reserve for later bargaining value. An exception to this general rule must be made in cases where management's proposals are so ambitious that to propose them without any proffered offsetting compensation or relief would make the proposals appear ludicrous.

In making its initial "pitch" in support of its proposals management should attempt to hold in reserve some of its supporting arguments and information for later discussions. If all the justifying points are made during the initial presentation, later discussions by management will be repetitious and momentum is likely to be lost.

Evaluating, and Determining Positions on, the Union's Agenda

After the union has presented and justified its proposals, management needs to take some time to analyze, evaluate, and determine its positions on each union proposal. Typically, this will be done in a management caucus or during a recess in negotiations following the presentation. Sufficient time should be allotted to do a thorough job. It is not unusual to take a one- or two-week recess in negotiations, or even longer, in order to do this.

Monetary Issues

The separation of items to be dealt with into the categories of monetary and nonmonetary (language) proposals may have already been made by the parties in their initial meeting(s), but if it has not, such a segregation should be made by management at this point. The monetary proposals should be identified and given to the designated cost estimator for a preliminary estimate of the union's total package proposal (details of cost estimating are discussed in Chapter 10). An undue amount of time should not be spent in this preliminary costing. The initial proposal comes at the "sun, moon, and stars" stage of negotiations and both parties realize that the final settlement will bear only a faint resemblance to the union's opening proposals. Avoiding undue costing effort is especially pertinent with respect to those proposals which are (1) so unrealistic that they will be given little or no serious consideration, and (2) so imprecise or speculative that realistic cost estimating is not possible. Nevertheless, it is helpful to have a rough calculation of the magnitude of the union's proposals as a means of gauging the starting point of the negotiations.

There may be several monetary proposals which deserve serious consideration, but whose cost may be difficult to determine. Examples of these are additional premium payments for certain types of job assignments, clothing and tool allowances, hours of work limitations, etc. Such items should be given attention at an early stage so that if research into payrolls, time records, or other documents is necessary it can be completed in sufficient time prior to preparing an economic offer. In some cases, adequate records may not be available and cost estimating will necessarily be somewhat speculative. In such cases, it is usually preferable to make informed assumptions as to unavailable basic information necessary to costing, rather than to have no estimate as to the cost impact of such proposals.

The union's initial agenda may also contain proposals which present new and/or complex concepts that are beyond the expertise of the members of the management negotiating committee. This is especially true of proposals dealing with pensions, health care benefits, and profit-sharing plans. In this event, assistance should be sought from other departments in the employer's management organization or from outside experts in the appropriate fields. Similarly, if any legal issues are raised by the union's agenda which are beyond the expertise of the management committee members, these should be referred to legal counsel for advice.

Nonmonetary Issues

Reviewing Each Proposal

Once the monetary issues have been assigned for preliminary costing and/or expert advice, the management negotiating committee should focus its attention upon the nonmonetary proposals. A useful starting point is for the committee as a whole to review each proposal and ask the following series of questions:

1. What change is actually being proposed?
2. What reasons or underlying problems has the union offered to justify the proposal's acceptance?
3. Do these reasons have merit and do the underlying problems actually exist? (Research and investigation may be required here.)
4. If the answer to number three is yes, is the union's proposal the best or only way to accomplish the objective? Is there a simpler or less burdensome way to accomplish the objective.

5. Who, if anyone, besides the management negotiating committee members can supply information or advice on the proposal?
6. What is the net effect or practical impact of the union's proposal on the employer's operation? How unfavorable (favorable) is that impact?
7. How important is the proposal to the union? If the employer does not agree, what is likely to be the effect upon negotiations?
8. What should management's *ultimate* position be on the proposal? Can and should it be accepted in some form? If so, in what form?
9. What should management's *initial* position be on the proposal? What reasons or arguments should be advanced to support that position?

In asking question 6, management should adopt a "worse case" analysis for each proposal. In other words, given the most unfavorable set of circumstances, what effect or practical impact will the proposal have on the employer's operations? This recommendation is based upon Murphy's Law, "If anything can go wrong, it will." With respect to labor contract administration, Murphy's Law is particularly apt.

A Devil's Advocate

When going through questions 6 to 9 above, the management committee will usually find it easy to reject the union's proposals and to find reasons why they would be harmful. Nevertheless, management representatives should remember that they are involved in a negotiation and if no significant concessions can be made, the negotiations will be very short and are likely to result in a work stoppage. To facilitate a more realistic appraisal, it is useful to have a member of the management negotiating committee play the devil's advocate by asking "management" why it cannot accept the proposal, what is so onerous about it, and other questions which will cause the management committee to thoughtfully examine each proposal and give reasons for its position. Even where the devil's advocacy approach does not reveal a possible concession, the process serves the additional function of testing the soundness of management's arguments in opposition to the proposal and assists the spokesman to formulate rationale, persuasive responses.

Developing Management's Positions

There are some practical aids the management negotiating committee can use to summarize the results of its analysis. The first aid is a form which is entitled "Union Proposal—Analysis and Position" (see Exhibit 5–2). This form contains most of the information elicited by the nine questions listed earlier in this section. The second aid which can be used in conjunction with, or in lieu of, Exhibit 5–2 is the "Union Agenda Summary" (see Exhibit 5–3). This form can be used to reflect simply a statement of the proposal, management's position, and the major reason(s) for that position. Exhibits 5–2 and 5–3, which reflect analysis and positions on each of the union's nonmonetary proposals, also can serve the function of advising top management of the negotiating committee's evaluation of the union's proposals and, where necessary, facilitate top management's approval of the positions to be taken by its negotiators at the bargaining table.

It should go without saying that forms shown as Exhibits 5–2 and 5–3 must be kept completely confidential. They reveal management's positions, and if they were to fall into the union's hands, no real negotiating on management's part would be possible. Strict security will also be required when offers are being prepared and final positions developed. It might be argued that too great a risk is taken by reducing such sensitive information to writing. However, if management negotiators neglect to organize and record information solely out of fear of having it fall into the union's hands, management will be greatly disadvantaged. Management negotiators simply have to adopt procedures to ensure the confidentiality and security of their bargaining information.

Once the management negotiating committee has evaluated and established positions on each of the union's proposals, management's spokesperson should confirm that these positions are sound and that they reflect the position which the employer's top management wishes to take. All management persons involved, however, should realize that at this stage of negotiations no positions should be set in concrete. Since serious bargaining has not yet taken place, the depth of union sentiment has not been fully ascertained, and opportunities for alternatives and counterproposals have not been seriously explored. It would be a grave mistake at this early stage of bar-

Exhibit 5–2. Worksheet on Union Proposal

UNION PROPOSAL—ANALYSIS AND POSITION

AGENDA NO. 18

A. UNION PROPOSAL

Establish sick leave benefit; earn 1/2 day per month with maximum accumulation of 15 days.

B. UNION'S SUPPORTING ARGUMENTS

1. Employees should not suffer loss of pay for legitimate illness.
2. Common benefit within the industry.
3. Very little cost to employer; employees seldom use sick leave.
4. Employer can require employee to submit M.D. slip to qualify for benefit.

C. MANAGEMENT ANALYSIS

1. Open to abuse; employees feel they are entitled to use all sick leave and use it whether or not needed—treat as holiday; M.D. slips are easily obtained.
2. Present sickness and accident indemnity plan covers nonoccupational illness.
3. Does not appear to be a high priority to union.

D. MANAGEMENT POSITION

1. INITIAL

   Reject on basis of lack of need and reasons 1 and 2 under Section C above.

2. ULTIMATE

   If this becomes a significant issue, consider some improvement under weekly sickness and accident program (e.g., additional $10 to $15 per week or increase weeks from 26 to 39).

Exhibit 5–3. Worksheet on Union Agenda

	UNION AGENDA SUMMARY		
NO.	PROPOSAL	MANAGEMENT POSITION	REASONS
1	Superseniority for union representatives	Reject	1. Creates favored class of employees 2. No relationship to skills or experience 3. Can be a divisive influence
2	Distribute overtime in order of seniority	Reject; consider if limited to certain types of O.T.	1. Senior employees can "hog" all O.T. 2. No recognition of skill, experience, and familiarity with job in progress
3	Increase period for filing grievances from 10 days to 30 days	Accept on basis that there is no backpay liability prior to filing of grievance	1. 30 days ok if management not prejudiced by delay
4	Provide pay for OSHA inspections	Accept subject to limitations on number and frequency	1. Can benefit company in some situations 2. Don't want to write a blank check
5	Post job bids for 10 days rather than 5 days	Reject	1. Delays filling of job vacancies 2. Not necessary; interested employees will see posting in 5-day period as easily as 10 3. Problems of absence due to vacation can be nearly as bad with 2 weeks as with 1 week

gaining to fix positions to the extent of not allowing any room for further consideration and movement. Nevertheless, recognition of the need for, and willingness to consider, a change in position must not dissuade management from the initial evaluation and position determination process discussed in this section.

Initial Response to the Union's Nonmonetary Proposals

Although the game plan developed by management that was discussed in Chapter 3 can have an influence on the manner in which management makes its initial response to the union's proposals, as a rule the response to each of the union's proposals will follow the order of those proposals as set forth in the union's agenda.

Kicking the Tires

Management's spokesperson often will preface his or her responses with a general statement about the nature and magnitude of the union's proposals. Usually the statement will point out how unrealistic the union's agenda is, and perhaps announce the total cost estimate the employer has calculated for the union's package of proposals. Mention should also be made of management's negative reaction to proposals which would reduce its rights to effectively manage its enterprise. Such a statement is not likely to have much impact on the union's negotiating committee members, for they realize that the union's opening agenda typically is excessive, and that management would never agree to anything like it. Nevertheless, failure of management's spokesperson to criticize the size and nature of the opening proposals advanced by the union could easily be interpreted by the union committee as meaning that management believes the proposals are not as ambitious or exorbitant as the union committee had thought. In other words, the union expects management to "kick the tires," and can be misled if it does not do so.

Categorizing Proposals

Management's spokesperson should then proceed to respond to each of the union's nonmonetary proposals. If the parties have not previously agreed upon a division between nonmonetary and monetary proposals, the union may disagree with the way in which management has characterized a particular proposal. Since a large percentage of proposals can be shown to have some economic impact, the union can seldom quarrel with designating a particular proposal as monetary unless it clearly has no direct bearing on compensation (e.g., recognition clause, dress code, no-strike clause, safety rules). It is usually to management's advantage to characterize borderline issues as "monetary" since such issues are usually treated as part of a package offer, and not frequently discussed as separate issues. Less crucial issues can sometimes "slip through the cracks" when package offers are being made. In any event, a serious disagreement seldom develops over a particular monetary/nonmonetary designation made by management, as long as it is understood that the particular issue in question will be addressed by management before the negotiations are concluded.

Initial Signaling

The initial responses the management spokesperson gives are designed to indicate to the union which union proposals are generally acceptable, possibly acceptable (usually in some other form), or unacceptable in any form. Of course, management should not, unless it has an unusual strategy in mind, reveal its bottom-line position on all issues at this early stage of negotiations. But on relatively innocuous proposals, early acceptance may be indicated, particularly where arguments in opposition thereto are few or nonexistent. Movement on such issues will help to cushion the negative impact caused by management's rejection of the union's more substantive proposals and are likely to create a positive tone conducive to union concessions.

It is especially important during this initial response that management's acceptance of any significant union proposals be linked in some fashion to acceptance or satisfactory resolution of management's proposals (if they have been made) or related to the elimination or "dropping" of other union proposals. In fact, during this initial response, repeated reference should be made to management's proposals and the necessity of favorable union consideration of them as the response management expects on the part of the union in exchange for management's agreement on the union's proposals.

Eliminating Issues

As each union proposal is reviewed, the management spokesperson should attempt to dispose of as many issues as possible. Some reduction in the number of issues can frequently be accomplished by consolidating several separate proposals. Others can sometimes be eliminated with explanations that the present contract already provides the result which the union seeks through its proposal. Some proposals may parallel limitations or provisions already imposed by law, and can therefore be eliminated on the basis that they are redundant. The objective here is to reduce the size of the union's agenda as much as possible without making any significant concessions.

Reflecting Basic Positions

The initial responses must also include clear and unequivocal statements with respect to proposals that are completely unacceptable to management. There should be no suggestion of bluff or bargaining table posturing. For example, if the issue is one over which the employer will take a strike or lockout, the union should be told that the proposal is totally unacceptable to management. It is seldom useful to use the words strike or lockout at this stage of negotiations, but the message can nevertheless be conveyed in such a way that the union has no doubt about management's position. For example, the management spokesperson might say, "This proposal is one with which we are in complete disagreement. I cannot overemphasize our opposition to it. We will not sign a contract containing this clause or anything like it."

With regard to union proposals which may be acceptable, ut which management wishes to hold back for more bargaining ılue at a later time, the management spokesperson must careılly frame a response to indicate rejection, but avoid making the rejection so definite that credibility will be lost if and when the proposal is later accepted. An appropriate response might be, "We see no merit in this proposal. It has no advantage whatsoever to us and has the following drawbacks: ________."

Such a response indicates a rejection, but does not over-emphasize the point at the risk of misleading the union. A hardening of positions at such an early stage of negotiations on issues which are ultimately soluble is not usually helpful.

The primary objectives of the initial responses are to make the union aware of those issues which are potentially dangerous ("strike issues") in order to avoid later miscalculation by the union, and to generate movement on the union's part, i.e., acceptance of management's proposals and/or dropping of union proposals. If the union perceives that management has made no significant effort to compromise, movement on the union's part will likely be commensurately insignificant. One of the key skills of negotiating is, of course, to concede little while appearing to concede much. This skill is important when initially responding to the union's proposals, and it will be no less important throughout the negotiations.

Getting Negotiations off the Ground

One of the more difficult phases of labor contract negotiations occurs after the parties have each presented their opening proposals and received the initial responses from the other side. At this point, novice negotiators are often at a loss as to how to "get the ball rolling." At the early stage of negotiations, neither party is inclined to grant concessions for fear they might give something of too great a value too soon in the process. Likewise, there is often a concern that early concessions will lead the other party to believe it will be a one-sided negotiation—all take and no give.

A convenient way to get over these hurdles is to select a group of issues raised by both sides that do not have significant consequences, and to work out satisfactory resolutions to them. In effect, work on the "easy issues." These may be relatively innocuous "housekeeping" items, i.e., updating of obsolete terms, correcting typographical or computational errors, and clarifying clearly ambiguous but noncontroversial terminology. By getting agreement on a number of such issues and making the agendas shorter, the parties are able to develop some bargaining momentum and hopefully enhance mutual trust early in the process. At the same time, they are able to claim to their respective constituencies that "some progress is being made."

Although the progress is on matters where there was little or no disagreement in the first place, it is less important than the fact that disagreements are being postponed until later.

The corollary to this advice is that issues involving serious disagreement should be bypassed at the outset of negotiations. There is no merit in trying to cope early in the process with hardrock issues such as union security, contracting out, pay, and benefits, etc. There will be plenty of time to come to grips with the tough issues. For now, the parties should ease into the process in order to develop some momentum that could make the way smoother for the more contentious issues later in the negotiations.

6

Practical Tips for the Management Spokesperson

Effective negotiating is, to a considerable extent, a matter of individual style, habit, and technique. Traits and techniques used to good effect by one negotiator may cause another to fall flat on his or her face. This is not to say that good negotiating techniques are purely intuitive. On the contrary, many effective negotiators have developed their own style by watching others and selectively imitating their approach or at least adapting that approach to suit their own personality. The purpose of this chapter is to provide certain ideas on negotiating style and practical techniques which have proven useful to the author and to other negotiators. Not all will prove satisfactory to any single reader, but most bear consideration and trial. Hopefully some will "fit" and prove useful to the reader.

Arranging and Conducting Meetings

It is important to consider the physical arrangements for negotiation meetings before the meetings commence. A great deal of time is usually spent in these meetings, so they should be conducive to reaching an agreement—an agreement favorable to management.

Seating Arrangements

It is common for management and union representatives to sit at opposite sides of a table. Management's spokesperson should make sure that he or she is seated in the approximate center of the management bargaining committee. This position is the natural location for the person who has the authority to speak for management. While this is obviously not a crucial aspect of the negotiations, the failure of the spokesperson to be in the center position of management's committee will raise questions in the minds of the union representatives as to who wields management's authority in negotiations. This uncertainty can detract somewhat from the spokesperson's clout at the bargaining table.

An awkward situation occasionally arises when the union spokesperson does not position himself or herself at the center of the union's side of the table, precluding good eye to eye contact if the management spokesperson is in the center. In such cases, the management spokesperson should remain in the center. The union counterpart will likely reposition at that meeting or in a subsequent meeting.

Meeting Times

Some general considerations regarding meeting schedules were covered in Chapter 5. Along the same lines, it is important to ensure that negotiating meetings are held at times which are most advantageous to management. When considerable travel by management's spokesperson is involved, morning meetings may be disadvantageous. Also, sufficient time between meetings should be allowed in order to make adequate preparation. For instance, management should not agree to consecutive morning meetings if this means burning the midnight oil will be necessary in order to be adequately prepared for the following day. Many unions use the tactic of pressuring management to meet frequently and at inconvenient times in the hope that concessions or errors will be made because of the pressure generated by such schedules.

The inadvisability of late night-early morning or marathon negotiations cannot be emphasized too strongly. Unless arrangements for meeting physical needs, including the need for sleep, are more favorable for the management negotiators than for union negotiators (and they usually are not), management's spokesperson and the employer is placed at a serious disadvantage by agreeing to meet at such hours. Of course, as negotiations approach a strike/lockout deadline, such meetings may become necessary. Until then, however, they should be avoided at all costs.

Response Timing

When parties meet more or less on a day-to-day schedule, a burden falls on the party which is obligated to respond to the other on the following day. Even if the next meeting is scheduled for the following afternoon, the party owing the response will probably have to work well into the evening in order to prepare its response. In effect, "the ball is in their court." In this situation, it is not a bad idea for management to time its responses in such a way as to leave the ball in the union's court by the end of the day. If the representatives of one of the parties have to work during the evenings to be prepared for the following day, shouldn't it be the union representatives?

Caucus Room and Equipment

More time during negotiations is spent in the caucus room than in face-to-face negotiating meetings, and as the negotiations proceed to a conclusion the percentage of time spent in caucus increases dramatically. Consequently, the caucus room should be carefully selected and equipped. It should be located reasonably close to the room where negotiations take place, and should be completely secure from eavesdropping, telephone intercepts, computer tampering, or entrance by unauthorized persons. Care should be taken that discarded work papers, draft proposals, and the like are not left in the room or in wastebaskets. All such papers should be immediately shredded or kept in a common container for destruction by someone on the management committee.

The caucus room should be equipped with the necessary equipment, which might include a telephone, typewriter or word processor, copying machine, calculator, facsimile machine, and computer. The facsimile machine can be used to send and receive documents and drafts of contract language from other management facilities and legal counsel. The computer can be used to make cost estimates and to store relevant bargaining data and contract language from other contracts.

Bargaining Table Talk

Hundreds of thousands of words are spoken during a typical negotiation. Some are used to persuade, others to bluff, and still others to resist. What is said and how it is said can have a significant effect on the outcome of negotiations.

Setting the Proper Tone

The way in which the parties will generally address one another during the course of negotiations is usually established in the first hour or so of the negotiations. The management spokesperson who treats his or her counterpart with respect and consideration is more likely than not to receive the same treatment from the union spokesperson. The same holds true for the other side of the table. In essence, the parties by the end of the first hour usually "set the tone" for the negotiations. To be sure, there are always certain union representatives who know only one style of negotiating—bargaining by bluster, threat, and the demeaning of management. In the author's experience, however, the "blusters" constitute a very small minority of union negotiators.

Dealing With Abusive Table Talk

Novice management negotiators sometimes become perplexed in those relatively rare instances where union representatives become profane and abusive. They are not sure how much of the rough and tumble is par for the course, or whether they are being taken advantage of because of their inexperience. They agonize over whether they should tolerate it or somehow try to put a stop to it. And if they feel the latter is appropriate, they are not sure how it should be done.

There are no simple or universal answers to these questions since each person has his standards and expectations. Certainly, labor negotiations are not tea parties, nor are union negotiators always polite. Oftentimes abusive language from the union's spokesperson is politically motivated—as a "show" for local union representatives. Attempts to "cut down" the union's spokesperson for using such language may be counterproductive, forcing the union negotiator into a corner from which he will try to extricate himself with even more abuse.

But there is a line beyond which union representatives may not cross if management and/or its spokesperson is to avoid losing respect, and each spokesperson must decide where that line is to be drawn. Once it is crossed, the spokesperson should calmly advise the union counterpart that management is not willing to tolerate such abuse and expects to receive the same degree of respect that has been afforded to the union. The meeting should then be recessed until a later time when, hopefully, a more conducive atmosphere prevails.

A Rational Approach

Management's spokesperson can also set a positive tone by exhibiting reasoned consideration and calm judgment when responding to exorbitant union proposals, claims of management's contract violations and/or bad faith, and other emotionally tinged communications. An effective management negotiator projects an image of a calm, thoughtful, and reasonable person by what he says and the way it is said. This means avoiding such things as

- Extreme statements
- Answering without having the facts
- Accusing the other side of bad faith (even if the same accusation has been made of management)
- Blaming "top management" or "careless supervisors" for existing problems.
- Interrupting the union's spokesperson before he or she has finished speaking
- Using abusive or profane language
- Sounding like a preacher giving a sermon
- Becoming emotional and/or losing one's self-control.

This is not to say that the management spokesperson should be shy and retiring, or simply act pleasant in the face of a barrage of accusations against management. On the contrary, the spokesperson for management needs to be strong in defending management's position and must project an image of firmness and resolve, but that strength should come across in a calm and reasoned manner, not in an emotional and uncontrolled way. Indeed, there will be times when the management spokesperson finds it necessary to raise his or her voice, criticize the union, and/or make a point in the most clear and convincing manner possible. If this is done on an occasional basis, however, it will have a much greater impact upon the union representatives than if this approach is part of his day-to-day rhetoric.

A Place for Humor

When discussing the proper tone for negotiations, it is difficult to overestimate the value of humor. Nothing can ease tension, nor create an atmosphere conducive to agreement, quite like a humorous remark or a funny story. Care should be taken, though, to assure that the remark or story is not patently offensive to anyone in the room. For this reason, sexual, racial, and ethnic jokes should be avoided. Similarly, the timing must be considered. If management has just responded negatively to a series of union proposals and an air of hostility pervades the room, humor will not be well received. With these caveats, however, humor has a very important place in successful labor negotiations.

Word Selection

The choice of words used by the management spokesperson has a surprisingly great effect upon the course of negotiations. It conveys messages which will be given great weight by the union representatives. Even if the spokesperson may not intend to convey any special message by the choice or juxtaposition of words, listeners on the other side of the table will often receive one. As a consequence, the spokesperson should choose words carefully, especially when crucial stages of negotiations are reached. For example, if the union makes a new proposal on an important issue, the following responses will convey different messages:

- "It's an interesting proposal—we'll seriously consider it."
- "We'll consider your proposal in our next caucus."
- "We'll get back to you on it."
- "We see little merit in your proposal, but we'll review it."

None of the responses indicates acceptance or rejection of the proposal, but each one conveys a different degree of receptivity.

The words one chooses to use when rejecting a proposal can be even more significant, since they can convey a message which can affect the union's bargaining strategy. Consider the following responses:

- "We cannot agree with your proposal at this time."
- "We are unwilling to agree to that."
- "We reject your proposal."
- "The answer is *no*."
- "We told you yesterday we would not agree to your proposal. The answer today is still no, and it will be the same tomorrow, next week, next month, and next year."

Negotiators often characterize such varying negative responses as "soft no's" or "hard no's." Of course, the tone and volume of voice, facial expression, and context of negotiations will also influence how the message is perceived. The spokesperson's words will be closely listened to by those on the other side of the table, and it is important that the message received be the one that is intended. In this regard, it is helpful to keep in mind the following saying: "I know you believe you understand what you think I said, but I am not sure you realize that what you heard is not what I meant."

The Spokesperson as a Persuader

A popular impression of labor contract negotiations is that economic force and threat or fear of work stoppages are the only factors determining the outcome of negotiations. Little is said about the degree to which parties change their positions based upon factual information, logical arguments, and friendly persuasion. However, short of sheer economic force, persuasion is what collective bargaining is all about and one of the most important roles of the management negotiator is that of a persuader—one who must convince union representatives by facts, logic, trust, or any other means that they should change their minds and, therefore, their positions.

In order to be an effective persuader, the spokesperson must have a good working knowledge of the subject matter and workplace factors about which he is negotiating. Although the spokesperson need not know all the details of the work performed by bargaining unit employees, he or she should have a reasonably good familiarity with the nature and problems of the work involved, know the terminology or shop terms which are common to the industry and work environment, and have a reasonably good knowledge of the economics of the employer's enterprise. If the spokesperson is new to the organization or the industry, sufficient time should be taken prior to the beginning of negotiations to become familiar with these matters.

Another aid to the spokesperson is to know the background, work history, personalities, and interests of each member of the union's bargaining committee. By knowing these facts, more personal and meaningful arguments, examples, and explanations can be formulated. For example, if the spokesperson knows that several members of the union's negotiating committee were victims of serious industrial injuries, he or she can make a more specific and persuasive proposal for a joint union-management safety program that management may wish to institute.

Types of Persuasion

There are several varieties of persuasion that an effective spokesperson should master. Each one has its own advantages and all should be utilized at one time or another to alter the positions taken by union representatives.

Persuasion Based on Factual and Statistical Information

An old saying goes "I've made up my mind, don't bother me with the facts." Although this is often the case in labor negotiations, there are times when the only way to change minds is through facts. For example, there are numerous times when a union justifies a proposed contract language change on the grounds that a supervisor has abused an existing management right, and therefore some contractual limitation should be placed on that right. The union spokesperson will cite one or more situations to exemplify the alleged abuses. Management is largely defenseless against such arguments unless it can show that the abuses did not occur or that they can be explained as being reasonable under the circumstances. Only facts can serve this purpose. Management must investigate, if it has not already done so, the alleged abuses and determine if it can counter the union's claims. Otherwise, the only rebuttals will be either (1) that the incidents were isolated (if they were), or (2) the weak old standby explanation, "We're sorry about it, it won't happen again, but we're not willing to change the contract."

Employers are fond of presenting statistical information during negotiations to support economic positions. Frequently, the data is presented in the form of graphs or charts and projected on a screen along with an oral explanation. As a general rule, such presentations seem to have little, if any, persuasive effect upon union representatives. The reasons for this are many and varied, but probably include one or more of the following:

1. They are not willing to be persuaded.
2. They do not believe the information is truthful or accurate.
3. They do not understand the presentation.
4. They feel they are being propagandized.
5. They are inattentive and do not follow the presentation.

This is not to say that management should refrain from any factual or statistical presentation of information, but only that management negotiators should understand the limitations of such forms of persuasion and attempt to avoid some of the obvious pitfalls. The following suggestions are offered for those who believe that they have an important story to tell, and are convinced that it cannot be effectively told without statistical and/or graphic support:

1. Keep it simple. To the extent possible, have each graph or chart depict only one idea, and simplify the method of portraying the information as much as possible.
2. Use everyday terminology, not technical jargon, except where such jargon is regularly used in the workplace and fully understood by the audience.
3. Use a simple, low-key presentation with aids such as a blackboard or flip charts; don't use flashy paraphernalia such as color slides with multiple projectors and prerecorded audio.
4. Make the presentation very short—15 minutes or less—but go slowly through the explanation of each point.
5. Follow the well-known rule for all presentations: tell them what you are going to tell them, tell them, then tell them what you already told them.
6. Offer to make the source documents of the data available to the union for verification of their accuracy.
7. Point out the significance of the data to particular issues being discussed in negotiations.
8. Repeatedly refer in subsequent meetings to the information contained in the presentation.

9. If appropriate, repeat selected segments of the presentation in subsequent negotiating meetings.

Following these suggestions will not ensure that anyone will be persuaded, but it may help.

Rational Persuasion

It is surprising sometimes how effective a carefully conceived, rational argument can be during negotiations. The argument, however, must proceed from the premises accepted by the listener, not those held by the speaker. Thus, for example, if the management spokesperson is arguing for a relaxation of a seniority provision regarding the selection of lead persons on the basis that it is an important management right, the chances of persuasion are very slim. Union representatives do not easily accept the notion of management rights, and therefore, no matter how logical or persuasive the subsequent argument is, the failure to agree with the basic premise will thwart acceptance. In this situation, a more effective premise is that each worker's job is made easier if the lead person who directs the work is an effective leader and is able to get along with the crew. From that point it can be argued that the qualities of leadership and compatibility with others are not always related to seniority and, therefore, selection of lead persons should not be solely a function of seniority.

An effective management spokesperson must put himself or herself in the place of the union spokesperson and the other members of the union bargaining committee by asking himself, "If I were in their shoes, what argument or reasoning would make sense to me?" Other members of the management negotiating committee can be helpful in formulating arguments and in role playing to test out the viability of various arguments. The sole test of the value of a solid, rational argument is not simply whether it persuades a union representative, for there are many other reasons why unions agree to a specific point (e.g., valuable tradeoff, economic pressure, etc.). Nevertheless, if an argument advanced by management to support a proposal or position is effective, union representatives will often subsequently use that same rationale to explain to the union's rank and file why management's proposal was accepted or the union's proposal dropped. In many such cases, management's arguments are passed on to the union's membership when union leadership attempts to sell a package settlement. Any effective persuasive argument to support a given position or proposal gives union negotiators ammunition to shoot down opposition from subordinate union officials or rank and file members.

Effective use of questions can also be a means of rational argument. Although more subtle and indirect than the straightforward rational argument, this Socratic technique's subtlety is its strength. Such questions as "What benefit would that be to your membership?", "How could we operate if all employees exercised their right to refuse overtime?", and "How often has that situation occurred?" can be as effective in casting a shadow on a proposal as an outright argument based on the same logic. Of course, when such questions are asked, the possible answers should already be known to management.

Emotional Persuasion

Emotional persuasion is, in some ways, the least effective way to change minds in a negotiation. The term "emotional" as used here does not necessarily mean tears and pleas for cooperation. It means an appeal to union representatives' feelings rather than to their minds. The appeal may rely upon their sympathy, trust, affection, or fear. While it has its place in labor negotiations, it can only be effective when used sparingly, and usually only for certain kinds of issues. For example, emotional arguments are usually not effective when one is attempting to convince the union that it should accept a lower pension benefit than that which is being demanded. Conversely, the author has seen it used to good effect in several negotiations to resist union demands for more restrictions on supervisors performing bargaining unit work. In most cases, the owner of a small business or a spokesperson can make a more effective presentation relying on emotional persuasion than the spokesperson for a large corporation. The key to this type of persuasion is credibility. A newcomer to a particular bargaining relationship can seldom achieve the necessary credibility to make an emotional appeal very effective.

Another type of emotional persuasion is based upon fear. The rules which apply to other types of emotional persuasion do not necessarily apply to this type. Usually this form of persuasion is based upon some type of threat, such as a strike or lockout, plant or facility closure, competing union election or decertification campaign, or other type of adverse consequences. Such threats may be overt or simply implied. They may border on being an unfair labor practice. To the extent that they constitute realistic possibilities, they may prove to be useful means of persuasion. However, the spokesperson should use them with great caution. The threat may be taken as a challenge and induce resistance rather than agreement. Likewise they must be used judiciously. "The boy who cried wolf" syndrome has real application in this area. When such emotional persuasion is used, it is most effective when supported with factual and rational persuasion. For example, an argument that continued wage escalation could result in a plant closure can also be supported by data indicating other plant closures in the same industry and/or geographical area as well as wages paid in competing countries or by competing nonunion firms. Similarly, rational arguments which show the impact of excessively high wage costs on product costs and market share can be very supportive and lend credibility to the presentation.

Limits of Persuasion

Regardless of how many facts or logical arguments are marshalled to support or reject a position, there will be many occasions when nothing works, and minds are simply unable or unwilling to be changed. In such cases, if management has determined to hold to its position, the only alternative is to cease trying to persuade and simply announce management's position. Frequently this will be in the form of a simple and firmly stated "no." In other cases, the statement is, "Our position has not changed; we retain our previous proposal." Management should never completely abandon its quest to achieve agreement through persuasion. It should continually return to the arguments and information which it initially advanced to support its position. Nevertheless, there will be times when a clear, simple statement of management's position, along with the admonition that such position will not change, are the only words which will be persuasive. If it is not possible to change the minds of your union counterparts, then at least you should convince them of your resolve not to change your own mind.

The Spokesperson as a Listener

Just as the spokesperson must be a persuader, so too must he or she be willing to be persuaded. If union negotiators perceive management to be unwilling to compromise, their own receptivity to compromise will disappear. The starting point for any persuasion, or for that matter any discussion, is listening.

Listening as an Art

Effective listening means not only hearing the words which are spoken, but attempting to sense the feelings behind the words. The following excerpt from a book of essays published some years ago captures the essence of that aspect of listening essential in labor contract negotiations:

> THE ART OF LISTENING
>
> I am convinced that a good deal which bugs us in our dealings with our fellows would be lost if we listened to each other.
>
> Someone has said that talk was an invention to conceal thought. It might as truly be said that serious conversation, as usually conducted, is an invention to scuttle agreement.
>
> When two people have a point of difference—whether in business, in love, or in games—and enter into a discussion about it, they nearly always emerge with the same equipment they entered with.
>
> That is to say, their defenses. Each man thinks, of course, that he is right, and develops an impressive armory of rationales—some rational and some not—to sustain his conviction.
>
> In "discussion" (which is a polite name for argument) this man is not likely to let his defenses go lightly. Nor is the other man, and for exactly the same reasons.
>
> They end up talking to themselves, not listening to each other. They do not listen until economic pressures, or emotional pressures, or the entry of a third impartial party, compels them to use their ears.
>
> When two sets of defenses flail away at each other we simply have debate, or argument. This is a primitive form of communication. Almost never does anything conclusive emerge from it.
>
> A great enemy to communication is the logical or syllogistic approach. This assumes that feelings between people are rational. They are not. Feelings and rationality are far too often contradictory, by definition.

The rational fellow, when he runs into feelings contrary to his own, tends to explain things. Explanation ignores the existence of feelings. It plows ahead, patiently and with a relentless rationality.

In the end, because he does not understand he is dealing with feelings, he gets nowhere. He irritates himself because he has failed at explanation. And he downgrades the feeling person, who does not respond because he did not want explanation. He wanted communication.

A great many labor disputes, it has been ascertained, derive not from wages and hours, but from wounds to the *amour propre* of the worker. The employee feels he is being undervalued as a human being. These feelings are very hard to put into words, especially when talking to the one who has wounded the feelings.

This is where skilled listening comes in.

The good listener must throw away a lot of rubbish of rationality. He must understand that he is dealing with feelings instead of facts, and that feelings are far more important than facts. * * *

Listening brings people together, explaining tears them apart. The good listener allows the speaker to flower, and be accepted as a human being. * * *

Unless you are one of the rare persons who was born with the talent, you have to learn it. Learning it is largely unlearning the gospel that every cause has its effect, etc., etc. You will never get very far in dealing with your fellows if you assume that human conduct—yours or theirs—is rooted in reason. If you do not know this is so, just listen.[1]

Listening for the Source of the Problem

The value of listening goes beyond simply being open to persuasion and conveying that impression to the union. It also serves the vital purpose of allowing management to pinpoint the source of problems and to lead the way to possible solutions. It is very common in labor negotiations for management to take an adamant position against what appears to be an unreasonable union proposal. From that point on, serious consideration of the union's supporting arguments often stops. Careful listening, however, can often lead to an understanding of the underlying problem, irritant, or objective upon which the proposal is based. From there it is often possible for management to fashion a counterproposal to deal with the underlying cause in a way acceptable to management. Without effective listening, however, this process never gets started.

Specific Listening Techniques

Although the art of listening comes naturally to some persons and not to others, there are some time-tested techniques which can be used to improve listening skills. Among them are the following:

1. Maintain eye contact with the speaker.
2. In addition to listening to the words spoken, note the tone, facial expression, and other characteristics of the way in which the words are delivered.
3. Ask questions about points which are not completely clear.
4. Periodically rephrase a statement or restate it using your own words to confirm your understanding.
5. From time to time, let the speaker know that you are following his thought by interjecting "I see" or "I understand." Be careful, however, not to imply agreement with the words spoken unless that is intended.
6. Curb the tendency to form opinions on things as you hear them. Judgments and decisions should be reserved until after the speaker has finished, and due consideration has been given.
7. Build a habit of "hearing out" the speaker, rather than thinking of rebuttals or what you are going to say when he stops talking.
8. Refrain from mentally criticizing the speaker because of his or her mannerisms, attire, attitude, accent, etc.
9. Sift each main point from supporting points. Learn to recognize and dismiss irrelevant material quickly.

Listening to Everyone

In addition to listening to the union's spokesperson, it can be enlightening to listen to comments from other members of the bargaining committee, especially those comments which appear to be spontaneous. These often reflect, to a greater extent than what is said by the union's spokesperson, rank and file sentiment. For this reason, some management negotiators make it a point to direct questions and comments to persons on the union's bargaining committee other than the spokesperson. The union's spokesperson will seldom restrain the committee member, and valuable information can sometimes be obtained. However, the personality, biases, and reputation of the speaker must be taken into consideration. Some union bargaining committee members represent no one but themselves and are no closer to rank and file opinion than is management. The adage "consider the source" applies here.

Making Concessions

Few successful labor negotiators are instilled with the spirit of Christmas; i.e., "it is better to give than to receive." Nevertheless, concessions are part and parcel of any negotiation. The secret is to maximize the value of each concession. The following suggestions are offered toward that end:

1. *Do not concede a point unless you are sure it is still an issue.* In the course of moving from one meeting to the next, it may not be clear if the union continues to cling to an issue. Make sure the proposal is still "on the table" before you agree to it. You do not want to give away something in which the union has lost interest.
2. *Never make a concession without consideration and/or caucus.* No matter how insignificant a concession may appear to be, never make it until advance consideration and discussion have been given to it. This usually requires a caucus. Explore all the possible ramifications of the concession before making it.
3. *Always try to get something in return.* Whenever something is given to the union, try to get something in exchange—even if it's only the withdrawal of some other union demands. Sometimes it is possible to reduce or modify an existing benefit when another is being improved, or to improve contract language from management's standpoint in the same section of the contract as that where a concession is being made to the union.
4. *Do not give the whole cake when half a cake might suffice.* Where the union has sought an improvement, do not concede the entire issue until you are sure that the union will not accept less. This is true even if you are ultimately willing to concede the whole issue. For example, if the union wants layoffs to be based solely on plant or facility seniority, you can attempt to obtain a concession to apply seniority only to certain jobs during the layoff or to have it apply only for extended layoffs before you agree to grant a complete concession.
5. *Make the union earn concessions.* Do not give away any easy concessions on significant issues. As stated earlier, try to get something in exchange. At a minimum, make the union supply considerable justification and supporting arguments before making a concession on a significant issue. Occasionally some bargaining mileage can be gained by making some minor concessions at an early stage of negotiations. This can

have the effect of "getting the ball rolling" and prompt the union into making its own concessions sooner than it would otherwise have done.

6. *Save major concessions for last.* Both parties to labor negotiations usually have the same perception as to which issues are the major ones. If management makes concessions on major issues early in the negotiations, the union may be misled into believing that there will be many more to come. Likewise, if management grants a major issue too early, it loses the chance that the union might have withdrawn it or traded it for another issue later in negotiations. If you have any "big gives," hold them until the end. That is when they will have the most trading value and the most value in achieving a final settlement.

Effective Use of the Caucus

Caucuses in labor contract negotiations serve a number of purposes. They allow each party to discuss pending issues, obtain necessary information, plan strategy and tactics, draft proposals and offers, estimate costs, and obtain approval from higher authority. They also serve as a release from tension which has built up at the bargaining table.

Tactical Significance

In addition to the above-listed functions, caucuses can be used to tactical advantage or disadvantage. They sometimes reveal a weakness on the part of one side or another. For example, if management is asked to give its *final* position on an issue which management has heretofore taken an adamant position, such as refusing to weaken its no-strike clause, and management announces that it wishes to caucus, the union might very well come to the conclusion that management's position was not as firmly established as previously stated. Similarly, the length of a caucus often has tactical implications for both parties. If management makes an offer which is extremely low in relation to the union's last announced position, a lengthy caucus by the union is likely to be interpreted by management negotiators as a sign that the offer was not as far from the union's position as was originally thought.

Calling for a Caucus

Some inexperienced negotiators call caucuses each time they are asked to respond to a point and they need input from others. This can result in numerous caucuses, and conveys the impression that the negotiator is not completely in charge or needs to be given a script before responding. To avoid this, the spokesperson should simply postpone an immediate response and save the discussion until the next caucus; e.g., "We'll get back to you on this," or "We'll consider this in our next caucus." Often in the interim the union will call a caucus of its own and that time can be used by management for its own deliberations.

As indicated in Chapter 2, caucuses should only be called by the spokesperson. The reason is that the spokesperson needs to orchestrate management's side of the bargaining, and interruptions caused by caucuses called by members of the negotiating team can easily sidetrack the plan. An exception to this general rule must be reserved, however, for the situation where the spokesperson is headed in a very dangerous direction and about to make a commitment or take a position which one of the other management negotiators knows to be a mistake. In such cases it is essential that a caucus be called immediately to avoid a serious blunder. This should not occur if the spokesperson has, as suggested earlier, reviewed each concession in advance with the committee. Aside from this type of situation, however, the general rule should be followed, i.e., only the spokesperson calls caucuses.

Length and Frequency of Caucuses

It is frequently difficult to estimate just how much time will be needed for a particular caucus. Althought it is not necessary to tell the union spokesperson how long management estimates a caucus will last, the management spokesperson needs to plan the negotiating timing. For planning purposes the amount of time necessary should be overestimated, for caucuses invariably take longer than originally thought.

If it is mid-to-late morning or into the afternoon when management's caucus is to begin and the work to be done in caucus is significant, it is often wise to simply recess for the day and agree to meet the following morning. Another technique is to allow a generous period of time for the caucus and ask the union to "stand by" or be "on call" at the end of that period. This approach shows consideration for the union representatives by not having them wait around for a call at any minute and resume negotiations. More importantly, however, it conveys the impression that management is in good control of its bargaining affairs, and knows that it will need several hours or more to complete its work in caucus. Frequent unanticipated, lengthy caucuses throughout negotiations can give the union the impression that management "doesn't have its act together."

When negotiations are close to conclusion, however, and management wishes to keep a certain amount of pressure on the union, it is frequently preferable to have the union constantly "on call" while management is in caucus. This technique does not allow the union negotiators to relax too much, and is apt to heighten their sense of anticipation as to what will emerge from management's caucus.

Managing the Caucus

More important than the timing of caucuses is the activity which occurs in them. The opportunities for wasted time and misused time in a caucus are numerous. Too many caucuses wind up as bull sessions, or in nonproductive debates. The spokesperson must manage the caucus just as he or she manages the negotiations. Whenever management calls a caucus, the spokesperson should have a definite reason for calling it and a plan as to how the necessary assignments will be accomplished. When the union calls a caucus, management's spokesperson should take advantage of that time to attend to necessary matters or to anticipate matters which need discussion or attention in future meetings. As each caucus approaches, the spokesperson should have a list of the items which need to be covered, and a list of the names of the individuals on the negotiating committee to whom they are to be assigned. Each person should fully understand what he is expected to accomplish and when it is to be completed.

Prior to ending the caucus, the spokesperson should review with the negotiating committee the information obtained, the decision(s) made, and the action/position to be taken in the next negotiating meeting. The committee should be permitted to critique, play devil's advocate, offer suggestions, and in any other way seek to improve the course of management's bargaining. The spokesperson should never feel that he or she is such an expert that the committee cannot give help in caucus. In the final analysis, of course, the spokesperson must choose which course of action to take, subject to overall directions determined by the employer's management.

Presenting Offers and Proposals

While each separate offer or proposal may call for unique methods of presentation, the following are some general tips that apply in a variety of situations:

1. *Written offers carry more weight.* There is something about the formality and permanence of the written (typed) word which causes most people to give it more attention and credence. Unless the negotiations are being conducted on a very informal basis, a written offer should be made if the offer is a serious one, i.e., one intended to settle the negotiations or to come very close to doing so.
2. *Read written offers.* If a written offer is made, it should be read aloud by the spokesperson. The spokesperson may first read the offer, and distribute copies after the reading, or distribute copies and then read it. In any event, copies should not simply be passed out without a reading; this gives the impression that the offer isn't very important.
3. *Explain management's position and considerations on key elements.* To the extent possible, management should foreclose questions and criticisms which the offer is likely to generate. If the offer contains only a fraction of the demands sought by the union, the spokesperson should explain management's reasoning as to why the offer contains what it does, or why it does not contain other items. For example, "You will not see anything in the offer in response to your proposal for double-time pay. Management is totally unwilling to agree to double time in any form." Where certain union requests are not in the offer, the spokesperson should point out (if able) where the underlying need sought to be met by that request is satisfied by some other means in the offer or is already adequately addressed in some other way.
4. *Accentuate the positive.* Although it is sometimes helpful to explain the absence of certain items, the overall tone in presenting an offer should be positive. The features of the offer which are attractive should be highlighted. Data can be used to show, for example, (1) how much an average employee under the new contract will earn, (2) the total cost outlay of the settlement to the employer, and (3) the number of paid

days off (vacations, holidays, and other paid leave) the average employee will receive during the contract year. While the presentation should focus on the positive, it should avoid the aura of "hard sell." Blatant or obvious salesmanship usually is not effective at the bargaining table.

5. *Expect acceptance.* Except for preliminary offers that are usually "trial balloons," a serious offer should be presented in a way that reflects management's view that it will be accepted by the union. If management conveys an attitude that the offer will not be accepted, the union can hardly be expected to do so.
6. *Invite questions.* After presenting an offer, the spokesperson should invite the union spokesperson or its committee to inquire about any aspects of the offer. This reflects a certain pride and confidence by management in its offer.

Traits and Characteristics of an Effective Management Spokesperson

Although the personalities, habits, and styles of good labor negotiators differ markedly, there are certain traits or characteristics which make for effective negotiating. It is helpful for the management spokesperson to cultivate these traits.

1. *Be well-prepared.* The spokesperson who does homework has a distinct advantage over the one who "wings it." This homework includes completing all the preparations discussed in Chapters 1 and 2, reviewing the material to be discussed before each meeting, having a plan as to where the bargaining should be headed, and all other actions which will keep the spokesman on top of the negotiations.
2. *Know the territory.* One aspect of being well-prepared is "knowing the territory"—knowing the employer's business, including products, production or service processes, competition, technology, profit and loss, operating problems, and the like. Unless the spokesperson can speak from a knowledgeable employer viewpoint, he or she will not be able to marshal the kind of arguments necessary to support management's proposals or positions.
3. *Have patience.* Labor contract negotiations can sometimes be compared to flying an airplane—"hours of boredom interspersed with moments of terror" (or in this case, tension). Sometimes days or even weeks are spent on a single subject. Intricate proposals carefully drafted and close to final agreement can be rejected by the other side at the last moment. Settlements reached with the union's negotiating committee after marathon bargaining prior to a strike deadline are sometimes rejected by the membership. The

spokesperson cannot afford to lose patience. A premature settlement prompted by impatience will usually be an unduly costly one.

4. *Inspire confidence.* The frustrations and disappointments inherent in negotiations are apt to discourage even the most stout-hearted. Nevertheless, the spokesperson must maintain the poise and confidence that an agreement will be reached. While being realistic, he or she must persuade management that a satisfactory agreement can be achieved without a work stoppage and must lead the negotiating committee in that effort. Likewise the spokesperson must be an inspiration to the union that the parties will reach agreement.
5. *Do not burn the candle at both ends.* After a hard day of negotiating, there is a great temptation to unwind with good food and drink. It is, after all, a way of rewarding oneself for the hard work and tension of that day. Unfortunately, there can be a tendency to overindulge. While the tension may be eased by wining and dining, performance at the bargaining table the next day can be impaired. Yes, many of the stories of the hard-drinking, hard-driving labor negotiators are true. However, it is suggested that such negotiators were effective in spite of the alcohol, not because of it. Contract negotiation is a form of competition, and as with all competitive activities one must keep in shape. (Only moderation, not abstinence, is necessary.)
6. *Be congenial.* The old saying that "you can sell more with sugar than with soap" applies in labor negotiations just as it does in sales.
7. *Be organized.* It is not unusual for a spokesperson to be dealing with 50 to 100 separate bargaining issues. While all are not of critical importance, each must be dealt with in some fashion. The opportunities for confusion and error are great. The spokesperson must have a system for keeping bargaining information, notes, proposals, cost estimates, and other materials organized on paper and in his or her head.
8. *Talk straight.* Although there will be times where subtle and indirect suggestions are necessary to protect management's position, for the most part, the management spokesperson should use plain and straightforward language. Listeners should not have trouble understanding what he or she says. It is especially important that when the spokesperson means *no*, he or she says "no."
9. *Be positive.* Just as some people see half a glass of milk as being "half-full" while others see it as being "half-empty," the management spokesperson should focus on areas of agreement rather than on areas of difference between the positions of the union and management. In responding to

the union's proposals, stress what management is willing to do, not what it is rejecting.

10. *Recognize your own ignorance.* Nobody likes a "know-it-all," nor does anyone ever have full information about all matters. The spokesperson should acknowledge an ignorance where it is appropriate to do so and should not be embarrassed to use such phrases as "I don't know," "I don't understand," or "I'll have to find out." This does not mean, however, that a seasoned veteran should play the role of the naive "poor old country boy." Union representatives will quickly see through the disguise.
11. *Have integrity.* Although bluffing is a legitimate bargaining tactic, it should not be confused with deceit or untruthfulness. It is vitally important that management's spokesperson be honest and true to his word. The saying "a deal is a deal" is as important now as it ever was. If the spokesperson says he will agree to a particular proposal or states "you have our word on that," he is bound to stand by the statement. The spokesperson's own credibility as well as that of the employer are on the line.
12. *Avoid unnecessary ultimatums and confrontations.* Although the final stages of negotiations may require the use of ultimatums and direct confrontation, they should be avoided until absolutely necessary. Since the aim of negotiations is to reach a settlement, roadblocks should not be set up where they are not necessary.
13. *Be magnanimous.* In order to reach agreement, more often than not one party has to back away from a position previously taken. Where union representatives must back down, the management spokesperson should allow them to do so with grace, letting them save face. This may require some words to help justify the position, although silence may be sufficient. In any event, one should never "rub it in."
14. *Deal constructively with pressure.* Labor negotiations inherently generate pressure on the respective negotiators. This is especially true in the concluding stages of bargaining. An effective spokesperson must become accustomed to it, and make it work for, rather than against, management's interests. Although the pressure may be felt, it should not cause the spokesperson to make drastic deviations from the plan. It is especially important not to display signs of pressure. Just as in a poker game, each player needs to avoid giving any signals which will tip his hand.
15. *Keep your eye on the ball.* In virtually all negotiations, there are several key issues which will make or break a settlement. The spokesperson cannot let himself get distracted or bogged down by minor or peripheral issues. This is not to suggest that minor issues should simply be conceded to the union. Not in the least. One should deal appro-

priately with all outstanding issues, but not get hung up by those issues which are not important enough to either party to block a settlement.

16. *Be flexible.* As important as it is to have a game plan, it is equally important to be prepared to change that plan. There are many roads to settlement. If roadblocks prevent the use of one or another of them, one must use a detour. Negotiators should not sacrifice vital goals or principles to reach a settlement, but they must be flexible enough to try new approaches when others will not work.
17. *Be tenacious.* Sometimes the impediments to reaching a settlement seem endless. Just when one roadblock is removed, one or more new ones take its place. An effective spokesperson, and the committee, cannot become discouraged. The spokesperson must continue to strive to reach an agreement, no matter how far away it seems to be.
18. *Take prudent risks.* Unless management is prepared to concede everything that a union is demanding, the risk exists that an agreement will not be reached and that a strike will occur. Of course, there are varying degrees of risk associated with various positions. Management's spokesperson needs to make accurate assessments of the risk factors associated with various alternatives and must be willing to take calculated risks when it is prudent to do so.
19. *Be an educator.* When key bargaining decisions are to be made by members of management not present at the bargaining table, the spokesperson must be a good educator in advising management as to the precise nature of the union's position, and the union's rationale for taking such a position. While it is not possible, nor even advisable, for the union's message to be translated without some value judgments by the spokesperson, management needs to know the what's and why's of the union's bottom-line position before critical decisions are made. The spokesperson must communicate this information in such a way that the best possible decision can be made.

The Other Negotiation

When one envisions a labor contract negotiation, the vision of union and management representatives seated at opposite sides of a long table, arguing their respective positions, comes to mind. What is often overlooked, however, is what might be called "the other negotiation," i.e., each party "negotiating" with its respective principals or constituencies to reach a consensus on the major position(s) to be taken at the bargaining table. This section assumes that the management spokesperson does not have full and unencumbered authority to make any and all agreements he or she wishes. The principal normally retains the right to make final decisions on key issues. If this is not true in the reader's case, this section may be skipped.

In the author's experience, the negotiation between the management spokesperson and his or her principal(s) is frequently as difficult as that with the union. There are a number of reasons for this. First, the principal does not have to persuade the union as to the justification for a given position. It is usually enough for the executive to say to the employer's spokesperson, "We won't agree to that—it's a foolish idea. Tell the union 'no'." The spokesperson is the one who must appear rational and reasonable to the other side. Second, the spokesperson has heard firsthand the arguments and rationale advanced by the union and is often influenced by the sincerity and justification expressed. In most cases, the management spokesperson's translation of that rationale and those arguments will be less convincing than that made by the union spokesperson or union committee member who made the point.

In effect, the management spokesperson must effectively convey to the principal the language, tone, innuendo, and atmosphere that exists at the negotiating table. At the same time, he or she must analyze, interpret, and evaluate what is going on for the principal's benefit and cannot be simply a listening post and a mouthpiece. At the same time the spokesperson has an obligation to prevent management from making mistakes in negotiations that could be costly or which could result in a strike. This may mean, and often does, that he or she must cajole, convince, dissuade, and argue with his principal. This is where the "other negotiation" becomes the difficult one.

The key point is that the principal should have all facts necessary to make a decision. Those facts should be presented in as objective, unemotional way as possible, with the spokesperson presenting the pros and cons of major decisions to be made. Following these, the spokesperson needs to make a recommendation. It is not enough to say, "It's your decision." In the final analysis, the key decisions should be made by the principal. Once they are made, the spokesperson should carry them out as closely as possible to the principal's directions. Until then, the spokesperson should give the principal the full benefit of his or her expertise and analysis.

7

Strategies for Bargaining Over Economics

In Chapter 3 the value of a game plan was discussed and models for establishing economic parameters were outlined. Assuming that management has decided the maximum amount it is willing to spend for wages and benefits during a new contract term, it must now determine how to obtain a settlement within those limits. This chapter discusses the general forms of economic bargaining, the strategies of constructing and presenting initial and subsequent offers, the role of tradeoffs in bargaining, and other strategies related to bargaining over wages and benefits.

General Forms of Negotiating Wages and Benefits

Auction or Traditional Bargaining

This form of bargaining consists of an initial offer which is relatively low in relation to the final settlement, and is followed by a number (usually two or more) of successively higher offers. The successive package offers are usually made in response to union counteroffers which are higher in value than the employer's last previous offer but lower than the union's previous position. This "bid and ask" bargaining form is used by a majority of employers in the United States.

"Boulwarism"

This type of bargaining, in its pure form, consists of a single "first and final" or "take it or leave it" offer made after the employer has conducted extensive research and surveys concerning competitive trends, economic conditions, and employees' preferences, and after it has heard union demands and supporting presentations. The offer is changed by the employer only if it obtains new information or if facts change after the offer is made. It does allow for rearranging the components of the offer without increasing its total value. In this type of bargaining the offer will not be increased as the result of a threat or occurrence of a strike. It is named after its author and leading practitioner, Lemuel Boulware, a vice president at General Electric during the 1960s. Boulwarism has not been used to any significant extent outside the General Electric Company, and the NLRB has ruled in at least one instance that this approach constituted an unfair labor practice.[1] Boulwarism does not recognize the political necessity of labor unions being able to claim credit for having obtained higher wages and benefits for its members. In most cases use of Boulwarism leads to confrontation.

"Ballpark Offer" With Minor Adjustments

This type of bargaining falls somewhere between the traditional form of multiple offers and the single-offer approach of Boulwarism. Using this approach, the employer makes an initial offer which is very close to its final position although it is not characterized as a "final offer." The employer leaves enough room to make minor improvements or rearrangements in the offer; the improvements may be made in several different offers, although such events are more accurately termed "moves" rather than offers in that the general magnitude of the offer does not significantly change. This form of bargaining attempts to get away from the "bid and ask" system traditionally followed by labor contract negotiators, but avoids the more harsh, confrontational approach of Boulwarism.

Piecemeal Approach

This type of bargaining varies considerably from the first three discussed in that it does not rely on the package offer concept. Instead, this is a piecemeal approach whereby economic issues are addressed and disposed of singly or in groups of several issues. For example, in bargaining across the table the parties may agree that the employer will spend 6 cents per hour to improve vacations and 4 cents per hour for holidays and will continue paying the cost of medical and health benefits. They may also agree that the balance of the economic package will be spent on wages and pensions. Thus, all further bargaining is devoted solely to those two issues. This does not necessarily make negotiations any easier, for traditional bargaining might similarly have narrowed the parties' differences to those two issues.

This type of bargaining has a number of pitfalls in that it causes the employer to commit itself to certain economic improvements before knowing the full scope of improvements which may be necessary to obtain union agreement. However, where the parties have a mature relationship and have utilized this form of bargaining in the past it can prove satisfactory.

Pattern-Following Approach

In reality, this is not a true form of economic bargaining in that the parties' settlement, or something very close to it, has actually been determined in some other negotiation. In this form of bargaining, the employer agrees to "follow the pattern" of a settlement negotiated (usually) by a major employer or group of employers in the same industry or line of work. Unfortunately, in some pattern-following negotiations the union seeks to bargain for "add-ons" or special provisions to which the pattern-setting employer did not agree. In this form of bargaining the message to a prudent employer is clear—don't agree to follow a pattern settlement until the union makes absolutely clear what it will accept as a *full settlement* in your negotiation.

Traditional Economic Bargaining: Offer and Counteroffer

While the five types of economic bargaining just discussed have taken place, and do take place, in the United States, it is the traditional form of auction bargaining which predominates.

For this reason, the various strategic aspects of this form of bargaining are discussed in depth in this chapter.

The traditional form of economic bargaining is sometimes characterized as "bid and ask," similar to the prevailing form in the stock or commodity markets. Some managers, especially those not experienced in labor relations matters, abhor this form of bargaining because it is slow, inefficient, not completely forthright, and akin to a game. Indeed, it is all of these. Nevertheless, these drawbacks should not be so distasteful as long as the technique results in satisfactory contract settlements without a strike. Decades of successful contract negotiations conducted within this framework suggest that it does work reasonably well.

The traditional form of auction bargaining has a number of distinct advantages. It allows each party to seek its ideal settlement while taking into account the needs and desires of the other party. It allows each party to feel the other out as they both move to an area where a settlement can be reached. By progressing in relatively small movements, each party can make the measured concessions necessary for an agreement without undue risk of sacrificing other desired objectives (i.e., without management "giving too much away" and without the union "leaving too much money on the table"). When utilizing this form of bargaining, management must proceed with caution and good judgment. This begins with the strategy concerning the initial offer.

Management's First Economic Offer

One of the most crucial aspects of a labor contract negotiation is management's initial economic offer. Its timing, size, design, and presentation will have a major impact on the progress, or lack thereof, in the balance of negotiations. It is usually the first concrete signal to the union as to the approximate magnitude of what management believes a final settlement should be and indicates what management is prepared, or not prepared, to do in the negotiations.

Timing of the First Offer

As discussed in Chapter 5, it is customary to address and seek to resolve nonmonetary or contract language issues before beginning serious bargaining on monetary or economic issues. The initial economic offer should not usually be made until all or nearly all nonmonetary issues have been resolved or dropped by the union. The reason for this is rather obvious. The union's principal goal in negotiations is usually higher wages and benefits. The performance of the union bargaining committee will typically be judged by the union's membership based upon the size of the employer's final economic offer. Consequently, in the normal course of events, the union bargaining committee is highly motivated to progress from noneconomic issues to the subject of wages and benefits, provided the union committee does not have to sacrifice too many noneconomic objectives in doing so.

If the employer begins "putting money on the table" prior to settling nonmonetary issues, there is normally little incentive for the union to drop or make concessions on the nonmonetary issues. For this reason, most experienced management negotiators will, as a general rule, seek to delay their first economic offer until all nonmonetary issues are resolved or dropped from consideration.

Exceptions to the General Rule

As with all general rules, however, some exceptions exist. If the nonmonetary issues are contract changes proposed by management (i.e., union concessions) and such proposals have not been accepted by the union by the time a first monetary offer would otherwise prudently be made, the offer might nevertheless be made, with the express condition that the economic improvements are contingent upon the union's acceptance of management's nonmonetary proposals. Likewise, if the union continues to cling to one or a few nonmonetary issues despite exhaustive discussions, and despite management's firm position not to concede such issues, a first economic offer can be made, if otherwise prudent to do so, provided management makes clear that it is contingent upon a complete settlement which does not include the union's proposed noneconomic changes. These exceptions must be allowed for, because strict adherence to the general rule could result in an impasse being reached and a work stoppage occurring without an economic offer ever having been made. It may be that the union's membership is willing to accept a settlement on the same economic terms management is willing to offer, without the union's proposed noneconomic changes, but unless an economic package is put on the table, settlement can never be reached.

In one of the first negotiations conducted by the author, the union's bargaining committee sought extensive contract changes in the seniority section of the contract. This was its overriding goal. Several weeks of negotiations were spent attempting to resolve those issues, but a number of them were still outstanding as the contract expiration date grew near. The bargaining committee adamantly avoided any discussion of monetary issues out of fear that once management opened those subjects, management's attention to, and the union's membership's interest in, the seniority issues would disappear. The committee was, of course, correct in harboring such fears. After approximately three weeks of bargaining on noneconomic issues, the union was advised that management had reached the limit on seniority concessions and other noneconomic issues and that economic issues would thereafter be addressed. With that, a written economic offer was promptly presented to the union committee. It was received with great reluctance, but with the realization that the union's membership would not have countenanced their elected representatives' refusal to consider a bona fide money offer. Although the union did not immediately drop its remaining noneconomic issues, from that juncture of negotiations the focus of both parties was clearly on dollars and cents.

Timing Factors to Consider

Aside from ensuring that nonmonetary issues are essentially resolved, management's evaluation of the correct timing of the first offer should take into account the days or weeks remaining before the contract expiration date, the complexity of economic issues which need to be addressed, and the amount of time reasonably necessary to get to a settlement or final position.

The first offer should be made sufficiently before the contract expiration date to permit meaningful bargaining. Thus, it is common in negotiations where the parties are not meeting on a daily basis to make the first offer two to three weeks before the contract expiration date. This allows them to meet a number of times before the expiration date to fully explore the offer, make counteroffers, and narrow or eliminate any differences between them. If the parties are meeting on a daily basis and their perceived positions are not widely divergent, a first offer 7 to 15 days prior to the contract expiration date may be sufficient. However, where there are numerous and/or serious differences in the parties' positions, it is risky to delay an initial economic offer so that it is presented just shortly before the bargaining deadline. A case in point is the contract negotiations between the National Football League owners and the Professional Football Players Association in 1982. Management's first complete economic offer was made only one week prior to the strike deadline, and with a wide range of issues still unresolved. The offer fell far short of the union's expectations, and a strike lasting more than two months ensued. Although there were numerous other factors to explain the strike, an earlier initial offer would have given union officials and players a longer time before the strike deadline to get used to the idea that they could not achieve all of their goals.

The timing of a first offer must be coordinated with the size and design of the final anticipated offer. If, for example, the strategy is to make an initial offer which is relatively close to the employer's final settlement or "wall" position, the first offer should not be made too far in advance of the contract expiration date. To do so could mislead the union into believing that management is prepared to go to a much higher level to obtain a settlement. On the other hand, if very complex economic issues such as a different formula for pension benefits or a productivity-sharing pay plan are involved, a first offer should be made well in advance of the contract expiration date to allow for extended discussions of, and exploration of alternative means to achieve, such complex changes.

Extraneous circumstances may dictate variations in timing. For example, simultaneous negotiations at other facilities of the employer, public announcement of the employer's quarterly earnings report, introduction of a new product, or acquisition of another business may all affect the time when the first offer should or should not be made.

Constructing Management's First Economic Offer

A first offer can serve a number of purposes. Among these are the following:

1. It can indicate to the union what management is *clearly willing to grant* in a final settlement.
2. It can suggest what management *might accept* as part of the final settlement.
3. It can announce what management feels, from its own standpoint, it *must have* in a final settlement.

What is, or is not, in the initial offer can convey each of these messages. The first offer cannot exclude elements management feels are vital to a final settlement on the presumption that they can be later added in counteroffers; such opportunities may never arise. Moreover, the union will never believe that management is very serious about a proposal that was not included in its initial offer. Likewise, areas in which the employer may be prepared to ultimately make concessions can be signaled in the initial offer with tentative proposals tied to corresponding union concessions.

It must be assumed that the employer's first offer represents the lowest level at which a settlement can possibly be reached. Furthermore, it must be assumed that any management concessions contained in the initial offer cannot later be removed. While it is sometimes possible to withdraw a concession from the initial offer or to substitute another concession for it, construction of the initial offer should not be premised on either of those two situations occurring. Although a concession can be withdrawn if it does not evoke the proper response (i.e., corresponding union concession), it is nevertheless dangerous to put it on the table at a stage too early in the bargaining.

An easy trap to fall into in this regard is a first offer which is constructed on a three-year basis and includes features appropriate to a long-term contract (e.g., higher wages, and perhaps more benefits than would be offered for a shorter contract). If it is later determined that the union's agreement on a long-term contract is not possible, the employer may have some difficulty withdrawing the features associated with the long-term contract (or at least convincing union negotiators that those features are no longer available). Such features should not be introduced (at least in a formal way) until it becomes clear that a long-term contract is achievable.

Credibility of the First Offer

Realization that, once offered, an economic proposal cannot easily be retracted can lead to very conservative first offers.

Running counter to this tendency, however, is the fact that the first offer must be credible. It must be realistic in relation to the range within which a final settlement can reasonably be expected to fall. For example, if the union reasonably perceives an acceptable final settlement to be in the range of 7 percent to 9 percent per year and management's comparable reasonable perceptions are in the range of 5 percent to 6 percent per year, an initial package increase of 1 percent per year will not be a credible offer.

One of the major adverse consequences of an unrealistic offer is that it suggests to the union and its membership that a settlement is not desired by the employer (and therefore a strike is being invited), or that the parties are so far apart that an impasse is inevitable. Another and perhaps equally disadvantageous result of such a low initial offer is that it may not prompt a counteroffer or at least may not bring forth a realistic counteroffer. Any of these results will make it difficult to reach an agreement.

On the other hand, if the union's opening demands are preposterously high, an initial "low ball" offer by management may be called for as a means of demonstrating to the union that it must be realistic if an agreement is to be reached.

Objectives of the First Offer

When constructing the first offer, management should ask itself, "What is this offer supposed to achieve?" If the offer is intended to result in a settlement (which is rather unusual for a first offer), it will be constructed very differently than if it is simply expected to "smoke out the union." If there are only a few major economic issues in doubt, the offer will usually be much higher than one made in the context of numerous unresolved issues.

If there are real or perceived differences in the desired term of the contract or form of wage increase (e.g., fixed wage increase vs. COLA), or major differences on fringe benefits, management would be foolish to advance an offer which is relatively close to its final position. In doing so, it would not retain enough trading stock to maneuver the union to an acceptable settlement level. Likewise, for the same reason, if all noneconomic issues have not been cleared from the union's agenda, and the union continues to seriously push for agreement on troublesome noneconomic issues, management should not make an initial offer that is anywhere near its final position.

Answering Questions

The most common objective of the first offer is to test the basic premises of the employer's desired final settlement and to get responses to some basic questions. For example:

1. Will the union accept a three-year contract?
2. Can a settlement be reached without a basic change in the pension formula?
3. Will a modest proposal to expand vacations be a sufficient tradeoff to obtain agreement on a new program to control absenteeism?
4. To what degree must a final settlement grant special benefits for skilled trades employees?

If these types of questions need to be answered, the offer must be constructed in such a way as to elicit the answers. Of course, there will normally be considerable discussion about the issues in the proposal, and *what* is said, and *how* it is said, will provide some answers. However, frequently during negotiations, actions (formal counterproposals) speak louder than words (casual comments), and the form of a counterproposal will tell quite a bit about what can ultimately be achieved.

Too much, however, should not be expected from management's first offer and the union's first counterproposal. At this point it is, after all, still early in the negotiations and neither party is very willing to make serious concessions. Nevertheless, the questions must be answered before a final settlement can be reached, and the first offer, followed by subsequent offers, should be designed in a way that will lead to the answers and, ultimately, a settlement.

Size of the First Offer

There is no magic formula which will tell a negotiator the cost level at which the initial offer should be set. As a general proposition, however, the ideal first offer should be high enough to encourage significant union movement from its initial demands—in the form of a realistic counteroffer—yet low enough to permit management to make further meaningful offers before reaching its final position, or "wall." It should also be low enough to permit a possible settlement at a level that is less costly than management's "wall." In other words, there should be room to maneuver and reach a settlement for less than management originally thinks is necessary. Moreover, the first offer should contain those proposals management believes are essential for a final settlement.

Length of Contract Proposed

One of the key elements of any contract offer, and especially the first offer, is the term or length of the proposed contract. The proposed contract term should normally *not be shorter* than that term which the employer is actually seeking. For example, if management feels that a two-year contract is essential, it should normally not make an initial offer on a one-year contract basis even if it is an extremely low offer. Such an offer would signal the union that management is willing to settle for a one-year contract, at least at some economic level. On the other hand, it is usually safe for an employer seeking a two-year contract to initially propose a three-year contract.

Because of the long-term inflationary economy in the United States, unions have usually been willing to settle for shorter-term contracts, while managements have preferred longer-term contracts. However, unions which have negotiated liberal cost-of-living clauses have generally been quite willing, if they have not actually sought, to enter into contracts for three years or even longer. As a general proposition, it is easier for management to initially propose a longer-term contract and back down to a shorter length than the opposite situation. Of course, if a long-term contract is the only one acceptable to management, the first offer as well as all subsequent offers must be made on that basis.

Reviewing the First Offer Before Presentation

After constructing the first offer, but before presenting it, management should evaluate the offer on several bases. First, of course, a careful cost estimate should be made and the estimate double-checked for accuracy. Chapter 10 details methods for costing an offer. Next, the offer should be critiqued in terms of its impact on negotiations. One or more members of management's negotiating team should act as a devil's advocate. How will it be perceived by the union? Will it be seen as much higher or lower than expected for a first offer? Does it address in some fashion those issues the union considers essential? Does it indicate a desire to settle without a strike? Does it provide enough to encourage the union to make a realistic counteroffer? What kind of response and what type of counteroffer is it likely to elicit from the union? And finally, does the offer leave management with enough maneuvering room to reach the level of settlement it desires or is at least willing to grant? Taking the answers to all these questions into account, revisions in the first offer may be indicated. As a rule of thumb in constructing the first offer, management should follow, with respect to any concessions, the adage "when in doubt, leave it out."

Presenting Management's First Offer

Characterizing the Offer

The manner in which the first offer is presented can add to, or detract from, the effect the offer is designed to have. And the way in which the offer is characterized by management will influence the way it is received by the union. If the offer is essentially a "smoke out" offer used to gauge the seriousness of the union on certain issues, it should not be presented as a "serious offer to settle the negotiations." Both management and the union negotiators will know that it is not so, and little will be gained. But the same offer might be characterized as a "serious attempt to narrow the issues in order to arrive at a settlement."

Words used in conjunction with the presentation of a package offer are normally accorded great attention and significance by the party receiving the offer. Consequently, the terms used should be carefully selected. Some negotiators do not employ any descriptive language in presenting an offer. While this may sometimes be appropriate, it does leave open the possibility that the union will not fully understand management's position. For example, if the union has emphasized six major economic issues, and the offer contains only two of them, a nondescriptive presentation may be misinterpreted by the union. A presentation which explains that management has seriously considered *all* of the union's proposals but is unwilling to accept those not specifically included in the offer (and perhaps includes management's reasons for not accepting them) tells the union that the absence of its priority goals was not due to an oversight, and that the union may not be able to achieve them in the current negotiations.

If the first offer is a "ballpark offer" (i.e., reasonably close to management's final position), it is important that the management spokesperson express the seriousness of the offer and the expectation that it should "settle" or "come very close to settling" the negotiations. It should make clear to the union that management has left little or nothing in reserve. Without such a statement, the union could be seriously misled into believing that a much higher settlement is possible.

Form of Presentation

Whether the first offer should be made orally or in writing is often a matter of the negotiator's style, the complexity of the offer, and the parties' customary practices, although the form of the offer can convey a significance all its own. Written offers, being formal, convey an impression of finality. To that extent they can be useful in signaling to the other side that the end of negotiations is near.

If written offers are used earlier in the negotiations, their value as a signaling device of finality at the final stages of negotiations is impaired. This loss must be balanced, in some cases, against the chance for misunderstanding if the offer contains any complex and/or technical provisions which cannot be adequately explained orally. If the offer is relatively simple, an oral presentation of the first offer is usually preferable. Where some technical information (e.g., a new pension or COLA formula) is necessary for a complete presentation, that information can be supplied in writing while the balance of the offer is given orally.

The Union's Response to Management's First Offer

In a normal bargaining situation, management's first offer will be questioned, criticized, and promptly rejected by the union. This should not come as a surprise. (The absence of one or more of these steps may be a signal in itself.) Beyond this on-the-surface reaction of the union's negotiators, however, a great deal of analysis and discussion will take place within the union's caucus. If the employer's offer has been realistic and if the union is genuinely seeking a reasonable settlement, a counteroffer will be forthcoming. If a counteroffer is not made, a critical impediment has been placed in the way of a settlement.

Failure of the Union to Make a Counteroffer

The Marquis of Queensbury rules of negotiation require that if a party does not accept an offer made to it, that party should make a counteroffer. It is not too unusual for this rule to be violated sometime late in negotiations, but serious problems are presented when no counterproposal is forthcoming after rejection of management's initial offer. Some unions, however, like to use this tactic to force management to make back-to-back offers. Although such a position might be an unfair labor practice, from a practical standpoint no useful purpose is served by filing a charge with the NLRB at this point.

When a union has made exceptionally high initial demands in its bargaining agenda, an employer's initial relatively low economic offer (relative only, perhaps, to the union's initial high demands) is often characterized as "insulting," "ridiculous," or simply "inadequate" by the union. Occasionally the union will respond with nothing more specific by way of a counteroffer than the union's initial demands resubmitted as its current position. It is a naive management negotiator indeed who will, at such a point, begin preparations for making another offer. This would, in effect, be bidding against management's own offer. The danger in refusing to make another offer without an intervening union counteroffer is that it accelerates the potential for impasse, but in such cases management must place the blame where it properly belongs—with the union.

A premature impasse resulting from the union's failure to counter management's initial offer can be dealt with in several ways. One, of course, is simply to refuse to make another offer until the union counters. Another is to withdraw the first offer. This has the effect of saying to the union, "If you won't make a counter to our offer, our offer is no longer available to you." In effect, the parties go back to square one. Still another alternative is to segment the outstanding economic issues and any remaining noneconomic issues and deal with them separately. This permits the parties to resolve certain less contentious issues without getting stalemated over the more difficult ones. However, it leaves the door open for the possibility that management will make numerous concessions on less crucial issues without any assurance of resolving potential strike issues.

Another means of dealing with the union's failure to make an initial counteroffer is to induce the union's negotiator to identify priority issues. This permits the union to give management some direction without making specific concessions.

However, if management has made a credible and reasonably realistic first offer, the means described above of avoiding potential impasse are simply crutches for the union and are not recommended except in unusual cases. For example, occasionally a union will experience internal conflict which limits the authority and flexibility of the union negotiator. In such cases, management's attempts to compensate for the lack of a legitimate union counteroffer may be justified. In other cases, the inexperience of the union's spokesperson may be the cause for no counteroffer having been made. Aside from these and other rather unusual circumstances, management should not be placed in the unreasonable position of bidding against its own offer; pressure should simply be put on the union to respond with a realistic counteroffer.

In the course of normal bargaining, the union will respond to management's initial offer with a legitimate counteroffer. Its counteroffer is likely to be as significant for the outcome of bargaining as was management's initial offer.

Evaluating the Union's First Counteroffer

The reason the union's first counteroffer is so significant is that it usually establishes the union's first realistic upper range for further negotiations. Because most unions tend to present unrealistically high initial demands in their bargaining agendas or leave their exact wage demands unspecified, the union's opening agenda usually is not a practical guideline for ascertaining the range within which serious negotiations will take place. A union's first counterproposal is a much more reliable guide of the union's true aspirations than its bargaining agenda.

Judging the Union's Economic Expectations

Although some unions do not often act as rational economic entities (nor, for that matter, do some employers), there is, in most unions, a set of economic goals which underlie their actions in labor contract negotiations. These goals are not always articulated nor formally adopted in union councils. Nevertheless, they generally exist somewhere in the minds of the principal union decision makers and can be shown graphically as a range of settlement levels from the lowest acceptable settlement level to the settlement level the union realistically desires to achieve. For the sake of simplicity, they are shown here based on percentage increase in total labor costs and on negotiations for a one-year contract as shown below.

Figure 7–1

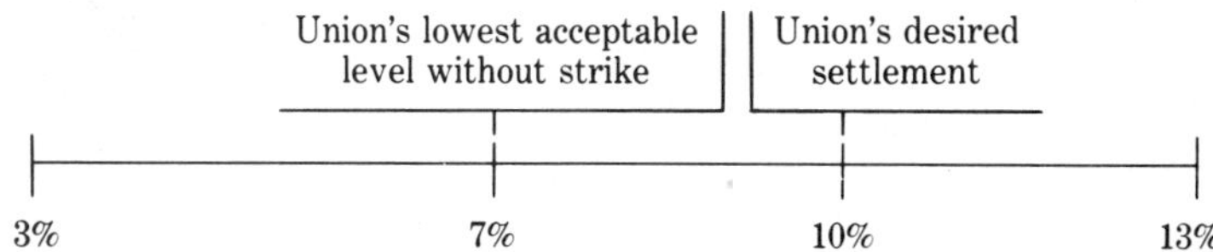

At the outset of negotiations, the union desires to negotiate a settlement which has a value of 10 percent in increased wages and benefits. While it would be most pleased with anything in excess of 10 percent, it recognizes that it is not realistic to expect it. On the other hand, the union also realizes that it probably will not get as much as 10 percent, and would be willing, although reluctant, to accept a 7 percent settlement if it could obtain one without a strike. Of course in actual negotiations the numerical targets are not always so precise, and factors other than just total wages and benefits come into the picture.

With the range of goals illustrated in Figure 7–1, the union will not, of course, make an initial counteroffer which is any less than its desired level of 10 percent, and its initial counteroffer will be somewhat higher than that level. The level of its first counterproposal will be dependent upon the size of management's initial offer and, to a somewhat lesser extent, upon the union's initial bargaining agenda demands. For example, if the union originally requested a 15 percent increase and management offered only 2 percent, the union is not likely to budge much, if at all, from its 15 percent demand. If, however, management offers a 5 percent or 6 percent increase, the union may counterpropose 11 percent or 12 percent. Because of the difficult position in which unions are often placed in having to back down from exorbitant initial bargaining agenda demands, many unions simply propose in their opening agenda "a substantial wage increase." This gives them a great deal more flexibility, particularly in responding to management's initial offer.

Management's Economic Expectations

The union's initial counteroffer cannot be fully evaluated unless management has identified its own goals. Management's economic goals in this example can be represented as shown in the following figure:

Figure 7–2

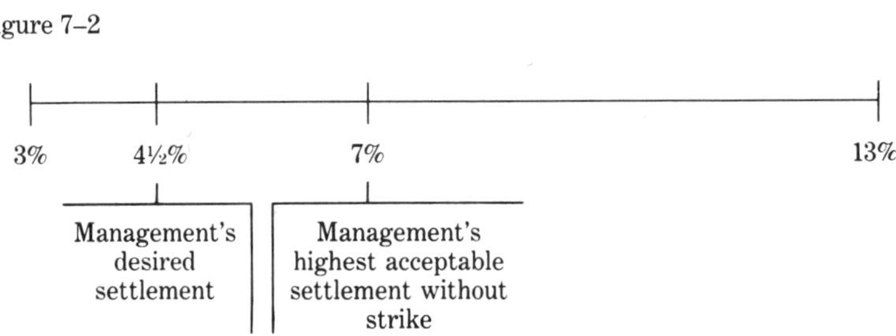

Based on these initial settlement goals, management should not make a first offer of 5 percent to 6 percent since it would, of course, foreclose any opportunity of settling at its desired level of 4½ percent. With the range of goals shown in the diagram, it is doubtful that management should initially offer any more than 3 percent to 3½ percent.

If management makes an initial offer of 3 percent against the union's bargaining agenda demand of 15 percent, the union may be unwilling to drop more than 1 percent or 2 percent from its initial demands. Therefore, an initial union counterproposal of 13 percent to 14 percent in the face of an initial offer of 3 percent does not appear very encouraging in terms of reaching a settlement without serious difficulty. Nevertheless, even if the parties do not readjust their goals, in the course of negotiations there is at least one level of settlement—7 percent—at which both parties are willing to agree. However, it will take skillful negotiating on both sides to reach that point.

Although 7 percent may be the ultimate settlement reached, it is also possible that one (or each) of the parties will adjust its sights during the course of negotiations and conclude that it is willing to grant more or accept less in order to avoid a strike or lockout. Thus, for example, a 6 percent or 8 percent settlement is also possible without a strike. This is, of course, what collective bargaining is all about, i.e., to cause the other party to modify its position to match one's own.

Given the hypothetical positions of the parties described above, the dilemma for management at this point is how to respond to an "outrageous" 13 percent counterproposal by the union in response to its "realistic" 3 percent offer.

The Potential Early Impasse

Faced with a gap of 10 percent between its first offer of 3 percent and the union's first counteroffer of 13 percent, management negotiators can easily become discouraged and feel that a settlement may not be attainable within management's preestablished parameters of 4½ percent to 7 percent. Although such a conclusion is premature, there is certainly cause for concern if the union truly believes that it will be able to negotiate something close to its 13 percent counteroffer.

Applying Pressure

One tack taken by some negotiators in such situations is to stop the progression of successively higher offers. When the union countered with 13 percent it likely expected management to raise its offer from 3 percent to perhaps between 4 percent and 6 percent. If management does not respond in such a fashion, it is likely to cause the union serious concern and to reexamine its negotiating premise. If, for example, management raises its offer by only ¼ percent or ½ percent, it is likely to cause the union to feel that management may be approaching its final offer and that the likelihood of a strike has been substantially increased.

Another course is for management to leave its offer at the same level, in this case 3 percent, and perhaps make certain other cosmetic changes in the offer. Coupled with this approach can be a statement or speech to the effect that, in view of the union's unrealistic position of 13 percent, management cannot afford to put more money on the table, *even though more money is available.*

Such an approach is designed to put some pressure on the union to modify its last counteroffer before another management offer is made. By advising the union that the employer has more money to offer if the union's position becomes more realistic, management seeks to give the union some incentive for further reducing its demands. In effect, however, this approach is designed to gain a bargaining advantage for management, by having the union make two reductions in its position while management has made only one. The success of this approach will depend greatly upon the relative bargaining leverage possessed by the negotiating parties. If management's bargaining power is relatively strong and the union's is relatively weak, the chances of having the union further reduce its demands are fairly good. The converse is equally true.

However, this approach discards the Marquis of Queensbury rules of alternative offer and counteroffer, and can backfire. If the union feels that management is attempting to gain an unfair bargaining advantage, it may simply refuse to further change its position until management has made another offer. If the union adamantly holds to this position, management must decide if it will continue the game of "chicken," or relent and make another counteroffer with a significant increase. If it chooses the former course it risks the possibility of an early impasse, whereas if it chooses the latter it hands the union an early tactical victory which could be significant in subsequent stages of negotiations.

Adhering to Conventional Bargaining

Unless management is fairly confident of its bargaining position, forcing an early confrontation is not wise. In most cases, it is advisable to continue the traditional offer/counteroffer sequence, although management must be careful about the magnitude of its subsequent offers as they compare to the union's counteroffers.

If management decides to proceed with another counteroffer in the face of an unrealistically high union counterproposal, it should not do so without first engaging in a rather frank discussion about its view of the union's position. Management needs to lower the union's expectations about what the union can achieve in the current negotiations. This is best done through the size and composition of the next offer, but also can be done by what is said across the bargaining table.

Formal Response to the Union's First Counteroffer

Communicating Through Offers

Regardless of the manner in which management orally responds to the union's first counteroffer, a message will be sent. Reception with little or no comment ("soft response") will generally be interpreted by union representatives as a sign that its counteroffer has been reasonably well received, whereas a response indicating disappointment, displeasure, and/or serious disagreement ("hard response") will obviously tell the union that its counteroffer is far off the mark. Of course, individual bargaining styles cannot be ignored.

Where parties have dealt with each other over a series of negotiations, subtle changes in facial expression, tone of voice, and selection of words may convey just as definite an impression as a vehement outburst among parties less familiar with each other. Nevertheless, the union will usually expect management to be dissatisfied with the union's first counteroffer, so the absence of some expression of dissatisfaction will normally be interpreted as a positive sign by the union.

Also to be considered, aside from the surface reaction to management's offer exhibited in the union's counteroffer, is the reception given to management's offer in a more substantive way. Does the union's counterproposal recognize the fundamental premises (e.g., the employer's profit/loss picture and other comparable labor contract settlements) upon which management's first offer was based? Is it within the cost range in which realistic bargaining can take place? Does it recognize that changes desired by management will be incorporated into the final settlement in some form? Unsatisfactory answers to these questions should be highlighted by management as soon as possible after receipt of the union's counteroffer and discussed openly across the bargaining table.

The Need for Candid Dialogue

Too frequently in the process of bargaining, management and union negotiators exchange offers and counteroffers without sufficient questioning, discussion, persuasion, or explanation of rationale. Management must explain to the union what aspects of the union's counteroffers are unsatisfactory and why they are unsatisfactory. The process of collective bargaining is intended to change the other party's perception in order to bring its position closer to one's own while being open to having one's own perception changed. It is difficult to do this without direct communication about one's own needs, desires, and limitations.

While sufficient consideration should be given to the union's counteroffer before a definitive response is made, a more immediate initial response giving management's reaction may be appropriate where the counteroffer is significantly out of line in relation to the size and makeup of management's initial offer. A delayed response will necessarily lessen the impact of the response. However, a thoughtful and appropriate response should not be sacrificed simply for such impact.

The question in the minds of the union's negotiators after they present their counterproposal will be essentially the same as that which occupied management negotiators after the initial offer was made: "Will they make a counteroffer, and if so, how much closer will it be to our position?" Advising the union as to when and how management will formally respond to the union's counterproposal is best postponed for the time being.

Intermediate Economic Offers

It is hoped that the employer's initial offer and the union's initial counteroffer will have sufficiently "framed the range" of economic bargaining so that they may proceed in a more or less orderly fashion to reach a settlement. Returning to the figures utilized earlier in this chapter, one can see that the parties' relative positions at the outset of negotiations were as shown in the following figure:

Figure 7–3

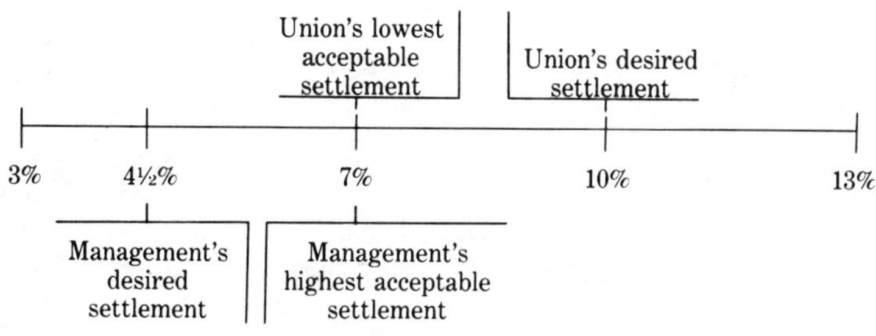

It appears from Figure 7–3 that a settlement can be reached (at 7 percent), although the initial formal positions are quite far apart, as shown below.

Figure 7–4

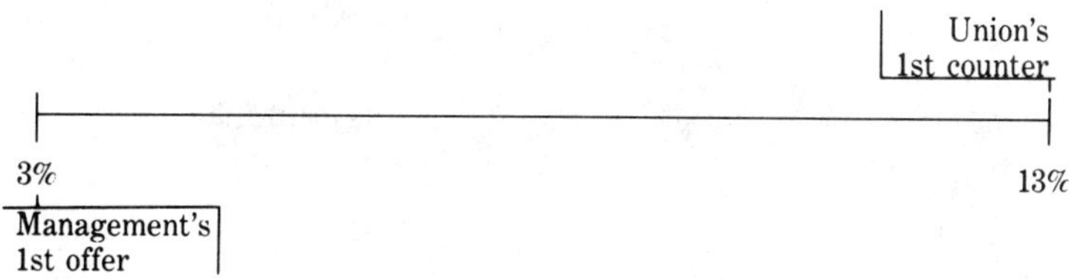

If the parties were to proceed by equal "moves" (i.e., offer and counteroffer, 2 percent per move for example), impasse will be reached, with the results shown below.

Figure 7–5

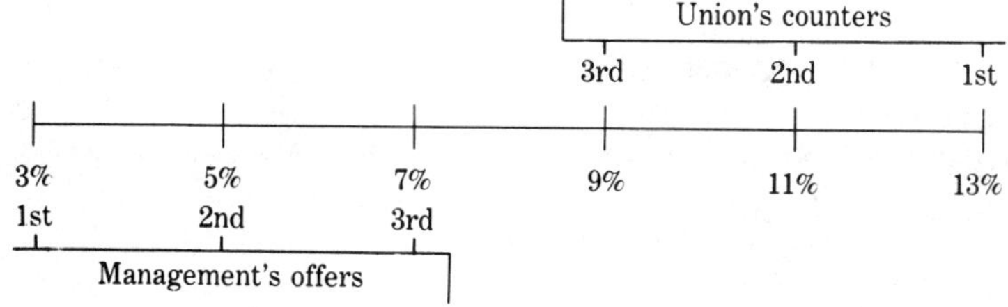

Looking Ahead

After each side has made three economic offers apiece, the parties would be apart by 2 percent with management having reached its outside limit or "wall" at 7 percent and the union being 2 percent above its last-ditch settlement position of 7 percent. Of course, in this hypothetical case management was extremely foolish to have offered its last increase of 2 percent at a point when the union's last position was 11 percent and no settlement was in sight.

Management, in such a situation, was additionally foolhardy in increasing its offer in equal increments as it proceeded to its wall position. By doing so, it gave the union a signal that each reciprocal move by the union (i.e., each 2 percent reduction) would be met by a correspondingly valued move by management. Once management saw after its first offer that the union was lowering its demands by an equivalent amount, it could have quickly calculated that an agreement would not be reached at an acceptable level of 7 percent or less. Moreover, management neglected to give the union a proper signal through its offers that management's wall was being approached. A more effective way for management to move to its final position would be as shown below.

Figure 7–6

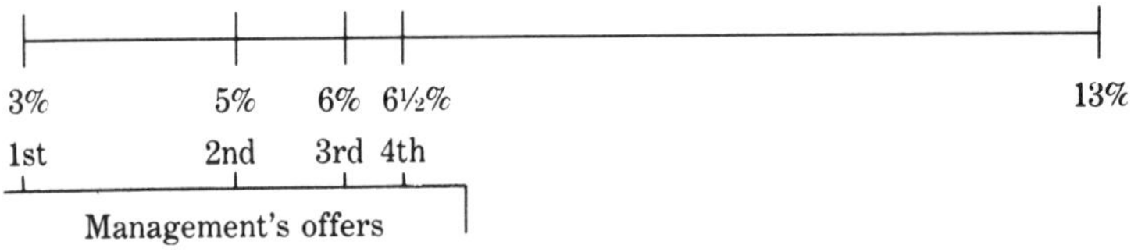

3% 5% 6% 6½% 13%

1st 2nd 3rd 4th

Management's offers

Inching Toward Agreement

By making successively smaller increases in its offers, management signals the union that it is quickly reaching its final position. Of course, such successive moves must be met with corresponding moderations in the union's position in order for management to justify approach so close to its wall. By the time the 6½ percent level is reached, the union must understand that management has reached its limit or is very close to it.

This message should be reinforced by the way in which the offers are presented and by other discussions at the bargaining table. However, no matter what is said by management, the union will place much greater weight on management's actions than on its words. By management's moving in successively smaller improved offers, it is hoped that the parties can arrive at a settlement within their respective ranges as shown below.

Figure 7–7

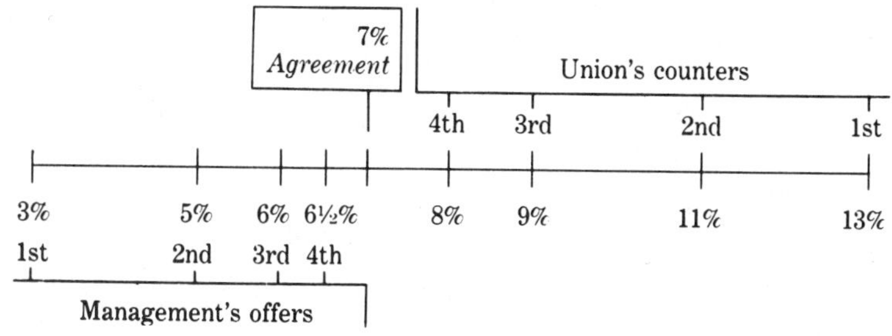

Complexity of Actual Negotiations

These figures greatly oversimplify the real world. Not all negotiating parties precisely identify, even to themselves, their desired settlement levels, let alone their minimum and maximum positions. Furthermore, the options available for movement are infinitely greater than shown in the diagrams. For example, in real negotiations multiyear contracts are usually involved. Consequently, variations in offers can be made by shifting money from one year to another to make the package more acceptable to the other side. This often means, for management, bringing increases from later to earlier years in the contract term, or for the union, making concessions effective earlier rather than later in the contract.

Real bargaining options are also increased by the variety of issues which are being negotiated. It is not unusual for 10 or more separate economic issues to be changed within a single offer. Offers can be varied by the inclusion or exclusion of certain of these economic items and by the degree to which the item is included, i.e., in whole or in part. To the extent that noneconomic issues are still on the table, these too can be used to vary subsequent offers. Notwithstanding the oversimplification of the figures, they do help to illustrate what can be a rather complex process of offer and counteroffer as negotiations proceed.

Custom Versus Innovation

Where union and management representatives have negotiated over a long period of time and have become used to each other, a pattern of economic bargaining usually develops and each party can more or less anticipate the moves of the other. This has considerable advantage to the extent that it minimizes the risk of miscalculation on both sides and makes the possibility of blundering into a work stoppage more remote. However, each labor contract negotiation is a unique event—no two are exactly alike. It should never be assumed, therefore, that the other party will necessarily respond in a given way simply because it has done so in the past.

The Trap of Habit

Management too should consider whether it has fallen into the habit of negotiating in a programmed way, based upon what it has done in the past. For example, does it always make an initial "low ball" offer, and then follow up with three or four higher offers to reach a point about double the size of its first offer? If so, then it has left itself little room for real bargaining since its "wall" package can probably be predicted by the union at the outset of negotiations.

While innovation in labor contract negotiations, or perhaps any other field of endeavor, is not inherently valuable simply for its own sake, it can prove to be a useful tool as negotiations proceed. In Chapter 12, innovation is discussed under "Creative Bargaining" as a means to avoid impasse. Here it is discussed as a means of constructing and presenting intermediate offers.

Changing the Approach

Customary bargaining approaches may not always be suitable where conditions have changed. For example, where management has customarily made an initial "low ball" offer followed by three or four successively higher offers, continuing such an approach is not feasible where economic conditions have become more difficult since earlier negotiations and management can only afford to grant, say, a 4 percent increase over two years. Although the employer's customary bargaining style might suggest an initial offer proposing a cut, followed by successive offers slowly advancing to a modest increase, a more credible approach may be to make an initial offer of, perhaps, 3 percent over two years and to move very gradually to a final position.

If such a new approach is adopted, it is important that management alert the union to the fact that the current negotiations do not reflect "business as usual." In fact, unless it is perfectly obvious, a reference might be made to how bargaining has previously been conducted and a contrast made to management's current intentions. The reasons for the new approach must be spelled out in great detail, lest the union believe that management is attempting to punish, trick, or otherwise "do a number" on it.

Despite taking great pains to explain that a new approach is being taken and to outline the reasons for the change, management may find union representatives do not believe management's words or accept them as reasonable. Management must know the union with which it is dealing before adopting a new approach to negotiations. Some old dogs simply cannot be taught new tricks, and it may be counterproductive to attempt to do so. On the other hand, it would be a mistake for management to conclude that past negotiating approaches must be used simply because of perceived union rigidity. Just as many facets of life and business change, so too collective bargaining must be amenable to change.

The *Quid Pro Quo* or Tradeoff

One of the stereotypes of the negotiator is that of the "horsetrader" or the "wheeler-dealer." According to that view of the negotiating process, everything has its price, and anything can be negotiated if one is willing to offer or concede enough; the *quid pro quo* (literally translated as "this for that") is the order of the day. In reality, there is probably a lot less horsetrading in labor contract negotiations than most outsiders would imagine. Nevertheless, tradeoffs do have their place in labor negotiations, and can be an extremely valuable means to achieve an agreement. They must be used, however, with great caution and finesse. In the simplest terms, a tradeoff consists of an offer of a concession or change of position by one party in exchange for a concession or change in position by the other party.

Advantages of Tradeoffs

The advantages of tradeoffs are rather obvious; they encourage the other side to concede an issue which may stand in the way of an agreement. Even in cases where the value of the issue to be conceded is far less than the one for which it is traded, it provides a face-saving device for the other party, which may have already been willing to concede the issue but could not find a reason to justify the concession to its principals. From the standpoint of the initiator of the trade, it permits a change in position, often in order to avoid impasse, but ties the change to some corresponding change in position by the other party. For example, where management sees that the union will not accept a three-year contract under any circumstances, management's willingness to accept a two-year contract might be conditioned on the union's acceptance of a cap (maximum payment) on the contract's cost-of-living adjustment formula.

Disadvantages of Tradeoffs

The disadvantages of tradeoffs are somewhat less obvious. The most serious drawback is that they indicate a possible unilateral concession, since normally there is no assurance that the *quid pro quo* will be forthcoming. Thus, management may indicate a willingness to increase its wage offer in the first year of a multiyear contract in exchange for a new type of medical insurance plan (which offers the prospect of lower premiums for management), only to discover that the revised insurance plan is unacceptable to the union. In so doing, management has tipped its hand that it is willing to increase the size of its offer in the first year, the only question being what, if anything, the union needs to concede to obtain it. This tipping of the hand is particularly troublesome if management has previously stated that its offer for the first-year wage increase was final.

Another related disadvantage of the tradeoff is that, in certain circumstances, it may indicate that management is not guided by principle, but solely by bottom-line economics. For example, management may have resisted a change in the seniority section of the contract on the grounds that such a change would interfere with important management rights and affect the efficiency of the employer's operations. If a tradeoff of the seniority issue is subsequently offered by management in exchange for a modification in scheduling vacations which will save the employer money, the union and its bargaining committee members may come to believe that the rights which management was so keen on preserving were not as valuable, or as much a matter of principle, as management had claimed. This may also foster an attitude of cynicism about employer positions on other management-rights issues.

Along the same line, another problem with tradeoffs is that the traded issues frequently do not appear to relate to the same subject matter, and therefore an exchange of one for the other can only be rationalized on the basis that it solves a negotiating problem, not on the basis that a concession in one area justifies a concession in the other area. For example, the union seeks to improve its union security position by changing from an agency shop to a union shop clause. Management resists based upon its strong belief that employees should not be forced to do anything more than help to financially support a union which represents them, and that they should not be forced against their will to join a union. On the other hand, management also wishes to rid itself of a burdensome contract limitation on contracting out work. A tradeoff of these two issues might make sense to the negotiators. However, management can hardly rationalize to its employees who do not wish to join the union, or to its supervisors who have supported management's position on the agency shop, that the union's willingness to concede on the subcontracting issue has somehow justified compulsory union membership.

Principle vs. Pragmatism

Notwithstanding the apparent cynicism that can be portrayed in the process of bargaining tradeoffs, the negotiation of a labor contract is fundamentally a pragmatic process. Like politics it is "the art of the possible." While genuine principles should be strictly adhered to, it is not unusual for certain issues to be clothed in the sacred garb of "principle" when in fact the naked reality shows them to be simply custom or tradition. And even when a true principle is involved, there may be ways of making a concession to circumvent disagreement without destroying the underlying concept. For example, in the agency shop example, management might agree to require that all newly hired employees be covered under a union shop agreement while "grandfathering" all existing employees under the agency shop clause. This preserves management's principle that employees who joined the company believing they would not have to join the union should be able to continue their nonmembership status.

Some employers have adhered to matters of "principle" in labor contract negotiations to the point where they no longer had a business within which the principle could be preserved. To some employers, the principle may be more important than the business itself, and if this is the case, management should certainly stick to its guns. If not, or if some compromise is possible, tradeoffs offer one way to avoid impasse.

Types of Tradeoffs

Direct Tradeoff

There are several variations on the tradeoff theme. The simplest is the "direct" tradeoff; e.g., "We will increase our wage offer by 2 percent in exchange for your agreement to make acceptance of overtime work on weekends mandatory for employees." Each side concedes on an issue which worsens its own position in exchange for a valued improvement.

Concession for Dropping a Demand

Another type of exchange, while not truly a tradeoff, is often characterized as such. It involves the exchange of an actual concession for withdrawal of a demand, or, in other words, for the avoidance of a *potential* burden. This would occur, for example, where a union which has initially proposed that management agree to convert from a departmental seniority system to plant-wide seniority and to pay double time for work on

Sundays, modifies its position by offering a "tradeoff" whereby it will drop its demand for plantwide seniority if management will agree to double-time pay for Sunday work. These "trade-offs" can be somewhat like one where the robber agrees to refrain from taking the life of his victim provided the victim turns over his wallet to the robber. In the negotiating example, the union has neither plantwide seniority nor the double-time provision, but agrees to "trade" management's concession on one issue for the union's withdrawal of its demand for the other. Obviously management would not receive anything tangible for its concession on double-time pay other than the union's agreement to refrain from attempting to change the seniority system. Such a ploy is not unethical or improper in any way, and if the union can find a management so naive as to accept such a trade, it is well advised to make it.

By the same token, management should not overlook such a strategic position. For example, if management proposes to reduce the number of paid holidays by two per year, and to incorporate a "zipper" clause (i.e., waiver of negotiable matters not included in the agreement) in the contract, it may induce union receptivity or acceptance of the zipper clause by agreeing to drop its proposal for eliminating the holidays.

For the most part, an offer to trade a concession by the other party relating to one demand in exchange for withdrawal of another demand by the offering party will only be successful to the extent that (1) the proposal to be dropped is regarded as a very major issue in the negotiations, and (2) the party offering to withdraw the proposal has the economic leverage and the perceived will to strike/lock out over that issue.

The "Blocking Issue"

A slight variation from the trading of a concession for consideration on another issue is the tactic of identifying a "blocking issue" proposed by the other party. In this situation, management refuses to give any favorable consideration to a proposal or a series of proposals as long as the union adheres to some other demand which is abhorrent to management. For example, a union proposes that a contract be for only a one-year period. In addition, it has a number of proposals for work practice changes on which management is prepared to make certain concessions. Management may wish to induce movement by the union to a longer-term contract on the basis that management is unwilling to consider any work practice changes as part of a one-year contract. By doing this, management has identified the union's one-year contract proposal as an issue which "blocks" any possibility of changes in work practices. The union realizes that it must remove the roadblock in order to achieve its desired changes, even though management has given no definite assurances that removal of the block issue will trigger concessions on work practices. Management must be careful, however, not to mislead the union by suggesting that changes will be made in work practices in exchange for removal of the blocking issue, unless that is what management intends to do.

There is a certain risk in identifying the blocking issue. By doing so, management attaches a great deal of significance to the issue, which may lead the union to believe that the issue is of much greater trading value than it is in management's mind. Another possible consequence is that the union may take as a challenge management's refusal to consider other valid proposals because of some other (and perhaps unrelated) issue. In effect, the union's committee may take the position, "We'll show them they can't blackmail us into dropping our one-year contract."

Notwithstanding such drawbacks, the blocking issue can be used effectively, particularly where management rationalizes the relationship between the blocking issue and the issues tied to it. For instance, in the example discussed earlier, the management spokesman might explain that liberalized work practices can only be justified by management if its labor costs can be locked in for an extended period of time. While this logic may not be fully understood or accepted by the union, it at least provides the appearance that management is not simply trying to foreclose negotiations on other issues important to the union simply in order that management can get its way on some other unrelated issue.

The Stalking Horse

It occasionally occurs in negotiations that a union desperately wants management to accept a proposal which management is readily willing to concede. It might be concluded that such an issue therefore will be quickly and easily resolved in the early stages of negotiations. If it is, however, management has not negotiated wisely. Once management is aware that the union places a high value on a concession, it should never concede the issue until it receives a union concession of equal or greater value.

Some years ago the author was negotiating in upstate New York. The labor contract contained an arbitration clause and a seniority provision which permitted the exercise of seniority by qualified employees for promotions and transfers, but contained the proviso that "management's decisions shall be final." It appeared on the face of the language that an arbitrator could not review management's judgment about such personnel moves, although this had never been put to the test in arbitration. This was the only contract the employer had in any of its operations which contained such language, and there were serious questions as to (1) whether an arbitrator would refrain from reviewing management's decision in spite of the language, (2) whether such a provision was a "healthy" one from the standpoint of union-management relations, and (3) whether the contract's no-strike clause would apply in the case of a wildcat strike under the *Boys Markets* rule[2] if seniority decisions were not reviewable in arbitration. In any event, management decided to agree to liberalize the language at the appropriate time during the negotiations. Throughout the negotiations, the author vehemently defended the language in question and refused to budge. However, as negotiations were reaching a conclusion and management needed a vital union concession on an important but unrelated issue a tradeoff of the two issues was suggested. In relatively short order an agreement was concluded. The moral of the story is that the value of a concession must be viewed through the eyes of the party *seeking* the concession. Once identified as important to the other party, the issue should be reserved until the moment when it can achieve its maximum value.

If the union should drop the issue before it can be traded for another of equal or greater value, the lost opportunity should not be mourned. If it truly is of great importance to the union, it will resurface in a subsequent negotiation. Besides, if the union dropped the issue before the final stages of negotiations, perhaps it was not as valuable to it as originally perceived by management, and may not, after all, have fetched such a valuable concession from the union.

Timing and Technique of Trading

The opportunity for an advantageous tradeoff may present itself at any time in negotiations. Frequently, however, it will be most useful during the closing stages of negotiations. Because trades frequently involve valuable concessions on both sides, it is often only in the concluding stages that each side has had an opportunity to fully explore the other's respective positions and come to some conclusions as to what is possible and what is not. Also, trades become more feasible at the point where the number of unresolved issues is limited, and this point is usually not reached until the final bargaining meetings.

The management negotiator should be careful not to suggest a trade too early in the negotiations, for doing so may indicate that the employer is willing to concede an issue before the time when a concession is usually necessary to avoid impasse. Similarly, the possibility of a trade should be advanced in as subtle a way as possible. Because, as stated earlier, the suggestion of a trade tips management's hand, the tipping should be done in a way which best preserves management's position if the trade is not accepted.

Private Discussions

Probably the safest way to propose a trade is through a private off-the-record discussion between the management and union spokesperson. Such discussions are commonly used by many negotiating parties, and are treated in greater detail in Chapter 12. While a private discussion does not guarantee confidentiality, it does afford a better opportunity to protect management's position than if the proposal is first advanced at a formal meeting. Whether the suggestion is made at a formal or informal meeting, it should be made in a tentative way, such as, "We have not yet fully considered the pluses and minuses of this proposal, nor do we have any authority from our top management to make this an offer, but you might wish to consider the following idea: (statement of the trade). If you think it has some merit, let us know and we will consider it in more detail and determine if management is willing to agree to it." Of course at this point the spokesperson should have evaluated the concept sufficiently to know whether it is worth offering and should know, or be able to predict, what top management's position will be.

Mediators and Trading

Mediators use tradeoffs as one of the tools of their trade. Because the mediator can be the author of the tradeoff (or at least be identified as the author), neither side has jeopardized its position by proposing a tradeoff through the mediator. However, the party to whom the tradeoff is proposed can often deduce that the other side has devised or at least approved the trade, and its position is revealed. Nevertheless, a skilled mediator can usually explore a possible tradeoff with both parties without overtly revealing the position of either until he has received responses from both sides.

Leaving Room to Move

As with any other type of proposal, it is prudent to assume that the union will not accept the entire tradeoff lock, stock, and barrel. Consequently it is usually wise to leave some room for movement in the trade proposal. The concession sought from the union should be somewhat greater than necessary and the concession offered by management in return should be a little less than management is willing to give. Often this is difficult to accomplish because trades are considered in the waning hours of negotiations where little time and patience remain. Nevertheless, management must assume that the union will continue to bargain hard until the contract is signed and should leave itself some negotiating currency (bargaining chips) for that eventuality.

The Total-Package or "Bottom-Line" Concept

Management negotiators sometimes suffer from tunnel vision by adopting a view of the "right settlement" composed of various contract changes which add up to a particular total cost figure over the period of the contract. They tend to view the key elements of the package—wages; holidays; vacations; medical, life, and pension benefits—as fixed. Unfortunately, the union with which they are dealing often does not hold the same view of the ideal package. This disagreement is distinct from one over the overall value of the package. It is more a difference on how the settlement pie is going to be sliced.

With certain important exceptions noted later, management is best advised to view a possible settlement from a "bottom-line" standpoint; i.e., what is the cost impact on the employer for each year of the contract regardless of the makeup of the package? By viewing the bargaining in this fashion, the negotiators allow themselves a great deal more flexibility in constructing a package which will be acceptable to the union and its members and yet keep management's costs within an acceptable limit. This is not to say that management should simply establish the bottom line and let the union determine how the money is to be allocated. Such negotiations can lead to disastrous results. But the union should be told that management does have its own bottom-line limits, and that regardless of what changes the union feels are vital, the final settlement must be within those limits.

More importantly, management and its negotiators must constantly examine the bottom line of each package offer and be willing to make changes in the composition of the package in order to achieve the most acceptable settlement.

The value of this approach is that, more than simply achieving a package acceptable to the union and its members, it demonstrates to the union that each improvement has a cost, and each concession has a value. It demonstrates that, as in other forms of human experience, "there's no free lunch"; if the union seeks to negotiate significant improvements in pension plan benefits, the money must come from some other part of the package. Even minor modifications can have a value placed on them in order to reinforce this concept.

Important Exceptions to the Bottom-Line Concept

There are some notable and important exceptions to the bottom-line concept. Management may wish to limit certain economic portions of the settlement package regardless of the amount of money available for them. For example, a multiplant employer usually must be careful to assure that wages in its various plants are within a given range. Otherwise, pressures will build in one or more plants to achieve parity, and countervailing pressures will be created in the other plant(s) to retain existing pay differentials. American auto makers have experienced these pressures between manufacturing facilities located in Canada and those in the United States. Management may also want to avoid allocating available money for wages in such a way as to benefit certain segments of the work force, e.g., unskilled workers. When a cents-per-hour across-the-board wage increase is negotiated, unskilled workers are proportionately better off than their skilled counterparts. Management may be concerned that such increases will have a negative influence on employees' motivation to progress and acquire greater skills.

Another area where management may wish to place limits regardless of the total size of the monetary package is that of medical insurance benefits. Expanded benefits may serve to escalate usage of the plan, which can result in greater-than-expected costs in subsequent years. Consequently, a policy decision may be necessary to limit expenditures in this area.

Policy Issues

There are also certain types of benefits which, aside from their cost, can have a negative effect upon work performance, attendance, and attitude. Because of this, management may, for policy reasons, refuse to entertain them. Predominant among these are certain types of pay for time not worked. Some employers absolutely refuse to agree to sick leave benefits on the basis that employees regard them as entitlements such as holidays, and therefore such benefits result in greater absenteeism than would otherwise be experienced. Pay for time spent by union representatives on union business within the employer's facility is another benefit which can produce negative results (i.e., lower productivity of other employees and more grievances), aside from the direct cost of the payments.

Loading the Package

The bottom-line concept becomes somewhat clouded in a multiyear contract. Depending upon how the bottom line is stated, it may not always be clear what settlement packages are greater or less than the established bottom line. For example, if management establishes a maximum bottom line of 5 percent in cost increases in each of three years, does a settlement of 6 percent the first year, 4 percent the second year, and 5 percent the third year exceed the bottom line? Probably not, although a thorough costing along the lines of the cost analyses shown in Chapter 10 should be made to assure that this conclusion is correct.

Some negotiators consider only cents-per-hour over the term of the contract and feel justified in moving improvements from the latter years of the contract to the earlier years without recognizing or admitting that they have made the package more costly. If managements permit their negotiators to do cost calculations on "the back of an envelope" with no more analysis than such simple noncompounded cents-per-hour additions, they are likely to pay for higher settlements without ever realizing that their bottom line was exceeded.

Contract Term Strategy

One of the most critical factors in the give and take of bargaining is the term or length of the contract. By varying the contract's term, offers can be substantially restructured, new ingredients can be introduced, and elements completely dropped. In some cases, a switch to a different length of contract can open up an entirely new phase of negotiations.

In the period since the early 1960s, mature industries in the United States have developed the custom of negotiating three-year contracts. Because of the economic uncertainty associated with the second and, especially, the third year of three-year contracts, cost-of-living adjustment (COLA) clauses were usually incorporated into these contracts. In such negotiations, the term of the contract was seldom an issue. Both parties sought extended periods of labor stability, and dreaded the prospect of annual or biannual negotiations (and the usual strike threats) which always proved to be costly, time consuming, and disruptive.

In less mature industries and in less sophisticated bargaining, the term of contract has continued to be a major variable in negotiations. As a general matter, at least in industries without COLAs, employers have usually sought longer-term contracts and unions have argued for shorter contracts. In the give and take of bargaining, management has usually been willing to spend more money for a longer-term contract.

Avoiding Coincident Contract Expirations

In some cases, employers find it imperative that a contract be only for a specific term or at least that it avoid a given expiration date. This is often the case where the employer has other facilities with contracts expiring in certain years and is not willing to have contracts at a substantial portion of its facilities expire in the same year. An illustration of this is the West Coast forest products industry, with which the author is quite familiar. Major employers have religiously avoided any agreement which would permit labor contracts in their wood products (i.e., lumber, plywood, particleboard, etc.) manufacturing facilities to expire in the same year as their pulp and paper manufacturing facilities. In cases such as this, management cannot use the term of contract as a bargaining variable—it is a must. Each offer must be framed within the same contract term, and the union must be put on notice that insistence on a different term will result in a strike or lockout. For all intents and purposes, bargaining ceases on this issue, unless the union feels so strongly that it is willing to engage in economic warfare over the issue.

A Possible Trap in the Long-Term Contract Offer

In the more typical case, bargaining takes place concerning the term of the contract, and management must be careful in constructing its longer term offers to avoid being trapped. For example, in constructing a three-year contract offer, management should initially develop the package so that each year can stand on its own if it were negotiated as its own contract. Stated another way, management should not, until it is sure of its ability to get a long-term contract, put particular contract improvements in the first or second years of a three-year contract offer that it would not be willing to agree to in a one- or a two-year contract. The reason is obvious. If management "shows" special improvements in the first or second year of a three-year contract, the union is likely to attempt to cut off the second and/or third years and lock in the special improvements, even though management has premised its special improvements on the union's agreement to a three-year contract.

While management can legitimately withdraw the special improvements if and when a shorter-term contract is offered, damage has been done to management's position in that it has surfaced significant improvements in an early year (or in early years) of the contract. Union negotiators will not lose sight of the fact that the employer was willing to grant special improvements in some portion of a long-term contract. It will be difficult to persuade them that the same improvement cannot be had in a shorter contract. It is much preferable to "show" the special improvements only in the third year (if at all) and, if necessary, advance them to an earlier year once it has been ascertained that the union will agree to a longer-term contract.

Discouraging Short-Term Contracts

One ploy sometimes used by management negotiators to discourage unions from adhering to demands for a one-year contract, despite management's clear rejection of same, is to make an offer for a one-year contract with obviously unacceptable terms. For example, if management has made an offer for a three-year contract with labor cost increases of 7 percent in each of the three years and the union continues to adhere to a demand for a one-year contract, management might propose a one-year contract containing labor cost increases of 3 percent to 4 percent. By doing so, management sends a clear message to the union that a one-year contract is not worth very much to management and that the union will have to make a great sacrifice in wages and benefits in order to obtain such a short contract.

The danger of this ploy is that it concedes the point that management will accept a one-year contract at least on some basis. In many cases, management may want to make no counterproposal for a one-year contract in order to make it clear that a one-year contract is totally unacceptable and that management will not accept one at any price.

Wage or Other Limited Reopeners

One alternative to a long-term contract is a "reopener" on certain limited subjects after one or two years. The most common type of reopener is for wages only. However, there is nothing to preclude the parties from designating any contract section as open to negotiations when the contract is reopened. The wage reopener is essentially a substitute for a COLA clause, or perhaps vice versa. It is usually regarded as protection for the employees against greater than anticipated inflation during the term of the contract. However, it might be motivated by the employer's concern about overextending its wage offer for subsequent years of a multiyear contract.

Insecurity of Reopeners

It must be pointed out that a reopener during the term of a three-year contract means that the employer does not truly have a long-term contract even though the nominal "expiration date" is three years. The employer is normally subject to a strike at the time of the reopener just as if the contract expired on that date. The only difference is that the subject(s) over which the union can strike are more limited. At the same time, there is less subject matter which can be used to trade off for the expected exorbitant wage increase proposals by the union.

Tactics of Reopening Clauses

A danger of reopeners is that the subjects (or subject) germane for bargaining are not always the only ones eventually discussed and/or changed. Once the parties sit down at the bargaining table, it is often difficult to avoid having other subjects raised and discussed. In some cases this enlarging of topics being considered is to the employer's advantage since negotiations limited solely to wages can lead to undue pressure being applied solely in that area.

If management finds itself confronted with a situation where acceptance of a reopener appears to be the only feasible alternative to a short-term contract, the following suggestions are offered:

1. Make the reopening language as specific as possible. If wages are to be reopened, specify if the reopener is limited to negotiations on a general wage increase or if other wage items are to be included, such as shift differentials, premium pay, and special wage adjustments for particular jobs.
2. Include in the reopener bargaining subject(s) in which management may wish to obtain offsetting concessions. For example, the reopener could, in addition to a general wage increase, include the subject of a no-strike clause which management wishes to incorporate or improve.

3. Require that any work stoppage which might result from a breakdown in reopener negotiations be preceded by a written notice sufficiently in advance of the work stoppage to permit management to alert customers and make other strike preparations.

Bargaining Strategy—Epilogue

A comprehensive discussion of collective bargaining strategy and tactics could easily consume this entire book. The permutations and variations are countless. This chapter and Chapter 12 simply attempt to cover the highlights of strategic and tactical considerations. One can never feel that he or she has mastered this subject, no matter how many labor contracts have been negotiated. More than any other phase of labor contract negotiations, this aspect requires the most thought, creativity, skill, and experience.

8

Negotiating Health and Welfare Benefits

One of the key components of any labor agreement is the section(s) covering medical, life, disability, vision, dental, and other benefits commonly referred to as "health and welfare" benefits. These benefits, in recent years, have consumed an increasing proportion of each dollar of labor costs and have become a much more significant aspect of labor contract negotiations.

As with the subject of pensions, dealt with in the next chapter, negotiation of health and welfare benefits is a complex and extensive subject which, in and of itself, could easily consume all the pages of this book.[1] The treatment given in this chapter is necessarily in summary fashion but will give the reader some foundation and guidelines on how the topic should be addressed within the overall framework of labor contract negotiations. It must also be kept in mind that this subject is one of the most dynamic and changing areas of employee compensation and benefits, and what applies as of this writing (in the early part of the 1990s) may not be true when this book is being read.

Use of Experts

Because of the value of technical knowledge concerning health and welfare benefits and the very significant sums of money involved in these benefit plans, it is usually advisable to have a benefits specialist sitting at the negotiating table when this subject is being discussed. This specialist may be the employer's Director or Manager of Benefits, an outside benefits consultant, actuary or broker, or a representative of the benefits carrier. If, for tactical or practical reasons, it is not feasible or advisable to have that person attend negotiations, the specialist should be within easy communication so that prompt and accurate advice can be obtained. Moreover, it is vital that the benefits specialist assist in the preparation of the employer's opening proposals and review the union's opening proposals, as well as analyze, develop cost estimates, and prepare recommendations on each item being negotiated.

If the benefits specialist is to be present at the bargaining table, it is important to define the extent to which he or she is authorized to speak. As a general proposition, the author favors an approach wherein any comments by the specialist are agreed upon in advance with the spokesperson and the specialist does not respond to questions unless cleared by the spokesperson. This will vary, however, based upon the level of experience of the benefits specialist in labor negotiations, the management spokesperson's own expertise in benefit matters, and whether or not the union has its own benefits specialist at the bargaining table.

Regardless of the use or availability of a benefits specialist by the employer, it is important that management's spokesperson be quite conversant with health and welfare benefit plans and costs. This negotiating subject is simply too important to be left completely to others.

General vs. Specific Contract Language

It is rather common for a labor agreement to spell out in some detail the extent of benefits provided to employees under the agreement. Frequently, it is not feasible to avoid negotiating such details into the agreement or to remove them once they are there. However, if it is possible to do so, the preferred method is to include as few specifics as possible in the agreement. An ideal clause from an employer's point of view would read as follows:

> The company will provide a plan which provides health and welfare benefits to employees covered by this agreement. The

benefits provided shall be those described in a booklet periodically issued by the company to employees.

The reasons in favor of vagueness rather than specificity are obvious. To the extent benefit details are not set forth in the contract, the employer is better able to modify and interpret them. With a general benefit provision in the labor agreement, it can be argued that the union bargained solely for a health and welfare plan, but not specific benefit provisions. Therefore, the argument goes, the employer is entitled to modify or interpret plan provisions at least to the extent they do not materially reduce benefits in effect when the contract was signed.[2] While the ideal level of vagueness or generality described above is seldom achievable, the management spokesperson should endeavor to come as close as possible by leaving detailed benefit provisions to the insurance contract or summary plan description, both of which are normally unilaterally determined documents.

Employer-Sponsored vs. Joint-Trusteed Plans

Even though health and welfare benefit plans are negotiated by the union and management, it is common that the employer administers the benefit plans, either directly or through a claims administration agent—typically an insurance company. An alternative to an employer-administered or employer-sponsored plan is a "joint-trusteed" plan in which the plan's administration is placed in the hands of a board of trustees with equal representation from the employer and the union.

Joint-trusteed plans are most common where a group of employers, usually in the same industry, who have labor agreements with the same international or national union join together to establish a multiemployer trust. Such plans are specifically authorized under Section 301 of the NLRA. Such plans are often referred to as "Taft-Hartley Trusts." They are more common in industries where there are a large number of small employers and one or a few large unions. Examples of industries in which these joint-trusted plans are often found are trucking (Teamsters), construction (carpenters, bricklayers, and other trades), retail sales and food service (United Food and Commercial Workers), and the entertainment industry (Screen Actors' Guild).

In many cases, an employer's participation in a joint-trusteed plan began years earlier, and continued participation is not seriously questioned. Such participation may have grown out of membership in a multiemployer bargaining unit where the employer members of the unit are signatory to the same labor agreement and to a joint-trusteed plan, and continued participation in the multiemployer negotiations is contingent on, or closely tied to, continued participation in the trust. Smaller employers who have participated in these joint trusts often find that they cannot obtain, on their own, comparable benefit coverage at the low cost available to the large multiemployer trust. In addition, they cannot reasonably assume the administrative burden and costs associated with administering their own plans.

Advantages

The advantages of such plans are that they consolidate significant buying power that often enables the trust to negotiate more favorable rates than could be achieved by any single employer. In addition, administrative overhead can be spread over a large number of participants, thus potentially lowering the employer's costs. In addition, such plans usually have a fixed employer contribution, and if benefit costs exceed the negotiated contribution level during the term of labor agreement, benefits will be reduced rather than increasing contributions.

Disadvantages

These advantages, however, are outweighed by a number of disadvantages. First, a joint-trusteed plan usually becomes identified as a "union plan," and the considerable costs absorbed by the employers are seldom recognized or acknowledged by their employees. Thus, the union usually gets the "credit" for such benefits. Second, matters of interpretation and administration become subject to debate and negotiation between union and management trustees. What might otherwise be a routine matter of management interpreting an insurance contract provision can become a major point of controversy. Third, a single employer has little or no individual control over key decisions concerning benefit design and administrative practices. The union will have a major role in this process as will those employers who have representatives on the board of trustees. Many unions persuade employer representatives on these boards that because the employer's financial contributions to the plan are fixed, employers should have little concern or involvement as to how the contributions are used. This is an erroneous and foolhardy trap to fall into. Fourth, because day-to-day benefit administration is usually within the control of the union, benefits are often paid without sufficient scrutiny as a way of keeping union members satisfied, usually to the detriment of cost control and the financial stability of the plan. Fifth, to the extent that the plan may be insufficiently funded as required by recognized accounting practices, the employer may be responsible to meet plan liabilities in excess of assets.

Types of Health and Welfare Benefits

The number and types of health and welfare benefits are quite numerous, and increasing each year. Nevertheless, it is possible to categorize the general types of benefits typically provided in labor contracts. This section will list these categories and the manner in which benefits are normally and most advisedly provided.

Life Insurance

This group benefit is similar to individual life insurance policies except that it is virtually always "term life insurance," i.e., insures against the risk of death with no investment or "cash value" component. It is negotiated as a stated absolute amount per employee (e.g., $50,000 per employee), as a percentage of the employee's income (e.g., one and one-half times annual salary), or as a hybrid of these two by providing a table of absolute dollar amounts of coverage related to pay levels. The following are examples:

Rate of Pay	Coverage
$7.50–10.00	$20,000
10.01–12.00	30,000
12.01–14.00	40,000
14.01–16.00	50,000
16.01 and above	60,000

From a negotiating standpoint, it is much preferable to negotiate a stated amount per employee or a table of stated absolute amounts. In this way, the union has to negotiate to obtain higher amounts of insurance. Of course, the level should be set only once during the term of the agreement, based on pay at the beginning of the labor agreement. If the benefits are stated as a multiple of earnings (e.g., coverage equal to two times annual earnings), the amounts escalate automatically when pay increases without any recognition on the part of the employee or the union that the employer's insurance costs have increased. Therefore, the employer gets no "credit" or benefit in negotiations for having provided greater and more costly benefits.

Accidental Death and Dismemberment

This benefit is an adjunct to life insurance by providing an additional benefit if a death occurs accidentally. It also provides payments if the covered party survives an accident yet loses a limb(s) or certain vital organs. The cost of this coverage is usually quite low, and the level of coverage provided typically parallels the amount of life insurance benefits.

Hospital-Surgical-Medical Coverage

Hospital-surgical-medical benefits are the heart of any group insurance program. They are the most costly and most important part of such programs. The cost of these coverages has been escalating at a more rapid rate than any other aspect of insurance coverages.

The benefits provided in this category include payment of services rendered by physicians and other medical practitioners, hospitals, and clinics, and for other expenses incident to these services such as medical supplies, prescription drugs, and ambulance charges. While the scope of coverages, means of funding, and plan administration characteristics are so varied that a general description is impossible in the space available, the following description outlines the major subcategories:

Indemnity Plans

The traditional, and still predominant, type of medical insurance in most areas is the "indemnity plan," which provides reimbursements for services rendered according to a predetermined formula. The most common formula currently found in employer-sponsored plans is a payment which is some percentage (typically 80 percent) of the "usual, customary, and reasonable" ("UCR") charges generally received by service providers for the same service in the same geographical area. The percentage not paid by the insurance coverage (typically 20 percent) is called a "co-payment." This amount must be paid by the employee.

A small minority of other plans provide for full payment of the UCR amounts and still others provide for a table of payments for designated surgical procedures and maximum daily hospital room charge reimbursements. The design of a majority of indemnity plans is that the covered employee will bear some portion of the medical charges.

Another common feature of indemnity plans is "deductibles" similar to those found in automobile collision policies. These provisions require that the covered employee assumes a certain level of initial costs before reimbursements will be paid. For example, a plan with a $200 annual deductible per covered person requires that person to accrue more than $200 in covered medical expenses before any reimbursement applies. Most plans have deductibles that apply to each covered employee and to each family member. A number of these plans also have a "family maximum deductible" which allow expenses of all family members to be aggregated and, once the family maximum is exceeded, entitles each family member to qualify for reimbursements even though each family member did not himself "satisfy" the deductible.

A related feature commonly found in indemnity plans is an "out-of-pocket maximum" or "stop loss." It is found in those plans with a co-payment feature. The stop-loss is an amount of incurred medical expenses beyond which employees no longer have to make a co-payment. Thus, if a $2,500 stop-loss is established, employees who pay out of their own funds $2,500 in medical expenses need not pay any additional medical costs since all costs above that amount will be paid solely by the plan.

Plan Design

One of the critical issues in health insurance is the selection of benefits to be provided and the level of coverage for each of those benefits. In the parlance of benefits specialists, this is known as "plan design." The reason it is so crucial is that it is the main determinant of the cost of a plan. If very costly procedures are not covered or only partly covered, plan expenses are thereby reduced. What exclusions does the plan contain? Are services provided by chiropractors, osteopaths, and podiatrists covered? How extensively are maternity expenses covered? Must certain medical procedures be authorized in advance? These and other questions are posed in the process of designing a medical plan.

It is most common for collective bargaining to determine the coverages provided under a medical plan, although the extent to which negotiations deal with very specific elements of plan design varies considerably. It is not unusual for labor negotiations to focus on the major elements of a plan, e.g., coinsurance, deductibles, and employee contribution, and to leave to the employer or insurance administrator the determination of the more detailed elements of the plan. Nevertheless, medical plan design is unquestionably a mandatory subject of bargaining.[3]

The degree to which the management negotiator can avoid opening up the detailed provisions of a plan for bargaining, the more cost effective will be plan design. An employer is more likely to be able to do this if the administration of existing plan benefits has been fair, efficient, and generally responsive to the needs of employees and their families. If an inordinate number of problems have been encountered during the term of a contract, the next contract negotiations are apt to focus on the specific elements of a plan and how the problems can be cured.

Sickness and Nonoccupational Disability Benefits

A normal part of most health and welfare benefit plans is income protection for time lost from work due to sickness or accidents unrelated to the employee's work. Such benefits typically take the form of sick leave, weekly indemnity payments, and short-term or long-term disability benefits.

Because regular attendance is a high priority with most employers, there is a strong incentive not to provide too much income protection for fear of prolonging absences due to sickness or injury or motivating employees to claim sickness or injury when none exists. On the other hand, employers realize that there can be great financial hardship on employees who cannot come to work due to disabling conditions. The key is to provide sufficient income protection to avoid a hardship, yet also provide adequate administrative controls to avoid abuse and/or malingering.

Except in work groups where there is an extremely high level of job satisfaction, a plan that provides 100 percent income replacement without any controls upon the receipt of such income almost certainly will encounter excessive use. Plans that pay only a proportion of regular income (two thirds is common in many plans) seem to have the best success in maintaining good employee attendance records. This is particularly true where some form of verification of disability (e.g., doctor's confirmation) may be required.

The primary opportunities for cost control for these kinds of benefits are (1) requiring a "waiting period" of some days prior to payment of benefits or (2) paying the employee only a portion of regular earnings so that the employee has to "share" in the cost of fully replacing lost income. A common waiting-period length is three days in the case of illness without hospitalization. Under such plans, the waiting period is to discourage employees from using the disability plan for supplementing paid vacation (i.e., using it when there is no true disability) and to encourage employees to come to work when the illness is but a minor indisposition.

As mentioned earlier in this chapter with regard to life insurance, management negotiators are advised to negotiate specific dollar amounts of disability benefits rather than percentages of normal pay. Payments as a percentage of pay automatically yield higher amounts (and therefore costs) as pay increases without recognition by employees or unions of an increased benefit, and without the employer receiving any negotiating value for what would otherwise be a benefit increase or negotiating concession.

The following table illustrates the type of graduated flat dollar sickness and accident benefit that acknowledges different pay levels, but does not automatically escalate:

Category*	Regular Pay Rate	Weekly Sickness & Accident Benefit
1.	Up to $9.00	$235
2.	9.51–10.50	260
3.	10.51–11.50	280
4.	11.51–12.50	300
5.	12.51–13.50	325
6.	13.50 and above	350

*Whatever pay category an employee is in at the beginning of a contract will be his category for the entire contract period.

Dental Plans

Reimbursement for expenses for dental work came to the fore in the 1960s and 1970s and were more common initially in the western states than in other parts of the country.

One of the key elements in plan design and negotiating strategy is to install cost controls on the most expensive procedures. This means flat dollar limits or higher co-payments for such procedures as orthodontia, crowns, and root canal therapy. Another significant cost control feature is an annual maximum payment per participant.

Because regular dental visits and preventive dental care are believed to reduce overall dental costs, some plans pay for routine office visits and lower employee co-payments when regular annual dental visits have been made. For example, if an employee gets an annual dental checkup, the co-payment may be increased from 80 percent to 90 percent. These types of arrangements are called "incentive plans" because they provide financial incentive to employees to encourage regular dental checkups.

Vision Care

Another relatively recent addition to the panoply of health care benefits is vision care or optical plans. These plans reimburse employees and dependents for eye examinations, lenses and frames, and contact lenses. Typically, there is a relatively low annual deductible (e.g., \$25–\$50) with percentage co-payments of reasonable and customary charges or specific dollar amounts for each procedure or appliance. From a negotiating standpoint, the specified dollar amounts (set at reasonable levels) are preferable to the percentage co-payment approach, since they encourage employees and dependents to select lower cost alternatives.

Prescription Drug Plans

Historically, prescription drugs were included as a covered expense under major medical plans wherein deductibles and co-payments were applicable. As the efficacy of less costly generic drugs became known and as more efficient drug delivery and claims processing systems (e.g., mail order systems and automated claims systems) were developed, separate or "carved out" prescription drug plans were introduced. These plans typically have no or low deductibles or flat amount dispensing fees such as one to five dollars per order filled, and otherwise pay the full cost of the prescription filled. Depending on the design of the plan and the organization administering the plan, both employers and employees can benefit from the establishment of prescription drug plans, particularly where employees regularly choose to use generic rather than name brand drugs.

Mental Health Benefits

Closely related to hospital, surgical, and medical benefits is mental health care. This involves treatment rendered by a psychologist, psychiatrist, social worker, or other mental health specialist on an in-patient or out-patient basis. The treatment may be for anxiety, depression, stress, or one of the many forms of mental disorders. Alcoholism and substance abuse are frequently covered as part of mental health care arrangements. The costs of mental health care have risen at rates substantially higher than other medical benefits. According to one group consulting firm, mental health rates in the early 1990s have been rising at twice the rate as other medical costs.[4]

Possible negotiating alternatives are to design benefits so as to discourage inpatient treatment (the most costly) in favor of intermediate and out-patient care. The way this is commonly done is to shift a disproportionate portion of the cost to employees for the more expensive treatment. Thus, by increasing employee co-payments (e.g., from 20 percent to 50 percent) or establishing maximum payments per year or per lifetime for inpatient treatment, mental health costs can be reduced. Use of Employee Assistance Programs ("EAPs") is another strategy to reduce costs. By providing, at an early stage, less intensive, less costly advice and counseling, it is sometimes possible to reduce later use of more extensive and costly treatment. Moreover, EAP counselors can serve as utilization reviewers and direct employees and dependents to more efficient and more cost-effective treatment than if the employee or dependent is left to select a provider on his own.

Another means to address mental health costs is to negotiate a "carve-out" plan whereby a separate mental health organization administers and delivers all mental health services.

By arranging a separate insured program, the employer can shift the risk to the mental health provider. This solution may not, however, be a permanent one in that premiums will increase if the benefits are not administered in a cost-effective manner. Even under this approach, plan design is essential.

Retiree Medical Benefits

Due to the tremendous escalation of health care benefits in the last several decades of the twentieth century, the issue of company-paid or subsidized medical benefits for retired employees has come to be one of the most sought-after, costly, and contentious benefits in the health and welfare arena. In its simplest and most common form, these benefits provide for hospital-surgical-medical benefits for retired employees from the date of their retirement until they are eligible for Medicare (age 65 as of this writing). Many plans continue coverage beyond age 65 as a supplement to Medicare. The benefit may be completely or partially paid by the employer, and the deductibles and co-payments to retirees may be the same as, or less favorable than, those provided for active employees.

Bargaining Obligation—Retiree Benefits

A unique feature of this benefit is that employers are not required, as a matter of law, to negotiate with respect to retirees as they are for benefits for active employees. In 1972, the U.S. Supreme Court ruled in *Pittsburgh Plate Glass*[5] that retired employees are not "employees" as defined by the National Labor Relations Act, and therefore, pension benefits for former (retired) employees are not a mandatory subject of bargaining. While that case involved pensions, it is equally applicable to other benefits for retired employees, including health benefits.[6] Nevertheless, once such benefits have been agreed upon, they must usually be continued for those who retired when the benefit was in effect. The contract language granting such retiree will control the changeability of such benefits. Any changes for future retirees must be negotiated if the retiree coverage is part of the labor agreement.[7]

FASB 106

While retiree health insurance has long been a contentious issue at the bargaining table, it took on dramatic new proportions in 1990, when the Financial Accounting Standards Board ("FASB") passed its Rule 106, which specified that prudent accounting practices require that an employer treat as a current expense the actuarial value of the liability it assumes when it obligates itself to pay for retiree's medical expenses.[8]

The impetus for FASB to pass Rule 106 was the common practice of employers to pay for retiree medical benefits as a normal current operating cost. In contrast to pensions which, by law (ERISA), must be prefunded, retiree medical benefits were typically paid from the same pool of funds as for active employees. This created a situation where long-term liabilities were not being accurately reflected on the employer's balance sheet, and where adequate financial reserves were not properly allocated to meet those liabilities.

One of the results of FASB 106 was to bring employers' attention to the extremely costly liabilities to which they had obligated themselves and to take the necessary steps to fund them. It also created a strong motivation to reduce the size of the liabilities by reducing retiree benefits, shifting costs to retirees, and instituting additional cost controls.

COBRA

Apart from any negotiated obligation to provide medical benefits for retirees, employers with 20 or more employees have a legal obligation to continue medical benefits for a period of at least 18 months following a termination, whether that termination be a retirement or for other reasons.[9] Although the employer may charge the retiree the "full cost" of these benefits plus an additional 2 percent to cover administrative expenses, the "full cost" rarely, if ever, compensates the employer for the *true* cost of these benefits. Because the employer may only charge retirees the same costs that apply to active employees, and because the average retiree's experience in the usage of medical benefits invariably exceeds that of the average active employee, the true costs are significantly higher—in some cases two to three times as high.

Nevertheless, COBRA benefits cannot be reduced by labor negotiations—they can only be increased. To that extent, they constitute a floor from which the union may seek to increase benefits at the employer's cost.

Quasi-Health and Welfare Benefits

The general notion of health and welfare benefits is that they protect employees and their dependents from the financial impact of illness, injury, and death. There are, however, other types of benefits which are not directly tied to physical health and well being, but which are often classified as health and welfare benefits, and about which an employer is required to negotiate.

Legal Services

Creative union negotiators, with the aid of lawyers' associations, in the late 1970s and 1980s prompted a benefit to assist their members to defray legal costs which, prior thereto, had received little attention. Plans providing legal services benefits vary considerably in scope, levels of coverage, and costs. The most common programs entail a specific cents per hour contribution to a group plan or to a network of lawyers for which a specific level of legal services is provided. The types of legal problems typically addressed by such plans include bankruptcy, divorce, wills, adoption, traffic violations, condemnation, real estate, debt collection, and property damage. Generally, these plans provide levels of advice, consultation, and legal services up to a predetermined number of hours. Thereafter, the employee participant is required to pay out-of-pocket for more extensive legal advice or services, often provided at a discount from the lawyer's normal billing rates.

Such plans have received considerable criticism from participants based on inaccessibility of the lawyers and perceived attempts to expand the work so that fees beyond plan limits can be charged. Despite initial enthusiasm on the part of some unions and their members, this benefit has not been widely negotiated into many labor agreements. The reasons for this lack of proliferation are numerous, but at least one major reason appears to be the limited bargaining monies available for what is generally considered as a luxury benefit at a time when more vital, essential health benefits have been escalating at a very rapid rate. Management is well advised to avoid the initial low cost lure of these programs. At best, they serve a marginal group of employees and a marginal need of employees with the near certainty of significantly higher costs.

Child Care

Another relatively new nonhealth benefit is child care. This benefit has become one of the most sought-after benefits in the 1990s. It is primarily a creature of the two wage-earner family which has become such a predominant phenomenon of the U.S. work force in the last quarter of the twentieth century.

Child care benefits take many forms, the most common types of which are as follows:

1. *Information and Referral Services*—This is perhaps the simplest form of child care which normally involves making available lists of licensed or approved child care facilities sometimes accompanied by additional personal advice and/or assistance. Usually, the referral service is provided by a firm or agency that contracts with the employer to provide the information/consulting with costs assessed on a per capita employee basis. In some cases, the employer's own staff does the screening and referral.
2. *Flexible Spending Accounts*—As authorized by Section 125 of the Internal Revenue Code, employers may establish accounts to which employees contribute through payroll deduction on a pretax basis from which fees for child care are paid. This benefit is frequently part of a broader group of benefits provided under a "flex plan" where employees may choose from different combinations of benefits based on the particular needs of themselves and their families. Employees who avail themselves of this benefit lose their entitlement to federal tax credit for child care expenses.
3. *Discounts*—Arrangements may be made by employers with local day care centers to provide discounted fees to their employees.
4. *Vouchers or Financial Subsidies*—Employers may provide direct financial assistance to cover or defray a portion of the expenses of a child care facility, selected by the employee.
5. *On-Site Day Care*—Perhaps the most ambitious of the child care alternatives, the on-site approach is one where the employer operates, directly or through contracted services, a child care facility at or near the workplace. A variation is that the employer joins with a group of other employers to

provide the service. The cost may be borne solely by the employer(s), or it may be partially subsidized with employees required to make a contribution.

6. *Sick Child Care*—A form of child care that can potentially alleviate absenteeism is to provide directly, or through subsidy, temporary care for employees' children who are ill and cannot attend their normal day care facility. This may be in addition, or as an alternative, to regular day care facilities.

With as much enthusiasm as is generated for this benefit in many work forces, it must always be kept in mind that, for the most part, it favorably impacts only those employees who have children between 6 months and 12 years, or those who contemplate starting a family in the near future. At the same time, the cost to the employer will be limited by the number of employees who will use this benefit. A detailed analysis needs to be done well in advance of negotiations to determine the absolute number and percentage of the work force who will conceivably utilize this benefit during the likely term of the next agreement. This is the potential "interest group."

Controlling Costs

The current dominant theme in the determination of health and welfare benefits, whether that determination be by collective bargaining or by unilateral employer actions, is cost control. In an era where 15 to 25 percent annual cost increases have been experienced, it is no wonder that this would be a primary focus. Despite the attention to, and concern for, cost control, employers have been largely unsuccessful in stemming the inflationary tide. Nevertheless, minor achievements have been made, and when overall inflationary rates are in the double-digit range, any possible savings are significant. Employers have some options in a favorable negotiating environment as to how to mitigate cost inflation.

Self-Insurance

Insurance companies that provide health care insurance require premium payments based upon an assessment of the risk. Because renewal premiums are based on experience under the prior contract, medical insurance contracts tend to be cost-plus arrangements. Nevertheless, the insurer requires that a certain percentage of the premium be allotted to reserves for claims and that a sufficiently high premium be paid in advance of the time when claims will be submitted. The time value of those funds can be significant. Because insurance contracts are essentially cost-plus arrangements and because of the time value of funds held in reserve, many employers have elected to assume the risk themselves (at least up to a certain level of claims) and thus "self-insure." The savings that can often be achieved by converting to a self-insured program are in the range of 3 percent to 10 percent.

Under these self-insured arrangements, employers frequently will transfer the risk of individual claims to the degree they exceed certain amounts (e.g., $50,000, $100,000) to an insurance company or consortium of companies that is better able to spread the risk over a greater number of persons than a single employer could do. This type of insurance is commonly referred to as "excess" or "stop loss" coverage.

Most employers who elect to self-insure continue to use an insurance company to administer the plan and pay claims since these firms are usually better organized to cost effectively administer claims. Moreover, they lend a certain professional objectivity or "third party" determination which is actually, or perceived to be, more expert and objective. Under this arrangement, the insurance company becomes a third party administrator, or simply "TPA." The contract or arrangement for doing so is called an "administrative services only" or "ASO" agreement. From the standpoint of the employee, it typically appears to be the same as a conventional insured plan since claims continue to be submitted to, and paid by, an insurance company. Nevertheless, the employer is directly paying the claims (only through the insurance company), and any excessive or wasteful usage of plan benefits must be borne by the employer. This fact should be made known to all employees since it will ultimately impact their benefits, contributions, or other forms of compensation.

Cost Sharing

Another means of reducing an employer's cost of health and welfare costs is to have employees share some of the costs of providing benefits. This is done through one or more of the following means:

1. *Employee Contributions*—This involves having employees make a contribution to cover some portion of the medical costs for themselves and/or their dependents. When this is done, the plan becomes a "contributory" plan. Normally the contributions are deducted from the employee's paycheck each month, and prior to 1978 were always made with after-tax dollars. Even today, that is frequently the case. However, as of this writing, it is possible to utilize provisions under IRC Section 125 to make employee contributions with pretax dollars.
2. *Deductibles*—These are among the most common forms of cost shifting. By requiring the employee to pay 100 percent of a given level of initial costs (e.g., first $100, $250, $500 per year), the benefit plan is relieved of the burden of those expenses. The cost-saving strategy of deductibles is not only to shift the amount of the deductible to the employee, but to provide a disincentive to the employee and dependents from using the medical plan for less than necessary purposes. Thus, for example, an employee who has not yet satisfied his annual deductible may elect not to seek medical treatment for a simple cold, whereas one who has satisfied the deductible or one who is in a plan with no deductible at all may choose to visit the doctor even though rest and home remedies may be sufficient to achieve a cure. By increasing deductible amounts, the employer further discourages use of the plan.
3. *Co-Payments*—Another common provision in medical plans to shift costs away from the plan is an employee co-payment, i.e., the obligation of the employee to pay some percentage of a medical bill after the deductible has been satisfied. For certain kinds of benefits that can be very costly and/or very frequently used (e.g., mental health, chiropractic care, etc.) a 50 percent co-payment is sometimes found. Again, as with deductibles, the purpose is only partially to shift costs. The potentially greater effect is to discourage unnecessary usage of the plan. Because the employee must always pay some portion of the medical cost (unless there is an "out of pocket maximum" which when reached relieves the employee of any additional expenses), he will seriously consider whether or not to purchase the medical treatment or care.
4. *Coordination of Benefits ("COB")*—This is a process whereby an employee who is covered by more than one medical plan (usually by the employee's own plan and as a covered participant by his spouse's plan) is precluded from receiving more than 100 percent of covered medical expenses. Thus, for example, even though each plan normally provides 80 percent of the usual and customary charges, the employee or dependent would not receive 160 percent from the two plans, but only 100 percent. The logic is, of course, that the employee should not receive a windfall just because he is

covered under two plans. An even greater cost-conserving process is involved in a "maintenance COB" clause whereby the employee and spouse are limited to receiving only that amount which would be provided by the employee's plan. Thus, in the above example, the employee would receive only 80 percent of the usual and customary charges rather than 100 percent even though he and his spouse were covered under plans which each provided 80 percent of covered expenses.

Managed Care

A number of other means have been developed in recent decades to control the usage of medical benefits. They involve a wide array of different techniques but generally come under the broad heading of "managed care." Some of the techniques are designed to reduce or eliminate unnecessary or marginally necessary medical treatment, and others are designed to take advantage of lower-priced services that may be available due to group discounts. These techniques include the following:

1. *Preadmission Certification*—This is a requirement for certain types of procedures (usually surgeries) to be authorized by the insurer, the insurer's claims processor, or the insurer's utilization reviewer prior to the employee or dependent having the procedure performed. The purpose is to assure that the treatment is medically necessary and that the length of hospital confinement is designed to be no longer than necessary. By knowing the nature of the intended medical treatment, the expense can sometimes be avoided completely or minimized by means of alternative and less costly treatment or alternative facilities. This review is typically done by nurse practitioners, nurses, or physicians employed by the utilization review organization.
2. *Second Surgical Opinion*—This is normally a recommended, voluntary step of obtaining an independent medical opinion prior to certain types of surgeries that have proven to be overused when other treatments may suffice (e.g., coronary bypass, hysterectomies). Although it has not proven to be an especially effective means of controlling costs, it can, in some cases, eliminate needless surgeries. When the employee or dependent seeks the second opinion, coverage is always at 100 percent reimbursement of the cost of the second opinion in order to avoid discouragement of its use.
3. *Preadmission Testing ("PAT")*—Costs of hospital stays for surgery and for other reasons can be reduced by having X-rays, lab tests, and other diagnostic procedures done on

an out-patient basis prior to scheduled hospital admission. Reimbursement is made so that the employee is at least as well off from a cost standpoint as if the tests had been done when he was admitted. In this way, employees and their dependents can be treated as soon as they enter the hospital, rather than to wait until the test results are completed. This saves the cost of hospital confinement when the tests are being conducted as well as the cost of hospital confinement while awaiting the tests' results.

4. *Reduced Percentage Reimbursement*—To discourage the use of high cost or unnecessary use of certain overused and/or high-cost procedures or facilities, lower percentage reimbursements may be helpful in discouraging their use (and abuse). For example, emergency room visits, mental health treatments, and chiropractic care are oftentimes reimbursed at 50 percent rather than 80 percent of the usual and customary charges.
5. *Case Management*—This is the process of having the insurance carrier, employer, or a utilization review firm monitor the progress of a patient following surgery or serious illness to ensure that the most cost-effective, yet sufficiently beneficial, means are employed to achieve recovery. For example, the case manager may recommend recovery or rehabilitation of a patient who has recently undergone surgery be done at home or in a custodial care unit rather than in an acute care facility.
6. *Incentives for Less Costly Treatment*—The converse of reduced co-payments for overused and/or high-cost procedures is the financial incentive for use of lower-cost alternatives. Some plans, therefore, waive deductibles and increase co-payments (e.g., 100 percent rather than 80 percent) for having minor surgeries performed in doctors' offices or surgical centers not part of an acute care hospital. Likewise, such enhanced benefits may be used to encourage employees to use skilled nursing facilities, birthing centers, hospices, and home health care as alternatives to acute care hospitals. These same lower cost alternatives may also be utilized as a result of effective "case management."
7. *Preferred Provider Organizations ("PPOs")*—The concept of "quantity discounts," so common in the selling of merchandise, forms the basis of "preferred provider organizations" or simply "PPOs." These are contractual arrangements between employers or networks of employers (often organized by common insurance carriers or claims administrators) and various hospitals, physicians, and other providers. Under the typical PPO arrangement, the insurer provides a financial incentive to employees to use the preferred provider organization, with that provider supplying medical services at a discount. In essence, the group of employers and/or insurers has purchasing power which translates into lower medical

costs—a portion of which the insurer realizes and a portion of which is passed on to employees, usually in the form of lower co-payments or expanded coverage. For example, employees who use a preferred provider organization may have to make co-payments of only 5 or 10 percent whereas those using any other providers might have to pay 20 or 25 percent. Obviously, the discounts from the providers would have to exceed sufficiently their regular costs (from nonpreferred providers) in order for the employer to achieve any monetary benefit from the PPO.

8. *Point of Service Plans*—These plans utilize the concept of a network of designated or preferred providers whose fees are discounted as with the previously discussed PPOs, but which limit patients' access to medical specialists by requiring the patient to be referred by a primary care physician. The primary care physician is often called a "gatekeeper." On the theory that most indemnity plans experience high costs due to unnecessary or excessive treatment by specialists, the point of service plans utilize the primary care physical to control access to specialists by rendering the treatment directly or referring the patient to that specialist who will provide the most efficacious and cost efficient treatment. The point of service plan is designed with a financial incentive to the primary care physician if predetermined plan cost parameters are achieved.
9. *Health Maintenance Organizations ("HMOs")*—As discussed earlier in this chapter, the traditional, and still predominant, type of medical insurance plan is an "indemnity" plan whereby the covered participant is assured of a given level of reimbursement for specific, or for certain categories of, medical services. In effect, the employee and his covered dependents are insured or indemnified against a loss or expense exceeding the level of benefits provided in the insurance policy. A contrasting approach is that of a "health maintenance organization" or simply "HMO" in which all, or virtually all, of the medical expenses are covered. In practice, the HMO does not bill the recipient for the services but provides the necessary covered services, whatever the cost. There may be a small administrative or processing fee that the employee or dependent must pay, but thereafter it is virtually cost free. The employee or dependent is limited to physicians and hospitals that are part of the HMO, and therefore, the employee or dependent is not free to select any provider he or she wishes as under an indemnity plan.

The cost or "premium" for HMO coverage may be higher than, lower than, or the same as that of an indemnity plan depending on the breadth of coverage under each plan, the cost effectiveness of the HMO provider, the usage rate of benefits by employees under each plan, and a number of other factors. Some employers will subsidize their employees' participation in HMOs up to the employer's cost of providing an indemnity plan. Thus, if a particular employer pays under its indemnity plan the full cost of its employees' coverage and 50 percent towards the employees' dependents' coverage, and the combination of such coverages costs that employer an average of $325 per family, the employer would pay up to, and including, that amount if employees select HMO coverage. The balance, if any, between the employer's subsidy and the full HMO cost must then be paid by the employee. Many employees are willing to pay a monthly "premium" for HMO coverage over and above the monthly cost of the alternative indemnity plan because they are not subject to any significant additional costs that are associated with an indemnity plan such as deductibles and co-payments.

From the employer's perspective, an HMO alternative may not provide the employer with any cost savings and may, in fact, increase its costs because low-risk employees (younger and more healthy ones) may disproportionately select HMO coverage. To the extent that, on average, these younger, more healthy employees and their families select HMO coverage, their favorable experience (i.e., low usage rates) is lost to the indemnity plan, and the costs of the indemnity plan will therefore increase.

The list of managed-care alternatives listed above is not exhaustive. A number of other techniques have been, and will be, developed as a means of attempting to achieve some control over medical costs which, in the last quarter of the twentieth century, have been simply out of control.

Health and Welfare Negotiating Strategies

As with all other portions of the labor agreement, an employer must determine what its objectives are with respect to the health and welfare section of the labor agreement. Once these are identified, a plan needs to be developed on how to achieve those objectives.

Analyze Experience

In developing health and welfare negotiating objectives, the employer needs to thoroughly review and analyze its experience during the previous five to seven years. Piercing questions need to be asked. Which benefits experienced the greatest cost increases? Were cost increases more pronounced in one geographical area than another, or in some facilities or divisions than another? How did our experience compare with other comparable employers? What feedback are we getting from employees about their benefits? What types of large claims were experienced, and do these seem to be related in any way to the way the plan is designed?

The employer's group consultant, broker or in-house insurance specialist needs to do a thorough analysis of data to summarize this experience and to recommend changes in the plan that may need to be negotiated. From that point, priorities need to be set, based largely on what type of financial payback each change can provide.

Negotiating Costs vs. Benefits

In employer-sponsored medical plans, it is quite common to negotiate benefit levels and to not specify the costs associated with those benefits. Joint-trusteed plans, on the other hand, typically negotiate a given level of employer contribution (e.g., X¢ per hour or X$ per week or per month). Under the joint-trusted plans, the benefit levels are determined by a board of trustees.

One key to successful negotiation of health and welfare benefits is to negotiate both benefits *and* costs. An employer's agreement to provide a given level of benefits should be conditioned by the fact that those benefits do not exceed a specified cost. For example, the employer may agree "to continue the benefits of Plan 'A' during the term of the agreement provided they do not exceed a composite cost[10] of $250.00 per employee per month." What if the costs actually exceed that amount? There are three alternatives: (1) reduce and/or redesign benefits to achieve lower costs, (2) have employees pay some portion or a greater portion of the plan's costs, or (3) divert some portion of wages or some other benefit to health and welfare benefits to cover the cost increase. The labor agreement should contain provisions that spell out just what will occur if costs exceed the negotiated limit. It may be sufficient to allow employees to vote on which of the above alternatives they wish to see implemented, although it is usually preferable to have a predetermined means of making up the difference.

An employer who merely negotiates benefits without any cost controls is signing a blank check. In an era of high inflation of medical costs, the blank check may turn out to be a very substantial amount.

Design Plan to Encourage Cost Control

The employer's objective in negotiations should always be to achieve the most cost effective means of providing a given level of benefits. This may frequently mean that a financial incentive needs to be provided for employees to select the less costly alternative either by having employees share some portion of the expense of the more costly alternative or by having employees pay less for the less expensive alternatives. For example, if certain types of minor surgeries can be performed in clinics or "surgi-centers" at significantly less cost than at a hospital, the employee co-payment for these less costly procedures may be decreased from 20 percent to 10 percent or perhaps be eliminated altogether. Similarly, employees may be required to pay 20 percent for brand name drugs but nothing for generic drugs.

Although it may seem perfectly obvious from the earlier sections of this chapter, it is important for management to look continually for opportunities in negotiations to include provisions that encourage employees to use medical and other benefits with discretion and cost conservation in mind. Each employee should see a personal benefit from judicious use of health and welfare benefits. Whether that translates to "shopping" for the least expensive, yet effective, care or whether it causes an employee or dependent to question a medical provider about the necessity of a particular procedure or confinement, the plan should reward cost conservation and penalize cost carelessness.

Certainly placing a cap on the employer's contribution to medical coverage, as described in the preceding sections, will be an incentive for employees to keep costs low so as not to trigger an employee contribution (or greater contribution) or a pay reduction. Nevertheless, the threat of a future employee contribution for medical coverage, or a future increase in the employee's contribution, is probably less effective than the spectre of an immediate out-of-pocket expenditure due to a higher deductible or co-payment. An increase in employees' contributions is dependent on the experience of the total employee group ("the other guys"), whereas deductibles and co-payments result from one's own or dependent's usage.

Retain Key Operating and Administrative Decisions

Another management negotiating priority should be the retention (or recapture) of the decision-making authority with respect to key health and welfare operating and administrative decisions. For example, an employer should possess the right to select the insurance carrier or claims administrator (if self-insured) for medical benefits. This is an essential decision that impacts plan costs, efficiencies and quality. It should not be a matter of bilateral determination. Similarly, the employer should make other key decisions such as what types of medical or utilization excess review (preadmission certification, case management, etc.) should be utilized, what claim break points should be selected for transferring risk from the employer to an excess insurance carrier under a self-insured plan, and what administrative procedures should be followed for normal claims handling and COBRA compliance.

It is perfectly understandable that a union will want to negotiate benefit levels, but a wise management negotiator will not agree to provisions in a labor agreement that permit a union to have joint control over health and welfare plan administration.

When to Negotiate Health and Welfare Benefits

Examining recommendations in earlier chapters that, in selecting an order of bargaining, language should come first and economics last, it would appear that health and welfare issues should be toward the end of the negotiations. In most cases, the general rule should be followed. However, where employer-proposed changes are extensive or somewhat complex, it is probably advisable to introduce the subject at an earlier stage of bargaining. If the union negotiators must assimilate new concepts or approaches, or be asked to agree to sweeping plan changes, they will need time to digest the new information and get used to the new approach.

However, if the health and welfare issues for discussion are more conventional (e.g., normal changes in coverage), it is preferable to forestall discussion on these issues until economic subjects are on the table. After all, health and welfare benefits are truly economic issues, and the employer's ability to provide them is no different than its ability to pay wages and salaries.

Consequently, they should be dealt with alongside wages and other employee benefits that have calculable costs.

Enlisting Union Cooperation in Cost Control

The phenomenon of rampant medical cost inflation is well known to union representatives. The problem is that most of them believe it is the employer's problem, not theirs. A key objective of the management spokesperson should be to help union representatives realize that rising medical costs are just as much a problem for the union and for employees (union members) as they are for the employer, because medical costs are simply a part of overall labor costs and whatever amounts are spent for medical coverage will not be available for wages or other benefits. Consequently, when medical costs increase, employees, through collective bargaining, are simply spending more of their compensation package for medical coverage than for other forms of compensation. The more management's spokesperson can impress this message on the union counterpart, the easier it will be to keep benefits at tolerable levels.

9

Negotiating Pensions

There is perhaps no subject that presents more intellectual challenges to a labor negotiator than pensions. Because of complexities in plan design, cost and actuarial analysis, and applications of the law, understanding pension plans and negotiating changes in them can be very difficult tasks. A truly competent labor negotiator needs to devote a significant amount of time studying the pension plan(s) he or she is charged with negotiating. Moreover, a considerable amount of time needs to be spent with the plan's actuary or pension specialist in order to have a full grasp of the key plan characteristics and the plan changes that will have the greatest economic impact. Preparation is always an important part of labor contract negotiations. With respect to negotiating pensions, it is absolutely necessary.

Comparisons With Health and Welfare

There are certain aspects of negotiating pensions that are similar to bargaining of health and welfare benefits as discussed in the previous chapter. First, the use of experts in bargaining pensions is as important, if not more important, than for health and welfare. Because the concepts are more complex and cost and benefit calculations are virtually impossible without a competent actuary, a negotiator is foolhardy to attempt serious negotiations without the advice and assistance of a pension actuary or pension specialist.

As with bargaining over health and welfare benefits, it is a judgment call as to whether the pension specialist should sit, and fully participate, in negotiations or merely be on call to provide assistance when needed, away from the bargaining table. The comments on this decision in the last chapter apply equally to pensions.

There are other similarities with negotiating health and welfare benefits. The determination of when to open discussions on pensions is similar to that with health and welfare. Generally, the subject should be raised as part of the economic portion of negotiations, unless significantly new pension approaches and/or complex aspects of pensions must be covered, in which case, introduction of this subject at an early point of negotiations is advisable. And, as with health and welfare benefits, the less detailed plan provisions inserted in the labor agreement, the better.

Legal Constraints

Although federal and state law influence, to some degree, the character and provisions of negotiated health and welfare benefits, the overall impact of the law is not extensive. This is not true in the case of pensions. Beginning with the Internal Revenue Code and the Employees Retirement Income Security Act ("ERISA") passed by Congress in 1974, and continuing with the Omnibus Budget Reconciliation Acts ("OBRA") and the Consolidated Omnibus Budget Reconciliation Act ("COBRA"), the Age Discrimination in Employment Act ("ADEA"), and many others, the constraints of federal law on pension bargaining are significant. These laws regulate such matters as reduction of accrued benefits, relative benefits between high-income and low-income participants, preretirement spousal benefits, and maximum pension benefit payments. Indeed, the negotiator of pension benefits needs either to have a good grasp of pension law or a counselor who can provide advice as to the legal constraints.

Major Categories of Pension Plans

There are a number of different ways to categorize pension plans, but perhaps the most fundamental differentiation is between "defined benefit" or "DB" plans and "defined contribution" or "DC" plans.

Defined Benefit Plans

The more traditional, and by far the more prevalent, type of pension is the defined benefit plan. Under this type of plan, a participant earns credit for each year of service toward a predetermined benefit level based upon years of service under the plan. The level of benefit is determined by a formula which typically multiplies the years of service times a dollar amount per year of service or a percentage of earnings. For example, a benefit formula might provide $20 per month (or $240 per year) for each year of service. Thus, an employee with 25 years of service would receive a pension benefit of $500 per month or $6,000 per year. Another common variation is a percentage of earnings. Those earnings may be the total earnings over the employee's career or those earned during a specific period of time prior to the employee's retirement. The later is termed "final average earnings" and typically would be calculated as an annual average of the employee's final five years prior to retirement. Under a plan that pays 1½ percent of final average earnings, an employee who worked 25 years, and who earned an average of $40,000 over his last five years prior to retirement would receive a monthly benefit of $1,250 ($40,000 × .015 = $600 × 25 years ÷ 12).

With a defined benefit plan, the employer need only contribute each year a portion of the ultimate cost needed to fund the benefits accrued in that year because the costs may be amortized over a period of years. Because some employees will terminate before they become "vested" (i.e., entitled to a benefit) or will die before they reach retirement age, the true cost of providing benefits is less than if the employer were paying given amounts each year into employee accounts based on benefit credits earned that year.

From an employee's standpoint, the defined benefit plan has the advantage of ensuring a benefit upon retirement that can be reasonably estimated well in advance of the employee's reitrement date with virtually no risk on the employee's part. On the other hand, the employee and spouse could lose a very significant part of the accumulated pension credits if the employee dies or terminates prior to normal retirement date.

Under the defined benefit approach, the employer places a certain amount of money each year into a pension fund, which monies are invested in some combination of stocks, bonds, money market funds, real estate, guaranteed investment contracts, government-backed instruments, and a myriad of other investment vehicles. The amount of employer contributions is determined by an actuarial evaluation of the amount of money that will be necessary to provide future retirement benefits. Actuaries for the plan take into account the age, pay scale projections, service, and turnover profile of the employee group participating in the pension plan, estimate (using mortality tables) the number of employees who will die prior to retirement, and assume a rate of return on funds invested by the plan's investment manager(s). Based upon other plan features such as provisions covering early and disability retirements, death benefits, and employee contributions, the plan's actuary will develop cost projections to determine the necessary level of employer contributions each year. The levels of contributions that ultimately are made for which an employer will want to receive tax deductions will be influenced by the Internal Revenue Code and regulations issued under the Code.

The negotiation of a defined benefit plan focuses almost exclusively on the benefit formula and other major plan features rather than cost. Because the cost of providing a given level of benefits can vary tremendously, depending on the actuarial methods and assumptions used, the cost cannot be established with such a degree of certainty that both parties will always accept it. The company's actuary and the union's actuary (if it employs one) might come to different conclusions about the true cost of a given level of benefits and plan provisions. In any event, bargaining will clearly focus on benefits. This is not the case with defined contribution plans, and a union trying to compare the cost/benefit relationship between one employer's defined benefit plan and another employer's defined contribution plan will have a very difficult task indeed.

Principal Features of Defined Benefit Plans

The following sections describe the primary features of defined benefit plans and how they will be impacted by the employer's and union's desired objectives and by the negotiating process.

Eligibility

The criteria most commonly used to determine eligibility are minimum age and service requirements. Federal law has established a maximum period for delaying an employee's eligibility to participate as age 21 and one year of service. The plan may require that employees accumulate five years of participation in order to be eligible for a normal retirement benefit.

Eligibility may also be limited to employees in particular work groups such as certain designated facilities or skill groups (e.g., maintenance employees only). Of course, it is common to limit coverage under a particular collectively bargained plan to the employees in that bargaining unit.

Service

There are two basic categories of service. *Vesting service* is that period of time worked, or for which compensation is received, which is credited for purposes of vesting. *Benefit service* is time worked or paid for which is credited for purposes of accruing benefits under the plan.

Generally, under federal law, an employee must be given credit for one year of vesting and benefit service if he or she has worked or been compensated for one thousand hours of service within one year (plan year, calendar year, or employment year, depending on the language of the plan). ERISA provides somewhat different rules regarding crediting of service for vesting purposes than for benefit purposes.

Employee Contributions

While contributory defined benefit plans are more common for nonunion groups, they sometimes exist for collective bargaining groups. Participation in such contributory plans is voluntary. Some plans permit voluntary contributions to enhance the benefits under a noncontributory plan. The amount of contribution is a matter of bargaining, but it seldom exceeds 6 percent of regular pay. If the benefit is integrated with social security, the contribution will normally also be integrated. Thus, if a plan's benefit formula provides for 1 percent of earnings under $800 per month, and 1½ percent of earnings in excess of $800 per month, the employee contribution might be similarly structured to require one percent of earnings under $800 per month and 2 percent of earnings over $800 per month.

Vesting

The word "vest" means to have an ownership right, and in the lexicon of pensions, it means an entitlement to a pension benefit at a specified age or period of service or both. For plans that have an employee contribution, employees are always vested in that portion of the benefit resulting from their own contributions. Employees become vested in that portion of the benefit attributed to the employer's contributions according to a vesting schedule that is no longer than one of the following two vesting rules established by the IRS:

1. Five-year "cliff vesting"—after five years' service, the employee is 100 percent vested. Prior to that time, he is 0 percent vested.
2. "Graded vesting"—after three years the employee must be at least 20 percent vested and must vest an additional 20 percent per year and be fully vested by the seventh year.

Unquestionably, the five-year vesting rule is the easier to administer and understand, and hence it is the most common one in use.

Because the IRS has established these relatively short maximum vesting periods, there is little management can do in labor contract negotiations to make the pension plan less costly by modifying the vesting periods.

Normal Retirement Age

The normal retirement age under a pension plan is that age when a participant receives a full (unreduced) pension benefit or 100 percent of the amount resulting from the multiplication of years of service times the benefit per year. For most plans the normal retirement age is 65, although some plans have a normal retirement age less than 65.

Some plans provide for an unreduced benefit below age 65 based on a sufficient number of years of service. A somewhat common type of formula of this type of plan is that age and years of service equal 85. Thus, an employee 55 years of age could retire with full benefits after 30 years of service, and similarly, an employee with 25 years of service could retire at age 60 with full benefits. Such plans, except for those in public employment, seldom provide for full benefits for employees retiring below age 55.

Early Retirement Age

A very common feature of most defined benefit plans is an option for an employee to retire prior to the normal retirement age. Invariably, the benefit is reduced below that provided by the regular application of the benefit formula to account for the fact that the employee will be drawing the benefit for a longer period of time and that the plan will have those funds to invest for a shorter period of time.

The amount of the reduction is often based on the actuarial equivalent of the normal retirement benefit according to probabilities of longevity. For example, an actuarial equivalency table reflecting percentage reductions from the full retirement benefit might look like the following:

Years Prior to Normal Retirement	Percent Reductions	Amount of Early Retirement as a Percentage of Normal
1	10.1	89.9
2	19.0	81.0
3	26.8	73.2
4	33.6	66.4
5	39.7	60.3
6	45.1	54.9
7	49.9	50.1
8	54.2	45.8
9	58.0	42.0
10	61.5	38.5

Some plans, particularly negotiated plans, encourage early retirement by providing a subsidy; that is, the percentage reduction is less than a true actuarial reduction. Thus, a plan might reduce the benefit by 5 percent for each of the first three years prior to normal retirement age and 3 percent per year for each year prior thereto. Thus, an employee retiring five years prior to normal would have a 21 percent reduction (three years at 5 percent and two years at 3 percent), whereas a true actuarial reduction would be 39.7 percent, or nearly twice as much.

Of course, there is a cost to the plan and the employer for providing this subsidy, and depending on the number of employees who elect to retire early, the cost can be quite substantial.

Of course, even before applying the early retirement reduction, the employee's retirement benefit is already less than what his normal retirement benefit would have been because he has less benefit service accrued than he would if he had waited to leave employment until he reached the normal retirement age. The example in the next section will illustrate this twofold reduction.

Early Retirement versus Normal Retirement

Employees A and B are each 60 years old and each has 20 years service under a defined benefit, a plan with a normal retirement age of 65 and a benefit of 20 dollars per month per year of benefit service. The plan permits early retirement with a reduced benefit on an actuarial basis. Employee A decides to retire at age 60 whereas employee B decides to work until the normal retirement age of 65. The benefit calculations are as follows:

Employee A (Early)	Employee B (Normal)
20 years	25 years
× $20/month/year	× $20/month/year
$400/month (normal)	$500/month
× 60.3% early retirement factor	
$241.20/month	

Under these facts, the five-year difference in retirement dates results in a monthly benefit for normal retirement more than twice as great as that for early retirement. (Consider, however, that employee A will receive his monthly benefit for five years for a total of $14,472 while employee B receives nothing from the pension plan for those same five years.)

Defined Benefit Formulas

Although there are many defined benefit formulas, most negotiated pension plans have one of the following three types of benefit formulas:

(a) flat dollar amount per year of service,
(b) percentage of earnings per year of service, and
(c) Social Security integrated formula.

Flat Dollar Amount Per Year of Service

This is a very simple and eqalitarian benefit formula. The retiree receives a predetermined amount for each year of benefit service. There is no differentiation between the employee whose job pays $8 per hour and one whose job pays $20 per hour. It abandons the income replacement concept so common in pension planning in favor of equality based on years of service.

One of the advantages of this type of plan is simplicity. A simple multiplication of years of service times the flat dollar amount yields the monthly benefit.

Percentage of Earnings

In contrast to the egalitarian approach of the flat dollar formula is the percentage of earnings formula which recognizes the function of pension benefits to replace some portion of an employee's normal earnings. A common range of percentages in negotiated plans is 1¼ percent to 2 percent for each year of benefit service. Thus, a retiree with 25 years service and annual earnings of $32,000 would, under a plan with a 1½ percent benefit formula, receive an annual benefit of $12,000 or a monthly benefit of $1,000 calculated as follows:

$32,000	annual earnings
× .015	benefit
$480	benefit per year
× 25	years
$12,000	÷ 12 months = $1,000 per month.

A key differentiation among types of percentage of earnings plans is the period of time in which the earnings are received. The two most common variations are the average of annual earnings, (a) over the employee's employment career under the plan, and (b) over the employee's final five years prior to retirement. Because of the inflationary environment which has characterized the U.S. economy in the last century except for a few recessionary periods, the final five-year formula normally produces the higher (and more costly) benefit. A variation of the final ending pay formula is to select the average of the highest three out of the final five years prior to retirement. This takes into account the fact that a number of employees approaching their retirement may lose work due to illness and may have some low earning years that were not characteristic of their career pattern.

The percentage of pay formula presents the employee planning his retirement with a more difficult task of estimating his benefit compared to the flat dollar formula. This is especially true with the ending pay variations which require estimates of future earnings. Nevertheless, this disadvantage is offset, from the employee's standpoint, by the ability to receive a benefit that tracks increases in wages and earnings.

From the employer's standpoint, ending pay formulas have the disadvantage of automatically escalating pension expenses with little or no recognition by employees or the union that benefits have improved. A 1½ percent ending pay formula when wages average $12 per hour sounds the same six years later when wages average $15 per hour, even though the employer's nominal cost of providing that benefit has increased approximately 25 percent. Because the pension benefit is tied directly to wages, the cost of the benefit increases proportionately with wage increases even though the nominal benefit formula remains the same. For this reason, most unionized employers prefer flat dollar formulas.

Integrated Formulas

A type of benefit formula that was relatively popular in earlier years is the social security integrated formula. Although still in existence in a number of labor agreements, it has waned in popularity as Social Security contributions and benefits have increased. This type of plan takes into account the fact that one significant portion of postretirement income is Social Security benefits. Because the employer contributes part of the cost of such benefits, it is logical that the employer should receive some cost offset in the benefit formula.

Although there are several variations of integrated formulas, the most common negotiated formulas are the "flat percentage—stepped up" and the "unit credit—stepped up" formulas. Under both of these formulas there are two levels of benefits—1 percentage for earnings up to a stipulated amount and a higher level applicable to earnings above that amount. To illustrate, a plan might provide one percent of final earnings up to $10,000 per year and 1½ percent for earnings in excess of $10,000 per year. An employee with 25 years' service and final earnings of $30,000 would receive a benefit calculated as follows:

$10,000		$20,000	
× .01 (formula)		× .015 (formula)	
$100		$300	
× 25 years		× 25 years	
$2,500	+	$7,500	= $10,000 ÷ 12 months = $833/month

The requirements for integrated formulas established by the Internal Revenue Service are very comprehensive and complex. Pension attorneys should be consulted prior to establishing or modifying an integrated benefit formula.

Social Security Offsets

Another, and somewhat controversial, feature of pension benefit formulas also related to Social Security is that of the "offset" or reduction. Under this arrangement, an employee's pension benefit is reduced by the amount of his primary Social Security benefit (not including dependent's benefit). Stated another way, under the pension formula incorporating a Social Security offset, the retiree's pension benefit will be composed of benefits from the pension plan and from social security.

Such offsets are controversial because social security is regarded as a federal entitlement, and using it to reduce the benefit from a private pension plan may seem to be a penalty. However, the impact of the offset can only be fairly judged in relation to the benefit formula, since it is the total pension benefit that is a measure of the adequacy of a pension plan. Negotiated pension plans with social security offsets have become less and less common in recent years and are not permitted at all for plans not subject to collective bargaining.

Death and Disability Benefits

It is relatively common for negotiated plans to include special benefit provisions in the event of death or disability of a pension plan participant, and the federal government has imposed requirements for employee options for survivors' benefits in the event the employee dies either shortly before or sometime after retirement.

Disability benefits are commonly provided for total and permanent disability. One popular method of determining what extent of disability is necessary to qualify is to stipulate that the employee must meet the qualifications for receiving social security disability benefits. The level of such a benefit varies from a fixed, specified sum to the amount of projected benefits at normal retirement (with or without an actuarial reduction). Variations can be found within these two extremes.

Death benefits likewise take many forms from a lump-sum payout, sometimes funded through a group life insurance contract, to a percentage of the employee's (or retiree's) expected (actual) retirement benefit.

Joint and Survivor Provisions

One type of death benefit is the "joint and survivor" annuity. This is a method to provide income protection to the surviving spouse of an employee who dies after beginning to draw a retirement benefit. Under the common forms of joint and survivor provisions, a pension plan participant may select, upon retirement, to provide his surviving spouse with a lifetime monthly pension equal to 100, 75, or 50 percent of the employee's regular pension benefit. Under IRS rules, a participant who has been married for at least one year must elect a survivor's benefit of at least 50 percent of the employee's normal pension. The sole exception to this rule is if the spouse waives in writing a survivor's benefit.

IRS rules permit, and most negotiated plans provide, that the normal retirement benefit be reduced to pay the actuarial cost of the survivor's benefit. That cost is dependent on the cost of the normal benefit and upon the age spread between the retiring employee and the retiree's spouse. Employee "A," who has a spouse five years younger than he, will have his normal benefit reduced more (i.e., the survivor's benefit will cost more) than employee "B" whose spouse is only two years younger than he, since there is a probability of paying a survivor's benefit to employee "A's" spouse longer than employee "B's."

Preretirement Spousal Benefit

A form of survivor's benefit much like the joint and survivor provision is the preretirement spousal benefit. Under this arrangement, an employee who is vested under the plan is provided with a survivor benefit for his spouse equal to 50 percent of the employee's normal monthly benefit. The cost of this benefit may, as in the case of the joint and survivor provisions, be paid by actuarially reducing the normal pension benefit or by allowing the employee the opportunity to pay it "out of pocket" in the form of a monthly premium during the period the benefit is in effect. This benefit, too, may be avoided only by the written consensual waiver signed by the spouse.

Defined Contribution Plans

The newer and faster growing type of pension plan is the defined contribution ("DC") plan. Under this type of plan, the employer contributes a specific dollar amount per hour, per week, per month, or per year into a trust with individual employee accounts, and the contributions are invested to yield a given sum of money which translates (through an annuity or otherwise) to a monthly benefit. Under the DC plan, the employee is not assured of any specific benefit level upon retirement, but is simply assured that contributions made to the plan will be allocated to each employee's individual account and will be invested to produce an ultimate retirement benefit.

Funding of Defined Contribution Plans

The means of funding defined contribution plans typically are more varied than defined benefit plans. Whereas most negotiated defined benefit plans are funded solely by employer contributions, defined contribution plans are more likely to be funded with employee contributions only, a combination of employee and employer contributions (often the employer's contribution matching all or some portion of the employee's contribution), or employer contributions only.

Another essential funding difference between defined benefit and defined contribution plans is the means by which employer contributions are made. Under a defined contribution plan, the employer contributes a specific dollar amount, percentage of employee earnings, or percentage of profits into a trust, whereas the employer's obligations to contribute under a defined benefit plan are less specific. The cost of providing future benefits may be, and normally is, amortized over a period of time as long as 30 years. Thus, the cost of a new defined benefit plan which does not assume liabilities for previous years of service ("past service") will assume a relatively low cost burden in its initial years of existence compared to a defined contribution plan designed to produce comparable levels of retirement benefits.

401(k) Plans

A popular form of defined contribution plan is the "401(k) plan" named after the section of the IRS Code that authorizes it. Under a 401(k) plan, an employee may contribute, on a pretax basis, earnings up to a specific limit established each year by the IRS. Employers often agree to make contributions as well, usually related to the amount of the employee's contribution. Individual accounts are established for each participating employee, and investment decisions are made by the employee from among a limited number of options available under the plan. All contributions made by the employee are always fully vested, whereas the employer's contributions need only vest according to the vesting options applicable to defined benefit plans (see "Vesting"earlier in this chapter).

Withdrawals by employees while still employed are available on a very limited basis. IRS provisions allow for "hardship" withdrawals by employees who have specific types of immediate and heavy financial needs. Congress established a 10 percent tax penalty plus immediate taxability of withdrawals to discourage participants from utilizing such hardship withdrawals. Regulations permit employers to establish loan programs in their 401(k) plans to enable employees to utilize their contributions without paying the tax penalty.

Advantages and Disadvantages of Defined Contribution Plans

From an employer's and negotiator's standpoint, defined contribution plans represent a simpler and less complex method of providing retirement benefits. Once the employer has made its required contribution, it faces little or no additional financial responsibilities. There is no risk assumed by the employer in being able to achieve a given level of return on funds invested or a given level of retirement benefits as with a defined benefit plan. The employee carries the investment risk. Conversely, there is no investment reward available to the employer. If funds invested under a defined contribution plan yield a greater than expected rate of return, the employer is not able to realize the advantage of that good performance to reduce its subsequent pension contributions as it could under a defined benefit plan. Under a defined contribution plan, the employer is not required to have complex actuarial evaluations made each year or to pay per participant premiums to the Pension Benefit Guarantee Corporation ("PBGC") to insure benefit payments as it is required to do under a defined benefit plan.

Because defined contribution plans usually provide for cash-outs upon termination, they are essentially portable provided the employee is vested under the terms of the plan. To that extent, they are often favored by younger employees who see the cash buildup as a savings for purposes other than retirement. This can work to the employer's disadvantage in that the defined contribution plan provides less of an incentive for the employee to remain with that employer than does the defined benefit plan.

Perhaps the greatest advantage to an employer from a defined contribution, rather than a defined benefit, plan is the predictability of the financial impact. Because the amount or percentage of payroll needed to be contributed by the employer under a defined contribution plan can be estimated with a good deal of predictability, the employer faces less uncertainty and surprises than under a defined benefit plan. The variations in investment return, turnover, mortality, and early retirements that must be assumed by an actuary under a defined benefit plan are not required under the defined contribution plan.

Hybrid DB/DC Plans—"Target Benefit Plans"

In order to ameliorate some of the disadvantages of defined benefit and defined contribution plans, pension plan designers developed a hybrid type of plan that incorporates features of both types of plans. Employees' retirement benefits are projected ("targeted") based upon actuarial calculations using fixed employer contributions determined by IRS-required conservative investment return assumptions. Contributions are accumulated in individual employee accounts. Employees may receive pension benefits more or less than the targeted amounts, although reserves can be set aside by the employer to make up any shortfall that may result from less favorable conditions than those that were assumed.

The value of a target plan is that employees can plan on receiving a definite retirement benefit, yet have an individual account which can be taken by an employee if the employee terminates after vesting yet before retirement age. The employer has a high degree of predictability of pension costs, yet can receive the reward of greater than expected investment performance. Moreover, the employer can reduce its pension contributions by the amount of forfeitures (savings achieved by participants terminating prior to vesting) and may pay for the cost of the plan over the future working lives of the plan's participants.

The following shows the relative features of the defined benefit, defined contribution, and target plans:

Features	Defined Benefit	Defined Contrib.	Target
Set rate of employer contribution	No	Yes	No
Set rate of employee benefit	Yes	No	Yes
Employer carries investment risk	Yes	No	Yes
Portability of individual employee account	No	Yes	Yes
Forfeitures reduce employer's cost	No	Yes	Yes
PBGC premiums required	Yes	No	No
Amortize plan costs over a period of years	Yes	No	Yes

Joint-Trusteed or Taft-Hartley Trusts

Just as for health and welfare plans, there is a category of pension plans for which the sponsor is not the employer, but a combination of union-appointed and employer-appointed trustees. Because these plans are authorized by Section 301 of the National Labor Relations Act ("Taft-Hartley Act"), they are frequently referred to as "Taft-Hartley trusts."

These plans are typically a product of a multiemployer bargaining arrangement with the employer trustees representing the employers who are parties to the multiemployer contract and the union trustees selected by the union party to the contract. Characteristics of these plans are similar to target plans in that they have features common to both defined contribution and defined benefit plans.

Usually, contributions are made solely by the employers, and such contributions are typically in the form of a designated amount of cents per hour worked or paid for, or as a percentage of each eligible employee's compensation. The obligation to contribute and the specific amount of the contribution are usually set out in the labor agreement. The plan's actuary then estimates what level of benefits can be supported by the contributions, considering all relevant factors including the age and service characteristics of the group of employees covered, turnover rates, assumptions on future compensation, and work hours. A defined benefit formula is thereby developed, causing the plan to look like a defined benefit plan. To the extent that the defined benefit does not match the defined contributions, contributions and/or benefits must be adjusted to bring them into line.

The author's distinct aversion to joint-trusteed health and welfare plans, outlined in Chapter 8 above, applies to an even greater degree for pension plans. The disadvantage of the employer receiving little or no credit for providing a pension plan is as true with joint-trusteed pension plans as health and welfare plans. Likewise, the union-dominated plan administrators are likely to interpret the plan liberally, so as to increase plan costs. This can be particularly pronounced when it comes to approving disability retirements, which can be very costly.

Far and away, the biggest disadvantage, however, of the joint-trusteed plans is an employer's exposure to "withdrawal liability." This phenomenon was created by the Multiemployer Pension Plan Administration Act of 1980 ("MEPPAA") and was designed to keep multiemployer plans solvent by assessing employers who were leaving such plans a sum of money that represents a proportional share of a plan's shortfall in funding or "underfunding."

Because so many of the industries and occupations in which multiemployer bargaining are found (construction, trucking, retail trades, etc.) have fallen on bad times, the work forces have shrunk (or at least the unionized work forces are smaller) and the level of pension contributions has commensurately been reduced. Thus, the active work force for which contributions are being made becomes smaller and smaller but must, nevertheless, support a retiree group, which often is quite large. Underfunding results, creating a financial liability which, by law, must be made up at least partially by assessing a financial obligation on employers who leave the trust due to reorganization (acquisition, merger, etc.), business failure, abandonment of the multiemployer bargaining unit and its labor agreement, or decertification. Such assessments can be very costly and often hit an employer at exactly the time it is least able to afford it. This reason alone should be a sufficient deterrent to any employer from joining a multiemployer pension trust.

Pension Negotiating Strategies

Retain Management Flexibility

Consistent with recommendations regarding a number of contract subjects, management should attempt to retain a maximum of flexibility. While a union has every reason to make specific the level of pension benefits, i.e., normal, early, and disability retirement formulas, vesting schedules, eligibility and service rules, etc., there is not the same rationale for fixing the manner in which benefits are provided or administered.

What management should avoid is making contractual commitments as to how pension benefits under a defined benefit plan are to be funded. Such matters as the identity of the plan's actuary, the actuarial methods and assumptions employed, and minimum funding levels should not be made a matter of agreement or included in the labor agreement. So long as the employer carries the obligation to provide a given level of benefits, it should be the employer's prerogative to determine the manner in which they will be provided. Any concerns that funding may be inadequate are answered by ERISA's minimum funding standards. Management needs sufficient flexibility to employ different investment managers and strategies to meet its funding obligations. It is not wise to limit that flexibility in any way.

Avoid Automatic Benefit Increases

Consistent with advice given elsewhere in this book, management should generally avoid negotiating benefit levels that automatically increase with increases in compensation. Thus, defined benefit plans that provide benefits based on a percentage of pay (career earnings or some form of "ending pay") should be avoided in favor of benefits stated in specific dollar amounts. Likewise, employer contributions to defined contribution plans are best stated in specific dollar amounts rather than in terms of percentage of pay. The reason for this advice is that formulas in percentage terms automatically increase in cost as pay increases in the normal inflationary economy. As the costs and benefits increase under a percentage formula, the employer receives no recognition or bargaining trading advantage for the additional outlays. Nor are employees generally aware that their pension benefits have increased (and the employer's costs increased) when they receive a pay hike. In essence, it is a "freebie," not apparent to employees or their unions (and often overlooked by management as well). Benefits, therefore, should be dollar denominated rather than percentage denominated. The same principle holds true for cost-of-living adjustments ("COLAs") in pension benefits. These escalators can significantly drive up an employer's costs with little or no bargaining credit or employee recognition.

Beware of Assuming Increases in Past Service Liability

A common objective of unions in negotiating pension increases is to increase benefits for *all* years of service. Thus, if the current benefit level is $22 dollars per month per year of service, a union might seek to increase it to $24 or $25 per month for all years of service. The effect of such an increase would be to apply the new, higher benefit retroactively, i.e., increase "compensation" for service previously rendered. This can be rather costly where the employee work group has considerable years of service under the plan.

The wiser negotiating strategy is to negotiate improvements only for "future service," i.e., service after the signing of a new contract. To the extent feasible, "past service," i.e., service rendered prior to the signing, should be left at its previous level. Because pensions are simply one form of compensation, it is not advisable to increase the compensation for service previously rendered.

Avoid Dual Defined Benefit and Defined Contribution Obligations

As discussed above, joint union-management pension plans frequently have a defined contribution and a defined benefit. This results in the employee getting the best of both worlds. The defined benefit becomes a floor under a defined contribution plan. Sometimes employers negotiate such dual obligation plans in a single employer labor agreement. For example, the agreement may provide that the employer contribute 75¢ per hour worked and that each employee will receive a retirement benefit no less than $24 per month for each year of service. This is not wise, especially where the plan precludes the employer from recouping any contributions that are in excess of those necessary to fund the defined benefits. The plan should be *either* a defined benefit or a defined contribution plan.

Beware of Loose Disability Rules and High Disability Benefits

One aspect of pension plans that can become very costly very quickly is disability retirements. The definition of disability should be drawn rather tightly requiring that the employee be permanently disabled from performing work in any occupation reasonably available. Definitions that do not require a permanent disability or which provide benefits if an employee is merely precluded from performing his or her regular job are too broad and can become very costly. Some plans tie eligibility for disability benefits to qualification for social security disability benefits. This is a conservative approach.

In addition, disability benefits should not be so high in relation to normal retirement benefits for the length of service involved that they provide employees with an incentive to apply for disability pensions when they would not otherwise do so.

Consider Work Group Characteristics When Making Pension Benefit Comparisons

It is typical in labor negotiations for union and management representatives to compare wage and benefit levels in their own contracts with those of other employers and unions as a gauge of what is appropriate. In its most extreme form, this results in "pattern bargaining." This is discussed more fully in Chapter 1 under "Recent Comparable Settlements." When such comparisons are made in the area of pension benefit levels, caution must be the watchword. Because the age and length of service characteristics of a given work force have such a dramatic impact on pension costs, a particular level of benefits for an aging, long-service work group can be many times more costly than the same benefits for a younger, shorter-service work group. Most unions will simply demand a matching of benefits with little or no regard for the relative makeups of the respective work groups or for costs. Management representatives should not be swayed by such demands. Costs are indeed a critical factor in determining management's bargaining limits.

Do Not Be Misled by Short-Term Cost Estimates

As recommended above, it is essential that management have a pension actuary assisting in the preparations for pension negotiations. Most, if not all, pension cost estimates will be prepared by the actuary. In making these estimates, the actuary will normally provide for each benefit change an increment to the annual cost for each modification. The cost of benefits incurred in the current year is called the "normal cost." Additionally, a cost for previous years' service ("past service") must be paid and can be amortized over a long period of time, typically 30 years.

When a significant pension improvement is being considered, the estimated cost impact on the normal cost does not usually seem great. This is because the additional cost is amortized over such a long period of time. This is terribly misleading, because the employer's pension plan actually assumes a much greater financial liability than would be reflected in the normal cost impact. Another way to view pension costs is on a "plan termination basis," i.e., the liability for which the employer is responsible if the plan were to be terminated and annuities purchased to provide all vested benefits. While the employer may be financially sound with no termination of its business or its pension plan being contemplated, the plan termination cost basis provides a more realistic view of the true financial liability of a given pension change than does the normal cost calculation. For cost estimating purposes as outlined in Chapter 10, the author recommends the normal cost approach, but suggests that management also know and weigh the actual total cost impact as reflected in the plan termination cost calculation.

10

Costing Contract Demands, Offers, and Settlements

The meat and potatoes of any labor contract negotiations is the "money package." Probably 90 percent of labor negotiations succeed or fail on the basis of the parties' ability, or lack thereof, to reach agreement on the monetary aspects of their negotiation. An absolutely necessary ingredient in this process is cost estimating. It is difficult in a volume such as this to attempt to describe all possible methods of costing a labor contract settlement.[1] However, a number of basic techniques used by most labor negotiators are described in this chapter.

The Negotiator as a Cost Estimator

Because labor cost estimating is similar to other types of cost estimating, it is often assumed that the responsibility for it should be given to an accountant, controller, or someone else regularly involved in cost estimating such as a cost analyst or economist. Such an assignment is usually advisable, especially where the nature and amount of changes may necessitate complex and numerous calculations. Even if such a specialist is assigned the cost estimating task, however, it is vital for management's negotiator to have knowledge of the employer's labor costs and ability to compute cost changes.

No matter how skillful and accessible the cost estimating specialist assigned to the bargaining, the negotiator must be able to understand, and make, cost computations in order to fully carry out the job. In the give and take of bargaining, package offers must be juggled, compromises carved out from differing economic positions, and new approaches fashioned from previous proposals and counterproposals. The negotiator must have the numbers fully in command to be able to see potential solutions or make the kind of bargaining adjustments from which a settlement can emerge.

Another reason the negotiator needs to be a cost estimator is to be able to confirm the accuracy of the specialists' estimates. It is quite common for a cost specialist to misunderstand the application of a labor contract change and miscalculate the cost impact. Gross errors may be evident to all, but less obvious (yet still serious) miscalculations may go undetected unless the negotiator or someone on his committee checks the calculations to see that the estimates are reasonable. Having a working knowledge of cost calculations will also assist the negotiator in explaining to union representatives why a particular demand cannot be met.

As can be seen, the negotiator who shies away from the task of cost estimating will be placed at a great disadvantage. A prudent management spokesperson must assume that his or her counterpart on the other side of the bargaining table will be in command of the relevant cost information.

Use of Specialists

The fact that the negotiator needs to be fully involved in cost estimating does not mean that others who can be of assistance should be excluded. As suggested earlier, accountants, controllers, cost analysts, and the like can be very helpful in carrying out the detailed and "official" cost estimates upon which top management may rely. In addition, where pensions, medical insurance, and other benefits involving specialized data are being negotiated, actuaries, insurance brokers, consultants, or other specialists will be necessary. Likewise, if wage incentives, productivity bonuses, or other complicated pay plans are involved, industrial engineers or other specialists may be necessary. The negotiator will need the data and expertise they can provide, and at the same time should become educated as to how the results were obtained and how variations therefrom will be costed.

Use of Computers

Computers have become an essential tool for cost estimating purposes during labor contract negotiations. Computers can be especially helpful in doing the routine calculations and developing a complete cost estimate of a package proposal in a very short time. But just as the hand-held calculator eliminates the need for mental numerical calculations, the computer obviates the need for mental gymnastics which can often help the negotiator to see a solution or tradeoff that might not occur to him or her if the calculations are done by computer. This is not said to discourage the use of computers in labor contract costing, but merely to alert the negotiator not to rely unduly on computers any more than he or she should place full and unmonitored responsibility for cost estimating on specialists.

Maintaining security of bargaining information and cost estimates is always an absolute necessity in labor contract negotiations. Use of computers heightens the level of concern since vital data is within the computer's memory, and perhaps subject to unauthorized disclosure. Furthermore, there is a tendency of computer operators to generate multiple copies of printouts. As a result, crucial information can inadvertently fall into the union's hands. Special precautions should be taken to assure the security of management's cost information and cost estimates.

The Necessity of Cost Estimates

Cost estimating necessarily begins long before negotiations commence, continues throughout the bargaining process, and can be completed only after a final settlement is reached. Prior to negotiations, a large volume of data and information must be assembled (see Chapter 2 and Exhibits 2–1 through 2–3, as well as Appendixes 1 and 2). When economic parameters are being established and company proposals are being prepared, accurate cost estimates are essential. As soon as the union's demands are received, key proposals should be costed in detail, with rough estimates of the total initial package submitted by the union. Of course, each package offer made by the employer and each counteroffer by the union must be fully costed, and the cost of the final settlement must likewise be carefully estimated.

Occasionally in the heat of the battle, and particularly where a strike or settlement is hanging in the balance, a negotiator is tempted to settle an issue which has cost implications but for which no cost estimate has been made. This is to be avoided at all costs. A strict negotiating policy should be: *No offers or concessions are to be made without a careful cost estimate having previously been made.*

It is usually not difficult to determine when a wage or benefit change will have an impact upon costs. Continuation of a cost-of-living provision, a change in eligibility for medical insurance, or a liberalization of vacation benefits will obviously have a cost impact. Changes in such "nonmonetary" matters as seniority rules, work scheduling procedures, or leaves for union business may not appear on the surface to have any impact on labor costs. On closer reflection, however, changes in these contract provisions may very well have a cost impact—and in some cases the effect may be very significant. It is important, therefore, to carefully examine each union proposal, whether considered to be monetary or not, and to ask the question "could it have any measurable effect upon our labor costs, efficiencies, or profits?"

Even though cost estimates of certain changes may be extremely difficult to make and the results are likely to be speculative, estimates should be made. Frequently, assumptions can be made where actual data is not available or difficult to obtain. In any event, management needs a cost estimate of any and all contract changes that can have an impact on the cost of the employer's operations.

"New Money"

"New money" is a term used by labor negotiators to describe a newly negotiated wage or benefit improvement that has a cost impact. It is distinguished from previously negotiated wage or benefit provisions that continue to have a cost impact. For example, if management agrees to pay its employees 5 percent more than wages in effect under the previous contract, the 5 percent represents "new money." The wages paid under the previous contract are considered "old money." Also, the concept of new money means that an employer will only "take credit" for the additional wage or fringe benefit *for the first year* the new wage or benefit is in effect. Although the 5 percent wage increase in the first year of a three-year contract is paid each year, it is normally only counted for labor negotiations purposes in the first year of the contract.

The same concept applies to benefits. If, for example, a vacation benefit of 4 weeks after 15 years of service was negotiated several years prior to the contract negotiations at hand, but had no previous cost impact because there were no employees with 15 years of service, the fact that a number of employees might progress to 15 years of service during the term of the contract at hand would not cause the cost of the benefit to be classified as a contract improvement. It is not "new money." A union will argue vehemently against an employer's taking credit for the "4 for 15" vacation benefit in the current negotiations since it was agreed to in previous bargaining. However, if a vacation benefit is improved in the current negotiations to 4 weeks after 12 years of service, the cost effect of reducing the service requirement for the fourth week of vacation by three years would be new money, provided there are some employees who will earn additional vacation at the 12-year level who would not have at the 15-year level.

Applying the New Money Concept

The general costing rule is that if management negotiates any improvement in wages or benefits which has a cost impact during the term of the contract being negotiated, or agrees to continue a wage or benefit provision which will have a higher cost under the new contract than under the prior contract, that impact should be estimated and included as part of management's settlement package cost estimate. In the previous example concerning vacations, there is dubious validity in management's including in its package cost estimates the added labor costs resulting from employees attaining 15 years of service, since that cost is not the result of an agreement reached in the current negotiations. However, some employers do include such costs, and it is difficult to argue that the employer's costs have not increased because of its willingness *to continue* with the vacation schedule.

There are other areas where the new money distinction is particularly significant. For example, if a noncontributory medical insurance plan was previously negotiated, but its premiums are expected to increase during the term of the current contract, the added costs to the employer should clearly be included in the cost estimate. If the employer agrees to maintain the existing level of benefits and also agrees to continue paying the full cost or the same percentage of the premiums, any increased costs represent an additional burden, and one which should be taken into account in cost estimating.

Management's Needs Must Prevail

In making cost estimates, management should not be misled by any union characterizations of old money versus new money or taking credit versus not taking credit. Notwithstanding anything discussed earlier, if the agreement will result in higher labor costs than the previous agreement, those costs should be "charged to the package," i.e., included in the cost estimate prepared by management. Because the cost estimates are for management's own bargaining strategy and planning, there is no need for union concurrence with the way in which the estimates are prepared.

The "Rollup" Concept

What "Rollup" Means

Fundamental to any discussion of labor contract costing is an understanding of the concept of "rollup." Other terms used to describe the same concept are "impact," "multiplying fringes," "burden," "loading," "creep," or "add-on." Simply stated, rollup is the cost effect upon certain benefits caused automatically by a negotiated change in wages or salaries. Because certain benefits such as pay for overtime, holidays, vacations, and "call-backs" are normally established in terms of the hourly wage rate, an increase in the hourly wage rate will automatically result in an increase in the respective benefit costs. The "rollup factor" is obtained by adding up the cost of all benefits subject to the rollup effect and dividing by the total cost of straight-time wages, as illustrated by the following:

Benefits subject to rollup	Average hourly costs prior to negotiations
Overtime	$0.90
Holidays	1.00
Vacations	1.30
Reporting pay	0.05
Call-in pay	0.12
Sick pay	0.23
Total cost	$3.60
Straight-time wages (prior to negotiations)	$12.00
Rollup factor ($3.60 ÷ $12.00)	30%

Applying the Concept

Once the rollup factor is determined for a particular negotiation, the same factor will be used for all cost estimates throughout the negotiations.[2] The rollup cost effect of a wage increase is obtained by multiplying the amount of a negotiated wage increase by the rollup factor. The result is the additional cost of the rollup benefits which automatically results from a wage increase. A simple example of how the rollup factor is applied can be shown as follows:

Average negotiated wage increase	60¢/hour
Rollup factor	30%
Rollup cost ($0.60 × .30)	18¢/hour

Thus, a 60 cent per-hour wage increase results in an automatic additional cost of benefits of 18 cents per hour and a total increase in labor costs of 78 cents per hour (60 cents + 18 cents). Note that in this example there were no negotiated improvements other than the wage increase, and yet benefits characterized as "rollup benefits" increased by 18 cents per hour, or 5 percent ($0.18 ÷ $3.60). The percentage increase in those rollup benefits (5 percent) is, of course, the same as that for the wage increase ($0.60 ÷ $12.00 = 5%).

Which Benefits Roll Up

The particular benefits which roll up with an increase in wages will vary from one labor contract to the next, although the following are generally considered as the principal rollup benefits:

- Overtime pay (generally over 8 hours per day and 40 hours per week)
- Premium pay for work on weekends and holidays
- Holiday pay (pay for unworked holiday)
- Vacation pay
- Reporting or "show-up" pay
- Call or "call-back" pay
- Sick leave pay
- Funeral leave pay
- Jury duty pay
- Employer's Social Security payments*
- Premium pay for shift work*
- Life insurance*
- Pensions*
- Payments to state unemployment compensation funds*

The benefits marked with an asterisk are not always rollup benefits, or at least not to the same degree as are the other benefits in the list. Their classification as such is subject to the conditions under which the payments are made, this classification varying depending on the labor agreement, state law, and form of benefit involved. For example, if premium pay for night shift work is, prior to the negotiations, paid in a stated cents-per-hour amount, for the sake of discussion 25 cents per hour, an increase in general wage rates will not automatically have an impact on the cost of shift work premiums since shift premium pay is not calculated in terms of wage rates. If, however, the formula for shift premium pay is based upon the wage rate, for example 2 percent of the base rate in the bargaining unit, then it will automatically roll up with an increase in the base rate of pay.

The same concept applies to pensions. If the basic pension benefit is a flat rate for each year of service, for example, $20 per month per year of benefit service, then a change in wage rates will not automatically change pension costs. On the other hand, if the formula for paying pensions is based on a percentage of each employee's earnings during a predetermined period, for example 1.5 percent of the retiring employee's average earnings for the five years prior to retirement, then a change in general wages will have an automatic impact on pension costs.

Social Security (FICA) payments are also a rollup benefit to the extent that a general wage increase will increase the employer's contribution for those employees who earn less than the cutoff maximum contribution amount.

In determining whether any fringe benefit is a rollup benefit, one merely asks the question, "Will the cost of this benefit increase automatically if there is an increase in the general level of wages?" If the answer is yes, the benefit is a rollup benefit and should be included in the list of benefits for calculating the rollup factor.

The Useful But Deceptive Cents-Per-Hour Measurement

The Virtue of Simplicity

Virtually all management labor negotiators (and union negotiators, too, for that matter) talk, think, and negotiate in terms of cents per hour. The reasons for this are simplicity of calculations, comparability among bargaining units of different sizes, and inability to accurately predict future bargaining unit work hours and, therefore, the total dollar cost impact. But whatever the reasons, it is clear that the cents-per-hour measurement is the focal point in most labor cost estimating. Some exceptions to this general rule exist where labor costs are more closely related to weekly, monthly, or annual payments in the case of salaried and professional employees. In terms of the universe of all labor contract negotiations, however, these exceptions represent a small proportion.

The application of the cents-per-hour measurement is most easily seen in terms of an across-the-board general wage increase. A 60-cent-per-hour general wage increase applicable to all employees will, except for the rollup effect, cost the employer 60 cents per hour. If there are 300 employees in the bargaining unit and each employee works an average of 2,000 hours per year, the total annual cost of the 60-cent-per-hour wage increase, without rollup, will be $360,000 (300 employees × 2,000 hours per year per employee × $0.60 per hour).

Using the same basic numbers, the cents-per-hour cost of an additional holiday can be calculated. Based upon an average wage of $12.00 per hour, if each paid holiday is equivalent to eight hours per day, the cost of one additional holiday will be

\$96 per employee per year (\$12.00/hour × 8 hours) or 4.8 cents per hour (\$96.00 ÷ 2,000 hours).

The Dangers of Simplicity

While the cents-per-hour measurement is convenient and well understood on both sides of the bargaining table, the management negotiator must never lose sight of the magnitude of dollars being handled. A concession of 1 cent per hour may not seem like a great deal, particularly in the heat of the negotiating battle, but with a bargaining unit of 300 employees the 1 cent will cost the employer \$6,000 each year (300 employees × 2000 hours per year per employee × \$0.01 per hour). If the concession is in wages and there is a rollup factor of 30 percent, the total annual cost of the 1-cent concession will be \$7,800 (\$6,000 × 1.30).

A Handy Shortcut

It is useful for the negotiator, at the outset of negotiations, to make the simple cost calculation of the value of an increase of 1 cent per hour. By multiplying annual bargaining unit work hours times \$0.01, and rounding that answer, the negotiator will have a handy reference point to avoid losing sight of the magnitude of what is at stake. Thus, if there are approximately 800 employees in the bargaining unit and an average of 2,000 straight-time hours per employee, the annual work hours will be 1,600,000 and the cost for each 1-cent increase will be \$16,000. The annual dollar cost of a 1-cent increase in wages, including rollup, should also be calculated. Using the same data as in the examples above, a 1-cent-per-hour wage increase will cost the employer \$20,800 each year (1,600,000 hours × \$0.01 + 30%).

Cents Per Hour and New Money

The cents-per-hour unit of measure is additionally deceptive when combined with the new money concept. Because the new money concept considers wage and benefit increases only in the first year in which they go into effect, the total cost impact is not usually appreciated. Thus, it may be announced that an agreement has been reached which provides for a "\$3.50-per-hour package over three years." The new money is broken down (wage and benefits are combined) as follows:

1st year	$1.75
2nd year	1.00
3rd year	0.75
Total package	$3.50

If one remembers, however, that the costs incurred in the first year will continue to be paid in the second and third years of the contract and that the second-year costs will also be paid in the third year, the $3.50 package looks like this:

1st year ($1.75 × 3 years)	$5.25
2nd year ($1.00 × 2 years)	$2.00
3rd year ($0.75 × 1 year)	$0.75
Total cash outflow package cost	$8.00

Thus, on closer examination, the $3.50-per-hour three-year package actually costs the employer $8.00 per hour in terms of cash out of pocket (or cash outflow). In a bargaining unit composed of 800 employees who each work an average of 2,000 hours per year, the three-year cost of what was called a "$3.50 package" will be $12,800,000 ($8.00 per hour × 2,000 hours per year × 800 employees). When a $3.50-per-hour settlement package actually costs an employer over $12 million, it is easy to see how deceptive the cents-per-hour measure can be. The process of calculating the total cash outflow as a result of a multiyear settlement is discussed at greater length later in this chapter.

Ascertaining Key Costing Variables

To be able to make relatively quick cost calculations throughout the bargaining process, the management negotiator needs to know at least the following five key variables:

1. Total number of employees in bargaining unit.
2. Total bargaining unit work hours per year.
3. Average straight time hourly earnings ("ASTHE").
4. Rollup factor.
5. Average hourly labor cost ("AHLC").

These variables can be ascertained by having someone complete the Labor Cost Recap form. A blank form, including instructions on the reverse side, is shown as Appendix 2, and a sample form with the front side completed appears in this chapter as Exhibit 10–1. The key variables are highlighted and footnoted with numbers corresponding to the list above. Once

Exhibit 10–1. Labor Cost Recap Form

Location Centerville, OH Prepared by N. Oliver

Union Involved Widget Workers Date 6/15/19--

LABOR COST RECAP
(INSTRUCTIONS ON REVERSE SIDE)

A. Reference Period From 8/1/19-- To 5/31/19--

B. Total Employees in Bargaining Unit 350[1]

C. Total manhours worked 664,211 (12 mos.)

D. Total manhours used for estimating 665,000[2]

E. ROLLUP Fringe Factor 30 %*

Cost Categories	Total Annual Cost	Cost per Manhour	% of Straight Time Wages	% of Total Labor Cost
(1) Straight Time Wages Paid	$7,970,532	$12.00[3]	1.00	.70
(2) ROLLUP Fringes				
(3) Overtime Premium	232,473	.35	.30	.002
(4) Sunday Premium	66,500	.10	.01	.006
(5) Holiday Premium	13,279	.02	.002	.001
(6) Vacation Pay	418,453	.63	.05	.04
(7) Holiday Pay	332,105	.50	.04	.03
(8) Reporting Pay	12,932	.02	.002	.001
(9) Call Time	19,925	.03	.003	.002
(10) Funeral Leave	6,640	.01	.001	.001
(11) Jury Duty	5,970	.01	.001	.001
(12) Other paid leaves (specify)	15,032	.02	.002	.001
(13) Retirement Plan	471,532	.71	.06	.04
(14) FICA (ROLLUP Portion)	797,132	1.20	.10	.07
Subtotal ROLLUP Fringes	2,391,973	3.60	.30[4]	.21
NON-ROLLUP FRINGES				
(15) Night Shift Differential	39,853	.06	.005	.003
(16) Meal Allowances	12,500	.02	.002	.001
(17) Group Insurance	697,422	1.05	.09	.06
(18) Worker's Compensation	119,580	.18	.02	.01
(19) Unemployment Compensation	46,450	.07	.01	.004
(20) Other uniforms (specify)	14,020	.02	.002	.001
(21) FICA (Non-ROLLUP Portion)	—	—	—	—
Subtotal Non-ROLLUP Fringes	929,955	1.40	.12	.08
TOTAL FRINGE BENEFIT COST	3,321,928	5.00	.42	.29
TOTAL LABOR COST	$11,292,460	$17.00[5]		1.00

the key variable numbers have been identified, future cost calculations will be relatively simple.

Calculating Specific Contract Changes

General Wages

Calculating the cost of general wage increases is usually quite simple unless the formula under which employees in the bargaining unit are compensated itself is somewhat convoluted. A simple percentage wage increase applicable to all employees will normally be calculated as follows:

Average straight time hourly earnings	$12.00/hour
Wage increase	× 5%
Cost/hour	$ 0.60
Rollup factor	× 30%
Rollup cost/hour	$ 0.18
Total cost/hour of 5% wage increase (cost/hour + rollup cost/hour)	$ 0.78

Bracket or Wage Category Increases

Where neither a cents-per-hour across-the-board increase nor a percentage increase suits the parties' needs, intermediate formulas are sometimes developed. Typically these types of increases provide for stated cents-per-hour increases according to ranges of wages or salaries. An example of such an arrangement would be as follows:

Straight time hourly rate	Wage increase	Straight time hourly rate	Wage increase
$ 8.50 or less	$0.43	$11.51–12.00	$0.60
8.51– 9.00	0.45	12.01–12.50	0.625
9.01– 9.50	0.475	12.51–13.00	0.650
9.51–10.00	0.50	13.01–13.50	0.675
10.01–10.50	0.525	13.51–14.00	0.70
10.51–11.00	0.55	14.01 or more	0.725
11.01–11.50	0.575		

In effect, these types of pay formulas are percentage increases, but the interval increases are not perfectly proportionate. For example, in the illustration, an employee earning $9.52 per hour would receive a 5.25 percent increase ($0.50 ÷ $9.52) whereas an employee earning $10.00 per hour would receive only a 5 percent increase ($0.50 ÷ $10.00). However, the amount of difference is not great, and diminishes as the number of brackets or pay categories increase and the spread between brackets is reduced.

Computing the cost of this type of increase requires a table showing the number of employees in each bracket or pay category. This information can be obtained from data compiled in a format such as that shown in Chapter 2 under Exhibit 2–2. After that it is simply a matter of multiplying the amount of the wage increase for each category by the employee population in each respective category, adding the resulting totals, and dividing that amount by the total number of employees in all pay categories.

Special Job Adjustments

If the parties agree to grant special wage increases to certain job categories—for example, to skilled trades or to correct wage rate inequities—the amount set aside for such adjustments must be independently calculated. The calculation for a 15-cent-per-hour wage increase for skilled trades would be calculated as follows:

Base Data	
Number of skilled trades people	80
Average number of hours/year worked (skilled trades)	2,000
Amount of special adjustment/hour	$0.15
Total bargaining unit hours worked	600,000
Rollup factor	30%

Calculation

80 employees × 2,000 hours/employee/year × $0.15
= $24,000/year ÷ 600,000 hours/year
= $0.04 × 1.3 (rollup) = $0.052/hour

Thus a 15-cent-per-hour adjustment for skilled trades employees would cost the employer a total of 5.2 cents per hour worked.

Cost-of-Living Adjustments

A cost-of-living adjustment (COLA) clause typically provides for adjustments in wages related to changes in the Consumer Price Index (CPI) issued by the Bureau of Labor Statistics of the U.S. Department of Labor. The most common clauses provide for quarterly adjustments based on a formula consisting of a stated number of cents per hour for each stated change in the points of the index.

For example, a typical clause will provide for a 1-cent-per-hour change for each increase of 0.3 in the CPI over a given base index number.

Computing the cost impact of a COLA clause is relatively simple; it is the necessity for making assumptions about the future movements of the CPI which complicates the process. Obviously no one can predict with great accuracy what changes will occur in the CPI in a given year, nor, certainly, within the span of a two- or three-year contract period.

Employers tend to make estimates concerning the future movement of the CPI on one of two bases. The first is a worst case assumption, i.e., that the CPI will increase to the maximum allowed by the negotiated formula. The other is a "most likely case" assumption, i.e., that the CPI will change according to the employer's best estimate of future economic conditions.[3] Some COLA clauses contain a maximum payment or "cap" that precludes any increases above a stated amount. These caps will put a limit on the worst case assumptions and can also have an effect on assumptions made under the most likely case approach. Where a COLA clause does not have a cap, the employer must adopt a totally predictive approach without any limit to act as a guide.

If the CPI is at 137 on the last day of the old contract and the employer assumes that the cost of living will increase at the rate of 6 percent per year in even increments throughout the year, a formula of a 1-cent-per-hour increase per 0.3 CPI increase will result in the following calculation shown for a one-year contract:

CPI (estimated end of contract year)*	145	
CPI (start of contract year)*	137	
Difference (6% increase)		8 index points
Quarterly increase		2 index points
Quarterly cost (2 ÷ 0.3 × $.01)		6.6¢
1st quarter	6.6¢	
2nd quarter	6.6¢	
3rd quarter	6.6¢	
4th quarter	6.6¢	
Total increase per hour	26.4¢	

*BLS/CPI Index 1982–84 = 100

The simple arithmetic used to obtain the sum of 26.4 cents per hour is somewhat misleading in that the increases take effect on a staggered basis and the 26-cent-per-hour cost is not in effect for the entire year. For evaluating COLA increases, the "time-weighted" computation discussed later in this chapter is much preferable to the simple unweighted model. Nevertheless, at the end of the contract year average wages will have increased by 26.4 cents per hour as a result of a COLA clause.

Vacation Benefit Improvements

The most common type of vacation improvement that requires costing is additional time off with pay for employees having varying lengths of service with the employer. For example, the parties may agree that under the new contract employees with more than 10 years but less than 15 years of service will receive four weeks of paid vacation rather than three, which was the former vacation benefit for such employees. This agreement would be commonly phrased as "4 for 10" instead of "3 for 10." The basic data necessary is the number of employees who have between 10 and 15 years of qualifying service. This number is then multiplied by the number of hours to be paid per week of vacation. For example, if there are 80 employees with more than 10 but less than 15 years service, and vacation is paid at 40 hours per week times the average hourly wage rate of $12.00, and annual hours worked are 665,000, the computation is as follows:

80 employees × 40 hours/week × $12.00/hour
= $38,400 ÷ 665,000 hours = $0.0577 or 5.77¢/hour

This cost calculation assumes that the only additional cost is that of the employees who are off work and being paid and that there is no additional cost to replace them.

Costing for Multiyear Contracts

If the contract is a multiyear one, employees who would move into and out of the 10- to 15-year service bracket must be taken into account in determining the costs for all years of the contract. If the additional week of vacation for employees with 10 to 15 years of service is effective in the first year of the contract and there is a net increase in the number of new employees with that length of service of 10 employees in the second year and 10 in the third year, the additional cost each year will be as follows:

$$10 \text{ employees} \times 40 \text{ hours/week} \times \$12.00\text{/hour}$$
$$= \$4{,}800 \div 665{,}000 = \$0.0072 \text{ or } 0.72¢\text{/hour}$$

It is likely that wage increases will also have been negotiated for the second and third years of the contract, and therefore, the $12-per-hour average wage rate should be adjusted accordingly to yield an accurate result as described in the next paragraph.

Costing Concurrent Vacation and Wage Increases

Another minor facet of the vacation improvement cost calculation should be kept in mind. The rollup factor will take into account the effect of a wage increase on existing vacation benefits. If, however, vacations are improved in the negotiations while wages are also being increased, the rollup factor will not reflect the added cost of a wage increase as it effects the new, improved vacation benefit. Using the earlier example, if an additional week of vacation is given to employees with 10 to 15 years of service and a wage increase of 5 percent is given at the same time, an accurate estimate of the vacation improvement should include a calculation that takes into account the 5 percent wage increase. Thus, using the example in the previous calculation, the true cost is actually 6.06 cents (5.77 cents × 1.05). Again, the reason for this is that when the rollup factor was originally calculated, vacation benefit costs were lower because employees with 10 to 15 years of service received only three weeks of vacation.

If one applies the "old" rollup factor of 30 percent of the wage increase(s) negotiated into the new contract (i.e., 5 percent), the resulting amount will not automatically take into account the cost effect of the 5 percent wage increase on the new vacation benefits, and thus it must be calculated separately. This is also true of any other improvements in rollup benefits during the term of the new contract.

The cost estimator need not be overly concerned about absolute precision in estimating vacation and other elements of a cost package. The cost estimator should keep in mind that these are merely estimates and based on a number of assumptions about the size of the work force, number of hours worked and other significant variables. It will be impossible to use all correct assumptions, and therefore a significant margin of error must be presumed. Consistency is usually more important than absolute precision.

Holiday Benefit Improvements

The most common type of holiday improvement is the addition of one or more paid holidays. Assuming for the moment that all holidays are unworked, and the only additional cost of an extra holiday is the cost of the employee's wages for the unworked holiday, the calculation can be done in either of the two following ways:

8 hours × $12.00/hour × 350 employees
= $33,600/year ÷ 665,000
= $0.0505 or 5.05¢/hour

or

8 hours × $12.00/hour
= $96 ÷ 1900 hours/employee
= $0.505 or 5.05¢/hour

The only difference between these two calculations is that the first computation uses the work hours for the entire bargaining unit whereas the second is calculated on a per-employee basis using an annual average of 1,900 work hours per employee (665,000 total hours ÷ 350 employees). A third and somewhat simpler way to calculate the cost of an additional holiday is to examine the hourly cost of existing holidays on the Labor Cost Recap form (Exhibit 10–1) shown earlier in this chapter. One divides the hourly cost for all holidays by the number of existing holidays; the result will be the cost for each additional holiday.

To the extent that a wage increase is negotiated at the same time as a holiday improvement, the cost impact of the wage increase on the new holiday must be computed as discussed in the example of the vacation improvement.

Other Paid Leaves

Vacation and holiday benefits are generally the most costly types of paid time off from work, but there are other types of paid leave which can present costing difficulties. These include paid leave for sickness or attendance at a relative's funeral, paid lunches, paid work breaks, absences for union business or jury duty, and other types of excused absences for which pay is often negotiated. The difficulty lies not in the preparation of computations, but in ascertaining or estimating the frequency of usage of such benefits. Where historical data is not available, it is common to use the "worst case" assumption in calculating the cost of sick leave improvements. For other types of leave, best guesstimates are about all one can rely upon. In the case of a brand new benefit with which the employer has had no experience, other employers might be consulted to obtain some estimates as to what usage frequencies may be expected.

Indirect Costs of Paid Leaves

When an employee is off work and receiving pay, the cost of such pay is rather obvious and easily calculable. This is the direct cost of paid leave. Frequently there are indirect costs associated with paid leave, and also with unpaid leave. If employees who are off work must be replaced, and such work is performed by employees hired especially for such replacement, or by regular employees working at overtime rates of pay or receiving other premium payments, then additional "indirect costs" must be calculated. For example, if granting a fourth week of vacation to employees with 10 rather than 15 years of service will result in 80 additional weeks of vacation each year, and if it is estimated that replacements will be required for 75 percent of those vacation absences, then there will be a need to find replacements for 60 weeks of additional time. This is somewhat more than one employee-year, and may necessitate the hiring of at least one additional full-time employee. The work hours of the newly hired employee should not be included, since the work hours would be paid for regardless of who performs the work. However, the costs associated with hiring, training, and carrying another employee on the payroll are legitimate additional costs to consider.

In addition to these costs will be the fringe benefit costs of the newly hired employee, which normally would not be incurred if the vacation improvement was not granted and the work was performed by employees already on the payroll and already drawing fringe benefits.[4] In a bargaining unit with an average hourly wage rate of $12 per hour, it would not be uncommon for the annual fringe benefit costs of a newly hired employee to be in the neighborhood of $6,000 to $8,000 per year.

Some employers might elect not to hire an additional employee to cover the extra 60 weeks of vacation, but to cover it with existing employees, all or most of whom would be working overtime. If it is assumed that 90 percent of the 60 weeks of vacation relief work would require overtime pay, the cost calculation would be as follows:

Weeks of vacation relief	(60 weeks × 90%)	= 54 weeks
Hours of premium pay	(54 weeks × 40 hours/week)	= 2,160 hours
Cost of premium pay	($12.00/hour × 50%)	= $6.00/hour
Cost of vacation relief	($6.00/hour × 2,160 hours)	= $12,960

These estimates do not take into account the possible loss of work productivity or quality due to the replacement of experienced employees by newly hired employees or by regular employees who may be less skilled at the work they are performing as replacements for the vacationing employees. Such estimates are appropriate, although frequently speculative. Unless the loss of output per unit of work or the deterioration of quality as the result of replacing a vacationing employee is rather clear and ascertainable, it is suggested that estimating these indirect costs be avoided.

Estimating Costs of Premium Payments

Improvements in premium payments such as shift work differentials, call-in pay, holiday or Sunday premium pay, and reporting pay require knowledge of the frequency of occurrence of such work. This data will be available from the Labor Cost Recap form (see Exhibit 10–1 above) if hours associated with these benefits are stated on the form or are kept on backup worksheets. For example, if the differential for work on each of the swing and graveyard shifts is to be increased by 5 cents per hour per shift, the calculation would be as follows:

Swing shift hours	200,000	
	× $0.05/hour	
	$10,000	$10,000
Graveyard shift hours	133,000	
	× $0.05/hour	
	$6,650	$ 6,650
Total cost		$16,650 ÷ 665,000 hours
Cost per hour		$0.025 or 2.5¢/hour

The cost estimator should be careful to check historical frequencies for reasonableness as to future cost estimates. If, for example, the amount of work estimated to be performed on the swing shift and graveyard shift during the term of the current contract is expected to drop considerably due to a slowdown in business, then the hours of work for these shifts should be reduced to an amount which represents a best estimate of what the actual hours will be.

Noneconomic Provisions

As suggested in earlier chapters, there are few provisions in a labor contract which do not have some cost impact. Nevertheless, it is common for negotiators to segregate economic or monetary contract provisions from noneconomic or "language" provisions. While such a division is useful for determining the order of bargaining, it can be seriously misleading to the extent that the cost impact of "noneconomic" provisions are not taken into account. Certain changes in work scheduling procedures, applications of seniority rules, or limitations on the subcontracting or "outsourcing" of work can have very significant impacts on the employer's labor costs or other costs of doing business. To the extent possible, all contractual changes that have an ascertainable cost impact should be included in the settlement package cost estimates.

Some management negotiators resist inclusion of these noneconomic concessions as part of the cost package, perhaps because of a concern that their negotiating efforts will thereby be considered less successful. Such personal concerns, however, have no place in a professional environment. Moreover, the negotiator with such a reluctance should keep in mind that estimating the cost of work practice changes is a two-edged sword and that any success achieved in obtaining union concessions on noneconomic items will correspondingly be deducted from the total package cost estimate.

Cost Impact Beyond the Bargaining Unit

Although not strictly a part of the ordinary cost package, many employers take into account the cost impact of a given labor cost settlement on employee groups that are not part of the bargaining unit to which the negotiation applies, but whose wages and/or benefits are related or closely tied to those paid to bargaining unit employees. This is sometimes referred to as "spillover" or "indirect impact." The types of employee groups whose wages and benefits are related to bargaining unit employees include salaried employees who work in the same facility as bargaining unit employees, supervisors of bargaining unit employees, and nonunion employees in facilities comparable to those in which bargaining unit employees work. If the employer recognizes at the time of labor contract negotiations that whatever it negotiates with the union, it will undoubtedly grant, in equal or greater measure, to related employee groups, then it is only prudent to include the impact of such increases in overall cost estimates.

To simplify this process, it may be feasible to develop, at least with respect to wage changes, a factor which will reflect the relative impact on the nonbargaining unit groups. For example, if the entire nonbargained work group directly effected by the negotiation is one fourth the size of the bargaining unit, any estimated costs of contract improvements can be multiplied by 1.25 to arrive at a rough estimate of the total cost impact of a given offer or settlement.

Costing the Total Package

A Useful Format

After cost estimates for each of the individual items in a package offer or settlement have been calculated, they need to be accumulated into one overall cost statement. In the course of a typical negotiation, dozens of such package cost estimates will be prepared. While the particular format chosen is not critical, it is important that the same format be used throughout the entire negotiations. The format the author has found most useful is shown by applying it to a hypothetical settlement as shown in Exhibit 10–2.

A number of specific points about this format should be noted. First, except for the last line shown as "cash outflow," the estimate reflects the cost of an additional wage or benefit only in the year in which it was granted. As discussed earlier, this format covers only "new money," i.e., wages or benefits not

Exhibit 10–2. Settlement Summary and Package Cost Estimate

Summary of Offer/Settlement—3 years

Wages: 1st year, 60¢; 2nd year, 6%; 3rd year, 70¢
Shift Differential: 1st & 3rd years, additional 5¢ per hr. each shift
Holidays: 2nd year, one additional holiday
Vacations: 1st year, increase from 4 for 15 to 4 for 10
1st year, increase from 5 for 30 to 5 for 25
Pensions: 1st year, increase normal retirement benefit from $13.00 per month to $14.50 per month for all years of service.
Health & Welfare: 1st & 3rd year, add $1,000 life insurance; Company to maintain the existing level of benefits up to a maximum cost increase of 10% per year

Package Cost Estimate

Number of Employees: 350 Total Work Hours: 665,000 Rollup Factor: 30%

	Base	*Estimate at End of Year* 1st yr.	2nd yr.	3rd yr.
ASTHE[a]	$ 12.00	$ 12.60	$ 13.356	$ 14.056
AHLC[b]	$ 17.00	$ 18.083	$ 19.262	$ 20.366

Negotiated Changes	*1st yr.*	*2nd yr.*	*3rd yr.*	*Total*
Wages	$0.600 (5%)	$0.756 (6%)	$0.700 (5.2%)	$2.056 (17.1%)[c]
Rollup	0.180	0.227	0.21	0.617
Shift Differential	0.025	—	0.025	0.050
Holidays	—	0.051	—	0.051
Vacation—4/10	0.058	0.007	0.003	0.068
5/25	0.019	0.006	0.006	0.031
Pensions	0.065	—	—	0.065
Health & Welfare				
Life Ins.	0.010	—	0.010	0.020
Maintenance of Benefits	0.126	0.132	0.150	0.408
Total Cost Per Hour	$1.083(6.4%)	$1,179(6.5%)	$1,104(5.75%)	$3.366(19.8%)[c]
Annual Cost Increase	$720,195	$784,035	$734,150	$2,238,390
Cash Outflow	$720,195	$1,504,230	$2,238,380	$4,462,805

[a]Average straight time hourly earnings.
[b]Average hourly labor costs.
[c]Reflects percentage increase in costs over base.

previously received. In other words, the 60-cent-per-hour wage increase in the first year is counted only in that year even though it is paid in each year of the contract. In effect, the first wage increase will cost the employer $1.80 over the term of the contract since it is paid in each of the three years of the contract. The cash outflow line at the bottom of the estimate does, however, reflect these repeated annual payments and shows the resulting cash outflow in each year of the contract.

It should also be noted that percentage increases are shown in parentheses for the wage increase in each year, even though the wage increases in the first and third years were negotiated in cents per hour. Such percentage calculations are for comparison purposes and do not serve a cost-estimating purpose. The percentage wage increase is shown as an increase over the previous year's average hourly wage rate, i.e., the average wage rate in effect during the prior year. Thus, the 60-cent-per-hour increase negotiated in the first year of the contract is divided by the previous year's average wage rate of $12.00 per hour to yield a 5 percent increase. The average hourly wage rate at the end of the first year is then adjusted to $12.60 to reflect the 60-cent-per-hour increase, and the new average hourly wage rate is multiplied by the second year negotiated increase of 6 percent to yield an average increase of $0.756 per hour ($12.60 × 6%). That second year wage increase is added to the $12.60 per hour average to obtain a new average rate of $13.356 ($12.60 + $0.756) by which the third year negotiated increase of $0.70 is divided to reflect a 5.2 percent increase.

The other percentage calculation shown is the increase in overall labor costs which is obtained by adding all wage and benefit cost increases in a given contract year and dividing by the average hourly labor cost at the end of the previous contract year. Thus the increase of $1.083 in the average hourly labor cost in the first year of the contract is divided by the base labor cost of $17.00 per hour to yield an increase of 6.4 percent. As in calculating the percentage increase in wages, the average hourly labor cost of $17.00 is adjusted to reflect the cost of the first-year wage and benefit increases and becomes $18.083 ($17.00 + $1.083). Then, the second-year increases totaling $1.179 are divided by the new average hourly labor cost of $18.083 to obtain a 6.5 percent increase in overall labor costs in the second year. The same process is followed to calculate the percentage increase in average labor costs for the third year.

The last item to be noted in this format is the "cash outflow" line. This number simply reflects the additional labor costs to be paid by the employer in each year of the contract as compared to labor costs existing prior to the new contract. As already explained, it is a cumulative total in that it recognizes that the additional costs of wages and benefits effective in the first year will continue to be paid in the second and third years, and that increases effective in the second year will also be paid in the third year. By examining the total of the annual cash outflows in the hypothetical settlement shown in Exhibit 10–2, management will realize that, although it negotiated only slightly more than $2.2 million in "new money," it will have spent a total amount of nearly $4.5 million in the three-year period of the contract as a result of the settlement over and above labor costs under the previous labor contract.

Time-Weighting and Present Value Costing

In considering multiyear labor contracts, negotiators frequently juggle wage and benefit changes from one year to another. Unfortunately for management, the movement frequently tends to be forward, i.e., to an earlier year of the contract. This is called "front-loading." Both inexperienced and seasoned negotiators recognize that front-loading means higher costs to the employer. However, they frequently neglect to calculate the full cost consequences of such maneuvering. Even where these more precise calculations are made, it is frequently after the negotiations are completed and the essential decisions have already been made.

Aside from the simple cents-per-hour package cost estimates, there are two types of cost analyses which are designed to reflect the real economic impact of the manner in which wage and benefit changes in a multiyear contract are spread over the period of the contract. One of these is "time-weighting" or "simple cash outflow" which simply takes into account the amount of time over which a contract change is in effect. The other method is the "present value" or "discounted cash outflow," which takes into account not only the period of time over which the payments are made, but also the time value of the money which will be spent as a result of the offer or settlement.

Simple Cash Outflow and Wage Negotiating Strategy

The simple cash outflow analysis was applied in the package cost estimate in Exhibit 10–2. Its most useful application, however, can be found at the time negotiating alternatives are being considered. Using the same wage increase amounts shown in Exhibit 10–2 for the negotiated package (except rounding to two decimal places for simplicity purposes), the simple cash outflow analysis can be useful in evaluating alternative offers. Hourly wage increases in that package were 50 cents, 6 percent (equal to 75.6 cents, or 76 cents after rounding), and 70 cents, giving a total of $2.06. Considering only the timing of the increases, but not the time value of money, the cost of these wage increases could be viewed as follows:

Time-Weighted Hourly Wage Increases

1st year	($0.60 × 3 years)	$1.80
2nd year	($0.76 × 2 years)	$1.52
3rd year	($0.70 × 1 year)	$0.70
Incremental increase	$2.06	
Cash outflow		$4.02

The net increase in wages over the three years is $2.06, but the time-weighted or cash outflow increase is $4.02. This is the manner in which the cash outflow line was computed in the package cost estimate shown in Exhibit 10–2. Although the union might be satisfied with the overall increase in wages, it may attempt to get more "up front" and counter with a proposal to shift 10 cents from the third year to be split equally between the first and second years. This would have the following effect:

1st year	($0.65 × 3 years)	$1.95
2nd year	($0.81 × 2 years)	$1.62
3rd year	($0.60 × 1 year)	$0.60
Incremental increase	$2.06	
Cash outflow		$4.17

The new wage incremental increase is the same, but the cash outflow is 15 cents per hour higher ($4.17 vs. $4.02). Obviously, this would not, other things being equal, be advantageous to the employer. Although some front-loading might be considered, management would presumably seek some other cost saving to offset the additional cash outflow resulting from the front-loading. The obvious answer would be to reduce the net overall increase by some amount to assure that the cash outflow is no greater than $4.02 per hour. This means that if the next counterproposal is to have no more costly effect on the employer's cash outflow, a reduction of 15 cents per hour in cash outflow must be made in one or more of the three years. If the entire 15-cent-per-hour reduction in cash outflow is to be made in the third year, it will require a 15-cent reduction from 60 cents to 45 cents.

The union will hardly be enthusiastic about reducing the wage increase in the third year since it will result in an incremental wage increase which is 15 cents per hour less over the term of the contract than the employer's original offer ($2.06 minus $1.91), shown as follows:

1st year	($0.65 × 3 years)	$1.95
2nd year	($0.81 × 2 years)	$1.62
3rd year	($0.45 × 1 year)	$0.45
Incremental increase	$1.91	
Cash outflow		$4.02

Given these options, the union might very well be content to remain with the employer's previous "balanced" offer rather than the front-loaded counterproposal. Union officials realize, as does management, that barring a cessation of the employer's business or a depression resulting in wage reductions, the net increase will be paid "forever" or at least for a very long time, and that 15 cents per hour sacrificed in one contract may never be recouped. If the front-loaded package was accepted and if the next labor contract is for three years without the 15-cent-per-hour wage differential being recouped, employees will have earned 15 cents per hour less than if they had accepted the balanced offer.

Another compromise, though, might be possible. The union's desire to move money "up front" might be offset by a net reduction which does not fully offset the full cash outflow disadvantage. For example, instead of reducing the third year's increase by 15 cents and increasing the first and second years by 5 cents each, the first year's wage increase might be increased by 4 cents per hour (to 64 cents per hour) and the second year's wage increase improved by 4 cents per hour (to 80 cents per hour) while the third year's increase is reduced by 10 cents. This would result in the following calculation:

1st year	($0.64 × 3 years)	$1.92
2nd year	($0.80 × 2 years)	$1.60
3rd year	($0.60 × 1 year)	$0.60
Incremental increase	$2.04	
Cash outflow		$4.12

This arrangement costs the employer 10 cents per hour more in cash outflow over the term of the contract than the earlier "balanced offer" of 60 cents—76 cents—70 cents ($4.12 versus $4.02). This may not seem like a terribly large amount, but if the bargaining unit consists of 350 employees and each one works an average of 1,900 hours per year, the total wage cost difference over the three-year contract will be $66,500 ($0.10 × 1,900 × 350). If there is a 30 percent rollup factor, the total cost will be $86,450 ($66,500 × 1.3). However, this arrangement results in a reduced amount of new incremental wages by 2 cents per hour over the three-year contract term ($2.04 vs. $2.06). This difference will not be lost on the union, for it will realize, as management also should, that when the next round of negotiations begins, the average wage rate will, other things being equal, be 2 cents per hour less than it would have been if the previous offer had been accepted. Beyond the fact that employees will earn 2 cents less for each hour worked, this lower average wage has special significance in future years in that any percentage wage increases will be based upon the then-existing wage rates. To the extent they are lower, subsequent percentage wage increases will be proportionately lower in value.

Present Value Analysis

The foregoing time-weighting or simple cash outflow analysis takes into account the amount of time an increase will be in effect, but it does not recognize the investment or time value of the wages spent or not spent. In other words, it does not fully recognize that the possession of money has a financial value in and of itself. This type of costing is accomplished through a "present value analysis" which recognizes the time value of money by acknowledging that money not spent now can be (1) invested at a given rate of return or (2) used for other capital needs of the employer so as to avoid borrowing at a given rate of return.

Present value analysis is, of course, common in many types of investment analysis and decision making. It can likewise be a valuable tool for labor contract costing.[5] Very simply, it says that, considering the rate of return one can expect for investing money, the value of capital possessed is greater now than it will be at some future time. Present value tables, more sophisticated hand-held calculators, and computer software are readily available to compute the relative values of money over given periods of time based upon various rates of interest.

Returning to the two alternative wage packages reviewed earlier, a present value analysis based on a 10 percent rate of interest and coupled with the time-weighting or cash outflow analysis would yield the results noted in Table 10–1 for the three-year contract term. Again, Option B, which provides for front-loading part of the 10 cents per hour taken from the third year, reflects a higher cash outflow of 8 cents per hour ($3.30 vs. $3.22) even though the incremental wage increases were 2 cents per hour less.

It is doubtful that most negotiators use a cash outflow costing method, let alone a present value analysis. It does not follow, however, that such costing techniques are not valuable. The infrequency of utilization of these methods is more an indication that most labor negotiators are still mired in the dark ages of simple, unweighted cents-per-hour calculations

Table 10–1. Alternative Wage Offers Under Different Cost Analyses

	Wage Increase	Cumulative Hourly Cash Outflow	Present Value Factor*	Cumulative Discounted Cash Outflow
Option A				
Year 1	$0.60	$0.60	0.909	$0.55
Year 2	0.76	1.36	0.826	1.12
Year 3	0.70	2.06	0.751	1.55
Total	$2.06	$4.02		$3.22
Option B				
Year 1	$0.64	$0.64	0.909	$0.58
Year 2	0.80	1.44	0.826	$1.19
Year 3	0.60	2.04	0.751	1.53
Total	$2.04	$4.12		$3.30
Difference	– $0.02	+ $0.10		+ $0.08

*Based upon an assumed interest rate of 10%.

made "on the back of an envelope." The time has long since passed when any employer should accept such unsophisticated cost estimates from its labor negotiators.

Sharing Cost Estimates With the Union

During or at the conclusion of negotiations, some union negotiators will ask the management negotiator if they can see the employer's cost estimate of an offer or settlement. The reason for such a request is not usually made clear, although it is seldom for a purpose which will benefit management. As pointed out in Chapter 4, the union is legally entitled to actual labor cost data and other information within the control of the employer which is relevant to a mandatory subject of bargaining. Most cost data about existing wages and benefits falls into that category. Similarly, cost information about possible improvements in medical insurance, pension plans, and other benefit programs is fair game for the union provided the employer has such information in its possession.[6] However, once the union has the basic cost information upon which calculations can be made, the employer would appear to be under no legal obligation to supply the union with its own estimates of the additional costs it will incur as a result of a given contract offer or settlement.[7]

Absent a legal obligation to supply such estimates, the employer is ill-advised to share its cost estimates with the union, for the union may wish to use them to push for comparable "cost" packages at other locations where key factors may be different. For example, an employer may negotiate an increase it estimates will cost 8 cents per hour in the premium pay for work on Sunday at one of its facilities operating on weekends. It agrees to the same provision at another of its facilities which has only occasional weekend work, and estimates the cost at this facility to be only 1 cent per hour. Seeing the employer's cost estimates, the union may push for the employer to spend the 7-cent-per-hour difference on some other wage or benefit improvement. Although the union is entitled to the basic cost data which will permit it to estimate the cost of the Sunday premium improvement itself, it may arrive at a lower figure or may simply not make the calculation. In any event, a cost estimate made by the employer will have a much greater impact on the union's negotiating committee than one prepared by the union itself. Therefore, it is wise for management to keep its cost estimates to itself.

11

Drafting Labor Contract Language

What remains after the long and tedious days of negotiation, the hours of tension facing a strike deadline, the euphoria of resolving a potential impasse, and the smiles and handshakes signifying total agreement, are the cold, unemotional words written to confirm an agreement that has been so arduously achieved. Months after the ink has dried on the new contract, few will remember the arguments and tension which were so vivid at the time. The words and sentences which memorialize that agreement, however, will remain for many years to come. In fact, over the years, those words will be read and interpreted by many who have no idea who their authors were, what the circumstances surrounding their creation were, nor what the intent behind the words was. For this reason, it is of the utmost importance that the language of the labor agreement be drafted with the greatest care.

This chapter will focus on the preparation of language for a renewal labor agreement, and deals with general drafting techniques and concepts as opposed to suggestions on specific contract language. Chapter 15 covers the drafting of a first labor contract and contains recommended language for selected key contract sections. Appendix 7 contains a checklist of provisions normally found in labor contracts.

Language Drafting

When Language Should Be Drafted

Some draft sections and paragraphs of a contract can be prepared in advance of actual bargaining, especially where the desired language duplicates that found in other contracts. As a general rule, however, the detailed drafting of contract language must be done during negotiations or shortly thereafter. Unless the negotiating parties have a history of successfully preparing and agreeing to contract language following negotiations, it is strongly recommended that all contract language be drafted, proposed, and agreed upon contemporaneously with, and as part of, the negotiating process. Oral agreements, agreements "in principle," or "understandings" in nonspecific terms are often understood differently by each party. Unless words embodying the agreements are reduced to actual contract language, it is very likely that subsequent disagreement will develop when "the meat is put on the bones."

Some years ago, a major West Coast employer in a commodity industry strayed from its normal practice of negotiating language at the bargaining table. General written summaries of proposals were exchanged and oral agreements were made. A final settlement was reached only after a six-week strike. After production was resumed, the negotiators met again to put their agreement in writing. Whether by design or accident, union representatives had a considerably different understanding from management as to what had been agreed upon. Because the employer could not stomach resumption of the strike, it acceded to most of the contract language drafted by the union. Needless to say, that company soon returned to its former practice of negotiating contract language at the bargaining table.

It should be recognized that drafting contract language and obtaining agreement at the bargaining table can, to a certain extent, slow down bargaining. Likewise there is a risk that proposals drafted "in the heat of battle" may contain some loopholes or be otherwise less carefully drawn than if more time had been available. These disadvantages can, however, be overcome by having patience and by taking the necessary time to do a thorough job. In any event, such disadvantages are far outweighed by the advantages of having, upon the conclusion of negotiations, a settlement agreement which resolves all matters and which does not require the parties, or their attorneys, to argue and negotiate about the words which express what union and management actually agreed upon.

Who Should Draft Language for Management?

There are several options as to who should draft contract language for management. Ideally, management's spokesperson should prepare the language. As the one who speaks for management at the bargaining table, the spokesperson will be expected to have the knowledge and articulateness necessary to write proposals and set down agreements that have been reached. This is not, however, always the case. Although the spokesperson may have good oral skills, he or she may lack the facility to write contract language in a careful and comprehensible manner.

Another option is to give the assignment to one of the members of the negotiating team who has good drafting skills. That person may be a lawyer or a layperson who has sufficient quasi-legal experience to realize the pitfalls in drafting language for a labor agreement. Such a person may have acquired valuable experience by representing management in grievance administration and arbitration.

Nonparticipants as Draftspersons

Another option is to rely upon the services of a lawyer or labor specialist who is not a participant in the negotiations. This is generally not advisable; the subtlety and nuances of the parties' positions, the examples used in the negotiating sessions to support their respective positions, and the sensitivity of both parties at the bargaining table to particular words and phrases cannot effectively be translated in most cases to the remote draftsperson. In seeking to protect management's position, the remote draftsperson will frequently prepare language which has little or no chance of being accepted. The gap in understanding between the bargaining table and the attorney's office is usually too great to bridge.

It is, however, often feasible to use the expertise of a nonparticipating attorney or labor specialist to *review* draft language prepared by one or more of the management negotiators. Errors in terminology, omissions of legal safeguards, inconsistencies, or conflicts with other contract provisions can often be spotted by such an objective reviewer, who may be able to suggest changes in phrasing while retaining the essence of that which the negotiating parties are attempting to achieve. The tremendous advances in communications, including fax machines, word processing, and overnight package delivery, permit rapid exchange of written material during negotiations so that bargaining need not be significantly delayed in order to accomplish such a review.

Handling Language Drafted by the Union

Once negotiations have begun, the process of considering proposals, exchanging counterproposals, and reaching tentative agreement begins. If management agrees to a proposal submitted by the union, it does not follow that management should necessarily accept the language offered by the union to embody that proposal. In fact, it is usually unwise to do so since the language will frequently be slanted in the union's favor. If the union is intent upon obtaining a particular contract provision, it will very often accept management's phraseology so long as its desired result has been achieved. Of course, if the language proposed by the union is, after careful consideration, felt to be satisfactory, management should not be reluctant to accept the language offered. Where the union's offered language needs to be revised, management will enhance the opportunity for agreement by retaining as much of the union's language as is prudently possible.

Writing for the Readers

As the draftsperson prepares contract language he or she must, as should any good author, keep the readers in mind and consider how the words will later be understood. The drafter is only successful if the readers understand and correctly apply what the negotiating parties intended. Who are the readers? Obviously they include management representatives such as department heads, foremen, and supervisors, as well as union representatives, including local union officers, shop stewards, grievance committee members, and the like. Also to be considered are hourly employees who may read the contract themselves and/or have its provisions conveyed to them by union or management representatives. The contract is also apt to be read and interpreted by arbitrators, administrative law judges, civil court judges, and other hearing officers.

The drafter must keep all of these parties in mind while writing, and should always ask, "How will these words be understood and interpreted by someone who did not participate in the negotiations?" The words must be sufficiently clear and simple to be understood and correctly applied by the first-line supervisor, yet legally sound enough to withstand attack in arbitration or in other legal forums. It must be assumed that none of the readers will know the arguments advanced or positions taken by either party which resulted in the language agreed upon. Nor should it be assumed that the readers will know who initially proposed the contract change or what counterproposals were exchanged along the road toward agreement. In other words, the *language must stand on its own.* Read alone, it should convey the mutual intentions of union and management. This is not always an easy task.

Cosmetic Language Changes

A labor contract should not be changed unless a change in its meaning and/or application is intended. Such a statement may sound foolish, yet is is surprising how often union representatives will urge that a change be made in the contract under the guise of "clarifying" or "simplifying" the contract. Such changes might be termed "cosmetic changes." Management should not be misled. If the words of the agreement are changed, regardless of the rationale, it will be assumed by a third party (e.g., arbitrator or judge) that a change in the meaning and/or application of the contract was intended. A later defense that the intention was merely to clarify or simplify the language will not be given much, if any, credence by the third party.

Notwithstanding the pitfalls just described, management may find itself in a position where a cosmetic change appears, for negotiating reasons, to be necessary. In such cases, there is a way to avoid the trap that a cosmetic change will later be interpreted as a substantive change. The technique for doing so is known as using a "statement of intent." For example, the union proposes that the employer's regular practice of notifying the union in advance of work to be contracted out be included in the labor agreement. The employer is not reluctant to obligate itself in this way, but is fearful that such a statement could be interpreted as limiting the right to subcontract it has enjoyed. The following two sentences could accomplish both parties' objectives:

> The Company will, where it is feasible to do so, notify the Union in advance of having bargaining unit work performed by an outside contractor. It is understood that the agreement to provide such notice does not limit the Company's right to contract out work.

The important point is that management has ensured that it has not given away a valuable right by agreeing to put into the contract a practice it has already been following. The general rule, however, is no less true: Don't change contract language unless you intend to change the effect or application of that section of the contract.

General Guidelines for the Draftsperson

The proficient labor contract draftsperson should write language which is simple, clear, and cautious, i.e., language that concedes no more than it intends and nails down the particular points that are essential to preserve management's rights. The following guidelines are given to assist the writer in accomplishing these objectives.

Simplicity and Clarity

1. *Avoid different terms for the same person or entity.* The draftsperson should try to use the same word when referring to terms appearing throughout the contract, such as "the Company," "the Union," "job classifications," "job assignments," "work week," and the like. An "employee" should always be an "employee" and not sometimes a "worker" or "person."
2. *Avoid different meanings for the same term.* Writers should be careful to cross-check the meaning and use of the same term in different parts of the contract. A "regular job" should have the same meaning in the seniority section as it does in the wage or vacation sections. If a term does have different meanings for different purposes, then a clarifying provision should be used as follows: "For purposes of this section, the term '______' means __________."
3. *Avoid redundant or needless phrases.* A labor agreement is a contract to which two parties have mutually agreed. It is therefore not necessary to repeat throughout the agree-

ment such terms as "The parties mutually agree" or "The Company and Union agree." Also, unless a particular provision is to have a limited duration, or extend beyond the contract term, all provisions of the agreement will be in effect for the period of the agreement. Hence, it is not necessary to include the words "During the life of the agreement" or "While the contract is in effect."

4. *Avoid legalisms.* No one but a lawyer feels comfortable with such terms as "whereas," "heretofore," and "provided however." Considering that there are simpler and more understandable equivalents, such as "because," "previously," and "except," there is really no good reason to use the more complicated expressions. Unless a simpler word cannot be found or will not convey the same meaning, the contract drafter should use the simpler word.

5. *Use headings where possible.* Just as road signs are helpful when one is trying to locate the correct route to a destination, paragraph or section headings are useful in helping supervisors and others find pertinent contract provisions. Therefore, where possible, parties should use headings to describe the contents of sections and articles. For example, rather than having a seniority section with numerous untitled paragraphs, the parties could use the following headings:

   - Accumulation and Loss of Seniority
   - Determination of Seniority Units
   - Probationary Periods
   - Transfers Within Plant
   - Promotions and Job Bidding
   - Filling Temporary Job Vacancies
   - Layoffs and Recalls.

6. *Be precise in the use of numbers and units of time.* For sections of the contract containing specific numbers or time references, the draftsperson should be precise with regard to the scope and extent of the application. For example, a clause in the vacation section might be phrased as follows:

   > Employees will receive a vacation after 1,600 hours.

   Does the 1,600 hours include only hours worked or does it also include holiday and vacation hours? What is the period for counting the 1,600 hours—calendar year or vacation year? A clearer sentence would be:

   > An employee will be entitled to a vacation if he or she has actually worked 1,600 hours in the 12 months preceding the beginning of the vacation period.

A common problem is the failure to denote whether "days" are calendar days or work days. This is especially true in regard to probationary periods, grievance procedures, and seniority provisions. When the term "days" is used it should always be preceded by either "calendar" or "work" or by another similar modifier.

7. *Clarify references to other contract provisions.* To avoid repetition, drafters often use the terms "such," "that," and "above" to refer back to previous contract provisions. Thus, one might see in a contract a sentence as follows:

   > In that event, such employee may file a bump notice in accordance with the above procedure in order to bump an employee with less seniority.

   Depending on what has appeared prior to the quoted sentence, the reference terms may be ambiguous and/or misleading. A better sentence would be:

   > An employee who is displaced from his or her job may file a bump notice in accordance with the procedure in paragraph (a) above. After filing the notice, he or she may bump the most junior employee then in the same department, provided he or she is fully capable of performing the job held by the most junior employee in that department. All of the bumping described in this paragraph shall be based on department seniority.

   Although considerably more words are used, the agreement is much more likely to be correctly understood and applied.

8. *Enumerate multiple terms.* Where a series of significant terms or conditions are listed, it is often helpful to highlight them with an enumerated list rather than a narrative series. For example, the sentence "Promotions will be based upon skill, experience, seniority, and attendance record" may be more effectively stated as:

   > Promotion will be based upon:
   > 1. Skill,
   > 2. Experience,
   > 3. Seniority, and
   > 4. Attendance Record.

   This type of enumeration is especially useful where it is intended to prioritize the items in the series. In such cases it is advantageous to add words such as "in the following order of priority" just before the list.

9. *Insert new provisions in the proper locations.* When additions are made to a contract, it is helpful, for purposes of clarity, to insert the new provisions where they logically fit. It makes no sense to put an agreement on premium pay for

work on Sunday into a seniority clause which describes how weekend work is distributed. The provision logically fits in the section of the agreement where other premium pay provisions are found. Some negotiators simply tack new provisions on to the end of a section regardless of whether they fit there or not. This can result in confusion and costly mistakes in contract administration. A convenient way to draft changes to ensure they are properly positioned in the contract is to use a pasteup of the previous contract and write in the changes. Exhibit 11–1 illustrates how this is commonly done.

10. *Use consistent sequential numbering of paragraphs.* Many contracts contain erratic and inconsistent numbering of paragraphs and subparagraphs. This tends to be confusing and can result in erroneous cross-referencing. There are various numbering systems, but consistent use of a system is more important than the particular system selected. One of the most common systems used for labor agreements is as follows:

    ARTICLE I
      Section 1.
      Paragraph A.
        (1)
          (a)
          (b)
          (c)

    Although not quite as popular, the decimal system used in the following example works just as well:

    ARTICLE 6
      Section 6.1
        Paragraph 6.1.1

11. *Use examples or charts for conceptually difficult provisions.* Certain agreements do not easily lend themselves to a narrative description. This is especially true of seniority, hours of work, and certain unusual pay or benefit formulas. In such cases, examples, diagrams, tables, or charts are often helpful. For example, a labor agreement might include the following diagram to illustrate the filling of temporary vacancies by means of overtime work:

	Shifts			
	(a)	(b)	(c)	(d)
Job A	__	__	__	__
Job B	N	V	Y	__
Job C	N	↑	N	__
Job D	Y →	↑	← Y	__
	__	__	__	__

Key	
V	vacant job
N	employee not willing to split shifts
Y	employee willing to split shifts

Exhibit 11–1. Insert of New Provisions in a Contract

Section 2. PROMOTION LADDER

1. The Promotional Ladder shall be recognized for employees of the Company in the Power House and shall be in descending order as follows:

   Shift Engineer
   Asst. Shift Engineer
   Recovery Boiler Operator
   Evaporator Operator
   Power Boiler Operator
   Turbine Oiler
   Hog House Operator
   Shift Utility
   Day Utility

   A. Present promotion ladders shall continue unchanged unless either:

      (1) a change is mutually agreed to between the Union Standing Committee and the Company, or

      (2) compelling manufacturing reasons necessitate a change; provided, however, that this exception shall not permit unreasonable designation of such compelling reasons and the Union Standing Committee is privileged to carry the issue through all further steps of the grievance procedure in which such unreasonable designation is claimed to exist ← (add:) , or

      (add:) (3) new products or new manufacturing processes are introduced which require substantially new or different job duties than those previously performed or required of incumbents

When employees are promoted on the promotion ladder, the senior employee in each classification shall have the right, provided he is qualified, to move up the promotion ladder.

   A. The Company shall consider an employee qualified for advancement if such employee has qualified himself for the next step on the promotion ladder by satisfactorily passing the required tests. ~~The Signatory parties shall agree on the required tests.~~ ← (delete)

   B. The Company will provide reasonable and adequate training on all jobs.

Section 3. HIRING PROCEDURE

1. The number of employees in the Power House will be designated from time to time as the work load may change. When a vacancy occurs, the Company may fill the vacancy in the following manner:

   A. Hiring a new employee:

   B. Transferring an employee from the Yard Labor Pool with less than ~~thirty (30)~~ sixty (60) days of service.

   In the case of hiring a new employee, consideration will be given to prospective employees referred to the Company by International Union of Operating Engineers, Local #302.

2. The Company will promptly notify the Union of all transfers and hires in the Power House.

3. The Company will also notify the Union of all terminations or other changes in hourly personnel in the Power House.

12. *Highlight most recent changes.* Some unions and employees have found it useful to highlight contract language changes by having the changes printed in bold type or underlining. Thus, when the contract is being reviewed, the reader can easily ascertain those changes made in the most recent negotiations. Likewise, deletions are reflected by dual diagonal lines (//) where the deletion occurs. An example of this technique is as follows:

    4. Weekly work schedules shall be posted no later than 3:00 p.m. on the Thursday prior to the week in question. Changes in such work schedules may be made without penalty payments if the cause of the change is due to late orders received, equipment malfunctions, //, employee illness or injury, or other factors beyond the control of the Company.

    Besides showing what changes have occurred since the previous negotiation, this kind of highlighting is valuable in producing a historical record of how particular contract clauses developed over the years. This is especially helpful in addressing questions concerning contract interpretation and in preparing for grievance and arbitration hearings.

Conservative Drafting

While clarity and simplicity are helpful in terms of enabling the users of the agreement to correctly understand and apply it, what is more important is that the labor agreement and supplemental agreements provide no more, or less, than is intended. Consequently, the draftsperson must be thoughtful, cautious, and conservative. Nothing should be conceded by management in the contract which was not conceded at the bargaining table, and any advantage obtained by management at the bargaining table should not be lost or weakened by the way it is expressed in the contract.

Considering the Worst Case

Labor contract language has a tendency to be etched in stone, particularly where it favors the party with the greatest bargaining leverage. Consequently, the drafter must assume that the new provision he or she is drafting will remain in the contract for many years to come, if not forever. The writer should envision what circumstances could possibly occur in the years to come which could make the agreement burdensome or unlivable for management, and attempt to "write around" the problem areas. Of course, the negotiator should not, in the first place, be entering into any agreements which can turn sour in years to come. But pitfalls are not always apparent until the concept is reduced to writing.

The failure of management negotiators and draftspersons to envision, and/or accommodate for the future, has been particularly evident in the railroad industry. Specific numerical restrictions regarding crew sizes, equipment movements, and other operating limitations were first negotiated in the 1930s and 1940s when trains ran at lower speeds. Improved technology and competitive conditions made work rules obsolete beginning in the 1960s. The rigidity of the railroad brotherhoods and their refusals to update the contractual limitations to suit the modern era is one of the prime factors which has caused the decline of the railroad industry.

"Hedge" Phrases

The draftsperson must continually ask "What if . . . ?" and envision the possible as well as the probable. Certain limiting phrases can be employed to keep management from being locked into unrealistic situations. Examples of such phrases are "insofar as practical," "provided there is no change in existing products, methods, or major equipment," and "provided circumstances reasonably permit." Phrases such as "whenever possible" or "in case of emergency" should be avoided since they leave little room for exception. Most things in life are "possible," and what may be considered an "emergency" by management may only be a "difficult situation" to an arbitrator.

Properly prepared "hedge" phrases incorporate the premise of reasonableness to obligations assumed by management. Needless to say, union negotiators will invariably resist such escape clauses since they give management an opportunity to avoid a contractual obligation and can deprive the union of a contractual advantage. Nevertheless, the possibility of management's being saddled with an obligation which it cannot practically fulfill, at least without great disadvantage, is incentive enough for management to press for such protective language despite union resistance.

The hedge phrases need not be so vague as those given above. They can be tied directly to some specific condition or set of circumstances. For example, an agreement to schedule fixed shifts (as opposed to rotating shifts) may be conditioned upon the level of production. Thus, the provision might read:

> So long as there are no more than ___ shifts of work per week in each department, employees will be scheduled to a fixed weekly work schedule.

Making Contractual Restrictions as Narrow as Possible

As stated earlier, most provisions in a labor contract impose some obligation or limitation upon management. For this reason, shorter labor contracts are, other things being equal, preferred over longer contracts. Since most of what is included in the contract is a limitation upon management, a key objective of the drafter becomes that of making the limitation as narrow as possible.

Many, if not most, nonmonetary provisions included in a renewal labor contract are in response to experiences (usually problems) during the term of the preceding agreement(s). In attempting to meet the requests of the union for remedial language to cure these "problems," the drafter should prepare language no broader than that necessary to deal with the situation identified. For example, the union has received complaints from regular employees that weekend work has been given to some seasonal employees rather than to them. Management agrees that the full-time employees should get first preference for the weekend work. However, management is not willing to give the weekend work to full-time employees if there are seasonal employees who have worked less than 40 hours during the week and can perform the weekend work as straight time (assuming weekend work "as such" is not paid at overtime rates). Consequently, a management-drafted proposal responsive to the union's demand might be written as follows:

> Work on Saturday or Sunday which will be paid for at the overtime rate (time and one half) will first be made available to full-time, regular employees prior to being made available to seasonal employees.

Management has thus met the union's demand, but has gone no farther than necessary and has retained the right to have weekend work performed at straight-time pay if that is possible.

Another example is a union demand that employees be permitted to bid to lower-paying jobs, a right not permitted by the labor agreement. Management is not opposed in principle to such a right, but is concerned that some employees in highly skilled jobs will bid to lower-paying jobs, causing the employer to incur additional training and break-in expense. Consequently, a limited responsive proposal might be the following:

> Employees in job classifications with job grades lower than ______ (no. of grade) may submit bids for jobs in lower paying classifications. Employees in job classifications with job grades above ______ (no. of grade) may submit bids in lower paying classifications only with the written approval of the employee's immediate supervisor and the appropriate department head.

Watching Out for Borrowed Language

One of the most common practices of experienced, as well as inexperienced, negotiators is to extract or "borrow" contract clauses from the other labor agreements. Union negotiators are notorious for pulling out clauses from other employers' labor contracts and proposing them as if the clauses had been blessed from above. There seems to be a tacit assumption held by many that if a clause has come from another contract, somehow it has value. Unfortunately, this is not always the case. The borrowed clause may have been the source of much dispute between the parties who negotiated it or it may have been the basis for erosion of management rights.

The important consideration in using language from another contract is to make sure both sides adopting the language understand what it says, and agree on what it means to them. If there is no meeting of the minds of the negotiating parties, language from another contract will not perform any magic and will likely lead to misunderstanding. Also, if it is possible to do so, the management draftsperson should check with the management of other employers which have had experience with the language in question, and determine how it has been applied and what the results of its use have been. If there have been any arbitration decisions interpreting the clause in question, these should be reviewed.

Borrowed language is not inherently good or bad. If it accurately reflects what the borrowing parties have agreed upon, it can be quite useful. The converse is equally true. The simple fact that a particular clause has found its way into other labor agreements is no assurance of its value. It should be evaluated on its own merits.

Catch-All Terms

In normal narrative writing it is common to use catch-all words or phrases such as "etc.," "and the like," and "other similar situations." In drafting contract language, however, such vague references can be extremely dangerous, although the orientation of the sentence will determine if management is benefited or burdened by the catch-all term. If the sentence is one which limits management, the catch-all is disadvantageous. For example, in the sentence "Part-time employees may not be assigned to day shift operational work, taking of inventory, maintenance work, etc.," the "etc." could virtually wipe out management's use of part-time employees. Conversely, if the contract is one which positively states management's right or limits employees' rights, the catch-all word or phrase can be helpful. The following is an example:

> Employees are not obligated to accept overtime work which is assigned with less than 2 hours notice unless the work is necessitated by an emergency, breakdown, unanticipated customer's order or other similar situation.

In all cases, a catch-all word or phrase should be used with great care.

Pitfalls of Mutual Agreement Clauses

Just as the catch-all word or phrase is a two-edged sword, so too is the mutual agreement condition. An example is the following:

> Outside contractors may not be used to perform bargaining unit work, unless the parties mutually agree otherwise.

Obviously, the union has an absolute veto over any subcontracting by management, and the employer has effectively precluded itself from subcontracting. On the other hand, the following example cuts the other way:

> In order to be timely, all grievances must be filed within 10 days following the occurrence out of which the grievance arose, unless there is mutual agreement to extend this time period.

Here, of course, the time limit works to management's advantage in that it can veto any extension which the union might propose.

As a general proposition, most mutual agreement clauses proposed in labor contract negotiations work against management's interests and are therefore to be avoided. The drafter must realistically assume that if the contract enables the union to veto a particular management action by failing to agree, the union will exercise that veto. There may be occasions when the union may not exercise its veto, but it is only a naive management negotiator who will insert such a mutual agreement clause in the contract with that expectation.

Avoiding Agreements to Agree

A corollary to the mutual agreement clause is an agreement to agree. This type of clause is sometimes used when the parties want to settle a matter but cannot find common ground. In essence, they put off until tomorrow what they have not been able to do today. The following is an example of this type of clause:

> An amount of money equal to 1¢ per hour will be set aside for the purpose of adjusting wage rates which are not equitable in relation to other jobs in the same seniority unit. Within 30 days following the ratification of the agreement, the parties will meet and agree upon the job classifications which shall be adjusted and the amount of each adjustment.

This is not an unusual labor contract provision; the delay mechanism is used because individual job rate adjustments can be politically difficult for the union to deal with during the ratification process, since there will be a number of jobs (and corresponding job holders) that will not receive a special wage adjustment. Nevertheless, the contract stipulates that the parties must agree. However, they have no assurance that an agreement can be reached, nor have they reached an understanding on what will occur if an agreement cannot be achieved. If such a provision is to be included at all, there should be a procedure to resolve differences if agreement cannot be reached. Arbitration is the most obvious choice, although the role of the arbitrator in such cases is not the normal one of interpreting the agreement, but rather one of determining what the agreement will be. This role is usually called "interest arbitration," and many employers violently object to having an arbitrator determine contract provisions with which management might or might not agree.

The better choice is to completely avoid any agreement to agree and settle all unresolved issues at the bargaining table. If this is not possible, the agreement to agree should be as narrow as possible, and any matters which might be left to an arbitrator should carry with them a formula or set of guidelines to limit the arbitrator. Returning to the example noted above, the following clause might be added:

> If the parties are unable to reach complete agreement, any unresolved issues may be referred to arbitration in accordance with section _____, and the arbitrator is limited as follows:
>
> 1. No job is to receive an increase of more than 5%.
> 2. Jobs are to be valued on the basis of required skill, experience, and responsibility.
> 3. Jobs in other industries or other geographical areas may not be considered as a basis of comparison.

Avoiding Overly General and High-Sounding Clauses

It is not unusual to find the following type of contract clause which has been excerpted from a labor agreement between a major national employer and one of the largest international unions:

> The Company and the Union encourage the highest possible degree of friendly, cooperative relationships between their respective representatives at all levels and with and between all employees. The officers of the Company and the Union realize this goal depends on more than words in a labor agreement, that it depends primarily on attitudes between people in their respective organizations and at all levels of responsibility. They believe that proper attitudes must be based on full understanding of and regard for the respective rights and responsibilities of both the Company and the Union. They believe also that proper attitudes are of major importance in the plants where day-to-day operations and administration of this Agreement demand fairness and understanding. They believe that these attitudes can be encouraged best when it is made clear that Company and Union officials, whose duties involved negotiation of this Agreement, are not anti-union or anti-company but are sincerely concerned with the best interest and well-being of the business and all employees.

This type of motherhood and apple pie language may represent a legitimate expression of good feeling between union and management, but it does not really belong in a labor agreement. It is best left to some joint memorandum or policy statement. As a provision in a labor agreement, it does not impose any real rights or obligations, and serves only as window dressing. However, in particular cases it may be used by one party or the other to support its position in arbitration or a court of law under circumstances where it was never intended to apply.

The conclusion to be drawn from this discussion is that labor agreements are not designed for recreational or uplifting reading. They are meant to spell out the respective rights and obligations of management, the union, and employees. Such rights and obligations should be spelled out in sufficient detail and clarity in order to express to supervisors, union representatives, and arbitrators what the negotiating parties intended to agree to. Anything beyond that is unnecessary, surplus, and possibly harmful verbiage.

Pinpointing the Effective Date

When new or changed wages, benefits, or significant working conditions are negotiated into an agreement, they are often not intended to be effective on the same date or at the same time as the labor agreement as a whole. Consequently, the draftsperson must always keep in mind the chronology of contract changes. This is especially true in the preparation of settlement agreements, which typically include only the changes negotiated in the most recent round of negotiations and which will be incorporated into the entire collective bargaining agreement when the settlement has been fully ratified.

A somewhat typical mixture of effective dates is as follows:

1. *Effective date of new contract*—first date following ratification vote.
2. *Effective date of wage increase*—expiration date of old contract.
3. *Effective date of medical plan improvements*—first day of month following date of ratification.
4. *Effective date of vacation improvements*—beginning of next vacation year.

Impact of Language Changes on Other Contract Sections

Labor contracts are loaded with interrelationships. The "hours of work" section has an impact on the wage section and vice versa. The seniority section can directly affect hours of work, vacation and holiday provisions, and a number of other contract sections. When a change is to be made in any section of the labor agreement, the drafter should ask, "Is there any other provision of the labor agreement which could be affected in any way by this change?" This question should trigger a search through a number of other sections, if not all sections, of the contract to see if any impact will result and if any other sections need to be changed to maintain consistency.

Dating and Labeling Each Proposal and Counterproposal

In the process of negotiations, numerous proposals and counterproposals are exchanged between the union and management. In order to avoid confusion, and to make a clear record of the negotiations for later reference purposes, each proposal or counterproposal received from the union should be dated and labeled. A simple handwritten notation such as "Received from union at 10:00 a.m. 3/26/93" will suffice. Similarly, each management proposal or counterproposal should be dated and labeled, e.g., "Management counterproposal 3/28/93." These types of notations often prove to be invaluable in later years when someone is attempting to determine the negotiating history of a particular clause for contract interpretation or arbitration purposes.

The Sidebar Agreement

The "sidebar" is a negotiated agreement which is not included in the collective bargaining agreement but which nevertheless normally constitutes a fully binding agreement. This type of agreement is normally in the form of a letter, memorandum, or other document separate from the labor contract. It may be, but usually is not, incorporated by reference in the labor contract. There are various reasons why such agreements are not included in the main agreement, but the following are the principal ones:

1. Desire of one or both parties to shield the agreement from the wider exposure it might receive if included in the collective bargaining agreement, and thereby to attempt to keep the agreement from spreading to other locations.

2. The belief that the sidebar agreement has limited life or significance, and that it should expire at the end of the current agreement.
3. The agreement is thought to be one of interpretation or administration of an existing provision in the collective bargaining agreement or a statement of general intention. As such, it is felt not to rise to the level of a formal agreement needing to be included in the contract.
4. The sidebar is agreed upon during the term of the labor agreement (after the contract was signed), and it is therefore not possible to include it in the collective bargaining agreement.

Several key points in drafting sidebar agreements should be kept in mind. First, the sidebar should not conflict with any provisions in the collective bargaining agreement, although it may clarify them. Second, the sidebar should have a termination date, usually to coincide with the termination of the current agreement, unless there is a desire by management to have it continue beyond that point. An example of typical self-destruct language would be as follows:

> This letter shall be in effect only for the term of the agreement that expires on (date), but not thereafter, unless specifically renewed in writing by the parties.

Finally, management should not put anything in a sidebar agreement that it would not, if necessary, be willing to agree to as part of the collective bargaining agreement. Some negotiators believe that a sidebar is something less than a full agreement, and might be willing to agree to an onerous provision if it is simply confirmed in a sidebar agreement rather than the collective bargaining agreement. Such an attitude is myopic in that a sidebar agreement creates a legally binding obligation just as the collective bargaining agreement does. Consequently, management should only agree to those provisions by which it is willing to be bound regardless of the form in which the agreement is stated.

Incorporating Changes

As the bargaining progresses, the respective negotiators will normally sign off, or initial, language changes in various sections of the agreement. As the language is drafted, its placement in the collective bargaining agreement should be determined and indicated on each proposal or counterproposal. When the negotiators begin to focus on monetary issues, typically most language or noneconomic issues fade into the background. However, when management prepares a complete economic offer, each initialed language change should either be included in the offer or at least referred to in the offer so that it is clear which noneconomic provisions are included and which are not.

As soon as a tentative agreement is reached, a summary of the agreed upon changes should be prepared and signed. Frequently this is simply a matter of signing the company's final settlement offer. As soon as the settlement agreement is ratified by the necessary parties, the collective bargaining agreement should be revised and executed. If the parties have, as suggested, negotiated and initialed specific contract language as the negotiations progressed, it will be a simple matter to insert the newly negotiated language into the appropriate sections of the collective bargaining agreement. Use of word processing equipment greatly simplifies the task.

After the settlement has been reached there is a natural letdown, and the process of incorporating the revisions into the collective bargaining agreement is sometimes delayed for weeks or even months. Such delays are strenuously discouraged. The sooner the collective bargaining agreement is finalized, the sooner supervisors, union representatives and employees can begin to adapt to the new contract. Undue delays can result in disagreements over what was specifically agreed upon. The new agreement should be signed as soon as possible.

Part III

Reaching a Final Agreement

12

Striving to Reach Agreement

Just as any good salesperson must know how to close a sale (i.e., get the buyer to commit himself), so too the labor negotiator must be able to bring the negotiations to an end and achieve a settlement. This is often the most difficult task in the entire process, particularly where important unresolved issues still remain on the bargaining table. Nevertheless, if impasse and a possible work stoppage are to be avoided, a conclusion and settlement must be reached. The management spokesperson must assume responsibility for making this settlement happen and, given the high stakes involved, cannot afford to count on the union spokesperson to engineer a settlement.

Proper Timing

There is surely no magic signal to alert the spokesperson as to when a move toward settlement should be made. The sense of timing in this regard is almost a sixth sense and one of the principal rewards to management for having an experienced negotiator at the helm. Clearly an early termination of the negotiations is a desirable objective, but the dangers of a premature attempt to settle are such that the end result can be devastating. If management's negotiator assumes that the union is ready to reach a settlement, but the necessary conditions have not been satisfied, the "hog" may simply attempt to continue "feeding at the trough." In other words, management's negotiator may make, or at least strongly suggest, valuable concessions in the hope of wrapping up the bargaining only to find that the union has benefitted from valuable management concessions without having made the reciprocal concessions necessary to reach a settlement.

Deadlines

The determination as to proper timing will obviously be influenced by any deadlines, most particularly the contract expiration date. This deadline should, however, only be accorded the respect warranted from the way it has been treated in the past by these same parties. If negotiators have in previous contract negotiations continued beyond the expiration date, there is little justification to regard it as a true deadline. On the other hand, if the union has a firm policy of "no contract, no work," the contract expiration date should be treated with respect, and the bargaining maneuvered in such a way that a conclusion *can* be reached by that time. In many respects it is to management's advantage to have such a mutually recognized deadline. Interminable negotiations seldom work to management's advantage.

Signals

Aside from the contract expiration deadline, there are other signals or indications that the union is ready either to settle or to reach some conclusion to the negotiations. Withdrawal of numerous and/or relatively important demands from the union's bargaining agenda is often an indication of such readiness. Tell-tale signs of greater-than-normal boredom or impatience can be a signal that a conclusion is desired. However, such signs should be carefully examined inasmuch as they may simply reflect lack of experience or a temporary state of mind and body rather than any genuine intention to end the negotiations. In some cases, private conversations between the respective spokespersons can be useful in ascertaining when a serious move toward settlement is appropriate. Management's spokesperson must be cautious that the information is not being conveyed as a ploy to put management at a bargaining disadvantage.

If it is management which is the moving party in seeking major contract changes, an indication on the part of the union of a desire to conclude the negotiations may, of course, be exactly what management does not want. Depending on how many issues are yet to be resolved and whether or not further discussion and negotiations are likely to bring the parties closer together, management negotiators may need to create ways to extend the negotiations. A timely recess may be helpful in reducing pressure and permitting both parties to catch their breath for further discussions. Similarly, a negotiated extension of the current contract may be a way of permitting further discussion without the threat of a deadline hanging over both parties.

Pressure to Settle

Care must be taken, however, to determine if pressure is working for, or against, management's interests. It may very well be that continued negotiations approaching a contract expiration date may put more pressure on the union than on management. Such situations exist where there is a possibility of a lockout, unilateral implementation of management's final offer, or a representation "raid" by a competing union (and the competing union is only waiting for the contract to expire and for the contract bar to an NLRB election to be removed). In these cases the incumbent union needs to get a settlement as much as or more than management. In these situations management should be able to reach a settlement in advance of the contract expiration date on terms favorable to management.

Assessing All Timing Considerations

In any event, the management spokesperson must be sensitive to (1) the union negotiators and signals they may be sending; (2) the status of bargaining in terms of relative positions of union and management; (3) the contract expiration deadline (and the time necessary for the union to conduct its ratification vote in advance of the contract expiration date); (4) the status of other negotiations involving other employers or other facilities of the same employer which may be influencing this negotiation; and (5) the potential dangers of trying to settle too early or too late. All of these factors must be carefully considered in determining when management should make a push to conclude the negotiations.

Methods of Moving to a Conclusion

Despite the variety of scenarios by which labor negotiations can advance toward a conclusion, there are two principal methods of working toward a conclusion which are found in a majority of labor contract negotiations.

Final Offer

In Chapter 7 the various styles of economic bargaining were reviewed. It was explained that the most common type of bargaining was "auction bargaining," whereby the parties propose successive offers and counteroffers to work toward a common ground. In this form of bargaining, neither party is prepared to "show its hand"—i.e., to reveal its maximum offer (employer) or its minimum acceptance level (union)—until it is sure that the other side has reached, or come very close to reaching, its final position. It is a true cat-and-mouse game. Within the context of this type of bargaining, management's final offer takes on great significance. It represents management's highest offer, which, if not accepted, is likely to precipitate a strike.

Precedents to a Final Offer

The key to making this type of closure approach succeed is to maneuver the bargaining, prior to the final offer, to the point where (1) the union indicates at what level it is willing to settle and that level is within management's acceptable limits, or (2) the relative positions of the parties are so close that (a) the final offer will be acceptable to the union or (b) the union would not be willing to strike over the difference. Of course, achieving either of these situations is much easier said than done, for the union is well aware that once it announces, or otherwise makes known, its settlement level it will never get more than that amount and quite likely will get less. Consequently, the union will normally be reluctant to take a formal position which is low enough to make a settlement easily achieved. In other words, it will want to have a cushion. Nevertheless, management must continue to pressure the union to lower its position to a point where that position is within management's desired settlement limits.

The Credibility Factor

The words "final offer" normally have, and should always have, a profound impact on negotiations. These particular words have a very special significance in labor negotiating parlance. In using such words, management in effect is saying "we're through bargaining" or "this is it." It is unfortunate that many employers have used these words as a bluff and that their bluff has been successfully called by the union often enough so that "final" has come to mean "near the end" or "just a little bit more." In fact, the term "final-final" has been coined to describe the next offer just after such a "final" offer. Credibility in such situations has been lost and, once lost, is not easily recovered.

Management must realize that unless it is prepared to make a "final offer" really final, it should refrain from using those words. Settlements can be reached without them. There are substitute words which can be used to signal to the union that the end of negotiations is at hand, yet not put management's credibility on the line when the offer is subsequently increased.

Such words as "best," "complete," and "total" all carry a connotation of finality, but still lack the uncompromising nature of the word "final." After all, a "best offer" can simply mean that it is higher than all previous offers. This is not to suggest that a "final offer" should not be made or should not be denoted as such. The only point here is that if you do not mean to stand behind your words and make the final offer truly final, you should not use them.

Finality as an Aid to Both Sides

While the words "final offer" may appear to carry a confrontational connotation, they certainly need not do so. In fact, many union negotiators will freely admit that they need management to say that an offer is "final." Otherwise, their constituents at the bargaining table or in the bargaining unit will not believe that everything possible has been obtained. This is particularly true of unsophisticated union representatives who are themselves members of the bargaining unit, who may participate in one negotiation every three years, and who believe, unless management says "it's final," that there is "more money in the sack."

Exceptions to Finality

In order to allow for the flexibility which may be necessary for a settlement, yet retain management's credibility, the presentation of a final offer should always carry an explanation that the word "final" refers to the overall cost of the offer for each year of the proposed contract. It does not mean that management would not consider some readjustments within the package as long as the overall cost is not increased. This would not, however, include advancing wages or benefits from a later to an earlier year since that would increase the cost of the package (on a time-weighted basis). Similarly, the explanation of finality with respect to noneconomic issues can include a statement that management is willing to "dot an 'i' or cross a 't' " if necessary, but that any substantive changes are not acceptable.

Aside from these limited expectations, management's final offer must be final. For this reason, it must be made at the proper time and contain the necessary ingredients.

Piecing the Settlement Together

Another form of working toward a conclusion, also discussed in Chapter 7, is the "piecemeal approach." This is a method by which the parties deal with isolated issues or groups of economic issues, reaching agreement on some issues while leaving others unresolved. It avoids the package offer concepts. The danger of this approach, from management's standpoint, is that agreements on certain cost elements can be reached without knowing the magnitude of other portions of the economic package. This disadvantage can be mitigated somewhat by emphasizing to the union that commitments made on such economic issues are contingent upon agreement being reached on the balance of the package. In other words, if the union's demands on one of the last unresolved issues (e.g., pensions) are too costly, management may have to reduce the tentative agreement on wages in order to pay for the higher pension benefits sought by the union.

Bringing the negotiations to a conclusion under this type of bargaining differs from the "final offer" approach in several ways. One difference is that the range of issues is usually narrower and therefore the range of options possible for a settlement is more limited because there are fewer possible variations. The movement toward a settlement does not involve putting total packages together. It is more like two people trying to find the right pieces to complete a jigsaw puzzle. The parties more or less ignore those portions of the package on which they have reached agreement and focus only on the few remaining unresolved issues. This is not to say that the total package cost is overlooked. It is simply that the elements, singly or in small groups, of the package are treated independently. In doing so, management must always be keeping an accurate account of how much the union is putting into its shopping cart. Accurate cost-estimating is continually required.

In most cases, the last pieces of the puzzle will be the most difficult ones, and management will usually have to make clear what its final offer is on those unresolved elements of the package.

Techniques for Avoiding or Resolving an Impasse

The management negotiator's primary function is to reach an agreement with the union within the economic and other parameters established for the negotiations. Numerous roadblocks will be encountered throughout the bargaining, and it is the negotiator's job to remove or circumvent them one by one. As the negotiations move toward a conclusion, however, the roadblocks become more troublesome. The easy problems get solved first, while the most difficult ones remain. Unless these roadblocks are eliminated or avoided, impasse is likely to result. It is in dealing with the particularly difficult roadblocks that management's spokesperson earns his or her keep. In this respect, the spokesperson must be a problem solver. And because each negotiation presents its own set of roadblocks, what may be successful in one negotiation will not necessarily work in another. Nevertheless, there are some time-tested techniques which can be useful in a variety of contexts to avoid impasse.

Private or Off-the-Record Meetings

A majority of negotiations are conducted in a formal, arm's-length setting. That is to say, the parties come together only in meetings where each side is represented by a bargaining committee, notes of the meeting are kept by each side, and proposals and counterproposals are exchanged. This is the traditional setting. There are, however, other types of negotiations where the above-described meetings are conducted but the real bargaining takes place in private meetings attended only by the spokespersons for the respective parties. In some cases, the spokespersons may also have one or two other trusted aides in attendance at such meetings. These meetings might be called "private," "back-room," "side bar," or "off-the-record" meetings.

There are some negotiations in which these meetings are held regularly throughout the course of bargaining and others in which they are held only periodically—usually near the conclusion of negotiations. The meetings might take place in an office, a hotel room, a bar or restaurant, or any other convenient location. In most cases, these meetings are secret in the sense that most constituents of both parties are not aware that they are occurring. In other cases, the occurrence of the meetings may be known, but the substance is not disclosed. The use of the private meeting is discussed in this section not so much in regard to its use as a type of ongoing bargaining, but rather with respect to its occasional use as a means to remove or circumvent bargaining roadblocks.

Ethics of Private Meetings

At the outset, it should be understood that there is nothing illegal, immoral, or unethical about these meetings, as such. Although it is possible for them to be used as a means to reach illegal or "sweetheart" agreements, the meetings themselves are perfectly legitimate. The secret or semiclandestine nature of such get-togethers can carry a connotation of impropriety, but as long as the participants properly represent their respective principals/constituents and their agreements conform to the law and to ethical standards, there is nothing improper about them.

Extension of Formal Meetings

The real value of the private meeting is that it permits the negotiators to explore possible concessions and areas of settlement as well as to explain politically sensitive matters and rationales which could not be expressed in an open meeting. By speaking off the record, neither negotiator gets locked into a position merely because he expresses a position different from the one taken in formal negotiations. Management's spokesperson, though, must not be misled into believing that such meetings are so off the record that all defenses can be dropped, or that nothing is lost by revealing management's final parameters or possible concessions. In fact, the private meeting is simply an extension of the negotiations conducted at the bargaining table. Although somewhat more candor can be used in the private meeting, the management negotiator should make no mistake about it: the union counterpart is still bargaining. In reality, one can give away as much in such informal discussions as in a formal meeting.

Trust Is Crucial

The potential for success of private meetings is essentially dependent upon the relationship between the respective negotiators. The trust, confidence, and respect they have for one another will largely determine whether the technique will be successful. Both persons must have the confidence that opinions and ideas expressed will be kept confidential. And there must be a mutually held belief that the other person is using the meeting to seek a path toward agreement, and not merely using it to gain a bargaining advantage.

The management spokesperson should be careful in off-the-record meetings not to make commitments or even suggestions of commitments that are not within the established parameters or not previously cleared with his principals. This does not mean that he or she cannot explore new areas or discuss new concepts as long as the union counterpart is told that the discussions are purely exploratory and that the ideas have not even been reviewed with, let alone approved by, management's principals.

It is important that management's spokesperson or an aide who is in attendance make notes of these meetings. If it does not seem appropriate to do so while the meeting is taking place, it should be done as soon thereafter as possible. Although the meeting is truly off the record, it does not mean that later reference will not need to be made to clarify a questionable point or refresh a recollection.

Although some unions religiously avoid such meetings for fear that they could be accused of having colluded with management, most mature and sophisticated union representatives are willing to participate in such meetings. Some years ago the author was bargaining with a union that had an unwritten policy against private meetings. At the latter stages of negotiations several thorny issues were still unresolved, and the need for off-the-record discussions was obvious. At the suggestion of the union spokesperson, two members of each committee moved to one end of the negotiating table and all note taking was stopped. Informal discussion in near whispers took place at one end of the table while the remaining members of the two bargaining committees engaged in small talk. The technique proved useful in advancing those difficult negotiations to a successful settlement. While such an awkward arrangement is not recommended here, it does show that, no matter how reluctant a party may be to engage in off-the-record negotiations, the private meeting does serve a most useful function in avoiding impasse.

Oral Agreements

Sometimes off-the-record meetings result in the parties making an oral agreement which is not to be set forth in the labor agreement or in any other written document. In effect, it is a "gentlemen's agreement."

The pitfalls of such an agreement cannot be overstated! First, if the agreement is not in writing and signed by the parties, there can be a dispute over whether it was ever made. Second, without a writing there can be numerous disagreements about what was actually agreed upon. Third, even if both parties concede that an agreement was reached and do not dispute the terms of that agreement, the agreement may be nullified by a court if it is contested by some other interested party, i.e., employees. In *Merk et al v. Jewel Food Stores and Unified Food and Commercial Workers Union, Local No. 881,*[1] a secret agreement was entered into by a food chain and food workers union that the employer could reopen the subject of wages if another supermarket chain entered the Chicago area market. This agreement was not disclosed to the employees and was not a part of the contract settlement ratified by the union's membership. When a new competitor entered the market, the parties reopened the contract and agreed to reduce wages. Affected employees challenged the wage cut agreement, and their case was upheld by a federal appeals court on the basis that it violated federal labor law and the union's constitution which required ratification of significant contract provisions.

While significant trust and confidence can develop between union and management negotiators, that trust and confidence should not go so far as to enter into oral agreements that are not reduced to writing, signed by the parties, or made a part of the final settlement package.

Creative Bargaining

During the late 1970s and early 1980s the term "creative financing" became popular in the real estate field. It was a term used to describe various techniques in financing the sale and purchase of real estate which went beyond conventional financing methods. By using new financing devices (such as wraparound mortgages, variable-interest mortgages, and shared-equity ownership) and/or a combination of existing financing tools (such as assumable loans and seller financing), deals could be put together under conditions where conventional financing was simply inadequate. A great deal of ingenuity and flexibility went into the development of these programs.

The opportunity for creativity exists in any type of negotiation. The essential ingredients are that the negotiating parties must be sufficiently motivated to reach an agreement, that they must be able to use their ingenuity to explore new ways of doing business together, and that they must be willing to make certain accommodations in their respective affairs in order to reach an agreement and make it work. Although the scope of possible creative arrangements in labor contract negotiations is almost infinite, some examples of creative approaches are given below.

Varying the Variables

Not so much an example of a creative arrangement, but rather a concept which underlies many such arrangements, is what might be called "varying the variables." This simply means that when a roadblock appears, one should consider changing one or more of those elements which can be varied.

Shifting Numbers

One of the main variables in a labor contract is *time* or *duration*. Consequently, when the parties are at loggerheads on a given economic package, they should consider changing the length of time of the contract and the length of time various improvements are in effect. If an offer for a three-year contract with 5 percent wage increases in each year is unacceptable because the union is seeking a higher increase in the first year, but the employer is unwilling to increase the overall cost of the package, an offer of 7 percent–3 percent–4 percent may be more acceptable to the union and may even be more palatable to management, especially since the overall increase in wages is 14 percent rather than 15 percent. Another variation would be to use a midyear increase in the first year, for example a 4.5 percent increase on the new contract date, 2.5 percent six months later followed by another 2.5 percent in six months, and 5 percent for the last 12 months of the contract. Using the same time-weighting method of costing described in Chapter 10, the weighted average percentage increase in each case is approximately 5 percent per year. Although none of these variations represent any startling creativity, they do illustrate the potential value of flexibility in putting a package together.

Shifting Time

Another possible variation involving time is a contract term not evenly divisible by 12 months. Most contracts are in full-year increments, e.g., one year, two years, or three years. Under this arrangement, the anniversary date of the contract remains the same (e.g., July 1), and the expiration date naturally falls on that same date. Where an impasse is approaching or exists, however, a contract term of 28 months or 32 months may offer some opportunities for each side to move from its previous position which was based upon a 24- or 36-month contract.

For example, an offer for a 24-month contract with an expiration date of July 1 may be unacceptable to the union because it does not include any increase in the number of holidays or the vacation entitlement schedule. Management, on the other hand, has reached its economic limits with that offer. Management, however, may desire a contract expiration date of October 1 because it would remove the next round of contract negotiations (and hopefully all subsequent rounds) from the employer's peak demand season. Moving to this contract expiration date would also mean that economic increases under the contract would be forestalled for three months beyond the date they would normally be increased (i.e., from July 1 to October 1), which would constitute a savings. The union might agree to a 27-month contract if management would be willing to improve holidays and/or vacations in order to "buy" the additional three months. While such odd-length contract settlements are not common, the management negotiator should not become so locked into 12-month increment packages that he or she does not even see or explore a different contract term as a way to avoid or resolve impasse.

Reaching Beyond the Contract Term

Altering the time when contract changes go into effect, either by advancing or delaying time, is one of the most common ways of varying the variables to make an offer more saleable. However, there is a tendency for negotiators to regard the term of a labor contract as setting the outer limits on effective dates. This need not be so.

Contract changes can be made effective prior to the beginning of a new contract, and closure of issues can be extended beyond the terminal date of the contract. Using the earlier example of a three-year offer of wage increases of 5 percent–5 percent–5 percent, the union's need for more money "up front" can be met without increasing overall negotiated wage rates (although with an increase in cash outflow) by making the first year's wage increase retroactive to a date prior to the first day of the new contract. This would amount to a lump sum payment when the new contract is signed. For example, if the average wage was $12 per hour and the increase was made retroactive for four months, the average employee would receive a lump payment of approximately $550 ($12.00 × 0.05 = $0.60 × 173 hours per month × 4 months). Although the cost to the employer is greater than in the previous offer, an agreement without an increase in the wage levels beyond those already offered and avoiding higher wage levels going into the next contract negotiations (i.e., not providing a higher base from which to negotiate increases in the next contract) is preferable to an agreement with higher conventional wage or benefit increases.

Another way of reaching beyond the contract term is to move forward. This is sometimes done by trading a concession in the current contract for the union's willingness not to negotiate on that subject for some period in the future. For example, management may agree to grant significant improvements in its pension plan during a three-year contract in exchange for the union's willingness to agree that pensions will be closed as a subject for bargaining for three years beyond the end of the contract being negotiated. This way the union is able to obtain improvements in pensions in the current contract that it might not otherwise be able to obtain, while management is able to assure that its pension costs (or at least pension benefits) will remain fixed for a six-year period. In effect, there is a separate agreement on pensions, the term of which is six years.

Shifting From Wages to Fringes

Although the exchange of a wage increase, or portion thereof, for a fringe improvement may not appear to be creative, it does have an aspect which can creatively avoid an impasse. It is a valuable technique because of the rollup effect. As explained in Chapter 10, the rollup effect is an automatic increase in certain fringe benefits as a result of a wage increase. Because of this, each 10-cent-per-hour increase in wages will normally result in an automatic increase of two to four cents per hour in fringe costs (assuming a rollup factor of 20 percent to 40 percent). Thus a 10-cent-per-hour wage increase actually costs the employer 12 cents to 14 cents per hour.

While a large number of union negotiators, at least sophisticated union negotiators, are well aware of this phenomenon, there are many who do not know or fully understand it.

Even those who do know and understand it are apt to overlook it in the heat of negotiations. Consequently, it is sometimes possible to take money out of wages and buy additional fringes, giving the appearance of management's having increased the size of the offer. For example, assume that the union tells management that its last offer of a two-year contract with wages increased by 50 cents per hour in each year is acceptable except that the union needs to have a dental plan, which is known to cost an additional 26 cents per hour. Management responds that it will not increase the size of its overall offer, but by reducing the wage increase in each of the first and second years by 13 cents per hour (i.e., to 37 cents per hour), the dental plan can be put into effect in the second year of the contract. The union responds that it will only agree to reduce management's previous wage offer by 8 cents per hour per year (to 42 cents per hour) to obtain the dental plan. Assuming a rollup factor of 30 percent, management could offer a compromise offer of wage increases of 40 cents per hour (10 cents per hour less in each year) without increasing the overall cost of its previous offer. Because each 10 cents per hour in wages actually costs 13 cents per hour because of rollup ($0.10 × 1.3), a reduction of 20 cents per hour in the wage offer over the two years will equal the 26-cent-per-hour reduction in the package offer necessary to fund a dental plan ($0.20 × 1.3). In this example, management must be sure that any inflationary costs of the dental plan during the term of the contract are included in the 26-cent-per-hour cost, or that if the cost goes beyond this amount, employees will pay the additional amount.

Importance of Appearances

One cannot overestimate the importance of appearances. So often how things look is as important as, or more important than, what they are. The Japanese concept of "saving face," which plays such a vital part in labor negotiations, is based on the notion that the side making concessions should not be embarrassed by the impression others may have of the way in which the concessions were made. Thus, an essential technique for the management negotiator in avoiding or resolving an impasse is to learn how to make the union negotiator look good to his constituents.

Form of Wage Increases

One of the key appearance factors in negotiations is the way in which a wage increase is expressed. A 5 percent wage increase may be expressed as an average hourly increase of 60 cents per hour (assuming an average wage rate of $12.00 per hour) or as an average weekly increase of $24.00 per week ($0.60 per hour × 40 hours per week), or as an average increase of $103.80 per month ($0.60 per hour × 173 hours per month). As the period of time used for the computations increases, the attractiveness of the figure increases.

Because a percentage increase benefits employees who are in the higher wage brackets, and an across-the-board, cents-per-hour increase benefits lower-wage-bracket employees, a union will normally be sensitive to the group having the greater political clout within the union and the group which will have the most impact in a contract ratification vote. Consequently, if the unskilled lower wage group is larger and more politically powerful than the higher skilled, higher wage group, the union's emphasis will be on an across-the-board increase. The danger of this to the employer is that, if followed for a succession of years, the difference between wage rates of low- and high-skilled employees becomes smaller, creating a compression of wage rates. This, in turn, fosters a disincentive for employees to upgrade their skills and makes the employer less competitive in recruiting skilled employees in the labor market because its wage rates for skilled employees are less attractive.

The trap that sometimes creates a push for the union to negotiate across-the-board wage increases is the appearance factor. A 60-cent-per-hour wage increase somehow seems to sound better than a 5 percent increase. However, to a skilled employee earning $17.00 per hour, a 60-cent-per-hour increase amounts to only a 3½ percent increase ($0.60 ÷ $17.00). A 5 percent increase to such a highly skilled employee would yield an 85-cent-per-hour increase. The skilled worker has sacrificed 25¢ per hour to meet the union's needs.

Meeting Both Sides' Needs

As can be seen, the form of a wage increase sometimes has to be tailored to meet the needs of both sides—the employer's need to maintain a sufficient wage spread between low-

and high-skilled employees, and the union's need to look good to its constituents and to keep powerblocks in its membership happy. This is often done by percentage increases and across-the-board increases given in alternate years. For example, in a three-year agreement, annual wage increases could be 5 percent–60 cents–5 percent. Another technique used to deal with the appearance problem is the graduated bracket approach, whereby the increases are expressed in cents per hour but vary with the levels of wages so that the increases are actually on a percentage basis. Hence, a graduated bracket wage increase roughly equivalent to a 5 percent increase in a bargaining unit where the average hourly wage rate is $12.00 would look something like this:

Wage Rate Group	Amount of Increase	Wage Rate Group	Amount of Increase
Below $10.00	48¢	$13.50–$14.00	70¢
$10.00–$10.50	51¢	$14.00–$14.50	73¢
$10.50–$11.00	54¢	$14.50–$15.00	75¢
$11.00–$11.50	57¢	$15.00–$15.50	78¢
$11.50–$12.00	60¢	$15.50–$16.00	80¢
$12.00–$12.50	63¢	$16.00–$16.50	82¢
$12.50–$13.00	65¢	$16.50–$17.00	84¢
$13.00–$13.50	68¢	Over $17.00	86¢

The cost of this arrangement can only be determined by knowing the number of employees or work hours in each wage grouping. However, if there is a relatively even distribution of work hours throughout the bargaining unit, the overall cost of the schedule shown above would approximate a 5 percent increase. While it might appear to be a game of mirrors, this kind of presentation does have some advantage for the union in helping employees to see the settlement in terms of cents per hour rather than as a 5 percent increase.

Following an Apparent Pattern

The importance of appearances can be illustrated by citing a negotiation in which the author was involved some years ago. In this case the union was seeking to match a pattern which its sister local unions had negotiated with several other employers. In previous years the employer had given this plant the "pattern settlement" established at other plants, but it was determined not to do so this year. The employer had come to realize that the pattern had been set at its other plants which had basic economics different from those of this particular plant. The union failed to accept this reality, and, for a number of reasons, the negotiations were delayed for many months.

By the time serious bargaining took place, nearly one year had elapsed since the contract expiration date. At that point, the union was still holding out for the pattern wage settlement, which was 10 percent, 9 percent, and 8 percent respectively in three years, while management's final offer was 6 percent, 6 percent, and 5 percent. The union struck. This particular plant was not crucial to the company's overall operations and the union leadership knew it. However, the union could not gracefully accept a "substandard" settlement after many years of parity with its sister locals. Pride was as important as economics. The dilemma was to make management's 6 percent–6 percent–5 percent offer look as good as the union's 10 percent–9 percent–8 percent goal without costing the employer any more money. To break the impasse and because nearly a whole year had gone by sincc thc contract expiration date, management decided to offer the first year's wage increase as a bonus, and not include it in the wage rates. In this way, employees could receive a lump sum equivalent to 10 percent, but the employer's wage costs would not permanently increase thereby. The second year's wage increase of 9 percent could then be put into effect upon the signing of the contract (which was the second year of the contract) and added to the wage rates, and the union's desired third-year increase of 8 percent could subsequently be granted.

By so doing it was possible to grant a settlement of "10 percent–9 percent–8 percent" which cost the employer roughly the same amount as a 6 percent–6 percent–5 percent wage package because the first year's 10 percent increase was simply a bonus and was not paid in any years beyond the first year.

Mathematically the two packages looked approximately as shown in Table 12–1.

The prestrike offer saved management 2.6 cents per hour in the long run ($1.77 vs. $1.796), whereas the strike settlement offer cost 4 cents more per hour in cash outflow over the three-year term ($3.67 vs. $3.63). However, since the 10-cent bonus did not become part of the wage rate there was no rollup effect.

Table 12–1. Strike Settlement Package and Associated Costs Utilizing Bonus

	*Incremental wages (rollup not included)**			
Prestrike offer	Year 1	Year 2	Year 3	Total
(6%–6%–5%)	$0.60	$0.636	$0.56	$1.796
Strike settlement offer				
(10%–9%–8%)	—	$0.90	$0.87	$1.77
	*Cash flow analysis (rollup not included)**			
Prestrike offer	Year 1	Year 2	Year 3	Total
6%	$0.60	$0.60	$0.60	$1.80
6%	—	0.636	$0.636	1.27
5%	—	—	0.56	0.56
				$3.63
Strike settlement offer				
10% (bonus)	$1.00	—	—	$1.00
9%	—	$0.90	$0.90	1.80
8%	—	—	0.87	0.87
				$3.67

*Average straight time wages = $10.00/hour.

Consequently, taking rollup into account (with a rollup factor of 30 percent), the strike settlement package cash outflow was 30 cents per hour less than it would otherwise have been ($1.00 × 0.30). Therefore, even on a cash flow basis, the settlement offer was less costly than the prestrike offer.

There was no trickery involved in that negotiation because the union negotiator and the membership fully understood that the first year's increase was merely a bonus and that the settlement offer of 10 percent–9 percent–8 percent was not the same as the pattern settlement which the union had negotiated with other employers. However, the two packages *sounded* alike, and to satisfy whatever political needs it had, the union leadership was able to represent that it had gotten a "10–9–8 settlement." The publicity concerning the settlement, however, made it clear that the first-year increase was only a one-time event, and it was generally understood in the community and by business and labor in that industry that the union had not gotten any more after the strike than it had been offered before the strike. Appearances were, however, important to the union so that it and its members could save face.

Creative Writing

Bargaining impasses arise not only over economic issues, but over failure to agree on noneconomic or contract language matters. Basic concepts held by one party often collide with those of the other, and a stalemate may develop. On the employer's side, management rights issues are frequently at stake, whereas on the union's side, seniority and union security are frequently key issues.

A way chosen by some negotiators and some mediators to avoid such a stalemate is to do some "creative writing." This is a technique whereby the parties who have not reached a complete meeting of the minds attempt to come up with language that will carry the essence of those aspects upon which they have reached agreement, but leave vague the items on which they still disagree. In an international relations context, this vagueness has been given the intriguing title of "constructive ambiguity."

Finessing Disagreements

This device is simply a way of avoiding an impasse by finessing the disagreement. For example, parties who have still not come to a common understanding may be willing to dodge the issue by writing language that concedes something to each side, but which leaves the confrontational aspects somewhat ambiguous so that each party will have some latitude to make an argument at a later time.

This technique could be used, for instance, in a negotiation where the union has made a major issue of the employer's extensive use of subcontractors to perform work which, the union argues, rightfully belongs to the bargaining unit, and the existing contract is silent on the subject. The union seeks an outright prohibition on subcontracting, whereas management wants the contract to remain as it is. After many days of arguing on the subject, the parties are at loggerheads. All other issues have been resolved save the thorny issue of subcontracting, and a strike over this issue seems like a distinct possibility. As the eleventh hour is at hand, the following constructively ambiguous clause is agreed upon:

> It is recognized that the integrity of the bargaining unit should be preserved to the extent possible. Notwithstanding such recognition, this contract does not preclude the subcontracting of bargaining unit work where such considerations as skills, costs, proper equipment, available time to complete work, number of qualified bargaining unit employees on layoff, and past practice indicate that it is reasonable and prudent to do so.

It must be perfectly obvious to both sides that they have simply "passed the buck" to an arbitrator, who will have to interpret such vague language in relation to a specific set of facts when subcontracting issues arise. Nevertheless, the union has achieved some limitation on management's right to subcontract, and management has retained flexibility to subcontract where appropriate circumstances warrant. Moreover, a strike has been avoided. No doubt management and supervision at the facility involved will be faced with a most difficult task of having to determine when they may or may not subcontract work.

Creative writing need not always be so ambiguous. Frequently it is possible to draft language which captures enough of the essence of areas of mutual interest on a disputed issue that the areas of disagreement are minimal. Such draftsmanship is a true art. Regardless of the degree of ambiguity in the language, management negotiators should realize the pitfalls of creative writing. By inserting vague language in a labor agreement, management runs the risk that its operating managers and supervisors will interpret it so loosely that more of management's rights will be given away than if more restrictive, but specific, language had been agreed upon. So too, an arbitrator may unduly restrict management when given such an open field within which to run. Creative writing as described in this section is a device which should be used sparingly, and only when absolutely necessary.

Reexamination of Principles

The contentious issues which often necessitate creative writing (e.g., management's rights, seniority, union security), often involve matters of "principle" to each side. From management's viewpoint, the right to make basic decisions about how the business is to be run, how services to the customer are to be rendered, and the like are guarded with justifiable jealously. These should never be given away.

Basic Principles

The dividing line between basic principles and *not so basic* principles is, however, rather fuzzy. For example, would it be a basic principle that management should have the unilateral right to select bargaining unit leadpersons or working leads as opposed to having seniority be a factor in the selection? How basic is it to management's rights that employees may be assigned to work in departments in which they hold no seniority? And how basic is the right of employees to work in the employer's facility without the requirement that they join the union? Obviously, such questions will elicit different answers depending upon management's philosophy on labor relations, the type of industry and work process involved, the geographical location of the facility, the tradition within the workplace, the degree of management's bargaining leverage, and many other factors. It is submitted that, with the exception of certain very crucial subjects, the determination of basic or essential principles is a relative judgment.

Careful Examination

If this is so, management should take great pains to examine each of the principles it is trying to protect or recapture before its activities in this regard result in an impasse and/or strike. It is simply too easy to proceed through negotiations on the premise that vital management's rights or other principles are at stake, and to allow such premises to lead management into, or to the brink of, a strike, without a thorough examination of the principle(s) at stake. This is not to suggest that such principles do not exist, or are not worth taking a strike for. Not in the least. Indeed, there are too many employers who have failed to recognize vital management's rights and other principles, and have foolishly bargained them away.

The only advice offered here is for management to carefully and thoroughly consider each principle which it is seeking to protect or recapture and which is creating, or likely to create, an impasse. It is necessary to identify the essence of the principle, and what would be sacrificed if some compromise or concession were to be agreed upon. If the principle is worth fighting for, go for it. If not, do not get bloodied over something which is not worth the fight.

Optional Offers

One of the difficulties with the "final offer" approach to closing negotiations is that it does not offer much, if any, choice. It is usually presented on a "take it or leave it" basis. Besides, the somewhat confrontational tone of a final offer (no matter how professionally it may be offered) presents special problems when the union is seriously seeking several changes from management's previous offer and all of these changes cannot be incorporated in the final proposal.

A technique that is sometimes helpful in such a situation is the optional or "A vs. B" offer. With this approach, management prepares two separate offers, usually of equal or approximately equal value and gives the union bargaining committee the opportunity to select either. For example, an offer for a two-year contract valued at a 9 percent increase over two years might be offered as option "A," while a three-year contract valued at 15 percent over three years might be offered as option "B." The three-year offer is more valuable on an annual basis, reflecting management's desire to obtain a three-year contract. The bargaining committee can select one of the two proposals and present that offer to the membership in a ratification election, or it can present the membership with both offers, allowing them to vote for either option or for neither.

This technique appeals to the natural human desire to have choices. On the other hand, it can be confusing, and it can suggest to the union negotiators that maybe the best of both offers is possible if they simply persist long enough. Considerable advance conditioning is advisable before presenting this kind of offer in order to guard against such a reaction.

The options need not necessarily be between two complete offers. Some aspect of a single offer may contain optional provisions. For example, an offer may permit the union to select between two different types of medical insurance plans. The union leadership may even wish to pass the choice on to its membership rather than make what could be a politically difficult choice.

In addition to its value as a means of avoiding impasse at the bargaining table, the optional offer approach has a value in diverting attention away from the choice between acceptance and rejection. With this approach the principal choice is between A and B (i.e., between two positives), rather than between a positive and a negative.

Splitting the Difference

When two parties are relatively close to making a deal but some difference remains between their positions, the natural course of compromise is to "split the difference"—to have each party move halfway along the distance separating them. In doing this, there will be a feeling that the burden of compromise has been shared equally. In fact, this may not be the case. One party may have previously moved relatively much farther from its bargaining objective than the other party. Nonetheless, when the final deal is being made, splitting the difference sounds like the "fair" thing to do. With this in mind, management should prepare its offer strategy in such a way that room will be left at the end to split the remaining differences.

Contingent Commitment

Because of the difficulty in forecasting what may happen in the course of the typical two, three, or sometimes five years of a labor contract, one party or the other may be unwilling to commit itself to a long-term agreement. Nevertheless, such agreements are helpful from the standpoint of labor relations stability. A solution to this problem is to make a contingent commitment, i.e., an agreement to do something if something else happens. Probably the best (and in many ways the worst) example of this is the cost-of-living adjustment (COLA), which obligates management to pay a given amount of additional wages if the cost of living, as measured by the U.S. Consumer Price Index (CPI), increases by a given amount.

Although the author has a very strong aversion to COLAs, there are other types of contingent commitments which he finds not so disadvantageous. Consider, for example, a situation in which the union seeks to increase the number of weeks of vacation an employee may be able to take during the summer months while the employer wishes to limit summer vacation time because of heavy production or service requirements during those months. An agreement might be reached whereby the number of weeks of vacation which can be taken during the summer months will be increased if the level of orders scheduled to be run during such months falls below a predetermined amount.

Relate Contingency to Employer's Needs and Capabilities

The key to a successful contingent agreement is to relate the contingency to management's need or ability to pay, not to some other event. The reason COLAs have proven to be so devastating to management is that under such arrangements labor costs automatically increase according to the cost of living, not according to the employer's ability to pay. Architects of COLAs no doubt assumed that an employer's prices and profits would follow the CPI, and therefore there would be little risk in agreeing to increase wages proportionately with that index. Unfortunately, they were seriously off the mark. During the 1970s, due largely to generous COLAs, wages went through the roof in many industries in which employers were incurring losses. To be useful, the contingency must be tied to the employer's needs or capabilities. In the vacation example given above, a decrease in orders during the summer would reduce management's staffing needs during those months. Hence, it would be feasible for management to allow more vacations at times when staffing needs are reduced.

The contingent commitment can be a dangerous way to avoid an impasse. It should be used very sparingly and only when management is prepared to live with a "worst case" scenario. In other words, when considering such a provision, a management negotiator should assume that the event or condition upon which the contingency is based will occur, and assume the worst set of circumstances which could reasonably exist at the time the event could occur. Can you live with it? If you cannot, do not enter into a contingent agreement.

Tying Agreements

When union and management are able to work out most aspects of a potential agreement, but are still apart on one or a few items, impasse can sometimes be avoided or resolved by tying the unresolved provision(s) to some other negotiation(s). For example, if the negotiating parties cannot agree on the level of pension benefits to be in effect during the second and third years of a three-year contract for bargaining unit X, they might agree that the benefit will be that which the employer provides to bargaining unit Y, the contract for which will be negotiated the following year. This allows management to obtain a settlement for bargaining unit X now, yet retain control over the level of pensions for bargaining unit X through its negotiations with bargaining unit Y the following year. If the employer has more leverage in the negotiations with bargaining unit Y, it will have enhanced its position vis-a-vis bargaining unit X. If, however, the union which is negotiating for bargaining unit Y is in a stronger bargaining position than bargaining unit X, the employer may have simply postponed the moment of truth.

"Most Favored Nation" Clause

A special form of tying agreement is the "most favored nation" clause. Under such an arrangement in a labor negotiating context, the employer agrees to grant a particular bargaining unit the wage, benefit, or contract provisions which are at least as favorable as any one of a defined group of other bargaining units. An example of a most favored nation clause is as follows:

> Employees shall be entitled to receive vacation benefits (i.e., weeks of entitlement and vacation pay) which are no less favorable than those provided under any labor agreement between the union and any employer in the food processing industry in the state of Florida.

In this example, the employer has virtually signed a blank check, in that it has allowed the union and some other employer (no matter how small or atypical that employer's business may be) to determine its vacation benefits. Such open-ended agreements are ill-advised because the employer has yielded the right to negotiate its vacation benefits to a third party. A most favored nation clause, if used at all, should tie the agreement or provision to one or more bargaining units, the negotiations with which are conducted by the employer itself.

Tying to Other Contracts

Because of an employer's small size and/or lack of comparable bargaining units, it may not be possible to use one or more of that employer's other units as the reference unit. The next best alternative is to tie the unresolved contract provision(s) to the *average*—not the highest—of the same contract provision in the labor agreements of a defined group of comparable bargaining units. By selecting an average, the employer can avoid the harsh effects from aberrations which sometimes emerge from other employers' negotiations. The larger the number of bargaining units from which the average is calculated, the safer the result. An example of such a provision would be as follows:

> The general wage increase to be effective in the third year of the labor agreement shall be equal to a weighted average of the hourly general wage increases negotiated by employer-members of the Widget Manufacturers Association and the United Widget Makers International Unit during the year 19___. The computation of the weighted average will be based upon the number of employees in each respective bargaining unit multiplied by the average hourly general wage increase for each bargaining unit.

If the employer competes in the widget manufacturing industry and is confident that the members of the widget association will negotiate responsibly, the agreement may not be burdensome. No matter how careful an employer is in agreeing to such a tying arrangement, however, the employer must be realistic in recognizing that it has delegated its negotiating responsibilities to others and will have to live with the results of their bargaining—favorable or unfavorable. To the extent that the agreement is tied to a sufficiently large number of other bargaining units of comparable size which are in the same industry or product market, and cover the same type of employees and job classifications in the same geographical area, the tying agreement should not put the employer at any serious competitive disadvantage.

A tying agreement often has the particular advantage of permitting the employer to negotiate a longer-term contract than would otherwise be the case, and it avoids the potentially hazardous results which accompany a COLA clause, which is the major alternative for pegging future wage increases. Because COLAs are based upon the rate of inflation rather than other indices more related to the employer's ability to pay, they are usually riskier to the employer than a tying arrangement of the type described above.

Using Others to Avoid Impasse

Up to this point, the suggested ways of avoiding impasse have been those within the sole control of the management and union negotiators. Unfortunately, the efforts of these two people may not be sufficient, and the help of others may be required. Egos of the respective spokespersons should not be allowed to stand in the way of getting such help.

Mediation

It is usually difficult to know just when, and if, mediation is appropriate. As a general rule, mediation is resorted to when all else has failed to resolve an impasse. This puts a rather heavy burden on mediators, but it is a role they are accustomed to assuming.

Mediators may be employees of the federal government (Federal Mediation and Conciliation Service), employees of a state government (state mediation service), or privately employed. They are usually persons who have had significant experience in the field of labor-management relations, either on the employer or the union side of the table. The services of federal and state mediators are available at little or no charge, and these individuals usually offer their services without any specific request having been made.

As a matter of law, federal mediators are given a copy of FMCS Form F-7 (Exhibit 2–11) which notifies that agency of the contract renegotiation. Generally, the mediator contacts both negotiating parties sometime prior to the contract expiration date to see if his services are required. Mediation services are also available upon request through the appropriate state or federal mediation office. When a mediator is assigned to one's negotiation, it is a good idea to find out something about that person if one has had no previous experience with him or her. This can be done by contacting other management negotiators in the same geographical area and obtaining their evaluations. Knowing his characteristics and leanings ahead of time can prove valuable.

The function of a mediator is to conciliate, counsel, persuade, dissuade, and assist the negotiating parties in any legitimate way so that they are able to reach an agreement. The function of a mediator is not to judge, decide, or arbitrate disagreements between the two sides. Having the assistance of a government or private mediator is completely voluntary on the part of union and management. Either one or both sides may reject offered government mediation services, although as a practical matter this is not frequently done. Instead of using a federal or state mediation service, the parties may choose to use a private mediator they may select by mutual agreement.

Objectives and Modus Operandi *of Mediators*

It should always be kept in mind that the sole objective of a mediator is to see that an agreement is reached and a work stoppage is avoided or stopped. A mediator has no inherent concern for management's rights, the viability of the employer's business, or effective representation of the membership by the union. This is not to suggest that a mediator is hostile to these objectives, but simply that they are not the mediator's concern. Consequently, the mediator will let management (or the union for that matter) negotiate away almost anything to get an agreement if management (or the union) is willing to do so. In other words, if you are management's negotiator, do not count on a mediator to protect your interests, except to the extent that a settlement may assist in that regard. The mediator will assume that you are looking out for management's best interests, and that your union counterpart is doing likewise for the union's members.

Different mediators have different modes of operations, although there are certain common techniques which most mediators, public or private, employ. As a general rule, the mediator will initially meet with the full union and management bargaining committees. At that time, or shortly thereafter, the mediator will meet with smaller groups and have each side state its current position in the negotiations and which issues each side perceives to be unresolved. The next meetings are usually held separately with the respective bargaining committees, or several members from each committee. Some mediators skip the initial joint meeting and simply begin with separate meetings.

From this point, the mediator will seek to isolate the key issues and probe for possible concessions and areas of compromise on these issues. In so doing, the mediator must be very careful not to indicate to one side that the other side is willing to make a concession until he is sure that the necessary *quid pro quo* or tradeoff can be secured. The process generally has the mediator shuttling from one caucus room to the other carrying different proposals, ideas, and packages in an effort to hammer out an agreement.

Working With a Mediator

Mediators are usually very personable and understanding people. It is very easy for management to regard the mediator as a friend—someone who is listening in confidence to management's position, and who is working diligently to persuade the union of the wisdom and necessity of accepting management's proposals. No doubt the union feels the same way. One should be on the alert, however, and keep in mind the following advice. Remember that the mediator's sole objective is to get an agreement. The mediator is not above taking your "off the record" comments and testing them out on the union to see if an area of compromise is possible. This is not to suggest that the mediator is dishonest or unethical; it is simply a way to get the negotiating parties together. Consequently, you should adhere to the following guideline: *Say nothing to the mediator that you are not willing to have the union representatives hear.* You should assume that any comments or exploratory suggestions will be passed on to the union in some form.

For the same reason, you should treat the mediator as the eyes and ears of the union with respect to selling your position. Take every opportunity to persuade the mediator of the soundness, reasonableness, and firmness of your position. To the extent that you can convince him, the mediator will help to convince the union.

If you are prepared to offer a concession, determine what concession you need to have in return. Leave some room for bargaining purposes. This proposal should then become the "mediator's suggested compromise" so that if it is rejected, it has not weakened management's position. Experienced mediators are usually adept at handling such maneuvers.

A mediator can be quite helpful in explaining to the union bargaining committee that a particular proposal made by management does not have a booby trap hidden inside. Likewise, a mediator's honest opinion to the union that management has made its best and final offer can go a long way toward convincing an unbelieving union committee that nothing more can be expected from management. The committee can, in turn, use the mediator's opinions and observations when it presents management's offer to the membership.

Mediation can be a valuable tool in avoiding or resolving impasse, depending upon the skill of the mediator, how the parties take advantage of the services, and the difficulty of the unresolved issues. Management should look upon a mediator as an additional means for achieving an agreement, keeping in mind that the agreement has to be one with which management can live over the contract's term, and not one into which management was pressured by a zealous mediator.

Interest Arbitration

The conventional means for resolving disputes between management and labor over the interpretation and application of a labor agreement is final and binding arbitration. Arbitration has not, however, been widely accepted in the United States as a means for setting the terms and conditions of a labor contract. Used in this manner, it is called "interest arbitration," and has found some favor in the public employment area and in professional sports to settle individual player contract conditions, and has been used occasionally in certain manufacturing and service industries. In general, however, the use of interest arbitration has been very limited in this country, probably due to the general aversion of unions and managements to having a third party make their agreement for them.

Limited Scope and Authority of Arbitrator

Arbitration should not, however, be dismissed out of hand as a means for avoiding or resolving impasse in a conventional contract renewal negotiation. It may have value in certain situations where agreement cannot be reached, and where the degree of economic pressure on both sides is such that the situation offers little hope for resolution and promises to levy a very high toll on the respective parties. Perhaps the most feasible use of arbitration is to resolve parts of a contract package rather than the entire agreement. For example, the parties might submit to an arbitrator a choice between several types of medical plans or particular provisions of an incentive bonus plan. As with the contingent commitment discussed above, management should make its decision on whether to proceed keeping a worst-case result in mind. Can management live with the worst possible decision an arbitrator could reasonably make? If not, arbitration should not be utilized.

If arbitration is to be used, boundaries should be specified within which the arbitrator's decision must fall. For example, if the item to be determined is a wage increase in the third year of a three-year contract, the submission to the arbitrator should state a maximum amount and the criteria the arbitrator should consider (e.g., wages in the same industry and area, wages in the employer's other facilities, cost-of-living changes). In other words, the arbitrator should not be given a blank check.

Furthermore, the neutral party selected to decide the issue must be selected with the greatest care. The arbitrator should be someone of great integrity, with knowledge of the industry and type of work involved, and should preferably have a somewhat conservative bent (at least from a fiscal standpoint). Also, the person should have a track record, and management should determine the nature of that record. Particular attention should be paid to past performance in interest arbitration.

Variations on the Arbitration Theme

There are a number of variations in arbitration techniques which have been utilized to settle contract negotiations. One is called "final offer selection." Under this technique, following an impasse in negotiations each party submits its last and best offer to an arbitrator who selects one of the two offers presented. The arbitrator is not permitted to "split the baby", i.e. the arbitrator may not select an amount or a package in between the two final offers. The basic premise of this method is that both parties are forced to formulate final offers which are realistic, and hopefully not widely divergent. Furthermore, it has the advantage that the final settlement is one selected by one of the parties, and not one simply conjured up by the arbitrator. Nevertheless, it does have the distinct disadvantage of permitting an unrealistically expensive settlement to result if the arbitrator selects the union's final offer which was an exorbitant one.

Another variation on the arbitration theme is a technique known as "Med-Arb," a blending of mediation and arbitration. Under this process, if the parties have been unsuccessful in reaching agreement, the third party acts initially as a conventional mediator in conciliating and helping them to reach an agreement. If mediation fails, this third party then becomes an arbitrator and has the power to render a final and binding decision. The submission to the third party for arbitration may simply consist of the unresolved issue(s), or it may be in the form of the two final offers, with the arbitrator selecting only one of the two. The loss of control over one's destiny in using Med-Arb is obvious.

Other variations of arbitration include advisory arbitration and fact-finding whereby the judgments and review by a third party are obtained, but are not binding upon either side. While these techniques may have some value in clarifying complex issues, they seldom offer much assistance in avoiding or breaking an impasse. They are used almost exclusively in public employment labor relations.

Bypassing the Union Spokesperson

Resorting to others beyond the bargaining table to avoid impasse is not always limited to use of third-party neutrals. Occasionally, the relationship between the union's spokesperson and management's spokesperson becomes so hostile and/or counterproductive that meaningful bargaining becomes impossible. If and when this point is reached, the negotiations are truly in jeopardy. If management's spokesperson is in a position where he or she cannot communicate or bargain with the union counterpart, he or she must look elsewhere.

Initially, access might be obtained to the union spokesperson's boss, assuming he or she is a paid representative within the union organization. Hopefully there is a preexisting relationship or at least an acquaintanceship with this person. If the difficulty with the union's spokesperson is only one of personality, some cooperation may be forthcoming. If the difference is over issues of substance, it is unlikely that a different position will be taken at the higher level unless the union's spokesperson has taken a clearly unreasonable or unauthorized position.

If the problem with the union's spokesperson is that the local union and/or the membership is not being properly represented, the recourse may have to be to a lower, rather than a higher, authority—the local union. In some cases, international union representatives push for their own personal goals or the international union's goals, rather than for what is best for the local union, the membership, or the facility. In such cases, communicating with local union leadership may be a better means of clearing away the logjam than going over the head of the spokesperson. Care must be exercised not to bypass the "authorized" bargaining agent lest the employer commit an unfair labor practice.

Bypassing the union's spokesperson is obviously a drastic step, and one which should only be resorted to as a last-ditch measure when all else has failed. By making an "end run," management's spokesperson virtually ensures that the union's spokesperson will be alienated and efforts to improve the relationship will be futile. Nevertheless, if the union's spokesperson is totally unreasonable and an impediment to settlement, and if the negotiations are apt to result in a strike as a result of his or her position, there is little choice but to find someone in the union organization who will understand and deal with the problem.

Before coming to the conclusion that the relationship with the union spokesperson is an impediment to settlement, however, the management spokesperson should also examine his or her own conduct and position. Is it reasonable and justified? It may be that all the problems are not emanating from the other side of the bargaining table.

13

Strike Preparation, Decision Making, and Management

The Role of Strikes in the Bargaining Process

It has been said that a strike is a sign of failure of collective bargaining. This is not completely true. To a large extent, strikes are part and parcel of the collective bargaining process. If strikes never occurred, the threat of an actual strike would not exist and serious bargaining would seldom take place. Nevertheless, strikes are a sign that the parties have not used the bargaining process to good effect and, therefore, have had to resort to brute economic force to try to change each other's position.

The relative frequency of strikes in a particular industry or in a particular bargaining relationship highlights the relative economic leverage possessed by labor and management. If few or no strikes have occurred in a collective bargaining relationship, one might suspect that there is an imbalance in bargaining power, and that one side or the other is dominating the relationship. Often industries or bargaining units with either very high pay rates and benefits (i.e., airline pilots) or low pay and benefits (i.e., garment workers) are characterized by a relatively low number of strikes. One of the reasons for this is that one side has most of the economic leverage and strikes (at least long strikes) are either unnecessary or futile in achieving a bargaining objective.

Just as an infrequency of strikes may reflect a problem of bargaining imbalance, excessive strikes point out another problem. The inability of negotiating parties to conclude their negotiations, with any regularity, without a work stoppage reflects, to a large extent, an underlying hostility and mistrust in the collective bargaining relationship which precludes the negotiating process from functioning as it should. The abysmal record of the copper industry and the United Steelworkers Union reflected such a mutual attitude; in the course of the six contract negotiations between the major copper manufacturers bargaining as a unit and the unions in the copper industry which took place between 1967 and 1983, five strikes occurred. In other words, 83 percent of the time those parties went to the bargaining table over a 15-year period, their negotiations ended in strikes. Obviously, they had been doing something wrong. Fortunately, the copper industry is not typical of most industries in the United States where the vast majority of contract negotiations are settled without work stoppages.

The statement "no one wins a strike" is almost a cliché. And, as with most clichés, it is only partially true. To the extent that both union and management suffer, as do employees, customers, and the public, it is a true statement. However, it is not true that strikes do not have winners and losers. In fact, most strikes have clear winners and clear losers—the final settlement reflects a position closer to the final prestrike position of either management or the union.

That strikes are a normal part of the collective bargaining process is of little consolation to the employer who is faced with a strike threat. For the employer, a work stoppage will mean serious financial losses, and perhaps may place the future of its entire business at risk. Because the consequences can be so devastating, management must make complete and careful preparations in the event a strike should occur. It must also carefully weigh its options prior to making the final decision to take a strike. The next two sections of this chapter discuss these steps.

Strike Preparations

A strike is somewhat like a public emergency or disaster in that it disrupts the normal way of living for many people and inflicts great financial and psychic damage on those directly affected by it. As with an emergency, the damage caused by a strike can be minimized, or at least made more tolerable, if advance planning has taken place and necessary precautions have been taken to mitigate its effects. And as in the case of a potential emergency, preparations for a strike are made with the fervent hope that they will not be necessary.

When to Begin

Some labor relations specialists suggest full strike preparations should begin before negotiations commence. They reason that the impact such preparations can have on negotiations is valuable to the bargaining process. The author disagrees. Strike preparations can become a self-fulfilling prophecy. If management begins to overtly prepare for a strike before bargaining has even begun, the union can draw no other conclusion but that management is seeking a confrontation. Employees who are not directly involved in the bargaining process, but who can usually see visible signs of preparations (notices to customers, extra security patrols, interviewing, and/or training potential replacements, etc.), are apt to conclude that a fight is in the making.

There is seldom any necessity to make *overt* strike preparations until it appears that negotiations are headed for an impasse. This will usually be at least three to four weeks prior to the strike deadline. This amount of time will usually be sufficient to accomplish the overt actions necessary to prepare for a strike. This is not to say that nothing else should be done before that time. On the contrary, management needs to have a plan that can be put into effect when the time comes. Such a plan should be developed early in the course of negotiations, if not prior thereto.

Assigning Responsibility

Responsibility for overall strike planning and coordination should be assigned to one person, the "strike coordinator." Although a committee may be appointed to ensure that all components of the organization are working together, one member of that committee should be given overall responsibility to see that all efforts are coordinated. It is generally preferable that the person given this coordinating responsibility not be on the negotiating committee, or at least not be the management spokesperson in the negotiations. The job of attempting to reach a negotiated settlement is simply too time consuming and intellectually demanding to allow the spokesperson to do a thorough job of preparing for a strike as well. Moreover, the spokesperson and the committee must be fully committed to reaching a settlement. Preparing for a strike at the same time is inconsistent with that commitment.

Developing a Strike Plan

The first responsibility of a strike committee or strike coordinator is to develop a plan which will be the road map by which management will be guided during the course of the strike. As a means of ensuring that all necessary points are covered in the plan, a checklist should be developed that will become an integral part of the plan. Appendix 5 is an example of such a strike checklist. The key elements in any good strike plan are as follows:

1. *Decision whether or not to operate during a strike.* This is probably the most crucial decision management will have to make since it will affect nearly all other decisions and actions. If the decision is made to operate, numerous follow-up decisions will be required including when and to what extent operations should resume. Considerations underlying the decision to operate or not during a strike as well as procedures for implementing this decision are discussed later in this chapter.
2. *Customer arrangements.* In virtually all private businesses and public institutions, a product or service is provided to customers or users. The viability of an employer's enterprise depends upon satisfying the customers' or users' needs. Hence, the customers' needs must be paramount in a strike plan. The plan must incorporate regular and timely communications with customers as well as a workable means of meeting the customers' needs during a strike. It is also particularly important that the employer's sales or service representatives or others who have regular contact with customers be briefed on the progress of negotiations so that they can intelligently keep customers informed. Too often, sales representatives unduly frighten customers about interruptions in supply or service or fail to adequately alert them to potential interruptions simply because the representatives lack adequate information and therefore misinform the customers.

3. *Supplier arrangements.* In some businesses, relationships with suppliers and vendors can be as important as those with customers. This is especially true in situations where supplies of the product or raw material needed by the employer may be scarce, and loss of a critical supplier can seriously injure the employer's business. In any event, the employer needs to keep suppliers alerted to the potential of a strike and the anticipated strike deadline to ensure that supplies can be terminated at the proper time. If they are terminated too early, production problems could develop if a strike does not occur. If they are terminated too late, unnecessary and costly inventories could accumulate. Such inventories can be particularly troublesome where perishable supplies are involved. If there are plans to operate during a strike, planning will be necessary to assure that picketing does not interrupt deliveries of supplies.
4. *Security.* Unfortunately, strikes are frequently accompanied by violence, vandalism, threats of bodily harm, etc. Even the most cooperative and loyal work force may become militant and hostile in a strike situation. Therefore, a good strike plan should assume the worst. Local law enforcement agencies should be contacted and guidelines established as to when and under what circumstances they will become involved. If the employer has a private security agency at the facility threatened by a strike, it should be alerted and special plans should be developed to increase and/or upgrade the normal security force. If there is no regular security service in place, several private agencies should be contacted in order to determine which are best prepared to deal with a strike situation. A number of security service firms specialize in strike security. Other security precautions may be necessary, such as construction or reinforcement of fences, installation of television monitors at critical locations, lighting of areas around the facility where vandalism would be most likely to occur, and appointment of strike monitors to observe picket line activity and discourage intimidation of persons entering or leaving the facility.
5. *Communications.* Explanation of management's views on the issues involved in the strike, the positions it takes, events during the strike, progress of negotiations to end the strike, and other information should be provided to customers, suppliers, striking and nonstriking employees, stockholders, and the public. Means of communication can include letters, paid media advertisements, feature newspaper articles, radio and television interviews, news releases, leaflets, and telephone hot lines (i.e., recorded messages regularly updated). A good strike plan should always include a section on communications. One person should be in charge of communication to all parties outside of the organization in order to ensure

consistency. This person should be experienced in communications and public relations matters. It is important, however, that information concerning contract negotiations not be disseminated without the express authorization of the chief management negotiator.

6. *Legal matters.* Because strikes frequently require resort to legal processes and because they expose the employer to legal liability (for unfair labor practices, strike-related injuries, etc.) it is important that the employer's labor law counsel be intimately involved in the planning and execution of the strike plan. A court injunction to limit the extent and location of picketing and to control strike violence and unlawful interference is required in a large number of strikes. Legal counsel should have the necessary preliminary work completed in advance to permit an early appearance in court if picketing or related activities get out of hand. Questions regarding permissible limits of employer surveillance of picket line activity, allowable communications with striking employees, obligations of the employer to make vacation payments and contributions for medical insurance coverage during the strike, and numerous other legal questions make it essential that legal counsel be consulted frequently and review and clear all strike plans and actions.
7. *Employee and industrial relations.* The employer's human resources, personnel department, or the person in charge of personnel or industrial relations should be assigned the task of developing policies and procedures to deal with employee-related issues which typically arise during a strike. Such questions include eligibility to receive accrued but unpaid vacation pay; continued eligibility for medical, life, and disability insurance during the strike and who is responsible for payment of premiums for such insurance; and status of striking employees with regard to other company benefits including stock purchase plans, company-provided recreational facilities, and disability payments which began prior to the strike. Likewise, arrangements with local offices of the state employment service regarding claims for unemployment insurance should be planned. This would include the drafting of notices to employees who are members of nonstriking unions at the same facility to advise them as to whether or not work is available during the strike, to ensure that no unjustifiable unemployment benefits are paid.
8. *Fact-gathering and recordkeeping.* The excitement and confusion which accompany a strike make it difficult to obtain and record information. All too frequently, the carrying out of disciplinary action, processing of insurance claims, or simply the reconstructing of events are thwarted because no one determined, or subsequently made a record of, what happened, when it happened, and how it happened. Thus, a plan

is necessary to ensure that essential recordkeeping is accomplished. *A strike log is absolutely essential.* The log should be used to record all pertinent actions taken, telephone or other conversations, incidents of violence, damage reported, and all other significant occurrences which take place during the strike. The log should be compiled under the supervision of the strike coordinator and should be reviewed daily to assure that it is complete. The log can be kept in the employer's data bank with inputs made by various persons. However, all entries to the data bank should be reviewed at least daily by the strike coordinator to ensure the entries are appropriate and that necessary actions and responses are undertaken. The security of the log must be protected. Videotaping equipment, movie cameras, and still cameras, as well as audio equipment, should be available to make photographic and sound recordings of any mass picketing, picket line violence or damage to property, equipment, employees' automobiles, etc., and to record any other significant events. Prompt investigation should be made of any and all untoward events, and a complete record made of the investigation.

It is important that the strike plan designate the specific persons who will be responsibile for carrying out each element of the plan, and that completion dates be attached to those tasks as necessary.

The Strike/Settlement Decision

Although strikes are called by unions, not employers, the employer will almost always have an option to concede to the union's demands or to take a strike. Even though the union's final prestrike demands may be so exorbitant or otherwise unreasonable that little choice seems to be offered, the option of settlement exists in nearly every case.

The decision as to where an employer is going to take a stand is usually made long before negotiations reach the impasse point. When economic parameters are set prior to, or at the early stages of, negotiations they are usually established with the idea that anything demanded by the union beyond those amounts will result in a strike. In the process of bargaining, however, it is not unusual for the parameters to change. Often this is for good reason. Circumstances may have changed since negotiations began, new facts may become available, cost-saving concessions may have been made by the union, or compromise language or concepts may have emerged from the bargaining, resulting in changes which do not violate management's original objectives. Changing positions is what bargaining is all about.

There comes a time, however, when management must determine the point beyond which it will not go in order to achieve a settlement. As indicated earlier, this is frequently called "the wall" by negotiators. This wall should contain the total amount of new money (or the total amount of labor cost increases per year of the contract) which management is willing to spend in order to get a settlement. It should also contain management's final position on all noneconomic issues being negotiated. The difference between this wall and the union's final prestrike position will be the "gap" over which management must decide whether or not to take a strike. It will also be the amount against which the cost of a strike must be compared.

Estimating the Cost of a Strike

The cost to the employer of a strike will, of course, depend upon the type of business or enterprise in which the employer is engaged. A manufacturer may be able to produce at an accelerated rate prior to a strike and stockpile inventories in order to supply customers during a strike. However, a service business such as a restaurant, an airline, or a bus company cannot inventory its product, and once business is lost it is generally lost forever. Regardless of the type of business, the employer and the employer's accountants should be able to calculate the cost of a strike on a daily, weekly, or monthly basis. To be sure, assumptions will have to be made. Will operations be continued and, if so, to what extent? How long will the strike last? Will any shipments be made? Will salaried employees continue to receive full pay during the strike? The answers to these and other questions will permit the accountants to develop rough estimates.

Assumptions of Operating Levels

It is usually advisable to compute estimates based upon sets of different assumptions. A sample cost estimate using different assumptions concerning operation levels is shown in Table 13–1.

Table 13–1. Sample Strike Cost Estimate

Assumptions	Estimated pretax losses per week (in thousands of dollars)								
	1	2	3	4	5	6	7	8	9
No operations	780	525	525	525	400	400	400	400	400
(Cumulative cost)	780	1305	1830	2355	2755	3155	3555	3955	4355
No operations 1st 2 weeks, then 50%	780	525	120	120	120	120	120	120	120
(Cumulative cost)	780	1305	1425	1545	1665	1785	1905	2025	2145
No operations 1st 3 weeks, then 75%	780	525	525	120	120	120	40	40	40
(Cumulative cost)	780	1305	1830	1950	2070	2190	2230	2270	2310
No operations 1st 2 weeks, then 75%	780	525	40	40	40	40	40	40	40
(Cumulative cost)	780	1305	1345	1385	1425	1465	1505	1545	1585

Within each of the sets of assumptions, there might be subcategories based upon other variables such as production or efficiency levels, market conditions, price levels, etc. This matrix is valuable as an aid not only in selecting a course of action (e.g., operating versus not operating during a strike), but also in bringing home to management just how much is at stake in a strike situation. Such estimates are also valuable as a means of alerting top management as to what financial resources may be necessary in order to carry the employer's business through the strike period.

Intangible Costs

The cost of a strike, however, cannot be measured simply in dollars and cents on a profit and loss statement. There are other costs to which a value cannot be immediately attached, but which can have a severe impact on the business. Where competition for the employer's product or service is keen, a strike frequently means the loss of customers. It may mean the loss of market share which the employer has achieved after many years of hard work. It can also result in a loss of the confidence and support of banks and other lenders. Although such lenders may sympathize with the employer's situation, they seldom understand the justification when losses are incurred and their money is placed at serious risk. Where the struck employer is a contractor or subcontractor, failure to operate during a strike may also mean the resulting inability of that contractor or subcontractor to fulfill its contractual obligations with government or private industry. Even though *force majeure* clauses may financially protect a business from noncompliance, its reputation as a reliable contractor will be damaged.

In addition, one cannot overlook the effect of a strike upon the employer's relationship with its employees. The inevitable consequence of a strike is bitterness on the part of employees. No matter how necessary and justifiable management's position is, employees will nearly always view a strike as having been caused by management's unreasonable unwillingness to agree to the union's "just demands." To the extent that employees return to work without any improvement in the agreement from management's final prestrike offer, the bitterness will simply be that much greater. The bitterness typically lasts for a number of years.

Enumeration of the tangible and intangible costs of a strike is not for the purpose of suggesting that management should never let a strike take place, or that the costs of a strike will always outweight the benefits. That is not the case. It is important, however, that management enter a potential strike situation with its eyes wide open, knowing all the "down-side" risks, and make an informed judgment as to whether a strike (assuming it will be successful from the employer's point of view) is preferable to a settlement.

Estimating the "Payback" of a Strike

Rather than considering that there is a payback from a strike which the employer successfully takes, it is probably more accurate to say that there is a payback from not making further concessions to a union beyond management's wall position. In either case, management must weigh what it hopes to achieve from a strike against the costs of the strike.

Period for Measuring Payback

Assuming that a strike will result over economic issues, the potential tangible benefits from a strike are measured by the difference between the union's final prestrike demands (whether expressed in public or in private) and management's final prestrike offer (the "gap"). The key factor in assessing the true value of the payback is the period of time used in the calculation. If the payback is to be evaluated only for the period of the current contract, the payback from taking a strike will seldom be great enough in relation to the costs of a strike to justify the employer's refusal to concede. For example, management makes a final offer for a two-year contract. The amount of the offer exactly matches management's wall. The union rejects the offer and says it will settle if management adds 10 cents per hour more in the first year and 5 cents per hour more in the second year. Management's calculations, based on a bargaining unit population of 350 employees and 1,900 hours of work per year per employee with a rollup factor of 30 percent, show additional labor costs of $86,450 ($0.10 × 1.3 × 1,900 × 350) in the first year and $43,225 ($0.05 × 1.3 × 1,900 × 350) in the second year. On a cash outflow basis, the employer will have spent, under the union's final offer, an additional $216,125 ($86,450 × 2 + $43,225) in labor costs during the two-year contract over what it would have spent under management's final offer.

When management calculates the costs (losses) of a strike using such figures, it will be the unusual situation where the payback from not agreeing to the demanded increase and, therefore, taking a strike, will be greater than the costs resulting from the strike, particularly if it is not feasible to operate during the strike.

But is it reasonable to evaluate the payback solely over the duration of the contract under negotiation? Probably not, unless management expects to concede the difference or "the gap" during the next contract negotiation. If it does expect to make up the difference to the union then, the wisdom of taking a strike would appear to be very dubious. However, if management is successful in the strike to the extent that it avoids moving to the union's side of the gap, the chances are that it can avoid paying back the gap in subsequent negotiations. This means that management should not pay more in subsequent contract negotiations than it would have paid in those negotiations had the gap been closed and a strike avoided during the contract term in question. If this is the case, management should calculate the payback from a strike over a longer period of time than one contract term. How long should that period of time be? There is no definite "amortization period." For purposes of discussion, one may arbitrarily select a period of eight years, or roughly three contract terms (i.e., two three-year contracts and one two-year contract).

Calculating the Payback

If a strike takes place over a gap of 10 cents per hour the first year and 5 cents the second, and the employer successfully takes the strike and withstands closing the gap in subsequent years, the payback for a bargaining unit of 350 employees would, over an eight-year period, be nearly $1 million, calculated as follows:

Wage difference		+ Rollup	×	Annual hours	=	Annual savings	×	Years in effect	=	Savings
				First Year						
$0.10	+	$0.03	×	665,000	=	$86,450	×	8	=	$691,600
				Second Year						
$0.05	+	$0.015	×	665,000	=	$43,225	×	7	=	$302,575
										$994,175

Thus, what appears to be a payback of $216,125 from a two-year perspective turns out to be a payback of nearly $1 million on an eight-year basis. Nor does this analysis include any credit for the time value of these funds.

The estimate shown above assumes that management will be completely successful in the strike and will be able to resist any closing of the gap for a long period of time. This may not be a completely realistic assumption since many strikes result in some compromise being worked out which results in a closing of the gap to one degree or another. A strike in which the ultimate settlement improves upon management's final pre-strike offer teaches a very bad lesson to the union and its membership, i.e., that management will increase its offer if the union strikes. Nevertheless, in the real world it does happen, and in terms of management's effort to make a realistic cost/benefit analysis, it may be more prudent to assume that the gap will be closed to some degree, if not during the term of the current contract, then at some point in the eight-year period.

Assessing Intangible Paybacks

As with the evaluation of strike costs, the determination of a strike payback must include intangible as well as tangible factors. Credibility is the principal intangible benefit of a strike to management. By taking a strike, management demonstrates that its "final offer" is truly final, and that it is willing to back up its word with muscle. The credibility value of a strike to management can only be measured, however, at the end of a strike. If management capitulates and the union improves significantly upon management's last offer prior to the strike, management's credibility has been seriously damaged. If, on the other hand, the union ceases the strike and returns on management's terms, management's credibility has been greatly enhanced.

The Long-Term Strike Impact

The occurrence of a strike, therefore, involves not only a financial risk, but a credibility risk as well. What is more, the reward for winning, and the punishment for losing, a strike will not be dissipated in one year or during one contract term. The impact will be felt for many years to come. It is not unusual, in the author's experience, for representatives of one or the other party in a negotiation to hark back as far as 20 to 25 years to when the "big strike" occurred and "management [the union] taught them a lesson." The lessons of a long, bitter strike are not easily forgotten. Management's willingness to take a strike over a legitimate issue, and its ability to hold to its position through a long strike, will often preclude the need for it to do so again for some time, for the memory of management's determination will remain with union representatives and employees for many years. Conversely, the memory of management's capitulation and the joys of a victorious strike experienced by the union and its members will remain just as long.

Cost/Benefit Analysis of a Potential Strike

Having projected the potential costs of a strike and the potential paybacks of avoiding further concessions, management needs to put the data into an equation that will permit a rational, informed judgment. But the judgment process is complicated by the fact that it is impossible to ascertain the union's final prestrike position until it is actually taken. In other words, management negotiators cannot predict the exact settlement level which must be achieved in order to keep the union from striking. This level will not be known until the final offer is made and voted on by the union's membership. Similarly, management cannot predict with great accuracy how long a strike may have to last before the union accedes to management's position. Despite the difficulties of predicting these key variables, however, management needs to have some estimates upon which to base a decision as to whether a strike should be taken. In this situation, some estimate, no matter how speculative, is better than none at all.

Estimating Probability and Duration

One way of estimating and depicting the likelihood of a strike occurring and its estimated duration relative to the employer's final offer is to use interrelated graphs such as those shown in Figure 13–1.

Figure 13–1

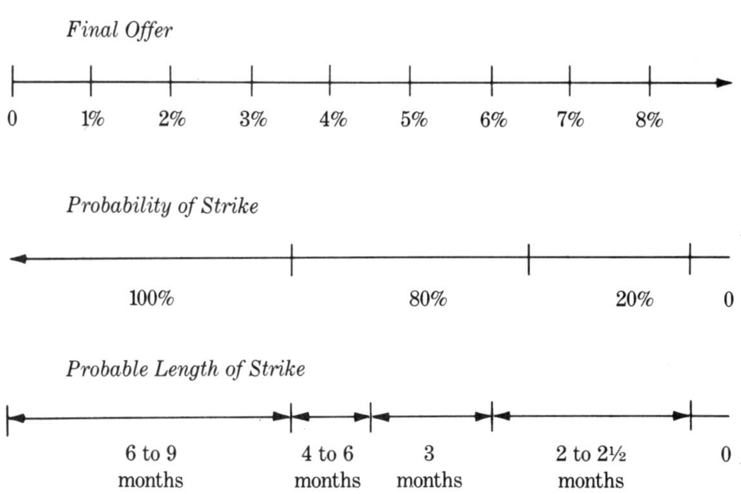

The graphs should state the assumptions upon which they are based, such as the following:

- Comparable settlements within the industry are running at 7 to 8 percent.
- The facility will not operate for the first two weeks of a strike, and thereafter will not operate at more than 50 percent capacity.

- The union's strike fund will pay no more than $40 per week for 20 weeks.
- The strike begins after September.
- There are no significant unresolved issues other than the cost of the package.

The graphs show the relationship between the cost of the employer's final offer and (1) the estimated probability that a strike of any duration will occur and, if one does occur, (2) the probable length of the strike. For example, if the employer's final offer is estimated at 6.5 percent, the probability of a strike occurring is estimated to be 80 percent. It can also be estimated that a strike occurring after such an offer is made is likely to last for two to two and one-half months before the union accedes to management's position.

These types of graphs are certainly not scientific in any sense. In fact, they are little more than best guesstimates of the management spokesperson and/or other management personnel who have a good feel for the union's political needs, union rank and file attitudes, bargaining dynamics, and other factors which bear upon the probability of a strike. As a general rule of thumb for realistically estimating the length of a strike, management should figure how long a strike *should* last given the variables of management's offer, the union's demands, and the various political considerations. Once this figure is determined, it should usually be *doubled.* Invariably management grossly underestimates the determination and staying power of the union and the allegiance of rank and file members to the union during a strike.

The Complete Payback Calculation

With such guesstimates in hand, management can at least make some cost/benefit judgment as to whether the potential labor cost savings are worth the risk of a strike. Using the strike cost estimates for week 9 of the second assumption in Table 13–1, management can estimate the cost of a 10-week strike (assuming the level of operations is nil for the first two weeks and no more than 50 percent thereafter) to be $2,145,000, or roughly $2 million. If the union accepts management's final offer at the end of the 10-week period, the payback would be calculated as follows, assuming management and labor would otherwise have agreed on a final settlement representing an 8 percent increase:

Payback percentage	(8% − 6.5%)	1.5%
Payback per hour	($17.00 average hourly labor cost × 0.015)	$0.255
Annual payback	($0.255 × 350 employees × 1900 hours/year/employee)	$169,575
Eight-year payback	($169,575 × 8)	$1,356,600

Of course, there is nothing magic about the eight-year payback period. One might argue for a longer period or even a shorter one. The important point is that some estimate should be made, and that the estimate should go beyond the period of the contract term, even though the employer has no assurance of avoiding a closure of the gap beyond the contract term. The decision to accept a strike must be viewed as a long-term commitment. Both the burdens and the paybacks of a strike will remain for many years to come.

Before placing too much reliance on its calculations, however, management must closely examine its estimates. How likely is it that the union would strike for only two to two and one-half months? Is there a significant chance that the strike could last for three to four months or even six to seven months? If so, perhaps the $2 million cost figure is grossly understated. Such questioning should be done from a reverse standpoint as well. Could the estimated 80 percent chance of a strike be pessimistic, and are the odds that the 6.5 percent offer will be accepted without a strike actually better than this? Perhaps there is at least a fifty-fifty chance that the union will accept the offer, particularly if some of the noneconomic portions of the offer are improved.

Balancing the Intangibles

The difficulty of making a rational decision regarding a strike is increased exponentially when all intangible factors are taken into account. For instance, what will be the short-term and long-term impact of a strike on labor-management relations? Will the immediate bitterness felt by the union and its members be replaced with greater respect for management's determination or will it simply mean months or years of union-management enmity? What is likely to be the impact on customer relationships? Will most customers return when the strike is over? Will they understand what management was attempting to accomplish, or will they merely complain about their interrupted shipments or service? Will the strike have any lasting effect upon employee morale and/or loyalty to the company? What will be the effect on emplyees' confidence in the union? Will the strike affect the employer's image with its lending institutions, stockholders, or the public, and, if so, what is the effect likely to be? Each of these factors, and others, must be weighed before a final decision is made to take a strike.

Beyond Logic

The foregoing discussion concerning the option of taking a strike as opposed to acceding to the union's demands tacitly assumes that both parties are acting in a rational manner guided by the logic of maximizing their economic welfare and working conditions. In the real world, however, organizations and those who control them do not always act out of reason or logic. Frequently, emotions are the driving force. Unfortunately, this is sometimes as true of management as it is of unions. The union may be attempting to make up for what it perceives as past abuses or inequities, trying to punish management by using a strike as a weapon to inflict economic pain for its own sake, not just to achieve a better settlement. While this is not a common occurrence, it does happen. In such cases, management needs to be able to detect this motivation, for otherwise it may make many needless concessions only to find itself enmeshed in a strike despite its honest and expensive, but misguided, attempts to avoid one.

On the other hand, if it is management which is driven by emotion or irrationality, it is the responsibility of someone in the organization to ask the often difficult, but necessary, questions. Why are we going to strike? What do we expect to achieve from it? How do we explain to the owners, principals, or stockholders why the strike occurred? What is standing between a settlement and a strike? Are we prepared to take a long strike in order to achieve our goals? The answers to these and similar questions must be answered forthrightly in order to assure that management is not undertaking a risk that cannot be justified by the potential paybacks.

Final Offer and Strike Decision Strategy

The question of whether management should accept the union's final terms or take a strike usually presents itself after management has made its "final offer" and that offer has been rejected. Typically, the union is seeking a settlement which is beyond management's wall in terms of the size of the economic offer or based upon one or more noneconomic issues which usually involve management's rights in one form or another.

Some negotiators prepare a final offer in such a way as to save a small amount in order to permit the union to add some "frosting on the cake" in obtaining a settlement. This, they feel, gives the union bargaining committee an opportunity to feel that it squeezed the last drop of blood from management. Some negotiators retain a small amount even when a strike is about to occur, in order to have something with which to settle the strike—to "bring them back." The logic of this strategy breaks down somewhat if the additional amount, or "frosting," would have been sufficient to bring a settlement without a strike. If it would have been sufficient, then a needless and costly strike could have been avoided by offering this additional amount before the strike began. (In actual bargaining, however, the additional amount which management may have reserved to settle the contract is frequently insufficient to close the gap between management's final offer and the union's final demand.)

A further complication can arise because of the adversarial nature of negotiations. For example, while the minimum acceptable settlement level required by the union if it is to refrain from striking may in fact be somewhat less than its announced final prestrike position, the union generally would be reluctant to take such a position formally by specifying exactly what it will accept because the level is still higher than what it has been told is management's final offer. No universal strategy can be suggested for dealing with this dilemma, but several guidelines can be recommended in such situations.

1. In general, management should avoid using the term "final offer" unless it truly intends to stick to that position.
2. Management should exceed its last or final offer, if at all, only when it is absolutely certain that it will secure an agreement.

3. Holding back some portion from the final offer in order to settle an anticipated strike simply ensures that the union will be able to claim at least a partial victory from the strike.
4. If the parties are in disagreement over a matter of contract language or principle, as opposed to the economics of the offer, a solution may be found by changing one or more of the economic issues of the offer in order to "buy out" the issue in dispute.
5. Management should be as certain as it can be that it knows the exact nature of the issue(s) threatening to cause a strike.
6. The decision to take a strike rather than to concede should not be made until all persons in management connected with the negotiations have voiced an opinion about the issue(s). There should be no intimidation or threat of adverse consequences inhibiting a candid expression of opinions.

Legal Questions Involving Strikes

As suggested earlier, legal counsel should be consulted at all stages of strike preparation as well as during the course of a strike. Beyond this, management should be aware of the paramount legal principles which apply in strike situations. These principles are discussed in the section below.

The Right to Strike and to Picket

A strike is perfectly legal if the labor agreement has expired or is open by virtue of a contract reopening which permits strikes. Similarly, the law permits striking employees or other persons acting for the union to peacefully picket the workplace of the employer in which the striking workers have been employed.

Secondary Picketing

It is often said that a striking union can picket the struck employer "anywhere it can find him." This means that the employer may be picketed at any of its facilities or when it is present at other employer's facilities, such as when making pickups or deliveries. An exception exists, however, to this rule. If the other nonstruck facilities of the employer at which the union seeks to place pickets are part of a subsidiary corporation or a separate operating division that is unrelated to the operations of the division that is being struck, the picketing is considered to be directed at a separate or "secondary" employer and is, therefore, illegal under the National Labor Relations Act. This is the so-called "Hearst doctrine," named after two cases involving separate divisions of the Hearst Corporation.[1] In order for this exception to apply, there must be separate control over the operations, including a considerable degree of general management and labor relations autonomy exercised by the struck and nonstruck parts of the employer's organization.

"Common Situs" Picketing

As a general rule, the union may not picket a neutral or secondary employer, i.e., any employer other than the one that has been struck. Here again, however, some exceptions apply. Where the struck or "primary" employer and the nonstruck or "secondary" employer share the same work site ("common situs"), as is common in the construction industry, the striking union may picket the primary employer as long as it has employees on the site, even though other (secondary) employers are there as well. The picketing must be confined to times when the primary employer is present and must specifically and clearly identify the primary employer that is being picketed, and the picketers must not verbally or otherwise urge employees of secondary employers not to work. If a separate or "reserved" gate is maintained for employees of the secondary employer, the striking union may picket only the gate used by employees of the primary employer. Similarly, if the union is striking a transportation company or supplier providing services to a secondary employer, the union may only picket the secondary employer at those times when the primary employer's employees are rendering the services on the site of the primary employer provided, the services are rendered when the primary employer is engaged in its normal business operations, the picketing is conducted reasonably close to the situs of the primary employer, and the picket signs clearly identify the struck primary employer.[2] Thus, if the union is striking a bakery, and deliveries are made by the bakery to a grocery store, the striking bakery union may picket the grocery store only when the bread is actually being delivered.

The "reserved gate" rule has another application when a struck employer wishes to have contractors perform work at its facility while a strike is in progress. This frequently occurs because an employer wishes to have capital improvements made or maintenance work performed while a facility is not operating, due to a strike. In these cases a separate gate must be established for the nonstruck or secondary contractor and its employees. This separate gate is sometimes called a "contractor's gate" and must be posted with a notice stating that it is only to be used by the contractor, its employees, suppliers, and subcontractors. The union may not legally picket such a gate, so long as work done by the contractor is not related to the normal day-to-day operations of the struck employer.[3]

"Ally Doctrine"

Another exception to the rule that a union may not picket a neutral or uninvolved employer is the so-called "Ally doctrine," whereby a secondary employer assists the struck employer in such a way as to aid the employer in withstanding the effects of the strike. This typically occurs where the secondary employer at the request of the primary employer manufactures products or provides services on behalf of the struck employer. In these cases, the secondary employer has become an "ally" of the struck employer and is, therefore, subject to being picketed.[4]

Limits on Violent or Threatening Picketing

Aside from the issue of whether a separate facility or employer may be picketed, the right to picket the struck employer is protected under the "free speech" portion of the First Amendment to the Constitution. However, that right can be limited by state courts where the conduct of the picketers is violent or picketing is done in large numbers or in such a way as to constitute a threat to safety or to block entrance to or exit from the struck facility. If the picketing cannot be kept within bounds by local law enforcement agencies, courts may issue injunctive orders placing limits on the number of picketers, their placement, and the types of conduct in which they may engage. The degree to which the courts will limit mass and violent picketing will vary from one jurisdiction to another.

If an employer has good reason to believe that picketing is, or will be, getting out of hand, its attorney should be prepared to file a lawsuit in state court for a temporary restraining order and subsequently for an injunction to place limitations on the picketing.

Legal Rights of Striking Employees

"Economic" versus Unfair Labor Practice Strikes

The key determinant of the extent of rights of employees who are on strike, as well as the rights of their employers, is the legal characterization of the strike, as determined under the National Labor Relations Act. For this purpose there are two basic categories: "unfair labor practice strikes" and "economic strikes." As discussed in Chapter 4, an unfair labor practice strike is one which is caused or prolonged, at least in part, by an employer's unfair labor practice(s). For example, if an employer has bargained in bad faith by refusing to meet and negotiate with the union, such refusal could cause a resulting strike to be characterized as an unfair labor practice strike. An economic strike, on the other hand, is any strike which is not an unfair labor practice strike, even though the issues in the strike may not involve subjects that are truly economic in nature. The consequences of these two types of strikes can be most significant for employer and employee.

Regardless of whether a strike is an economic or an unfair labor practice strike, an employee may not be discharged or disciplined for going on strike, since under the law it is "protected activity" (i.e., protected by the National Labor Relations Act), and therefore beyond legitimate sanctions by the employer. An exception to this occurs where a collective bargaining agreement contains a no-strike clause, meaning that the union has waived the right of its members to strike during the term of a labor agreement.

Replacing Economic Strikers

Where, however, the labor contract has expired the no-strike clause is of no effect, and employees may legally strike without fear of retaliation. This does not mean, though, that strikers do not jeopardize their jobs when they exercise their right to strike—even where the labor contract has expired. If the strike is an economic strike (i.e., neither caused nor prolonged by an employer's unfair labor practices), the employer may permanently replace striking employees with newly hired employees.[5] Furthermore, when the strike is over, the employer may retain the newly hired replacements in preference to strikers who offer to return to work.

Striking employees who unconditionally offer to return to work but who are not reinstated, because they have been permanently replaced, must be placed on a reinstatment list for recall to work when permanent job vacancies occur. Throughout the strike and while on a reinstatement list they continue to be employees of the employer. During this period they retain their seniority in the bargaining unit, even though they may not exercise that seniority to displace newly hired replacement employees. Once a permanent vacancy occurs, an employee on the reinstatement list must be recalled prior to the hiring of a brand-new employee, provided the employee on the reinstatement list is capable of performing the available work. Also, for one year from the start of an economic strike, strikers are eligible to vote in an NLRB representation election, including any decertification election.

Unfair Labor Practice Strikes

If, on the other hand, the strike is found to be caused by an employer's unfair labor practices, replacements hired by an employer may only be temporary and may not be retained by the employer in the face of unconditional offers by striking employees to return to work. Where the employer's unfair labor practice occurs after the strike has begun but is held to have prolonged the strike, any replacements hired after the commission of the unfair labor practice must give way to striking employees who offer to return to work.[6] An employer in an unfair labor practice strike who insists on retaining replacements rather than reinstating striking employees who unconditionally offer to return to work, is liable for back pay accruing after the strikers' offer to return to work.

Striker's Misconduct

Regardless of whether the strike is an economic strike or an unfair labor practice strike, an exception to the right of a striking employee to be reinstated exists where the striking employee has engaged in serious misconduct during the strike. An employer has the right to terminate a striking employee who has engaged in violent conduct such as physical assault or significant property damage, or other actions or statements, such as threats of bodily harm, that can reasonably tend to coerce or intimidate other employees.[7] However, an employer must apply the standards for serious misconduct in an even-handed way, and may not single out certain employees, such as union officials, for termination while allowing others who have engaged in similar misconduct to return to work.

Offer to Return Must Be Unconditional

In any case where an employee wishes to return to work following an economic strike, the employee must not place any conditions upon his willingness to return. There cannot be an "if," "provided," or "on condition that" attached to the offer. The employee must offer to return on the employer's terms. Of course, if there has been a settlement agreement between the employer and the union as to the terms and conditions under which striking employees are to return to work, fulfillment of that agreement by the employer becomes a legitimate condition on the employee's availability to return to work.

Employers' Rights and Obligations in Strike Situations

As just explained, an employer has a right to permanently or temporarily replace striking employees. These replacements may be salaried or hourly employees of the struck employer from the same facility or some other location. Likewise, the replacements may be newly hired persons who have been employed solely for the purpose of replacing striking employees on a temporary or permanent basis. The law thus permits employers to continue doing business even though a strike is in progress.

Unilateral Implementation of Final Offer

An employer also has a right to put into effect, on a unilateral basis, part or all of the terms of its last offer to the union provided an impasse in bargaining was reached prior to the implementation. The term "impasse" has a special significance in labor contract negotiations, meaning that both sides, after having negotiated for a reasonable period of time, have reached their respective final positions and that neither one is willing to budge from its stated position. From the point of impasse, management is permitted to unilaterally put its final offer, or a portion thereof, into effect.

Although a strike typically follows an impasse in negotiations, it need not always be so. It is possible, for example, for a union to strike prior to the concluding of negotiations, as a means of pressuring an employer to increase its offer even before the employer announces its final offer. In such cases an employer may commit an unfair labor practice if it unilaterally implements the last offer it made before the strike.[8]

In the more normal case, however, a strike signals that an impasse has been reached in negotiations. Thus, the employer may pay newly hired strike replacements those wages and benefits which were in its last offer prior to the bargaining impasse. Similarly, if there are employees who elect to work rather than to strike, they may be compensated under the terms of the employer's final pre-impasse offer. In addition, the employer may make unilateral changes in compensation and working conditions for strike replacements, provided the labor agreement has been terminated.[9]

Communicating With Strikers

During a strike the employer has a right to communicate with striking employees, to advise them of its last offer, to explain and justify management's position in negotiations, and to express opinions as to the futility and senselessness of a strike. However, the employer may not bargain directly with the employees, for example, by offering wages, benefits, or other considerations beyond its last offer if employees will return to work and abandon the strike. Nor may the employer bargain directly with them in any other way.

Continuing Bargaining Obligation

The union continues to be the bargaining agent for the striking employees as well as for strike replacements, and the employer is obligated to continue dealing with the union on all bargainable subjects. This obligation to bargain with the union continues even after the strike has commenced. Although it is not necessary that the employer agree to meet immediately after a strike has started, the employer cannot simply say that it is finished with bargaining since the union has elected to strike. The bargaining obligation continues as long as the union legally represents employees at the struck facility. Any changes in terms and conditions of employment which an employer desires to make during the course of the strike and which were not in the employer's final pre-impasse offer must be offered to, and bargained with, the union prior to being implemented.

Changes in Position

As stated in Chapter 4, withdrawn offers or regressive proposals are taken as indications of bad faith bargaining. However, when offers are withdrawn or reduced after a strike has begun, such bad faith motivations are not usually imputed. It is understood that the financial and other impacts of a strike on the employer may justify a reduced offer or a new approach to bargaining.[10] Beyond this, the simple fact of an employer's enhanced bargaining position following a union's unsuccessful strike has been held to justify a lower contract offer.[11]

Legal Caveats

The above discussion of the legal issues involved in strikes is but a brief overview of an extensive and complex body of law concerning the economic warfare which is a strike. Even in this brief outline it should be apparent that the rules are not absolute and numerous exceptions exist. While it is entirely possible for a nonlawyer to conduct a labor contract negotiation from start to finish without the aid of legal counsel, it is the rare strike which management can successfully endure without competent legal counsel.

The Decision on Whether to Operate During a Strike

If not sooner, at least as soon as it is clear that a strike will become a reality, management should make the decision as to whether it will operate its business during the strike. Most employers must consider the option of operating well in advance of an apparent bargaining impasse. This is particularly true in the case of public service employers where interruption of service would cause grave results. It may also be true in the case of employers which have a history of operating by having supervisors and salaried employees take over striking employees' functions during a strike, and who have a well-designed plan for maintaining or resuming operations after a strike has begun.

Prestrike Bargaining Positions

For other employers, however, the decision on whether to operate during a strike may not be so automatic or easy. Numerous considerations must be taken into account. The relative positions of the negotiating parties at the conclusion of negotiations prior to the strike are significant. If the parties are quite close to reaching a settlement, and if there is a reasonable likelihood of a short strike, it might be foolhardy to begin operations behind the picket line. Such operations could cause hostility and solidify positions to the point where the chances of an early settlement would be thwarted. On the other hand, if the parties' positions are far apart, and a long strike is a virtual certainty, commencement of operations may be clearly indicated.

Nature of Struck Operations

The nature of the employer's operations will have a great influence on the decision of whether or not to operate. If the operations are capital intensive, and the skills needed to operate machinery are not too demanding, or if the necessary skills are possessed by supervisors or others readily available in the labor market, continuing operations may be more feasible than if the work is labor intensive with high skill demands and experienced potential replacements are not readily available. For example, employers in the oil and chemical manufacturing industries, telephone communications, and broadcasting industries have normally operated during strikes, whereas employers in the steel, automobile, and trucking industries have not. Not all of these decisions were dictated by the work requirements, but clearly it is easier to operate a highly automated oil refinery with supervisory personnel than a more labor intensive automobile assembly plant.

Feasibility Factors

There are other factors which influence the feasibility of operations. The ability to receive sufficient amounts of raw materials and/or operating supplies, the capability to make regular deliveries of products, and the expected level of interference by unionized employees with customers, suppliers, and transportation companies will all influence the ability to maintain or resume operations *in a successful manner*. These last words must be emphasized, for the employer can suffer a great tactical as well as financial loss by attempting to operate during a strike and failing in the attempt. By considering the labor factors just described, plus the technical and logistical considerations, an employer should be able to determine if operations, at least at some level, are feasible.

Many employers and industries, however, underestimate their ability to operate during a strike. The pulp and paper industry, with which the author has been intimately involved, for the most part did not attempt to operate during strikes which occurred in the 30-year period prior to 1978, despite a number of years of relatively high strike activity. In 1978, however, operation during a strike was accomplished very successfully by several major West Coast plants. The realization that struck facilities could operate successfully induced other employers in the same industry throughout the United States to follow suit in subsequent years.

Impact on Labor-Management Relationships

An employer contemplating operations during a strike cannot overlook the impact such operations will have on the short- and long-term labor-management relationship at the struck facility. The impact cannot be predicted with certainty, but it is the rare situation where an employer operating during a strike does not experience significant hostility and animosity, particularly where replacements are newly hired employees rather than supervisors and other salaried employees who were already working for the employer prior to the strike. The impact of such operations on union-management relationships, however, is not totally negative. The realization on the part of the union and its members that they are replaceable and that management has the resolution and fortitude to successfully resist a strike can add up to a greater respect and deference on the part of the union for management's position in future negotiations.

Of all aspects of the decision to operate during a strike, none is more critical than that of determining who will perform the work of the striking employees. As stated above, this decision will dramatically affect the reaction of the striking employees and the long-term union-management relationship. Furthermore, the distinction between temporary and permanent replacements will have an important effect that can be either a catalyst to ending the strike or a destructive influence on the parties' ability to settle the strike.

As an example, some years ago employees at an Arizona plant operated by the author's former employer went on strike. The plant employed approximately 100 persons. Two weeks after the strike started, help-wanted ads for permanent replacements were placed in local newspapers. On the first day after the advertisements appeared, over 200 applicants appeared at the plant to file applications. Three days later, before any significant number of replacements were hired, the strike ended under the terms of management's final prestrike offer.

Impact on Bargaining Leverage

Finally, management must consider what impact continuing operations during a strike will have on the amount of leverage possessed by the union on one side and by management on the other at the bargaining table. If the level of operations is significant in comparison to the normal level, and if operations are otherwise successful, management can be significantly advantaged. The ability to earn income and write off overhead means that the employer is not being hurt financially as badly as if operations ceased. Moreover, customers can be supplied and loss of market share is minimized.

The significance of these factors will not be lost either on the union or on its members. They will realize, regardless of who has replaced them, that the impact of the strike has been nullified or at least blunted and that their loss of earnings is not being matched by those of the employer. And while members may be told by their union representatives that the employer is operating at only a fraction of normal levels and is losing money, the members nevertheless will know that the union has not landed a knockout blow by engaging in a strike.

Managing Operations During a Strike

If the decision is made not to continue operations during a strike, management's task is relatively simple. Proper precautions will be necessary for adequate security; mothballing of equipment; notices to customers, suppliers, and other interested parties; and monitoring of picket lines. If, however, the decision is made to operate, the job is infinitely more complex, and management must undertake a concerted program to prepare for and carry out an operating plan during the strike. If the employer expects to continue operations immediately following the strike or within a short period of time thereafter, planning and preparations will be particularly necessary well before the labor contract expires.

Labor Sources

The need to identify the source(s) of labor during a strike has already been reviewed. The choices are among one or more of the following:

1. Supervisors and other salaried employees at the struck facility.
2. Supervisors and other salaried employees from other facilities of the employer.
3. Hourly employees (preferably nonunion) from other facilities of the employer.
4. New employees hired on a temporary basis.
5. New employees hired on a permanent basis.
6. Bargaining unit employees who choose to work rather than to strike.
7. Contract labor.

Supervisors and Other Salaried Employees

Each labor source has its advantages and disadvantages. Supervisors and other salaried employees from the struck facility have the advantage of being familiar with the facility, equipment, product, service, and customers of the struck facility. However, if the facility is to operate efficiently, their presence is usually needed in their regular capacities. And while using these people to replace striking employees could be considered advantageous in that they obtain a better hands-on knowledge of the work ordinarily performed under their supervision, their future effectiveness and rapport with their subordinates could be adversely effected by their having replaced striking employees.

The advantages and disadvantages of using supervisors and other salaried employees from the employer's other facilities are almost inverse to those of using the local supervisory/salaried group. Although they normally do not know the work process, equipment, product or service, and other facets of the operation as well as salaried and supervisory personnel from the struck facility, their replacement of strikers is less apt to create long-term hostility in the struck workplace.

Hourly Employees—Other Facilities

Hourly employees from other facilities can be effective replacements provided the work is the same as, or similar to, their normal work and provided they are not represented by a union at their regular locations. Their services, as well as the services of supervisory and salaried employees from other facilities, should always be voluntary. Also, it is generally preferable that the tour of duty be for a limited time if the struck facility is an inconvenient distance from their homes. Extended tours can be disruptive to the facility from which the employees came, and can also be disruptive to their personal lives. If the employees from the employer's other facility(ies) are unionized, few of them are likely to volunteer to work in the struck facility. The inter-union conflict and inter-personal animosities likely to result are serious enough to discourage that source altogether.

Use of Strike Replacements

Strike replacements, particularly if they are permanent replacements or if their employment status is not specified, are considered by the union and its members in a much different light than are other company employees used to perform struck work. In the eyes of the strikers, replacements are true "scabs." In most instances this means that their working conditions will be more difficult than those of employees who are transferred from other jobs. Entrance into the facility will be met with epithets and frequently more. Telephone threats at home and broken automobile windshields can be expected.

Special security efforts will almost certainly be required, and management should go to great lengths in order to provide protection for strike replacements as well as to police and prosecute criminal activity directed at the replacements. The type, size, and location of the community in which the struck facility is situated obviously will have an influence on the degree of reaction to newly hired strike replacements. When strike replacements are hired, it is vitally important that they be forewarned about the type of treatment they can expect. Furthermore, they should be selected at least in part on their apparent tenacity and ability to withstand threats and intimidation.

In some cases, employers do not specifically state whether strike replacements are permanent or temporary and so keep their options open to treat them either way when the strike ends. In other cases, employers may specifically want to announce in advance that any strike replacements hired will be permanent, in order to induce striking employees to return to work. Indefiniteness on the part of the employer as to the status of strike replacements will adversely affect its ability to recruit a competent replacement work force. Potential strike replacements may be willing to endure the hostility and risk of bodily harm in order to secure regular employment. They are much less likely to do so for temporary jobs.

Contract Labor

Contract labor may be the best type of competent temporary replacement labor. Some firms make a business of supplying nonunion labor to replace striking employees. Although the struck employer is likely to pay a premium for such labor, the employees obtained in this manner are less apt to be intimidated by strikers than normal replacement employees. Some states limit the means of recruiting strike replacements, requiring, for example, that newspaper advertisements and recruitment literature specify that a labor dispute is in progress, and/or restricting the use of state employment services. A struck employer should know which, if any, limitations on recruitment exist in the state(s) where the strike will take place.

Multiple Labor Sources

Management should not feel that it must rely only on one or two of the previously listed sources of labor to make up its replacement work force. A combination of supervisory and salaried employees from the struck location and from other locations of the employer can be utilized along with hourly employees from the employer's other facilities and a selected number of newly hired strike replacements and/or contract labor.

Once a sufficient number of persons have been transferred, assigned, or recruited to operate the employer's facility, a list of the available workers should be correlated with a list of the jobs to be filled. The most highly skilled and critical jobs should be given top priority and filled with the persons best qualified to perform those jobs. Backups or alternates should be designated to ensure that all critical jobs will be filled regardless of absences due to illness, unexpected terminations, or for other reasons.

Training

It is almost certain that training of replacements will be required. The extent of the required training will vary considerably depending upon the nature of the work, the number of supervisors and salaried employees utilized from the struck location, the availability in the labor market of persons with the required skills, and other factors. The process suggested above of matching the replacement work force with the jobs to be filled will make the major training requirements evident. Because bargaining will normally be in progress up to the time of the strike, and because the negotiators will not want to disturb the atmosphere for achieving a settlement, there will normally be little opportunity in advance of a strike for on-the-job training in the facility concerned. This does not mean, however, that some advance training and preparation cannot be accomplished.

It is important that there be job training manuals and job instruction video tapes for each job or group of related jobs. These manuals and video tapes should already be in existence as part of normal working operations. If not, they should be prepared. They can be distributed in advance to the persons designated to perform the job(s) in the event of a strike. The period prior to a strike then can be used for studying these manuals and video tapes. Other training devices such as other audio-visual aids, classroom instruction, and computer-based training can also be utilized in advance of a strike. If the employer has other operations similar to the one likely to be struck, those operations can perhaps be utilized for hands-on training of selected personnel.

It will be difficult to conceal from bargaining unit employees the fact that recruitment and training activities are in progress. To the extent that the activities are treated as contingency measures and not given undue publicity by the employer, they can often have a salutary effect upon union negotiators and rank and file members. The knowledge that the employer will be prepared to operate in the event of a strike can often encourage more realistic bargaining. To the extent that such strike preparations are blatant and arrogant, however, the strike can become a self-fulfilling prophecy.

Care and Feeding of Strike Replacements

In a sense, strike replacements can be compared to soldiers. They are involved in an economic war between union and management. Many will be working long hours away from home, and will have to live in a community where they are targets of hostility from strikers and their families. Just as an army "marches on its stomach," so too do strike replacements need good food and housing. Management should make an extra effort to see that high-quality food is served at the work site and is available after work hours.

Similarly, secure and comfortable housing and transportation should be provided. Recreation and entertainment should be provided if not otherwise within easy access. If the replacements are to be housed within the confines of the employer's property to avoid picket line violence, special attention will need to be paid to see that suitable accommodations are arranged. Trailers or temporary housing will be necessary. Usually it is more practicable to have replacements lodged away from the work site as long as precautions are taken to protect them.

Scheduling Work

It is somewhat unlikely that there will be a completely adequate number of sufficiently skilled replacements available. This will often necessitate long work hours. Care must be exercised to ensure that overly long periods of work are not scheduled so that fatigue, accidents and employee burn-out can be avoided. If the strike is a short one, long hours may be tolerable. However, it is virtually impossible to predict the length of a strike, and therefore work schedules should be geared so that operations can be sustained over a long period of time. Long weekends or leaves should be programmed into the work schedules so that replacements can get away from the job and the community in which they are working.

Compensation and Benefits

Just as strike replacements should be fed well and housed well, so they should be compensated well for their efforts. Working as a strike replacement imposes much greater burdens on salaried employees and supervisors than does their normal work, and they should be appropriately compensated. Because the work they will be performing will normally be nonexempt under federal wage and hour laws, they will legally be entitled to time and one half for work in excess of 40 hours per week. In addition to this, the employer should consider some type of premium or bonus with which to reward replacements for their efforts. It is recommended that such bonuses be paid on a daily, weekly, or biweekly basis rather than at the end of the strike. The morale of replacements is likely to be much better if they are aware of the added compensation while they are performing the struck work.

In addition to the standard benefits, management should provide a per diem living allowance for those who are working far from home. Also, some travel allowance or means of transportation should be provided to permit relatively frequent trips home or to other locations during long weekends or leaves.

Security

Security during a strike is always a major concern. It is especially essential when the employer is operating behind a picket line. Aside from the need for security for the struck facility and for vehicles owned and operated by the employer which are vulnerable during a strike, the presence of strike replacements presents additional security demands. Each time someone crosses a picket line there is a possibility of violence. Replacements should, where possible, enter the employer's facility in secure vehicles, and preferably in groups. Police or hired security guards should monitor facility entrances, especially when replacements enter and leave. If the replacements are housed in groups away from the employer's facility, such housing should be selected with the safety of the replacements in mind. Local law enforcement officials should be alerted to possible threats and private security guards should be assigned to the housing occupied by replacements.

If the employer finds that its normal security protection and/or local law enforcement is not adequate and it is therefore necessary to hire a private security guard service, the service selected should be screened on the basis of its experience in strike situations. Many agencies are staffed by persons who are simply watchmen and who are totally unprepared to cope with the type of violence and confrontations accompanying strikes. The firm selected should be able to demonstrate that it has experience with difficult strike environments and is capable of dealing with the attendant problems.

Another word of caution is in order. In many communities, the local police force is itself represented by a labor union. Incidents have arisen where members of a unionized police force have been less than zealous in enforcing the law against striking union members. If management is not sure if the police in the locality of the struck facility are organized, that information should be obtained. If they are unionized, other employers in the same area who have had experience with strikes should be contacted to determine whether the laws were properly enforced. If a potential problem in this regard is anticipated, the employer should obtain more private security than would otherwise be the case.

Services, Supplies, and Deliveries

In order to operate during a strike, the employer must ensure it has a sufficient flow of services and supplies and that it will be able to deliver or provide its product or service to the customer. Invariably, normal means will not be adequate, and therefore special arrangements will be necessary.

Deliveries of raw materials and supplies may be hindered by the reluctance or unwillingness of delivery drivers to cross a picket line. Advance alternative arrangements should be made with the supplier in anticipation of such problems. For example, regular drivers can park their trucks outside the facility and supervisors can drive the trucks across the picket line. The same procedure is advised for deliveries by rail, where necessary. If the quantities involved are not too great, shipments can also be routed to an intermediate facility not being picketed, where the struck employer can pick up the goods. The same procedure can be used to deliver the struck employer's finished products when the customer's driver is unwilling to cross a picket line. Because common carriers are obligated to accept deliveries from any shipper and cannot refuse service, the common carrier's management will have a special obligation to cooperate in making necessary arrangements if their drivers are unwilling to cross a picket line and the right of the drivers to refuse to do so is protected by a labor contract.

Services provided by contractors on the premises of the struck employer present additional difficulties. Tradespeople or other employees of contractors often refuse to cross a picket line and their labor contract may very well give them the right to do so. The struck employer's only practicable recourse in such a situation is to establish a "reserved gate" or "contractor's gate," to be used only by specifically named contractors and their employees and suppliers. A sign so stating must be clearly posted at the contractor's gate and the striking union must be notified in writing of the existence and location of the reserved gate. If properly established, such a gate cannot legally be picketed by the striking union, provided the work done by the contractor and its employees is not work normally done by striking employees and is not work related to the struck employer's normal operations. An employer who intends to use a contractor during a strike and who has reason to believe that the contractor's employees will not cross a picket line should contact labor law counsel to ensure that the proper steps are taken to establish a valid reserved gate. The NLRB decisional rules on reserved gates are so demanding that experienced labor law counsel is usually necessary.

Management's Bargaining Posture During a Strike

Regardless of whether the employer is or is not going to continue operations once a strike has commenced, management's main objective must be to have the strike terminated as soon as possible. This does not mean, however, that in attempting to do so management should abandon its basic economic goals or principles which were at issue when the strike began. Nevertheless, the strike will eventually end, and the sooner it ends the better.

Initial Bargaining Position

Unfortunately, the shortest distance between a strike and a settlement is not a straight line. That is to say, prompt resumption of negotiations after a strike has commenced will seldom lead to a quick settlement. If both parties measured their respective positions vis-a-vis the other side and commenced the strike with their eyes wide open, it is very doubtful that a quick settlement would be possible. In most cases, it will be necessary for one or both sides to feel the economic pressure of the strike before a change in position(s) is possible. This, of course, takes time.

For this reason, it is seldom useful for management to seek resumption of negotiations for at least several weeks following the commencement of a strike. In fact, to do so is often counterproductive. A premature attempt by management to commence negotiations is likely to be interpreted by the union as a signal that management is ready to make concessions on positions taken before the strike began. To the extent this is not true, an early attempt by the employer to commence negotiations could have the effect of prolonging the strike. Management's normal posture at this point, therefore, should be to sit and wait.

Communications

Undoubtedly there will be numerous questions regarding the strike, from supervisors, employees, customers, suppliers, stockholders, the news media, and the public. They will want to know what issues are involved in the strike, what management's final offer was, how the employer's offered wages and benefits compare with comparable employers, whether any negotiating meetings are scheduled, and they will have numerous other similar questions. Management should be prepared to respond. If the bargaining unit is of substantial size and significance within the community, a news release should be prepared. Furthermore, questions and answers should be prepared in anticipation of inquiries from the media or others. These questions and answers should lay out the issues in the strike and management's position on each issue.

Direct Communications

Management needs to consider whether it should communicate directly with striking employees. To the extent it believes that employees are not fully aware of the issues or differences in position that caused the strike and/or may not be completely in sympathy with their union's position, an immediate communication may be advisable. Such a communication, probably in the form of a letter mailed to the home of each employee, should be factual, straightforward, and "soft-sell" in tone. It should not have an obvious sound of propaganda, but should explain the respective positions of the parties in as objective a manner as possible. It should also clearly express management's rationale for the positions it has taken in negotiations.

Management may wish also to consider the establishment of a "hot line"—a recorded telephone message linked to a series of telephones having a common number. Interested parties can dial the number and hear a prerecorded message about the progress of the strike, facility operations, eligibility for insurance continuation, and other matters. Some employers like to publicize the hot line as being directed to supervisors, although, of course, there is no restriction as to who can dial the number to reach the recorded message. If management initially establishes such a line, it is quite likely that the union will do likewise as a defensive measure. Of course, if the union already has set up such a hot line, management risks having its side of the story go unheard if it does not follow suit.

Hot lines require a great deal of time and creativity. The messages must be changed frequently enough to maintain interest. Likewise, they must contain information of sufficient interest and objectivity to encourage repeat calls. Many times as a strike continues it will be difficult to say anything of interest or importance. Changing the message and keeping it lively can be almost a full-time job.

Media Communications

If the strike is significant enough to warrant media attention, management is encouraged to work closely and cooperatively with media representatives. To the extent that these persons understand management's position, they will be in a better position to agree with it and convey that feeling in their publications, broadcasts, and telecasts.

Management's contact person with media representatives must be knowledgeable about the negotiations and strike, and must be completely credible. Whether management's bargaining spokesperson should speak directly with media representatives is a matter to be decided early in the process. In most cases it is important that he do so at least on a periodic basis. Media representatives may believe management has something to hide if its chief speaker is not made available to talk directly with them. Obviously, the individual must speak carefully, for what is printed in the newspapers or said on radio or television could come back to haunt management at the bargaining table.

There is a school of thought that the management spokesperson should never communicate directly with the media for fear of extending the negotiations beyond the bargaining table and into the media. Another concern is that the spokesperson may inadvertently say something, or be attributed as saying someting, that could harm management's position at the bargaining table. As a general proposition, the author supports this school of thought.

Resuming Negotiations

At some point following a strike negotiations must resume. The exact time will be a matter of judgment. Frequently, a mediator will have been involved in the negotiations prior to the strike and can call a negotiating meeting on his or her own initiative when appropriate. Management negotiators may not feel that the mediator's judgment is correct. They may believe that the union is not yet ready to move toward management's position and may ask him to delay a meeting, or they may indicate that management negotiators are not available to meet until a later date. Management cannot be forced by the mediator to meet, although considerable informal pressure to do so can be exerted. Management should strenuously avoid being characterized in public as unwilling to meet and bargain with the union.

If management believes that an earlier resumption of negotiations would be useful, it may wish to arrange for a meeting with the union. In order to avoid weakening its position, in such a situation management can contact the mediator and suggest that the mediator call a meeting without revealing that management requested it.

Bargaining a Strike Settlement Agreement

It is not possible to spell out the myriad ways in which a strike can be settled. No two strikes are identical, and the right combination of actions and contract terms is unique to each situation. Creative techniques for resolving an impasse are reviewed in Chapter 12. In Chapter 14, a series of techniques are suggested to put pressure on a union to settle. A number of these techniques are also applicable in strike situations.

Beyond the various means of resolving the differences which caused the strike, management needs to consider a number of points which are essential in putting together a strike settlement agreement.

Order of Recall to Work

Consideration must be given as to when work will be resumed, whether it will be on a complete or staggered basis, what work schedules will be in effect, and what order of recall of striking employees will be applied. Similarly, management should secure an agreement from the union that penalties and payments for certain types of work scheduling set forth in the labor agreement will be waived during the recall period. Such penalties and premiums are designed to prevent, or compensate employees for, scheduling inconveniences. They do not apply when management is seeking to get all striking employees back to work as soon as possible. Due to the typical nature of work patterns during resumption of regular operations with bargaining unit employees following a strike, management may also seek a grace period during which the union waives contract penalty and premium provisions during the recall.

If permanent replacements have been hired and will be retained after the strike, a strike settlement agreement should address the status of returning strikers, their seniority status vis-a-vis replacement employees, procedures applicable to recall from the reinstatement list, and numerous other questions attendant to terminating such a strike.

Eligibility for Benefits

In almost every poststrike period, questions arise concerning the eligibility of striking employees for (1) holidays which occurred during the strike; (2) credit for work time lost during the strike toward vacations, pensions, and other benefits which are dependent upon time actually worked; and (3) medical benefits or reimbursement for medical expenses incurred during the strike. These and other similar questions should be anticipated before a strike settlement is reached. Unless management has no bargaining leverage to do so, it should insist that striking employees receive no credit for time or benefits lost as a result of the strike. To allow credit for time not worked or benefits not earned during a strike only rewards them for having gone on strike.

Seniority Status of Strikers

Closely related to the question of benefits is that of seniority status. Will employees be considered to have accrued seniority during the period of the strike? If some employees in the bargaining unit worked during the strike, did their seniority accrue during the strike, and will they be able to bypass from a seniority standpoint striking employees who did not work during the strike? The strike settlement agreement must address all aspects of the questions of the seniority status of returning strikers, as well as the seniority status of strike replacements.

Disciplinary Action for Strike Misconduct

If the strike resulted in violent acts or other significant misconduct by striking employees, management may have taken disciplinary and/or discharge action against the offending employees or may be intending to take such action upon termination of the strike. If so, the parties should frankly discuss the actions or intended actions. If no special provisions are included in the strike settlement agreement, management is free to act as it sees fit within the confines of the law. The union will usually seek to negotiate some protection for its members and/or seek reinstatement for discharged members. The party with the greatest bargaining leverage will control the results on these issues. Immediate arbitration of discharges for strike misconduct is a common resolution reached in strike settlement agreements where neither party completely capitulates.

Union Disciplinary Action Against Picket Line Violators

Just as the union will seek to protect its members from disciplinary action by the employer, so too will the employer attempt to protect any employees who during the strike chose to cross the picket line and come to work (i.e., "cross-overs"). Union constitutions and bylaws frequently contain sanctions against employees who do not honor the picket lines established or authorized by their union. The degree to which the union will or will not enforce its constitutional sanctions should be addressed in the strike settlement agreement. It is vital for the employer to shield cross-overs from any union sanctions, lest it discourage such activity again in some future strike.

Pending Litigation

During the course of a strike, the parties frequently file lawsuits or unfair labor practices against each other. The status of these legal actions can have a bearing on the ability of union and management to reach a final agreement. Although it is common for a strike settlement agreement to contain a provision whereby both parties agree to abandon all legal claims and actions, many employers refuse to drop lawsuits for violence directed at person or property. The rationale here is that violence should not be considered an integral part of a labor dispute, and that to drop such actions would be to condone strike violence and encourage its future use.

Poststrike Posture

It is the unusual strike that does not create bitterness and resentment on the part of the union, management, employees, and supervisors. One of the most unfortunate legacies of a strike is the continuing hostility between the parties which persists during the poststrike period despite the most concerted efforts to remove it. Nevertheless, management must do everything within its power to restore and improve good union-management relations. It must instruct its supervisors to abandon any signs of bitterness toward the union and the striking employees. Furthermore, they should be as sympathetic as possible to the feelings of employees who themselves are bitter. Lingering hostility can only have an adverse effect on work performance and can harm the employer.

Management should attempt to bind up the open wounds left by the strike. A letter of conciliation or other communication in the same vein may help in this regard. Notwithstanding this and other attempts at reconciliation, the memory of a strike is not easily erased. Usually only the passage of time will heal the wounds left by a strike.

14

Bringing the Negotiations to a Conclusion

In Chapter 12, "Striving To Reach Agreement," the significance of an employer's final offer in bringing negotiations to a conclusion was reviewed. Also suggested in that chapter were various means for avoiding or resolving an impasse in negotiations. Aside from clearing away specific roadblocks as discussed in Chapter 12, the management negotiator needs to bring an end to the bargaining and achieve a settlement. In effect, the negotiator must "close the deal." This requirement exists prior to the contract expiration and prior to any work stoppage. It can also exist where a strike is in progress when management is seeking ways to achieve a settlement in order to end the strike.

This chapter addresses ways to bring negotiations to an end. Specifically, it covers ways to bring pressure on the union to settle, common pitfalls in reaching a settlement, and techniques for improving the odds that a tentative settlement will be ratified by the union's membership. It will conclude with a discussion of the important tasks to be undertaken following bargaining.

Applying Pressure to Settle

No matter how interested a union is in reaching a settlement, union negotiators are often reluctant to leave the bargaining table for fear that they might "leave money on the table," i.e., accept anything less than the maximum amount that an employer might have been willing to grant under pressure of a strike. In addition, there may be lingering and unsatisfied union demands that the union's negotiators genuinely feel are essential to a settlement. To the extent that management is not willing to increase the total value of its last offer or accede to the union's "must" items, the bargaining is over from management's standpoint. Unfortunately, where complete agreement has not been reached by this time, management must sometimes apply pressure on the union to conclude the negotiations and to submit management's final offer to a membership vote or to whatever contract ratification procedures exist within the union. There are a number of techniques that can be employed to apply such pressure.

Deadline for Acceptance

A useful way to exert pressure on the union to act upon management's final offer is to place an expiration date on the offer, which therefore establishes a deadline for acceptance/ratification. If the offer is not accepted by the designated date, it expires. Typical language to establish such a deadline in an offer reads as follows:

> This offer will continue in effect until April 1, 19__. If written notice of acceptance and ratification is not received by the employer by 12:00 midnight April 1, 19__, the offer is withdrawn in its entirety.

Although this condition may make union negotiators uncomfortable if they are unaccustomed to it, an offer deadline is nevertheless a businesslike way of negotiating, and a union cannot reasonably accuse management of unfair tactics by its use. Management is entitled to have a timely response to its offer, and if the union chooses not to accept the offer by the stated time and date, there is no good reason why management should leave the offer on the table. As long as the period for acceptance is a reasonable one, the technique is entirely proper.

If the offer deadline is not employed, the union may simply let the offer sit for a period of time while management is left hanging. Moreover, without such a condition, the union may be led to the conclusion that it can reject management's final offer and have negotiations resume, yet still have the final offer to fall back on if the resumed negotiations do not bear fruit. With the suggested deadline, however, the union is put on notice that if the final offer is not accepted, the union has nothing, and it cannot be certain that management will subsequently match that offer, let alone exceed it.

Following this same reasoning, if the union rejects management's final offer and goes on strike, that final offer should be formally withdrawn by written notice to the union.

Deadline on Offer of Retroactivity

It is quite common for labor contract negotiations to continue beyond the formal expiration date of the existing contract. Under ordinary conditions, when bargaining extends beyond the contract expiration date the contract continues to be in effect by virtue of the terms of that contract, because of a separate specific agreement to do so, or simply because of a tacit understanding by the negotiating parties. Moreover, under the NLRA, the terms and conditions of the preexisting agreement must be maintained until impasse is reached or until a new agreement becomes effective. While the negotiations continue, there is frequently an explicit or tacit agreement that any economic improvements in the first year of the contract will be effective on a retroactive basis back to the first day following the expiration date of the previous contract.

Just as placing a deadline on a final offer is a strong encouragement for a union to act upon (and hopefully accept) management's final offer, so too is a deadline or cutoff date on any offer of retroactivity. Typical language to provide such a condition in a final offer is as follows:

> The economic improvements of this offer (except those affecting life and medical insurance) shall be retroactive to March 1, 19__, provided written notice of acceptance and ratification of this offer is received by the employer no later than 12:00 midnight, March 25, 19__.

One may reasonably ask how this condition differs significantly from the deadline for acceptance by which the entire offer is withdrawn. If the entire offer is withdrawn, isn't the retroactive payment of the first year's economic improvements automatically withdrawn? The obvious answer is *yes*. However, explicit withdrawal of retroactivity alone may be a more credible condition. The union may not believe that the employer would take back its entire offer and never make it available again. It is entirely plausible, however, that management might remove the retroactive feature of the offer while leaving the rest of the offer intact. After all, the employer will probably not be able to retroactively increase the prices, fees, service charges, or fares it charges to customers to reflect the added cost of a labor contract settlement. Consequently, any offer to make retroactive wage and benefit increases will normally come directly out of profits.

Any employer might be reluctant to guarantee retroactivity for a significant period of time; therefore, a condition in a final offer to limit the retroactive aspect of the offer to a specific date certainly is a logical and reasonable one. For this reason, a union may be quite apprehensive about not accepting an offer by the established deadline if it seriously fears that the retroactive increases will be jeopardized.

Added Benefit for Acceptance by Deadline

The two previous deadline techniques for applying pressure on the union might be considered as a "stick" (i.e., punishment or sanction) for not accepting an offer. A "carrot" can be used in addition to, or in lieu of, the stick. A benefit or advantage, not otherwise present in the offer, can be provided to induce the union to accept by a certain date. This technique is not commonly used, although it is employed in some cases where a contract has been reopened considerably in advance of its expiration date, and the employer wants to get a new contract ratified well in advance of the expiration date. Language in a final offer providing this condition could be as follows:

> Provided the employer receives notice of acceptance and ratification of this offer no later than September 1, 19__, each bargaining unit employee who is on the active payroll of the employer as of September 1, 19__, shall receive a one-time bonus payment of $300.00.

This type of incentive should be used on rare occasions. The carrot for acceptance can become, if it is not used properly and only rarely, an expected gratuity for accepting an employer's final offer. Also, an employer's final offer should be presented in such a way that it does not need a bonus or other special consideration for its acceptance by a given date. For these reasons, a carrot should normally be offered only where there is some special consideration or concession on the part of the union or the employees involved in accepting by a given date.

Breaking Off Negotiations

A union that wishes to act like a pig feeding at the management trough is usually not ready to leave the bargaining table so long as management is still willing to bargain. Often the only way to deal with such a union is to break off negotiations. Of course, management must be careful that its exit from the bargaining table is not premature and its unwillingness to resume is not unreasonable or it may find itself the recipient of a meritorious unfair labor practice charge.[1] Aside from this caveat, however, there is nothing improper about management's taking the position that its final offer has been made, the union's response thereto has been considered, and management has nothing further to propose.

This gambit can put pressure on the union to act on management's final offer. It can, of course, also put the union in an untenable political position whereby management's posture may seem to look like a "take it or leave it" one. And that may be the exact message that management wants to deliver. Contrasted with the gentle nudge of an offer deadline, breaking off negotiations can appear to be confrontational. Much depends on the timing of the break, the speeches or statements explaining it, and the tone of the negotiations which preceded the cessation of talks.

If the union has not been publicly embarrassed by the break in negotiations, the technique can result in the offer being submitted to the union membership. And if management's manner of presentation of the final offer convinces the union that it *is* the final offer, the union negotiators may very well present it to the membership with the explanation that it is the very best offer that management is going to make. In any event, breaking off negotiations will send a clear and unmistakable signal to the union that the status quo of the bargaining cannot be maintained, and that management has put the ball squarely in the union's court.

Unfair Labor Practice Charge

Another technique sometimes used to apply pressure on one or both negotiating parties is the filing of an unfair labor practice charge (ULP). Unions can file a charge that the employer has refused to bargain in good faith by alleging a violation of Section 8(a)(5) of the National Labor Relations Act. The employer can similarly charge the union under Section 8(b)(3) of the Act. Because of the NLRB's slow pace in processing and hearing charges, and because of the relatively mild remedies imposed (i.e., usually an order to bargain in good faith), this tactic is seldom very effective for either party. It is used more often by unions than employers, and seldom against employers who are bargaining renewal contracts with unions whose legitimacy they do not contest.

Because the filing of a ULP is usually done for tactical reasons, the charging party should be quite sure that the charge has merit. If it does not, the refusal by an NLRB regional director to issue a complaint, or the failure to prevail before the NLRB, can prove to be a tactical loss. A case in point is the strike by the NFL Players Association against the National Football League in 1982. The union sought to gain a bargaining advantage and public support by filing an unfair labor practice charge alleging that the owners were refusing to bargain in good faith about a minimum wage scale. Although the NLRB's general counsel determined that the Board would seek a court injunction to force bargaining on that issue, the full panel of NLRB members rejected the counsel's recommendation.[2] Because union leadership and the players themselves had placed great stock in the charge, and because the NLRB decision came at a crucial point in the negotiations after the union had been on strike for about seven weeks, the union was dealt a severe tactical defeat. Within a week of the NLRB's decision the union conceded on most major issues, and the strike was over.[3]

If management is persuaded that the union has not bargained in good faith, and if pressure needs to be applied to move the union from a status quo position, an unfair labor practice charge might generate some momentum. However, the chances of achieving any significant advantage are so remote that management should very carefully consider its legal and tactical positions before exercising this option.

Elimination of Checkoff

If negotiations continue beyond the expiration date of the contract, and if the contract has not been extended (i.e., it has expired), another potential means of exerting pressure on the union exists. Section 302(c) of the National Labor Relations Act provides that an employer may only deduct union dues from employees' pay and pay them to the union where a written assignment by each employee from whom dues are deducted is in effect, and such assignments are normally revocable when a collective bargaining agreement has been terminated.[4] Therefore, if the contract has expired, employees may revoke their dues deduction authorization. Management may inform them of this option, and employees may elect to revoke assignments, which could seriously affect the union's financial resources. Also, since there is no contract in effect, management may legally refuse to comply with the checkoff provisions of the contract since that clause is dependent upon the existence of a valid union contract.[5]

Ceasing the checkoff of union dues is probably useful only in a situation where the union does not wish to strike, but is delaying reaching a settlement. This might occur, for example, where other negotiations are in progress and the union wishes to stall in order to see what settlement is reached in the other negotiations, or where the union does not believe it has sufficient clout to wage a successful strike. Management may wish to pressure the union to submit management's final offer to a membership vote in order to get a settlement. Under these circumstances, the threat of ceasing the payroll deduction of union dues could provide a meaningful sanction and an effective impetus for the union to submit management's offer to the membership. Management should fully appreciate that such a tactic will undoubtedly be perceived by the union as a "hard ball" maneuver.

Strike Preparations

As suggested in the preceding chapter, management should begin preparations for a strike well before the contract expiration date. Such preparations should normally be as unobtrusive as possible while negotiations are in progress. The value of keeping the preparations under wraps, however, diminishes as the negotiations bog down. In fact, management can apply some pressure on the union to settle by allowing information about strike preparations to come to the attention of union officials and employees. This information should not be disseminated in such a way that it appears to be a challenge but in a more subtle way. For example, the installation at facility entrances of remote control television cameras, sufficiently out of reach that they cannot be easily damaged but close enough to allow clear pictures of the scene, can be observed by employees as they enter and leave the facility. No announcement of their installation need be made for all employees to be aware that the employer is preparing for a strike.

Likewise, management can issue strike preparation instructions to supervisors, which will inevitably become known to bargaining unit employees, sending a signal that management is gearing up for a strike.

Hiring Strike Replacements

If management has not now, or in the past, operated its enterprise while a strike has been in effect, or if it has operated under the strike conditions only with supervisory and salaried personnel, additional pressure can be applied to obtain a settlement by an announcement of management's intention to utilize replacements, especially permanent replacements. As explained in Chapter 13, permanent strike replacements can be retained in preference to striking employees who offer to return to work at the end of a strike, provided the strike is an "economic" one, i.e., not caused or prolonged by unfair labor practices on the part of the employer. An employer's announcement in anticipation of, or during, a strike of an intention to hire permanent replacements puts employees on notice that they might suffer permanent loss of their jobs if the strike continues.

This technique, especially if it is presented as a threat, can sometimes backfire and simply stimulate greater resistance and resolve on the part of the union and the striking employees. However, under proper conditions, it can be a powerful incentive to motivate union negotiators to seek a settlement before or during a strike. For example, the notice can be quite effective where a strike has continued for some period of time; where there is a ready, willing, and able potential supply of labor to replace strikers; and where the news of planned hiring of replacements is completely credible.

Representation Election

When a collective bargaining agreement has expired (with or without a strike), NLRB rules provide that there is no longer a bar (i.e., preclusion) to a representation election.[6] In more common terms, the "contract bar" has been removed. Thus, it is possible for a competing union(s) to petition the NLRB to conduct a representation election. In order to do so, any competing or "raiding" union would need to supply the NLRB with signed authorization cards from 30 percent of the employees in the appropriate bargaining unit. Likewise, if 30 percent of the employees in the bargaining unit simply wish to oust the incumbent union, a decertification petition can be filed once the contract has been terminated.

If there is substantial objective evidence that the union no longer represents a majority of employees in the bargaining unit, management can file an "RM" petition which can also result in a representation election.[7] The RM petition is the means by which the employer brings before the NLRB its good faith doubts that the union represents a majority of its employees. An RM petition, unlike the petition filed by employees or a competing union, is not supported by signed cards, but rather must be supported by objective evidence that the union no longer represents a majority of the employees, results of a lawfully conducted poll,[8] and/or evidence of inactivity of the union in representing employees coupled with the filing of a decertification petition.[9] However, the evidence must be very persuasive, and the employer must not have interfered in any way so as to have caused the union's loss of representation.[10]

There is not a great deal which management can legally do to create the conditions which would cause a representation petition to be filed. However, if some dissatisfaction with the union exists on the part of employees and/or if a competing union has shown some interest in raiding the unit, there is nothing to prevent management from bringing these facts to the union's attention, and reminding union representatives that as long as a labor contract is not in effect, the union is vulnerable to an NLRB petition that could result in its loss of representation rights for the bargaining unit. This could be a strong inducement for the union to reach a settlement.

Common Pitfalls in Reaching a Settlement

Despite careful planning, effective strategy, and proper execution by the negotiator, a successful negotiation cannot be assured until the contract is signed. Not infrequently, critical errors are made at the concluding stages of negotiations. The following sections are devoted to pointing out some of the more common errors made, even by experienced negotiators.

Being Pressured Into Settlement

Strike Threat

Just as management frequently has reason to apply pressure on the union to reach a settlement, so too the union often exerts pressure on management to settle. The techniques used are based largely on the union's primary weapon, the strike. By printing and displaying picket signs; having employees remove tools, clothing, and personal effects from the threatened facility; and by spreading strike rumors, the union can create an aura of strike imminency which can cause management negotiators to believe that the union is intent on "pulling the trigger" as soon as the strike deadline arrives.

Although management cannot ignore the risks imposed by a strike, neither can it afford to allow itself to negotiate with a gun to its head. Of course, the ideal solution is to reach a settlement sufficiently in advance of a strike deadline so that the ultimate pressure is obviated. If it is possible to reach an early settlement, that solution is best for all parties. However, a management negotiator who is anxious to settle early may simply have spent everything available without having obtained a settlement. A skilled union negotiator will want to use all the time available to wring out every last cent management may be able (or eventually willing) to spend. The union loses nothing by taking management up to "the moment of truth" to see how much more it can get.

Anticipating the Worst Case

The most feasible method to avoid undue pressure is for management to plan for a strike and to assume that it will be necessary to bargain all the way to the strike deadline, and possibly even beyond. It should also be assumed that the union will threaten a strike in every way possible. Such threats may even take the form of premature scattered walkouts before the contract has expired. The union's purpose in such cases is to point the gun at management's head in the hope that it will blink. Only by convincing itself that such union tactics are for the purpose of putting pressure on the employer will management effectively discount their significance and avoid the pressure that can cause serious mistakes.

Another way to deal with a union's pressure tactics is for management to have established for itself a true final position before the final bargaining stages. If the ultimate positions on economics and contract language issues are not firmly locked in place, union strike threats are apt to cause self-doubt, confusion, and a failure of resolve that can be discerned by the union. Management should remember that, despite what the union negotiators say, there is no single package that the union must achieve to reach an agreement. The union's willingness to accept management's final offer will largely depend upon its perception and belief that management will allow a strike to commence rather than go beyond its final offer. Unless the management spokesperson has locked that final offer into his or her own negotiating psyche, and prepared top management to "stay the course," the spokesperson will not be able to convince the union that management will remain firm.

The irrevocability of management's final offer position should not, however, cloud management's judgment to the extent that it is unwilling to pursue alternative packages that may differ in form or arrangement from its final offer, but which cost the employer no more in a monetary or management-rights sense. If it is possible to substitute, modify, or help the union save face without significantly changing the cost of the final offer or sacrificing any negotiating objectives, this avenue should be left open. However, in exploring alternative packages, management's spokesperson needs to make it clear that the total cost of the package is fixed and that further bargaining, a strike, or any other union gambit will not cause management to increase its final offer.

Bargaining Deadline

Closely related to the strike pressure designed to induce management to increase its final offer is the pressure applied by the union on management to conclude negotiations by a specific bargaining deadline—usually a strike deadline. In most cases the deadline is a real one in that the union has likely issued instructions to commence the strike at a particular time on a particular day, and presumably intends to strike at that time if no agreement has been reached.

Extending the Deadline

In virtually all cases the union's strike deadline can, and will, be extended if union negotiators are convinced that they can reach a settlement without a strike. Management negotiators should keep in mind that it is just as advantageous to the union as it is to management to avoid an unnecessary strike. Consequently, pressure to fully conclude a settlement in advance of a bargaining or strike deadline should not cause management to agree to what would otherwise be unacceptable terms, if it is possible that additional bargaining time could result in terms that are truly satisfactory to management. This means that management's spokesperson must remain optimistic and persuade the union counterpart that although the current positions of the parties are apart, further bargaining can realistically resolve the differences and that in order to give time for further bargaining, the strike deadline needs to be postponed. The union's negotiator may need to be reminded that once a strike begins, management's final offer or last position will no longer be available, and that all the progress that both sides have made to that point will have been lost.

"Stopping the Clock"

A traditional device used in some industries to extend a deadline without officially extending it is to "stop the clock." This is a self-deceptive technique of actually pulling the plug on a clock in the negotiating room or corridor (or acting as though that was done if no wall clock is available). The idea is that the parties are "officially" adhering to a deadline but actually extending it. The author has not personally found it necessary to use this transparent subterfuge, but if it helps negotiating parties to reach a settlement it is worth using.

Extra Value of Additional Time

In addition to the trap of being forced to agree to otherwise unacceptable terms, time pressure to conclude a settlement by the union's strike deadline is likely to cause errors of judgment and in the wording of terms of agreement. Because such "eleventh-hour" settlements are often finalized after marathon bargaining and frequently in the middle of the night, mistakes can easily be made. The combination of pressure and exhaustion can easily lead one to overlook key points, make arithmetic miscalculations, draft erroneous contract terms, and the like. A postponement of the strike deadline can allow the negotiators to get needed sleep, food, and time to enable them to approach the wrap-up phase of negotiations with clearer heads.

Problems Presented by the Union's Acceptance and Ratification Process

As a general rule, management negotiators have authority to conclude a final and binding agreement at the bargaining table without any further approval or ratification by their principals. Unions, on the other hand, must usually submit a tentative settlement to a ratification vote by the rank and file membership or by a representative body selected by the membership. This difference between management and union methods of finalizing negotiations introduces great complications into the bargaining process. It also gives the union a bargaining advantage in that the union negotiators can consistently "pass the buck" by blaming the membership for unreasonable or excessive demands and bargaining positions. The phrase "we couldn't sell *that* to the membership" is the type of response unions commonly use in this regard to try to improve their bargaining position.

In all fairness, however, the union's need to obtain membership ratification imposes significant burdens on union negotiators as well. They can never be certain that the terms they are able to wrest from management will ultimately be acceptable to their membership. Although their membership has usually indicated in some manner what they wish their negotiators to obtain in bargaining, those goals are seldom clearcut and are rarely attainable in all respects. Union negotiators must trust their own judgment or must estimate the membership's bottom-line positions as the tentative settlement is being hammered out. Theirs is not an enviable task in this regard.

Knowing and Dealing With the Union's Ratification Process

Notwithstanding union negotiators' burden in dealing with the ratification process, management must be aware of the pitfalls imposed by this process. Initially, management must be informed well in advance as to exactly what the union's ratification process is. Is it simply a membership vote or are there additional levels of approval? For example, some unions require a vote of the membership of the local union and acceptance by the international union. Other unions have a regional organization that must approve contracts. Although such approvals are often simply rubber stamps, management should be aware of their existence and of any possible problems they may present.

Beyond the mere knowledge of the union's ratification/acceptance process is the development of a strategy to deal with it. For example, if, in addition to ratification by the union's membership, approval by some higher level within the union's organization is going to be necessary, and if there is a serious question as to obtaining that approval, management negotiators need to get an informal confirmation of the settlement's acceptability to union officials at that level before a final offer is made and before the membership votes. Likewise, if there are separate votes taken among different segments of the union's membership (e.g., votes counted on a local-by-local basis, or separate tallies for production workers and skilled-trades workers), that factor should be taken into account when the bargaining is being conducted and especially as a final settlement is being reached.

Final Authority by the Committee

Occasionally, management may be able to induce a union negotiating committee to get its membership to grant the negotiating committee the authority to conclude a final agreement without a ratification vote. This is often, however, precluded by the union's bylaws. If it is not, or if a grant of final authority to the committee is done by a full membership vote (and therefore treated as a form of ratification), it is a useful technique for concluding difficult negotiations. It is especially useful, if not necessary, after an offer, fully recommended by the union committee, has failed a ratification vote.

Buying a Recommendation

Where a tentative settlement or management's final offer must be submitted to the union's membership for ratification, the most management can expect from the union's bargaining committee is a full recommendation in favor of acceptance and a commitment that the committee will do everything within its power to have the membership vote in favor of the tentative settlement or final offer. In the jargon of collective bargaining, the committee agrees to "sell the package." In the majority of labor contract negotiations, a fully recommended settlement is tantamount to having a final ratified settlement.

Recognizing the value of a full recommendation by the union's bargaining committee, management should make a determined effort not to leave the bargaining table without a commitment of a full recommendation by the union's negotiating committee. From a strategic standpoint, this often requires management to plan its offers or positions in such a way as to reserve some portion of its maximum wage, benefit, or contract language offers in order to "buy a recommendation" if necessary. Thus, for example, management, at the final stage of bargaining, might hold back enough to tack on an additional small wage increase or some other incidental benefit in order to obtain a fully recommended offer. This additional "sweetener" should come before any "final offer" statement is made. If it follows the final offer, it will break down management's credibility, thus adversely affecting future negotiations.

Should Management Have to Pay for a Recommendation?

It might seem superfluous for management to negotiate in good faith to reach an acceptable settlement only to have to offer something in addition in order to get the union bargaining committee's favorable recommendation. In many cases it is not necessary. The process of hammering out an acceptable agreement is frequently sufficient in itself to have the union's bargaining committee fully recommend its acceptance.

In other cases, however, the settlement may not have reached the level the bargaining committee feels should have been achieved or the level the committee members believe is necessary to satisfy the membership. Despite this, the committee may not wish to urge a strike because the offer is not too far off the mark or because the union leaders may not believe a strike can be won. Under these conditions, the committee may simply want to submit management's final offer to a vote with no recommendation, and let the members make their own choice without being influenced. The reason for taking such a position is usually due to the committee members' concern for the political jeopardy in which they might place themselves by going on record as supporting a settlement package which is not too attractive and which might be rejected by the membership. It is in these situations that management may need to "buy a recommendation," i.e., add one or more additional features to the offer solely on the condition that the union's bargaining committee then will fully recommend the offer.

Reliability of Bought Recommendation

A legitimate question might be raised as to whether management can truly induce an honest recommendation if the members of the union's bargaining committee are not genuinely enthusiastic about the offer. In other words, won't a recommendation that is "bought" be a hollow one? There is no simple answer. In some cases it probably is; the author is aware of instances where management negotiators were told that the union negotiating committee would recommend an offer, only to learn afterward that in the preratification meetings (where the employer's final offer or tentative settlement is explained to the membership), the members of the bargaining committee criticized the offer or recommended against approval.

On the other hand, if the additional features used to buy the recommendation are greatly desired and valued by the bargaining committee, and if the balance of the offer is not too far from the committee's expectations, a final offer which the union committee agrees to recommend will usually be sincerely recommended. Often such a recommendation can spell the difference between a favorable and unfavorable ratification vote.

Locking in the Recommendation

Is there any way for management to assure that once it buys a recommendation it gets what it paid for? Probably not, at least not with absolute assurance. However, there are some techniques which experienced negotiators use to get as close as possible to such an assurance. One way is to include a written statement on the face of the tentative settlement, or summary thereof, that the union's negotiating committee fully recommends that the settlement be ratified by the membership. Each member of the committee can then sign below the statement to verify this commitment. Union negotiators are sometimes wary of doing this, however, unless the price the employer is paying to buy the recommendation is substantial.

Another technique is for the management's spokesperson to poll the union's committee. The spokesperson looks each member of the committee in the eye and individually asks, "Will you fully recommend the package?" The idea here, of course, is to create a moral obligation for each member to carry out what he or she has said would be done. Neither of these techniques is foolproof, however, and in the final analysis, management's negotiator must trust the good faith of the union's committee members as well as the fairness and attractiveness of the settlement itself, to carry the day.

Last Minute Add-Ons

Some union negotiators have a nasty habit of attempting to get minor improvements in a tentative settlement by waiting until the last minute, when management has stretched itself to the limits in an effort to reach a settlement and avoid a strike, to demand them. Such a tardy "Oh, by the way" approach used to resurrect an issue on which discussion had ceased, or to add a totally new demand, can sometimes catch an unsuspecting management negotiator off guard.

In the quest for a settlement, there is sometimes a temptation for management to avoid "killing a deal" by refusing such a small "sweetener," particularly since the cost is usually not great. Invariably, such add-ons would not be considered strike issues by management, and therefore there is a reluctance by some management negotiators to say no. But just as such last minute add-ons are not usually strike issues with management, neither are they the kind of issues over which the union is apt to strike. They are simply extras which, if obtained, union negotiators can boast about to their colleagues in the bar after an agreement has been reached.

If the bargaining has resulted in a package that the union's spokesperson had previously indicated would be satisfactory, management should avoid the temptation or pressure to give in to such last minute add-ons. This type of union bargaining is little more than chiseling, and deserves nothing more than a firm "no." Ethical union negotiators will not stoop to such tactics, and the unethical ones who do should never be rewarded for their temerity.

Premature Implementation

Because there can be delays in final acceptance caused by protracted negotiations, extensive union ratification procedures, time required to prepare contract language, and other factors, there is sometimes a request by union representatives to place into effect a particular wage or benefit change or other provision of a tentative settlement before agreement is finalized. Such a request is often coupled with assurances that the matter causing the delay (e.g., ratification vote or finalization of contract language), is merely a formality and that there is no reason to forestall implementation of the newly negotiated terms of the new contract.

Management should never place any contract terms or provisions into effect before one of the following conditions has occurred: (1) the new contract text is signed; or (2) a written settlement agreement is signed and all conditions thereto (e.g., ratification) have been satisfied; or (3) management has received a written notification from the union that it has accepted management's final offer, and that final offer was in writing and was given to the union in written form. The order in which the conditions are listed is the order of preference. If it is feasible to do so, management should have the complete revised written labor agreement signed before any new contract provision is put into effect. If that is not feasible, and frequently it is not, one of the next two conditions listed above should be required.

There are several reasons for adhering to this guideline. First, unless it is certain that agreement is truly finalized, it is possible that one or more of the terms of the settlement could change. If any of these terms have been placed into effect, it will be extremely difficult to retract them. Second, once any of the terms of a settlement have been put into effect, the union's incentive to expedite finalizing of the contract is gone. The process can drag on for weeks or even months. Even worse, the union may attempt to force management to "change its interpretation" of one or more of the contract terms or add a "sweetener" in order to assure that the process is finalized.

In some cases the revised or clarified "interpretation" sought by the union may be an attempt to clarify a provision to match the interpretation which the union honestly had in mind when the agreement was reached. On the other hand, it may be an attempt to extract additional concessions. If management has begun to implement the settlement before the final contract language is completed, the union may refuse to sign the contract until the "correct interpretation" and corresponding contract language have been accepted by management.

Rather than implement any portion of a new settlement before it is finalized, management can assure union negotiators that the terms of the new settlement will be applied retroactively to the effective date agreed upon, and that management will keep records to ensure that it is properly applied. For contract terms that do not lend themselves to retroactive application (e.g., changes in work rules, seniority provisions, etc.), there is little that can be done to permit the union or employees to receive the new benefit(s) back to the effective date of the new contract. This inability to make such terms retroactive can be a factor motivating the union to finalize the contract without excessive delay. In such cases, management must take pains to see that the employer is not the party responsible for the delay.

Tentative Settlement and Ratification

If a settlement has been reached by the negotiating parties at the bargaining table subject only to ratification by the union's membership, there is usually a state of euphoria, and the parties congratulate each other on having successfully completed their respective assignments. All is not over, however, for there are several important steps which remain to be completed to ensure a successful negotiation.

Written Memorandum of Agreement

Although there are few absolutes in labor contract negotiations, there is one to which the author subscribes without variation: *Never leave the bargaining table without a written and signed memorandum of agreement.* Where the bargaining has gone back and forth with oral proposals and counterproposals crisscrossing at a fairly rapid rate, settlements sometimes emerge without one piece of paper changing hands. When agreement is reached, both parties have a clear idea in their minds as to what was just agreed upon. When they shake hands to seal their agreement there is no question in their minds that they will be able to formalize their agreement the next morning, the next day, or the following week. In some cases they may be able to do so. In many other cases, however, they will find that what was apparently clear at 3 a.m. when they shook hands in a hotel room is not as clear the following day when they consider it in their respective offices. When they later attempt to reduce the agreement to writing, each party may find that what was in the mind of the other party at the time was not what it believed the agreement to be. In legal terminology, there was not a complete "meeting of the minds."

Importance of a Written Summary

The value of a written and signed memorandum is that it forces the parties to put into specific words exactly what is in their minds. In so doing, it requires, or at least helps, them to consider certain factors which they might otherwise have overlooked. Opportunities for misunderstanding are numerous. What is the effective date of the new insurance plan? Is it the same as for all other contract changes? Is retroactive pay to go to all employees who were with the employer during the retroactive period, or will it simply be paid to employees who are on the employer's payroll on the day when the contract is ratified? If a new type of benefit (e.g., a "floating holiday") is negotiated, are the qualifications to earn it any different from those for a regular or "fixed date" holiday?

Although the discipline of writing out the agreement is a substantial aid in arriving at a true "meeting of the minds," it is not a guarantee that questions or disputes will not arise regarding the interpretation and application of certain agreements. This is to be expected, and it is these types of disputes which are regularly submitted to arbitration during the term of a contract. Notwithstanding the availability of arbitration, however, the parties should make every effort when they conclude their negotiation to minimize the areas for dispute and disagreement by making their settlement agreement and new contract language as clear and complete as possible.

Some negotiators prefer to avoid the memorandum of agreement, and simply incorporate the agreed-upon changes directly into the contract document. Although this may be largely a matter of style, the author recommends the additional use of a memorandum for several reasons. First, preparation and proofreading of the full contract document may take, even with the use of word processing equipment, at least several days to prepare. Until that can be done, there is no written statement of what the parties' agreement was. Second, once the agreed-upon changes are incorporated into the contract, they are blended in with the provisions that were previously in the contract. Thus there is no single document which reflects only those specific points agreed upon in the most recent negotiations. From a historical standpoint, a memorandum of agreement will assist both parties in reconstructing just what was agreed upon in the total package in a given negotiation. Third, if the union needs to conduct a ratification vote, a memorandum of agreement will be helpful to union officers to explain the settlement being voted upon.

Memorandum Format

There is no single memorandum format which is universally used. Different industries and different employers within those industries use different forms of agreement. The important points to remember are that the memorandum should:

1. Specify all agreements reached, no matter how minor.
2. Indicate any agreements that were reached in negotiations, but that are not to be included in the contract document.
3. Include, usually by way of attachments, the actual contract language for those agreements that are to be included in the labor contract.
4. State the effective dates of all changes in wages, benefits, and working conditions.
5. Describe any conditions, exceptions, or limitations applicable to any agreements reached.
6. Include places for the signatures of union and employer representatives who are empowered to obligate the respective parties who will sign the memorandum, and a line on which to insert the date the memorandum is executed.

An example of one format which can be used for a memorandum of agreement is shown in Appendix 6.

Proceeding From Agreement to Ratification

Once a tentative settlement, subject only to ratification by the union's membership, has been reached, the ball is squarely in the union's court. The union must assume the responsibility for seeing that the ratification step is successfully completed. While the picture is changed somewhat if no tentative settlement has been reached and the vote is being taken on the employer's final offer (with or without a recommendation), nevertheless the matter is, for the most part, out of the employer's hands. Despite all of this, there are certain steps that management can take, and certain actions management should avoid, that can improve the chances of an affirmative ratification vote.

Assist in Preparing Written Materials

The union needs to communicate the tentative settlement or management's final offer in such a way that it will be understood by, and appear attractive to, the union's membership. Management can assist the union by providing sufficient copies of easily understood summaries of the settlement and examples of how the new contract would be beneficial to the members (e.g., showing how the income of the average employee would increase over the term of the contract). Although some of the larger and more sophisticated unions have the know-how and facilities to prepare such materials, most unions do not have the capabilities or creativity to develop effective ones. Of course, the union must be receptive to management's assistance in this regard. Union representatives may decline such assistance for fear that the materials will be identified by the members as being management productions, or simply as slick propaganda, and the representatives may feel that the materials would weaken, rather than strengthen, the chances of ratification. On the other hand, the union may welcome such assistance. In either event, the union's wishes must be respected.

Facilitating Explanatory Meetings and Voting

In addition to providing explanatory materials, management can sometimes assist the union in its ratification procedures by making time and/or space available for explanatory meetings and voting. While use of paid work time for such activities is not recommended, the employer can make facilities such as a cafeteria or auditorium available for explanatory meetings before or after work. It can also make available ballot boxes or polling places near the work site for voting to take place. Many unions abhor conducting union affairs in such close proximity to the employer's facilities, while other unions are happy to take advantage of such assistance. Where a union is receptive to the use of the employer's facilities, it usually works to management's advantage in that a greater, and therefore a more representative, number of employees are likely to know the terms of the settlement and vote on it.

Avoiding Publicity

Except in rare instances (one of which will be discussed immediately below), management is well advised to remain silent about the terms of a tentative settlement. The instances of publicized tentative settlements being rejected by union memberships are legion. One of the major reasons for avoiding the disclosure of settlement terms is that the media can easily misunderstand the terms and therefore erroneously report them. Likewise, casual discussion of the terms by union members before the union can adequately explain the settlement is often based on misinformation and therefore frequently negative.

Management's best course of action is simply to issue a statement along the lines of the following: "A tentative settlement has been reached between management and the union's negotiating committee. The union is scheduled to conduct informational meetings with, and a ratification vote of, its members."

The Publicity Exception

As all rules have exceptions, so too does the no-publicity admonition have an exception. There may be cases where management's final offer is received by the union and is either (1) not to be submitted at all to a vote by the membership, (2) submitted to the membership with a recommendation to vote against it, or (3) submitted to the membership for a vote with no recommendation either way. In these cases, management may be wise to disclose the terms of the offer in such a way that the membership is aware of the contents of the offer. But the advisability of disclosure of a final offer will vary depending upon the tenor of negotiations, the union's own forthrightness in communicating with its members, and management's credibility with its employees.

Caution About Direct Communication

If the union was hostile to management's final offer or did not reveal it to its members, and the employer is largely respected by its employees, a factual account of the offer should probably be communicated by management to employees in the most effective way possible. If, on the other hand, the union plans to submit management's final offer to a vote without a recommendation and has scheduled informational membership meetings in which management believes its final offer will be fairly presented, and if management has only marginal credibility with its employees, publicizing the final offer could backfire.

Caution and good judgment must be exercised. Management's support of its final offer could be "the kiss of death." On the other hand, if it is clear that employees are in the dark or misinformed about management's offer, proper disclosure by management could be most beneficial. This is especially true in a strike situation or potential strike situation, where union leadership may consciously be attempting to hide or misrepresent management's position for fear that if employees are aware of it, they will be unwilling to support, or less enthusiastic in supporting, union leaders.

Be Absolutely Factual

If management does decide to disclose or publicize its offer, the communications should be entirely factual, and not subject to any reasonable attack. Some years ago a West Coast employer was struck after it had made a very generous offer that the union refused to submit to its membership. Management then issued a bulletin containing the highlights of the offer with a cents-per-hour valuation of the entire package. Unfortunately, the cents-per-hour figure was based upon some estimates that were very subjective and could not be verified. The union subsequently issued its own bulletin effectively attacking management's "phony numbers." From that point, management was on the defensive, was unable to prove its case, and lost most of the credibility it had prior to the ill-advised publicity. Any presentation of information thus should be absolutely factual and straightforward, devoid of obvious or hard salesmanship, and free of derogatory language. If management's position and offer are good ones, they will generally speak for themselves.

Means of Direct Communication

The means of communication chosen will vary considerably depending upon the geographical location, size of the bargaining unit, and content of the communication. A direct letter to employees mailed to their homes may be most effective in some situations, whereas in some other situations notices in newspapers, on plant bulletin boards, or in fliers handed to employees may be preferable. Where subtlety is important, one tactic used by some employers is to send a written memorandum to supervisors informing them of the offer. In the normal course of affairs, such memoranda easily find their way into the hands of employees. In this way, employees are informed as to the contents of the employer's offer without having it appear that management has made a direct appeal to employees.

Legal Caveat

There is nothing illegal about an employer communicating accurately and directly with its employees about its contract offer.[11] It must be understood, however, that from a legal standpoint any direct communications with employees about the employer's offer or position cannot substantively contain anything more or different than what has already been communicated and offered to the union. If management tells employees that it is willing to offer more or less than it told the union it would agree to, the employer is bypassing the authorized bargaining representative and commits an unfair labor practice.[12]

The Negative Ratification Vote

There is probably no greater disappointment to a management negotiator than to work doggedly to achieve a settlement only to have it rejected by the union's membership. The initial reaction is usually a mixture of anger, frustration, despair, and self-doubt. Weeks, if not months, of hard work seem to have been in vain. If the final offer or tentative agreement is one which the union's negotiating committee fully endorsed, the anger and frustration felt by management's negotiator is likely to be shared in equal measure by the union counterpart, who also had a stake in seeing the settlement ratified. The union negotiator's political stature has been blemished in that the membership has rejected the settlement he or she negotiated and endorsed. After the initial emotional reaction has subsided, however, both union and management negotiators have much work to accomplish. Although the union must carry out the work necessary to identify and correct the voting deficiency, management can prod, make recommendations, and assist the union in the legwork necessary to turn around the unfavorable vote.

Identifying the Cause(s)

Initially, it must be determined what factor(s) appear to have caused the contract rejection. Selected union members should be polled. Critical questions must be asked. Was the offer clearly explained? Did most members seem to understand the settlement's terms? Did the union's bargaining committee fully support and recommend the settlement? Do the members of the union respect and believe their representatives on the union's negotiating committee? How many members voted as a percentage of the total membership? Were there portions of the settlement to which the members were particularly opposed, and if so, which ones are they and why were they opposed? Was it clearly explained that management had made its final offer, and that if the union sought anything more, it would have to strike? These and other questions should reveal the main crux of the problem. What to do about it is a much more difficult task.

Correcting the Problem

Management's bargaining position must be that the settlement agreement previously reached was a fair one and the highest which management was, and is, willing to offer. While management may consider some rearrangement of the elements of the offer, it should not increase the economic value of the settlement or grant any additional concessions on working conditions. Any action other than maintaining this position would simply reward union members for their refusal to accept the recommendation of their bargaining representatives and destroy the credibility of a management that said it had made its final offer.

In some cases, rank and file members may have been misled by suggestions from representatives of the union's bargaining committee or others that management had not "reached the end of its rope," and that a better offer was possible if management's final offer was rejected. In other cases, union members may not have been given an adequate explanation by union representatives as to why one or more of the union's (or members') priority demands were not met. But whatever the causes for the rejection, it is important that management and union negotiators identify and eliminate them as soon as possible so that another vote can be taken—hopefully with better results.

In a number of cases, the alleged cause of the contract rejection will simply be that "it wasn't enough." This presents a serious problem both to management and to the union. It attacks the credibility of management in supporting its claim of having made its final offer, and the credibility of union negotiators in having said to management that "a deal is a deal" and having said to its own members that "this is the best we can get." The parties may try to reshape the offer to make it more appealing in those areas where criticism was the greatest without increasing the total value of the offer. In doing this, some of the techniques for avoiding and resolving impasse discussed in Chapter 12 may prove useful. In the final analysis, however, management may simply have to improve its offer or take the calculated risk that the next ratification vote will also be rejected. If management elects expediency over steadfastness, however, it must be prepared to accept the consequences of this decision in future contract negotiations.

Avoiding Another Misfire

When a second or subsequent ratification vote is scheduled, management should do everything possible to ensure that the union has done its homework in (1) sounding out dissident elements of its membership and selling the offer to them, (2) preparing a clear and thorough presentation of the offer, (3) seeing to it that as many members as possible vote, and (4) ensuring that local unions and their members realize that they have only one choice between two alternatives, i.e., to settle or strike. Given only this choice, the chances for acceptance at the next vote should improve significantly.

Preparing and Executing the Revised Contract Document

Once the contract has been ratified, management should receive a written notification from the union affirming that the settlement has been ratified, and that complete and final agreement has been reached. At this point, it is usually safe to implement the terms of the settlement which are to be effective immediately. The admonitions listed earlier in this chapter (under "Written Memorandum of Agreement") should be noted. Some managements refuse to put the settlement into effect until a completely revised contract has been signed. It is difficult to find fault with this approach, especially if exact contract language was not finalized by the time the settlement was submitted for ratification. If the text of the entire labor agreement has not yet been revised to incorporate the terms of the settlement, no time should be lost in having this done.

Incorporating Contract Language Changes

Hopefully, both parties worked out specific contract language to be placed in the labor agreement as the negotiations took place. If not, there remains the difficult task of drafting contract language to fit the more general terms agreed upon by the negotiating parties. If, however, as recommended previously in this book, specific contract language was agreed upon as each subject or proposal was negotiated, the task remains simply to insert the language in the appropriate sections of the agreement. If the parties agreed earlier upon the language to be included in the contract, they also should have agreed upon the section of the contract in which it was to be placed. As discussed in Chapter 11, some companies and unions like to highlight (by underlining or using bold type) all changes in contract language from the previous agreement. This is a useful practice, especially when either party wishes to trace the evolution of a particular contract provision or section.

As each clause is inserted in the contract, great care should be taken to ensure that it does not conflict with or modify any other terms of the contract (this too should have been checked earlier when contract language was negotiated). Also, numbering of subsections, articles, and paragraphs should be carefully done to ensure continuity. Additionally, all sections and articles of the contract should be checked for cross-references to make sure that any revisions necessitated by inclusions or exclusions resulting from the settlement are made. While some of these chores may seem obvious or overly detailed, failure to do a careful job can cause confusion and disputes in the future.

Incorporating Economic Changes

Revising the contract to incorporate changes in wages and benefits is not particularly difficult. Again, however, absolute care is vital. Revised wage rate tables and job classification wage schedules must be carefully computed. Computations of rates should be checked three or four times to ensure accuracy. The contract wage schedule will be the official one used for payroll purposes; errors in the schedule can be perpetuated for many years to come.

Questions such as whether percentage changes in hourly wages are to be rounded to the nearest whole cent or half cent and what cutoff point is to be used for rounding should be answered. Generally speaking, renewal contracts follow the procedure used in previous years. When addressing these issues in a first contract, the best course may be to follow the procedure used in the employer's other plants or by other employers in the same industry.

If significant changes in pensions or in health, accident, or life insurance were negotiated but full contract language has not been finalized, close attention will need to be paid to such language. Usually it will be necessary to obtain the advice and counsel of specialists in these areas.

Where economic changes are deferred (i.e., they will go into effect in subsequent periods of the contract), it is important that the effective dates be included in the contract. A calendar should be consulted in order that the changes can be made, insofar as possible, at the beginning of a pay period or a week, or at another logical starting point.

Finalizing the Revised Contract Document

Once the economic and contract language changes have been incorporated into a revised complete labor agreement, the resulting document should be retyped. Prior to preparing the revision, someone should review the previous contract for typographical or other nonsubstantive errors; necessary corrections should be made while the new contract is being typed. A list of any such nonsubstantive changes should be kept so that they can be reviewed with the union prior to the signing. Once the contract has been retyped, it should be carefully proofread.

Signature lines should be included so that the appropriate persons "execute" or sign the contract. If the labor agreement is between the employer and an international union, it is important that an official of the international union sign the contract. If, by custom, local union officials also sign the contract, that is perfectly acceptable, but it is essential that the union which is the formal party to the contract have its authorized official sign the contract document. Conversely, if the contract is with the local union, an official or officials of that organization should sign the contract.

Many employers like to have a formal signing of the labor contract where both parties meet and sign multiple copies of the contract in an atmosphere of some ceremony. To enhance the ceremony, sometimes special pens are obtained for the signing and distributed to each of the signatories and other participants in the negotiations. This is a matter of style. If the parties have had a difficult negotiation and/or are both resolved to enter into a new, and hopefully more enlightened, period of labor-management relations, a formal occasion with some ceremony could provide a good starting point for such a relationship.

In many industries, it is customary to have copies of labor agreements printed in a convenient booklet size so that they can be distributed to employees and supervisors and used on a day-to-day basis. Some employers, however, avoid issuing printed contracts because of a belief that if a copy of the contract is too convenient and available, employees will use it more often and more grievances will be filed. There does not seem to be any hard evidence of this, although it is certainly possible.

If copies of the contract are to be printed, it is important that the parties agree in advance on who is to pay the cost of printing. This is sometimes the topic of a proposal included in the union's original agenda of contract proposals. If the contract is to be typeset, and not just photocopied from the typed version, an additional proofreading will be necessary. Again, a careful job is a must. Although the original typed and signed contract will be the official document, the printed contract will be used almost exclusively throughout the term of the labor agreement, and errors therein can cause problems of interpretation and application.

Postnegotiation Wrap-Up

When the ink is dry on the contract, there is a tendency to sit back and relax. There are, however, several additional important steps that should be attended to before too much time passes following contract negotiations.

Informational Meetings for Management and Supervisory Personnel

Throughout the negotiations, managers and supervisors who were not involved in negotiations could not be informed of all items being negotiated, due to the sensitivity of negotiations plus the lack of available time, which precluded sufficient briefings. Now that an agreement has been reached, it is the managers and supervisors who must administer the contract. It is vital that they understand what changes in the contract were agreed upon, what the intent of the parties as regards these changes was, and how the new contract provisions are to be administered.

Probably the best means to explain new contract provisions is to apply them either to specific actual or hypothetical cases during informational meetings. If the changes are particularly complex, written guides should be distributed for each manager or supervisor to use for later reference. These informational meetings should be held as soon as possible after the contract settlement has been ratified. It is desirable that they be held before the new contract provisions are placed into effect. In some cases, refresher meetings within 6 to 12 months after an initial meeting may be useful.

Beyond being given an explanation of the new contract provisions and their application, supervisors and managers should be given some of the flavor of the negotiations and management's rationale for reaching the agreement it did. Too often, managers and supervisors are not told *why* management took a particular course of action, or why it agreed to a particular provision. Without this knowledge, they are often quick to criticize the outcome of the negotiations and to lack a full understanding of the intent of new contract provisions. It is not unusual to hear that "management gave away the store" or "they made it harder for us to supervise." Some of these criticisms may be legitimate, but they can be less frequent and less bitter if management's rationale is known.

Critique and Analysis

After just having completed weeks or months of negotiating, management's negotiators will not be in the mood to rehash what just happened in the negotiations. This disinterest will be heightened if the negotiation was not as successful as had been expected. Nevertheless, it is vital that management negotiators review the recently completed negotiation with the goal of critically and objectively analyzing what happened, why it happened, and what lessons can be learned for the future. This exercise should be undertaken no later than one to two months following the completion of negotiations. After that point, memories fade and much useful thought and reflection will be lost.

All members of management's bargaining committee should participate in the critique. Better results can often be achieved if it is conducted away from the normal workplace. Some of the points to be covered include:

1. Review original economic parameters and bargaining goals. How many were achieved? How many were not? What explanation is there for both results? Were the original goals and parameters realistic or not? Could we have reached a settlement at less cost? If so, how?
2. Were the preparations made for the negotiations adequate? Was the information and data sufficient? What, if any, additional information would have been useful? What, if any, was unnecessary? Were all other aspects of preparation adequate? What could have been improved?
3. Was the original assessment of union leadership and the union's spokesperson and representatives accurate? What new facts about the union and its leaders did we learn from this negotiation? Was the original assessment of the membership's feelings and priorities accurate? If not, what caused us to misread them? How can we get a better reading of our employees in the future?
4. Was our bargaining strategy well formulated? Given the economic parameters and bargaining goals established, could our negotiating moves have been better planned to achieve more effective results? Were our offers well structured and effectively timed? Did we correctly anticipate the union's responses to our moves? Did the union follow the pattern it has in the past?
5. Did we execute our strategy properly? Were there signals we tried to give which just weren't understood? How was the tenor of negotiations? Was it too relaxed or too hostile? Did we fully take into account what the union's spokesperson was trying to tell us? Did we take any unnecessary risks? Should we have taken risks which we didn't?
6. What were the turning points in the negotiations? Did they turn in our favor or the union's? Why? What could we have done to achieve a better result? Could we have avoided any of the roadblocks we encountered? How? Did we successfully overcome potential impasse issues? How?
7. Did the way we managed or supervised during the last contract term create unnecessary negotiating problems? If so, how can we avoid them in the future? Did we lose any significant management rights in negotiations? If so, which ones, and how can we minimize their impact through more effective management and supervision? Did we recapture any management rights? If so, which ones and how can we hold on to them during the term of the contract?

This list of possible questions could continue for pages. Many are not easy to answer, and most require the kind of critical self-analysis which most persons find difficult to make. There is real value in doing so, however, since there is much profit in learning from mistakes and recognizing the reasons for successes. A written summary of the critique and analysis will be extremely valuable in preparing for the next contract negotiations with the same bargaining unit.

Finalizing Minutes and Notes

A record of the recently completed negotiations will become more valuable as time goes on. As memories fade, the value of the written record of negotiations will increase. Thus, while memories are still fresh and time is available, minutes or notes of negotiations should be reviewed by the spokesperson and other members of the negotiating committee, and corrections should be made where necessary. The notes should be organized by date and time, and an index should be prepared by subject matter and by contract section. Although this will be a tedious task, it is one which can yield abundant benefits in the future as an aid in contract interpretation and in supporting management's position in grievance-arbitration disputes.

Finalizing Cost Estimates

In addition to finalizing minutes and notes of the negotiations, a final cost estimate of the settlement should be prepared. All assumptions should be checked for reasonableness, and all computations double-checked for accuracy. Also, labor cost estimates on a per-hour or per-year basis should be translated into more meaningful terms such as cost per ton, per revenue passenger mile, per barrel, per car, or in relation to any other unit of measure commonly used in the employer's enterprise.

Additional consideration should be given to the implications of the labor cost changes resulting from the settlement. Can productivity be improved to offset additional costs? Can staffing reductions be achieved? Can labor-intensive operations be replaced by more capital-intensive ones? In addition, an audit schedule should be established to evaluate, at the end of each contract year, the accuracy of the original labor cost estimates. Actual labor costs at the end of each contract year should be compared to the estimates prepared at the end of negotiations. Explanations should then be prepared to explain all major variances.

Effect of the Settlement on Other Employee Groups

A settlement with a significant bargaining unit invariably has an impact upon other persons who work for the same employer. Supervisors for whom the bargaining unit employees work will quickly learn the terms and the value of the settlement. To the extent that the settlement narrows the gap between their monthly income and that of their subordinates, management must seriously consider such impact, and determine if any actions are necessary. Similarly, salaried employees who work in conjunction with, or at least at the same facility as, bargaining unit employees may compare the equivalent hourly rate of their salaries to the hourly rate received by the bargaining unit employees. Thus, the impact of the settlement on these employees should also be considered.

Nonunion hourly employees who work at other facilities or at the same facility of the employer will be among the first to learn of the recent settlement with bargaining unit employees. To the extent that they fall behind their union counterparts, they may begin to contemplate the value of union representation. A prudent employer cannot overlook, and if necessary should act upon, the impact of the settlement on this group of employees.

What, if any, actions should be taken with respect to these other employee groups can only be answered by management under the particular circumstances facing it at the time. There can, however, be no doubt that it is a foolhardy management indeed which negotiates a labor contract for any organized bargaining unit and neglects to recognize the settlement's impact on its other employee groups.

15

Special Bargaining Situations

The most common type of labor contract negotiations in which employers engage is the contract renewal negotiation, which takes place each time an existing labor contract is about to expire. Most of the information in this volume relates to this type of negotiation. There are, however, several variations from the standard contract renewal negotiations that have certain characteristics that set them apart, from a planning and execution standpoint. Because of their unique characteristics, the following types of labor negotiations have been singled out and treated as special bargaining situations: negotiations for an initial labor agreement, concessionary bargaining, plant closure negotiations, and bargaining over joint union-management programs. Each presents its own unique opportunities and challenges.

Negotiating the Initial Labor Agreement

When a bargaining unit is certified or recognized for bargaining purposes, union and management must sit down and negotiate for the first time the basic labor contract language under which they will, under normal circumstances, co-exist for many years to come. In most instances, this will be their most important negotiation, for it will normally set the dominant tone of their relationship for years to come and establish the basic provisions and language of their labor agreement, that are apt to remain largely intact through the years, renewal negotiations notwithstanding. *Management should assume that whatever it agrees to include in the first contract with respect to work practices and basic contract provisions will remain there forever.* For this reason it is particularly important that a careful job be done in this first negotiation.

Unique Characteristics

Besides the fact that the parties do not have an existing agreement to govern wages, hours, and working conditions, there are other aspects of initial contract negotiations that are unique. Because there is no contractual relationship at the time these negotiations take place, there is no contract expiration date, and therefore no natural deadline for completing bargaining as there would be in normal contract renewal negotiations.

Also, because there is no existing contract expiration date, the termination date of the contract about to be negotiated is as yet undetermined. This gives management some flexibility in seeking a favorable month of the year in which the contract will expire. For example, if the employer's business normally slows down in February and March, the employer may seek a January 31st expiration date. The obvious reason for this is to minimize the potential damage to the employer if a strike were to occur when the contract expires. Although negotiating parties normally have expiration dates in 12-month increments from the date the contract is signed, it is somewhat more feasible in an initial contract (as contrasted to a renewal contract) for the employer to bargain for an uneven contract term having an expiration date occurring at an interval other than 12, 24, or 36 months from the date the agreement was reached.

Another unique characteristic of an initial contract negotiation is the likelihood that the parties have just completed an election campaign in which they campaigned against each other, and in which the union probably gave assurances that it would obtain certain specific wage and benefit improvements. In a postcampaign postelection atmosphere, negotiations are likely to be strained. If the initial bargaining resulted from voluntary recognition by the employer or an election in which the employer did not oppose the union, a more amicable negotiating atmosphere should prevail.

However, if the employer is a successor employer, and not bound by the predecessor's contract, the bargaining atmosphere may be different than it had been under the prior employer, yet generally more (or less) conducive to agreement based upon the present management's attitude toward unions in general and its predecessor's labor relations experience with the union having representation rights.

Special Preparations

Although preparations for negotiating the initial contract will generally follow most of the steps outlined in Chapters 1 through 3, management should place emphasis on the following aspects of its preparation:

1. *Research the union.* Management should learn as much as possible about the international as well as the local union, their respective histories, priority bargaining goals, and constitutional and bylaw provisions, and especially the personalities, characteristics, and tendencies of their leaders.
2. *Research other contracts.* Management should obtain copies of as many labor contracts as possible between the union with which it will be bargaining and other employers in its industry and in allied industries. Management should also obtain copies of labor agreements between other companies and other unions in its industry, and wage, benefit, and working condition data covering nonunion employers.
3. *Prepare a draft contract.* Management should prepare a draft of the labor contract as it would like to have it. Clauses may be borrowed from other contracts in the industry, although it is important to know how the borrowed language has been interpreted in the industry or by arbitrators. As a way of checking the adequacy and completeness of the initial draft, the draftsman may find the contract checklist in Appendix 7 of assistance.

Bargaining Suggestions

Work From Management's Draft Contract

It is common for both union and management at the outset of negotiations to present their respective proposals for a complete labor agreement. Occasionally one hears the horror story of the manager of a small shop or the owner of a business who is presented with the union's boilerplate or "model" contract and who simply signs it as one might sign a standard form for the purchase of supplies. Few unions expect that an employer will buy their boilerplate language lock, stock, and barrel, and, therefore, they load this "model" contract with provisions inordinately favorable to the union to use as trading stock in negotiations. These model contracts are meant to be negotiable and should be used in the way in which they were intended.

However, rather than going through the difficult and time-consuming process of trying to change the union's proposed contract piece by piece, management should work from its own draft. In negotiating each section of the contract, reference should constantly be made to the company's draft. If some portions of the union's draft are acceptable to management, they should be incorporated into the appropriate portion of management's draft contract. Each updated redraft should follow the original management format, incorporating those changes which have been agreed upon. By using its own draft as the "working draft," management can see to it that portions of the contract which are not yet resolved will be stated in terms of management's proposed language.

The union is likely to resist this approach and will probably seek to focus the negotiations on its own contract language. The union's language should be considered and accepted if appropriate, but it should always be incorporated into management's draft. If management's negotiators are sufficiently persistent, gradually the union negotiators will get used to the organization and numbering system in management's draft and accept it as the working document.

Use Union Security Concessions to Maximum Advantage

Of vital importance to the union is a contract that contains the optimum union security provisions achievable. Usually this will include a "union shop" clause (required union membership after 30 days of employment) and a checkoff clause (mandatory payroll deduction of union dues). If management is prepared ultimately to grant the union these or other types of union security provisions, it should maximize the trading value of these concessions.

Logical *quid pro quos* for union security provisions are provisions vital to management's interests, e.g., management-rights, no-strike, and arbitration clauses. Another logical tradeoff is a zipper or waiver clause, in which the union waives its right to bargain, during the term of the contract, over subjects which were bargainable during the negotiations leading to a settlement. But the tradeoffs need not be limited to these. Management should also seek flexibility in work assignments, staffing, and scheduling, as well as maximum autonomy in all other aspects of managing the enterprise.

Specific Contract Language Objectives for an Initial Contract

Regardless of whether management is prepared to grant the union the type of union security provisions being sought, management must attempt to have included in the first contract those provisions that may be important to it in the years to come. The following are suggestions that should prove useful in this regard.

Less Is Usually Best

With just a few exceptions (e.g., managements rights, zipper and no-strike clauses), most clauses in a labor contract are for the benefit of the union or the employees covered by the contract. Consequently, as a rule of thumb, the greater the number of provisions in a contract, the less favorable it is to management. Therefore, keeping a labor contract short and simple is generally a good idea.

Avoiding Undue Specificity

Avoid putting into the contract provisions management is likely to want to modify at some time in the future to meet changing conditions. Examples of such provisions are the following: specific work schedule times, rules governing employees' conduct, and staffing levels. Because changes in these provisions require mutual agreement if they are included in the agreement, it is best to exclude them entirely. To protect against unfair labor practice charges in the event of unilateral changes by management, it is preferable to refer to these subjects in the management-rights clause as being within the sole discretion of management.

A Strong Management-Rights Clause

Management's spokesperson should seek to make the management-rights clause as strong as possible. Although labor specialists sometimes disagree on whether it is preferable to enumerate the specific rights reserved to management or to use the more simple version which simply states that all rights not limited by the contract are reserved to management, the author prefers a combination of the two. The following is an example of a rather strong management-rights clause for a manufacturing facility:

> The management of the plant and the direction of the working force are vested exclusively in the Company and, except as limited by specific provisions of this agreement, the Company shall continue to have all sole and exclusive rights customarily reserved to management, including the right to hire, promote, suspend, discipline, transfer, or discharge for proper cause; the right to relieve employees from duty because of lack of work or other proper reasons; the right to schedule operations, shifts, and all hours of work; the right to assign work and require overtime work; the right to select supervisory personnel and control their conditions of employment; and the right to establish rules pertaining to the operation of the plant and permissible conduct of employees. The Company shall have the sole right to decide the process of manufacture, types of machinery and equipment to be used, types and quantities of products to be made, quality of material, quantity and quality of work required, selling prices and products, as well as the methods of selling and distribution of products. The Company also retains the right to close all or a portion of the facility covered by this agreement or to sell, relocate, transfer work, or in any other way to dispose of or alter such facility and the work performed therein.
>
> The above-mentioned management rights are not to be interpreted as being all-inclusive, but merely indicate the type of rights which belong to and are reserved to management. It is understood that any of the rights, power, or authority the Company had prior to the signing of this agreement are retained by the Company, except those specifically abridged or modified by this agreement.

Such a clause will not usually be easily negotiated, but it is not a bad starting point.

Avoiding Veto Clauses

Management's negotiators should avoid "mutual agreement" or union-veto clauses which limit management's ability to act or places an obligation on management to obtain union agreement before doing so. The type of clause to avoid would read as follows:

Work schedules may be changed only by mutual agreement of the parties.

Under this type of contract provision, the likelihood of obtaining union agreement during the term of the contract on some action that could have an adverse impact on any employee or on the union is not great. If management is willing to limit one of its rights in a particular manner, agree to do so. If it is not, do not insert a limitation with a proviso that it can be avoided by mutual agreement to the contrary. You will probably never get such an agreement.

Automatic Escalators Are Dangerous

To the extent possible, management should avoid inclusion of automatic escalators. These are economic provisions whose cost goes up automatically when some other factor increases. The most common example of such a provision is the cost-of-living adjustment (COLA). Wages are increased automatically as the cost of living—or more precisely, the Consumer Price Index—increases.

There are other, and somewhat less obvious, escalators. Benefits paid in terms of the hourly wage rate automatically escalate as wages are increased over time. For example, overtime pay, call or call-back pay, vacation pay, and holiday pay are normally stated in terms of the hourly wage. Hence, when general wage rates are increased through negotiations, the cost of these benefits automatically increases. Because of the long-established and widely accepted tradition of paying certain benefits in terms of hourly wage rates, it will be difficult to avoid such automatic escalators. However, efforts to break with tradition can result in significant cost savings.

Moreover, there are other benefits such as shift differentials, meal allowances, and reporting or "show-up" pay where forms of payment are less entrenched and where efforts to state the payment in dollar amounts are more achievable. For example, providing a shift differential of 50 cents per hour is recommended rather than providing one of 2 percent of the employee's hourly rate (or facility base rate). Also a flat rate of, say, $30 or even $35 for show-up pay is preferable to a guaranteed payment of four hours pay where the average hourly wage rate is $8.00 per hour.

The advantage of using specific payment amounts over percentage or per-hour payments is that the cost does not increase automatically as does a rate based on some variable. Where specific dollar amounts are stated, if the cost is going to be increased, it must then be negotiated instead of being increased automatically. Consequently, the union must spend some of its negotiating currency or bargaining power to achieve an increase. Stated another way, the employer "gets credit" for agreeing to the increases, and there is a charge to the settlement package each time a specifically stated benefit is increased, rather than an automatic increase in the amount, with no charge to the package, as the standard (i.e., wage rate) upon which it is based increases.

Zipping Up the Contract

Management negotiators should seek to include a "zipper" or waiver clause in contracts. Such clauses are designed to preclude the union from attempting to bargain during the term of the labor agreement. Under such clauses, the union waives its right to bargain over subjects not included in the contract and also waives its right to bargain further on subjects covered in the contract. While zipper clauses are not 100 percent effective as a defense against an unfair labor practice charge for refusing to bargain in good faith, such clauses can prove useful as a means of avoiding liability for unilateral actions by management during the term of a contract. The following is an example of a typical zipper or waiver clause:

> It is agreed that this labor agreement contains the full and complete agreement on all subjects upon which the parties did bargain or could have bargained. Neither party shall be required, during the term of this Agreement, to negotiate or bargain upon any other issue. All matters not included in this Agreement shall be deemed to have been raised and disposed of as if covered herein. All subjects referred to in the management's rights clause shall likewise be deemed to have been raised and bargained to a conclusion.

Protection Against Strikes

Management negotiators should seek to make the no-strike clause as broad as possible. In addition to prohibiting strikes during the term of the agreement, the clause should cover all forms of work stoppages as well. The following is an example of such a clause:

NO INTERRUPTION OF WORK

There shall be no strike, walkout, picketing, concerted refusal to report for work, slowdown or any other interruption of work by the Union or by any employee during the term of this Agreement. The Company agrees not to lock out during the term of the Agreement. Furthermore, it is understood that no union officer, representative nor agent may authorize, encourage, or assist in any picketing, strike or concerted work stoppage in the Company's facility(ies) or on any premises of the Company, nor will the Union or its officers, representatives, or agents participate in, counsel, or induce any concerted interruption of work. This clause also specifically prohibits any employee from refusing to report for work or refusing to work due to the existence of a picket line.

The Company agrees to waive its rights to collect damages against the Union in the event of a strike only if the following conditions are met. The Union will:

a. Notify all employees immediately in the event of an interruption of work that it is unauthorized and in violation of the contract;
b. Publicly announce through a major local daily newspaper and on at least one major local ratio station that the work interruption is unauthorized and not condoned by the Union, and that employees are to return to work;
c. State in writing addressed and delivered to employees that the work interruption is in violation of the Agreement; and
d. Make every other possible and reasonable effort to have employees cease violations of this Article.

It is further understood that any employee who participates in a violation of this Article shall, in the sole discretion of the Company, be subject to immediate discharge.

Arbitration

As with the no-strike clause, management negotiators should attempt to make the arbitration clause as broad as possible, since it is desirable to avoid work stoppages during the term of the agreement. In the decision of the U.S. Supreme Court in the *Boys Markets* case,[1] it was held that in order to obtain an injunction to terminate a strike in violation of a no-strike clause, the dispute underlying the work stoppage must be subject to the grievance/arbitration provisions of the labor contract. Consequently, the arbitration clause should be very broad and should cover "all alleged contract violations and all disputes and disagreements between the parties." This will provide a better opportunity to enforce a no-strike clause than a more narrowly drawn clause.

Perfection Not Attainable

Of course, all of the points just mentioned represent more or less the ideal situation. In the real world of collective bargaining, the normal give-and-take of bargaining necessarily forces acceptance of less-than-optimum contract provisions. Seldom will the suggested language be completely achievable. Nevertheless, management should begin with the ideal if it is to achieve maximum results. One can always pull back, but seldom is it feasible to improve upon the language after it is initially proposed. In bargaining a first contract, achieving a "good" contract is of the utmost importance. If a little more money needs to be spent in order to achieve favorable language, it is usually well worth the price.

Concessionary Bargaining

The late 1970s and early 1980s spawned a phenomenon which came to be known as "concession bargaining" or "concessionary bargaining." In its simplest terms, it represents a type of bargaining in which management seeks (1) net reductions in wages and benefits and/or less favorable working conditions (from the union's perspective) or (2) less costly wages, benefits and/or working conditions than would be negotiated under "normal conditions."

In general, such bargaining was a response to distressed economic conditions being experienced by employers. During the recession of the early 1980s, the automobile, steel, rubber, trucking, newspaper, and commercial airline industries, among others, experienced considerable financial losses, business failures, curtailment of production and services, and severe layoffs and terminations of employees. In many cases, the losses and curtailments were not due solely to the general economic recession, but were also due to such factors as government deregulation (in the case of the trucking and airline industries) and foreign competition (in the case of the automobile, steel, and rubber industries). Unions could hardly be held responsible for the results of deregulation or foreign competition. However, with respect to foreign competition, union-negotiated labor costs in many industries in the United States exceeded those of foreign competitors by 50 to 100 percent. But regardless of the specific causes of the depressed economic conditions, unions in many industries recognized the plight of employers with whom they had collective bargaining relationships and negotiated absolute or relative reductions.

Concessionary bargaining as practiced in the early 1980s did not represent a totally new concept in labor contract negotiations. Many employers had, for a number of years, negotiated contract provisions which reduced labor costs and/or increased management's flexibility in running its business. What changed was the extent and magnitude of the acceptance and use of such bargaining. Beginning with the 1980s, there were very few industries which did not engage in some form of concessionary bargaining. In concessionary bargaining situations, employers simply recoup wages, benefits, and management rights that were given away, through negotiations or sloppy operating practices, during earlier and more prosperous times.

Necessary Ingredients for Concessionary Bargaining

It cannot be said that the process and techniques used for concessionary bargaining differ in any fundamental way from the same elements in traditional labor negotiations. The preparation for, and conduct of, concessionary bargaining follows the basic pattern of contract renewal negotiations. However, there are distinct differences in union and management bargaining climate, attitudes, and timing. The task shifts from that of deciding how the profits are to be shared to that of deciding how the losses are to be allocated. More importantly, the efforts become focused on what the parties can do to make the employer more competitive in order to survive as an employer and as a source of jobs. It is survival rather than prosperity that is the principal objective of both union and management in such cases.

Based upon the experience of the 1980s, there appear to be a number of factors that need to exist or take place in order for concessionary bargaining to succeed. While all factors need not be present, it is essential that most of them exist.

A Financially Distressed Industry and/or Employer

This is a universal necessary condition. However, some employers in troubled industries may escape financial distress themselves due to diversification, competitive advantages, or some other factor(s) peculiar to their operations. Even though their industry may be faltering, they manage to make a profit. Such employers will normally not find a receptive partner in negotiating concessions. Nevertheless, concessions granted to other employers in the same industry will make the healthy employer relatively less competitive and hence it can make a strong argument for concessions.

The Imminent Threat of Job Loss

Financial losses, in and of themselves, are not usually a sufficient cause to prompt concessions unless they are accompanied by the imminent threat of loss of jobs due to facility closure, relocation, or sale, or other threatened major structural change. The union and employees usually must see possible concessions as the only alternative to avoiding loss of employment. In other words, they must have the attitude that "less is better than nothing."

The Likelihood or Guarantee of More Jobs if Labor Costs Are Lowered

For concessionary bargaining to take place it is not sufficient that unemployment in the employer's business be high or that loss of jobs be threatened. What is usually necessary is that the union perceive that concessions which will lower the employer's labor costs will also result in more jobs. Thus, in the automobile, steel, and rubber industries, where foreign competition from companies having substantially lower labor costs was a major cause of high unemployment in the United States, a connection could logically be made between lower labor costs and more jobs. In fact, a few of the concessionary pacts in the automobile industry conditioned the concessions on lower sales prices for the employer's products which would stimulate sales and, therefore, production. In the early 1980s, however, appeals for concessions were often rejected at least in part because the unions could not see that lower labor costs could significantly improve employment opportunities where business suffered because of generally poor market conditions and not because of competitors having lower labor costs.

Data Sharing

In addition to being in a financially distressed condition, the employer must be able to demonstrate to the union that the situation is as bad as it is represented to be. In short, the employer must be willing to "open the books" in one form or another. This may often go beyond the mere review of balance sheet and profit-and-loss statements. It may also include review of investment data, competitors' cost data, and executive and salaried employees' compensation. And once the door has been opened, it may be difficult to close it. However, unless the information is made available for review, there is usually no way that sufficient credibility can be established. It may be possible to limit the review to one carried out by an independent outside party who can report on a limited basis. In some fashion or other, however, a credible plea of distressed financial conditions must be substantiated.

Equality of Sacrifice

If management is going to seek sacrifices from its unionized work force, it must show that employees in other parts of the work force are also making sacrifices. This includes other groups of hourly employees, both union and nonunion, and salaried and executive employees. The importance of this factor was brought home to General Motors Corp. and International Harvester Co. in 1982, when their concessionary proposals were originally rejected due, in part, to the fact that these companies had granted bonuses to management employees at approximately the same time the concessionary settlements were being considered by the union's membership. Although management may have previously foregone salary or benefit increases, enhancing compensation programs for management and/or salaried employees while concessionary proposals are being offered to union members will almost certainly jeopardize the chances of the proposals' success.

Secure Union Leadership

Union leaders who negotiate concessionary settlements do not win any medals. In fact, such agreements can jeopardize their political future. Consequently, it is not too likely that a union can engage in meaningful concessionary bargaining unless its leaders are well entrenched, have the political clout to make and fulfill commitments, and are willing to take the necessary political risks inherent in this type of bargaining.

Timing of Concessionary Bargaining

In conventional contract renewal negotiations, the normal time for commencement of negotiations is usually determined by the contract expiration date. The parties will typically begin negotiations sufficiently in advance of the contract expiration date so that they can be completed by that time. Because concessionary bargaining is usually survival bargaining, it cannot normally wait until the contract expiration date; by that time the business may fail or unemployment may increase to intolerable levels. Consequently, negotiating during the term of the agreement is common in this type of bargaining.

Of course, there is no legal obligation on the part of the union to participate in such bargaining during the term of the contract. It is purely consensual on the union's part. By the time they sit down at the bargaining table, therefore, union representatives will have to be well aware of the problems being experienced by the employer and the severe unemployment suffered by their members which warrants a possible opening of the contract during its term.

Conducting concessionary bargaining during the term of a contract has another advantage for the employer besides the tacit acknowledgement by the union of the seriousness of the situation and of the need to change the labor contract terms. Because such negotiations have the best chance of success where there is a cooperative climate, the avoidance of the typical contract expiration meeting time is helpful in itself. Negotiations conducted just prior to a contract expiration date can, if from nothing more than habit, easily take on a confrontational tone. The potential failure to reach an agreement at that time forces the parties to consider the normal consequences of an impasse, i.e., a work stoppage. Concessionary bargaining, however, succeeds best where economic warfare is not a consideration. Therefore, concessionary bargaining during the term of a contract rather than at the end of the term is usually recommended.

Another optimal time for concessionary bargaining occurs when a distressed business or facility is being considered for closure, relocation, or sale to a new employer. Where the alternative to sale is closure, management has maximum leverage to negotiate concessions. Where a sale has definitely been determined to be the only alternative, and where concessions are needed to make the sold facility economically viable, the bargaining should be done by the prospective buyer. Only that individual can speak to the union in terms of what concessions are necessary to operate the business profitably, and only the prospective buyer can play the role of the decision maker in regard to whether the business will survive. It must be credibly shown, however, that unless the business is sold to a new employer and unless labor costs are reduced, the business and the jobs that it provides will not survive. It is not a happy story to tell, but the union and the employees are best advised of the available options while some options still exist.

Quid Pro Quos

Although the term concessionary bargaining implies that the union makes all the concessions, in practice that has seldom been the case. As in most forms of bargaining, you do not get something for nothing. In concessionary bargaining, unions have usually sought to obtain, and have often been successful in obtaining, management concessions that do not have an immediate monetary cost to the employer, but that have strategic and/or long-term monetary value. The author is not attempting to evaluate the wisdom or lack thereof of granting such concessions in providing the following list of the types of tradeoffs various managements have made in concessionary agreements.

1. *Participation in corporate governance*. Several concessionary agreements, including the much-publicized agreement in 1979 between the Chrysler Corporation and the United Auto Workers, have placed a union official or union-desig-

nated representative on the employer's board of directors or have given the union some quasi-official role in management.

2. *Agreements on how to allocate concessionary savings.* In an attempt to have its sacrifices used to preserve jobs or create new jobs, some unions have been successful in negotiating agreements which specify that labor cost-savings realized from concessions be used to reduce prices of the employer's product or to invest in new capital equipment with the intent of making more jobs available. In one case, failure of an employer to live up to its agreement to use concessionary savings for investment purposes and a subsequent closure of the plant in which the investment was to take place resulted in a court judgment of $2 million against the employer.[2]

3. *Limitations on contracting out of work.* In a similar attempt to preserve jobs, some concessionary agreements, particularly in the automobile industry, have limited contracting out or "outsourcing." Such agreements require the employer to have certain work done by bargaining unit employees even though it might be done cheaper, faster, or better by a subcontractor. A somewhat similar limitation was negotiated in the over-the-road trucking industry which precluded the participating employers from establishing nonunion trucking subsidiaries ("double-breasted" operations).

4. *Trigger mechanisms to restore wages and benefits.* A number of concessionary agreements are limited to that period of time when they are absolutely necessary. Such agreements often referred to as "snap back" agreements contain provisions which reinstate the conceded wages and benefits when a stated condition or "trigger point" exists. The condition or situation is frequently a certain level of profits achieved by the employer.

5. *Expanded seniority protection or bumping provisions.* In exchange for concessions, some employers, including those in the trucking industry, have agreed to extend the period of layoff absence from work during which seniority is preserved. Agreements in which an employee retains his seniority for one or two years while on layoff might have this period extended to three or four years. Other concessionary agreements provide that laid-off employees may exercise their seniority at other facilities of the employer.

6. *Improved unemployment benefits.* Although it amounts to a type of trading of dollars, the steel industry agreed to expand the period for supplemental unemployment benefits (SUBs) in exchange for wage and other benefit concessions in its 1983 concessionary pact with the United Steelworkers.

7. *Work guarantees or assurances.* In exchange for union concessions, some employers have agreed to keep facilities operating and/or open. Such guarantees can backfire, however, if the employer's business is not viable for reasons other than high labor costs. Failure to fulfill such guarantees can subject an employer to substantial back-pay liabilities.
8. *Gain-sharing and profit-sharing programs.* Another tradeoff consists of a type of benefit wherein employees receive a portion of the gain realized from lower costs, higher productivity, or higher profits. A variety of gain-sharing plans and formulas exist, including the Scanlon Plan, Rucker Plan, and various types of profit-sharing plans.
9. *Stock ownership plans.* One way to provide something of value in exchange for wages and benefits is to provide stock in the employer's business. A myriad of plans exist for doing this including the well-publicized Employee Stock Ownership Plan (ESOP) which receives favorable tax treatment.
10. *Two-tiering.* Some concessionary agreements do not result in immediate pay or benefit reductions for employees then actively employed, but union and management agree that all employees hired after a given date will be subject to lower job classification, wage, or salary rates and/or reduced benefit levels. In effect, current employees' wages and benefits are to be frozen or "red-circled" for the period of time they are employed. The employer does not benefit immediately from lower labor costs, but as time progresses and attrition in the work force occurs, labor savings are realized.

Concessionary Bargaining in the Future

Concessionary bargaining as practiced in the 1980s was a product of a recessionary economy, increased foreign competition, and government deregulation. To the extent that these phenomena continue to exist in the economy, concessionary bargaining will continue to exist, at least in some form. The lessons of this period for employers generally should be clear—excessive wages and benefits cannot continue to be granted without regard to foreign competition, regional competition, nonunion competitors, and competition from substitute products and services wherein labor and/or other costs are lower. Likewise, agreements limiting management's rights that may be tolerable during prosperous times may force the employer out of business during highly competitive and recessionary times. Employers should not permit their labor contracts to become so generous and so riddled with limitations upon their right to manage that when the economy dips they must go to their unions in order to seek relief from the economic and management constraints to which they foolishly submitted themselves at times when conditions were more favorable.

Negotiating Over the Closure, Sale, or Relocation of a Facility

Another type of special bargaining situation occurs when an employer finds it necessary to close (partially or completely), sell, or relocate a facility or to make some other major change in its business that affects the bargaining unit. Those employers covered by the National Labor Relations Act, as amended, are under a legal obligation to bargain over such a change. Bargaining under these circumstances differs considerably from the usual type of contract renewal negotiations covered in the rest of this book.

Union Bargaining Waivers

Explicit Waivers

Although it is possible that bargaining over the closure, sale, or other disposition of a facility can be avoided, it is not very likely. In order to avoid this, the union must have waived its right to engage in such bargaining. This may be done in several ways. One way is for the union to have previously agreed in contract negotiations to a clear and unequivocal provision in the management-rights clause or in some other contract clause giving management the right to close, sell, relocate, or otherwise divest itself of the facility or business.

Ideally, coupled with this would be a zipper or waiver clause in which the union explicitly waives its right to bargain over any actions the employer might take pursuant to the management-rights clause. While such clauses are not always foolproof defenses to an unfair labor practice charge alleging a violation of Section 8(a)(5) of the NLRA (i.e., refusal to bargain in good faith), they will be of substantial assistance in that regard.[3] Persuading the union to agree to such contract provisions is not an easy task, however, and only by substantial bargaining leverage or use of valuable tradeoffs can such explicit waiver language normally be achieved.

If, however, management agrees in a labor contract to grant severance pay and/or other benefits in the event of a plant closure or other disposition, it is in a strong position to seek a union waiver to bargain further when the closure or disposition actually occurs. If a severance or termination pay clause is negotiated, it is advisable to include with it language in the agreement to the effect that the pay "is in consideration for the union's waiver to negotiate on any aspect of closure, sale, relocation, or other disposition of the facility."

Failure to Request Bargaining

Another way in which the union can waive its right to bargain is to fail to request such bargaining after it has been notified of the intended disposition.[4] This, of course, presumes that the union has been notified in a timely manner of the change. It is recommended, therefore, that management notify the union in writing of its intention well before a final decision and commitment to dispose of the facility has been made. The notice should, of course, be sent by registered mail, return receipt requested. The following type of notice can be used:

> Dear _____,
>
> This is to advise you that XYZ Corporation is considering the possible closure of our facility located at _______. The principal reason for considering this action is the severe financial losses incurred at this operation in recent years.
>
> If you wish to discuss this matter, please contact me no later than _____ in order to set a mutually satisfactory date for a meeting.

If the union fails to respond to this type of notice, it will have waived its right to bargain. If the union responds, which it is almost certain to do, there is a legal obligation to bargain.

Duty to Bargain Over Work or Facility Relocation

One of the more frequent and troublesome issues that arises in the process of concessionary bargaining is the intended relocation of a facility or the relocation of work from one facility to another. The issue typically presents itself where an employer is losing money manufacturing products or providing services in a particular facility or location, and believes that a change in the work site can result in a profitable operation.

From the union's standpoint, the work is likely to be removed to a facility so remote or distinct, with a new work force, that its representation rights will be lost. The union is quite likely to challenge the facility or work relocation. The union will contend that the employer has (had) a duty to bargain over the relocation and that bargaining can resolve whatever difficulties exist.

The employer is often faced with a dilemma—should bargaining be undertaken even if it is unlikely that union compromises will be sufficient to make the facility profitable, or should the employer initiate discussions in the hope that the conditions causing the unprofitability can be remedied. What is the employer's exposure from a legal standpoint if it does not bargain over the closure?

In *Dubuque Packing Co.*,[5] the NLRB developed new and more comprehensive guidelines than had ever before been available to determine an employer's bargaining obligations under these circumstances. The guidelines are premised on the matter ultimately being litigated before an NLRB administrative law judge. The guidelines require the NLRB's General Counsel (on behalf of a union) to establish a *prima facie* case of a mandatory bargaining obligation by showing that the relocation of work was not accompanied by a "basic change in the nature of the employer's operation." If it is shown that the basic operation is the same, the employer must proceed to rebut the charge on one of the following bases:

1. The work performed in the new location differs significantly from that in the previous location, in that
    (a) The previous facility has been discontinued entirely and not simply moved or
    (b) The relocation involves a change in the scope and direction of the business, or
2. Labor costs (which are subject to bargaining) were not a factor in the employer's decision to relocate; or even if they were a factor, the union could not have offered concessions sufficient to affect the employer's relocation decision.

These guidelines are difficult to apply in any relocation situation, and an employer's unwillingness to bargain about a facility or work relocation places it in jeopardy of violating

Section 8(a)(5) of the NLRA (i.e., refusal to bargain in good faith about a mandatory subject of bargaining). As discussed in earlier sections of this book, where borderline issues exist with regard to an employer's obligation to bargain in good faith, the prudent course of action for an employer is to notify the union of the contemplated change (while reserving in writing the right to claim that no such obligation exists) and being willing to negotiate to impasse if necessary, over the change. While this approach is likely to entail additional delay, effort, and expense, it is ultimately the wisest course of action. The employer can always say "no" to union proposals. But an outright refusal to meet and discuss the issue places the employer at risk of being found to have not bargained in good faith.

Scope of Bargaining Obligation

Once it is clear that bargaining will take place, one of the key decisions to be made by management is whether it will bargain only about the *effects* of the closure, sale, etc., on bargaining unit employees or whether the bargaining will also encompass the *decision* underlying management's action.

Effects Bargaining

"Effects bargaining" typically centers around such matters as severance pay; transfer to, or preferential hiring at, other company facilities; supplemental unemployment benefits; vesting of certain benefits such as pensions; waiving of hours-worked requirements for vacations, holidays, etc.; extended coverage for displaced employees and their families for medical insurance; and a myriad of other subjects. The focus of the negotiation is on mitigation of the adverse effects upon employees.

Decision Bargaining

"Decision bargaining," on the other hand, is directed toward management's fundamental decision to close, sell, or relocate the business, and presumes that the question of whether the closure, sale, or relocation action to be taken is subject to mutual determination. The rationale for this form of bargaining is that the cause(s) of the action may be subject to amelioration through the collective bargaining process, and that before any action is taken, efforts should be made to see if the contracting parties can negotiate an agreement that would obviate the need to close, sell, or relocate the facility. For example, if the employer is going to close the plant due to unprofitable operations, wage and benefit concessions by the union might permit the employer to operate profitably instead.

Most employers prefer to avoid decision bargaining over facility closures on the basis that such decisions are a critical part of the function of management and are complicated by so many factors that are beyond the ken of union-management negotiations, involving such matters as product pricing and competition, location of markets for the employer's products, raw material supplies and prices, and operating costs other than labor. Unless they are legally required to bargain about the decision, employers normally want to avoid it. The U.S. Supreme Court has significantly limited the types of fundamental business decisions over which management must engage in bargaining prior to taking action.[6]

The Prudent Course

Notwithstanding the absence of a legal bargaining obligation in closure situations, it is suggested that, just as in the case of relocation discussed above, management not refuse to engage in at least a limited form of decision bargaining. The reason for the suggestion is that the NLRB continues to issue complaints and prosecute cases in various types of facility disposition cases, and an employer is often obligated to expend thousands of dollars and hours of management's time to defend its position in having refused to engage in decision bargaining.

Moreover, in so many situations unions have little or nothing of significance to offer when actually afforded the right to bargain over the decision. More often than not, a union will focus on the effects of a closure, sale, or relocation even though it has been given the right to bargain over the decision. Management usually has little to lose, except time, by engaging in decision bargaining.

If management elects to open the door to decision bargaining it is suggested that it condition its willingness with reservation of rights language (preferably given to the union in writing) somewhat along the lines of the following:

> We will agree to listen to and fully consider your ideas and any proposals you wish to make regarding our tentative decision to dispose of this facility. However, we do so only on the condition that the employer does not waive the right to decline to engage in decision bargaining, and that management has reserved the right to terminate such bargaining at a later time and to assert its rights as a defense in any administrative or judicial proceeding which might take place.

The purpose here is to allow decision bargaining to take place without waiving any of management's legitimate defenses if the matter is later contested before the NLRB or in the courts.

Union Bargaining Leverage

Economic Action

In traditional contract negotiations, the union's ultimate bargaining leverage is determined by its ability to successfully wage a strike against the employer, and the employer's leverage is based upon its ability to take a strike or to lock out. In a facility closure, sale, or relocation situation a strike threat is usually meaningless or of little effect. A strike, at least at the affected facility, will simply hasten the demise of the facility and accelerate the concomitant loss of jobs. Consequently, the union's bargaining leverage is severely reduced. This is not to say, however, that it is nonexistent.

Public Relations

If the employer has other facilities, particularly in the same geographical area, pickets from the plant targeted for disposal could cause work stoppages at such other facilities. Another point of some leverage is the value the employer places on its public image in the community in which the targeted facility is located. An unwillingness on the part of management to negotiate reasonable provisions for displaced employees could be brought to the attention of news media, and therefore to the attention of the public, by the union.

Litigation

A third point of bargaining leverage in favor of the union is the threat of potential litigation through the NLRB, arbitration, or the courts. A signed agreement concerning a plant closure, sale, or relocation will normally contain, or at least should contain, a waiver by the union of all further claims in connection with the disposition. This frees the employer from any legal liability and also ensures that legal expenses will not be incurred, nor management time wasted, in defending against union claims. Freedom from litigation will be especially valuable if the employer has not properly notified and bargained with the union. This is an additional reason for management to agree to decision bargaining. By doing so it provides the union less bargaining leverage, since the possible consequences of a union's threat to litigate are less serious.

In any event, management should be aware of the various forms of bargaining leverage the union possesses as it approaches closure negotiations. It should also consider the fact that the failure of employers generally to recognize the legitimate needs of employees created by the permanent loss of jobs resulting from a facility closure or its equivalent will, in the long run, only serve to prompt the government to pass legislation to force employers to meet such needs.

The Timing of Negotiations

Consistent with the legal considerations discussed earlier, it is essential that decision bargaining take place before a final decision is made and before the employer is committed to a particular course of action. It is not absolutely necessary that effects bargaining take place prior to a closure, sale, or relocation, although it is recommended that management, after giving advance notice, be prepared to negotiate in advance of the action to be taken. This is especially important where the facility is to be operated by a different employer or the business is to be relocated. Advance negotiations will enable the union to bargain about work opportunities at the newly constituted facility. To permit such bargaining is not to suggest that the employer will agree, or is even capable of agreeing, to offer jobs at the newly constituted facility. It is only the opportunity to bargain that is being made available.

The Precedential Effect of Agreement

Management should recognize that, for the most part, whatever it agrees to provide in a given facility disposition situation it will be expected to match in future facility disposition situations. Although there may be distinguishing features about a particular situation which may warrant special treatment, it will be difficult to rationalize such variable treatment to employees, the union, or the public. Consequently, management should formulate its strategy and bottom-line positions on the basis that it will grant the same treatment to its other facilities if they meet the same or a similar fate in the future.

Negotiating Joint Union-Management Programs

Closely related to, but conceptually distinct from, concessionary bargaining is the general subject of joint union-management programs ("joint programs"). These programs are referred to by many different terms, and take many different forms such as quality of work life improvement ("QWL"), employee involvement, participation teams, quality circles, gain-sharing plans, Scanlon plans, and profit-sharing. In essence, they are programs that seek union cooperation and some form of employee involvement in increasing production, product and service quality, customer satisfaction, operating efficiency, cost reduction, and other positive results that can benefit the employer, its employees, and the union.

Distinction From Concessionary Bargaining

As discussed earlier in this chapter, employers' economic difficulties and the resulting threat of job losses frequently stimulate concessionary bargaining which, in turn, often results in joint programs being proposed (usually by the employer) to improve the employer's economic circumstances. A number of joint programs were born in the 1980s as a result of threats of plant closures, job losses, and bankruptcies. These joint programs were usually trade-offs for union concessions. For example, a number of gain-sharing, profit-sharing, and employee stock ownership programs were instituted in exchange for union agreements to accept wage, benefit, and work rule concessions.

While many of the same programs that were a product of concessionary bargaining are the same ones to now be discussed under the rubric of "joint programs," the difference is that true joint programs are negotiated for their intrinsic value to the employer, the union, and the employees, not merely as a *quid pro quo* for other contract changes. This is a critical distinction for it sets the framework for the timing and negotiating process as well as the rationale used to enlist the support of rank and file employees and supervisors. Where joint programs are initiated as a trade-off for union concessions, their continued existence is threatened when the employer's economic situation improves and previous wage and benefit levels are restored. This is not the case where the joint programs stand on their own. In a true joint program, both management and union representatives want to work cooperatively on one or more programs because they each see an ultimate advantage to them and their respective constituencies, irrespective of any other contract provisions. Under these circumstances, it is not necessary for either party to give something in return for an agreement to participate in a joint program. Both parties value the program for its own merits.

Types of Joint Programs

The range of joint programs is considerable. Some types of "jointness" affect relatively noncontroversial subjects such as charitable contribution campaigns (e.g., United Way), safety, and apprenticeship while others address more politically sensitive and economically crucial subjects such as work practice determination, production design and control, profit sharing, gain sharing, and stock ownership plans.

Many of the less sensitive types of programs have been in existence for many decades, whereas the more politically and economically sensitive ones did not generally appear with any frequency until the late 1970s and 1980s. For example, joint health and safety and joint apprenticeship programs go back to the 1930s and 1940s, whereas QWLs and employee involvement programs were products of the 1970s and 1980s.

The following is a list of the most common types of joint union-management programs in existence in the United States:

- Health and safety
- Substance abuse and employee assistance
- Apprenticeship and training

- Quality circles
- Quality of work life/employee involvement
- Productivity improvement
- Gain sharing
- Profit sharing
- Employee stock ownership
- General labor-management committees.

Benefits and Burdens to Management

Any employer considering joint programs needs to analyze what benefits such cooperative programs offer versus what burdens they may impose.

Benefits

The benefits, at least of some joint programs, are fairly obvious. Quality and productivity improvement programs offer the possibility of greater production, lower costs, and enhanced product quality. Similarly, gain sharing and profit sharing, at least when tied to employee involvement activities, offer the potential for these same results and greater profits. Joint welfare, safety, employee assistance ("EAP"), and training programs can increase employee morale and productivity while reducing turnover, product defects, and workers' compensation costs.

One might argue that the same results can be achieved by instituting the same programs as unilateral employer programs. That may sometimes be true except that unilateral programs generally are not accepted as readily by employees as those that have union endorsement and participation. In fact, the lack of union cooperation may result in union resistance and opposition, which are apt to make unilateral programs even less effective than they would otherwise be. Lack of union involvement could result in outright hostility which could seriously impair the effectiveness of any such program.

Beyond the potential for greater employee receptivity due to union involvement, participation by the union is likely to result in better input, information, and identification of pitfalls. Many union representatives are in a position to offer a perspective of the work culture and environment that may not be possible by management representatives. Such perspectives may significantly enhance the design, presentation, and implementation of these programs.

Perhaps the greatest benefit to management from joint programs is the effect upon the overall union-management climate. While such a climate is often a necessary prerequisite for the institution of such programs, there seems little question that a likely product of such programs, at least of successful ones, is enhancement of labor-management relationships. The mutual trust and respect necessary to make such programs function effectively spills over into the more traditional areas of union-management interaction such as grievance processing and contract negotiation.

Those with experience in joint programs in the auto, steel, glass, metal-working, and communications industries repeatedly tell of how their positive experiences with joint programs set the stage for more amicable relationships at the bargaining table. This is not to say that hard bargaining vanishes with the institution of joint programs, but the parties are less likely to see each other as enemies or adversaries and more likely to view each other as legitimate players in a high-stakes enterprise where neither party wins unless both win.

Burdens

Despite all the noble feelings that accompany discussions of joint programs, employers should not be misled into believing that there are all pluses and no minuses associated with union-management cooperative programs. Without question, the highest price employers pay for joint programs is loss of control and dimunition of management's ability to make unilateral decisions and changes. It is axiomatic that making programs subject to joint determination means that management cannot act alone in the areas encompassed by the joint program. This means some dilution of management's rights which most employers covetously protect. Joint programs require a leap of faith that the other side will exercise its new-found influence in management decisions in a responsible and productive manner.

Another burden of joint programs is the likelihood of increased nonproductive time and failed efforts. Such activities as quality circles and other employee involvement programs mean time away from the job for those who participate. That lost time should, if the programs are at all effective, be offset by efficiencies from new methods and other improvements resulting from their involvement. There are likewise real risks that employee involvement, gain-sharing, and other joint programs will not achieve their objectives, will be regarded as failures by participants, and ultimately may be more harmful to union-management relationships than if such programs had never been introduced. Most published reports of joint programs relate success stories. For each success there is probably an equal, if not greater, number of programs that floundered for lack of enthusiasm, insufficient commitment, inadequate resources, or any number of other reasons. Joint programs require large quantities of good faith, trust, commitment, persistence, creativity, and follow-through.

Despite these burdens, the author believes that the potential benefits to management compared to the potential burdens are sufficient to embark on one form of joint program or another—provided the program(s) fit the organization involved. Not all types of joint programs are a good fit in every work environment. Those situations that may be ideal for gain-sharing programs may not be equally fertile ground for quality circles. Management needs to thoroughly analyze its own management orientation and philosophy, the union and its attitudes, the makeup of the work force, the nature of the production or service facility(ies) to be involved, and a number of other factors that will influence the success or failure of the programs.

Union Perspective

Employers sometimes presume that they are the only ones who take any risks in entering into joint programs. Nothing could be further from the truth, for unions assume major political risks in entering into cooperative programs. Sometimes, employers use joint programs as a means to co-opt or weaken a union by enlisting employee cooperation and involvement for greater productivity without fully involving the union. In other cases, unions see cooperation with management as relinquishing the union's role as a champion of employee rights and interests. For example, the International Association of Machinists and Aerospace Workers ("IAM") has taken an official position against such programs as evidenced by a letter and accompanying "White Paper," which states the following:

> Government and industry are currently engaged in a serious effort to undermine our collective bargaining rights by promoting "team concept" programs under the guise of labor management cooperation. These programs by their very nature interfere with our duty to protect the interests of all bargaining unit members. We *must* challenge management's implementation of these kinds of programs. * * * It is, therefore, the policy of the IAM to vigorously resist any team concept programs.[7]

Other unions, however, have taken a completely contrary position and embraced the cooperative approach. The position of the United Auto Workers as articulated by one of its key vice presidents is as follows:

> The whole thrust of the United Auto Workers' program has been to win greater influence in the decision-making process that affects the workers the union represents. There is no better way to achieve this result than by involving not only union representatives, but when possible, the workers themselves in the process.
>
> * * *
>
> [A]llowing individuals to participate through joint programs is a natural way to improve the quality of their work lives. Working through joint committees has afforded the union greater opportunities to serve the membership and solve many of the problems faced in the plants in a more sensible and timely fashion than through crisis bargaining when logical, sensible answers to problems are not always possible.[8]

Bargaining Strategies and Tactics

Having determined to embark on a joint program, management needs to assess the strategies and tactics it will employ to achieve agreement.

Separation From Other Negotiations

Consistent with the analysis above that the most effective joint programs are justified on their own merits rather than being linked to concessions or other *quid pro quos*, it is usually advisable to separate the negotiations on joint programs from general contract negotiations. If the two are combined, it will be too tempting for one party or the other to seek some advantage in exchange for an agreement to embark upon a joint program. The separation can be achieved in several ways. A separation in time is probably the most effective. By entering into an agreement well before or after general contract negotiations, it is easier to avoid the lure of tradeoffs. If that is not feasible, the parties should attempt to hold the negotiations on a joint program at a different site and preferably by a different set of representatives than those who are negotiating the labor agreement. These talks will be enhanced even further if both parties agree in advance that the joint program is not to be linked with any contract issues.

Equal Access to All Information

If jointness is to work after an agreement is reached, it must be successfully employed when the agreement is being negotiated. Therefore, each party must have full access to data and information held by the other party. Relevant cost, productivity, profit, and other data must be equally available. Once one party feels that the other is holding back, trust (which is essential to a successful program) will be lost.

Trial Period

When either party or the work group involved has not had previous experience with the joint program being negotiated, it is frequently advisable to institute the program on a trial basis. This is especially true if the joint program has significant economic consequences such as a gain-sharing or profit-sharing plan. By having an opt-out feature for either or both parties after one or two years, both parties can enter into the agreement with much less apprehension than if bound to continue it in its initial form unless both parties agree otherwise.

Top and Mid-Level Management Support

It is one thing for the management negotiator, human resources executive, or even the CEO to see the value of, and desire to implement, cooperative union-management programs. It is quite a different matter to have the full range of management be committed to such programs.

Consequently, it is essential that management get its entire team (or at least the key players of that team) on board with the concept and commitment to joint programs before it attempts to negotiate such programs with its union. If that is not accomplished, the union will sense the lack of management cohesion and commitment and refuse to participate in such a half-hearted venture. Even if the union can be persuaded to participate, the venture is unlikely to be successful without concerted and sustained management support. Do not try to sell the union on a joint program that cannot be sold to management. Do not be sold on a joint program by the union that cannot be sold to your own management.

Joint Programs and Traditional Contract Negotiations Not Mutually Exclusive

One of the fundamental issues in management cooperation is whether union and management must, can, or should abandon traditional collective bargaining (i.e., zero sum bargaining, distributive negotiations, "business as usual" labor negotiations) in order to successfully establish joint union-management programs. Different parties have widely divergent opinions on this subject.

Irv Bluestone, former Vice President of the United Auto Workers, articulates the UAW's general view as follows:

> Literally hundreds of joint-action processes exist in U.S. industry at the present time while the traditional bargaining process continues (even involving occasional strikes), attesting to the feasibility and viability of the parallel approach to solving labor-management problems. In the years to follow, it is a reasonable assumption, based on current practice, that managements and unions will, on the one hand, continue to engage in contract negotiations concerning tough issues in controversy and, on the other, continue to devote their mutual attention to the resolution of problems of a noncontroversial nature through the QWL process. In short, experience indicates that normal collective bargaining and the QWL process can and do exist and fulfill their respective roles side by side.[9]

A number of academics and management consultants preach that "you can't go home again" and that once unions and managements learn to cooperate on joint programs, they can never return to the give and take of traditional labor negotiations with threats of strikes, lockouts, and possible unilateral implementation that are part and parcel of traditional labor contract negotiations. The author disagrees with this assessment. While joint programs allow the door of mutual trust and common interest to be opened to the fresh air of new approaches and reduced confrontation, the economic needs of, and internal political pressures within, unions and managements are likely to result in both parties adhering to the traditional mode of collective bargaining for the major portion of their relationships. This is not necessarily negative, for this form of union-management relationships has served employers and unions in this country very well for more than a half century.

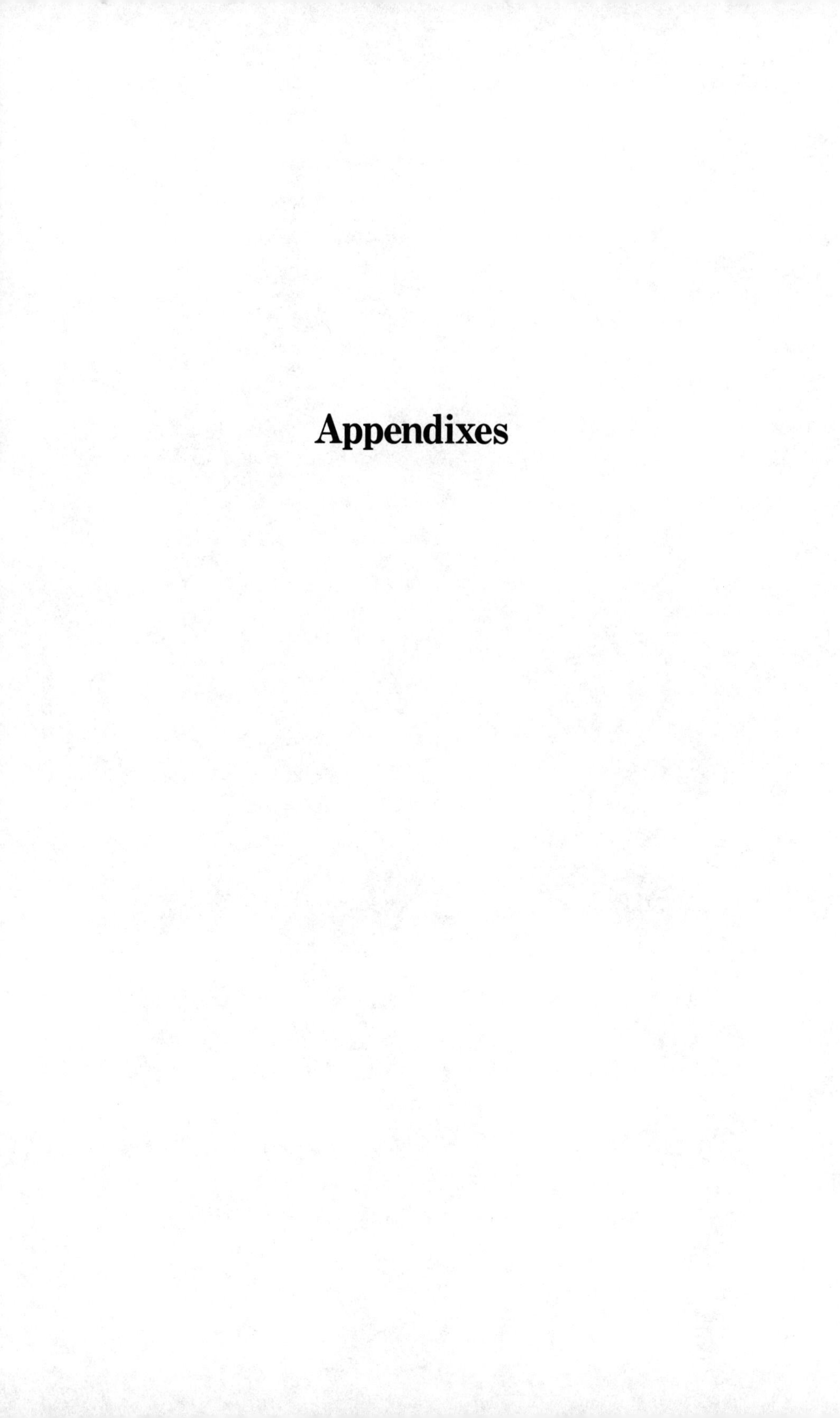

Appendixes

Appendix 1

Summary of Labor Contract Provisions

American Paper Institute, Inc.
260 Madison Avenue, New York, N.Y. 10016 / (212) 340-0600
cable address: AMPAPINST New York

Date
Region

CONTRACT DATES (if appropriate)	Company				Location		
Effective	Contact		Location		Telephone No.		

Expires	NUMBER OF PROD/MAINT. EMPLOYEES	Paper Mill	Pulp Mill	Power	Recovery	Maintenance	Others	Total

Re-opens	Union/International Reps.	Probation Period (calendar or days worked)

Termination Notice 10-day? ______ Other? (Specify): ______	Office Union?	Guard Union?	Woodlands Union?	Total Exempt Salaried	Total Non-exempt Salaried

MILL CHARACTERISTICS:

Machine No.	Cylinder/Fourdrinier/Twin Wire	Product	Trim (inches)	Speed (Fpm)	Capacity (Tpd)

Number of: Batch Digesters ______ Continuous Digesters ______ Number of Operating Crews ______
(e.g. Southern swing, 3, other?)

WAGE CHANGES BY EFFECTIVE DATES:

Date	Changes	Job Adjustments	Hire Rate	Base Rate	Top Maintenance Rate	A S T R

COLA (Specify):

BENEFIT CHANGES BY EFFECTIVE DATES:

Page 2

Company	Location

PREMIUMS AND OVERTIME:

Shift Differential(s) 2nd 3rd	Meal Allowance	Wire Time	Call-in	Report-In

Over 8 Hours	Over 16 Hours	24 Continuous	Saturday	6th Day	Sunday	7th Day	Other

Paid Holidays (List, Underlining Production Restricted) — Total Paid Holidays

Holiday Rates (If Worked)

Holiday Hours Paid Used in Computing Weekly Overtime Yes ☐ No ☐ If Yes, explain: ____

May Employee Receive Pay in Lieu Of Time Off? Yes ☐ No ☐ If Yes, explain: ____

Jury Pay Yes ☐ No ☐ Maximum No. Days ____

Witness Pay Yes ☐ No ☐

To Receive Holiday Pay, Must Employee Work? Day Before ____ Day After ____ Other ____

Vacation (wks/yrs service) — Vacation Pay/Wk — May Employee Receive Pay In Lieu Of Time Off? Specify:

Funeral Leave Pay (Max. Days) — Members Of Family (List)

Severance/Layoff Pay Yes ☐ No ☐ — If yes, specify:

Hand Tools

Co. Furnish? ____ Employee Furnish? ____ Allowance $ ____

Safety Shoe Allowance $ ____ Wearing Mandatory? Yes ☐ No ☐

WAGE INCREASES SINCE 1979:

STRIKES SINCE 1979:

INSURANCE PLANS:

LIFE & AD&D		LIFE	AD&D
1. Flat Amount (all employees):		$ ____	$ ____
2. Schedule:			
Minimum Wage Rate Bracket	$ ____	$ ____	$ ____
Maximum Wage Rate Bracket	$ ____	$ ____	$ ____

3. Earnings Basis:

1x ____ $1\frac{1}{2}$x ____ 2x Annual Earnings ____ Other ____ Maximum $ ____

4. Optional Life/AD&D (Specify) ____

DEPENDENT GROUP LIFE Yes ☐ No ☐ If yes, specify: ____

Page 3

Company	Location

ACCIDENT AND SICKNESS

1. Flat Amount (all employees) $ ______
2. Schedule:

	Rate/Earnings	Weekly Benefit
Minimum	______	______
Maximum	______	______

3. Percent of Weekly Earnings: ____ %
Minimum Benefit $ ______
Maximum Benefit $ ______

Maximum Weeks Paid Per Disability ______ Per Year.

Waiting Period (days) For Illness? ____ Accident? ____ If Hospitalized? ____ Retroactive after ____ days

Benefit Integrated With:
Social Security? Yes ☐ No ☐ Workers Compensation Supplement? Yes ☐ No ☐

State Statutory Benefit? Yes ☐ No ☐ Maximum Weekly Benefit ______

Paid Sick Leave? Yes ☐ No ☐ If yes, specify: ______

LONG TERM DISABILITY Yes ☐ No ☐ If yes, specify: ______

DENTAL: Yes ☐ No ☐ Dependent Coverage? Yes ☐ No ☐

Type of Plan: R&C ______ Schedule ______ Integrated with Major Medical? ______

COVERED BENEFITS	Deductibles Annual	Deductibles Life	Benefit Max. Annual	Benefit Max. Life	Co-Insurance Formula
Preventive Procedures					
Basic Procedures					
Major Procedures					
Orthondontia					

Pre-determination: Yes ☐ No ☐ Amount $ ______

If dental is integrated with regular major medical, explain deductibles, co-insurance, and inside limits: ______

HEALTH CARE:

PLAN: Circle TYPE(s) offered and show the NUMBER OF HOURLY EMPLOYEES enrolled.

BASIC + MAJOR MED ______ (# emp.) COMP ______ (# emp.) HMO ______ (# emp.) PPO ______ (# emp.)

Other/Specify: ______ (# emp.)

Below provide data for the Plan in which MOST HOURLY EMPLOYEES are enrolled.

MAXIMUM LIFETIME BENEFIT: $ ______

DEDUCTIBLE: Individual: $ ______ PER YEAR Family Maximum: $ ______ PER YEAR

COINSURANCE: (Ratio of Company/Employee payment of medical expenses) ______ % / ______ %
Company Employee

STOPLOSS: (Maximum amount employee is obliged to pay towards medical expenses. If no stoploss, so state.)

Individual: $ ______ PER YEAR Family Maximum: $ ______ PER YEAR

Stoploss limits do ____ / do not ____ include initial deductibles

Hospital Room & Board (Daily Benefit/Max. Days): $ ______ / ______

Deduc./Stay Yes ☐ No ☐ $ ______ Misc. Extras: In Full ______ Other ______

Surgical Benefit: R & C ____ Schedule ____ Max. $ ______ Other (Explain) ______

Vision Care (separate plan)? Yes ☐ No ☐ Prescription Drugs (separate plan)? Yes ☐ No ☐

DOCTOR VISITS In Hospital: Daily Benefit ______ Max Days Covered ____ Other ______

Office & Home: Daily Benefit ______ Max Days Covered ____ Other ______

Is Care For The Following Covered?	Hospitalized		Out-Patient	
Psychiatric	Yes ☐	No ☐	Yes ☐	No ☐
Alcoholism	Yes ☐	No ☐	Yes ☐	No ☐
Drug Abuse	Yes ☐	No ☐	Yes ☐	No ☐

COST MANAGEMENT FEATURES:

____ Outpatient Diagnostic/Lab/X-Ray
____ Outpatient Surgery
____ Pre-admission Testing
____ Second Surgical Opinion
____ Utilization Review
____ Large/Med. Case Mgmnt.
____ Hospital Bill Auditing
____ Home Health Care
____ Hospice Care
____ Employee Assistance Plan
____ Wellness Program
____ Other (Specify Below)
______

Page 4

Company	Location

BENEFIT/CONTRIBUTIONS/PREMIUMS:

	AMOUNT OF ACTIVE EMPLOYEE CONTRIBUTIONS/MONTH			TOTAL PREMIUM/MONTH		
	Employee Only	Employee Plus One Dependent	Family	Employee Only	Employee Plus One Dependent	Family
Life	$	$	$	$	$	$
AB & D						
A&S						
Long Term Disability						
Hospital, Surgical, Medical						
Dental						
Vision Care (separate plan)						
Prescription Drugs (separate plan)						
TOTAL						
HMO Dual Choice (Explain)						

PENSION:

Eligibility Age ____ Service __________ Does Service Prior to Eligibility Count for Benefits? Yes ☐ No ☐

Vesting Method ____________________

Benefit: Flat $ __________ Final Average Earnings __________ Career Average Earnings __________

Other (Explain) ____________________

Normal Retirement Age ____ Service __________ Early Retirement Age ____ Service __________

Disability Retirement Age ____ Service __________

Percentage Of Accrued Benefit Payable Early

Age 64 ______ Age 61 ______ Age 58 ______

Age 63 ______ Age 60 ______ Age 57 ______

Age 62 ______ Age 59 ______ Age 56 ______

No Reduction In Accrued Benefit (early retirement):

Age ______ Service __________

Disability Criteria (check as appropriate):

☐ Unable to Perform Any Work

☐ Unable to Work for Company

☐ Unable to Work in Paper Industry

☐ Social Security Definition

☐ Other (specify): __________

Accrued Benefit Reduced: Yes ☐ No ☐

Benefit Options (check as appropriate)

☐ ERISA
☐ Joint & Survivor
☐ Life Annuity
☐ Years certain
☐ Lump Sum payment
☐ Social Security Offset

Post-Retirement Death Benefit (other than benefit options described above and other than group life insurance)

Yes ☐ No ☐ Benefit Formula ____________________

OTHER COMPENSATION/INCENTIVES:

(Where yes, indicate essential features below)

Thrift Plan Yes ☐ No ☐
401(K) Plan Yes ☐ No ☐
Profit Sharing Plan Yes ☐ No ☐
Stock Purchase Plan Yes ☐ No ☐
Gain Sharing Plan Yes ☐ No ☐
ESOP Yes ☐ No ☐

RETIREE LIFE/HEALTH:

Life Insurance Continued: After Normal Retirement? ______ At Early?/Age? ______ At Disability?/Age? ______

Amount $ __________ Reduction Formula? ______ Contribution by Retiree $ __________

Hospital, Surgical, Medical Continued: Retiree? ______ Spouse? __________

Type Coverage And Contribution	Same As Active?	Medicare Supplement?	Other? (Specify)	Contribution/Month (Amount or Percent) Company	Retiree
Normal Retirement					
Early Retirement					
Disability Retirement					

WAGE RATES

Page of

Company					Location				
CLASSIFICATION	Effective Dates			No. of Workers	CLASSIFICATION	Effective Dates			No. of Workers

Appendix 2

Labor Cost Recap

Location ______________

Union Involved ______________

Prepared by ______________

Date ______________

(INSTRUCTIONS ON REVERSE SIDE)

A. Reference Period From ______________ To ______________

B. Total Employees in Bargaining Unit ______________

C. Total hours worked ______________ (12 mos.)

D. Total hours used for estimating ______________

E. Rollup Fringe Factor ______________ %

Cost Categories	Hours	Total Annual Cost	Cost per Hour	% of Straight Time Wages	% of Total Labor Cost
(1) Straight Time Wages Paid					
(2) Rollup Fringes					
(3) Overtime Premium					
(4) Sunday Premium					
(5) Holiday Premium					
(6) Vacation Pay					
(7) Holiday Pay					
(8) Reporting Pay					
(9) Call Time					
(10) Funeral Leave					
(11) Jury Duty					
(12) Other ______________ (specify)					
(13) Other ______________ (specify)					
(14) FICA (Rollup Portion)					
Subtotal Rollup Fringes					
Nonrollup Fringes					
(15) Night Shift Differential					
(16) Pension Plan					
(17) Group Insurance					
(18) Worker's Compensation					
(19) Unemployment Compensation					
(20) Other ______________ (specify)					
(21) FICA (Nonrollup Portion)					
Subtotal Nonrollup Fringes					
TOTAL FRINGE BENEFIT COST					
TOTAL LABOR COST					

INSTRUCTIONS

This data on this form should be completed prior to the beginning of labor negotiations. It will be used in making all cost estimates during negotiations.

Although the form does not require that hours applicable to each fringe factor be noted, it is suggested that these hours be accumulated for later use in making cost estimates.

A. Reference Period—Select a representative period during which current wage rates were in effect. If current rates were not in effect for part or all of the period, adjust the amounts to reflect current labor costs. If the reference period is not a 12-month period, adjust data to a 12-month period. **Eliminate months which are not at all representative.**

B. & C.—Self-explanatory.

D. Total Annual Manhours for Estimating Purposes—Use same number as reference period unless you anticipate significant changes. Reference period manhours may also be rounded to facilitate calculations.

E. Rollup Fringe Factor—This is arrived at by dividing the sum of all rollup fringes (items 3-14) by straight time wages paid (item 1).

COST CATEGORIES

1. Straight Time Wages Paid—The straight time portion of all payments for hours actually worked. This includes the straight time portion only of Overtime, Sundays and Holidays worked. It does not include night shift differential.
2. Rollup Fringe—A fringe benefit the cost of which is automatically increased as a result of a wage increase.

ROLLUP FRINGES

3. Overtime Premium—Include only the premium paid as a result of working over 8 hours per day and 40 hours per week. The straight time portion of overtime hours worked is to be included under No. 1 above.
4. Sunday Premium—The premium portion of wages paid for work performed on a Sunday because it is a Sunday. The straight time portion of hours worked on Sunday to be included under No. 1 above.
5. Holiday Premium—The premium portion of wages paid for work performed on a holiday. The straight time portion of hours worked on a holiday to be included under No. 1 above.
6. Vacation Pay—Pay for time not worked while on vacation.
7. Holiday Pay—Pay for the holiday as such, whether or not work is performed on that day.
8. Reporting Pay—Allowance for failure to provide work when employee reports and work is not available.
9. Call Time—Only the premium payments for responding to a call-in or call-back to work.
10. Funeral Leave—Pay for time not worked when death occurs in the "immediate family."
11. Jury Duty—Pay for time not worked when on approved jury duty.
12. Other—Include here other fringe benefit payments such as sick leave, wire time, percentage shift differential, or other payments which vary with the hourly wage.
13. Other—as above.
14. FICA—Determine the number of employees with an annual income of less than the Social Security annual maximum; divide that number of employees by the total number of employees in the bargaining unit. The resulting percentage should then be multiplied by the total annual FICA payments made. This yields a total dollar figure which is the rollup portion of FICA. The balance, if any, is to be included under No. 21 below.

NONROLLUP FRINGES

15. Shift Differential—Premium payment, if it is a simple cents per hour amount.
16. Pension Plan—Contributions to Pension Plan
17. Group Insurance—All Group Insurance and Sickness & Accident costs including Health Service Plan costs. (In California, include company payments for UCD.)
18. Workmen's Compensation—Total payments for Industrial Accident Insurance or out-of-pocket cost where self-insured.
19. Unemployment Compensation—Amount paid to State and Federal governments for unemployment insurance taxes.
20. Other—Include here any other fringe payments which do not automatically increase with an increase in wages.
21. FICA—The balance which is not recorded under item 14 above.

Appendix 3

Review of the Development of a Clause

DEVELOPMENT OF SUBCONTRACTING CLAUSE

1960–1972

"Nothing in this agreement shall be interpreted to restrict the right of the Company to contract for services of independent contractors, nor shall this agreement be interpreted to restrict the right of the Company to employ specialists from outside its regular plant organization on work not regularly performed by Unit employees."

1972–1981

"It is the intent of the Company to fully utilize employees at the Plant. Work traditionally and normally performed by Company employees will be performed by these employees unless:

1. Appropriate skills are unavailable, or
2. Necessary equipment is not reasonably and timely available, or
3. Manhours necessary to complete the job are unavailable within the time period during which the Company feels the job must be completed."

1981 to date

"It is the intent of the Company to fully utilize employees at the Plant. Work traditionally and normally performed by Company employees will be performed by these employees unless:

1. Appropriate skills are unavailable, or
2. Necessary equipment is not reasonably and timely available, or
3. Manhours necessary to complete the job are unavailable within the time period during which the Company feels the job must be completed, or unless use of Company's personnel would curtail or delay necessary work.

If necessary work is to be contracted while employees are on layoff management and union representatives will meet, discuss and make an honest effort to determine what, if any, part of that necessary work can be performed by laid-off employees."

Appendix 4

Negotiations Preparation Checklist

LABOR CONTRACT NEGOTIATIONS PREPARATION CHECKLIST

(check only those items that are necessary and/or useful)

Facility Involved ______________________

Union ______________________

Contract Expiration Date ______________________

Assigned To	Completion Date

A. REVIEW OF PREVIOUS NEGOTIATIONS

___ 1. Review union agendas from previous negotiations.

___ 2. Review notes or minutes of previous negotiations if available. Study arguments made and answers given. Mark and index subject areas anticipated in upcoming negotiations.

___ 3. Evaluate successes/failures in past negotiations—tactics, timing, concessions, gains, etc. What can be learned from experience? Were bargaining objectives met? If yes, how? If no, why?

___ 4. Review settlement agreements and any "side agreements."

___ 5. Collect all oral or written commitments made during prior negotiations and since the last contract. Have all commitments been carried out? Do any need to be revised, eliminated, and/or incorporated into the basic agreement?

___ 6. What were the key issues in recent negotiations? Are they likely to surface again? Determine necessary preparations to deal with these issues.

___ 7. Who were the dominant personalities in recent negotiations? Will they again be involved? Will their presence or absence likely be a factor in the forthcoming negotiations? What can be done to maximize or minimize their influence?

Assigned To	Completion Date

B. REVIEW OF EXPERIENCE DURING TERM OF LAST CONTRACT

___ 1. Thoroughly study the present contract to identify any provisions that require modification (include as part of the review memoranda of intent, supplemental agreements, letters, etc.).

___ 2. Review the contract and any supplemental agreements to determine if there are any illegal provisions (consider laws prohibiting discrimination, federal and state labor laws, and recent court decisions). Propose changes where necessary.

___ 3. Solicit input from salaried supervisors as to needed changes in the labor contract, side agreements, work rules, etc.

___ 4. Analyze grievance/arbitration experience during the term of the contract. Consider the origin of grievances, subject matter, patterns of grievances granted and denied. Study arbitration awards as to changes in contract application or interpretation.

___ 5. Review minutes or notes of union-management meetings which occurred during the terms of the contract.

___ 6. Consider personnel problems during the term of the contract to determine if the contract or past practices are a cause or possible solution. Consider such factors as absenteeism, turnover, recruitment difficulties, productivity rates, quality control, etc. Develop proposals and/or strategy to deal with such problems.

___ 7. Review and analyze any disruptive incidents, problem areas, signs of discontent (e.g., walkouts, petitions, anonymous bulletin board "squalks") to determine if they will or should influence negotiations.

C. CONSIDERATION OF UNIT FOR BARGAINING

___ 1. Are there any employer groups which management should consider joining for bargaining purposes?

	Assigned To	Completion Date
___ 2. Evaluate the track record, composition, cohesiveness, and bargaining leverage of the employer bargaining group(s) being considered.		
___ 3. Consider the pros and cons of a single-employer—multi-facility bargaining group if the employer has more than one contract with the same union.		
___ 4. Estimate the union's interest in bargaining this contract within a multi-employer or multi-facility framework.		
D. <u>DATA COLLECTION (INTERNAL HISTORICAL)</u>		
___ 1. Prepare a wage chronology showing base, average, and key wage rates over the last 10–15 years.		
___ 2. Prepare a benefit chronology of the most significant benefit changes in the last 10–15 years.		
___ 3. Prepare a historical summary of key economic factors of the employer's enterprise such as productivity rates, prices, production levels, sales or revenue volumes, profits, etc.		
___ 4. Prepare a chronology of key labor costs such as health insurance, pensions, vacation pay costs, etc.		
___ 5. Prepare a chronology of unit labor costs (e.g., total labor cost per hour) for the last 10–15 years.		
___ 6. Prepare a chronological evolution chart of contractual language in key sections of the contract.		
E. <u>DATA COLLECTION (INTERNAL CURRENT)</u>		
___ 1. Prepare a recap of labor costs on a gross and hourly basis under the current labor contract. Show the cost of each element of labor cost. Select a sufficiently long and representative period for which data is obtained.		

	Assigned To	Completion Date
___ 2. Assemble hours-of-work data (estimate, if actual data is not available).		
___ a. Average weekly hours.		
___ (1) Entire bargaining unit.		
___ (2) Each work shift.		
___ (3) Each department.		
___ (4) Each job classification (if appropriate).		
___ b. Unworked paid hours on the job.		
___ (1) Paid lunch period.		
___ (2) Paid break periods.		
___ (3) Paid wash-up time.		
___ (4) Paid time off for union business.		
___ (5) Other (specify) ________		
___ c. Overtime hours worked.		
___ (1) Entire bargaining unit.		
___ (2) Each work shift.		
___ (3) Each department.		
___ (4) Each job classification (if appropriate).		
___ (5) Overtime hours offered but refused (if such option is available).		
___ (6) Show all overtime as a percentage of straight-time hours worked.		
___ d. Premium hours worked and paid for based upon:		
___ (1) Over 8 hours per day.		
___ (2) Over 40 hours per week.		
___ (3) Work performed on a holiday.		
___ (4) Work performed on Saturday and Sunday.		

Assigned To	Completion Date

___ (5) Early call-in or hold-over.

___ (6) Other bases (specify) ___.

___ 3. Compare current hourly labor costs (obtained from #1 above) with those which were estimated during the last labor contract negotiations. Account for any major differences. Revise costing techniques and/or assumptions if necessary.

___ 4. Identify any current labor costs which appear to be out of line in relation to the same cost categories in other comparable employee groups. Develop proposals and/or a strategy to deal with serious problem areas.

___ 5. Prepare a summary description of economic provisions of the current contract for quick reference. Prepare the same summary for the employer's contracts at other comparable operations.

___ 6. Prepare a list of all job classifications, the wage rate for each classification, and the normal number of employees (or hours worked) in each classification (note any "red-circle" or "grandfathered" rates).

___ 7. Prepare a chart showing hourly wage brackets in even increments (e.g., 25¢, 50¢) from the lowest to the highest and the number of employees normally receiving wages within each wage bracket.

___ 8. Prepare a matrix showing the number of employees in the bargaining unit according to age and years of service.

___ 9. Prepare detailed cost breakdowns and analyses of key labor cost items such as medical, life, and sickness insurance, pensions, etc. Obtain cost estimates from specialists of potential changes in such areas.

___ 10. Obtain labor cost data and hours-of-work information for other employee groups of the employer that are likely to be influenced by negotiations.

___ 11. Estimate the impact of given labor changes on product/service costs.

Assigned To	Completion Date

___ 12. Collect copies of all work schedules to which bargaining unit employees are normally assigned.

___ 13. Assemble seniority information (as appropriate).

  ___ a. Seniority lists for all seniority units.

  ___ b. Copies of all seniority lines of progression.

  ___ c. Number of jobs filled by job bid procedure.

  ___ d. Number of promotions granted to other than the most senior applicant or bidder (also show as a percentage of all promotions).

  ___ e. Layoff information—numbers of employees effected and seniority range of those laid off.

  ___ f. Frequency and impact of "bumping" during layoff.

  ___ g. Average period of Layoff for those employees who have been laid off.

  ___ h. Data reflecting frequency and impact of job transfers, promotions, and other types of turnover.

___ 14. Collect copies of all employer-issued policies, rules, insurance booklets, etc.

___ 15. Prepare a "contract language book" for key contract provisions by assembling copies of the same contract sections from the contracts of other comparable employers and comparable facilities of the same employer.

F. DATA COLLECTION (EXTERNAL)

___ 1. Accumulate data on the key gross economic indicators.

  ___ a. Rate(s) of inflation—U.S., local area.

  ___ b. Rate(s) of unemployment—U.S., local area, industry.

Assigned To	Completion Date

__ c. Rate(s) of production, revenue, sales—industry, employer.

__ 2. Prepare a comparison spread sheet showing wage rates paid by other employers for comparable job classifications in comparable facilities (note effective dates; include nonunion facilities).

__ 3. Prepare a comparison spread sheet showing major benefits provided by comparable employers in comparable facilities (note effective dates; include nonunion facilities).

__ 4. Prepare a summary of recent contract settlement terms for comparable facilities within the same industry in the relevant geographical areas.

__ 5. Where appropriate, prepare a summary of recent contract settlement terms of negotiations in other industries and/or other geographical areas.

__ 6. Select the most representative and comparable settlement(s) from the summaries described in #4 and #5 above and prepare a cost estimate based upon the basic cost data for the facility for which you are negotiating.

__ 7. Collect copies of labor contracts for a representative number of comparable bargaining units; collect contracts covering all of the employer's other bargaining units.

__ 8. Talk personally with management representatives of other companies in the area (particularly those having recently negotiated a contract) to determine unpublished practices, concessions, etc.; recent union demands; attitudes and personalities of union negotiators; terms of last settlements; etc.

__ 9. Determine if any innovative measures have been instituted by other employers in the same or other industries to control labor costs. Obtain information about such innovations and develop appropriate proposals and/or strategy.

Assigned To	Completion Date

___ 10. Obtain a copy of the union's current Constitution and By-Laws, a list of officers, and recent issues of the union newspaper or other publications.

___ 11. Obtain the most recent copy of the union's financial report filed with U.S. Department of Labor, Labor-Management Services (forms LM–1 and LM–2).

G. DEVELOPMENT OF EMPLOYER'S BARGAINING AGENDA—BARGAINING STRATEGY

___ 1. Establish overall objectives for negotiations.

___ 2. Establish the approximate range of the desired economic settlement.

___ 3. Determine what, if any, changes in non-economic terms and contract language need to be made. Consider:

   ___ a. Adverse arbitration awards.

   ___ b. Costly work practices.

   ___ c. Misapplied contract provisions.

   ___ d. Grievance producing contract language.

   ___ e. Unproductive and/or wasteful contract requirements.

___ 4. Prepare drafts of needed changes identified in #3 above.

___ 5. Determine what, if any, proposals identified in #1, #2, or #3 should be part of the initial bargaining agenda or reserved for counteroffers or counterproposals.

___ 6. Prepare background material, data, arguments, and/or other information to support all of management's proposals. Consider charts or visual aids as appropriate.

___ 7. Prepare a rough negotiating timetable.

   ___ a. Starting date of negotiations compared to expiration date.

   ___ b. Available dates to meet.

Assigned To	Completion Date

___ c. Ideal frequency of meetings.

___ d. History of negotiations (e.g., extending negotiations beyond expiration date, frequency of meetings, etc.).

___ e. Timing of first offer. (How many offers were made in the past?)

___ 8. Prepare management's opening statement for negotiations.

___ 9. Establish guidelines for the management bargaining team to follow throughout negotiations.

H. PREPARATIONS REGARDING UNION PROPOSALS

___ 1. Well in advance of beginning negotiation, anticipate union's proposals (consider results obtained from checklist items A. 1 and 6; B. 5, 6 and 7; and F. 4 and 8 above). Investigate, research, and obtain all necessary information on those which are new, complex, and/or significant.

___ 2. When the union's agenda is received, thoroughly analyze each demand.

___ a. What does it mean? Do we need more information?

___ b. What are the immediate effects if granted?

___ c. What are long-range and indirect effects?

___ d. How strongly does union feel about item? How strongly are employees likely to feel about it?

___ e. What prompted this request?

___ f. Is there really a problem? If so, can it be solved by the union's proposal? Is there another and better solution?

___ 3. Estimate the cost of each economic proposal made by the union.

Assigned To	Completion Date

__ 4. Determine how a situation concerning the union's demand is handled at other locations (of the same employer and of other employers).

__ 5. Prepare the employer's position on each union agenda item:

__ a. Initial

__ b. Intermediate.

__ c. Final.

__ 6. Prepare statements, arguments, alternative solutions, counterproposals for each position in #5 above.

__ 7. Draft contract language where necessary.

I. <u>COMMUNICATIONS AWAY FROM THE BARGAINING TABLE</u>

__ 1. Consider information obtained through, and future use of, "pipeline" or "grapevine" to and from rank-and-file union members (no surveillance permitted).

__ 2. Develop a plan for communicating necessary information to supervisors and receiving information from them.

__ 3. Consider possible formal communications to employees and public (no by-passing of union as to actual bargaining).

__ 4. Develop a plan for communicating during negotiations with the appropriate line executive(s)—determine the method, frequency, amount of detail, need for clearances, etc.

__ 5. Develop a plan for communicating with others (employer's other facilities, or others, e.g., sales personnel) who have a "need to know" about the progress of negotiations.

__ 6. As appropriate, select the person(s) who will communicate with news media representatives. Establish guidelines for limitations on information to be disseminated, clearances required, and communications objectives.

Assigned To	Completion Date

J. BARGAINING REPRESENTATIVES AND ARRANGEMENTS

___ 1. Select a management negotiating team.

  ___ a. Spokesman.

  ___ b. Operations manager.

  ___ c. Contract language draftsman.

  ___ d. Cost estimator.

  ___ e. Note taker.

  ___ f. Other (Specify) ______________.

___ 2. Establish the limits of authority of the employer's chief negotiator.

___ 3. Prepare and send contractual reopening notices to the union and required notices to federal and state mediation agencies.

___ 4. Determine the locale of negotiating meetings.

  ___ a. Is it large enough? Consider the size of the union and management committees.

  ___ b. Is it quiet enough? Free from interruptions?

  ___ c. Are communications and support services available?

  ___ d. Are there adequate caucus rooms?

  ___ e. Is it available for the probable duration of negotiations?

___ 5. Coordinate with the union as to the acceptability of the proposed meeting locale and sharing of costs as necessary. Establish initial meeting date(s).

___ 6. Arrange for communications and support services.

  ___ a. Word processing equipment.

  ___ b. Telephones, fax, copier.

  ___ c. Secretarial services.

  ___ d. Computer/calculator.

	Assigned To	Completion Date
___ e. Audio-visual equipment.		
___ f. Dictating equipment.		
___ g. Other (specify) ______________.		
___ 7. Arrange for outside assistance/experts.		
___ a. Legal counsel.		
___ b. Pension and benefit actuary consultants.		
___ c. Communications specialist(s).		
___ d. Other (specify) ______________.		
K. MISCELLANEOUS		
___ 1. Estimate the likelihood of a strike and the necessity of a strike plan. If necessary, appoint a strike plan coordinator and develop a strike contingency checklist.		
___ 2. Determine the availability of a mutual assistance pact or other form of strike insurance. If available, analyze the value of such a program.		
___ 3. Identify the key issues in the negotiations raised by the employer's or the union's proposals. Develop a plan to deal with these issues.		
___ 4. Other (specify).		
___ a. ______________________.		
___ b. ______________________.		
___ c. ______________________.		

Appendix 5

Strike Contingency Checklist

SAMPLE STRIKE CONTINGENCY CHECKLIST
(Manufacturing Facility)

	Assigned To	Due Date

I. NONOPERATING MODE

A. CUSTOMER-SUPPLIER RELATIONS

1. Notify customers and suppliers of the impending work stoppage and probable date it will occur.
2. Assist customers in securing products from alternative sources (other Company plants and/ or competitors).
3. Secure needed warehousing space for the transfer of selected items in finished-goods inventory to ensure availability to customers.
4. Prepare a timetable for transfer of orders, raw materials, equipment, finished goods inventory, etc. to other Company plants or warehouses, or to other employers' facilities.
5. Notify suppliers of the impending strike in order that items can be delayed, cancelled, or routed to an outside warehouse or other facilities for the duration of the strike.
6. Notify service suppliers (railroads, trucking firms, guard service, maintenance services, etc.) in order that they can prepare for termination or modification of services.
7. Notify utility companies of the impending strike, if necessary.

B. PLANT SECURITY

1. Prepare a diagram of the entire facility showing key areas and equipment for use in security planning.

Assigned To	Due Date

2. Notify appropriate law enforcement agencies to ensure prompt response in the event of picket-line violence or other unlawful conduct.
3. Advise the Fire Department of the shutdown and the resulting increase in potential for undetected fires.
4. Develop a facility security plan with a specially trained guard service to ensure 24-hour protection of Company equipment and property from pilferage, violence, or fire.
5. Establish a policy of payment or nonpayment for damage inflicted on cars or other personal property of persons who will be crossing picket lines.
6. Determine the need for special high-intensity lighting around the perimeter of the facility.
7. Obtain special security "hardware" as needed:
   a. Two-way radios—special frequency.
   b. Infrared cameras (nighttime photography).
   c. Closed-circuit and portable video equipment.
   d. Other equipment recommended by the security agency.
8. Develop a plan to secure breakable objects and remove, to the extent possible, valuable, combustible, and/or delicate objects.
9. Determine if any additional physical barriers (fences, window grates, gates, doors) need to be installed.
10. Ensure that all personal property of striking employees is removed before the strike commences and that any property belonging to the employer, but in the custody of employees (e.g., keys, credit cards, etc.), is returned before the strike begins.

C. FACILITY PLANNING

1. Develop a plan and timetable for an orderly shutdown.
2. Develop a plan to "mothball" equipment based upon the most reasonable estimate of the strike's duration.

	Assigned To	Due Date
3. Consider the leasing of valuable equipment and the sale of raw materials and supplies which will not be needed during the strike.		
4. Develop a timetable to remove as much of the finished-goods inventory as possible prior to the strike deadline.		
5. Ascertain the manpower needed to conduct watchman and possible maintenance-worker duties; develop a work schedule and plans for their entering/leaving the plant, food service, and other necessary arrangements.		
6. Determine retention, assignments, transfer, etc. of non-striking nonexempt and exempt salaried employees during strike.		
II. OPERATING MODE		
A. CUSTOMER-SUPPLIER RELATIONSHIP		
1. Notify customers and suppliers of the impending work stoppage and the probable date of occurrence.		
2. Advise customers of intended operations, when these will be in effect, and what, if any, changes in the product or service will result during the strike.		
3. Develop a plan to make shipments to customers. Have backup plans if the primary means is not feasible.		
a. Contact all existing transportation companies and determine which ones can be depended upon in a strike situation.		
b. Contact any additional transportation companies to determine their attitudes and capabilities to service the Company's needs during the strike.		
4. Ascertain if any additional off-premises warehousing may be needed (particularly to avoid a situation where strikers follow trucks to customers' facilities).		

Assigned To	Due Date

5. Notify suppliers and review needs for operations during the strike. Develop nonroutine shipping and receiving schedules if necessary. Ensure that trucks, trains, etc. will continue to make deliveries through picket lines.

B. PLANT SECURITY

1. Follow items 1–9 under items I.B. above.
2. Develop a plan for strike replacements, salaried employees, and others to enter the plant.
    a. Private cars: staggered times, special parking arrangements?
    b. Private cars: convoy, special parking arrangements?
    c. Bus or van: arrange parking system and pickup arrangements?
    d. Arrangements for living within plant premises?
    e. Need for law enforcement presence at shift-change times?
3. Develop a coordinated plan with local law enforcement officials to obtain quick responses in emergency situations, presence at selected times.
4. Develop a plan for picket-line or other surveillance with particular attention to the use of infrared scopes and cameras, video equipment, long-range (shotgun) microphones, still cameras with telephoto lens. Plan sites for positioning surveillance persons and equipment.
5. Ensure that the guard service is sufficient in terms of the number of personnel and their experience in strike-period operating situations. Ask for information about prior experience.
6. Check to make sure communications systems (phones, fax, two-way radios, mail, etc.) are secure from tampering, interception, and bugging and that they are otherwise sufficient for strike-period operating needs.

Assigned To	Due Date

7. Determine if any guard or surveillance services are necessary at auxiliary employer locations, e.g., sales offices, warehouses, depots, etc., or if such services may be warranted at employers' or managers' houses.

8. Consider the use of guard dogs where the normal guard service may be inadequate.

C. OPERATIONS

1. Develop a timetable for continuation or resumption of operations following the strike.

2. Prepare operations schedules. Be conservative and realistic.

   a. Prepare daily and weekly targets; consider learning curves.

   b. Cut frills where possible in terms of product or service.

   c. Produce products most in demand and easiest to produce.

   d. Consider farming out more complex or labor-intensive work.

3. Estimate personnel availabilities.

   a. Estimate the number of returning strikers (be conservative).

   b. Estimate the number of supervisors and non-bargaining unit personnel available.

   c. Estimate the number of new-hire replacements necessary, temporary or permanent.

   d. Consider the use of outside contractors, especially for maintenance.

4. Match personnel availabilities with requirements.

   a. Determine critical skills needed and who will supply them.

   b. Survey all supervisors and salaried employees as to skills and experience.

   c. Assess training needs and how these can be met.

   d. Consider cross-assignments and cross-training not done under normal conditions.

	Assigned To	Due Date
5. Prepare staffing charts and work schedules.		
a. Have backups for each key position.		
b. Coordinate the work schedule with the operating schedule.		
c. Develop a schedule that can be sustained; avoid burnout.		
d. Leave nonessential jobs unfilled or intermittently filled.		
6. Determine policies for unusual personnel needs.		
a. Plan for more extensive food service.		
b. Develop, where appropriate, special pay/benefit policies:		
1. Overtime pay for supervisors and salaried employees?		
2. Per diem allowances and paid leaves for employees working away from home.		
3. Reimbursement for unusual expenses, e.g., transportation.		
c. In-plant facilities for rest and relaxation.		
7. Hiring strike replacements.		
a. Determine recruiting sources (state employment service not available).		
b. Contact former employees and determine their availability and interest.		
c. Prepare newspaper recruiting ads.		
d. Determine whether replacements will have the status of permanent or temporary workers.		
e. Develop a schedule for interviewing, screening, reference checks, etc.		
f. Prepare an orientation program for new hires; cover special considerations for strike-period operations.		
g. Determine and communicate all policies regarding pay and benefits for strike replacements.		

Assigned To	Due Date

8. Miscellaneous policies and actions.
   a. Determine what action is to be taken against non-striking non-bargaining-unit personnel who refuse to cross the picket line.
   b. Determine how and in what manner striking employees who wish to return to work will be treated vis-a-vis new employees (e.g., return to old job or take whatever job is available?).
   c. Develop special policies and activities to encourage safety and minimize industrial injuries.
   d. Develop a firm policy that those who cross the picket line and those guarding the plant are not to react (unless in self-defense), respond, provoke, or otherwise exacerbate picket-line hostility.
   e. Plan periodic events or treats for those working during the strike, to keep morale high.

III. OPERATING OR NONOPERATING MODE

A. STRIKE MONITORING AND COORDINATING

1. Appoint a "strike coordinator" who will be responsible for coordinating all aspects of strike-related activities.
2. Strike log—Assign the task of entering all pertinent occurrences (recording date, time, and incident) and collecting pertinent documentation.
3. Schedule regular coordination meetings to assure all responsible persons are fully briefed.
4. Schedule persons responsible for monitoring picket-line activity.

Assigned To	Due Date

B. COMMUNICATIONS

1. Prepare a letter to striking employees advising them of the employer's position in negotiations. Prepare a letter to nonstriking employees.
2. Designate a person who will maintain contact and relations with all public news media.
3. Develop a communication plan to get the employer's position to the public, employees, customers, etc. in the most favorable way possible.
4. Plan regular briefings for key management personnel, including sales personnel, to advise of the status of the strike, negotiations, etc.
5. Consider the advantages of a telephone "hot line" (recorded messages) to communicate with employees, customers, supervisors, etc. about the strike, negotiating issues, etc.
6. Provide information to strikers as to their right to return to work and limitations on union sanctions for their doing so.
7. Have mailing lists and preaddressed envelopes for sending letters to employees on short notice.

C. ADMINISTRATION OF PAY AND BENEFITS

1. Ensure that all strikers have been paid wages which were earned prior to strike.
2. Designate a person who will handle all claims or questions by strikers concerning pay and benefits.
3. Determine the eligibility of striking employees for medical insurance benefits, sickness and accident benefits, life insurance, etc.
   a. Are there different provisions for different classes of employees?
   b. Are opportunities for self-pay available?
   c. What are the state laws governing benefits for strikers?

Assigned To	Due Date

d. Determine whether employees who were off work due to disability when the strike began have any special status. Check the expected date of their return to work.

4. Notify insurance carriers of the strike and ensure no unjustified benefits are paid.
5. If the employer participates in any Taft-Hartley trust funds, determine the cutoff date for employer contributions and cutoff date for employee benefits.
6. Determine the status of strikers with respect to pension and profit-sharing plans.
7. Notify the state employment service of the strike and file necessary forms to protest payment of unemployment insurance benefits.
8. Determine the policy to be followed regarding payment of vested, but unused, vacation pay. (Caution: the employer must treat strikers as favorably as nonstrikers where vacation is vested.)
9. Determine the policy to be followed on continued participation in use of stock purchase plans, 401(K) plans, credit unions, employer-provided recreational facilities, cafeterias, transportation services, etc. (Caution: discriminatory treatment of strikers vis-a-vis nonstrikers may be an unfair labor practice.)
10. With regard to policy decisions concerning pay and benefits, check records to determine policies followed in any previous strikes.
11. Cease checkoff of union dues unless otherwise prevented from doing so.

D. <u>LEGAL MATTERS</u>

1. Ensure that the employer has competent labor law counsel, with experience in strike situations.
2. Ensure the availability of counsel on a day-to-day basis.

	Assigned To	Due Date
3. Determine permissible actions/statements concerning: a. Communications to employees. b. Hiring strike replacements (especially pay/ benefits). c. Surveillance of picketers. d. Scope of legally permissible conduct of picketers (speech, actions, signs). e. Rights of strikers to return to work and the extent of permissible union sanctions against those who return to work. f. Obligations under wage-hour laws to exempt employees who perform nonexempt work during a strike. g. Bargaining or refusal to bargain during a strike.		
4. Determine the type of evidence legal counsel will need to obtain court restraining orders or injunctions to control mass picketing and/or picket-line violence.		
5. Review property-line boundaries and public roads around the facility to determine legally permissible areas for picketing.		
6. If not previously done, brief legal counsel on the status and history of negotiations preceding the strike.		
7. Alert counsel as to operating conditions that could enmesh other employers in the strike. Seek advice and counsel as to ways of minimizing risk of other employers being picketed.		
8. Determine the scope of permissible disciplinary or discharge action against striking employees who engage in picket-line violence.		
9. Determine legal requirements for a "reserved gate" or "contractor's gate" in the event a contractor is to be employed during the strike on work other than that normally done by striking employees.		

Appendix 6

Sample Memorandum of Agreement

MEMORANDUM OF AGREEMENT

Widget Manufacturing Inc., Des Moines Iowa Plant ("Widget") and the Metalworkers International Union ("MIU") on behalf of its Local Union 345 agree to renew their collective bargaining agreement for a period of two years based upon the contract changes set forth below. This agreement is subject only to ratification by the members of Local 345. The retroactive improvements in this agreement are contingent upon Widget receiving from the union written notification of ratification of the agreement no later than midnight, September 20, 19__. All changes to be made in the first year of the agreement will be effective on the first regular workday following ratification of the agreement unless another effective date is set forth in this memorandum. The terms of the labor agreement which was in effect from August 1, 19__ through July 31, 19__, shall continue in effect except as specifically changed by the terms of this memorandum of agreement.

The parties agree as follows:

First Year (through 7/31/__)

1. General Wages—Effective August 1, 19__, all job classification wage rates set forth in the last labor agreement will be increased by 5%, rounded to the nearest half cent. This percentage increase shall be applied prior to the wage adjustment described in paragraph 2 below. Any and all retroactive wage payments shall be paid only to employees who are actively employed by Widget on the first workday following receipt of written notice of ratification.

2. Special Wage Adjustments—Effective August 1, 19__, the wage rates of the job classifications of "journeymen mechanics," "tool and die makers," and "lead persons" shall be increased by 35¢ per hour. Any and all retroactive wage payments shall be paid only to those employees who held the above-listed classifications on a regular basis during the retroactive period and who are actively employed by Widget on the first workday following receipt of written notice of ratification.

3. Health and Welfare—The present hospital, medical and surgical benefits shall remain in effect with the employer paying the full premium costs of such benefits, provided the monthly premium cost per employee on a composite rate basis does not exceed $ _____ per month. If the cost exceeds that amount the following will occur:

   (a) Within 30 days after receiving notice of the increase from the insurance carrier, the parties shall meet for the purpose of negotiating changes in benefits to reduce the monthly premium cost on a composite basis to $ _____ ; or

(b) Employee shall contribute a monthly amount which when added to the employer's contribution of $ _____ per month shall equal the monthly premium composite cost per employee charged by the insurance carrier; or

(c) A combination of (a) and (b) above which will assure that the employer's contribution does not exceed $ _____ per month per employee on a composite basis.

4. Shift Differentials

(a) The shift differential for the second shift shall be increased from ___¢ per hour to ___¢ per hour, and for the third shift from ___¢ per hour to ___¢ per hour.

(b) Shift differential shall no longer be included in the hourly rate for purposes of calculating holiday pay, vacation pay, funeral leave pay and jury duty pay. It shall, however, continue to be included in the hourly rate for purposes of calculating overtime pay (Contract language to implement this change is attached as Exhibit "A").

5. Vacations

(a) Commencing in the vacation year January 1, 19___ , through December 31, 19___ , employees who have completed ten (10) or more years of service but less than fifteen (15) years of service with the Company shall be entitled to receive four (4) weeks of paid vacation.

(b) Commencing in the vacation year of January 1, 19___ through December 31, 19___ , employees who have completed fifteen (15) or more years of service but less than twenty-five (25) years of service shall be entitled to receive five (5) weeks of paid vacation.

6. Call-Back Pay—Call-back pay shall be paid only to those employees who have punched out from their work area and have left the plant premises, and are recalled to work within the same workday (Contract language to implement this change is attached as Exhibit "B").

7. Other Contract Changes—In addition to the changes described above, the following additional changes have been agreed upon, and implementing contract language is attached in Exhibits "C" through "H" to this memorandum and made a part of the settlement agreement:

Exhibit C—Section 6—Break Periods

Exhibit D—Section 8—Seniority-Probationary Employees

Exhibit E—Section 10—Hours of Work—Daily work maximum

Exhibit F—Section 13—Tools—replacement of broken tools

Exhibit G—Section 15—Grievance Procedure—Modification in Step 3

Exhibit H—Section 27—Transfers of Work

Second Year (8/1/__–7/31/__)

(All changes to be effective August 1, 19__ unless otherwise specified)

1. General Wages—All wage rates set forth in the labor agreement shall be increased by __ ¢ per hour, except for unskilled jobs (i.e., those having a wage rate of $ ____ or less), which shall be increased by 3%.

2. Holidays—One floating holiday shall be deleted from the contract. In consideration thereof, all employees on the employer's payroll as of August 1, 19__ who have qualified for a floating holiday shall receive a lump sum payment of $150. This payment shall be made only once and is to be considered as a "buy-out" for the elimination of the paid floating holiday. Neither party makes any commitment as to negotiations on the subject of holidays for any future contracts.

3. Health and Welfare—Hospital, medical and surgical benefits in effect during the first year of this contract shall remain in effect provided the monthly premium cost per employee on a composite rate basis does not exceed $ ____ + 5% (i.e. 5% above the rate in effect during the first year of the contract). If the premium cost increases beyond this figure, the actions described in paragraph 3(a), (b) and (c) in the summary of the first year's contract changes shall be taken to assure the employer's contribution does not exceed $ __ + 5%.

4. Pensions—The basic benefit for normal retirement shall increase to $ ____ per month per year of service for employees who retire on or after January 1, 19__. Benefits for all other forms of retirement shall remain unchanged.

5. Shift Differentials—The shift differential for the second shift shall be increased from __ ¢ per hour to __ ¢ per hour and for the third shift from __ ¢ per hour to __ ¢ per hour.

6. Holiday Pay—Employees who are on layoff status shall qualify for holiday pay only for a period of 60 days from their last day worked prior to the beginning of the layoff. In no event may an employee receive payment for more than three holidays while on layoff during any one contract year, i.e., August 1 through July 31 of the following year. (Implementing contract language attached as Exhibit "I")

The above contract changes have been agreed upon by the representatives of the below-signed parties. All Union bargaining representatives agree to fully recommend ratification of the settlement to their membership.

Widget Manufacturing Inc.	Metalworkers International Union
By: ____________	By: ____________
Date ____________	Date ____________

Appendix 7

Labor Contract Checklist

The following outline/checklist sets forth a comprehensive list of provisions commonly found in collective bargaining agreements. The checklist can be a useful tool in the preparation and review of labor contracts. The fact that the checklist contains particular provisions should not be interpreted as a recommendation that they should be included in a labor contract—only that they are commonly found there.

PREAMBLE

- A. Statement of purpose of this agreement
- B. Any pledge of cooperation between parties to the agreement? To what end?
- C. Parties to the agreement
  - 1. Union
    - a. International
    - b. Local
    - c. Regional Union Organization
    - d. Combination of the above or one "on behalf of" another
  - 2. Employer
    - a. Corporation, sole proprietor, partnership
    - b. Division
    - c. Plant/Facility
    - d. Combination of the above or one "on behalf of" another

I. MANAGEMENT RIGHTS

- A. Enumerated Rights
  - 1. Hiring
  - 2. Production/Service Standards
  - 3. Work Scheduling
  - 4. Facility closure and relocation, subcontracting, etc.
  - 5. Staffing and crew sizes
  - 6. Decisions regarding all aspects of product and service
  - 7. Promulgation of rules and policies regarding conduct, dress, attendance, etc.
- B. Reserved Rights—All rights reserved to employer which are not specifically limited by labor contract

II. RECOGNITION

- A. Limit coverage to those employees working at specific geographical location(s)

B. Included job classifications or types of employees—list by job title or function
C. Excluded job classifications or types of employees (e.g., technical, managerial, supervisory, clerical, guards, etc.)—list by job title or function

III. UNION SECURITY

A. Type of union security:
    1. Open Shop
    2. Maintenance-of-membership
    3. Union Shop
    4. Agency Shop
    5. Other
B. Length of probationary period
C. Limit union shop obligation on employees solely to payment of duly authorized dues and initiation fees
D. Check-off of union dues
    1. Hold Harmless clause for management
    2. Period for revocation by employees

IV. HOURS OF WORK

A. Definition of workday
B. Definition of workweek
C. Definition of shifts
D. Statement as to no guarantee of hours of work
E. Right of management to change hours and schedules
F. Right of management to determine the numbers of hours per day & per week

V. OVERTIME

A. State the specific conditions which qualify employees for premium pay (time and one-half or double time):
    1. Over eight hours in one day?
    2. Over 40 hours in one week?
    3. Saturdays, as such?
    4. Sundays, as such?
    5. Sixth or seventh day in workweek?
    6. Work performed on a contractual holiday?
    7. Before or after scheduled workhours?
    8. Other
B. Exceptions to above:
    1. Maintenance work
    2. Guards, cleaners, janitors, etc.
    3. Power supply employees
    4. Other classifications
C. Employees not to be laid off to offset overtime hours?
D. Employees required to work overtime? Any conditions?
E. Distribution of overtime:

1. On basis of best qualified. Who determines?
2. On basis of seniority only
3. On basis of who normally performs work
4. On basis of seniority from among those qualified or from among those within a particular work group
5. Equal distribution? Over what period? As equal as practicable—not exact
6. Different rule of priority for overtime during week than on weekends?
7. Rotation plan. Count as work if offered but refuses?
8. Any records required. Open to union?

F. Pay limited to only one basis for calculating overtime, i.e., "no pyramiding."
G. Other

VI. <u>HOLIDAYS</u>

A. What days are holidays? When observed?
B. Requirements to be eligible for holiday pay:
   1. Length of service with employer or hours worked.
   2. Work day before and after; any exceptions? (e.g. industrial injury leave, layoff, etc.)
   3. Obligation to work if scheduled? Forfeiture of holiday pay?
C. Amount of holiday pay
   1. What rate?
      a. Straight time
      b. Rate of pay of regular job
      c. Rate of job worked during preceding week
   2. How many hours per day?
D. Time off work only if holiday falls on a scheduled workday.
E. What if holiday falls within a vacation period?
   1. An extra day off and holiday pay
   2. Just holiday pay
   3. Nothing
F. What if holiday falls on a weekend? Pay and/or extra day off?

VII. <u>SENIORITY</u>

A. Types of seniority:
   1. Job classification
   2. Departmental
   3. Plantwide
   4. Plantwide with labor pool
   5. Other
B. From what date is seniority calculated?
   1. Date of hire
   2. Date started to work
   3. Date of last hire
   4. Supervisory and/or salary personnel:

a. Only if promoted from bargaining unit job
b. Salaried retain full seniority rights from date of hire in bargaining unit job, and accumulate while in salaried position
c. Retain seniority only for time in bargaining unit before promotion out of bargaining unit
d. Retain only for specified period of time following exit from bargaining unit job (e.g. 6 mos. or 1 year)
e. Other arrangements

C. Filling Job Vacancies
1. Company decision on all new hires:
a. How many to employ
b. Whom to employ
c. Obligation to notify union of names of new hires?
2. Job openings are posted for bids? Exceptions for skilled trades or other key jobs?
a. Qualified bidder with most seniority. Any exceptions?
b. Employer selects bidder who is most qualified. Employer determines qualifications, subject to grievance procedure if union disputes selection.
c. Trial period?
d. Length of trial period?
e. Who determines qualifications during or at end of trial period?
f. What happens to employee if unsuccessful during trial period?
g. How long are bids posted?
h. How long are bids open?
i. Any time limit for bidder to be placed on bid job?
j. Any restrictions on eligibility to bid?
(1) Time since last change of jobs
(2) Qualifications
(3) Minimum length of service
(4) No bids, or limitations on bidding, to lower-rated jobs
(5) Other

D. Job Preference System
1. In addition to, or in lieu of, bidding
2. Employee indicates job preference before vacancy arises
3. Advance selection and training of potential replacements

E. Temporary vacancies
1. What is temporary? Length of time, specific causes of vacancy, other?
2. Are temporary jobs posted? If not, how filled?
3. What happens when employee whose absence caused temporary vacancy returns? What if he doesn't return?

F. Temporary transfers:
1. Any limitation on company rights to transfer employees?
2. Any maximum length of a temporary transfer?

a. To higher-paid job
b. To lower-paid job

G. Layoffs:

1. Any waiver of exercising seniority for short periods of layoff?
2. Must union be notified before employees are told?
3. Any minimum period of notice before layoff?
4. Who is laid off?
   a. By seniority only? Job? Department? Plant? Other?
   b. To what extent are qualifications determining?
5. Does laid-off employee have bumping rights?
   a. Who notifies employee?
   b. What restrictions on bumping rights?
      (1) Number of bumps?
      (2) Time limit for exercising bumping rights?
      (3) Jobs excluded from bumping?
   c. May employee refrain from bumping? Any penalty for doing so?

H. Recall after layoff:

1. Notify union before notifying employees?
2. Basis for recall
   a. Qualifications
   b. Seniority
   c. Combination of a. and b.
3. Consequences of employee not accepting recall?
4. How employees notified of recall?
5. Any provision not to hire until all laid-off employees have been recalled? Any exceptions because of qualifications?
6. What terminates seniority?
   a. Discharge
   b. Unexcused absence—how long?
   c. Tardiness
   d. Layoff in excess of specified period of time
   e. Failure to return when recalled from layoff within specified period of time
   f. Failure to return from a leave on schedule
   g. Working on another job while on leave without prior approval.
   h. Quit
   i. Other

I. Seniority list

1. Prepared how often?
2. Posted or distributed to whom? How often?
3. Types of seniority shown on list? Job, plant department?

VIII. <u>GRIEVANCE AND ARBITRATION</u>

A. Who is on union grievance committee?

1. Represent department or craft?

2. Plantwide?
3. Other
4. Limitation on number of persons on committee?
5. Minimum length of service in bargaining unit to qualify?

B. Is time off work allowed to investigate and process grievances?
1. With pay?
2. Without pay?
3. With pay only for working time lost?
4. Must get permission of foreman to leave job?

C. Definition of grievance
1. Limited to violations and interpretation of the contract
2. No limitations
3. Other

D. Does employer have right to file a grievance? Same or different basis than employee grievances? Right to grieve alleged violation of no strike clause?

E. Time limit within which a grievance must be filed?

F. Describe steps in the grievance procedure and the time limit at each step. At what point must grievance be in writing?

G. At what point does a grievance go to arbitration?

H. Procedure for expedited arbitration? Work stoppage cases? Other?

I. Describe arbitration procedure
1. How Arbitrator selected? Permanent arbitrator, panel, FMCS or AAA list?
2. Who pays arbitrator? 50/50? Loser pays all?
3. Use of transcripts or tape recordings of hearings?
4. Any limitation on authority of arbitrator? Interpretation of contract only; can't add to, delete from or modify?
5. Other provisions

J. What happens if either party refuses to arbitrate or comply with Arbitrator's award?

IX. LEAVE OF ABSENCE

A. Reasons for leave of absence
1. Illness; industrial or non-industrial
2. Personal reasons
3. Death in family
4. Union business
5. Military service
6. Maternity
7. Jury Service; trial or grand jury?
8. Other

B. Who decides whether a request for a leave will be granted or denied?

C. Written request required? Written confirmation?

D. Time limits (minimum and maximum) of a leave?

E. Penalty if employee does not return from a leave on schedule. Any exceptions?

F. Does seniority accrue during a leave of absence?
G. Limitation on other employment while on leave?
H. Other

X. WAGES

A. Job content
   1. Are job descriptions used?
      a. Prepared by whom?
      b. Approved by whom?
   2. Do job descriptions limit assignments of other duties not included in description? Permit other duties to be assigned by supervisor?
   3. How often are job descriptions reviewed or updated?
B. How job rates determined by
   1. Straight bargaining. Opportunity to renegotiate rates if substantial changes in job content or new jobs instituted during contract term? What if no agreement reached?
      a. Arbitration?
      b. Defer to next contract negotiation? If increase agreed to is it retroactive?
      c. Right to strike?
   2. Based on job evaluation:
      a. Prepared by whom?
      b. Approved by whom?
   3. Other.
C. Rate schedules
   1. Single rates; per hour, per week, per month
   2. Rate ranges? Basis for determining rate paid within range?
   3. Production Incentive Rate/Bonus
      a. How determined? Changed?
      b. Participation by union?
      c. Detailed or summary description of plan?
      d. Arbitrability of rates, plan changes, etc.?
D. Shift differentials
   1. Rate for designated hours or shifts?
   2. Provisions for odd shifts or mixed shifts?
   3. Limited to scheduled shifts or hours actually worked during applicable shift?
E. Any lead-person rates?
F. Any "red-circle" rates? How established? Eliminated?
G. Wage increases within rate ranges based on
   1. Length of service only.
   2. Merit only. Determined by whom?
   3. Length of service if work is satisfactory
   4. Time schedule for increases or consideration of increases
H. Any provisions for wage decreases within rate ranges? On what basis?

I. Pay for temporary jobs, other than regular jobs?
   1. Higher-paying jobs
   2. Lower-paying jobs
   3. Employee solicits assignment vs. employer designates assignment
   4. Time limitations on rate retention

J. Call-in or call-back pay
   1. Conditions under which it is paid? Not paid?
   2. Minimum hours to be paid? Include time worked in determining minimum?
   3. Limitations on payment? Jobs, conditions necessitating, call, etc.?
   4. Definition of call-in or call-back

K. Reporting or "Show-Up" Pay
   1. Conditions under which it is paid? Not paid?
   2. Minimum pay—include time worked as an offset to minimum payment?
   3. Exception for extenuating circumstances beyond employer's control

L. Paydays:
   1. Weekly
   2. Bi-weekly
   3. Other. Consider legal requirements

M. Termination of Severance Pay:
   1. Payment of accrued but unpaid vacations; pro rata pay
   2. Basis of severance payment.
      a. Flat sum
      b. Percentage of earnings
      c. Years of service
      d. Other
   3. Reasons causing or affecting termination pay
      a. Plant or facility closure
      b. Technological change
      c. Work permanently contracted outside bargaining unit
      d. No notice given
   4. Receipt of termination pay triggers loss of all employment rights

XI. VACATIONS

A. Eligibility:
   1. Length of service
   2. Number of hours worked in given period
   3. Credit for time accrued during Layoff
   4. Credit for time lost due to accident or illness
   5. Credit for time related to pay for compensated non-work time, e.g. vacations, holidays, etc.

6. Completion of hours worked (or credit therefor) requirements by specified date

B. Employees leaving company to receive accrued vacation benefits?
   1. Death
   2. Discharge
   3. Quit
   4. Layoff for extended periods
   5. Basis for calculation
      a. Pro rata for accrued time
      b. Full pay as if all qualifications met

C. Part-time and seasonal employees:
   1. No rights
   2. Computed on basis of hours worked
   3. Pay based on specified ratio of hours worked

D. Vacation periods
   1. Non-uniform periods—Individual employee year
      a. Based on date of hire
   2. Uniform vacation period
      a. From ____________________ to ______________________
      b. Plantwide shutdown at company's option
      c. Choice of vacation by seniority; limit on number per job/department/plant
      d. Limitation on time off; e.g., weekly increments; maximum number of consecutive weeks

E. Vacation rights of laid-off employees

F. Option to work instead of taking vacation

G. Vacation pay. How calculated?
   1. Flat amount per week of vacation
   2. Hours per week of vacation entitlement
   3. Straight time rate
   4. Average rate; regular job? Rate of job held just prior to vacation
   5. Percentage of annual earnings, gross or net

H. Returning servicemen:
   1. Vacation time accummulates
   2. Entitled to present year's vacation only
   3. Military service counts toward years worked

I. Arrangements for holiday falling during vacation period
   1. Pay only
   2. Additional time off

J. Amount of vacation time
   1. One week after X year(s) of service
   2. Two weeks after X years of service
   3. Three weeks after X years of service
   4. Four weeks after X years of service
   5. Other

XII. LIMITATIONS ON UNION ACTIVITIES

A. No union meetings during working time or on company property
B. No access by union business agents, except with approval of employer
C. No distribution of literature on company property
D. No solicitation of members for union or other non-employer matters during working time
E. How are meetings with Company arranged?
   1. Regular schedule
   2. On call. By Whom?
   3. Other combinations

XIII. DISCIPLINE

A. Warnings
   1. Verbal
   2. Written
   3. Number
   4. Penalties provided for each act?
B. Disciplinary action:
   1. Union notification prior to action required?
   2. Company sole judge
C. Discharge requiring no warning:
   1. Specific list
   2. General policy determined by management
D. Suspension during investigation
E. Subject to grievance procedure. Any time limit to file a grievance?

XIV. DISCHARGE

A. Causes:
   1. Violations of specific rules in contract
   2. Violation of posted rules or company policies
   3. Causes not limited to those listed
B. Types:
   1. Without notice.
   2. With notice and after warnings
C. Rights of employer:
   1. Full and unquestioned
   2. Subject to union review
   3. Subject to submission to grievance procedure
   4. Other
D. Notice and explanation of discharge:
   1. Prior notice
   2. Exceptions
   3. Union notified

XV. MILITARY SERVICE

A. Applies only to draftees or members of reserve called to duty
B. Retain seniority during service
C. Accumulate seniority during service
D. Offer same or comparable job on return, provided employee still has ability
E. Receive all general increases granted during absence
F. Credit military service for vacation benefits or other benefits based upon length of service

XVI. PUBLIC ELECTIONS

A. Employees vote on own time where possible
B. Specified number of hours granted for voting when can't be done on own time
C. Other. Consider state laws

XVII. BULLETIN BOARDS (for use of union)

A. Number per plant or department
B. Placement
C. Posted notices to be approved by company
D. Who does posting?
E. Limitations on type or content of notices

XVIII. SAFETY

A. Company requires that specified safety equipment be worn or used
B. Company determines all safety practices adopted
C. Company and union appoint safety committee to work together:
   1. Composition
   2. Authority
D. Discipline or discharge for violation of safety rules
E. Who pays for personal safety equipment?
   1. Eye and hearing protection
   2. Shoes
   3. Special clothes
   4. Other

XIX. "SAVING" CLAUSE

A. Provide for preservation of lawful portions of contract when one or more provisions are illegal
B. How is legality to be determined?

XX. STRIKES AND LOCKOUTS

A. No-strike, no-lockout provisions
B. Grievance procedure and arbitration must be relied upon
C. Employees to continue working pending grievance processing

D. Union cooperation in wildcat strike. State obligations of union to end wildcat
E. Dismissal of leaders and/or participants in wildcat strike
F. Provisions for cooling-off period
G. Notification required before legitimate strike called
H. Include slowdowns and refusals to report for work
I. Include specific prohibition against honoring of "stranger picket line."
J. Possible provision for expedited arbitration of employer-initiated grievance for violation of no-strike clause

XXI. DURATION OF CONTRACT

A. Length of term
   1. Specify beginning and expiration date
   2. At what time on expiration date does contract expire?
B. Automatic extensions
C. Other extensions
D. Any provision to reopen or cancel before end of term?
E. When and how is contract reopened for negotiations prior to expiration date?
F. What is status of contract if negotiations extend beyond expiration date?
G. Are re-opening and termination notices both required?
H. Any particular requirements as to form, address, or means of transmission of required notices

Notes

Chapter 1

1. D. McDonald, Union Man 265 (1969).
2. It is, of course, possible for the employer operating multiple facilities to structure its business and management organization in such a way as to influence the NLRB decision on which type of bargaining unit it finds appropriate. Such factors as common labor relations management, integration of product and work force, and similarity of working conditions will be important determinants.
3. Bureau of Labor Statistics, U.S. Dep't of Labor, Bull. No. 2095, *Characteristics of Major Collective Bargaining Agreements—January 1, 1980* (table 1.8) (1981).
4. Charles D. Bonanno Linen Serv., Inc. v. NLRB, 454 U.S. 656, 109 LRRM 2257 (1982); NLRB v. Custom Wood Specialties, Inc., 622 F.2d 381, 104 LRRM 2530 (8th Cir. 1980). The limitation on withdrawal may, however, be negated by "unusual circumstances," such as the union's execution of a separate agreement with one member of the multiemployer unit. Corson & Gruman Co., 284 NLRB 1316, 126 LRRM 1279 (1987); Marbro Co., Inc., 284 NLRB 1303, 126 LRRM 1281 (1987).
5. Although this is the general rule, if the employer's other facilities are sufficiently separate from the standpoints of geography, general management, labor relations management, and other criteria, it may be illegal for the union to picket such employer's other facilities; Electrical Workers (IBEW) Local 2208 (Simplex Wire and Cable Co.), 285 NLRB 834, 128 LRRM 1143 (1987); Newspaper Guild, Local 69 (Los Angeles) (Hearst Corp.), 185 NLRB 303, 75 LRRM 1014 (1970), *enf'd*, 443 F.2d 1173, 77 LRRM 2895 (9th Cir. 1971); Television & Radio Artists (Hearst Corp., Baltimore News Am. Div.), 185 NLRB 593, 75 LRRM 1018 (1970), *enf'd*, 462 F.2d 887, 80 LRRM 2001 (D.C. Cir. 1972).

6. Teamsters Local No. 560 (Curtin Matheson Scientific), 248 NLRB 1212, 104 LRRM 1003 (1980); NLRB v. Electrical Workers IUE, Local 459, 228 F.2d 553, 37 LRRM 2219 (2d Cir. 1955).
7. For a study of productivity improvements in a large paper mill that was operated by salaried employees during a strike *see* Riggs, *Part I, Productivity Improvements: Learning From a Strike Situation*, INDUS. ENGINEERING (May 1980), and *Part II, Lessons From a Strike—Productivity Cluster and Progressive Productivity Index*, INDUS. ENGINEERING (June 1980).
8. Airline Deregulation Act of 1978, 49 U.S.C. Sec. 1301, et. seq.
9. Kennedy v. Long Island R.R., 319 F.2d 366, 53 LRRM 2545 (2d Cir.), *cert. denied*, 375 U.S. 830, 54 LRRM 2313 (1963).
10. Operating Engineers, Local 12 (Associated Gen. Contractors), 187 NLRB 430, 76 LRRM 1033 (1970).
11. Omnibus Budget Reconciliation Act of 1981, Pub. L. 97-35, 95 Stat. 357 (OBRA) §109; Lyng. v. Automobile Workers, 485 US 360, 127 LRRM 2977 (1988).

Chapter 2

1. Timken Co., 301 NLRB No. 84, 137 LRRM 1184 (1991); United Gilsonite Laboratories, 291 NLRB 924, 131 LRRM 1034 (1988).
2. SE-MA-NO Elec. Coop., 284 NLRB 1006, 125 LRRM 1349 (1987); Anchorage Laundry & Dry Cleaning Ass'n, 216 NLRB 114, 88 LRRM 1219 (1975); Sawyer Stores, Inc., 190 NLRB 651, 77 LRRM 1434 (1971).
3. Royal Packing Co., 198 NLRB 1060, 81 LRRM 1059 (1971), *aff'd*, 495 F.2d 1075, 86 LRRM 2571 (D.C. Cir. 1974); Fort Smith Chair Co., 143 NLRB 514, 53 LRRM 1313 (1963), *aff'd*, 336 F.2d 738, 55 LRRM 2290 (D.C. Cir.), *cert. denied*, 379 U.S. 838, 57 LRRM 2239 (1964).
4. United Artists Communications, Inc. 274 NLRB 75, 118 LRRM 1353 (1985), *aff'd sub nom.*, IATSE v. NLRB 779 F.2d 552, 121 LRRM 2237 (9th Cir. 1985), *cert. denied*, 477 U.S. 904, 122 LRRM 2656 (1986).

Chapter 3

1. For example, if concessions can be obtained in seniority and scheduling which are estimated to result in labor cost savings of .5% per year over a three-year period, the total savings would be 1.5% (not compounded), and therefore a "dividend" of 0.75% in labor cost improvements could be granted.
2. F. ELKOURI & E. ELKOURI, HOW ARBITRATION WORKS 357 (4th ed. 1985).

Chapter 4

1. For the most comprehensive of these, *see* THE DEVELOPING LABOR LAW (T. O'Reilly 2d ed. 1989).
2. Temple-Eastex, Inc., 228 NLRB 203, 96 LRRM 1424 (1977).
3. NLRB v. Truitt Mfg., 351 U.S. 149, 38 LRRM 2024 (1955).
4. Johns-Manville Sales Corp., 252 NLRB 368, 105 LRRM 1379 (1980). White Furniture Co., 161 NLRB 444, 63 LRRM 1277 (1966).
5. Oregon Coast Operators Ass'n, 113 NLRB 1338, 36 LRRM 1448 (1955).
6. Sylvania Elec. Prods., 154 NLRB 1756, 60 LRRM 1178 (1965).
7. Johns-Manville Prods., 171 NLRB 451, 69 LRRM 1068 (1968).
8. Detroit Edison Co., 218 NLRB 1024, 89 LRRM 1515 (1975).
9. General Elec. Co., 192 NLRB 68, 77 LRRM 1561 (1971).
10. General Elec. Co. v. NLRB, 466 F.2d 1177, 81 LRRM 2303 (6th Cir. 1972).
11. International News Serv., Div. of Hearst Corp., 113 NLRB 1067, 36 LRRM 1454 (1955).
12. Hughes Tool Co., 100 NLRB 208, 30 LRRM 1265 (1952).
13. This does not include the subject of possible retention by supervisors of seniority within the bargaining unit.
14. An exception to this exists where the union has proposed a dues checkoff clause. An employer may lawfully insist on an indemnification provision in a clause requiring payroll deduction of union dues.
15. Teamsters Local 515 v. NLRB, 906 F.2d 719, 134 LRRM 2481 (D.C. Cir. 1990) *enforcing in part, denying in part* 288 NLRB 69, 127 LRRM 1265 (1988); Boise Cascade Corp. v. NLRB, 860 F.2d 471, 129 LRRM 2744 (D.C. Cir. 1988), *enforcing* 283 NLRB 462, 124 LRRM 1391 (1987).
16. Associated Bldg. Contractors of Evansville, Inc., 143 NLRB 678, 53 LRRM 1395 (1963), *enf'd as to this issue sub nom.* NLRB vs. Painters Union, 334 F.2d 729, 56 LRRM 2648 (7th Cir. 1964).
17. General Elec. Co., Battery Prods. Dep't, 163 NLRB 198, 64 LRRM 1312 (1967).
18. Griffin Inns, 229 NLRB 199, 95 LRRM 1072 (1977).
19. Bartlett-Collins Co., 237 NLRB 770, 99 LRRM 1034 (1978).
20. Colfor, Inc., 282 NLRB 1173, 124 LRRM 1204 (1987); Interstate Paper Supply Co., 251 NLRB 1423, 105 NLRB 1480 (1980); Federal Pac. Elec. Co., 203 NLRB 571, 83 LRRM 1201 (1973), *enf'd in pertinent part sub nom.* Electrical Workers IBEW, Local 2338 v. NLRB, 499 F.2d 542, 86 LRRM 2814 (D.C. Cir. 1974).
21. Tennessee Chair Co., 126 NLRB No. 160, 45 LRRM 1472 (1960).
22. Co-Jo, Inc. d/b/a/ Clinton Food 4 Less, 288 NLRB 597, 130 LRRM 1441 (1988); General Motors Acceptance Corp. v. NLRB,

476 F.2d 850, 82 LRRM 3093 (1st Cir. 1973), *enforcing* 196 NLRB 137, 79 LRRM 1662 (1972).

23. Medical Towers, Ltd., 285 NLRB 1011, 127 LRRM 1152 (1987); National Amusement, Inc., 155 NLRB 1200, 60 LRRM 1485 (1965).
24. A.H. Belo Corp., 170 NLRB 1558, 69 LRRM 1239 (1968); General Elec. Co., 150 NLRB 192, 57 LRRM 1491 (1964), *aff'd*, 418 F.2d 736, 72 LRRM 2530 (2d Cir. 1969), *cert. denied*, 397 U.S. 965, 73 LRRM 2600 (1970).
25. Yearbook House, Subsidiary of Shaw Barton, 223 NLRB 1456, 92 LRRM 1191 (1976).
26. Pacific Grinding Wheel Co., 220 NLRB 214, 90 LRRM 1557 (1975); Big Three Indus., Inc., 201 NLRB 700, 82 LRRM 1454 (1973).
27. Howmet Corp., 197 NLRB 471, 80 LRRM 1555 (1972).
28. U.S. Gypsum Co., 200 NLRB 1098, 82 LRRM 1064 (1972).
29. NLRB v. American Nat'l Ins. Co., 343 U.S. 395, 30 LRRM 2147 (1952).
30. L. W. LeFort Co., 290 NLRB 344, 130 LRRM 1180 (1988); Aero Alloys, 289 NLRB 497, 130 LRRM 1383 (1988).
31. Prentice-Hall, Inc., 290 NLRB 646, 129 LRRM 1052 (1988); Reed & Prince Mfg. Co., 205 F.2d 131, 32 LRRM 2225 (CA 1, 1953).
32. Tri-Produce Co., 300 NLRB No. 137, 137 LRRM 1022 (1990); Loggins Meat Co., 206 NLRB 303, 84 LRRM 1270 (1973).
33. Pittsburgh-Des Moines Corp. v. NLRB, 663 F.2d 956, 109 LRRM 2089 (9th Cir. 1981).
34. Midwest Casting Corp., 194 NLRB 523, 79 LRRM 1098 (1971).
35. Atlas Metal Parts Co. v. NLRB, 660 F.2d 304, 108 LRRM 2474 (7th Cir. 1981). But compare to situation where employer withdrew all proposals and agreements following a strike. Trumbull Memorial Hosp., 288 NLRB 1429, 130 LRRM 1400 (1988).
36. Taylor Bus Serv., 284 NLRB 530, 128 LRRM 1073 (1987); NLRB v. Ralph Printing & Lithography Co., 433 F.2d 1058, 75 LRRM 2267 (8th Cir. 1970).
37. Clothing Workers v. NLRB, 324 F.2d 228, 54 LRRM 2477 (2d Cir.), *reversing* 140 NLRB 1292, 52 LRRM 1222 (1963).
38. Haddon Craftsman, Inc., 300 NLRB No. 100, 136 LRRM 1190 (1990); AAA Motor Lines, 215 NLRB 793, 88 LRRM 1253 (1975).
39. Chicago Tribune Co., 304 NLRB No. 62, 138 LRRM 1065 (1991); North Kingstown Nursing Care Center, 244 NLRB 54, 102 LRRM 1193 (1979); Rust Craft Broadcasting, 225 NLRB 327, 92 LRRM 1576 (1976); Wabash Transformer Corp., 215 NLRB 546, 88 LRRM 1511 (1974).

40. LaMousee, Inc., 259 NLRB 37, 108 LRRM 1356 (1981); Weather Tec. Corp., 238 NLRB 1535, 99 LRRM 1709 (1978); Peerless Food Prods. Inc., 236 NLRB 161, 98 LRRM 1182 (1978).
41. Madison Indus., 290 NLRB 1226, 129 LRRM 1323 (1988); J.I. Case v. NLRB, 321 U.S. 332, 14 LRRM 501 (1944).
42. Logemann Bros., 298 NLRB No. 155, 134 LRRM 1251 (1990); Dow Chem. Co., 215 NLRB 910, 88 LRRM 1625 (1975).
43. Lear Siegler, Inc., 283 NLRB 929, 126 LRRM 1073 (1987); Ampac, Subsidiary of Kane-Miller Corp., 259 NLRB 1075, 109 LRRM 1075 (1982); T.M. Cobb Co., 224 NLRB 694, 93 LRRM 1047 (1976).
44. United Technologies, 274 NLRB 609, 118 LRRM 1445 (1985) and 274 NLRB 1069, 118 LRRM 1556 (1985).
45. Airport Parking Management v. NLRB, 720 F.2d 610, 114 NLRB 3484 (9th Cir. 1983) *enforcing* 264 NLRB 5, 112 LRRM 1013 (1982).
46. NLRB v. Mackay Radio & Tel. Co., 304 U.S. 333, 2 LRRM 610 (1938).
47. Clear Pine Mouldings, 268 NLRB 1044, 115 LRRM 1113 (1984), *enf'd* 765 F.2d 148, 120 LRRM 2631 (9th Cir. 1985); NLRB v. Washington Aluminum Co., 370 U.S. 9, 50 LRRM 2235 (1962).
48. Laidlaw Corp., 171 NLRB 1366, 68 LRRM 1252 (1968), *enf'd*, 414 F.2d 99, 71 LRRM 3054 (7th Cir. 1969).
49. Belknap, Inc. v. Hale, 463 U.S. 491, 113 LRRM 3057 (1983).
50. American Ship Bldg. v. NLRB, 380 U.S. 300, 58 LRRM 2672 (1965).
51. Boilermakers Local 88 v. NLRB, 858 F.2d 756, 129 LRRM 2569 (D.C. Cir. 1988), *enforcing* 281 NLRB 593, 124 LRRM 1314 (1986); Harter Equip. Inc., 280 NLRB 597, 122 LRRM 1219 (1986), *enf'd sub nom.* Local 825, Int. Union of Oper. Engrs. v. NLRB, 829 F.2d 458, 126 LRRM 2337 (3d Cir. 1987).

Chapter 5

1. Litton Microwave Cooking Prods., 301 NLRB 30, 136 LRRM 1163 (1991); WPIX Inc., 293 NLRB 10, 131 LRRM 1780 (1989); NLRB v. Lloyd J. Taylor, 141 NLRB 765, 52 LRRM 1407 (1963), *enf'd*, 338 F.2d 1003, 57 LRRM 2560 (5th Cir. 1964).

Chapter 6

1. C. McCabe, THE FEARLESS SPECTATOR 81-82 (1970), copyright © San Francisco Chronicle. Reprinted by permission.

Chapter 7

1. General Elec. Co., 150 NLRB 192, 57 LRRM 1491 (1964), *enf'd*, 118 F.2d 736, 72 LRRM 2530 (2d Cir. 1969), *cert. denied*, 397 U.S. 965, 73 LRRM 2600 (1970).
2. In order to obtain an injunction to enforce a no-strike clause in a labor agreement, the *Boys Markets* rule requires that the dispute which caused a strike be subject to the grievance/arbitration provisions of the labor agreement. Westmorland Coal Co. v. United Mine Workers, 910 F.2d 130, 134 LRRM 3192 (4th Cir. 1990); Buffalo Forge Co. v. United Steelworkers, 428 U.S. 397, 92 LRRM 3032 (1976); Retail Clerks v. Boys Markets, Inc., 398 U.S. 235, 74 LRRM 2257 (1970).

Chapter 8

1. For further discussion of negotiating health insurance, see ———, NEGOTIATING HEALTH INSURANCE IN THE WORKPLACE: A BASIC GUIDE (1992).
2. Hertz Corp., 91 LA 261 (Frost, 1988); Plover Police Dep't, 89 LA 322 (Vernon, 1987); Polygram Distrib., Inc., 83 LA 249 (Gibson, 1984).
3. Hassett Maintenance Corp., 260 NLRB 1211, 109 LRRM (1982).
4. Martin E. Segal Co., Executive Letter Vol. 15, No. 1. 1991.
5. Allied Chem. & Alkali Workers Local 1 v. Pittsburgh Plate Glass Co., 404 U.S. 157, 78 LRRM 1433 (1972).
6. Anderson v. Alpha Portland Indus., 727 F.2d 177, 115 LRRM 2249 (8th Cir. 1984), *reh'g en banc*, 752 F.2d 1293, 118 LRRM 2265 (8th Cir.), *cert. denied*, 471 U.S. 1102, 119 LRRM 2248 (1985), *aff'd*, 836 F.2d 1512 (8th Cir. 1988).
7. *Smith v. ABS Industries*, 890 F.2d 841, 133 LRRM 2001 (6th Cir. 1989).
8. Financial Accounting Standards Board, *Statement of Financial Accounting Standards* No. 106—"Employer's Accounting for Postretirement Benefits other than Pensions."
9. Consolidated Budget Reconciliation Act, 26 U.S.C. 4980 B (1985).
10. A "composite cost" is simply a weighted average of the costs of all types of coverages, (i.e., employee only, employee and spouse, full family coverage).

Chapter 10

1. For an excellent detailed treatise on labor contract costing, *see* M. GRANOF, HOW TO COST YOUR LABOR CONTRACT (1973).

2. One minor caveat to this statement occurs when a change in one or more rollup fringe benefits is negotiated at the same time as a wage increase. To be completely accurate, either the rollup factor should be readjusted to recognize the additional benefit cost(s) or the percentage increase negotiated in wages should be multiplied by the cost of the additional benefit(s).
3. GRANOF, *supra* note 1, at 39-41.
4. This statement does not apply where fringe benefits contributions are paid as part of the normal hourly costs, as is common in the construction industry.
5. For an excellent explanation of this type of labor cost analysis, *see* GRANOF, *supra* note 1, at 83-126.
6. Globe Business Furniture, 290 NLRB 841, 130 LRRM 1492 (1988); Hall Indus., 285 NLRB 391, 126 LRRM 1162 (1987); Nestle Co., 238 NLRB 92, 99 LRRM 1241 (1978).
7. Although the author is not aware of any cases directly bearing on this point, it seems doubtful that an employer would be obligated to share its cost computations with the union when the union has the basic data from which it can make its own computations.

Chapter 12

1. 945 F.2d 889 (7th Cir. 1991).

Chapter 13

1. Simplex Wire and Cable Co., 285 NLRB 834, 128 LRRM 1143 (1987); Newspaper Guild, Local 69 (Los Angeles) (Hearst Corp.), 185 NLRB 303, 75 LRRM 1014 (1970), *enf'd*, 443 F.2d 1173, 77 LRRM 2895 (9th Cir. 1971); Television & Radio Artists (Hearst Corp., Baltimore News Am. Div.), 185 NLRB 593, 75 LRRM 1018 (1970), *enf'd*, 462 F.2d 887, 80 LRRM 2001 (CA DC, 1972).
2. Sailors Union of the Pacific, 92 NLRB 547, 27 LRRM 1108 (1950). (This is the "Moore Dry Dock" case.)
3. Electrical Workers IUE, Local 761 v. NLRB, 366 U.S. 667, 48 LRRM 2210 (1961).
4. NLRB v. Electrical Workers IUE, Local 459, 228 F.2d 553, 37 LRRM 2219 (2d Cir. 1955), *cert. denied*, 351 U.S. 962, 38 LRRM 2211 (1956).
5. NLRB v. Mackay Radio & Tel. Co., 304 U.S. 333, 2 LRRM 610 (1938).
6. Vulcan-Hart Corp. v. NLRB, 718 F.2d 269, 114 LRRM 2745 (8th Cir. 1983), *enforcing* 262 NLRB 167, 110 LRRM 1302 (1982) and 263 NLRB 477, 111 LRRM 1022 (1982); NLRB v. Pecheur Loz-

enge Co., 209 F.2d 393, 33 LRRM 2324 (2d Cir. 1953), *cert. denied*, 347 U.S. 953, 34 LRRM 2027 (1954).

7. Clear Pine Moldings, 268 NLRB 1044, 115 LRRM 1113 (1984), *enf'd* 765 F.2d 148, 120 LRRM 2631 (9th Cir. 1985); Washington Aluminum Co., 370 U.S. 9, 50 LRRM 2235 (1962).
8. Huck Mfg. v. NLRB, 693 F.2d 1176, 112 LRRM 2245 (5th Cir. 1982) *enforcing* 254 NLRB 739, 106 LRRM 1319 (1981) and 255 NLRB 170, 106 LRRM 1339 (1981); J. H. Bonck, 170 NLRB 1471, 69 LRRM 1172 (1968).
9. GHR Energy Corp., 294 NLRB No. 76, 133 LRRM 1069 (1989); Marbro Co., 284 NLRB 1303, 126 LRRM 1282 (1987); Imperial Outdoor Advertising, 192 NLRB 1248, 78 LRRM 1208 (1971), *enf'd*, 470 F.2d 484, 81 LRRM 2908 (8th Cir. 1972).
10. Walker Die Casting v. NLRB, 682 F.2d 592, 111 LRRM 2457 (6th Cir. 1982); NLRB v. Randle-Eastern Ambulance Serv., 584 F.2d 720, 99 LRRM 3377 (5th Cir. 1978).
11. Pittsburgh-Des Moines Steel Corp., 663 F.2d 956, 109 LRRM 2089 (9th Cir. 1981).

Chapter 14

1. Talbert Mfg., Inc., 250 NLRB 174, 104 LRRM 1543 (1980); Pan N Save Corp., 210 NLRB 311, 86 LRRM 1457 (1974).
2. *The Strike: The Winners, The Losers, and Who Did WHAT to WHOM*, SPORTS ILLUSTRATED 22 (Nov. 29, 1982).
3. *Id.* at 19.
4. Smithfield Packing Co., 303 NLRB No. 74, 137 LRRM 1404 (1991); Anheuser-Busch, Inc. v. Teamsters, Local 822, 584 F.2d 41, 99 LRRM 2539 (4th Cir. 1978).
5. Tampa Sheet Metal Co., 288 NLRB 322, 129 LRRM 1188 (1988); Robbins Door and Sash Co., 260 NLRB 659, 109 LRRM 1181 (1982); Bethlehem Steel Co., 133 NLRB No. 136, 49 LRRM 1016 (1961), *enf'd as to this issue*, 320 F.2d 615, 53 LRRM 2878 (3d Cir. 1963).
6. Deluxe Metal Furniture Co., 121 NLRB 995, 42 LRRM 1470 (1958).
7. *See* NLRB §9(c)(1)(B), 29 U.S.C. §159(c)(1)(B).
8. Thomas Indus. v. NLRB, 687 F.2d 863, 111 LRRM 2233 (6th Cir. 1982); Struksnes Constr. Co., 165 NLRB 1062, 65 LRRM 1385 (1967).
9. Colonial Manor Convalescent Nursing Center, 188 NLRB 861, 76 LRRM 1445 (1971).
10. NLRB v. Powell Elec. Mfg., 906 F.2d 1007, 134 LRRM 2732 (5th Cir. 1990) *enforcing* 287 NLRB 969, 127 LRRM 1239 (1987); Viking Lithographers, Inc., 148 NLRB 139, 74 LRRM 1407 (1970).

11. Madison Indus., 290 NLRB 1226, 129 LRRM 1323 (1988); Bennett Packaging Co., 285 NLRB 602, 129 LRRM 1245 (1987).
12. General Elec. Co., 150 NLRB 192, 194, 57 LRRM 1491 (1964), *enf'd*, 418 F.2d 736, 72 LRRM 2530 (2d Cir. 1969), *cert. denied*, 397 U.S. 965, 73 LRRM 2600 (1970).

Chapter 15

1. Boys Markets, Inc. v. Retail Clerks, 398 U.S. 235, 74 LRRM 2257 (1970).
2. Electrical Workers IUE, Local 461 v. Singer Co., 540 F. Supp. 442, 110 LRRM 2407 (D.C. N.J. 1982).
3. Columbus & S. Ohio Elec. Co., 270 NLRB 686, 116 LRRM 1148 (1984), *enf'd sub nom.* Electrical Workers (IBEW) Local 1466 v. NLRB, 795 F.2d 150, 122 LRRM 2948 (D.C. Cir. 1986).
4. Haddon Craftsman, Inc., 300 NLRB No. 100, 136 LRRM 1190 (1990); W. W. Grainger, Inc. v. NLRB, 860 F.2d 244, 129 LRRM 2718 (7th Cir. 1988).
5. Dubuque Packing Co., 303 NLRB No. 66, 137 LRRM 1185 (1991), *supplementing* 287 NLRB 477, 130 LRRM 1151 (1987).
6. First Nat'l Maintenance Co. v. NLRB, 452 U.S. 666, 107 LRRM 2705 (1981).
7. Memorandum and White Paper from IAM President George J. Korpias to union representatives, GL-6 (Sept. 14, 1990).
8. Donald F. Ephlin, Vice President and Director, G.M. Department, *United Auto Workers: Pioneers in Labor Management Partnership*, Ch. 10, in TEAMWORK, JOINT LABOR-MANAGEMENT PROGRAMS IN AMERICA (1986).
9. Irving Bluestone, *Joint Action and Collective Bargaining—and Vice Versa*, Ch. 4, in TEAMWORK, JOINT LABOR-MANAGEMENT PROGRAMS IN AMERICA (1986).

Index

A

Ability to pay 122, 469
Abusive language 180–81
Acceptance of management offer (*see also* Ratification of contract)
  added benefit for 426–27
  deadline for 424–25
Across-the-board increases (*see* Wages)
Agenda (*see also* Proposals and counterproposals)
  of management
    development 109–118
    for first contract 460–67
    pitfalls 113–16
    presenting 164–66
  of union
    advance receipt by management 157
    clarification 158–63
    evaluation 166–72
    limitation on additions 163–64
    pending grievances and 157–58
    pitfalls of clarifying 160–63
    responding 163, 172–75, 181–83
Agreement(s) (*see also* Offers and counteroffers; Settlements)
  clauses
    checklist 526–37
    mutual 336–37
  confirming when tentative 148–49
  contingent commitment 368–69
  costing of (*see* Cost estimating)
  effective dates of 339
  language of (*see* Drafting contract language)
  long-term (*see* Term of contract)
  memorandum of 441–44, 523–25
  "most favored nations" clause 370
  other employers' 29–31, 70–75
  preparing final contract 450–53
  ratification 150–51, 435–39, 444–50
  refusal to put in writing as ULP 134
  sidebar 82, 340–41
  strike settlement 419–21
  supplemental (*see* Sidebar agreement)
  tentative 148–49, 441–44
  to agree 337–38
  tradeoffs (*see* Tradeoffs)
  tying 369–71
  unilateral changes in as ULP 135
Ally doctrine 36–37, 399
American Ship Building 139
Analysis of negotiations
  of previous 6–13
  of recently completed 454–56
Arbitration
  advisory 377
  to avoid impasse 375–77
  clause 466–67
  final offer selection 376–77
  gathering data on results of 78–80
  interest 337–38, 375–77
  interpreting "borrowed" language 335
  interpreting creative writing 364–65
Arrangements for meeting (*see* Meeting arrangements)
Assessment of negotiations 3–49
Automatic escalators (*see also* Cost-of-living adjustments) 247–48, 251, 278, 287, 464–65
Automobile industry
  Chrysler Corp. 86, 472–73
  concessionary bargaining 467–70
  cooperative programs 489
  dual-level or two-level bargaining 17
  multi-plant negotiations 15–16
  parity with Canadian plants 237

B

Bargaining
  bad faith (*see* Good faith bargaining)
  book 63
  calendar 105–06

Bargaining—*(Cont'd)*
committee (*see* Management, bargaining committee)
concessionary 105, 467–75
critique and analysis 454–56
data (*see* Data for bargaining)
deadlines 104, 149–50, 433–35
forms of 202–05
good faith (*see* Good faith bargaining)
history
negotiators 7–10
review for assessment purposes 6–13
timing 102
joint union-management programs 482–90
leverage
assessment of 31–43
employer's 33–40
plant closure negotiations 480–81
strike situations 407–08
union's 40–43, 480–81
objectives
achieved in previous negotiations 7
economic 28–29, 94–102, 218–19
models of 94–102
non-economic 95–96
union's 217–18
pattern (*see* Pattern bargaining and settlements)
strike in progress 403–04, 416–21
traditional form 202, 204–05
trades (*see* Tradeoffs)
unit (*see* Unit appropriate for bargaining)
Beginning negotiations 4, 102–03
Bell cow (*see also* Pattern bargaining and settlements) 25–26
Benefits
bargaining objectives 98–101
chronology of changes in 64–65
comparative data 70–75
costing (*see* Cost estimating)
eligibility during strike 384, 420
mandatory bargaining subjects 125–28
tradeoffs with wages 235–36, 358–59
Blocking issue 231–32
Bonus payment(s) 357–63, 426–27
"Borrowed language" 335
Bottom-line bargaining concept (*see also* "Wall," Final offer) 235–38
Boulwarism 203
Boys Markets 233, 466
Breaking off negotiations 181, 427
Briefing management 60–61, 85–87, 200–01, 453–54
"Buying" recommendation 437–39
"Buy outs" 75, 98–99, 397
By-passing union spokesperson 135–36, 377–78, 403

C

Calendar for bargaining 105–06
Cash outflow 312–15
Caucus
effective use of 193–96
method of calling 152, 194
room 179
timing 194–95
Checkoff of union dues 428–29, 461
Chief spokesperson (*see* Spokesperson)
Child care benefits 257–58
Clauses in labor contract (*see also* Drafting contract language) 79, 82, 322–42, 462–67, 500, 526–37
Climate for bargaining
economic 28–29
employee attitudes as affecting 44–46
institutional (union) attitudes as affecting 43–44
management attitudes as affecting 46–48
public and governmental perspective as affecting 48–49
Closure of facility (*see* Plant closure, sale, or relocation)
"Common situs" picketing 398–99
Communications
with employees
before negotiations 44–46
before ratification vote 445–47
during strike 383–84, 403, 416–18, 520
unauthorized 153
with news media (*see* News media contacts)
Comparable settlements (*see also* Pattern bargaining and settlements) 29–31, 70–75
Computers 179, 293
Concessions (*see also* Tradeoffs)
as part of tradeoff 227–31
seeking of, by management 109–118, 467–75
techniques of making 192–93
on union security 461–62

Concessionary bargaining 109–10, 467–75
Constructive ambiguity 364–65
Consumer price index (CPI) (*see* Cost-of-living adjustment)
Contract
  bar (to NLRB election) 430–31
  clauses (*see* Clauses in labor contract)
  drafting (*see* Drafting contract language)
  expiration (*see* Expiration of contract)
  language (*see* Drafting contract language)
  ratification (*see* Ratification of contract)
  reopening notices (*see* Notices)
  term (*see* Term of contract)
Contracting work (*see* Subcontracting)
Cooper, R. Conrad 9–10
Cost estimating 291–321, 456
  basic data 302, 498–99
  cash outflow 312–15
  cents-per-hour technique for 299–301
  COLA (*see* Cost-of-living adjustment)
  computers used for 179, 293
  cumulative calculations 301, 312–15, 319
  final 312–21, 456
  health and welfare benefits 265–66
  holiday benefits 308
  impact on other employee groups 311–12, 457
  key variables 301–03
  new money 294–96, 300–01, 307–08, 312–13
  paid leaves 308–10
  premium payments 310–11
  present value 318–20
  recap form 302, 498–99
  rollup 66–67, 296–99, 302, 307, 313, 358–59, 498–99
  security of data 293
  settlement package 312–20, 363
  specialists used for 57, 292
  "spillover" 312, 457
  spokesperson's responsibilities 291–92
  strike vs. settlement 386–94
  time-weighting 315–19
  total package 312–21, 456
  union access to employer's estimates 320–21
  vacation benefits 306–08
  wage increases 303–06, 312–20, 358–59
Cost-of-living adjustment (COLA) 29, 238–39, 304–06, 369, 464
Creative bargaining 355–59
Creative writing 364–65
Credibility
  of management agenda 117
  resulting from previous strike(s) 390–91
Critique of completed negotiations 6–13, 454–55

D

Data for bargaining 61–85, 493–512
  costs (*see* Cost estimating)
  duty to supply to union 121–24, 320–21, 488
  economic
    external 28–29, 70–75, 506–08
    internal 63–70, 503–06
  noneconomic
    grievances and arbitration 78–80
    hours of work 75, 78, 504–05
    seniority 78, 506
    supervisor's survey 79, 81
Deadlines
  bargaining 104, 149–50, 433–35
  on employer's offer 424–27
Decision bargaining 478–80
Decision-making by management 200–01
Decorum of negotiations 180–82
Drafting contract language 322–42
  agreements to agree 337–38
  "borrowed" language 335
  catch-all terms 336
  cosmetic language changes 326–27
  creative writing 364–65
  dating proposals and counterproposals 340
  effective dates 339
  final contract document 450–53
  for first contract 458–67, 526–37
  general guidelines 327–39
  health and welfare clauses 244–45, 265–67
  "hedge" modifiers 333–34
  incorporating changes in contract 329–30, 341–42, 450–52
  management-rights clause (*see* Management-rights issues and clauses)
  mutual agreement clauses 336–37, 463–64
  pension clauses 286

Drafting contract language—*(Cont'd)*
responsibility for 58–59, 324–25
settlement memorandum 441–44, 523–25
"sidebar" agreements 340–41
time for 322–23
veto clauses 336–37, 463–64
Dubuque Packing Co. 477
Duty to bargain (*see* Good faith bargaining)

E

Economic climate for bargaining 28–29
Economic data (*see* Data for bargaining)
Economic issues
analysis of 96–102, 166–67
bargaining strategy 202–42
offers (*see* Offers and counteroffers)
order of bargaining 147–48
patterns (*see* Pattern bargaining and settlements)
Economic parameters (*see also* Final offer; "Wall")
establishment of 94–96
models 96–102
Economic strike 400–02
"Effects" bargaining 478
Employee benefits (*see* Benefits)
Employee stock ownership plan (ESOP) 474, 484
Employer (*see* Management)
Estimating costs (*see* Cost estimating)
Experts
cost estimating 292
drafting language 324
health and welfare benefits 243–44
pension benefits 269–70
Expiration of contract 103–05, 149–50, 239, 345–47, 471–72

F

Federal Mediation and Conciliation Service (FMCS) (*see also* Mediators) 90–92, 372–75
Final offer (*see also* Offers and counteroffers; "Wall") 125, 348–50, 396–97
added benefit for acceptance 426–27
"add-ons" 27, 439–41
alternative choices 367–68, 433
deadline for acceptance 424–25
recommendation by union 436–39
rejected by membership 448–50
relationship to strike 396–97
timing 345–47
First contract negotiation 458–67
Fringe benefits (*see* Benefits)
Front-loading (*see also* Loading the package) 315–20

G

Gainsharing plans 474, 483–84
Game plan 93–118
"Gap" 386, 388–94
"Give-backs" (*see* Concessionary bargaining)
Goals (*see* Bargaining)
Good faith bargaining
bad faith bargaining
by-passing union 135–36, 403
imposing conditions 132
inhibiting or delaying meetings 132–33
insufficient authority of negotiator 133
plant closure, sale or relocation 476–80
refusal to put agreement in writing 134–35
surface bargaining 133–34, 339
unilateral changes 135, 402–04
withdrawal of accepted offers 134, 404
during strike 402–04
furnishing information to union 121–24
generally 119–20
negotiating conduct 131–36
subjects
illegal 124, 128
mandatory 124–28
permissive 124, 128
totality of conduct 132
ULP as pressure tactic 427–28
Grievances (*see also* Arbitration)
gathering data on 78–79
negotiating on pending 157–58
Ground rules for bargaining
both parties
confirming tentative agreements 148–49
contract expiration treatment 149–50
meeting schedules 144–45

news media contacts 146–47
order of addressing issues 147–48
pay for union representatives 145
management
caucuses 152, 193–96
communications 153
inadvertent signals 152–53
spokesperson as sole speaker 151–52

H

Health and welfare benefits (*see also* Medical insurance) 243–68, 420
Hours-of-work data 75–76, 78, 504–05
Humor 10, 182

I

Impact of wage increases (*see* Rollup)
Impasse
definition 125, 403
potential early 219–21
techniques for avoiding or resolving 351–78
unilateral implementation after 402–03
Inability to pay
concessionary bargaining 469
data to support 122, 470
Initial contract negotiations 458–67
Interest arbitrating 337–38, 375–77
International Association of Machinists 486–87
Issues
economic 147–48, 166–67, 204–21
plans for responding to 108–09
in previous negotiations 10–12

J

Joint negotiations (multiple unions) 26–27
Joint trusteed benefit plans 245–47, 284–86
Joint union-management programs
automobile industry 489
benefits and burdens 484–86
concessionary bargaining distinction 482–83
general 482–90
machinists union 486–87
strategy and tactics 487–90

K

Key contacts 85
Key issues 10–12, 105–09
Key personalities in previous negotiations 9–10

L

Labor costs (*see also* Cost estimating)
compiling data 66–70, 301–03, 498–99
estimating changes in (*see* Cost estimating)
recap form for estimating 302, 489–99
union access to data 121–24, 320–21, 488
Labor law (*see also* National Labor Relations Act) 58–59, 324–25
general 119–20
impact on negotiations 136–38
requirements for bargaining 119–36
strikes 397–404
Language draftsperson (*see also* Drafting contract language) 58–59, 324–25
Lawyers
as draftspersons 58–59, 324
as spokespersons 53–54
strike counseling 384
Legal services benefits 256–57
Length of contract (*see* Term of contract)
Leverage (*see* Bargaining)
Life insurance 247
Listening 189–92
Loading the package
effects on costs 312–15, 361–63
generally 237–38
variations to avoid impasse 356–57, 361–63
Lockout 138–39
Lump-sum payments 357–58, 361–63, 426–27

M

Machinists union 486–87
Management
attitude toward unions 46–48
bargaining committee
cost estimating specialist 57
language draftsperson 58–59,

Management—*(Cont'd)*
324–25
note taker 57–58
operational expert 56–57
selection of 56–60
spokesperson (*see* Spokesperson)
bargaining objectives 7, 94–102, 218–19
briefings for 60–61, 85–87, 200–01, 453–54
decision-making 60–61, 96–97, 200–01, 385–97
positions on union proposals 169–72, 181–82
Management-rights issues and clauses 11–12, 127, 186–87, 334–35, 365–66, 462–63
Management spokesperson (*see* Spokesperson)
Mandatory subjects of bargaining (*see* Subjects for bargaining)
McDonald, David J. 9–10
"Med-Arb" 377
Mediators
during strike 418–19
notice to 90–92
techniques of 372–75
use of tradeoffs by 235, 374–75
Medical insurance (*see also* Health and welfare benefits)
clauses 244–45
COBRA 255–56
cost containment 258–64, 266
cost estimating 265–66
dental plans 252
disability benefits 250–51
during strike 384, 420
effective date of changes in 339
hospital-medical-surgical coverage 248–50
mental health benefits 253–54
negotiating strategies 264–68
prescription drug plans 252–53
retiree medical benefits 254–55
vision care 252
Meeting arrangements
equipment for management 179
pay for union representatives 145
private (*see* Private meetings)
schedules 144–45, 178–79
site 87–88
Memorandum of agreement 341–42, 441–44, 423–25
"Me-too" agreement (*see* Pattern bargaining and settlements; Tying agreements)
Minutes of negotiations (*see* Notes of negotiations)
Most-favored-nation clause 27, 370
Multi-employer negotiations 19–24
Multi-plant or multi-facility negotiations 18–19
Multiple-union situations 24–28
Multiplying fringes (*see* Rollup)
Mutual aid or mutual assistance pacts 38–40

N

National Football League (NFL) negotiations 208, 428
National Labor Relations Act (NLRA) (*see also* National Labor Relations Board; Unfair labor practices)
general 119–20
good faith bargaining 120–36
impasse 125, 403
mandatory subjects of bargaining (*see* Subjects for bargaining)
plant closure, sale or relocation 475–80
representation election 430–31
rights during strikes 397–404
voting eligibility of strikers and replacements 137–38
National Labor Relations Board (*see also* National Labor Relations Act)
determining good faith bargaining 131–36
effect on bargaining 137–38, 427–28
representation cases 430–31
Negotiator(s) (*see* Spokesperson)
"New money" 294–96, 300–01, 307–08, 312–13
News media contacts 146–47, 153, 418, 445
No contract-no work policy 149–50, 346
Noneconomic issues 95–96, 105–09, 147–48, 172–75
Nonunion facilities
data on wages and benefits 74
impact of settlement on ("spillover") 311–12, 457
No-strike clause 465–66
Notes of negotiations
finalizing 456
private meetings 353–54
responsibility for 57–58

spokesperson's 159–61
Notices
of contract reopening 88–90
to Federal Mediation and Conciliation Service 90–92
FMCS Form F-7 91, 372
of plant or facility closure 476
requirements prior to strikes and lockouts 138–39

O

Objectives (*see* Bargaining)
Offers and counteroffers (*see also* Proposals and counterproposals)
contingent commitments 368–69
creative bargaining 355–59
deadline on 424–25
final offers 348–50, 385–97
"add-ons" 439–40
"final-final" offers 349
optional offers 367–68
relationship to first offer 211–12
timing 345–47
first offer by management
construction 208–10
objectives 210–12
presentation 213–14
response by union 214–16
size 211–12
term 212
timing 205–08
first offer by union 214–16
response by management 221–22
innovative 226–27, 355–59
intermediate economic 222–26
optional alternative 367–68
presentation 196–97, 213–14
retroactivity 425–26
splitting the difference 368
strategy 202–42
tying agreements 370–71
withdrawal of accepted 134
written vs. oral 196, 214
Off-the-record meetings (*see* Private meetings) 118, 234–35, 351–55
Opening statements
by management 153–55
by union 156
Operations during strike 37–38, 382, 386–87, 404–15, 515–19
Optional offers 367–68
Order of addressing issues
ground rules 147–48
initial responses and 172–75
relationship to management's first offer 205–06
Outsourcing (*see* Subcontracting)

P

Pattern bargaining and settlements 25–26, 31, 70–75, 204, 359–63
"Payback" from strike 388–91, 393–94
Pensions 269–90
basic data on 68–70
benefit formulas 276–81
clauses 286
costing of changes 68–70, 289–90, 292
defined benefit plans 271–81
defined contribution plans 281–83
early retirement 275–76
hybrid DB/DC plans 283–84
legal constraints 270
as mandatory subject of bargaining 126
negotiating strategies 286–90
as nonmandatory subject of bargaining 128
Persuasion 183–88
Picketing 36–37, 397–400, 413–15, 420–21, 513–22
Planning negotiations 93–118
Plant closure, sale, or relocation 463, 469, 472, 475–82
Preparation for bargaining 50–118, 460, 501–22
Press releases 146–47
Previous negotiations analysis 6–13
Private meetings (*see also* Off-the-record meetings)
to avoid or resolve impasse 351–55
before commencing negotiations 117–18
proposing tradeoffs 234–35
Procedures for negotiations (*see* Ground rules for bargaining)
Productivity
data for bargaining 63, 66
during strike operations 38
negotiated plans 474, 482–90
Profit sharing programs 474, 483–84
Proposals and counterproposals (*see also* Agenda; Offers and counteroffers)
contingent commitment 368–69
creative 355–59

Proposals and counterproposals—*(Cont'd)*
- dating 340
- deadline to accept 424–25
- drafting (*see* Drafting contract language)
- first contract 458–67
- management agenda item as counterproposal 115
- opening (*see* Agenda)
- presentation 164–66, 196–97
- by union
  - draft, management handling of 325
  - evaluation of 166–72
  - limiting additional opening 163–64
  - responding to 172–75, 179
  - understanding and clarifying 158–63

Public opinion
- plant closure 480
- strikes 48–49, 520

Publicity for final offer 445–47, 520

Q

Quality of Work Life ("QWL") 484, 489–90
Quid pro quo (*see* Tradeoffs)

R

Railroad industry 333
Railway Labor Act xxiii, 119
Rank and file (*see* Union(s))
Ratification of contract 150, 435–39, 444–50
Recommended final offer 435–39
Recess in negotiations 181, 427
Red-circled wages 474
Relocation of facility (*see* Plant closure, sale, or relocation)
Reopener (*see* Wage reopener)
Reopening Notice (*see* Notices)
Replacements for strikers 37–38, 136–38, 409–10, 411–14, 430
Reservation of rights (*see* Management-rights issues and clauses)
Reserved gate 398–99, 415
Retirement benefits (*see* Pensions)
Retroactive increases 357–58, 425–26, 441
Rollup 66–67, 296–99, 302–03, 307, 313, 358–59, 498–99

S

Sale of facility (*see* Plant closure, sale, or relocation)
Scheduling of meetings 144–45, 178–79
Secondary boycott and picketing 36, 397–400
Security during strike 383, 413–14, 513–14, 516–17
Security of management's information 169, 179, 293
Seniority 78, 506, 528–30
Settlements
- cosmetic changes to obtain 359–63
- economic impact on other employee groups 311–12, 457
- memorandum of 341–42, 441–44, 523–25
- piecing together 350–51
- premature implementation 440–41
- pressure for
  - by employer 423–32
  - by union 432–35
- ratification by union membership 150, 435–39, 444–50
- recommendation by union committee 435–39
- rejection by membership 448–50
- strike-period negotiations 419–21
- summary of other employers' 74–77
- tentative 441–44
- timing for 345–47
- written, importance of 441–44

Sidebar agreement 82, 340–41
Site for negotiations (*see* Meeting arrangements)
Snapback provisions-concessions 473
Specialists (*see* Experts)
Splitting the difference 368
Spokesperson
- for management
  - authority of 60–61, 133
  - assessment and planning of negotiations 4–6
  - caucuses, use of 193–96
  - concessions, making of 193–96
  - cost estimating 291–92
  - executive as 54
  - lawyer as 53–54
  - listening 189–92
  - manner at bargaining table 180–83
  - note taking 159–61
  - opening statement by 153–56
  - persuasion 183–88

practical tips 177–201
selection of 51–56
as sole speaker 151–52
traits and characteristics 197–200
word selection 182–83
for union
avoiding embarassment of 199, 359
by-passing 135–36, 377–78, 403
hostility by 180–81
opening statement by 156
in previous negotiations 9–10
Spillover costs 311–12, 457
Steel industry 9–10
Steelworkers 9–10, 380
Strategy
analysis 6–9, 454–56
bargaining economics 202–42
contract term 238–42
game plan 93–118
health and welfare benefits 264–68
pension benefits 286–90
strike situation 382–85, 396–97
Strike(s)
agreement for settlement of 419–21
assessing ability to resist 31–43
bargaining during 403–04, 416–21
benefit payments to union members 41–42, 384, 420
coordinator for management 381–82
communications during 383–84, 403, 416–18
contingency checklist 382–85, 513–22
deadline 149–50, 433–35
decision to take 385–97
deliveries during 414–15
estimating costs 386–94
fund of union 41
"gap" between offer and demand 386, 388–94
insurance for employers 38–40
legal constraints 138–39, 397–404
log 384–85
negotiations during 403–04, 416–21
no-strike clause 465–66
operations during 37–38, 382, 386–87, 404–15, 515–19
"payback" from 388–94, 393–94
plan 382–85
preparations 380–85, 429–30, 513–22
replacements 37–38, 136–38, 409–10, 411–14, 430
reserved gate 398–99, 415
security during 383, 413–14
settlement of 419–21
threat as pressure to settle 432–33
and unfair labor practice finding 136–38, 400–01, 430
Strikers
alternative employment opportunities 42–43
benefits during strike 41–42, 384, 420
disciplinary action for misconduct 400–02, 420–21
order of recall following strike 419–20
rights in general 400–02
seniority status of 420
union discipline of 421
Stopping the clock 434
Subcontracting 36–37, 127, 311, 326–27, 336–37, 364–65, 410–11, 473
Subjects for bargaining
contract checklist 526–37
economic 147–48, 166–67, 202–42
illegal 124, 128
mandatory 124–31
noneconomic 95–96, 105–09, 147–48, 172–75
nonmandatory 128–31
Summaries of contract provisions 64–65, 82–84, 493–97
Supervisors
briefings after settlement 453–54
input for bargaining proposals 79–81, 110–11
replacing strikers 408–09, 413
support of joint programs 488–89
Supplemental agreements 82, 340–41
"Surface bargaining" 133–34

T

Taft-Hartley Act (*see* National Labor Relations Act)
Taft-Hartley Trusts 245–47, 284–86
"Take-backs" (*see* Concessionary bargaining)
Target settlement 100–02
Term of contract
agreements beyond 357–58
bargaining objectives for 96–102
of first contract 459–60
proposed in first offer 212
strategy 238–42
variations to avoid impasse 356–57
Timetable for bargaining 102–06, 144–45

Timing
  bargaining calendar 105–06
  bargaining strategy 102–05, 178–79
  beginning negotiations 4, 102–03
  caucuses 194–95
  concessionary bargaining 471–72
  ending negotiations 104, 345–47
  offers 104–05
  plant closure negotiations 481
  in previous negotiations 8
Total package
  concept 235–38
  costing 312–20, 363
Tradeoffs
  advantages and disadvantages 228–29
  concessionary bargaining 472–74, 482–83
  objectives 98–100
  mediator's use of 235, 373–74
  Quid pro quo 227–28
  timing and techniques 234–35
  types 230–33
  between wages and benefits 358–59
Training strike replacements 411–12
Trigger mechanisms 473
Two-level bargaining 18
Two-tiered wages and benefits 474
Tying agreements 369–71
Types of economic bargaining 202–04

U

Unemployment benefits to strikers 42
Unfair labor practices (*see also* National Labor Relations Act)
  bad faith bargaining (*see* Good faith bargaining)
  causing or prolonging strikes 400–02
  charge to apply pressure 427–28
  impact on negotiations 136–38
  remedies for violations 136
Union(s)
  agenda for bargaining 157–64
  bargaining committee pay 145
  bargaining habits 7–9
  bargaining power 40–43
  bypassing 135, 445–47
  cooperation (*see* Joint union-management programs)
  leaders 9–10, 43–44, 471
  opening statement of 156
  organization 43–44, 436
  language drafted by 325, 460–61
  multiple 24–28
  perspective on joint programs 486–87
  political pressures 43–44
  rank and file attitudes 44–46, 448–50
  ratification procedures 150, 435–39, 444–50
  recommendation on final offer 435–39, 444–48
  research of 43–44, 460
  response to employer's first offer 214–17
  security clauses 230, 461–62
  spokesperson (*see* Spokesperson)
Unilateral changes 135, 402–03, 476–80
Unit appropriate for bargaining 13–14
  multi-employer bargaining 19–24
  selection of 13–28
  single-employer—multi-facility 18–19
  single facility 14–18
United Auto Workers 489
United Steelworkers of America 9–10, 380

W

Wage reopener 240–42
Wages (*see also* Offers and counteroffers)
  across-the-board 360
  brackets 67, 303–04, 360–61
  cents per hour vs. percentage 360
  chronology 63–66
  comparative data 70–74
  costing changes 303–06, 312–20, 358–59
  effective date of change 339
  red-circled 474
  retroactive change 357–58, 425–26, 441
  two-tiered 474
Waiver
  avoiding by management 129
  of union's right to bargain over plant closure 475–76
  of union's right to receive information 123–24
  zipper clause 465, 475–76
"Wall" (*see also* Final offer)
  establishing before negotiations 100–02
  explanation of 100
  relationship to first offer 211–12

relationship to intermediate offers 222–25
and strike threat 385–86, 433, 449
"Whip-sawing" 18–19
Withdrawal of accepted offers 134
Work hours 75–76, 78, 504–05
Work practices or rules (*see also* Noneconomic issues)
multi-employer bargaining over 21–22
multi-plant bargaining over 17–18
Work stoppage (*see* Strike(s))

Z

Zipper clause 465, 475–76

About the Author

Charles S. Loughran is President of Seahurst Associates, a consulting firm in Seattle, Washington specializing in labor and employee relations. Previously, he was Vice President, Human Resources for Alaska Airlines, a major airline serving 40 cities in the U.S., Canada, Mexico, and Russia.

Mr. Loughran has spent over 30 years in the field of labor and employee relations having held managerial positions with Louisiana-Pacific Corporation, U.S. Steel Corporation (now USX), Trans World Airlines, and Crown Zellerbach Corporation. He is an attorney, and was previously engaged in the practice of labor law with the firm of Pettit and Martin, a large firm in San Francisco. He is a member of the California Bar Association as well as the federal bars for the Northern District of California and the Ninth Circuit Court of Appeals.

The author has served as chief spokesman in scores of labor contract negotiations in a variety of industries. Likewise, he has counseled managers and employers in conducting their own negotiations. He has also represented employers in a large number of grievance arbitration and NLRB hearings as well as in administrative proceedings before various state and federal agencies.

Mr. Loughran has a B.A. in Political Economy from the Johns Hopkins University in Baltimore, Maryland, an M.A. in Economics from the University of California in Berkeley, California, and a J.D. in law from Golden Gate University in San Francisco, California. He has written and lectured extensively on various subjects within the fields of Human Resources, Labor Relations, and Labor Law.

Mr. Loughran was born and raised in Pittsburgh, Pennsylvania, and now resides in Seattle, Washington. He is married and has four adult children.